BRITAIN'S PRIME MINISTERS

BRITAIN'S
PRIME MINISTERS

from Walpole to Wilson

E. Royston Pike

ODHAMS BOOKS

First published 1968

© 1968 E. Royston Pike

Published for Odhams Books by
The Hamlyn Publishing Group Limited
Hamlyn House, 42 The Centre
Feltham, Middlesex

Made and printed in Great Britain by
Morrison and Gibb Ltd., London and Edinburgh

CONTENTS

CONTENTS

ILLUSTRATIONS

ILLUSTRATIONS

Introduction

THE GREASY POLE

When Benjamin Disraeli, that most improbable of Britain's Prime Ministers, achieved at length the summit of his ambition, he went round telling his friends, 'I've climbed the greasy pole—I've climbed the greasy pole!'

He had good reason to be proud, for the way to the Premiership is indeed a greasy pole, and of the hundreds who have tried to climb it fewer than fifty have succeeded.

Some have climbed it more than once (Gladstone holds the record, with four times). Some have succeeded in remaining aloft for years on end, while others hardly got there when they lost their hold and slithered down again to the bottom.

In these pages we are going to meet them all, the men whose names are enrolled in the most splendid list of political personalities that any country can boast of. Some of them are household names, whose fame has come rolling down the centuries and will continue to roll for many a century to come. Others are remembered hardly at all, and most of them, perhaps, deserve nothing better. But in some few cases they are more generously dealt with here than in the political histories. The reason ? Because in these pages I am concerned with the Prime Ministers not only as political animals but as human beings.

Of course, there is a great deal of political history in what follows —enough, I trust, to enable the ' ordinary reader ' to understand the development of politics in the course of the last two and a half centuries. But there is much more. It has been my object to give as full and fair a description of each of the Prime Ministers in turn as it is possible to give within a single pair of covers, and that means including a number of things that the histories leave out. We will not begin our acquaintance with the man when he is already making his mark on the parliamentary stage, nor shall we desert him when he has retired into the shadows of private life; our concern with him will be from the cradle to the grave. We shall learn of the family into which he was born. We shall see him as a schoolboy and at university. We shall note whether he was born with a silver spoon in his mouth or whether he had to hack his way through a tangle of obstacles. We shall watch him in his business activities, his leisure pursuits. We shall note the books he read—and sometimes wrote. We shall see what he was up to when he put off the appearance of the public figure. We shall observe him at close quarters, remark what he looked like and his manner of speaking, and perhaps be able to decide whether he was a man we would like to have met.

There is still something else to be mentioned, and a very important something it is. We shall not make the mistake—so common, unfortunately, in historical writing—of omitting the feminine interest. In every Prime Minister's life there was a woman, and very often her influence was a powerful factor in determining his career. In nearly every case this woman was his wife—and indeed, it is one of the most remarkable things about our Prime Ministers that they were so fortunate in their marriages. But for Lady Hester, Chatham would have been immured in a mad-house. It is impossible to credit that Disraeli would have surmounted the immense drawbacks of his earlier years if he had not his Mary Anne to encourage and stimulate and solace. Gladstone would never have become the 'Grand Old Man' but for the woman who was for nearly sixty years his wife.

Returning, now, from the personal to the political, we may well spend a few minutes in considering just what the ' pole ' is that our subjects have spent so many years in trying to climb.

In the political set-up of modern Britain, the Prime Minister—Premier for short—is by far the most commanding figure. He is No. 1 in Parliament. He appoints Ministers—that they are appointed by the sovereign is one of the pleasant fictions of our Constitution —and he gives them the boot. True, he has to be assured of the support of a majority of members of the House of Commons; but since he, and only he, has the right to demand a dissolution, he holds their future in the hollow of his hand. He controls vast patronage, political and business, social and ecclesiastical. He makes speeches, and is pretty sure of a half-column at least in the morning papers. He appears on television whenever he wants to, and his face— benevolent or lowering—his voice, his manner and mannerisms, are familiar in millions of homes. Wherever he goes he is given V.I.P. treatment. Although in the terminology of the modern Commonwealth he is not 'Head of State', his position is such that the question, whether we are heading for a presidential type of Government, is being increasingly discussed.

All this is part and parcel of the political facts of present-day life, and it is therefore all the more surprising that the office of Prime Minister is a comparatively recent institution.

Of course, throughout the many centuries of our island story the sovereign has usually had one minister who has been the favourite and most trusted member of the royal entourage. Thus Henry VIII had Wolsey and Cromwell, Queen Elizabeth Lord Burleigh and his son Robert Cecil. Charles I put his trust in Strafford (or perhaps it was the other way round) and Charles II in Clarendon, and later on there were Shaftesbury and Danby, Sunderland and Harley, Bolingbroke and Stanhope. All these were, however, royal servants rather than Parliament's, and very often they found it their duty, or in line with their interest, to support their master in the exercise of his prerogatives against the hereditary or elected representatives in Parliament assembled. It was not until the Hanoverians came in early in the eighteenth century that there began to emerge one who established himself as the prime (first, or chief) minister in a government based upon the support of a majority of members of the House of Commons. That support was essential, since in Charles II's time it had been made clear beyond any doubt that the House of Commons controls the power of public taxation.

By common consent, the first Minister who so established himself was Robert Walpole, who was appointed First Lord of the Treasury in 1721. With every right, it is Walpole's name that heads the list of Britain's Prime Ministers.

Note, however, that Walpole was appointed First Lord of the Treasury: not Prime Minister. Not for nearly another two hundred years was that style officially recognized. For quite a time it was repudiated by other members of the Cabinet. In a great attack launched on Walpole in 1741 one of his chief misdemeanours was expressly described as his usurpation of the sole power of directing all public affairs and solely enjoying and engrossing the ear of his sovereign. The M.P. who led the attack in the Lower House put it most clearly. 'According to our constitution we can have no sole and prime minister,' this gentlemen declared; 'every officer of state has his own proper department, and no officer ought to meddle in the department of another'. The attackers were routed in both Houses, but in the Lords there was a minority who drew up a formal protest which is worth quoting. 'We are persuaded,' ran its opening statement, 'that a sole, or even a First Minister, is an officer unknown to the law of Britain, inconsistent with the constitution of the country, and destructive of liberty in any government whatsoever'.

Walpole himself, it may be noted, seems never to have used the title, even when he had been enjoying the *thing* for years. Twenty years later George Grenville, who was not one of the least opinionated of Prime Ministers, declared the title to be 'odious', and Lord North would never permit himself to be called *Prime* Minister among his friends and in his family circle. The first in the list who allowed himself to be so styled officially seems to have been Lord Beaconsfield when he negotiated the Treaty of Berlin in 1878: in the opening clause of that historic document he is described as 'First Lord of Her Majesty's Treasury, Prime Minister of England'. We shall probably be right in assuming that this was for the benefit of foreigners, who might otherwise have been puzzled by Queen Victoria's chief minister being apparently the functionary entrusted with her money-bags.

The British public might be expected to be better informed, and yet the fiction persisted until the turn of the century. In 1900 the *Court Circular* tripped up—or perhaps it was a calculated indiscretion —when it referred to Lord Salisbury as Prime Minister. Of course, he was, and had been for years and on several occasions, but the statement was received with raised eyebrows in official circles. Even four years later a member complained in the House of Commons that he had just seen in the newspapers a column of 'Birthday Honours' with the heading 'Prime Minister's list'. Prime Minister's list, indeed! Who *was* the Prime Minister? So far as he was concerned, he didn't recognize the fellow. Whereupon Mr. Balfour (who as Prime Minister was in the best position to know) uncoiled his long legs and in his most supercilious drawl informed the Hon. Member that *he* was not responsible for the term: it was one of those editors who had done it . . .

But a year later, when Sir Henry Campbell-Bannerman was forming his administration, the office of Prime Minister was at length given official recognition, and its holder accorded a place in the Table of Precedence. Not the most important place, however, not immediately after the sovereign and the royal family but following along behind the Lord Chancellor (whom he appoints as a member of his government) and the two Archbishops (in whose appointment he has a large, probably a decisive voice).

Ever since Walpole the Prime Minister has been usually the First Lord of the Treasury. This is because, firstly, the First Lord is the principal member of the Board of Commissioners which since 1714 has wielded the powers of the Lord High Treasurer, one of which used to be the disbursement of the 'secret service' money out of which bribes were paid to members of Parliament; and secondly, because the First Lord's position carried with it a substantial salary, whereas the post of Prime Minister, not being recognized under the Constitution, had of course no salary at all attached to it.

Not until 1937 was the matter put on a proper footing. By the Ministers of the Crown Act of that year the Prime Minister (who is now always First Lord of the Treasury) is paid a salary of £10,000 per annum, of which £4,000 is free of tax. He is provided with an official residence at No. 10 Downing Street, Westminster, rent free and free of rates, and he has the use of Chequers, a Tudor mansion in the Chilterns which was presented to the nation in 1917 by Lord and Lady Lee of Fareham for that purpose.

At the end of this brief summary, it may be pointed out that the power of the Prime Minister has grown steadily with every advance in the means of popular communication. Disraeli and Gladstone were brought into every home where a newspaper could be read; Stanley Baldwin made good use of the new technique of radio, and Harold Macmillan seized the opportunity of getting himself across afforded by television. Today the Prime Minister occupies the heights of power.

So much by way of introduction; now let us push open the door of the picture gallery and start looking at the portraits in their gilded frames—the eighteenth-century grandees, bewigged and beruffled, in their plum-coloured coats, fancy waistcoats, and knee-breeches— the frock-coated gentlemen of truly Victorian respectability, whose countenances emerge so stiffly from their high white collars—and the much more easily dressed Prime Ministers of today, who look as though they are just off to the golf-course (which indeed may be the case). What a collection they make! And for my part I must confess that the more I have found out about them the better I have come to like them.

E. R. P.

Hinchley Wood,
  Esher.

I

SIR ROBERT WALPOLE

BRITAIN'S FIRST PRIME MINISTER was a robustly jovial country gentleman from Norfolk, Robert Walpole by name, who made the position for himself in 1721 under George I, was confirmed in it by George II, and managed to hold on to it until 1742—thus creating a record of twenty-one years' unbroken occupation of the supreme situation in politics that none of his successors has surpassed, or, for that matter, come near to equalling.

Robert Walpole was born on 26 August 1676 when Charles II, the 'Merry Monarch', was King of England. He was the third son and fifth of the nineteen children born to Robert Walpole and Mary his wife, of Houghton Hall near Castle Rising in Norfolk. The Walpoles were good county stock, and although they had no grand aristocratic or territorial connections they were a cut above the squirearchy. They were wont to boast of their descent in a direct line from an ancestor who had come over with William the Conqueror, and in the library at Houghton they kept a pedigree on parchment to prove it.

For many generations they had been established at Houghton—perhaps it is true, as they claimed, that they were there in King Stephen's time—and their many hundreds of broad acres constituted an estate from which they derived a very substantial income: in Walpole's early days the rent-roll amounted to some £2,000 a year, and it was very much more by the time he had done with it. The Walpoles were indeed very comfortably off, and they spent their days pleasantly enough in country pursuits, shooting and fishing and horse-racing and the rest.

None of them seems to have been particularly distinguished—but for as long as men could remember they had taken an active interest in politics. Sir Edward Walpole sat in the Parliament which restored Charles II to the throne in 1660, and Sir Edward's son Robert (our Robert's father) was M.P. for Castle Rising for the last dozen years of the century. There was never any difficulty in getting elected, since they were the owners of three of those seats in the House of Commons that were very rightly described as pocket boroughs.

Robert Walpole the Elder seems to have had a good deal in common with Squire Western in Fielding's *Tom Jones*. He was big and burly, fond of farming and pretty good at it, so that his cattle fetched good prices when sent to market and his crops were above the ordinary. He was also fond—very fond—of the bottle, and one of the first things he taught his son was to be fond of it too. As the boy sat beside him in the parlour at Houghton, after the ladies had withdrawn, he would ply him with mug after mug of strong ale in the hope of making him tipsy. For, he explained, it was not fitting that his son should remain in a fit state to see what a silly old fellow his father appeared when deep in his cups.

Since Robert was a younger son not very much was expected of him. In the natural course of events the estates would devolve upon his eldest brother, and he would have to make his own way in the world. It was planned, therefore, that he should go into the Church, a customary refuge in those days for younger sons. Robert had not the slightest inclination in that direction but he was doubtless quite prepared to fit in with whatever was decided.

Years afterwards he was heard to remark that if the original plan had been followed he would never have become Prime Minister: he would have become Archbishop of Canterbury instead.

So after a year or two under a tutor in a neighbouring village he was sent at the age of fourteen to Eton, where he did not learn very much, and then in 1696 to King's College, Cambridge, where besides nearly falling a victim to an attack of smallpox he learnt a good many things that were not in the books.

But after all, he did not have to don a black gown and mount the pulpit steps. Both his elder brothers died within a short time of one another, and in consequence he became the direct heir to Houghton and all that went with it. His circumstances being thus greatly improved he was able to look around for a wife, and in the summer of 1700 he married Catherine Shorter, the good-looking and very well-dowered daughter of a Baltic timber-merchant in the City and the granddaughter of a Lord Mayor. She bore him three sons and two daughters. Later on, so the gossip ran, she was as addicted to ' gallantry ' with the men as her husband was with the women.

In the same year as his marriage, Walpole's father died, and he entered into his inheritance. He might then have settled down like so many of his ancestors before him; but devoted though he was to country pursuits and pleasures, he was not to live out his days in a rural backwater. He felt that he was made for much more important and satisfying things; and since the way now lay open to a political career—which is what he had long fancied—he hastened to embark upon it. In 1701, then, a few months after his father's death, he entered the House of Commons as member for Castle Rising, which had been his father's seat. Subsequently he exchanged this for King's Lynn, another of the boroughs in the family's control, and this seat he retained until he became a peer forty years later.

Walpole's first speech in the House was a failure, and this though he had taken great pains over its preparation. It was unlucky that he should have been immediately followed by a member who was much more fluent than he was, but it is recorded that at least one of those who listened to his maiden effort was by no means un-impressed. 'You may applaud the one and ridicule the other as much as you please,' this member is reported to have remarked, ' but depend upon it, the spruce gentleman who made the set speech will never improve, while Walpole will in course of time become an excellent speaker.'

And so it soon proved. Walpole mastered the arts of parliamen-tary procedure, showed exemplary diligence in the business of the House, spoke briefly but always to the point, and never lost an opportunity of demonstrating his loyalty to the party to which he had attached himself—the Whigs—the party to which his father and his grandfather had belonged in years gone by.

The two great parties in the State at that time were the Whigs and the Tories. Both had originated a generation earlier, about the time that Walpole was born, in the reign of Charles II. But before we describe their beginnings a word of warning is necessary, or we shall fall into the error of believing that ' party ' in those days meant very much what it means today. Whigs and Tories were not parties in the sense that Liberals and Conservatives and Labour are parties in the modern political set-up

The modern party has an acknowledged leader, a more or less definite set of political principles or a programme which is periodically discussed and reviewed at a national conference, and an organization composed of a central office and a network of local branches through which members are enlisted and continue to belong on payment of an annual subscription. These things are mostly Victorian inven-tions. For the best part of two hundred years after their first emergence the Whigs and Tories were not a bit like this. They were rather rival groupings of politically conscious aristocrats with their numerous collections of dependants and hangers-on, who found the game of ins and outs in politics not only interesting but potentially profitable. At any one time, the one party was composed of those who were primarily concerned with remaining ' in ', and the other of those whose chief endeavour was to turn the ' ins ' out and take their place.

Charles II's queen was barren—he had no difficulty in fathering a number of bastards—and the heir to the crown was his brother James, Duke of York, a man of forbidding personality who also laboured under the immense disadvantage of being a Roman Catholic, and a very bigoted one at that. The prospect of James's accession so alarmed a large body of politicians under the Earl of Shaftesbury that they proposed that he should be excluded in favour of some Protestant heir; but they were strongly opposed by another faction under the Earl of Danby who professed the belief that kings ruled by Divine Right, from which it followed that any interference with natural succession was nothing short of blasphemy.

As the great debate continued, and showed signs of ending in blows, the former became known as Whigs and the latter as Tories.

The origin of these names is curious. ' Whig ' is a shortened form of 'Whiggamor ', a nickname (supposed to have been derived from the peculiar sound used by the peasantry of the Scottish lowlands in driving their horses) that had been applied to the dour, intensely fanatical Presbyterians who had been so cruelly persecuted by James when he was acting as his brother's viceroy in Scotland, and who had the very best of reasons for dreading his succession to the throne. ' Tory ' is an anglicized spelling of an Irish word which had been applied to bands of wild outlaws, half-savage ' bog-trotters ', Roman Catholics in religion and robbers and cut-throats by occupation, who for years past had been waging guerrilla warfare against the Protestant English in Ireland.

Lord Shaftesbury dubbed his opponents Tories in the hope of arousing against them the anti-Irish, anti-Catholic prejudices of the mob; and Lord Danby retaliated in kind with an epithet which might serve to associate his rivals with gangs of obscure and despised Scottish fanatics.

Both nicknames caught on. Their opprobrious meanings were very shortly forgotten, and the two great parties in the State were proud to be known by names which had been terms of contempt and ridicule.

When Charles II died in 1685 he was succeeded by his brother James, and all the horrid things that had been anticipated came to pass. Then Whigs and Tories combined in an uneasy alliance, and James was kicked out and William of Orange was put in his place as William III—king not by Divine Right but by Act of Parliament.

Before long Whigs and Tories were fighting one another as before, struggling for seats in Parliament and in the Cabinet. There was as yet no idea of government by a single party, however, and William chose his Ministers from among the best men available, whatever party they nominally adhered to.

When Walpole made his entry into Parliament he joined the Whigs, probably because his family had been Whigs for years past. William III was still on the throne, but in 1702 he died and was succeeded by his sister-in-law Queen Anne. Both parties accepted her as their sovereign willingly enough—after all, she was James II's daughter—but the extremer Tories began to fix their eyes on her young brother, Prince James Edward, who had been an infant in arms when his father made his hurried exit from England in 1688. Since then the prince—whom the Tories called the Prince of Wales and the Whigs ' the Pretender '—had been living at the court of Louis XIV in France, exposed to all the influences of the most autocratic monarchy in Europe. Furthermore, he was a strict Roman Catholic, a fact which the Tories—who were all staunch Church of England men—did their best to minimize, when they could not put it out of their minds altogether.

Not surprisingly, it became the most settled principle among the Whigs to keep the Pretender from ascending the throne. The man *they* favoured was Prince George of Hanover, who was a distant cousin of Queen Anne, but had the distinct advantage of being the nearest Protestant heir. Walpole made this the principal objective of his parliamentary career.

The Tories had the majority in the House of Commons when he entered it, but as the years passed the Whigs gradually established their supremacy. Although Walpole had no powerful political connections or aristocratic backers he soon attracted the favourable attention of the party managers. He struck them as being a sound young fellow, clear-headed and stout-hearted, industrious, a man with a good head for business—particularly figures, not afraid of hard knocks given or taken and, what is more, not over-scrupulous. Clearly, he was good ministerial timber, and in 1705 he was given a seat at the Board of Admiralty. In 1708 he was appointed Secretary at War, and in the following year Treasurer of the Navy. But when things seemed to be going swimmingly with him, his Whig patrons lost their positions at the Queen's Council Board and were supplanted by Tories, and his former chief at the Admiralty was charged with mismanagement of naval affairs. Walpole defended him in a couple of well-argued pamphlets to such effect that the new Tory ministers took alarm. They brought an accusation against him that he had received a corrupt payment of £2,000 in connection with a contract for the supply of forage entered into when he was at the War Office. Whereupon in 1712 the House of Commons voted that Mr. Robert Walpole had been found guilty of a high breach of trust and of notorious corruption, and resolved that he should be expelled from the House and imprisoned in the Tower.

The charge has a nasty ring about it, and in fact Walpole *had* received the money—not for himself, however, but for a friend to whom he wanted to do a good turn. This may not sound much of an excuse to us but to his contemporaries it was taken as an almost complete exoneration. What surprised *them* was that he had not taken a rake-off for himself in addition. He became something of a popular hero, and ballads were hawked about the town in which ' the Jewel in the Tower ', who ' late adorn'd the Court, with excellence unknown before ', was extolled in doggerel which caught the popular mood:

> The day shall come to make amends,
> This Jewel shall with pride be wore,
> And o'er his foes, and with his friends,
> Shine glorious bright out of the Tower.

Walpole's sojourn in the Tower was by no means rigorous, and every day he was at home to admiring visitors. When the parliamentary session came to an end he was released, and in the general election which followed was returned again for King's Lynn as a matter of course.

Then in 1714 there was a complete reversal of the party fortunes. When Queen Anne was on her death-bed, and her Tory ministers were in active negotiation with James Edward for his succession to the throne, Lord Shrewsbury and other Whig magnates determined on a bold stroke. They forced their way into the royal bedchamber, and persuaded the queen to consent to their taking over the administration. The queen died on 1 August, and within a few hours the heralds were proclaiming from the gallery at St. James's not King James III but King George I.

The Tories had played for high stakes, and they had lost the last throw. The Hanoverians came in, and with them the Whigs who had made their arrival possible. The Tories went out into the political wilderness from which they were not to emerge for nearly half a century.

Walpole shared in his party's triumph. To begin with, he was made Paymaster-General. An apparently modest appointment, it was, or could be made to be (and in the hands of most Paymasters, generally was) the most lucrative of government appointments. The nominal head of the new administration was Lord Halifax, but the guiding spirits were Lord Stanhope and Lord Townshend (who had married Walpole's sister Dorothy). Since most of his colleagues were in the House of Lords, Walpole was entrusted with the leadership of the House of Commons, and he made an excellent job of it. Then Halifax died, and in October 1715 Walpole was exalted to the conspicuous position of First Lord of the Treasury and Chancellor of the Exchequer. It is still too early to speak of him as Prime Minister, but it might be appropriate to call him first minister, for that is what his merits made him.

On the whole, Walpole got on very well with the new sovereign. George I had never been taught to speak English, and Walpole knew not a word of German, but they managed somehow with what little Latin they remembered from their schooldays. But when the king put in an appearance in the council chamber, as his predecessors on the throne had been in the habit of doing, he was acutely bored, understanding hardly one of the torrent of words. In the circumstances it is not surprising that the king found, more and more often, that he had other and better things to do than listen to his ministers speaking in an unknown tongue. So he stayed away. Walpole slipped into the vacant chair, and was accepted by his colleagues as their chief.

A year or two passed, and the Whigs were now in such unchallengeable supremacy that they could afford to indulge in strife among themselves. After one such quarrel Townshend was forced to retire, and the next morning Walpole resigned out of loyalty to his friend and brother-in-law. King George was aghast, and when Walpole made to hand back the seals of his office the king refused to take them. Walpole insisted, and so did the king. The situation bordered on the ludicrous, as time after time—ten times in all— Walpole proffered the seals, the king put them in Walpole's hat, and Walpole took them out again and put them on the table. At length Walpole had his way. He left the royal closet with tears in his eyes, and the king, too, was deeply moved.

Walpole stayed out of office for the next three years, although his influence in the House of Commons was still so great that the ministers had to seek his assistance in getting their bills through. In 1720 the dissensions in the Government were smoothed out and he returned to office, but only as Paymaster, and without a seat in the Cabinet.

Before many months had passed, the country was plunged into that orgy of get-rich-quick speculation known as the South Sea Bubble. Like most other people with some money in hand, Walpole bought some of the South Sea Company's stock, but unlike them he saw the red light in time. When a friend expressed his surprise that Walpole should be selling his stock on a still rising market he is said to have rejoined quietly, ' I have made a profit of a thousand per cent—and I am satisfied.'

When the Bubble burst, thousands of people in all walks of life were ruined. An infuriated public called loudly for scapegoats. One minister of the Crown was expelled from Parliament with ignominy; another committed suicide rather than live to face the coming inquest. The Government was tottering. At this crisis all eyes were turned on Walpole, who had won golden opinions for his financial acumen.

In April 1721 the call came. On 3 April the king appointed him for the second time First Lord of the Treasury and Chancellor of the Exchequer, and he proceeded at once to take steps to restore the public credit. From that day he was Prime Minister, the first to be recognized as such without any question, and we should not be put off by the modest disclaimer that he is sometimes reported to have made.

For twenty-one years Walpole was at the head of affairs as Prime Minister. Their history may seem dull: no great and glorious wars, no splendid victories, no far-reaching measures of reform. But of this there is not the slightest doubt, that for the great mass of the British people they were, on the whole, good years.

As a man who had been brought up to work, Walpole took the greatest interest in the commercial aspect of government. He effected trade treaties with countries on the Continent, he stabilized the currency and cleared up the mess left by the South Sea Bubble, he instituted a sinking-fund for the reduction of the national debt, and above all, for most of the time he kept Britain at peace. Throughout his long administration the people were enabled to go about their ordinary business, free to develop industries, to farm their fields and introduce many improvements into agricultural practice, to build towns, to enjoy many of the good things of life. As a peace minister he ranks among the best, and his achievement in this respect is all the more remarkable when it is understood that the Whigs were traditionally the war party, looking upon France as their natural enemy; and that the fact that the king was also Elector of Hanover meant that he was generally only too eager to embroil Britain in continental struggles. But, said Walpole, ' My politics are to keep free from all engagements as long as we possibly can.' In the end, as we shall see, his hand was forced, and he had to allow Britain to go to war. But that was not until 1739, and until then the people were free from military service and war taxation. Wealth increased steadily in all classes, but especially in the trading community which with good reason was predominantly Whig in allegiance. The Nonconformists, or Dissenters, also did well, for although the repressive Acts were still left on the Statute Book their effect was nullified by annual Acts of indemnity. For the first time they were enabled to go about their daily business in peace and security, and in every town they constituted an element of God-fearing, hard-working citizens. They, too, gave Walpole and the Whigs their undeviating support.

Wages were kept up, prices were generally stable, so that over the years the standard of living was improved. Industry flourished, British shipping increased by tens of thousands of tons, the burden of taxation was lightened or given a fairer incidence.

But, it will be asked, did not Walpole practise corruption on a very large, even an unprecedented scale? Yes, he did: no doubt about it. He was the most astute manager of the House of Commons, and in order to maintain his majority he bought the support of its members with whatever they happened to value most—some of them with hard cash, others with titles and decorations, a share in a profitable government contract, a job in the Customs or in a government office for a son, a commission in the army or navy, a shove up the official ladder, a business tip, a chance of making money on the side. All these things he did, and many others that we might think reprehensible, even dishonourable. But his contemporaries thought nothing of them, or not very much. Almost the only people who complained were those who felt that their services had not been well enough rewarded.

' No man ought to be severely censured ', wrote Lord Macaulay, ' for not being beyond his age in virtue.' To buy the votes of constituents (he went on to argue) is as immoral as to buy the votes of representatives, and ' yet we know that, in our own time '— Macaulay was writing in 1833, soon after the passing of the great Reform Bill—' no man is thought wicked or dishonourable . . . because under the old system of election, he was returned, in the only way in which he could be returned, for East Retford, for Liverpool, or for Stafford. Walpole governed by corruption because, in his time, it was impossible to govern otherwise.'

In making our comparisons we should remember, what is generally not realized, that there was no Civil Service in those days. At the beginning of a new reign, the sovereign was voted a Civil List, out of which he was required to meet most of the expenses of government. All the officials, great and small, were appointed through patronage, and the Prime Minister as First Lord of the Treasury had most of the royal patronage at his disposal. A great deal of the funds which were employed on 'corruption' were in fact the wages and salaries of the clerks and other employees in the government offices.

Furthermore, members of Parliament in those days received no salaries or expense allowances—a situation which may be compared with the present, when every M.P. has a vested interest to the value of several thousand pounds per annum in seeing that his seat is not put at risk too often at a general election. Not only are our M.P.s paid, but there are about a hundred appointments in the administration which carry with them very much larger salaries. When Walpole was ministry-making, he had only a dozen or so of such appointments at his disposal.

As for the bribery of the individual electors, this continued well into mid-Victorian times, even later than Macaulay would suggest. Indeed, it may be argued that every general election since 1832 has been an exercise in mass bribery. It is forbidden, on pain of severe penalties, to slip coin of the realm into an outstretched palm, but there is nothing to prevent a political party soliciting the votes of millions by promises of social benefits, jobs, houses, and a whole heap more of the most tangible benefits.

One of the sayings most frequently attributed to Walpole, and for which he is so generally reprimanded is, 'Every man has his price'. In fact, he did not say this, although he said something like it. His actual words seem to have been, 'All *these* men have their price', when he was referring to some men of high and lofty pretensions but with itchy palms, who had been loudly declaiming against him.

There is something else that he said, and there is no doubt about it this time, since his son Horace tells that he often heard it from his lips. This was the maxim, '*Quieta non movere*', which may be translated, 'Don't disturb things at rest', or more simply, 'Let sleeping dogs lie'.

While George I lived, Walpole's career was one of uninterrupted prosperity. In 1725 he was given the red ribbon of a Knight of the Bath, and a year later the even higher distinction of the blue ribbon of the Garter, the first commoner to become K.G. since 1660. More than once he was offered a peerage, but he knew better than to allow himself to be pushed upstairs into the House of Lords. On the other hand, he preferred peers as Cabinet colleagues, and as often as not he was the only commoner in the Government.

Then George I died in 1727 during a visit to Hanover. The news reached Walpole a few days later, and he at once mounted his horse and rode down to Richmond, where the Prince of Wales was in residence at the Lodge. It seems to have been the general rule among the Hanoverians for father and son to be deadly enemies, and Walpole had been so closely attached to George I that he cannot have looked forward with equanimity to his first interview with George II. When he arrived at Richmond Lodge he asked to see the prince, but was informed that he had just dined and, as was his rule, had retired to his bedroom with Princess Caroline and must not be disturbed. Walpole insisted on being announced, whereupon the princess emerged, probably rather flustered, and urged him to await her husband's pleasure. But Walpole was not to be denied. He pushed open the bedroom door and fell on his knees before the little man lying on the bed. 'I am Sir Robert Walpole,' he said, 'and I have the honour to announce to your Majesty that your royal father died at Osnaburg last Saturday . . .'

'Dat is one big lie!' roared the prince in a rage, and it was some time before he could be convinced. Then he conducted himself most ungraciously. 'Go to Chiswick and take your directions from Sir Spencer Compton,' were his instructions; and Walpole, feeling no doubt that his career was very definitely at stake, bowed and went away to do as he was bade.

Because of their complete estrangement, the Prince of Wales had maintained a separate court from his father's, and in this establishment Sir Spencer was Treasurer. He was also Speaker of the House of Commons. His thoughts must have been very different from Walpole's. His master was now king, and he seems to have been quite of the opinion that he was the Prime Minister designate.

When Sir Robert waited on him at his Chiswick villa, he accorded Sir Spencer every courtesy and consideration. Might he be of any possible assistance to Sir Spencer, he inquired? Well, yes, came the reply, there was something he might do. Since Sir Robert had more experience of this sort of thing, perhaps he would be so good as to draft the speech which his Majesty would be giving to his Privy Council when he met them for the first time.

After a moment's hesitation, Walpole withdrew into an adjoining room and penned the draft, not forgetting to include a few lines of complimentary allusion to the way in which the previous Government—his Government—had conducted the nation's affairs.

Sir Spencer graciously accepted the paper, made a copy of it in his own handwriting, and took this along to the king. His Majesty read it through, approved it with only one slight alteration (which Compton consulted Walpole about, so as to get it right), and delivered it to his council in due course.

For the next few days Sir Spencer's sun appeared to be in the ascendant, and Walpole's to be sinking fast. Leicester House, the residence of the Prince of Wales, which in the late king's time had been shunned like the plague, was now thronged with visitors. If Walpole put in an appearance he was given the cold shoulder by men who only a short time before sought his favour; Compton, for his part, was condescending, full of smiles and promises.

But then in the council chamber at St. James's the question of money came up. Compton proposed that the new queen's jointure should be settled at £60,000 per annum. Walpole was on his feet at once: he offered to ask Parliament to grant Queen Caroline £100,000, and this was agreed. Then arose the question of the grant to be made to the king himself. George I had received £700,000, and Compton proposed that George II should receive the same. Walpole bobbed up again, and suggested it be increased to £800,000. The new terms were accepted, and the king turned to Walpole and took his hand.

'Consider, Sir Robert,' he said, 'what makes *me* easy in this matter will prove to your ease too; it is for my life it is to be fixed, and it is for your life too.'

As Walpole left the palace with a friend their way lay through St. James's Square, where Sir Spencer Compton's mansion was receiving a throng of courtiers. 'Did you observe', said Walpole to his companion as they went past, 'how *my* house is deserted, and how *that* door is crowded with carriages? Tomorrow this house will be deserted, and mine will be frequented more than ever.'

Before the news had leaked out, Lady Walpole went to Leicester House to pay her respects to the new queen. She was cold-shouldered as her husband had been. Then Queen Caroline saw her across the room and called out to her. 'I think I see a friend,' said the queen, for all to hear, and she received Lady Walpole most kindly. 'As I came away,' said the latter afterwards, 'I might have walked over their heads if I had pleased.'

So Walpole was confirmed in his office, and very soon he had established even better relations with the new sovereign than he had enjoyed with his father. As for Compton, he did become Prime Minister eventually, as we shall see; but not for a long time yet.

*   *   *

For fifteen years more, Walpole remained at the head of affairs as Prime Minister. For the first three years he shared power with his brother-in-law Townshend, but their relationship was to become less and less cordial. 'As long as the firm was Townshend and Walpole,' said Walpole later, 'the utmost harmony prevailed, but it no sooner became Walpole and Townshend than things went wrong.' As Walpole grew older he found it ever more difficult to brook a rival, and in 1730 Townshend, after a bitter quarrel between them, relinquished his appointments and retired to his estates at Raynham, in Norfolk, not far from Walpole's Houghton. There he spent the evening of his life in country pursuits, and it is to his credit that, unlike most of those who fell out with Walpole, he never joined in the opposition against him.

Now the 'firm' was Walpole alone, and things did not go so well as before. For years Walpole had been able to treat the House of Commons almost with indifference, but now a noisy and numerous opposition developed. Some were young men, inexperienced and impatient, others were former ministers skilled in intrigue—something that Walpole scorned—and smarting under rebuffs or refusals of the plums of office. One party among them boasted of the name of 'Patriots'. Walpole turned all his artillery on them.

'A patriot, sir?' he said in the House once. 'Why, patriots spring up like mushrooms! I could raise fifty of them within four-and-twenty hours. I have raised many of them in one night. It is but refusing to gratify an unreasonable or an insolent demand, and up starts a patriot.'

Those newcomers to the House who assailed him with their invective he dubbed 'the Boys': a leader amongst these was William Pitt, whose abilities Walpole did not appreciate until too late.

The House of Commons became increasingly restive and uncooperative. In 1733 Walpole's proposal to put an end to tobacco smuggling by putting a tax on tobacco when it was sold instead of when it was imported—in other words, an excise duty instead of a customs one—was so strongly resisted that it had to be withdrawn. The Gin Act of 1736 was a most praiseworthy attempt to grapple with what had become a national scandal, but the excise duty of 5s. per gallon that it imposed was furiously condemned as an unwarrantable interference with the right of a man to get drunk if he pleased. The Act gave rise to rioting and large-scale evasion, and it was left to Walpole's successors to bring the situation under control.

Another blow to his administration was the mishandling of the Porteous Riots in Edinburgh in 1736, the story of which is so admirably told in Sir Walter Scott's novel, *The Heart of Midlothian*.

In this and many another matter of policy, Walpole found a firm friend and supporter in Queen Caroline, and it was a grievous blow to him when she died in the winter of 1737. Walpole at least knew something of her real worth. In one of his letters to her he wrote, ' If I have the merit of giving good advice to the king, all the merit of making him take it, Madam, is entirely your own, and so much so, that I not only never did anything without you, but I know I never could.' Her dying words to him were, ' I recommend the king, and my children, and the kingdom to your care.'

Deprived of his best friend at court, Walpole was attacked with ever-increasing vigour and animosity by a host of foes—Patriots and Boys, and the fragments of the Tory party, all of whom found a rallying-point in the Prince of Wales. His hold on the House of Commons began to weaken. Elections went against him, and he found that the secret-service money did not go so far as it used to do in buying votes. His peace policy, sustained for so long and with such success, came under heavy fire. The king was thirsting for British intervention in the continental struggles, and the trading and moneyed interests which had been so long Walpole's main support were now shouting for war against Spain, whose South American colonies were closed against British traders. Horrible things were alleged to be happening over there. One day in 1738 an English merchant captain named Robert Jenkins put in an appearance at the bar of the House of Commons and complained that when trading from Jamaica he had been boarded by Spanish coastguards, who accused him of smuggling; he had been imprisoned and tortured and had an ear torn off. The members were greatly impressed when he produced what he alleged was the ear out of his pocket and offered to show it round. (Some unkind people said that if he had lost an ear it was in the pillory.)

Many years of peace had given rise to boredom. The public demand for war grew, and at length was irresistible. To his lasting discredit, Walpole, much against his will and altogether against his judgment, declared war on Spain at the end of October 1739.

When this was announced, the people received it with a frenzy of enthusiasm. But there was no gladness in Walpole's heart. 'Ah! they are ringing the bells today,' he muttered, 'but they will soon be wringing their hands.'

Of course, he ought to have resigned—he who throughout his political career had stood for peace. Why didn't he? Macaulay thought he knew the answer. 'No person was more thoroughly convinced than he of the absurdity of the cry against Spain,' he wrote in his essay on Horace Walpole. 'But his darling power was at stake, and his choice was soon made. He preferred an unjust war to a stormy session.'

A harsh judgment, and whatever substance there may be in it there were other reasons for Walpole's holding on. We may be sure that one of them was the conviction that, if war must come, then he could carry it on with more economy and less danger to the State than his rivals. Another, doubtless, was his sense of loyalty to the king.

George II had very soon outgrown the suspicions of Walpole with which he had begun his reign. The more he knew of him, the better he appreciated his excellent qualities, and in particular his courage. 'Walpole is a brave fellow,' he would say with an oath, ' he has more spirit than any man I ever knew.' He bestowed on the Prime Minister many marks of special favour, and it is worth recalling that among these was No. 10 Downing Street.

This sombre-looking mansion in a side street off Whitehall, one of four houses built in 1681 by George Downing—an Irish adventurer who was clever enough to serve as one of Cromwell's ambassadors and then at the Restoration to get a job at the Exchequer (where Pepys was his grumbling clerk) and be knighted by Charles II— was offered to Walpole by George II in 1731 as a personal present. Walpole declined it as such, but it was agreed between them that in future it should go with the office of First Lord of the Treasury. Walpole moved there in 1735 from his house in St. James's Square, and he lived at No. 10 until his resignation in 1742 when he removed to a house in Arlington Street.

The king's obvious partiality towards Walpole was one of the things that most incensed his rivals, but he retained the royal confidence even when he had become the object of popular execration. Walpole is said to have tendered his resignation but the king begged him to stay. 'Will you desert me in my greatest difficulties?' he said appealingly—and so Walpole stayed.

Before long British troops and ships were heavily engaged in various parts of the world, and generally with inglorious results. Great peace ministers make indifferent war ministers as a rule, and Walpole was no exception. His heart was not in the war, and yet, as he was heard to mutter, ' I dare not do what is right.'

The opposition—the opposition which he had himself created, through his jealousy of ability in others, his deep-seated reluctance to share his ' darling power '—intensified their efforts. In 1740 a motion appeared on the order-paper in the House of Commons urging that the king should be petitioned to remove Sir Robert Walpole '. . . from his Majesty's presence and counsels for ever ', and although this was negatived by a large majority the Prime Minister's position was shaken. At the general election in the next year a number of members were returned who were hostile to his regime, and when the new Parliament met the attack was pressed home.

The end came on 2 February 1742. The occasion of the great Minister's fall was nothing more than a miserable little affair of a disputed election. At Chippenham the bribery and corruption had been rather more in evidence than usual, and the House of Commons were called upon to decide whether Mr. Rolt, the candidate supported by the Opposition, should be allowed to take his seat. The Government favoured his opponent, and it was soon clear that they were heading for defeat.

As the fatal division was being taken, the Prime Minister sat and watched the procession of hostile members with his unfailing equanimity. Then he beckoned to Rolt to come and sit beside him. ' Young man,' he said, ' I will tell you the history of all your friends as they come in. That fellow I saved from the gallows, and that from starvation; this man's sons I promoted . . .', and so forth.

The vote went against the Government, and amid the wild cheers of his opponents Walpole, erect and calm, rose from his seat, bowed to the Speaker's chair, and (as Lord Morley relates it) '. . . walked away for the last time out of that famous chamber, where for forty years he had laboured so assiduously for the national good, which had witnessed so many of his triumphs, which had been the scene of so long and undaunted a struggle against his most formidable enemies, and for which finally he had acquired new prerogatives and an immovable supremacy in the constitution of the kingdom '.

A few days later it was published in the *London Gazette* that Sir Robert Walpole had resigned all his offices and had been created Earl of Orford. It was arranged that he should receive a pension of £4,000 a year. Also his illegitimate daughter by his mistress

Miss Skerrit (see below) was given the rank of an earl's daughter. Lady Mary Walpole, as the girl was now styled, was received at court shortly afterwards.

From his seat in the House of Lords, the new Earl of Orford looked down with amusement on the struggle for power. He maintained his good humour when he heard the shouting that he should be brought to trial for peculation, that he should be impeached for misgovernment, that he ought to be sent to the Tower, that it would only be what he deserved if he were hanged.... In March the House of Commons appointed a committee to inquire into his alleged misdeeds. Of its twenty-one members only two were of his own party, and it is hardly surprising that the report which was eventually drawn up and presented to the House was unfavourable. But Walpole still had plenty of friends, and before long the proceedings against him were quietly dropped.

Behind the scenes the fallen minister still maintained his influence on affairs, and he was successful in discrediting and so excluding from the supreme office the most formidable of his competitors. The second premier was a nonentity, the Sir Spencer Compton (now Earl of Wilmington) who fifteen years before had had his brief moment of glorious expectation. For the time being, at least, Walpole still pulled the strings.

*　　　　　*　　　　　*

Sir Robert Walpole was such a dominating personality in his day and generation that we are fully justified in speaking of the Age of Walpole. No man was more frequently described, nor so intimately discussed. Take up any volume of the memoirs of the time—and that was the age *par excellence* of memoir-writers—and his name crops up on page after page. Of course this is specially so in the writings of Horace Walpole, and particular interest attaches to the ' Parallel ' which Horace draws between his father and Henry Pelham (next but one in the succession of Prime Ministers), generally very much to the latter's disadvantage.

In this we are told that Sir Robert was bold, open, steady, never dejected; he loved power so much that he would not endure a rival; his eloquence was made for use—he never would shine but when it was necessary that he should; he loved magnificence, chiefly confined his friendships to such persons as were below him, and ' was forgiving to a fault—if forgiveness can be faulty '. Then we have the remarkable admission that Walpole ' durst do right—and durst do wrong too '.

Of even greater interest, perhaps, is what Lord Hervey says about Walpole in his *Memoirs of the Reign of George II.* Hervey knew Walpole well, both as a politician and as a courtier. For some years he was one of his supporters in the House of Commons, and it was through Walpole that he got his barony in 1733. As a writer, Lord Hervey must be given a high place in his special field of literature, since he had absolutely no inhibitions. In his pages he reveals a society living with tremendous zest, robust and raw, vigorous and vicious. So lively and scandalous is the writing, so witty and cruel its satire, that it is not surprising that the book did not appear until 1848, when Hervey and all the people he had stabbed at had long been dead. As for Hervey himself, it may suffice to note that when Alexander Pope introduced into one of his satirical pieces the figure of Sporus, the boy-lover of the Roman emperor Nero, his readers were left in no doubt that it was Lord Hervey he had in mind:

> This painted child of dirt, that stinks and stings;
> Whose buzz the witty and the fair annoys,
> Yet wit ne'er tastes, and beauty ne'er enjoys . . .

Writing in the privacy of his study, without any intention of letting the world see what he had written, this rather unpleasant homosexual made a penetrating analysis of the great statesman whom he had so often encountered and observed so closely, not only in the great world but in what may be termed undress.

Sir Robert Walpole, he begins, 'had a strength of parts equal to any advancement, a spirit to struggle with any difficulties, a steadiness of temper immovable by any disappointments'. Then, after mentioning Walpole's great skill in figures and extensive knowledge of finance, he proceeds:

'The weight of the whole administration lay on him; every project was of his forming, conducting and executing . . . and, considering the little assistance he received from subalterns, it is incredible what a variety and quantity of business he dispatched. . . . No man ever was blessed with a clearer head, a truer or quicker judgment, or a deeper insight into mankind; he knew the strength and weakness of everybody he had to deal with, and how to make his advantage of both. He had more warmth of affection and friendship for some particular people than one could have believed it possible for any one who had been so long raking in the dirt of mankind to be capable of feeling for so worthless a species of animal . . .'

Walpole was 'not one of those projecting systematical great

Britain's first Prime Minister was Sir Robert Walpole, and here we see him (above left)—portly and commanding, splendidly dressed and with the Garter ribbon across his chest—as he appeared in 1737 to the French portrait painter J. B. Vanloo.

Never was there a finer actor on the stage of politics than William Pitt (above right), the 'Great Commoner' who became an earl. In this portrait of him in earl's robes the gesture is theatric and there is fire latent in the hawk-like eyes.

Lord North (left), 'heavy, large, and much inclined to corpulency', possessed of an equanimity that only the worst disasters could shake.

Chatham's last speech in the House of Lords, as depicted by the American artist J. S. Copley. Inaudible for the most part, the dying statesman roused himself in a final spirited protest against the dismemberment of the Empire that he had done so much to build. Right: William Pitt the Younger, as Hoppner saw him—a portrait that his friend William Wilberforce found all too distressingly lifelike. Below: Spencer Perceval, shot in the lobby of the House of Commons—the only Prime Minister to meet a violent end.

geniuses who are always thinking in theory, and are above common practice '; he knew that ' those must often be disappointed who build on the certainty of the most probable events ', and so seldom turned his thoughts to warding off future evils which might or might not happen or the scheming of remote advantages, ' but always applied himself to the present occurrence, studying and generally hitting upon the properest method to improve what was favourable, and the best expedient to extricate himself out of what was difficult '.

' In all occurrences, and at all times, and in all difficulties, he was constantly cheerful . . . Whether his negligence of his enemies, and never stretching his power to gratify his resentment of the sharpest injury, was policy or constitution, I shall not determine; but I do not believe anybody who knows these times will deny that no minister was ever more outraged, or less apparently revengeful . . .

' There never was any minister to whom access was so easy and so frequent, nor whose answers were more explicit. He knew how to oblige when he bestowed, and not to shock when he denied; to govern without oppressing, and conquer without triumph.

' He pursued his ambition without curbing his pleasures, and his pleasures without neglecting his business; he did the latter with ease, and indulged himself in the other without giving scandal or offence. In private life, and to all who had any dependence upon him, he was kind and indulgent; he was generous without ostentation, and an economist without penuriousness; not insolent in success, nor irresolute in distress; faithful to his friends, and not inveterate to his foes.'

What kind of a *man* was Walpole ? A big, burly, boisterous fellow, with a big laugh. ' It would have done you good to hear him laugh ', said his son Horace; and another who knew him well spoke of his ' heart's laugh '. One of the finest tributes to him was penned by Alexander Pope, who hated his politics and was not too kindly disposed to him personally:

> Seen him I have; but in his happier hour
> Of social pleasure ill-exchanged for power;
> Seen him uncumbered with the venal tribe,
> Smile without art and win without a bribe.
> Would he oblige me ? Let me only find
> He does not think me what he thinks mankind.
> (*Epilogue to the Satires*)

Country sports and pastimes were always his delight. Until

almost to the end of his days he rode regularly to hounds. George II despised foxhunters: he said that the poor fox was generally a much better beast than those who pursued him, since he inflicted hurt only for subsistence, while they did it just for the pleasure they got out of it; but he forgave Walpole his indulgence in this deplorable relaxation. When he received his post-bag of a morning, the first letter he looked for was from his gamekeeper.

Beyond a doubt, Walpole was a coarse-fibred man. As we have noted, he was a heavy drinker, but we may be sure that he never allowed himself to become fuddled when serious business was afoot. In conversation, he was inclined to be broad. It is to Dr. Johnson that we owe the reminiscence that ' Sir Robert Walpole said he always talked bawdy at his table, because in that all could join '. What we are told of his talk with Queen Caroline suggests a degree of intimacy far transcending that of simple friendship. It might also be cruelly frank, as when he advised this middle-aged and no longer pretty woman that if she wished to continue to exercise control over her husband she must cease to rely upon the charms of her person and concentrate on her intelligence—that, he said, would never fail her. He also counselled her not only to tolerate but to encourage her husband's turning to mistresses—a matter in which she did not perhaps need much prompting, since she must have often been bored to distraction by the king's commonplace chatter, whether in the boudoir or in bed.

Lord Chesterfield declared that Walpole's ' prevailing weakness was to be thought to have a polite and happy turn to gallantry ', and that this was his ' favourite and frequent subject of conversation '. So generally was this recognized, that those ' who had any penetration ' played up to it with success. His amorous boastings were thought extraordinarily funny, and in one of the vulgar squibs that have been preserved we may read how Walpole,

> . . . to divert the sneering town,
> Is next a general lover grown,
> Affects to talk of his amours,
> And boasts of having ruined scores,
> While all who hear him bite the lip,
> And scarce with pain their laughter keep . . .

Of his mistresses the best known was Molly, or Maria, Skerrit whom he eventually made his second wife. She is said to have been the daughter of a London merchant, and to have been twenty-two when the affair between them began about 1724. Walpole is said to have paid her £5,000 ' by way of entrance money '. After about a year a child was born of the liaison, who was named after her mother.

Molly was the first of Walpole's mistresses to feature largely in gossip, and he seems to have really loved her. There is a passage in Lord Hervey's *Memoirs* that bears this out. It reports a conversation Hervey had with Queen Caroline in 1735, which began with the queen's remarking that she had never seen Sir Robert ' so much struck and cast down ', and that she supposed he was worried about some political matter. Whereupon Hervey told her that Sir Robert's concern was really about ' his mistress, Miss Skerrit, who was extremely ill of pleuritic fever, and in great danger '. Lord Hervey goes on:

' The Queen was glad to hear his embarassment thus accounted for, and began to talk on Sir Robert's attachment to this woman, asking Lord Hervey many questions about Miss Skerrit's beauty and understanding, and her lover's fondness and weakness towards her. She said she was very glad he had any amusement for his leisure hours, but could neither comprehend how a man could be very fond of a woman he only got for his money, nor how a man of Sir Robert's age and make, with his dirty mouth and great belly, could ever imagine any woman would suffer him as a lover from any consideration but his money. " She must be a clever gentlewoman," continued the Queen, " to have made him believe she cares for him on any other score; and to show you what fools we all are in some point or other, she has certainly told him some fine story of her love and her passion, and that poor man believes her. My God! What is human nature! " '

Walpole's eagerness to secure the rangership of Richmond Park has been ascribed to his desire to provide his mistress with a convenient country retreat. The Old Lodge in the park was rebuilt and refurnished in a style to form a ' bower of bliss ' (Hervey's phrase), at a cost of £14,500, and Walpole spent his weekends there with Molly and their little daughter. As early as 1727 Molly was holding a sinecure appointment bringing in £400 per annum, and others were added until in 1735 she was in enjoyment of about a thousand a year out of public money. This continued until 1738 when, Lady Walpole having died the year before, Walpole was at length able to marry her. She was received at court without delay or demur, but three months afterwards she died of a miscarriage.

Providing in this way for his mistress, it is not surprising that he used his official position to benefit members of his family, as well as himself. He secured the grant to himself of the post of Collector of the Customs, worth nearly £2,000 a year; and the patent provided that it should continue for the lives of his sons Robert and Edward. His eldest son was made Clerk of the Pells, another sinecure, with £3,000 a year, and later this was exchanged for the post of Auditor of the Exchequer, with a salary of more than twice as much, when the clerkship of the Pells was passed on to the next brother. Nor was Horace Walpole, the youngest son, left unprovided for. When he was still a boy his father got him appointed Clerk of the Estreats and Controller of the Pipe, a job with a salary of £300 a year attached to it but no duties worth mentioning; and when Horace was nineteen he was made Usher of the Exchequer. This was worth £900 a year, but not all of this was profit. The Usher had to furnish the clerks with paper, pens, sealing-wax, sand (for blotting), pen-knives (for sharpening their quill pens), and scissors. Horace saw nothing at all wrong in this. With no little complacence he informs us that from the age of twenty he was no burden at all on his family.

All the same, Walpole was not without his critics, and abuse of official patronage was only one of the charges brought against him. Most formidable was the accusation that he was dipping his hands into the public till. That 'palace' that he was erecting at Houghton in place of the house he had inherited—where did he get the money to pay for the new buildings, for his splendid picture-gallery and its contents, the landscaped gardens with their fountains and ornamental waters? According to the popular rumour, he had made large purchases of land in Norfolk; he had huge holdings of government stock; he had invested £150,000 in jewels and plate; he had transferred £400,000 in a single year to his accounts with bankers in Amsterdam, Genoa, and Vienna. Where had he got it all? To quote one of the lampoons that were current about him:

> But a few years ago,
> As we very well know,
> He scarce had a guinea his fob in;
> But by bribing of friends,
> To serve his dark ends,
> Now worth a full million is Robin.

How far were they justified, these allegations? It is impossible to say for sure; but while it may be allowed that Walpole was far from being scrupulous, he had other ways of filling his purse than jobbery. He was a large landed proprietor, and since he came into his property his rent-roll had increased from £2,000 to £5,000 a year. His first wife brought him a dowry of £7,000. His official emoluments from the various posts he held amounted (it has been estimated) to an average of £9,000 a year. He was also a successful speculator, as in the South Sea Company's stock. Admittedly his housekeeping expenses must have been enormous, when we have in mind those 'hunting congresses' at Houghton which involved keeping open house to half the county for weeks at a time. But even so, there should surely have been a substantial balance on the right side?

And yet, when he died, he was deeply in debt. There was a big mortgage outstanding on Houghton Hall, and his other debts amounted to £50,000. So heavily encumbered was his estate that in 1779 his grandson had to sell most of his pictures (which had cost Walpole £40,000) to the Empress Catherine of Russia, who hung them in the Hermitage palace at St. Petersburg.

So a big question-mark remains.

*   *   *

Not long after his retirement from office, Walpole's health began to fail and he withdrew to Houghton, where he tried to occupy himself with his pictures and gardens. He would have liked to take pleasure in reading, since, as he told a friend, '. . . it would be the means of alleviating many tedious hours; but, to my misfortune, I derive no pleasure from such pursuits'.

His last public appearance was in the House of Lords on the last day of February in 1744, when he expressed his grave concern over a report that a French fleet was prowling in the Channel and that the young Prince Charles Edward, the Young Pretender, son of the Prince James Edward (the Old Pretender) whom the Whigs had excluded from the throne so many years before, had arrived in France to join it.

On leaving the Lords he returned to his house in Arlington Street, but as soon as he felt fit enough he went back to Norfolk. He remained at Houghton until November, when in answer to repeated solicitations he proceeded to London. He was suffering agonies with the stone, and spent four dreadful days on the road. He arrived at length, and was consulted by the king and his ministers. Then he was obliged to undergo several operations, which he endured with unbroken fortitude. He died at his house in Arlington Street on 18 March 1745.

'His constancy, his courage, his temper, his unfailing resource, his love of peace, his gifts of management and debate, his long reign of prosperity will always maintain Walpole in the highest rank of statesmen ', wrote Lord Rosebery in a fine passage of his book on Chatham. ' Distinguished even in death, he rests under the bare and rustic pavement of Houghton Church, in face of the palace that he had reared and cherished, without so much as an initial to mark his grave. This is the blank end of so much honour, adulation, power, and renown . . .'

2

THE EARL OF WILMINGTON

THE MAN who stepped into Walpole's shoes was Spencer Compton, the Earl of Wilmington. Born in 1673 or thereabouts, he was a son of James Compton, third Earl of Northampton. The Comptons were an old and wealthy family settled in the Midlands. In the civil wars of the seventeenth century they had been Royalists, but in 1688 they switched from James II to William of Orange and it was one of Spencer Compton's uncles who, as Bishop of London, crowned William and his consort in Westminster Abbey.

Spencer Compton lost his father early, but he had influential friends and in 1698 he entered the House of Commons as member for the Suffolk borough of Eye. He at once identified himself with the Whigs, and became one of Walpole's closest friends and supporters. He was not brilliant, but he was a hard worker and set himself to master the intricacies of parliamentary procedure; with the result that in 1714, when the Whigs formed their government, he was chosen to be Speaker of the House of Commons. On the whole, he performed his duties competently enough. Not much is recorded of his tenure of office, but there is one incident that suggests that he was not without a sense of humour.

A member who had bored the House with his long-windedness, and was talked down in consequence, complained to Mr. Speaker that he had a right to be heard. 'No, sir,' rejoined Sir Spencer, 'you have a right to *speak*, but the House has the right to judge whether it will *hear* you.'

In addition to being Speaker, Compton was Treasurer to the Prince of Wales, and in 1722 he received from Walpole the much coveted post of Paymaster-General. Thus he was at one and the same time in favour with both court and Commons, and when the Prince of Wales became king in 1727, his expectations must have been great. When Walpole came to him with the message from the new sovereign—that he was to take his instructions from Sir Spencer—his appointment to the highest office seemed certain.

But nothing came of it, and it is very likely that the king had never had any real intention of making Compton the new premier.

He had had abundant opportunities of getting to know his Treasurer, and his opinion of his character may not have been very different from that sketched by Lord Hervey in his *Memoirs*.

'He was a plodding, heavy fellow,' Hervey writes, 'with great application, but no talents. He was always more concerned for the manner and the form in which a thing was to be done than about the propriety or expediency of the thing itself; and as he was calculated to execute rather than to project, for a subaltern rather than a commander, so he was much fitter for a clerk to a minister than for a minister to a Prince. Whatever was resolved upon he would often know how properly to perform, but seldom how to advise what was proper to be resolved upon. His only pleasures were money and eating; his only knowledge of forms and precedents, and his only insinuations bows and smiles.'

Before his accession, the king had not had much personal contact with Walpole, and that contact had not been altogether agreeable. But he was a shrewd judge of men, and Walpole was confirmed in the premiership.

Something was done for Sir Spencer, however. In the circumstances it was thought hardly right to ask him to continue to preside as Speaker over a House in which Walpole was to remain the dominating figure, and so he was 'kicked out' (Hervey's expression) of the Commons into the Lords as Lord Wilmington, and shortly afterwards his barony was converted into an earldom. He was also appointed Lord Privy Seal, and then Lord President of the Council. In 1733 he was installed a knight of the Garter. He was rich. He had a fine house in St. James's Square and a villa at Chiswick. He was a bachelor, with no family cares. On the face of it, his lot seemed an enviable one but he could not forget that he had come very near to being Prime Minister. He knew who had been responsible for the mischance. 'He hated Sir Robert in his heart,' Hervey tells us, 'and though he did not dare to speak against him himself he approved and caressed those who did.'

All the same, it is on record that on one occasion, when Wilmington was in bed with an attack of fever, he insisted on getting up and going to Westminster to record his vote for his hard-pressed leader.

Walpole had no doubt summed him up pretty accurately, but he was quite ready to make use of his talents, such as they were, although in private he might refer to him in most uncomplimentary terms. ' " Old woman " is the most honourable title I have heard is given to him by those who are most my enemies,' he said once. Horace

Walpole wrote that Lord Wilmington was ' the most solemn, formal man in the world, but a great lover of private debauchery '. Lord Hervey says that the royal princesses nicknamed him ' Privy Nasy ', and he describes how, ' with his open mouth, his eyes half shut . . . grinning horrible a ghastly smile, I hear him (snorting, belching all the while) tell you that " two and two " he's sure " makes four ".'

In 1739, when Walpole's position showed signs of weakening, Wilmington's name was canvassed as a possible successor. Nothing came of it then, but when three years later the great minister was at length brought down, none of those who had engineered his downfall were particularly keen on taking his place, and the king sent for Lord Wilmington. He gladly accepted the charge of forming an administration, and soon succeeded in doing so. Within sight of his seventieth year, he had at last realized his great ambition.

But after all, it was something of an anti-climax. On the face of it, there had been a political revolution; as Lord Rosebery describes it in his book on Lord Chatham, ' There is a great crash, and the spectators expect to see the world in ruins. But when the dust has cleared away it is seen that things are much as they were; Wilmington, scarcely visible, in Walpole's seat; Walpole . . . seated smug and dumb among the distant peers.' Wilmington was Prime Minister, but Walpole was the power behind the throne.

Lord Wilmington had formed his government in February 1742. Before many months had passed his health began to fail, and he was unable to transact any business. Towards the end of the year he left London for Bath. There he fell ill, and became steadily worse until his death on 26 July 1743.

3

HENRY PELHAM

AFTER SOME WEEKS of busy intrigue among the Whigs there emerged as Prime Minister the younger of two brothers who had long been eminent in the party's ranks. This was Henry Pelham; his elder brother was Thomas Pelham, Duke of Newcastle, who, as we shall see, also has his place among the Prime Ministers.

Only a generation or two before, the Pelhams had been quiet country gentlemen in Sussex. The great improvement in their fortunes was owing to a succession of marriages which brought them great wealth and also influential connections among the political aristocracy.

Thomas Pelham was born in 1693, and his brother Henry two years later. They were the sons of Thomas Pelham, of Halland Place, in Sussex, who after representing that county in the House of Commons for many years as a good Whig was created Lord Pelham in 1706. On his death in 1712 he was succeeded in the title by his elder son Thomas, who the year before had inherited large estates from his maternal uncle John Holles, Duke of Newcastle. Two years later Queen Anne died, and young Lord Pelham came out strongly in support of George I. His services on this occasion, and the fact that he was one of the largest landowners in the country, marked him out for advancement and in 1714, when he had just come of age, he was created Earl of Clare, and in the following year became the new Duke of Newcastle. The Garter followed in 1718, and in the same year he increased his already great influence among the Whigs by marrying Henrietta Godolphin, granddaughter of the great Duke of Marlborough.

Meanwhile Henry Pelham, with whom we are concerned in this chapter, had likewise been making his mark, although as the younger brother he had nothing like so many splendid prizes thrust into his hands. He had gone to Westminster school with his brother, and then on to Oxford while Thomas was at Cambridge. In 1715 there occurred the Jacobite rebellion and the brothers raised a troop of horse among their tenantry in Sussex. Thomas stayed at home but Henry, as a captain in Dormer's regiment, was under fire in the skirmish at Preston.

After Preston, Henry travelled for some time on the Continent, and on his return home was elected M.P. for the little borough of Seaford. He attached himself firmly to Walpole, and when in the next year Walpole became Prime Minister he appointed young Henry Pelham to a minor office in the administration. In 1725 he was given the much more worth-while post of Paymaster to the Forces, and it is notable that, unlike most of those who held that particular office, he was scrupulously honest and never guilty of graft. This was perhaps the more surprising in that he was a confirmed gambler, and lost considerable sums at the gaming-tables. In 1726 he married Lady Catherine Manners, daughter of the Duke of Rutland, and his brother Thomas, who was also doing very well in politics, made over to him half the property inherited from their father.

Now well supplied with funds, Henry purchased the mansion of Esher Place, in Surrey, about a mile from his brother's great house of Claremont beside the Portsmouth Road. The grounds at both were taken in hand by William Kent, founder of the English school of landscape gardening, and were provided with artificial waters, grottoes, stone ornaments and other romantic embellishments. But Parliament was where his real interests lay, and he comported himself there with courage, hardihood, and resource. In the fierce struggle over the Excise Bill he supported Walpole steadfastly, and one day he was required to render him assistance of another kind.

After the last debate on the bill, Sir Robert Walpole and Mr. Pelham left the House together, and as they passed through the lobby were surrounded by a mob of political opponents. When they had nearly reached the top of the steps leading to Alice's coffee-house, one fellow seized hold of Sir Robert's cloak, and as the collar was tightly fastened nearly throttled him. At this moment Pelham pushed Sir Robert into the passage leading to the coffee-house, and with drawn sword took up his place at the entrance, exclaiming in a resolute tone, 'Now, gentlemen, who will be the first to fall?' The assailants were cowed, and slunk away.

Lord Hervey says that 'Mr. Pelham was strongly attached to Sir Robert Walpole, and more personally beloved by him than any man in England'.

When Walpole resigned, Pelham was offered the post of Chancellor of the Exchequer under Lord Wilmington but he declined it, preferring to keep his old position at the Pay Office, with the leadership of the House of Commons. Walpole told him that he thought he had made a mistake: 'Lost opportunities are not easily retrieved,' he remarked sententiously. But Pelham was far-seeing, or perhaps just fortunate. Lord Wilmington died within a year, and Henry Pelham, with Walpole's backing, became Prime Minister. A year later he reconstructed his ministry on a broader basis, including in it not only the principal Whigs but a few Tories. For this reason it is usually referred to as 'the broad-bottom administration'. Most of the members of the Cabinet were dukes, and Pelham (who was a duke's brother) was the only member of the House of Commons in it. With an interval of only a few days, when he resigned to get his own way in face of the king's disapproval of a ministerial appointment, Pelham was Prime Minister until his death.

Mention has been made earlier of the famous 'Parallel' that Horace Walpole drew between his father and Pelham. The memoirist clearly had no very high opinion of the latter. He describes him as being timorous, reserved, fickle, apt to despair; a lover of power so well that he would endure anything rather than lose it; an obscure speaker, who had to 'lose his temper before he could exercise his reason'; a man of 'the most pride, with the least self-confidence', one whose friendships were almost all founded on birth and rank; who 'never forgave, but when he durst not resent'; who was guilty of much ingratitude, and was often deceived 'but not half so often as he suspected it'. Then, as regards corruption, 'Mr. Pelham would never have wet his finger, if Sir Robert Walpole had not dipped up to the elbow; but as he did dip, and as Mr. Pelham was persuaded that it was as necessary for him to be Minister as it was for Sir Robert Walpole, he plunged as deep . . .'

Compare this picture with the one drawn by Lord Waldegrave in his *Memoirs from 1754 to 1758*. Pelham, he writes, 'acquired the reputation of an able and honest minister; had a plain, solid understanding, improved by experience in business, as well as by a thorough knowledge of the world; and without being an orator, or having the finest parts, no man in the House of Commons argued with more weight, or was heard with greater attention. He was a frugal steward to the public, averse to continental extravagance and useless subsidies; preferring a tolerable peace to the most successful war; jealous to maintain his personal credit and authority, but nowise inattentive to the true interest of his country.'

From this it would seem clear that Pelham was by no means the ineffectual sort of fellow Horace Walpole tries to make out. And in point of fact his eleven years' administration was remarkable for a number of social reforms; indeed, in the eighteenth century there is no other administration with a better record in this respect, and it is only reasonable to suppose that Pelham himself had quite a lot to do with it. Very likely he would have done more, if he had not to provide in his budgets for lavish expenditure on a war (the War of the Austrian Succession) which had been forced upon him and which he did his best to bring to an end as soon as possible.

Of his social measures, perhaps the most important was aimed at the frightful evils of excessive gin-drinking. It was in 1751 that Hogarth published his famous plate of *Gin Lane*, in which the beastly degradation of the gin-soaked population of St. Giles's is shown in all its horrific detail. In the same year Pelham's government passed an Act that severely restricted the number of persons entitled to sell gin, and greatly increased the penalties for unlicensed retailing. Sir Robert Walpole had attempted something on these lines years before, and had been worsted by the threat of mob violence: Pelham succeeded where his master had failed.

Also in 1751 was passed the Act that introduced the new calendar into Britain. The matter was entrusted to Lord Chesterfield, who confessed that he knew nothing at all about it but was convinced that it was most necessary. He had the good sense to consult Lord Macclesfield, one of the most eminent mathematicians of the day. Pelham's brother, the Duke of Newcastle, begged Chesterfield not to 'meddle in new-fangled things' and 'not to stir up matters that had long been quiet'. His uneasiness was justified—for years afterwards unpopular politicians were pursued on the hustings by shouts of 'Who stole the eleven days ?', 'Give us back our eleven days ! ', in reference to the fact that to inaugurate the new calendar what would have been the third day of September in 1752 was taken as the fourteenth.

Mention must also be made of Lord Hardwicke's Marriage Act of 1753, which put a stop to the disgraceful scandals of the so-called Fleet marriages. Before the passing of this Act, a valid marriage could be celebrated by a priest in Anglican orders at any time and in any place, without registration and without the consent being obtained of parents or guardians. Atrocious abuses had grown up, and in London the neighbourhood of the Fleet prison was notorious for the numbers of persons (many of them prisoners for debt in the Fleet) who were prepared to perform marriages at a moment's notice, without questions and without a licence. Marriages were performed in public-houses, gin-cellars, attics and brothels, and many a young heiress was trapped into a union that led to a lifetime of shame and degradation. Under Hardwicke's Act no marriages might be celebrated in future (except those of Jews and Quakers) except by a priest in orders and according to the ritual of the Church of England; that banns must have been called in the parish church, and a special licence obtained if this was not observed.

Such measures as these reflect great credit on Pelham's government. But the work of administration was a sore tax on his constitution, which had never been strong. More than once he asked the king if he might retire, but King George had come to rely completely on his minister and would not hear of such a thing. He carried on, therefore, until early in 1754 he caught a chill after walking in St. James's Park and then standing at an open window. The chill developed into erysipelas, or what Lord Chesterfield describes as 'a fever and a mortification, occasioned by general corruption of his whole mass of blood, which had broke out into sores across his back'. On 6 March 1754 he died, suddenly, to the general dismay and grief. The king was very upset. 'Now I shall have no more peace,' he exclaimed.

Writing to his son two days later, Lord Chesterfield paid his own memorial tribute. 'A great and unexpected event has lately happened in our ministerial world,' he wrote. 'Mr. Pelham died last Monday . . . I regret him as an old acquaintance, a pretty near relation, and a private man, with whom I have lived for many years in a social and friendly way. He meaned well to the public, and was incorrupt in a post where corruption is commonly contagious. If he was no shining, enterprising Minister, he was a safe one, which I like better. Very shining Ministers, like the sun, are apt to scorch, when they shine the brightest.'

4

DUKE OF NEWCASTLE

WHEN HENRY PELHAM DIED, his brother Thomas, the Duke of Newcastle, went around telling everybody that he had 'suffered the greatest loss that a man can have', and that he had no other object in mind than 'to endeavour to pursue his late brother's measures, serve his friends, and particularly do everything that can best comfort his poor family'. But while he was making these professions of filial piety he was also busily engaged in securing the succession for himself. He pulled every wire that he could lay his hands on, and it was soon made clear that he had pulled them to advantage. In April 1754 Newcastle was appointed First Lord of the Treasury and Prime Minister.

The duke was no novice. As we have seen in the last chapter, he was born in 1693, and was only twenty-two when he was raised to the highest grade in the British peerage. His first political action was in 1714, when he 'paid a large crowd in the city to halloo for King George'. While his younger brother Henry had been making an honourable career for himself Thomas was also moving steadily up the ministerial ladder. His first political appointment was Lord Chamberlain of the Household in 1717, and then in 1724 Walpole chose him to be Secretary of State in place of Carteret. He held this post for thirty years, under Walpole and Wilmington and Henry Pelham, until now he followed his brother as Prime Minister. He formed his Ministry, for the most part out of Whig peers, and made one blunder, an extraordinary one for such an experienced political hand: he omitted to give any promotion to William Pitt, but merely confirmed him in the position of Paymaster-General, which he had been holding for the past ten years.

Pitt was bitterly offended and joined his friends in attacking the ministry of which he was still a member. Newcastle bore it as long as he could and eventually dismissed his unruly colleague. But Pitt in opposition was even worse than Pitt in office, and Newcastle was overwhelmed with work and worry. The Seven Years' War was going badly. His ministers were a poor lot, and the king was no help at all. In November 1756 he was constrained to resign, and was succeeded by the Duke of Devonshire who had Pitt as his chief lieutenant.

Horace Walpole had been watching the course of events with his usual keenness. It was quite clear to him that Newcastle was in hopes of making a come-back before long. The journals were full of obviously inspired stories to the effect that the fallen minister had quitted office without place or pension; and 'his enormous estate, which had sunk from thirty to thirteen thousand pounds a year, by every ostentatious vanity, and on every womanish panic, between cooks, mobs, and apothecaries, was now represented by his tools as wasted in the cause of government'. Walpole scoffs at the claim that the Duke had relinquished the administration un- rewarded; he might not have taken much for himself, but a 'catalogue of his disinterestedness' would include his dukedom entailed on his nephew, Lord Lincoln; a peerage for one of his 'creatures', and an Irish earldom for another; profitable sinecures for his cousin Thomas Pelham, his secretary, and a favourite clerk. 'All this being granted, his Grace retired to Claremont, where, for about a fortnight, he played at being a country gentleman. Guns and green frocks were bought, and at past sixty he affected to turn sportsman; but getting wet in his feet, he hurried back to London in a fright, and his country was once more blessed with his assist- ance.'

The Duke of Devonshire, meanwhile, was growing tired of his unsought elevation, and a few more months sufficed to fill him with disgust. He asked to be allowed to retire. This put his Majesty in a dilemma. Who should succeed Devonshire ? The king looked around and the first man he had in mind was the memoirist Lord Waldegrave, who was one of his closest friends and whom he had appointed some years earlier to be 'governor' to his grandson, the young Prince of Wales (later George III). But very soon Walde- grave had to be ruled out, mainly, it seems, because he had no parliamentary following. The king considered other names but while he was still trying to make up his mind Newcastle settled the matter for him.

After his damping experience at Claremont, the Duke had soon reached the conclusion that it was unfair to deprive the country of his assistance any longer. He had weighed up the political situation to a nicety, and now the time seemed ripe for a return to office. But he took care not to repeat his mistake of excluding Pitt from his calculations. He made overtures to his formidable rival, and they were not rebuffed. Very shortly the two had reached an understanding. Only when the matter was practically settled was it intimated to the king. He made no objections; or if he did, they were overruled. So in July 1757 the Duke of Devonshire bowed himself out and the Duke of Newcastle bowed himself in as First Lord and Prime Minister.

This was the beginning of one of the most successful coalition governments in our history. Each of the two partners knew his place, and kept to it. As Horace Walpole expressed it, ' Mr. Pitt does everything; the Duke gives everything.' Lord Macaulay, in his second essay on William Pitt, describes the arrangement in more detail.

The partition of the powers of government between the two ministers, Macaulay writes, was singularly happy. Newcastle took the Treasury, the civil and ecclesiastical patronage, and the disposal of that part of the secret service money that was employed in bribing the members of Parliament. Pitt as Secretary of State was concerned with foreign affairs and the direction of the war. ' Thus the filth of all the noisome and pestilential sewers of government was poured into one channel,' while ' through the other passed only what was bright and stainless.'

This is all very fine, and is an excellent illustration of the unctuous rhetoric that Macaulay delighted in. But it is a bit hard on Newcastle. He might well have asked, ' Where would Mr. Pitt be if his majority in the House of Commons were not kept together by the means at my disposal, and which I know better than anyone how to employ to the best advantage ? ' He might have pointed out, too, that his part in the arrangement was not an easy one by any manner of means. Pitt was shockingly extravagant. He poured out money like water, on military adventures (by no means all of which were successful), on naval expeditions, and in subsidies to foreign powers to maintain their armies in the field. Somehow the money had to be found, and Newcastle had the responsibility of finding it. This meant higher taxes, and M.P.s could be induced to vote for the increased taxation only if they were kept sweet by government contracts, profitable little sinecures, places of profit under the Crown, commissions in the army and navy, prestige appointments, ribbons and decorations and the rest.

If Newcastle occasionally grumbled at his colleague's high-handed ways and inconsiderate profusion, he was well content with the ' partition of Powers ' they had effected. The one thing that interested him—' his ruling, or rather his only passion ' as Lord Chesterfield calls it—was 'the agitation, the bustle, and the hurry of business . . . He was as jealous of his power as an impotent lover of his mistress. . . . His levees were his pleasure, and his triumph; he loved to have them crowded, and consequently they were so. There he generally made people of business wait two or three hours in the ante-chamber, while he trifled away that time with some insignificant favourites in his closet. When at last he came into his levee-room, he accosted, hugged, embraced, and promised everybody, with a seeming cordiality, but at the same time with an illiberal and degrading familiarity.'

For five years Newcastle was Prime Minister—four of them in conjunction with Pitt—and it was during those years that what is called the first British Empire was established in India and North America. The death of George II in 1760 deprived him of royal favour and support, however, since the new sovereign was young and foolish and determined to 'be a king' as his mother, the Princess Dowager, was never tired of urging. He looked with aversion on the old and tried ministers he had inherited from his grandfather, and was determined to have new ones of his own selection. Lord Bute was his first choice, and rather than serve under the royal favourite Pitt resigned from the Government in 1761. Newcastle continued to cling to office, displaying an ignoble subservience which in the end did him no good. He told the king that he thought he ought to resign, and the reply the young monarch made was, 'In that case I must fill your place as I can'. Still the old man lingered, and even so far demeaned himself as to plead with Lord Bute that he should use his good offices on his behalf. To no purpose, however, and on 26 May 1762 the Duke handed in his resignation.

Horace Walpole sneered at him for being so long in going, but once Newcastle had accepted the inevitable he comported himself with dignity. He was getting on for seventy, and had been continually in office, with the exception of those few months in 1756–7, for forty-five years. He was offered a pension, but declined it, although Lord Chesterfield states that the Duke 'retired from business above four hundred thousand pounds poorer than when he first engaged in it'.

This was not quite the finish of his ministerial career. He lived long enough to observe, with immense satisfaction, Lord Bute's ignominious fall after so spectacular a rise. He watched George Grenville's coming and going; and then in Lord Rockingham's ministry in 1765 he was Lord Privy Seal. But after only a few months Rockingham resigned, and Newcastle retired with him, this time for good. He was becoming senile, and in 1768 he died, at the age of seventy-five. He was buried at Laughton, in Sussex.

No English statesman has been more mercilessly satirized than the Duke of Newcastle. Most of the contemporary writers seem to have taken a delight in holding him up to ridicule, and Horace Walpole in particular covered page after page with cruel and malicious denigration.

According to him, nothing would have been heard of the Duke if he had not succeeded as a very young man to an estate of £30,000 a year. Walpole asserts further that, while the duke's ' person was not naturally despicable, his incapacity, his mean soul, and the general low opinion of him, grew to make it ridiculous. A constant hurry in his walk, a restlessness of place, a borrowed importance, and real insignificance, gave him the perpetual air of a solicitor, though he was perpetually solicited; for he never conferred a favour till it was wrested from him.'

' This disquiet and habit of never finishing,' he goes on, ' which proceeded from his beginning every thing twenty times over, gave rise to a famous *bon mot* of Lord Wilmington—a man as unapt to attempt saying a good thing, as to say one. He said, " The Duke of Newcastle always loses half an hour in the morning, which he is running after the rest of the day without being able to overtake it ".'

Jealousy, Walpole continues, was the great source of all his faults, with a ridiculous fear. ' There was no expense to which he was not addicted, but generosity. His houses, gardens, table and equipage, swallowed immense treasures; the sums he owed were only exceeded by those he wasted. He liked business immoderately, yet was only always doing it, never did it . . .'

Lord Waldegrave, who gives us a picture of Newcastle in 1758, when he was ' in his thirty-fifth year of ministerial longevity ', also fixes on jealousy as one of his prevailing passions, but adds to it ambition and fear. ' In the midst of prosperity and apparent happiness, the slightest disappointment, or any imaginary evil, will, in a moment, make him miserable; his mind can never be composed; his spirits are always agitated. Yet this constant ferment, which would wear out and destroy any other man, is perfectly agreeable to his constitution: he is at the very perfection of health, when his fever is at the greatest height.'

The Duke's character is ' full of inconsistencies ', so much so that ' the man would be thought very singular who differed so much from the rest of the world as he differs from himself . . . Talk with him concerning public or private business, of a nice or delicate nature, he will be found confused, irresolute, continually rambling from the subject, contradicting himself almost every instant. Hear him speak in Parliament, his manner is ungraceful, his language barbarous, his reasoning inconclusive. At the same time, he labours through all the confusion of a debate without the least distrust of his own abilities; fights boldly in the dark; never gives up the cause; nor is he ever at a loss either for words or argument.'

Then after uttering a warning that the duke's professions and promises are not to be relied upon, since 'though at the time they are made, he means to perform them, he is unwilling to displease any man by a plain negative, and frequently does not recollect that he is under the same engagements to at least ten competitors', Waldegrave goes on to say that 'if he cannot be esteemed a steady friend, he has never shewn himself a bitter enemy, and his forgiveness of injuries proceeds as much from good nature as it does from policy. Pride is not to be numbered amongst his faults . . . Neither can he be accused of avarice, or of rapaciousness; for though he will give bribes, he is above accepting them.'

Then there is Lord Chesterfield. Included in his *Characters* is an essay on the Duke of Newcastle, who was one of his 'contemporaries, near relations, and familiar acquaintances'. He thought that 'the public opinion put him below his level, for though he had no superior parts or eminent talents, he had a most indefatigable industry, a perseverance', and a knowledge of those things which 'will carry a man sooner and more safely through the dark labyrinths of a Court than the most shining parts would do without these meaner talents'. Chesterfield's summing up is that, 'Upon the whole the Duke of Newcastle was a compound of most human weaknesses, but unattainted with any vice or crime'.

5

DUKE OF DEVONSHIRE

IN BETWEEN Newcastle's two premierships came the Duke of
Devonshire. He was Prime Minister for little more than seven
months. He did not want the office, and he relinquished it as soon
as he could do so without leaving his royal master in the lurch.

Born in 1720, William Cavendish was the eldest son of the third
Duke of Devonshire, who died in 1755. The Cavendishes had been
one of the most powerful political families in the realm since the
Revolution of 1688, when the then Earl of Devonshire had taken
the dangerous lead in sending an invitation to William of Orange
to become King of England, and had been rewarded for his services
on this occasion with the dukedom. Ever since they had been among
the firmest supporters of the Hanoverian dynasty, and had claims
to be considered the chief of the Whig families.

As we are told by Waldegrave, the third Duke was 'a man of
strict honor, true courage, and unaffected amiability . . . sincere,
humane, and generous', a man ' with solid rather than showy parts',
of ' great credit with the Whigs ' and belonging to ' a family which
had eminently distinguished itself in the cause of liberty '.

Very much the same might have been said of his son, the fourth
Duke. For ten years the Marquess of Hartington, as he was styled
during his father's lifetime, sat in the House of Commons as member
for Derbyshire, where the family's territorial influence was paramount. In 1751 he was called to the House of Lords in one of his
father's baronies, and shortly afterwards he was given an appointment at Court as Master of the Horse and was sworn a Privy
Councillor. Then in 1755 the Duke of Newcastle, appreciating the
advantage of having a Cavendish in his administration, appointed
him Lord Lieutenant of Ireland. Eight months later Hartington
became Duke of Devonshire on his father's demise.

Already he had been spoken of as a possible Prime Minister, and
when Newcastle resigned in 1756 his name came up again. Pitt
strongly recommended him, both on account of his personal attain-
ments and abilities and his high standing among the Whigs, and on
4 November Devonshire kissed the royal hand as Prime Minister.

He proceeded to form an administration, in which Pitt was the dominant figure as Secretary of State.

From what we are told, it is clear that he agreed to accept the appointment only out of his sense of public duty. He had no personal ambition, and indeed, his high place in society, his immense wealth and accumulation of dignities made him indifferent to the prizes of a political career. Waldegrave states that 'he did not accept till His Majesty had given his word that, in case he disliked his employment, he should be at full liberty to resign at the end of the approaching session of Parliament'.

As a Prime Minister, he was undistinguished and ineffectual. Almost the only thing remembered of his period of office is the case of Admiral Byng, who was shot on board ship at Portsmouth in March 1757 for 'neglect of duty', and while the blame for this judicial iniquity falls more heavily on the king than on his chief minister, Devonshire's dislike of his appointment was such that after scarcely six months in office he asked the king to be allowed to retire. George was reluctant to let him go, but he had given his word and he asked only that the Duke should remain until he could find a suitable successor. Then, as we have seen in the last chapter, Newcastle seized his opportunity and effected the coalition with Pitt.

Devonshire must have breathed a great sigh of relief when he was permitted to retire. As Waldegrave explains, 'Though he had been disgusted by faction and perplexed with difficulties, he lost no reputation; for great things had never been expected of him as a minister, and in the ordinary business of his office he had shown great punctuality and diligence and no want of capacity.'

King George made him a Knight of the Garter, and he retained his position at Court until the accession of George III. As may be easily understood, he soon fell foul of Lord Bute, and when Bute became Prime Minister in 1762 Devonshire was among the first to experience the favourite's bitter hostility.

'The Duke of Devonshire,' writes Macaulay, 'was especially singled out as the victim by whose fate the magnates of England were to take warning. His wealth, rank, and influence, his stainless private character, and the constant attachment of his family to the House of Hanover, did not secure him from gross personal indignity. It was known that he disapproved of the course which the government had taken ' (in the matter of the negotiations for the conclusion of the Seven Years' War) ' and it was accordingly determined to humble the Prince of the Whigs, as he had been nicknamed by the Princess Mother. He went to the palace to pay his duty. " Tell

him," said the King to a page, " that I will not see him." The page
hesitated. " Go to him," said the King, " and tell him those very
words." The message was delivered. The Duke tore off his gold
key, and went away boiling with anger. A few days later, the King
called for the list of Privy Councillors, and with his own hand struck
out the Duke's name.'

Immediately afterwards Devonshire wrote to the Secretary of
State, Lord Halifax, resigning his lord lieutenancy of Derbyshire.
He had learnt, he said, that the Duke of Newcastle and Lord Rockingham had been deprived of their lord lieutenancies, which he took
as ' a clear indication that His Majesty does not think fit that those
who have incurred his displeasure should continue his Lord Lieutenants, and, as I have the misfortune to come within that description,
His Majesty having been advised to show me the strongest marks of
his displeasure that could possibly be shown to any subject, I look
upon it as a respect due to my sovereign, and I owe it to myself, not
to continue any longer in such an office . . .'

This was in 1762. Early in 1764 he was taken ill, and went to
Spa, hoping to gain relief from his dropsy. And there on 2 October
he died at the early age of forty-four, which makes him the shortest-
lived of all our Prime Ministers.

6

LORD BUTE

ALTHOUGH he was Prime Minister for less than a year, Lord Bute made a great noise in the world. The letters and memoirs and journals of the period are filled with references to him, both as a politician and as a man, and for the most part they are uncomplimentary. There is indeed no man in the list of Prime Ministers whose rise was watched with such jealous hostility, whose career as a minister made him the target for so much vulgar abuse, and whose fall was the occasion for such general jubilation.

John Stuart was the elder son of James Stuart, second Earl of Bute, a distant connection of the ancient royal house of Scotland, and his wife Lady Anne Campbell, daughter of the first Duke of Argyll. He was born 25 May 1713, and succeeded to the earldom at the age of ten. He was then sent to Eton but did not proceed to any university. In 1736, when he was twenty-three, he married Mary Montagu, whose mother was the celebrated letter-writer, Lady Mary Wortley Montagu. ' It was a runaway love match,' we are told by Lord Chesterfield, ' notwithstanding which they lived very happily together; she proved a very good wife, and did in no way *matrizare*. He proved *a great husband*, and had thirteen or fourteen children successively by her, in as little time as was necessary for their being got and born, though he married her without a shilling, and without a reasonable probability of her ever having two.'

The year following his marriage Bute was elected a representative peer for Scotland, but a vote he cast against Walpole's government prevented his election for a second term. He thereupon returned to Scotland, and, says Chesterfield, for the next eight or nine years lived ' in a frugal and prudent manner, in the Isle of Bute which was entirely his own property. There he applied himself to the study of agriculture, botany, and architecture, the employments of an industrious than of an elevated mind.'

Lord Shelburne, who in later years came to know Bute intimately and received his first political appointment through his influence, describes this period of withdrawal from the world as being the result of a ' gloomy sort of madness ' that affected him. In the Isle of Bute, writes Shelburne, ' he resided some years with as much pomp and as much uncomfortableness in his little domestick circle as if he had been King of the Island, Lady Bute a forlorn queen, and his children slaves of a despotick tyrant '.

About 1746 however he found that ' his patrimonial fortune was very unequal to maintain the figure befitting his rank in life ', and he revisited England and took a villa on the Thames near Windsor. This piece of information we owe to Sir Nathanael Wraxall, author of *Historical Memoirs of My Own Time: 1772-1784*, first published in 1815, a book which is one of the most valuable works of the kind and is specially rich in human detail. Very probably Bute had some hope of getting an introduction to the governing circles, and Wraxall tells us how this came about.

During his residence in the Thames valley Bute was induced one day to visit Egham Races ' But as he either did not at that time keep a carriage, or did not use it to convey him to the Race Ground, he condescended to accompany a medical Acquaintance; in other words, the Apothecary that attended his Lordship's family, who carried him there in his own chariot. Frederic, Prince of Wales, who then resided at Cliefden, honored the Races on that day with his presence; where a tent was pitched for his accommodation, and that of the Princess, his Consort.

' The weather proving rainy, it was proposed, in order to amuse His Royal Highness before his returning home, to make a party at cards: but a difficulty occurred about finding persons of sufficient rank to sit down at the same table with him. While they remained under this embarrassment, somebody observed that Lord Bute had been seen on the Race Ground; who, as being an Earl, would be peculiarly proper to make one of the Prince's party. He was soon found, informed of the occasion which demanded his attendance, brought to the tent, and presented to Frederic.

' When the company broke up, Lord Bute thought of returning back to his own house: but his friend the Apothecary had disappeared; and with him had disappeared the chariot in which his Lordship had been brought to Egham Races. The Prince was no sooner made acquainted with the circumstance, than he insisted on Lord Bute's accompanying him back to Cliefden, and there passing the night. He complied, rendered himself extremely acceptable to their Royal Highnesses, and thus laid the foundation, under a succeeding reign, of his political elevation, which flowed originally in some measure from this strange contingency.'

Invitations to Leicester House, the Prince of Wales's establishment in London, followed. Lord Chesterfield takes up the tale again: 'He soon got to be at the head of the pleasures of that little, idle, frivolous and dissipated Court. He was the *Intendant* [master of ceremonies] of balls, the *Coryphaeus* [director] of plays, in which he acted himself, and so grew into a sort of favourite of that merry Prince. The Scandalous Chronicle says, that he was still a greater favourite of the Princess of Wales: I will not, nor cannot decide upon that fact. It is certain, on one hand, that there were very strong indications of the tenderest connection between them; but on the other hand, when one considers how deceitful appearances often are in these affairs, the capriciousness and inconstancy of women, which makes them often unjustly suspected, and the improbability of knowing exactly what passes in tete-a-tetes, one is reduced to mere conjecture. Those who have been conversant in that sort of business, will be sensible of the truth of this reflection.'

From another source we learn that the Prince of Wales was not particularly impressed by Bute's talents. Waldegrave informs us that he used to say that Bute was ' a fine showy man who would make an excellent ambassador in a court where there was no business '. To which Waldegrave adds the remark, ' Such was his Royal Highness's opinion of the noble earl's political abilities; but the sagacity of the Princess has discovered other accomplishments of which the Prince her husband may not have been the most competent judge.'

Wraxall is nothing like so supercilious; clearly he was of the opinion that Bute was not such a booby as had been made out. When he was young, he says, ' Lord Bute possessed a very handsome person, of which advantage he was not insensible; and he used to spend many hours every day, as his enemies asserted, occupied in contemplating the symmetry of his own legs, during his solitary walks by the side of the Thames. Even after he became an inmate at Cliefden, and at Leicester House, he frequently played the part of " Lothario ", in the private theatricals exhibited for the amusement of their Royal Highnesses, by the late Duchess of Queensberry . . . a fact to which Wilkes alludes with malignant pleasantry in more than one of his publications. To these external accomplishments, he added a cultivated mind, illuminated by a taste for many branches of the Fine Arts and Letters. For the study of Botany he nourished a decided passion, which he gratified to the utmost; and in the indulgence of which predilection he manifested, on some occasions, a princely liberality.'

On the other hand, his disposition was naturally 'retired and severe; he was not formed for an extensive commerce with mankind, or endowed by Nature with talents for managing popular assemblies. Even in his family he was austere, harsh, difficult of access, and sometimes completely inaccessible to his own children.'

Frederick, Prince of Wales, died in 1751, but Bute retained his position in the Princess Dowager's household even though it had become decidedly equivocal. The young prince, the future George III, who was now the next heir to the throne, was brought up under the supervision of Bute and his mother until the death of George II. This event wrought an immediate change in Lord Bute's situation. On 24 October 1760 his position was the modest one of Groom of the Stole to the twenty-two-year-old Prince of Wales. On the 25th the old king died. On the 27th Bute was admitted to the Privy Council, to take his place among the old and tried advisers of the Sovereign. When the Prime Minister, the Duke of Newcastle, submitted his draft of the speech to be delivered by the king on his first meeting with his Council, George III calmly informed him that 'My Lord Bute will tell you my thoughts'. The Duke bowed, displaying a submissiveness that must have belied his feelings, and went off to consult the favourite as he had been bidden.

A few months later one of the Secretaries of State was induced to resign, and Bute was immediately appointed to the vacant post with a seat in the Cabinet. Now he was well placed for successful intrigue. In the autumn of 1761 Pitt resigned. Newcastle's fawning approaches to Bute were repaid with ignominy, and in May 1762 he was 'shoved out', as Horace Walpole put it. Bute succeeded him as Prime Minister.

Never in English politics—since, at least, the time of Cardinal Wolsey—had a man risen so fast and so high. And never, it may be said, has there been a Prime Minister who became in so short a time so generally suspected, derided, and detested.

Bute suffered under three disadvantages, each of which might have been sufficient to sink a character of far greater stamina. He was a Scotsman, he was a Tory, and he was the royal favourite. To these may be added something more—the widely held belief that he was the lover of the Princess Dowager, the king's mother.

Even in the first days of the new reign, reports Horace Walpole, ' papers were stuck up at the Royal Exchange and in Westminster Hall, with these words, No Petticoat Government ! No Scotch favourite ! ' And because of ' the gross and insulting apostrophes with which she was received from the galleries', the Princess was obliged to cease her visits to the theatre.

When Pitt, now out of office, rode through the London streets to dine with the Lord Mayor at Guildhall he was acclaimed by the crowds as a conquering hero; but Bute had to engage what Chesterfield calls 'a gang of *bruisers*, who are the scoundrels and ruffians that attend the Bear Gardens' to protect him when he went out in his chair. In the vulgar prints and wall-scribblings he was generally represented by a jack-boot, with a petticoat to indicate the Princess, sometimes fastened on a gallows and sometimes committed to the flames. Day after day libels were published exceeding in audacity and venom any that had been seen before, and for the first time the victims were named and not given the disguise of initials.

For a time Bute succeeded in maintaining a bold face, as though feeling quite safe and happy in the royal favour. Says Chesterfield, 'He placed and displaced whom he pleased, gave peerages without number, and pensions without bounds', hoping by these means to make sure of the permanence of his power. But unfortunately for him, he had made few personal friends, and indeed was unable to do so, since 'his natural temper was dry, unconciliatory and sullen, with great mixture of pride', and 'he never looked at those he spoke to, or who spoke to him—a great fault in a Minister, as in the general opinion of mankind it implies conscious guilt.' Most of the junior ministers whom he appointed were incapable; 'No man living had his entire confidence—and no man thinks himself bound by a half confidence.'

Still he continued with his bullying and bluster. One thing he had set his heart on—making peace with France and so bringing the Seven Years' War to an end. Why he did so has been much debated. Perhaps it was because, as Lord Chesterfield suggested, that he knew his own limitations—that he did not possess the makings of a successful war minister; moreover, that his credit in the City was so low that there was small likelihood of his being able to raise the vast sums necessary for carrying on the struggle. Perhaps he was envious of Pitt, whom the war had raised to such a pinnacle of popularity. There is also the shameful suggestion—made then and repeated since—that the French government gave him a large sum of money as an inducement to favour a peace that would not be too humiliating and crippling to their power.

Another reason that may be advanced is perhaps the most plausible, that Bute was simply doing what his royal master told him to do. The young king was set on establishing his personal rule, and he saw plainly enough that this could never be done while Pitt was at the head of affairs.

Is this is true it affords no excuse for Lord Bute. On the contrary, it adds to his burden of responsibility, since it was from him that the king must have got most of his ideas. He it was who had brought to the prince's attention the intoxicating arguments of Lord Bolingbroke's *Idea of a Patriot King*, and together they had read in manuscript Blackstone's *Commentaries*, in which antique conceptions of the royal prerogative were presented as though they were still practically valid.

In our mind's eye we may see the young man listening eagerly to Bute as he turns the close-written sheets in the study at Leicester House, while the Princess Dowager his mother leans fondly over the back of the privileged tutor's chair, and occasionally, in her gurgling German accents, urges her son, when the time comes for him to succeed his old grandfather on the throne, ' George—be a king!'

Lord Bute it must be allowed was extraordinarily successful. He got rid of Pitt, he got rid of Newcastle, he got rid of the great Whig dukes of Devonshire and Grafton, and he brought the Seven Years' War to an end.

The Peace of Paris was signed on 10 February 1763. It was Bute's hour of triumph. He had done what he had set out to do. He had beaten the politicians at their own game. And then, on 8 April of the following year he threw in his hand. He resigned.

Bute's only explanation of his action was, ' The ground that I stand upon is so hollow that I am afraid, not only of falling myself, but of involving my royal master in my own ruin.'

In point of fact, his stomach had taken more than it could stand. It seems clear enough that his hard-boiled exterior belied his real nature. He was a very sensitive man, and he must have felt most keenly the shafts of innuendo, the sneers and jibes, the black looks, the dirty jokes made about him and his patroness. If he had not come to politics so late in life he would have been better prepared; as it was his skin had not been thickened by years of political battle. And it must be allowed that the storm of opprobrium and obloquy that beat about his ears would have made the most experienced blench.

Another consideration must also have weighed with him. After all, he had done very well for himself. The Garter (and very prominently it appears in the portraits that were painted of him), a British peerage for his wife, some very lucrative sinecures for members of his family, and his followers rewarded with pensions amounting in all to £52,000 a year out of public funds. Furthermore, there had recently occurred a great improvement in his personal fortunes. Chesterfield was right when he declared that when Lord Bute married his wife had not a shilling—and all credit to him; but now Lady Bute's father had died and, rather than leave his money to a wastrel son, had bequeathed it all to her. Chesterfield put the figure at £600,000, but Horace Walpole estimated that it was £1,340,000.

What more could Lord Bute expect ? It would seem that when he resigned the premiership he still hoped to retain something of his old privileged position at court. He recommended as his successor a man whom he thought would prove amenable, and he must have been very much put out when George Grenville let him know that he was not playing second fiddle. And Wraxall preserves a rather sad story of an attempt he made, in conjunction with the Princess Dowager, to continue to see the dispatches that were sent to the king by the Secretary of State.

' On those occasions, when the green box, containing letters or papers, arrived, his Majesty always withdrew into another room, in order to peruse them with more attention. Lord Bute, as had been pre-arranged, upon the messenger bringing a dispatch immediately took up two candles and proceeded before the king to the closet, expecting that his Majesty, when they were alone together, would communicate to him its nature, and that he would thus begin again to transact business. But the king, unquestionably aware of the intention . . . when he came to the door of the room, stopped, took the candles out of Lord Bute's hand, and then, dismissing him, shut the door; after which he proceeded to examine the dispatches, alone. Lord Bute returned to the company, and the experiment was never repeated.'

While this was the real state of affairs, the public continued to believe that Lord Bute was still directing the wheels of government from behind the scenes. Wraxall knew that the imputation was without foundation, but all the same, ' it operated with irresistible force. A cry of Secret Influence arose. The Grenville administration was stigmatized as being only a machine, the puppets of which were agitated by concealed wires.'

Nothing that ' the power of malevolence could invent ' could be more damaging to the king in his people's estimation, but it was further augmented by ' another topic of abuse and declamation, founded on the extraordinary degree of favour enjoyed by Lord

Bute at Carlton House, and the predilection with which he was known to be regarded by the Princess Dowager . . . His visits were always performed in the evening; and the precautions taken to conceal his arrival, though they might perhaps have been dictated more by an apprehension of insult from the populace . . . than from any improper reasons, yet awakened suspicion. He commonly made use on these occasions of the chair and the chairmen of Miss Vansittart, a lady who held a distinguished place in Her Royal Highness's family. In order more effectually to elude notice, the curtains of the chair were close drawn.

'The repartee of Miss Chudleigh, afterwards better known as Duchess of Kingston, at that time a Maid of Honour at Carlton House, when reproached by her royal Mistress for the irregularities of her conduct, obtained likewise much publicity. "*Votre Altesse Royale sait*," replied she, "*que chacune a son But.*"

'As the King was accustomed to repair frequently of evenings to Carlton House, and there to pass a considerable time, the world supposed that the Sovereign, his Mother, and the ex-Minister met, in order to concert, and to compare their ideas; thus forming a sort of interior Cabinet, which controlled and directed the ostensible Administration.'

When he was at length made to realize that the king had no further use for his services, Lord Bute retired from the scene of his greatness, and took up residence in his great house of Luton Hoo, in Bedfordshire, that the Scottish architects the brothers Adam had built for him. His secretary describes him living there in 1764 'in the lowest dejection of mind, scarce speaking a word, complaining and in a gloomy mood'. Then he went abroad, travelling incognito as Sir John Stuart in Italy. Even when some years had passed, there was still no possibility of his returning to politics. As late as 1765 his house in South Audley Street was attacked by a mob, and a year or two later his effigy, along with one of the Princess Dowager, was burnt by a rabble of chimney-sweeps on Tower Hill.

But there were still many years before him, and he spent them chiefly at Luton Hoo in cultural pursuits. He was a man of scholarly tastes, and a visitor to Luton Hoo in 1773 reported that his library consisted of 30,000 volumes. He made a collection of pamphlets of the Commonwealth period which George III later bought and presented to the library of the British Museum. His cabinet of mathematical and scientific instruments was considered to be the most complete in Europe. The gardens at Luton Hoo were laid out under his direction, and after the death of the Princess Dowager in

1772 he erected a Tuscan pillar bearing a memorial tribute to his good friend and benefactress.

'This is one of the places I do not regret having come to see,' remarked Dr. Johnson to Boswell one day in the summer of 1781, when Boswell had obtained a ticket to visit Luton Hoo. 'It is a very stately place, indeed; in the house magnificence is not sacrificed to convenience, nor convenience to magnificence. The library is very splendid; the dignity of the rooms is very great; and the quantity of pictures is beyond expectation, beyond hope.'

Bute also built himself a marine villa near Christchurch, overlooking the Needles, which he named Highcliffe. Here he passed many happy days with his children, encouraging them to take an interest in those scientific pursuits which had been his constant delight. He was living at Highcliffe when on a day in November 1790 he had a serious accident: seeing a new plant on the cliff he reached up to pick it—and fell twenty-eight feet over the edge. He seemed to have suffered nothing worse than a sprained ankle, but the shock was followed by complications which eventually killed him. He died at his house in South Audley Street on 10 March 1792, when he was nearly seventy-nine. He was buried at Rothesay, in his ancestral island of Bute.

Of all the Prime Ministers, George Canning, seen here (right) as painted by Sir Thomas Lawrence, held the office the shortest time, a mere hundred days. But although the high hopes of his premiership were dashed by premature death, he will always be remembered as the brilliant Foreign Secretary who 'called the New World into existence to redress the balance of the Old '.

Below: Such is the Duke of Wellington's reputation as a military commander, it tends to be forgotten that he was Prime Minister for several years—which is just as well, perhaps. This painting by Sir Edwin Landseer, *A Dialogue of Waterloo*, shows him as an old man revisiting the battlefield—now the scene of rural pursuits and pleasures—in company with his daughter-in-law the Marchioness of Douro.

Lord Melbourne (right), who by a most fortunate circumstance was Prime Minister when the young Princess Victoria became Queen in 1837. When she received him first in audience she formed the opinion that he was 'very straightforward, honest, clever, and good ', while he for his part, as Greville put it in his Diary, ' acted in all things an affectionate, conscientious, and patriotic part'.

Most famous perhaps of London streets, Downing Street is shown in this old print as it appeared in Georgian times, before most of the houses had been supplanted by the Victorian piles of government offices. But on the right may be distinguished No. 10, which for more than 200 years has been the official town residence of the Prime Minister, and No. 11 next door, which is usually appropriated to the use of the Chancellor of the Exchequer.

Right, above: Altogether charming in her pretty bonnet and tailored riding habit, the young Queen Victoria goes out riding in the Park between Lord Melbourne, her Prime Minister (on the left), and the always jaunty Lord Palmerston.

Right: Lady Caroline Lamb, whom the future Lord Melbourne married as a young man and who died some years before he became Prime Minister. Brilliant, beautiful! and witty—she was not called ' the Sprite ' for nothing—she shocked as often as she charmed. For a time she held even Lord Byron captive. And yet, her innumerable escapades notwithstanding, it was true what she said of her husband, ' he has never failed me '.

7

GEORGE GRENVILLE

WHEN LORD BUTE handed in his resignation, he recommended to the king as his successor a member of his Cabinet—George Grenville, a man of long ministerial experience and proved capacity, and one who was, in Bute's words, ' in the foremost rank of the few friends I highly regard '.

On the face of it, this suggests that Bute was hopeful of continuing to play a part in the direction of affairs. But one of the first things Grenville did on being appointed Prime Minister was to send out a circular letter to his friends and associates in which it was stated that Lord Bute, ' out of regard to what he thinks will be most in his Majesty's interest has declared that he is determined to retire and to absent himself not only from the Counsels but from the presence and place of residence of his Majesty until the suspicion of his influence on public business shall be entirely removed '.

Grenville took the precaution—very wise in the circumstances— of persuading the king to approve the wording before the letter was dispatched. King George was not pleased; while still feeling that Lord Bute had let him down, he had no wish to see him humiliated. Whatever his faults, Bute had never faltered in his devotion to the royal family, while Grenville was a comparative stranger—and proved to be a bore. ' When he has wearied me for two hours,' the young king complained to the Duke of Bedford, ' he looks at his watch to see if he may not tire me for an hour more.' He was also a bully. He never hesitated to say what was in his mind; and all too often, it was such a very unpleasant mind!

George Grenville came of a long line of Buckinghamshire squires. He was born on 14 October 1712 at Wotton Hall, the second son of Richard Grenville, one-time M.P. for Wendover, and his wife Hester Temple, who belonged to a much grander county family whose seat was the fine house of Stowe. She subsequently became heiress to her brother Lord Cobham, and was created a viscountess, and eventually Countess Temple in her own right.

With his older brother Richard, George went to Eton, where he was in the Lower Fourth when William Pitt was in the Sixth Form, and then to Christ Church, Oxford. He read for the bar and practised for some years in London, until in 1741 he was given one of the Temple family boroughs, Buckingham, which place he represented in Parliament for the rest of his life. On entering the House of Commons he attached himself to the 'Boy Patriots' among whom his brother and Pitt were numbered, and aided them in bringing about Walpole's downfall.

Advancement was not slow in coming, since apart from his powerful connections he was a steady, plodding fellow, very industrious, and an excellent House of Commons man. The House was, indeed, his sole delight. Once he was taken ill in the House, and fainted. There were loud cries for ammonia and cold water; but George Selwyn, who was a bit of a wag, was heard exclaiming, ' Why don't you give him the *Journals* to smell ? '

In several successive governments, Grenville was Secretary of the Navy, and he was very popular with the sailors because he insisted that they should be paid the wages that were owing to them. Under Bute he was one of the Secretaries of State and leader of the House of Commons; but by this time he had fallen out with his brother-in-law Pitt, as most people did, at one time or another, and on one well-remembered occasion the great man made Grenville his butt. This was in the debate in 1762 on the Budget proposals which included a tax on cider-production, something which enraged the largely Tory population of the cider-lands of the West Country. Sir Francis Dashwood, the incompetent Chancellor of the Exchequer, soon got into difficulties defending the unpopular imposition, and Grenville was put up to effect his rescue.

Increased taxes were absolutely necessary, he urged, owing to the vast military expenditure for which the previous (Pitt-Newcastle) government had been responsible; the only question was, how and where they were to be levied ? With hand on heart he begged the gentlemen opposite to be good enough to tell him where. ' I say, Sir, let them tell me where. I repeat it, Sir: I am entitled to say to them, Tell me where.'

Pitt was sitting just in front of him. Irritated by the reflections on his government, and by Grenville's fretful repetitions, Pitt murmured, in a whining tone mimicking Grenville's, a line of a very popular song of the period, ' Gentle Shepherd, tell me where . . .'

Grenville turned on him in a fury. ' If gentlemen are to be treated in this way,' he began—but Pitt had made his point. Rising with slow deliberation, he bowed at Grenville with a supercilious civility, and walked out of the chamber, 'leaving his brother-in-law,' says Macaulay, 'in convulsions of rage, and everybody else in convulsions of laughter'. For a long time after that Grenville bore the nickname of ' the Gentle Shepherd '.

In April 1763 when he had just entered his fifties, he became Prime Minister, and in his administration he was not only First Lord of the Treasury but Chancellor of the Exchequer. He was in difficulties from the start. He had no solid backing of Whig groupings, and was hardly on speaking terms with Pitt and the rest of the Pitt-Grenville clan. No wonder it was generally supposed that he was having to rely upon the advice and assistance of Lord Bute, the displaced Prime Minister. This impression was, however, a completely false one. Grenville was resolved to be master and proceeded to make his own mistakes.

In the first place, he authorized the prosecution of John Wilkes, for having published in No. 45 of his periodical *The North Briton* a strongly critical article on the king's speech at the opening of Parliament. Although it was pretty generally understood that the speech on these occasions reflected the views of the Ministry rather than of the Sovereign, King George took personal offence and demanded that Wilkes should be brought to book. Grenville concurred, and made the huge mistake of issuing a ' general warrant ' for the apprehension of the ' authors, printers, and publishers ' of No. 45, instead of one directed at the author of the alleged libel. Forty-nine persons were arrested, and had to be released when the courts declared such warrants illegal. Wilkes had now been revealed as the author of the article in question, however, and he was promptly arrested and imprisoned in the Tower. This made him a popular hero. He found eager champions in Parliament, and the newspapers vigorously contested what they represented as an attack on the liberties of the press. Wilkes won all along the line, although the struggle went on for years, long after Grenville had ceased to have anything to do with it.

Grenville now committed a worse blunder. He introduced into Parliament proposals for taxing the colonies in America, and so set in train the course of events which led to the American War of Independence.

On the face of it, it seemed a very reasonable proposal. The Seven Years War which had just concluded had involved the mother country in a vast expenditure, much of which had been incurred in defending the English colonies from the French in Canada. Surely the colonists would not object to the impositions of certain stamp duties, to be levied on legal and commercial documents, which it was anticipated would bring in a revenue of £100,000—the whole of which sum, it was explained, would be applied to the purposes of imperial defence. But the colonists objected, and their representatives in London informed the Prime Minister that his proposals had aroused the sternest opposition.

Grenville, who had the nice, tidy mind of a good accountant, listened to their objections, but insisted that the Colonies must pay a contribution to the British military costs. ' I know of no better way than that now proposed,' he told the colonies' London agents, ' but if you can tell me of a better I will adopt it.'

The bill providing for the new duties was introduced into Parliament, and passed through all its stages almost unopposed. The House of Commons was nearly empty when the final vote was taken. The bill received the royal assent as the Stamp Act on 22 March 1765 and was to come into operation in the following November.

By that time, however, Grenville was no longer Prime Minister. In April the king had been attacked for the first time by the mental disorder which was to cloud so many of his latter years. It was proposed that Regents be appointed to serve during any period of his incapacity, and Grenville in drawing up the list expressly excluded not only Lord Bute but the king's mother, the Princess Dowager. When the king was able to understand what was being proposed he was naturally highly indignant. Grenville found himself in an impossible position, and the opposition did nothing to help him out of it. The Princess Dowager's name had to be added to the list of possible regents, but this did not allay the king's resentment. He determined to get rid of Grenville at the earliest possible moment and begged his uncle, the Duke of Cumberland, to sound Pitt and other political leaders with a view to forming a government. Grenville got wind of the royal move, and poor George had to submit to the humiliation of being told in his own room, by Grenville and the Duke of Bedford, the Lord President of the Council, that he had broken his word and had treated his Ministers with gross unfairness. The king had not fully recovered from his attack, and almost choked with rage as the two Ministers read out their protest. When they had gone, he again approached his uncle, and this time Cumberland was able to light upon a possible alternative Prime Minister in the person of the Marquess of Rockingham.

In the *Grenville Papers* we find a long document telling how, on

10 July 1765 ' Mr. Grenville received a letter from my Lord Chancellor at half-past ten, signifying to him the King's command to attend him at twelve o'clock at St. James's with the Seal of his office. When Mr. Grenville came into the Closet, the King told him that from what the Duke of Bedford had said to him the last time he saw him, he understood that the Duke had resigned himself, and in the name of the rest of the Ministers, and that he [the King] had therefore found himself at liberty to form another Ministry, which he had accordingly done. Mr. Grenville said . . . that for his part, he had *not* resigned, nor even if he had intended it, should have employed another person to do it for him.' He then reminded the king that about two months previously, when he saw that the king had withdrawn his confidence he had told him ' that he did not wish to continue in his service after he had lost his favour ' since ' the situation was in every way too responsible and irksome '. But he now ' most earnestly entreated His Majesty to apprize him by what means, either omission or commission, he had drawn down his displeasure upon him ?

' The King said in general that he had found himself too much constrained, and that when he had anything proposed to him, it was no longer as counsel, but what he was to *obey*.

' Mr. Grenville started at that word, said he did not know how to repeat it, that surely His Majesty could not mean that word to him, who knew that there was no power on earth in whom His Majesty ought to acknowledge superiority, but that it was the duty of his servants, sworn to that purpose, to deliver their opinions to him upon such things as were expedient for his Government . . .

' Mr. Grenville then entreated His Majesty, from his known justice and honour, to clear him from the malice of his enemies, who he found had ventured to spread about that he had been wanting in respect to His Majesty, so far as to threaten to quit his service, and to leave the Seals at the Closet door. The King with some emotion said, " Never, Mr. Grenville, never: it is a falsehood ", and repeated it once or twice.

' The King's whole conduct was civil, imputing no blame, but giving no word of approbation throughout the whole conversation . . . Mr. Grenville thanked the King for the justice he had done him in his appeal against the aspersions of his enemies, gave him his papers to sign, went through an account with him, which the King gave him his word should never go out of his own hands, for which he likewise thanked him, saying there were those now in his service to whose honour he should be sorry to trust, and withdrew.'

This is Grenville's own story of how he parted from his royal master. When in later years it was suggested to the king that, disagreeable as Grenville had been, he might be preferable to the then Ministers, George absolutely refused to have him back. ' I would sooner meet Grenville at the point of the sword than let him into my closet ', he is reported to have told Lord Hartford, and to Colonel Fitzroy, ' I would rather see the Devil in my closet than Mr. Grenville '.

Grenville continued active in politics, although he never again held office after his dismissal in 1765. In 1769 he lost his wife— she was Elizabeth Wyndham, daughter of Sir William Wyndham, and was reported to exercise great influence over his political conduct—and he felt her death most keenly. He died in November 1770. Many years afterwards one of his three sons became Prime Minister.

8

MARQUESS OF ROCKINGHAM

THE MAN who followed George Grenville in the premiership was the Marquess of Rockingham. Like Grenville, he was a Whig, but a much more orthodox one, and the leader of one of the principal factions or groups into which the once great Whig party had disintegrated. He was young as statesmen go—only in his middle thirties—and he had held no ministerial office before; but he was a man of high reputation, excellent intentions and fair capabilities, and one whose immense wealth and accumulation of honours and dignities raised him far above any suspicion of self-seeking.

The choice was nonetheless strange—obviously Pitt ought to have become head of a government: even the king, who disliked him, thought so. But Pitt was not available. He was ill, or he was shamming: it hardly mattered which, since in any case he was quite resolved not to accept office at that moment. His turn was approaching, but for a year Lord Rockingham, a child in experience and ability compared to Pitt, occupied the supreme place.

Charles Watson-Wentworth, second Marquess of Rockingham, was the youngest of five sons, but all his brothers died in childhood. He was born in 1730. His father, Thomas Wentworth, was a grandson of Edward Watson, Lord Rockingham, and his wife Lady Ann Wentworth who was the daughter and heiress of the Lord Strafford who was the chief minister of Charles I and died on the scaffold in 1641. Through Lady Ann the family had acquired vast estates in Yorkshire, and their influence was such that in a few years Mr. Wentworth became a Knight of the Bath, M.P. for the West Riding of Yorkshire, Lord Lieutenant of the county, Baron Haith, Viscount Higham, Earl of Malton, Baron Rockingham, and finally Marquess of Rockingham. So rapidly had these honours descended upon him that Sir Robert Walpole said jokingly, soon after he had been made an earl, 'I suppose we shall soon find our friend Malton in opposition, for he has had no promotion in the peerage for the last fortnight.'

Almost the first thing told of his son, Charles Wentworth, the

71

future Prime Minister, is that when he was a fifteen-year-old boy at Eton he ran away to join the Duke of Cumberland's army marching against the Young Pretender, Prince Charles Edward. It was the winter of 1745, and Charles had gone home to Wentworth for the Christmas holidays. One morning he went out hunting, attended only by a groom, and they had not returned by nightfall. The next day it was reported that Lord Higham, as he then was, and his man had been seen riding in a northerly direction, and before long a letter arrived from the truant, dated from Carlisle, where the Duke of Cumberland had his headquarters. Zeal for the Whig cause had impelled the boy to join the royal army against the Pretender. His parents were, or professed to be, much displeased at his escapade, but an aunt rejoiced that ' the monkey Charles had shown such a spirit '. Amongst the family papers a letter from Charles has been preserved, addressed to his mother, and written in a large schoolboy hand.

' Dear Madam ', it reads, ' When I think of the concern I have given you by my wild expedition, and how my whole life, quite from my infancy, has afforded you only a continued series of afflictions, it grieves me excessively that I did not think of the concern I was going to give you and my father before such an under-taking; but the desire I had of serving my King and country as much as lay in my power, did not give me time to think of the undutifulness of the action. As my father has been so kind as entirely to forgive my breach of duty, I hope I may, and shall have your forgiveness, which will render me quite happy. I am, Madam, Your very dutiful Son, Higham.'

From Eton the youth went to St. John's, Cambridge, and then he spent some time on the continent, as was the custom in those days for the sons of aristocracy and wealth. His travels took him to the south of Italy, where according to Wraxall, who tells the story in his *Memoirs*, he indulged in ' some imprudent gallantries ' which caused him to ' suffer severely in his frame and health, which had never been robust '. Wraxall continues: ' The Princess of Franca Villa was commonly supposed to have bestowed on him the same " fatal present ", which the " Belle Ferronière " conferred on Francis the First, King of France; and which, as we learn from Burnet, the Countess of Southesk was said to have entailed on James, Duke of York, afterwards James the Second. The Princess was still living when I visited Naples in the year 1779; and Sir William Hamilton [the British ambassador at the court of Naples] assured me that she always expressed the utmost concern for the unintentional misfortune which the Marquis's attachment had produced, as well as for its supposed results.'

Rightly or wrongly, the Princess's 'fatal present' was held to have incapacitated Rockingham 'for close or continued application' to business when he was head of the Administration.

In 1750 his father died, and at the age of twenty he succeeded to all his titles and estates. He was appointed Lord Lieutenant of the North and the West Ridings, and a Lord of the Bedchamber to George II, a post to which he was reappointed by George III on his accession. So great was his position and influence that he had only to ask for the Garter and he was given it. Although keenly interested in politics, and the staunchest of Whigs, he played no great part at Westminster. The place he liked best was his great country mansion at Wentworth, where he could act the lavish host and engage in a variety of rural activities. He was a frequent figure on the course at Newmarket, and liked play at the gaming-tables, something he could afford better than most. It is said that as a young man he once ran a match from Norwich to London between five geese and five turkeys.

Rockingham was no time-server, and when in 1762 King George struck out the name of the Duke of Devonshire from the list of the Privy Council, he ventured to defend his chief in the royal closet. As he wrote to his old commander, the Duke of Cumberland: 'I humbly informed his Majesty, that it was with great concern that I saw the tendency of the counsels, which now had weight with him; that this event fully showed the determination that those persons who had hitherto been always the most steadily attached to his Royal predecessors, and who had hitherto deservedly had the greatest weight in this country, were now driven out of any share in the government in this country, and marked out rather as objects of his Majesty's displeasure than of his favour: that the alarm was general among his Majesty's most affectionate subjects, and that it appeared to me in this light:—it might be thought, if I continued in office, that I either had not the sentiments which I declared, or that I disguised them, and acted a part which I disclaimed. His Majesty's answer was short; saying that he did not desire any person should continue in his service any longer than it was agreeable to him.'

As time passed, Rockingham's place among the Whigs improved, until he became acknowledged as their leader. When Grenville was thrust out, there were many names canvassed for the premiership before the Whigs nominated Rockingham. The king was surprised. 'I thought,' he remarked, 'that I had not two men in my Bedchamber of less parts than Lord Rockingham.' Perhaps Rockingham, too, was surprised, and it is clear that he had no great desire for the supreme post. But having been called upon, he was resolved to do his duty.

In Lord Albemarle's life of Rockingham, we are told that the causes of the attachment of the Whigs to Rockingham 'must be sought in the character of the leader himself. Lord Rockingham possessed by nature a calm mind and a clear intellect, a warm benevolent heart, of which amiable and conciliatory manners were the index. He was imbued with sound views of the principles of the Constitution, and with a firm resolution to make those principles the guide of his actions. If eloquence were the sole criterion of a great leader or a great minister, Rockingham would have but small claims to such a title. The malady which consigned him to the tomb, when he was little more than fifty years of age, had imparted to his frame a sensibility of nerve which only extraordinary occasions enabled him to overcome. He was a hesitating and an inelegant debater. His speeches commanded attention, not from the enthusiasm aroused by the persuasive arguments of the orator, but from the confidence placed in the thorough integrity and practical good sense of the man ... He lacked outward graces. He possessed the inward power.'

Rockingham formed his administration in July 1765 and since Pitt and other of the Whig chiefs refused office it was weak in personnel. Charles Townshend, who held the post of Paymaster to the Forces, wittily described it as 'a lutestring administration, fit only for summer wear'. All the same, Albemarle makes the claim that in no one year between the Revolution of 1688 and the Reform Bill of 1832 'were so many immunities gained by the people, or, more properly speaking, so many breaches in the Constitution repaired', as in the twelvemonth that was the term of the Rockingham administration, and this ' in face of one of the ablest and most unscrupulous Oppositions, of which the King himself was the head '. Rockingham might well have preserved the American colonies to the Empire if George III ' had but possessed common sincerity '.

General warrants, such as the one launched against Wilkes, were formally condemned by Parliament. Military officers who had been deprived of their rank because of their votes in Parliament were reinstated, and this kind of petty tyranny was never attempted again. The obnoxious cider tax was modified. A commercial treaty was concluded with Russia. Above all, the Stamp Act that Grenville had passed was repealed—an event, so declared Edmund Burke, then M.P. for Wendover, and Lord Rockingham's secretary, ' that caused more universal joy throughout the British dominions than perhaps any other that can be remembered '.

These things make a fair showing, but as the months passed Rockingham became increasingly disgusted with his position. There were divisions in the Whig party, and the king was obviously intriguing against him. Once more he tried to bring Pitt into the ministry, but was again unsuccessful. Then the Duke of Grafton, perhaps the most competent of the ministers, took it into his head to resign the seals of Secretary of State. Clearly, the Government was on the verge of dissolution, and at the end of July 1766 the king, having come to an arrangement at length with Pitt, gave Rockingham his dismissal.

For the next sixteen years Rockingham was in opposition, but not a factious one. Throughout he strove for a reasonable accommodation with the Americans, a limit to be put on the exercise of the royal prerogative, and a purification of the springs of government. After Chatham's death he was approached to form a ministry, and in 1780 Lord North invited him to enter his Cabinet, but on both occasions he declined. He would not compromise just for the sake of political advancement. But when Lord North's long administration came to an end, the king felt obliged to apply to Rockingham as the most likely of the elder statesmen.

Rockingham was now over fifty, his health was breaking up, and he had no real illusions over the king's real attitude towards him. But he answered what he felt was the call of duty, and on 27 March 1782 he kissed hands for the second time as Prime Minister.

In the new administration, Rockingham was First Lord of the Treasury, and among his colleagues were the Duke of Grafton, the former Premier, Lord Shelburne and the Duke of Portland, future Premiers, and Fox and Burke—a splendid collection of great names and political talent.

' Never was a more total change of costume beheld,' wrote Wraxall in his *Memoirs* under the date 8 April 1782, ' than the House of Commons presented to the eye, when that assembly met for the dispatch of business after the Easter recess. The Treasury Bench, as well as the places behind it, had been for so many years occupied by Lord North and his friends, that it became difficult to recognize them again in their new seats, dispersed over the Opposition benches, in greatcoats, frocks, and boots . . . To contemplate the Ministers their successors, emerged from their obscure lodgings, or from Brookes's, having thrown off their blue and buff uniforms; now ornamented with the appendages of dress, or returning from Court, decorated with swords, lace, and hair powder, excited still more astonishment . . .'

Before accepting office, Rockingham had told the king that he was convinced that ' the times require a speedy conclusion of peace and a rigid economy in the expenditure of public money '. As fate would have it, he had insufficient time to do the first, but he did manage to get through Parliament bills excluding Government contractors from membership of the House of Commons, disfranchising revenue officers (who were appointed by the Crown, and generally voted as they were told), and severely reducing or suppressing a large number of sinecure posts with which the king and the Government had been able to buy or reward parliamentary support. This was the first real attempt to tackle the evils of parliamentary corruption.

If he had had more time, Rockingham would surely have done far more in the way of introducing a liberal spirit into the machinery of government, but his physical strength soon began to fail. His last appearance in the House of Lords was in early June 1782, and shortly afterwards he left his house in Grosvenor Square and retired to Roehampton, where he was obliged to keep to his room. He was suffering from what Wraxall describes as ' decay, to which was added a slow fever, or as it was denominated, influenza ', which had ' for some time undermined his strength, without nevertheless appearing to menace his immediate dissolution '. His friends were confident he would get better, but on 1 July he died.

In the grounds of Wentworth Park, a splendid mausoleum was constructed to his memory by his nephew Earl Fitzwilliam, who since Rockingham left no issue succeeded to his estates. For this Edmund Burke composed a long inscription. ' Let his successors,' it concludes, ' who daily behold this monument, consider that it was not built to entertain the eye, but to instruct the mind. Let them reflect that their conduct will make it their glory or their reproach . . . Remember; Resemble; Persevere.'

9

WILLIAM PITT, EARL OF CHATHAM

WILLIAM PITT—often called William Pitt the Elder to distinguish him from his equally famous son—was looking back on more than thirty years in Parliament when, in an unfortunate moment, he accepted the king's invitation to form an administration. In little more than a year his premiership was over, and that was none too soon.

Born at Westminster on 15 November 1708 he was the younger son of Robert Pitt, a country gentleman of Boconnoc, near Lostwithiel in Cornwall, by his wife Harriett Villiers; and grandson of Thomas Pitt, a colourful adventurer who did very well for himself as a trader with India, was for twelve years governor of Madras under the East India Company and acquired a magnificent diamond which he sold at an immense profit to the French Regent. It was mainly through this fortunate transaction that Governor Pitt or Diamond Pitt, as he was variously styled, was enabled to raise his family from quite middling circumstances—his father was rector of Blandford in Dorset—to one of wealth and political influence, the latter being exercised through the purchase of several pocket boroughs, including Old Sarum, the most notorious of this species of political property. As regards his party he was a Whig, of the most violent sort.

Very little is known of William Pitt's early life. He went to Eton and then in 1726 to Trinity College, Oxford, but a recurrence of a malady which had attacked him in his schooldays and was never to leave him for long throughout his life, obliged him to leave the university before he had taken his degree. This malady is usually described as gout, but it seems to have been quite as much mental as physical, expressing itself as a form of mental instability which frequently bordered on insanity and on occasion went over the edge. Lord Shelburne, who knew the Pitts well, once said that there was ' a great deal of madness in the Pitt family ', and it has been surmised that this was something which was inherited from Governor Pitt, whose blood had been heated by the tropical conditions and excesses of his early life.

On leaving Oxford, Pitt seems to have studied for a while at

Utrecht, and then to have spent some time in France and Italy. His father died while he was abroad, and on his return in 1731 at the age of twenty-three, as the younger son he had to choose a profession. He fancied the army, and he obtained through the interest of friends a commission as a cornet (junior officer) in the First Dragoon Guards. But his military career was destined to be short, for in 1735 his brother Thomas, who had been returned as Whig member for both Okehampton and Old Sarum, passed on the latter seat to him.

Accordingly Pitt entered the House of Commons as M.P. for a seat which was a synonym for political corruption. He attached himself at once to the band of discontented young Whigs known as the Boys or Patriots, whom Walpole's selfish love of power had driven into opposition. In his first session he did not once open his mouth, but in 1736 he delivered his maiden speech in support of an address of congratulation to the king on the marriage of his son Frederick Prince of Wales. If we are to believe Pitt's flattering biographers, the speech was a veritable *tour de force*, worthy of comparison with the best efforts of Demosthenes and Cicero, and we can believe them if we wish. But in fact everything that we are told about the parliamentary debates of those days is just hearsay, since not until long afterwards were reporters allowed in the House of Commons to take down what was said. And yet there is not the slightest doubt that Pitt made a very deep and lasting impression on his hearers. In all the accounts that have come down to us, there is the most complete unanimity that he was a fine orator; indeed, we may well conclude that he was what his contemporaries claimed, that he was the greatest orator ever heard at Westminster.

When he made his first appearances in the House of Commons his figure was graceful and commanding, and so it remained when the shapely limbs had been distorted by gout and were swathed in flannel. His head was small, and his countenance thin. His nose was long and aquiline, his eye—and this was something which every beholder remarked upon—was 'like a hawk's', piercing, fire-flashing; while his voice was low and clear, melodious, and of the most wonderful compass. Sometimes it sank to a whisper, but even so it might be clearly heard on the farthest benches; sometimes it rose like the swell of a great organ, and then the chamber was filled with the tremendous volume of sound, the walls echoed and re-echoed and the very rafters seemed to shake.

'Mr. Pitt came young into Parliament,' writes Lord Chesterfield in his *Characters*, 'and upon that great theatre soon equalled the oldest and ablest actors. His eloquence was of every kind, and he excelled in the argumentative as well as in the declamatory way. But his invective was terrible, and uttered with such energy of diction, and stern dignity of action and countenance, that he intimidated those who were the most willing and the best able to encounter him.' Lord Lyttelton tells us that ' his words have sometimes frozen my young blood into stagnation, and sometimes made it pace in such a hurry through my veins that I could scarce support it '. Horace Walpole reports that Pitt ' crushed ', ' crucified ', ' lashed ', ' punished ', ' attacked ', one or other of the victims of his hostile eloquence.

Of course, he was an actor, as great orators generally are. Walpole put him on a level with David Garrick, and Macaulay says that he would have made the finest Brutus or Coriolanus ever seen. Pitt confessed that he was sometimes carried away by his own feelings. ' When my mind is full of a subject,' he told a friend, ' if once I get on my legs it is sure to run over.' And this though he took the greatest care over his speeches, arranging the paragraphs, selecting the most apt tags from the classics for quotation, choosing just the right word. Once he claimed that he had read Bailey's Dictionary twice through from beginning to end.

Of course, this was not achieved all at once, but even so that first speech of his made Sir Robert sit up and take notice. A young man in a hurry, he concluded; but a potentially dangerous one. ' We must muzzle this terrible cornet of horse,' he is reported to have said. Very soon it was announced in the *Gazette* that Mr. Pitt had been cashiered. Walpole could be very mean when he thought the occasion demanded it.

Pitt could ill afford the loss of his army pay, but the Prince of Wales, whose cause he had championed against his father, tried to make up for it by appointing him to a position on his personal staff as Groom of the Bedchamber.

As Walpole neared the end of his long reign the opposition intensified their efforts, and Pitt was always in the forefront of the battle. He was no respecter of persons. He criticized in the strongest terms the payment of Hanoverian troops out of the British exchequer, and he even ventured to imply that the king was wanting in courage. Small wonder that George II, who was a stout little fellow and had proved himself on the field of battle, swore that he would never forgive him.

When the Prime Minister dragged his heels in declaring war on Spain, Pitt rode the high horse of patriotic indignation. He thundered against the convention which Walpole had negotiated. 'This insecure, dishonourable convention!' he is reported to have described it. 'I wish we could hide it from the eyes of every Court in Europe. They see that Spain has talked to you in the language of a master!'

Walpole scowled, his supporters looked glum, the Opposition roared themselves hoarse. Outside the House reports spread, of a man who was determined that the English should no longer be pushed around by a gang of rascally foreigners. War was declared, but still Pitt kept up his onslaught. Even when the great man had been compelled to resign, Pitt pursued the fallen minister with a reckless venom. Sir Robert Walpole should be impeached, he should be made to pay for his raids on the public purse . . . But it was rumoured that only a short time before Pitt had been offering to use his good offices on the other side if he might be given some small indication of Government favour.

This particular charge has been denied but beyond a doubt there was a good deal that was disreputable in Pitt's long climb up to the heights of place and power. Unlike so many of the Whigs, he was entirely dependent on his own exertions; he was, comparatively speaking, a poor man, with no more than a hundred pounds a year of his own. Not until 1744 was his financial situation eased by the gift of £10,000 under the will of the old and eccentric Duchess of Marlborough, as 'an acknowledgment of the noble defence he had made for the support of the laws of England and to prevent the ruin of his country'. That is how she phrased it, but we may suppose that what she really meant was that he had stood up against her old enemy, Sir Robert Walpole.

Year after year passed and Pitt was still only a back-bencher. Walpole had scoffed at his pretensions, Wilmington had left him out in the cold, and the Pelhams seemed in no hurry to avail themselves of his proffered services. All of which is hardly surprising when we recall how insulting he had been to the king and his ministers. At last, however, he was given a job. It was not much to speak of, only the vice-treasurership of Ireland, whatever that may have meant. This was in February 1746 when he had been in the House nearly a dozen years already. But he must soon have made a favourable impression on his chiefs, for no later than the following June he was promoted to the much more important, and generally much more lucrative, post of Paymaster-General, which gave him a place in the Privy Council though not in the Cabinet.

Knowing what we know of the Pelhams, we must suppose that they thought that Pitt would take the opportunity of feathering his own nest as previous Paymasters had done, and were generally expected to do, and that this would keep him quiet. But Pitt absolutely refused to draw a shilling other than his official salary. The news leaked out, as doubtless Pitt had intended it to do. His apparently disinterested action was a splendid advertisement of his own virtues, and the public were led to believe that Pitt was a man of quite exceptional integrity and high personal honour.

For nearly eight years Pitt remained a member of the Pelham administration. Henry Pelham thought very highly of him. Writing to his brother the Duke of Newcastle in 1750 he said, ' I think him the most able and useful man we have among us, truly honourable, and strictly honest. He is as firm a friend to us as we can wish for, and a more useful one does not exist.' But when Pelham died and Newcastle took over the Government, Pitt was bitterly disappointed in not being given any promotion, although Newcastle could plead as an excuse that at the time he was making up his ministry Pitt was away ill at Bath and so was not available. Horace Walpole put the matter succinctly. ' Pitt has no health, no party,' he wrote, ' and has what in *this* case is allowed to operate, the King's negative.' Pitt was so disappointed that he talked of getting out of politics for good, but at this juncture his personal life underwent a great change: he got married.

Up to this time he seems to have shown no particular interest in women, although in his young days he is supposed to have lost his heart to a mademoiselle in Besançon and a little later to have had a tenderness for his friend Lyttelton's sister Molly. But that was long ago and here he was, a mature bachelor of forty-six, and apparently in love. His bride was Lady Hester Grenville, the thirty-three-year-old sister of Lord Temple and Richard Grenville. He had first met her on a visit to her home at Stowe in 1735 when she was a girl of fourteen. In the intervening years he must have met her often and there was probably no woman, other than his sisters, with whom he was better acquainted. Although she was no great beauty, her portraits reveal her as being by no means unattractive, with auburn hair, a long upper lip, and a slightly turned-up nose. She was reputed to be very good-natured, and beyond any doubt she was remarkably intelligent. Furthermore, she was a member of one of the most numerous, influential and tightly knit of the Whig families.

What made the middle-aged cripple—for that is what his gout

frequently made him—suddenly decide to take the plunge into matrimony ? According to his nephew Lord Camelford, he made his proposal when on a visit to George Grenville's place at Wotton, and Lady Hester at once declared that she would be unworthy of the honour he proposed if she should hesitate a moment in accepting it. So they were married on 15 November 1754, and she contrived to make herself a good wife by a devotion and attachment that knew no bounds. She lived only in her husband's glory. She was his nurse, his flatterer, his housekeeper and steward, and she would submit to any deprivation that would gratify his wants or his caprices. She bore him five children: three sons and two daughters.

Marriage was the making of Pitt. His gout took a turn for the better and very soon he was back in London, where he joined his friends in criticizing the Government of which he was still a member. Newcastle put up with this as long as he could, but eventually even he had had enough and he forced Pitt's resignation. But this only increased the duke's difficulties, and in the autumn of 1756 his ministry collapsed.

The next Prime Minister was the Duke of Devonshire, and Pitt accepted the invitation to join him—but only on the condition that the Duke of Newcastle should be excluded. Why he was so hostile to Newcastle at this juncture is not clear. Newcastle had shown him many favours in the past, and since 1746 Pitt had been sitting in the House of Commons for Seaford, one of the Newcastle boroughs. But whatever the reason Pitt absolutely refused to sit in the same Cabinet with the duke, and Devonshire was in no position to deny him. In the new government Pitt was the Secretary of State for the Southern department, and he was also appointed leader of the House of Commons; in fact, he was virtual Premier.

' My Lord,' he told Devonshire, ' I am sure that I can save this country, and that nobody else can.' And the country very much needed saving; the Seven Years War had opened and things were going badly for Britain both on land and sea.

But it could not be saved under such a well-meaning but ineffectual leader as Devonshire, even with Pitt's assistance; and in April 1757 after an uneasy existence of some four months the Devonshire ministry quietly expired.

For eleven weeks the country was without a government, while the Whig factions wrangled among themselves and the king was completely at a loss. No one shed any tears for Newcastle, but Pitt was a different matter. In our long political history it would be hard to find a fallen minister who was given in so short a time so many proofs of popular confidence and admiration. London and all the chief towns voted him addresses of support and conferred on him the freedom of their corporations. ' For some weeks,' reports Horace Walpole, ' it rained gold boxes.' And meanwhile a great war was waging, difficulties were accumulating apace, and the reputation of the country sank to a low ebb.

At length the political deadlock was resolved. Out of the muddy turmoil there emerged a new administration, in which Newcastle was First Lord of the Treasury and Prime Minister, and Pitt was Secretary of State with the controlling interest. As he used to say afterwards, ' I used the Duke of Newcastle's majority to carry on the public business.'

At the same time he made a bold assertion of political independence. He relinquished his Newcastle borough and got himself elected for the city of Bath, which had something of a popular franchise.

Essentially, the Newcastle-Pitt administration was a ' win the war ' one, just as much as Lloyd George's in 1916 and Winston Churchill's in 1940, and in the very different circumstances it was just as successful. From June 1757 until he resigned in October 1761 Pitt was the dominating figure in it, and his biography is submerged in the history of England. Those were the years when the British Empire was brought to birth, and it was Pitt who presided over the accouchement. He gave the nation an example of the most splendid patriotism. He breathed into others his spirit of relentless resolution and unyielding courage. As was said at the time, no man left Pitt's presence without feeling himself a braver man. He inspired and encouraged, he drew up the plans and chose the men to carry them into execution. Wolfe, who won Canada on the Heights of Abraham, was Pitt's selection over a number of officers senior and more experienced; and it was one of his generals who bestowed the name of Fort Pitt on the former French stronghold of Fort Duquesne where the great city of Pittsburgh now stands. ' I have used the freedom of giving your name to Fort Duquesne,' wrote General Forbes, who (with George Washington as his second-in-command) took possession of it, ' as I hope it was in some measure the being actuated by your spirits that now makes us masters of the place.'

' England has been a long time in labour,' wrote Frederick the Great of Prussia, who owed his survival to the subsidies that Pitt poured into his war-chest, ' but she has at last brought forth *a man*.'

One of the most forceful tributes to Pitt as war leader was paid by Edmund Burke in the *Annual Register* for 1761. ' No man was ever better fitted to be the minister in a great and powerful nation, or better qualified to carry that power and greatness to their utmost limits. There was in all his designs a magnitude, and even a vastness, which was not easily comprehended by every mind, and which nothing but success could have made to appear reasonable . . .

' Under him Great Britain carried on the most important war in which she was ever engaged, alone and unassisted, with greater splendour, and with more success, than she had ever enjoyed at the head of the most powerful alliances. Alone this island seemed to balance the rest of Europe. In the conduct of the war he never suffered the enemy to breathe, but overwhelmed them with reiterated blows, and kept up the alarm in every quarter . . . The spirit of the nation once roused, was not suffered for a moment to subside . . . In short, he revived the military genius of our people; he supported our allies; he extended our trade; he raised our reputation; he augmented our dominions; and on his departure from administration left the nation in no other danger than that which must ever attend exorbitant power.'

Then there is Horace Walpole. Like so many confirmed men of letters he felt an almost fearful fascination when he contemplated this great man of action. For the benefit of posterity he set about drawing an impartial picture. ' I am neither dazzled by the blaze of the times in which I have lived '—he was writing in 1759, when Pitt was still in the plenitude of power—' nor, if there are spots in the sun, do I deny that I see them. It is a man I am describing and one whose greatness will bear to have his blemishes fairly delivered to you—not from a love of censure in me, but of truth; and because it is history I am writing, not romance, I pursue my subject.'

Walpole found plenty of blemishes and disclosed them. ' Pitt lavished the last treasures of this country with a prodigality beyond example and beyond excuse . . . He drew magnificent plans, and left others to find the magnificent means . . . Secluded from all eyes, his orders were received as oracles; their success was imputed to his inspiration, misfortunes and miscarriages fell to the account of the more human agents . . . the more money was thrown away, the greater idea Pitt conceived of his system's grandeur . . .'

But having called attention to these Walpole felt bound to pay tribute to the greatness of the man's achievement. When Pitt entered upon his administration he had found the nation ' at the lowest ebb in point of power and reputation. His predecessors, the men who were now his coadjutors, wanted genius, spirit, and system. The fleet had many able officers, but the army had lost sight of discipline, and was destitute of generals in whom either the nation or the soldiery had any confidence. France was feared heartily, and the heavy burden of the national debt . . . served as an excuse put forward by those who urged the impossibility of the country making an effectual stand. Pitt roused us from this ignoble lethargy; he had asserted that our resources were still prodigious— he found them so in the intrepidity of our troops and navies . . .'

*   *   *

When George II died in 1760 Pitt occupied a situation which, so Macaulay averred, was the most enviable ever occupied by any public man in English history. He had conciliated the old king who had resisted for so long his admission to the Cabinet but had at length come to trust him completely. He was adored by the people, admired by all Europe; he was the first Englishman of his time, and he had made England the first country in the world. And then in October 1760 George III became king in succession to his grandfather, and almost the first object of his policy was the removal of his great minister. In October 1761 Pitt was outvoted in the Cabinet and forthwith resigned.

The young sovereign received Pitt graciously when he waited upon him to deliver up the seals of his office, and Pitt was deeply moved, even to the point of bursting into tears. It is not a very pretty picture, but then Pitt had often shown a strange servility in his relations with his royal master. The wits at court used to say that when he bowed ' you could see his hooked nose between his legs'. When he entered the king's room he used to fall on his knees. The least peep into the royal closet, said Burke, intoxicated him. Now he was full of gratitude for the king's goodness: ' such goodness overpowers, it oppresses me '.

Pitt was offered the governorship of Canada with a salary of five thousand a year, but he declined it. A peerage, then ? This, too, he respectfully declined, but he accepted one for his wife, who became Baroness Chatham. He also accepted a pension of £3,000 a year for his own and two further lives, and for this he has been severely blamed, perhaps too severely in the light of his financial embarrassments. Burke said that it was ' a shame that any defence should be necessary ' for the acceptance of a pension by a man who had deserved so well of his country.

For the next five years Pitt was out of office, although he was often pressed to return to it. From time to time he was afflicted by severe attacks of his gout and prevented from taking any part in public business. Much of his time was spent at Bath, tended with the utmost solicitude by his wife, and when he was not taking the waters there he was at his home at Hayes, near Bromley, a property he had purchased soon after his marriage, or at Burton Pynsent in Somersetshire, a fine place which had been bequeathed to him in 1765 by an aged and eccentric baronet, Sir William Pynsent, out of admiration for Pitt's services to his country. The value of the estate was said to be £3,000 a year, and there was also a lump sum of £30,000.

Then in the autumn of 1766, when the Rockingham ministry had been dismissed, Pitt was induced by King George to form a government. Now he was Prime Minister in name as well as in fact. He formed a ministry containing some distinguished names and some promising ones (there were three future Prime Ministers among them), but without any solid backing in the House. Edmund Burke described it as being 'utterly unsafe to touch and unsure to stand on'.

But there was something worse. In the new administration Pitt allotted the position of First Lord of the Treasury to one of his protégés, the young Duke of Grafton, who was clearly expected to do most of the donkey-work. Pitt himself accepted the almost sinecure office of Lord Privy Seal, which necessitated his removal to the House of Lords. With a few strokes of the royal pen, the Great Commoner was transformed into the Earl of Chatham. This was a fatal mistake.

'My Dear Friend'—it is Lord Chesterfield writing to his son Philip Stanhope, under the date of 1 August 1766—'The curtain was at last drawn up, the day before yesterday, and discovered the new actors, together with some of the old ones. Mr. Pitt, who had *carte blanche* given him, named every one of them: but what would you think he names himself for? Lord Privy Seal; and (what will astonish you, as it does every mortal here) Earl of Chatham. The joke here is, that he has *had a fall up stairs*, and has done himself so much hurt, that he will never be able to stand upon his legs again.

'Everybody is puzzled how to account for this step; though it would not be the first time that great abilities have been duped by low cunning. But be it what it will, he is now certainly only Earl of Chatham; and no longer Mr. Pitt in any respect whatever.

'Such an event, I believe, was never read nor heard of. To withdraw, in the fullness of his power and in the utmost gratification of his ambition, from the House of Commons (which procured him his power, and alone could insure it to him), and to go into that hospital for incurables, the House of Lords, is a measure so unaccountable, that nothing but proof positive could have made me believe it: but true it is . . . There is one very bad sign for Lord Chatham, in his new dignity, which is that all his enemies, without exception, rejoice at it; and all his friends are stupefied and dumbfounded . . .'

On the very day on which the new Prime Minister kissed hands, says Macaulay, three-fourths of that enormous popularity which he had long enjoyed, and to which he owed the greater part of his authority, departed from him. He was charged with having sold himself for a peerage and the highest place in the royal favour. When the citizens of London had heard that he had been sent for from Somersetshire and that he was closeted with the king at Richmond, there had been transports of pride and joy. Preparations were made for a grand illumination and entertainments on a lavish scale. The lamps had actually been placed round the Monument, all ready to be lit, when the *London Gazette* announced that the object of all this enthusiasm was now an earl. The lamps were taken down, the festivities were abandoned. The address of congratulation that the City Fathers had prepared remained on the table unread. The proposal to name a new bridge after him was forthwith abandoned. The newspapers were filled with the bitterest comment and ' pamphlets made up of calumny and scurrility ' filled the bookshops. Some of the most galling of these were written under the direction of Pitt's brother-in-law Earl Temple, who had by this time become one of his most malignant enemies. The spell which Pitt had exercised for so long a time over his countrymen was broken, and the idol collapsed into the dust amid a storm of derision.

Why did he take such a momentous step, without consulting even one of his friends ? The reasons are not far to seek. He was a sick man, sick in body and in mind; indeed, his health was so shattered that he never made anything like a full recovery. At the age of fifty-six he looked an old man and we may be sure that he felt it, in his bones and tormented brain. In these circumstances he might well be excused for preferring the comparative peace and quiet of the Upper House to the rough-and-tumble of the one below, and the almost complete freedom from official cares of the Privy Seal office to the constant preoccupations of the Treasury.

Over his premiership it would be kinder to draw a veil than to attempt to describe its blundering descent into anarchy. The House of Commons, deprived of his leadership, became a cockpit of factious intrigue and irresponsible behaviour. Pitt himself, in the novel surroundings of the House of Lords, cut a very different figure from the one he had shown in the popular assembly. He who had used to thunder now muttered and mumbled. His temper, always haughty, became ungovernable, and he engaged in angry altercations with other noble lords. Very soon he grew tired of the place and the people in it and went off to Bath, where he remained from October 1766 until the following March. During this period he managed to keep in touch with his colleagues through correspondence, but he scarcely ever saw any of them even when there was the most pressing and important business to decide. Of course, he was unable to exercise any proper supervision, and things were done in his name and by his authority which he would surely have prevented if he had known anything about them. Thus in 1767 Townshend, his Chancellor of the Exchequer, imposed those import duties on tea and other commodities which are generally regarded as being the first step that led to the separation of the American colonies.

As the months of that baneful year passed, Chatham's condition became worse and worse, and he who was understood to be the head of the Cabinet had as little share in the government of the country as an unenfranchised peasant. He was hardly ever seen in London, spending his time at Hayes where he set an army of gardeners to work planting a thick screen of trees, urging them on so that the work was continued by torchlight throughout the night, or at Burton Pynsent, where he had a barren hill covered with cedars and cypresses, brought regardless of expense from London. Sometimes he was able to go out riding, but at others he was reported to be ' in the lowest dejection and debility that mind or body can be in ', sitting ' all the day leaning on his hands, which he supports on the table; does not permit any person to remain in the room; knocks when he wants anything, and, having made his wishes known, gives a signal without speaking, to the person who answered his call '. At any mention of politics, he would start and tremble violently from head to foot. He could bear no noise and his children, to whom he was normally devoted, had to be removed to another house.

Such correspondence as he had with the outside world was made through his wife, to whom he had given a power of attorney. It fell to her to answer his letters and keep callers away, and she had to cope with the most awkward domestic requirements. Thus she had to keep a succession of chickens on the spit in the kitchen, as her husband's appetite was so fitful that a meal had to be ready immediately, just when he wanted it, at any hour of the day or night.

When Chatham was at Bath, he wished he were at Pynsent, and when he was at Pynsent he wished he were at Hayes. He sold Hayes Place, and hardly was the contract signed when he wished most passionately to have the place back. 'That might have saved me!' he murmured plaintively. At Lady Chatham's earnest entreaty Mr. Thomas Walpole, who had bought the estate, agreed to have the sale annulled.

All this time the young and inexperienced Duke of Grafton was at his wits' end to keep the administration functioning. He begged again and again for an interview with his chief, however short, and the king joined in the entreaties. Let Chatham see Grafton if only for a few minutes . . . The king very much wanted to see Chatham himself. In one month George wrote eight letters to his Prime Minister, all couched in the most friendly and considerate terms, asking for an interview of a quarter of an hour perhaps; if Chatham could not come to London to see him, then he was quite prepared to visit Chatham in his own home.

To every appeal there came much the same reply, in Lady Chatham's handwriting. Chatham was overwhelmed with the royal goodness; he laid himself at his Majesty's feet; he begged his indulgence . . . but such was his extreme weakness that he could not possibly sustain the weight of an audience, he could not make any useful suggestion, he was utterly incapable of making any effort whatever.

At last Chatham was permitted to do what he had been anxious to do for a long time. He forwarded his resignation of the premiership to the king on 14 October 1768. George had no alternative other than to accept it.

This was not the end of his career, though he never held office again. For another ten years he lingered on, appearing from time to time on the stage and playing a by no means contemptible part. In July 1769 he staggered the courtiers by putting in an appearance at a royal levee, and the next year he resumed his attendance at the House of Lords. When his gaunt, crippled figure appeared in the doorway, the ministers shivered; and they did not breathe freely again until he had made his stumbling departure. While only a wreck of his former self he could still sway men's hearts and minds with the relics of his eloquence. He protested whenever he was able against the train of events which were hurrying Britain into strife with her colonies across the Atlantic.

When war was actually begun, and the Americans asserted their independence, Chatham was again incapacitated; indeed, for two years from the spring of 1775 he was out of action, hardly aware of anything that was going on beyond his sickroom. All his affairs were managed by the devoted woman who was his wife, and not the least of her troubles was his extravagance in ordering 'improvements' of one kind or another in his properties. Fortunately she had a good head for business, notwithstanding what Lord Camelford said about her disregard for economy, and she had the advantage of being able to go for advice to Thomas Coutts, founder of the famous banking firm, who had a great admiration and affection for her. It was also thanks entirely to her that Chatham was not only preserved through his succession of illnesses but on occasion was able to return to public life.

At the end of May 1777 he reappeared in the House of Lords, wrapped in flannels and supporting himself on crutches. 'If an end be not put to this war,' he exclaimed, 'there is an end to this country . . . You may ravage the Americans but you cannot conquer them! It is impossible. I might as well talk of driving them before me with this crutch !'

When the news came of General Burgoyne's surrender at Saratoga in October he again went to the House of Lords and made another impassioned appeal to end the fratricidal strife. 'If I were an American, as I am an Englishman,' he declaimed, 'while a foreign troop was landed in my country, I never would lay down my arms— never—never—never!' Having said which, he went on to denounce in the strongest terms the employment on the British side of Red Indians as allies. 'Who is the man,' he demanded, 'that has dared to associate with our armies the tomahawk and scalping-knife of the savage ? To call into this civilized alliance the wild and inhuman savage of the woods . . . to wage the horrors of his barbarous war against our brethren ?'

One of their lordships ventured to argue that it was justifiable to use 'all the means that God and nature have put into our hands'. The old man turned on him in a fury of disgust. 'To attribute the sacred sanction of God and nature . . . to the cannibal savage torturing, murdering, roasting, and eating—literally, *eating !*—the mangled victims of his barbarous battles ! Abominable principles, and even more abominable the avowal of them . . . I am old and weak, and at present unable to say more, but my feelings and indignation are too strong to have said less. I could not have slept this night in my bed, and reposed my head on my pillow, without giving vent to my eternal abhorrence of such preposterous and enormous principles.'

But his words carried little weight, and no conviction. What did Lord Chatham advise ? What would be his policy if he had the opportunity of carrying it out ? He wanted peace—and so did they all; but the terms he suggested—the grant to the Americans of the right of internal taxation but with the acknowledgment of Britain's supremacy in everything else—was not practical politics. Far too much blood had been shed for any such friendly composition of their differences.

All the same, Chatham's name and fame were still so charged with power that in the early months of 1778 the question of his being called upon to form a ministry and see what he could do, was actively canvassed. But when the king was approached, he absolutely refused to have anything to do with the man whom he had once styled ' a trumpet of sedition '.

Chatham's last appearance in the House of Lords was on 7 April 1778, on the occasion of the young Duke of Richmond's motion for an address to his Majesty, requesting him to dismiss his present ministers, withdraw his troops from America, and negotiate with the Americans so as ' to recover their friendship at heart, if not their allegiance '. The principal reason for this change of policy was the news that France and Spain were about to join America in the war with a view to reversing the defeat of 1763, when Pitt had been the captain of Britain at war. No sooner had Chatham heard of what was proposed, than all his old hatred of the Bourbon monarchies, whom it had been the main object of his life to humble, was aroused and he resolved to raise his voice against it.

When he rose that morning he was in a state of high excitement, and his doctors strongly advised him not to venture out. But he spurned their counsels, and went down to Westminster in his coach, accompanied by his son William Pitt (not yet nineteen, but destined to be Prime Minister in a mere five years' time) and his son-in-law Lord Mahon (Lord Stanhope). He rested for a while in the Lord Chancellor's room, and then, leaning on his two young supporters, he made his entrance into the chamber. Some of the peers rose to make way for the little procession, and he bowed to them with great courtliness. He was holding his crutch in his hand. He wore, as was his fashion, a rich velvet coat, but his legs were swathed in flannel. His face was sunk and wan, and so emaciated that none of his features could be discerned from beneath his over-large wig, except the aquiline nose and his eyes, which still sparkled occasionally with their old penetrating brilliance. 'He looked like a dying man,' wrote one who was there, 'yet never was seen a figure of more dignity: he appeared like a being of a superior species.'

When the Duke of Richmond had presented his motion, Chatham rose to his feet with painful slowness. He began speaking, and for a time his voice was so low that it was impossible to catch his words. But as it went on it gained strength and assurance, and some among his audience thought that they could detect traces of his former majestic eloquence.

'I thank God that I have been enabled to come here this day to perform my duty . . . I am old and infirm . . . I have one foot, more than one foot, in the grave . . . I have risen from my bed to stand up in the cause of my country . . . perhaps never again to speak in this House . . .'

There was a deathlike stillness. A handkerchief dropping would have constituted a disturbance. He stammered, lost the thread of what he was saying, repeated himself, regained the thread and stumbled on. The assembled peers listened in solemn silence, and on every face might be read the feelings of profound respect and deepest courtesy. Men held their breath in wonder and compassion.

Towards the end of his speech he roused himself to denounce the follies and disasters of the war in America. 'My Lords,' came his peroration, 'I rejoice that the grave has not closed upon me—that I am still alive to lift up by voice against the dismemberment of this ancient and most noble monarchy! Shall this great kingdom now fall prostrate before the House of Bourbon? If we must fall, *let us fall like men!*'

As he subsided into his seat, the House breathed again. The Duke of Richmond replied with good sense and consideration. If Chatham himself were head of the Government—he, even he, would find it impossible to carry on. The old man listened, and seemed to be becoming increasingly indignant. He struggled to his feet, pressed his hand upon his heart, and then sank back in convulsions. As he fell, three or four of those nearest to him reached out to receive him in their arms. The House broke up in confusion, as the sorely stricken statesman was carried out and across the way to the house of one of the officials in Downing Street. When he was sufficiently recovered he was driven back to Hayes.

For a few weeks he lingered on, 'his bed watched to the last' writes Macaulay, 'with anxious tenderness by his wife and children; and he well deserved their care. Too often haughty and wayward to others, to them he had been almost effeminately kind. He had through life been dreaded by his political opponents, and regarded with more awe than love even by his political associates. But no fear seems to have mingled with the affection which his fondness, constantly overflowing in a thousand endearing forms, had inspired in the little circle at Hayes.' He died on 11 May 1778, when in his seventieth year.

At the time of his death he had not, in both Houses of Parliament, ten personal adherents, but with the exception of a few detractors who could not bury their animosities in his grave all men hastened to pay tribute to ' the lofty genius, the unsullied probity, the undisputed services, of him who was no more '. Lord North, the Prime Minister and a Tory, moved in the House of Commons a generous tribute: £20,000 was voted to pay the debts that Chatham had left behind him, and an address was presented to the king praying that the deceased statesman should be accorded a public funeral.

The Corporation of the City of London urgently entreated that ' as a mark of gratitude and veneration from the first commercial city of the Empire towards the statesman whose vigour and counsels had so much contributed to the protection and extension of its commerce ', he should be buried in St. Paul's, but Parliament had already decided in favour of Westminster Abbey, on the ground that he ought to be brought ' near to the dust of kings '. On 9 June therefore, Chatham's remains, after lying in state in the Painted Chamber, were carried to a grave in the centre of the north transept. Colonel Barré, an old supporter of Chatham's and who had been wounded at the taking of Quebec in 1759, bore the banner of the lordship of Chatham, and the Duke of Richmond and Lord Rockingham followed close behind. The chief mourner was the young William Pitt, who twenty-seven years later was to be buried in the same grave.

Chatham's widow—Lady Hester, a countess in her own right—survived him until 1803. She is buried in the same vault, together with other members of the Pitt family.

In due course a rather pompous memorial was erected above Chatham's grave at the public expense, and ever since the north transept has been appropriated to statesmen. Thus the words that ' Junius ' once wrote about Chatham have been literally fulfilled: ' Recorded honours still gather round his monument, and thicken over him. It is a solid fabric, and will support the laurels that adorn it.'

Lord Macaulay's essay on Chatham draws to its conclusion with a splendid passage. ' In no other cemetery do so many great citizens lie within so narrow a space. High over those venerable graves towers the stately monument of Chatham, and from above, his effigy, graven by a cunning hand, seems still, with eagle face and outstretched arm, to bid England be of good cheer, and to hurl defiance at her foes . . . And history, while, for the warning of vehement, high, and daring natures, she notes his many errors, will yet deliberately pronounce, that, among the eminent men whose bones lie near his, scarcely one has left a more stainless, and none a more splendid name.'

10

DUKE OF GRAFTON

WHEN IN THE SUMMER of 1766 William Pitt at length formed an administration of his own, he did not become First Lord of the Treasury, as most Prime Ministers have done, but appointed the Duke of Grafton to that post, while he himself took the comparative sinecure office of Lord Privy Seal. Before many months were out, Pitt withdrew to the House of Lords as Earl of Chatham, and it was on Grafton's young shoulders that the full burdens of the Government fell.

To look at his portraits—His Grace Augustus Henry Fitzroy, third Duke of Grafton—is to be irresistibly reminded of the saturnine countenance of Charles II. Which is hardly surprising, for the king was his ancestor. The first Duke of Grafton was one of Charles's bastards by the splendid spitfire Barbara Villiers, whom Charles made countess of Castlemaine and Duchess of Cleveland. The second duke, Charles's grandson, notwithstanding the Stuart blood in his veins became a firm supporter of the Hanoverians, and was a lifelong friend of George II. On his death in 1757 his grandson, Augustus Henry, succeeded as third duke.

There is a painting of him by John Hoppner which shows him as an old man, beaming benevolence and wisdom. As a young man, when he was a great figure in the Whig aristocracy—and particularly when he was Prime Minister from 1767 to 1770—he looked very different. In those years he demonstrated that he had inherited something more than his physiognomy from the Merry Monarch. An insatiable love of pleasure, an utter disregard for convention, a passionate lusting after women—these were among his most marked characteristics, as they had been among King Charles's. Even in those easy-going times it was thought rather shocking that the Prime Minister should put off a Cabinet so as not to miss a meeting at Newmarket, and should flaunt his mistress in public. ' An apprentice,' so Horace Walpole refers to him scornfully, ' thinking that the world should be postponed to a whore and a horse-race.'

When Grafton was born on 9 October 1735 there seemed little likelihood of his ever becoming duke, since his own father was a third son and he himself had an elder brother. But his father, who had been M.P. for Thetford and was an officer in the navy, died of malaria at the siege of Cartagena when he was only twenty-five, and death also removed those others who stood ahead of him in the succession. At the age of twelve he became next in line, and as Lord Euston he was sent to Westminster school and in due course to Peterhouse College, Cambridge, where by right of birth he graduated M.A. at sixteen.

One incident in his boyhood stuck in his memory. He was taken on a visit to Lord Cobham's great house at Stowe, and there he encountered William Pitt. The statesman patted him on the head, and prophesied a bright future for him. From that day onwards Grafton was Pitt's most fervent admirer.

After Cambridge, he set out on the Grand Tour. He had for his travelling companion and guardian a Monsieur Alleon, of Geneva, whom he describes in the autobiography that he wrote as an old man as ' a real gentleman, and a man of great honor, with much knowledge of the world, but who was more fitted to form the polite man than to assist or encourage any progress in literary pursuits'. However, ' I by no means neglected the little I had attained; and a natural inclination leading me to history, and to study those principles of government which were ever present to my mind from the time I first read the sound system of Mr. Locke, I lost no opportunity of improving myself in that science, on which the most essential interests of mankind in this world depend.'

Returning to London in 1754 he found ' the various parties of political men ambitiously struggling to advance their own power and that of their friends, and appearing to be less attentive to the state of the nation '. Mr. Pelham had recently died; the Duke of Newcastle was Prime Minister, but ' the two most distinguished statesmen of the time ', Henry Fox (Lord Holland) and William Pitt, were excluded from office. In 1756 Grafton came of age and he secured election to the House of Commons as member for the borough of St. Edmunds, and at once attached himself to Pitt. But a few months later his grandfather died, and he succeeded to the title. He took his seat in the House of Lords but was a silent member until 1762, when he delivered a slashing attack on Lord Bute. ' He is appearing in a new light,' wrote Horace Walpole, ' and by the figure he makes he will soon be at the head of the Opposition if it continues.' Already he was considered sufficiently formidable to be deprived of his lord lieutenancy of Yorkshire, when the great Whig lords, Newcastle and Rockingham, lost theirs.

In Rockingham's administration in 1765 he was appointed Secretary of State—a splendid opening for a mere novice. Pitt formed his government soon after and he offered Grafton the post of First Lord of the Treasury. This was an extraordinary preferment for a man only a little over thirty, and Grafton took a good deal of persuading before he ' yielded at length, tho' with reluctance, to Mr. Pitt's solicitation '. Pitt's views, he goes on, ' were great and noble, worthy of a patriot; but they were too visionary to expect that ambitious men would co-operate in promoting them. He had persuaded himself, that his weight as a statesman, together with his present popularity, and the cause well supported by his Majesty, would be able to reconcile every man to those posts which he had designed for them '. A few lines farther down the page he explains ' Mr. Pitt's plan was Utopian, and I will venture to add, that he lived too much out of the world to have a right knowledge of mankind.' To make matters infinitely worse, the Great Commoner promptly removed himself to the upper house as Earl of Chatham.

Grafton thought this a deplorable error of judgment on the Prime Minister's part, and he was more concerned when Chatham, ' a suppressed gout falling on his nerves, to a degree sufficient to master his resolution, became invisible, even to the Lord Chancellor and myself '. He retired to Bath, and let it be known that he wished to be ' allowed to attend solely to his health, until he found himself to be equal to any business. Here, in fact, was the end of his administration.'

Poor Grafton was left to carry on as best he could, trying desperately to keep a government in being, of which the chief had in effect abdicated and whose members were all at loggerheads. He wrote again and again to Lady Chatham, begging her to use her influence with her husband to grant him even the shortest of interviews. He did manage to see him once, and it proved a most painful experience. ' His nerves and spirits were affected to a dreadful degree: and the sight of his great mind bowed down, and thus weakened by disorder, would have filled me with grief and concern, even if I had not borne a sincere attachment to his person and character.' With this exception, all Grafton's appeals for an interview met with the same answer: Chatham was deeply appreciative of Grafton's solicitude, but he felt himself quite unable to attend to matters of business. King George himself wrote repeatedly to Chatham—begging him to see Grafton, but the reply was always the same. From the autumn of 1767 Grafton was accepted as Prime

Minister, and in the face of mounting difficulties and all too well aware of his own inadequacies he struggled along.

But he had no liking for what he called the 'drudgery of Parliament', and he left as much of it as he could to his subordinates. What really interested him were his hounds and his horses—and his women. And it so happened that a domestic crisis came to a head when he ought to have been giving the whole of his time and attention to affairs of state.

In 1756, the year in which he came of age, Grafton had married the Hon. Anne Liddell, daughter of Lord Ravensworth. They had three children, two boys and a girl, but before long what Horace Walpole styles a 'disagreement of their tempers' arose between them, and after a visit to the Continent in 1761, taken for the benefit of Lady Grafton's health, they decided on a separation. Still the marriage might have held together if the Duke had not become infatuated with a woman who called herself Mrs. Hoghton (or Haughton), although she is generally known as Nancy Parsons.

Other Prime Ministers have had their mistresses, but they have usually kept them in the background. Grafton took a very different course, as will be seen from this letter to George Grenville, the former Prime Minister, that bears the date 22 April 1768. 'It is impossible to conceive the disgust which the Duke of Grafton's appearance at the Opera with Mrs. Hoghton, last Saturday, has given: a Minister, a married man, the Duchess there in the pit— talking to her only, waiting upon her out, are the changes rung by everybody. Libertine men are as much offended as prudish women: and *it is impossible he should think of remaining Minister who thus defies all decency*, is almost the general conclusion.'

To this letter the editor of the *Grenville Papers* (W. J. Smith, 1852) appends an informative footnote. Anne or Annabella Parsons, he states, is said to have been the daughter of a tailor in Bond Street. She obtained the name of Hoghton from a West India captain and merchant of that name with whom she lived for some time, and accompanied to Jamaica—but she was not married to him. She soon wearied of the West Indies; she escaped from her lover by stratagem, and returning to London took lodgings at a perfumer's in Brewer Street, where by some chance she soon became acquainted with the Duke of Grafton.

Grenville's correspondent used the words 'impossible', but Grafton might well have got away with his shameless exhibition if it had not attracted the notice of Junius, the hardest-hitting journalist of the century. The famous Letters were published in the *Public*

Advertiser between January 1769 and January 1772, and were shortly afterwards reprinted in volume form. A number of them are addressed to the Duke of Grafton, or make his misdeeds their theme. Here is what Junius wrote to Grafton in a ' letter ' published under the date of 23 April 1768, a few days after the Duke's appearance with Mrs. Hoghton at the Opera House.

' My Lord, Permit me to congratulate your Grace upon a piece of good fortune which few men, of the best established reputation, have been able to attain to. The most accomplished persons have usually some defect, some weakness in their characters, which diminishes the lustre of their brighter qualifications . . . But yours, my Lord, is a perfect character: through every line of public and of private life you are consistent with yourself. After doing everything, in your public station, that a minister might reasonably be ashamed of, you have determined, with a noble spirit of uniformity, to mark your personal history by such strokes as a gentleman, without any great disgrace to his assurance, might be permitted to blush for.

' I had already conceived a high opinion of your talents and disposition. Whether the property of the subject, or the general rights of the nation, were to be invaded; or whether you were tired of one lady, and chose another for the honourable companion of your pleasures; whether it was a horse-race, or a hazard-table, a noble disregard of forms seemed to operate through all your conduct. But you have exceeded my warmest expectations. Highly as I thought you, your Grace must pardon me when I confess that there was one effort which I did not think you equal to. I did not think you capable of exhibiting your lovely Thais at the opera-house, of sitting a whole night by her side, of calling for her carriage yourself, and of leading her to it through a crowd of the first men and women in this Kingdom. To a mind like yours, my Lord, such an outrage to your wife, such a triumph over decency, such insult to the company, must have afforded the highest gratification. When all the ordinary pleasures of life were exhausted, this, I presume, was your *novissima voluptas.*

' It is of a lasting nature, my Lord, and I dare say will give you as much pleasure upon reflection, as it did in the enjoyment. After so honourable an achievement, a poet's imagination could add but one ray more to the lustre of your character. Obtain a divorce, marry the lady, and I do not doubt but Mr. Bradshaw [Grafton's private secretary] will be civil enough to give her away, with an honest, artless smile of approbation.'

Thus was the Prime Minister addressed, in a public print, by a pseudonymous journalist. There was more to come. Letter xiii, for instance, which was published on 30 May 1769.

'You have better proofs of your descent, my Lord, than the register of a marriage, or any troublesome inheritance of reputation. There are some hereditary strokes of character, by which a family may be as clearly distingusihed as by the blackest features of the human face. Charles the First lived and died a hypocrite. Charles the Second was a hypocrite of another sort, and should have died upon the same scaffold. At the distance of a century we see their different characters happily revived and blended in your Grace . . .'

And again, on 22 June of the same year: 'The example of the English nobility may, for aught I know, sufficiently justify the Duke of Grafton, when he indulges his genius in all the fashionable excesses of the age; yet, considering his rank and station, I think it would do him more honour to be able to deny the fact, than to defend it by such authority. But if vice itself could be excused, there is yet a certain display of it, a certain outrage to decency, and violation of public decorum, which, for the benefit of society, should never be forgiven. It is not that he kept a mistress at home, but that he constantly attended her abroad . . . When we see a man act in this manner, we may admit the shameless depravity of his heart, but what are we to think of his understanding?'

Junius, whoever he was, is reported to have been the author likewise of the scurrilous set of verses that were printed in Almon's *Political Register* in 1768, under the title, *Harry and Nan: an elegy in the manner of Tibullus*. The first two verses run:

> Can Apollo resist, or a Poet refuse,
>   When Harry and Nan solicit the Muse;
> A Statesman, who makes the whole nation his care,
>   And a Nymph, who is almost as chaste as she's fair.

> Dear Spousy had led such a damnable life,
>   He determin'd to keep any whore but his wife:
> So Harry's affairs, like those of the State,
>   Have been pretty well handled and tickled of late.

After this reference to Grafton's marital troubles and the nasty rumours that were circulating about his wife, we are told in the next verse that:

> From fourteen to forty our provident Nan
>   Had devoted her life to the study of man,

which indication of the lady's age is followed by the charge that
Grafton was providing for her out of public funds:

> Secret service had wasted the national wealth,
> But now . . . 'tis the price of the Minister's health:
> An expense which the Treasury may well afford,
> He who serves him in bed should be paid at the board.

And so on to verse six, the last:

> My friend holds the candle—the lovers debate,
> And among them, God knows how they settle the State;
> Was there ever a nation so govern'd before,
> By a Jockey and Gambler, a P . . p and a Wh . . . ?

The scandal continued for many months, to the dismay of
Grafton's friends and supporters, who feared the discredit that the
Prime Minister's behaviour was bringing not only on himself but
upon his administration. Eventually the affair was settled in an unexpected way. It came out that the 'beautiful and most accomplished' Duchess of Grafton, having striven in vain to effect a
reconciliation with her husband, had at length herself taken a lover
and was with child by him. He was John Fitzpatrick, Earl of
Upper Ossory, who was a nephew of the great Whig nobleman
the Duke of Bedford.

Grafton decided to seek a divorce, which in those days might be
had only by a special Act of Parliament. This was passed in March
1769 and in the following May he married—not Nancy Parsons
but Elizabeth Wrottesley, daughter of the Rev. Sir Richard Wrottesley, Dean of Windsor, who is described as 'not handsome, but
quiet and reasonable, and having a very amiable character'.

It is good to learn that the marriage turned out very well indeed.
In his *Autobiography* we may read Grafton's tribute to his second
wife's 'merit as a wife, tenderness and affection as a mother of a
numerous family'—she bore him twelve children—'and exemplary
conduct thro' life'.

And what of Mrs. Hoghton? Should we perhaps keep a tear
in reserve for the discarded mistress? There is no doubt that in the
early stages of the liaison she thoroughly enjoyed being the Prime
Minister's 'favourite Sultana' (Horace Walpole's term), and being
courted by his friends who hoped she would exercise her influence
on their behalf. But Mrs. Hoghton was easily bored, it seems. His
Grace was a fine catch but his worries made him gloomy and pre-
occupied. So she took herself off to the Continent, ostensibly for

the benefit of her health although there were some who supposed that the trip was only a ruse to keep Grafton's passion on the boil. The Duke seems to have had his suspicions. He put spies on her track, letters were intercepted, and it was soon made clear that Nancy was having an affair with the young Duke of Dorset who, so Walpole informs us, was ' unnusually handsome, well made, and had an air of sentimental melancholy, which more than atoned for a want of sense '. Nancy must have thought so, for she exchanged one duke for the other with the greatest of ease.

Nevertheless Junius, who not long before had been sneering at her ' faded charms ', had another fling at Grafton on her account. He asserts that after the Duke had separated from her, he ' proposed to continue united with her on some Platonic terms of friendship, which she rejected with contempt. His baseness to this woman is beyond description or belief.'

Junius need not have bothered. Nancy and Lord Dorset lived together as man and wife in France until 1776 when, the Duke having found a fresher attraction, she left him for young Viscount Maynard whom, says Walpole, ' she still had charms or art enough to captivate, and had hopes of marrying, and did actually marry before the end of the year '.

So the lady whom Horace Walpole calls ' the Duke of Grafton's Mrs. Hoghton, the Duke of Dorset's Mrs. Hoghton, everybody's Mrs. Hoghton ', became a peeress after all. And she lived a long time to enjoy it, since she did not die until the winter of 1814.

After noting that he had been honoured by the king with the Garter, and had been elected Chancellor of the university of Cambridge, Horace Walpole goes on to say that Grafton ' could not bear the thoughts of business ' but ' diverted himself in the country, coming to town but once a week or once a fortnight to sign papers at the Treasury ', with the result that ' everything fell into confusion '.

Even when he did manage to summon up enough energy to make a decision he perpetrated the most egregious blunders, as when he secured the expulsion of John Wilkes from the House of Commons, thereby making a popular martyr of him. ' Wilkes and Liberty! ' became the rallying-cry of the first organized bodies of Radical opinion. In the spring of 1769 there was an outbreak of mob violence, in which the royal palace was threatened. The king, it should be said, displayed on this occasion a courage and self-possession which contrasted strongly with his first minister's state of nerves.

By the middle of January 1770 Grafton had indeed reached the limit of his endurance. The scurrilous attacks made on him by Junius ' threw him into an agony', Wraxall reports. Defeated in his Cabinet, deserted by his friends, cold-shouldered by the king, his policies in ruins, and assailed, Wraxall states, ' with an acrimony and ability that have perhaps never been equalled' he went along to the palace on the evening of 27 January and handed in his resignation. The king, who had already decided on Lord North as his successor, received it without comment.

After a year's rest Grafton returned to politics and accepted the post of Lord Privy Seal under Lord North, but he retired in 1775 because of his opposition to the Government's American policy.

He now joined the Whigs in the Rockingham group, and took a strong line against the American war. Several times Lord North tried to entice him back into office, but he always declined. In 1782 however he agreed to serve as Lord Privy Seal under Rockingham and then under Shelburne. The young William Pitt offered him his old place for the third time, but now he preferred an existence of country pursuits passed mainly at his seat of Euston Hall in Suffolk. These were probably the happiest years of his life. In his *Memoirs* he is revealed as a benevolent old aristocrat, serenely happy in his home life, deeply respected by his friends and neighbours, and revered by the younger generation. In his latter years he took up the study of theology, which led him to become a Unitarian, and he worshipped at the Unitarian chapel in Essex Street off the Strand. He also collected rare books and it is said that he read quite a number of them. He died in 1811 at the age of seventy-seven.

II

LORD NORTH

LORD NORTH, the Prime Minister who 'lost America'. There he sits, on the front bench in the House of Commons, a man of 'the middle size, heavy, large, and much inclined to corpulency'. This is how Wraxall describes him; and he goes on, a man with 'a fair complexion, regular features, light hair, and bushy eyebrows, and grey eyes rather prominent in his head'. Another noticeable thing about him is his tongue, which 'being too large for his mouth, renders his articulation somewhat thick'. In speaking, walking, and in every other motion, he is 'to the last degree awkward'.

There is something else about him that should be mentioned, his 'constitutional somnolency'. Lolling there on the padded seat, with his eyes closed, he seems to be quite unaware of what is going on, and it would not be surprising if he were to snore.

But here we may be doing him an injustice, for there comes to mind the occasion when a member, who had been boring the House for a long, long time with his account of the Prime Minister's many sins of commission and omission, spluttered indignantly, 'Even now, in the midst of these perils, the noble Lord is asleep.'

'No, I am not,' protested the noble Lord, without opening his eyes. 'But I wish to God I was.'

The Hon. Frederick North, commonly called by the courtesy title of Lord North and who eventually succeeded as second Earl of Guilford, was born on 12 April 1732.

The Norths were a family of some distinction in politics and letters, who had been established in Cambridgeshire since Queen Elizabeth's time. One of them translated Plutarch, and Shakespeare became indebted to him for the plots of several of his plays. Another wrote lives of himself and his brothers—they flourished in the latter part of the seventeenth century—which some critics have pronounced to be worthy to stand on the same shelf with Boswell's *Johnson*. One of these brothers was made Lord Guilford by Charles II, but there was also a barony of North in the family dating from 1554. These two peerages were combined in the person of

Francis North, third Lord Guilford, who in 1752 had his barony converted into the earldom of Guilford. This Lord Guilford was Frederick North's father; his mother was Lady Lucy Montagu, daughter of the Earl of Halifax.

Both Lord and Lady Guilford were on terms of intimate friendship with Frederick Prince of Wales, the son and heir of George II, and Frederick, the Guilfords' eldest son, was named after the Prince who also stood godfather for him.

Five years later the Prince of Wales's own eldest son was born—the future George III. The two boys grew up together and were very good friends. There was also between them what Wraxall calls an ' astonishing resemblance ', which excited ' much remark and pleasantry ' on the part of the Prince of Wales. He ' often jested on the subject with Lord Guilford, observing, that the world would think that one of their wives had played her husband false '.

Lord Guilford had attached himself to what he called the ' Court of Great Expectations ' at the beginning of George II's reign, and we may suppose that he managed a subservient smile at his master's vulgar ' pleasantry ', but it must have required an effort, since he was reputed to be a man of high principle, devoutly Anglican in religion and a staunch Tory in politics, as most of the Norths had been for generations. He took pains to ensure that his son should imbibe all the correct principles, and in this he succeeded. Among all the hard things that were said of Lord North, never a word was whispered against his moral character.

He spent his youth at the family seat of Wroxton Abbey, in Oxfordshire, very much under his father's thumb. At the age of ten he was sent to Eton. The Master wrote to his parents that ' both the masters and the boys love him, and really by his behaviour he deserves it ', but his tutor—and this is something that he always recalled with a chuckle—once shouted at him, ' You're a blundering blockhead, and if you are ever Prime Minister it will always be the same ! '

From Eton he went on to Trinity College, Oxford, where ' he completed his academical studies with the reputation of being a very accomplished and elegant classical scholar '. At least this is what we are told by his daughter, Lady Charlotte Lindsay, in a biographical fragment which she composed in her old age. Lady Charlotte goes on to state that after taking his degree, ' My father passed three years on the Continent, residing successively in Germany, Italy, and France, and acquiring the languages of those countries, particularly the last. He spoke French with great fluency and correctness;

this acquirement, together with the observations he had made upon the men and manners of the countries he had visited, gave him what Mme. de Stael called *l'esprit Européen*, and enabled him to be as agreeable a man in Paris, Naples, and Vienna as he was in London . . . his figure was slight and slim; his face was always plain, but agreeable, owing to its habitual expression of cheerfulness and good humour, though it gave no indication of the brightness of his understanding.'

In 1752 Lord Guilford was made an earl, and Frederick was henceforth known as Lord North. As mentioned earlier, this was a courtesy title only. It carried with it no right to a seat in the House of Lords, and allowed its holder to sit in the Commons. For all the years of his parliamentary career only the thin thread of his father's life separated him from political extinction in the House of Lords. But Lord Guilford survived until 1790, when his son had passed into political eclipse.

Lord North was abroad on the Grand Tour when his father became an earl. Soon after his return home he was elected, in 1754, M.P. for Banbury, one of the family's pocket boroughs, which continued to return him to the House of Commons throughout his parliamentary career. In Parliament he soon made his mark. Said George Grenville, ' North is a man of great promise and high qualifications, and if he does not relax in his political pursuits he is very likely to be Prime Minister.' His first official appointment was in 1759 as a junior lord of the treasury in the great Newcastle-Pitt administration, and he remained in that position until Lord Rockingham took over office six years later. As a Tory, he declined to serve under Rockingham but in Chatham's ministry of 1766 he was joint Paymaster-General.

North had been only a few months in the Paymaster's office when he was offered the post of Chancellor of the Exchequer. He respectfully declined it on that occasion, but in October 1767 the offer was renewed and he was constrained to accept. He held the post for thirteen years, including all the time that he was Prime Minister; and in this capacity, at least, he earned golden opinions.

So well did he acquit himself that the king soon had him in mind for the highest position in the Government. Grafton's ministry was staggering from crisis to crisis, and was clearly doomed to collapse. Who should take his place ? The Whigs were hopeless, split as they were into quarrelling factions. The Tories were falling over themselves to display their loyalty, but they were not numerous enough to stand alone. For some time past the king had been busy building up his own party of ' King's friends ', composed of Tories, dissentient Whigs, and a number of political nondescripts, recruited through royal bounty and patronage and sitting, many of them, for boroughs at the disposal of the Treasury. All that was needed now was a leader, and in Lord North the king felt sure he had just the man he was looking for. He sent for him and made him an offer of the premiership. North hesitated, and it was not until January 1770 that he kissed hands and formed his administration.

Most of the political prophets gave it a short life and admittedly the new ministers, apart from Lord North himself, were nothing much to speak of. In the House of Lords the Government were sure of a majority but in the Commons, out of a total membership of 558, North could count on only just under two hundred ' placemen '. On the Opposition benches sat most of the best debaters in the House, and as the new Prime Minister looked across the gangway he may well have felt nervous. But he was much too experienced a parliamentarian to show it if he did. He put on a bold front, replied to his critics in terms that were firm but conciliatory, and managed to scrape home in the divisions. Each week that passed saw him more firmly in the saddle, and before long even the great Chatham was speaking well of him. ' Lord North is serving the Crown more sufficiently upon the whole,' he said, ' than any other man now to be found could do. His tenure seems a pretty good one.' Chatham was right. In the previous ten years there had been six Prime Ministers, but Lord North was premier for the next twelve.

Nominally it was a Tory administration and Lord North has been usually styled a Tory. No doubt he was, bearing in mind the traditional Toryism of his family. But he did not consider himself bound to any party but the king's; he was a ' King's man ' whose job it was to see that the King's Government was carried on. He even went so far as to repudiate the title of Prime Minister: there was no such thing in the Constitution, he asserted. As he saw it, *all* the ministers were the royal servants, and they owed their allegiance not to the man who took the chair at Cabinet meetings but to the king himself. In all things Lord North was his Majesty's most loyal and obedient servant, and in the light of history his chief fault is seen to have been that he obeyed his master too consistently. Particularly was this the case in everything connected with the American confrontation.

George Grenville had imposed the stamp taxes, Rockingham had taken them off. Chatham had openly sympathized with the American cry of ' No taxation without representation ', and would have gone out of his way to conciliate the colonists rather than drive them into rebellion. Grafton likewise might have exercised a moderating influence if he had not been so much occupied with other things. Now it was North's turn, and it fell to him to conduct negotiations with an increasingly suspicious, resentful, and hostile America, while being egged on to extreme measures by the monarch who looked upon the Americans as a landlord might look on tenants who refused to pay their rent.

North was no fool, and it was not long before he realized what a dreadful prospect lay at the end of the road down which he was being pushed. King George was a most pigheaded fellow, and against him Lord North never really stood a chance. After all, they had been boys together, and up to the present nothing had happened to disturb their friendship. North was also well aware of the king's constitutional malady, and he dreaded doing anything that might upset his precarious balance. As someone has remarked, Lord North lost America because he could not bear to think of the king being kept awake at nights with worry. Beyond any doubt he fully vindicated his master's trust. No statesman could have served the king with more zeal and devotion.

In debate in the House of Commons he was a skilled performer. Writes Wraxall, he was ' powerful, able, and fluent, sometimes repelling the charges made against him with solid argument, but still more frequently eluding or blunting the weapons of his antagonists by the force of wit and humour '. While he rarely rose to sublimity, he possessed ' vast facility and command of language '. He had the gift of speaking ' for a long time, apparently with great pathos, and yet disclose no fact, nor reveal any secret '. Furthermore ' the unalterable suavity and equality of temper, which was natural to him, enabled him to sustain, unmoved, the bitter sarcasms and severe accusations levelled at him from the Opposition benches. They always seemed to sink into him like a cannon-ball into a woolsack.'

As a statesman, North was often charged with irresolution, but Wraxall thought that he might rather have been taxed with indolence and procrastination. ' He naturally loved to postpone ', though when once he had made up his mind he stuck to it. He hated writing letters; ' I am the world's worst correspondent,' he confessed. He seldom took notes, but his memory seldom let him down. And he was so careless that it was considered positively unsafe to entrust him with State papers, since he would be sure to mislay or lose them. On one occasion, a member of his Cabinet told Wraxall, a letter of the first importance addressed by the king to Lord North was found to be missing and only after a long search was found lying open in the W.C.

Such was the man who for twelve years was Prime Minister, however often he might repudiate the title. To begin with, things went reasonably well with him and his government. He basked in the royal favour. In 1771 his wife was appointed to the rangership of Bushey Park, which carried with it an excellent house as official residence—the house which is now occupied by the National Physical Laboratory. This was North's home for the rest of his life. In 1772 the king made him a Knight of the Garter, and a few years later, when the wardenship of the Cinque Ports fell vacant, the king conferred that on him, although the appointment was not for life as North had hoped it would be. The salary attached to the position was £1,500 a year, and altogether North's official annual emoluments are estimated to have amounted to £12,000.

Surely a tremendous sum and yet, it would appear, North generally found it very hard to balance his accounts. His domestic budget was frequently in the red, and at length he was in such financial difficulties that the king felt it necessary to intervene. In a letter to Lord North dated 19 September 1777, the king recalled that North had told him that he had been in debt 'ever since your first settling in life and that you have never been able to get out of that difficulty'. His Majesty went on: 'I therefore must insist you will now state to me whether 12, or £15,000 will not set your affairs in order, if it will, nay if £20,000 is necessary I am resolved you shall have no other person concerned in freeing them but myself... and I want no other return but your being convinced that I love you as well as a Man of Worth as I esteem you as a Minister.'

A most kind and considerate letter on the face of it, and North was duly grateful. But although the twenty thousand pounds—it may have even been more—was not a bribe, it undoubtedly placed North under a deep personal obligation to the king.

Even before hostilities had begun in America in 1775 North had shown signs of wishing to retire, and as the war developed what had been a wish became a gnawing anxiety. While never wavering in his conviction that right lay on the British side, he was equally convinced that this was a war that Britain could never win. Time and again he urged attempts at a negotiated settlement, and always the king refused to consider it: the Americans were his subjects, and they must be brought to heel.

North allowed himself to be persuaded or at least overruled, but

he was quite sure that he was not the man to carry the royal policy
to a successful conclusion. He was getting old, he was tired, his
strength was exhausted, his capacity was worn to a shred, really he
could not carry on much longer. ' Every hour convinces me more
and more,' he wrote to his master, ' of the necessity Your Majesty
is under of putting some other person than myself at the head of
affairs.'

After the disaster of Saratoga in 1777, when Burgoyne's little
army was compelled to surrender to the Americans, North's plain-
tive appeals to be allowed to quit became monthly, almost weekly
occurrences, and an almost abject note was struck in some of them.
But George was obdurate. Sometimes he commanded, and sometimes he pleaded. He reminded North of the Duke of Grafton,
who had left his post when the danger clouds threatened. Surely
Lord North would not desert him as Grafton had done ? No, no,
of course not, replied the Prime Minister, who in that same year
had received the royal bounty: he would ' rather die than abandon
His Majesty in distress ', and he had ' no idea of deserting His Majesty
while his faculties of mind and body would enable him to continue
in his service '.

After every such protestation of continued loyalty, North must
have wished most fervently that he had strength of mind enough to
resist the royal blandishments.

In the House of Commons, while the war made its disastrous
progress, North was assailed with a fury such as no previous Prime
Minister had ever had to encounter, and of his successors only Peel,
perhaps, ever had to meet such a storm of vituperation. ' Resign!
Resign!' came the cry, after every revelation of mismanagement,
after every fresh disaster to the British arms in America. He was
blamed for everything; and although his majority kept together
they were sullen and discontented.

There was one famous evening when Fox taunted him beyond
endurance, and threatened him with impeachment. The Hon.
Gentleman, said North in his reply, had asked him why he had not
resigned at this or at that. ' I will tell the hon. gentleman why . . .
I was always determined never to resign as long as his Majesty
thought fit to accept of my poor services . . .'

All the same, the day arrived when he could stand no more. On
19 October 1781 General Cornwallis was compelled to surrender to
the Americans and their French allies at Yorktown. The news did
not reach London until 25 November. It was conveyed to the
Prime Minister at his house in Downing Street by Lord George

Germain, the Secretary of State for American Affairs, who had received it by special messenger from Falmouth. Wraxall asked Lord George afterwards how Lord North had received it.

'As he would have taken a ball in his chest,' replied Lord George Germain. 'For he opened his arms, exclaiming wildly, as he paced up and down the apartment during a few minutes, " Oh, God! it is all over!" ' Words which he repeated many times, under emotions of the deepest agitation and distress.'

Even so, it was not until the following March that the king let his servant go. He was very rude to North when he came to take his leave. 'Remember, my Lord,' he told him, ' that it is *you* who desert *me*, not I you.'

The scene in the House of Commons on 20 March 1782 is well described by Wraxall. ' I have rarely witnessed so full an attendance at so early an hour, as on that day; not less than four hundred Members having taken their seats before 5 o'clock . . . The only delay arose from the absence of the First Minister; and he being expected to arrive from St. James's, all eyes were directed towards the door . . . each time that it opened . . . At length Lord North entering in a full dressed suit, his Riband over his coat, proceeded up the House, amidst an incessant cry of " Order ", and " Places ". As soon as he reached the Treasury Bench, he rose and attempted to address the Chair; but Lord Surrey, who had given notice of a motion for that day, being consequently in possession of the right to speak first, and having likewise risen, a clamour began from all quarters, of the most violent description. It lasted for some moments, in defiance of every effort made by the Speaker to enforce silence; 'till in consequence of the earnestness with which the Minister besought a hearing, and some expressions relative to the importance of the communication that he had to make, which pervaded the tumult, the Members opposite allowed him the precedence. He then stated, after a short preface, that " his object was to save the time and trouble of the House, by informing them that the Administration was virtually at an end; that His Majesty had determined to change his confidential servants; and that he should propose an adjournment, in order to allow time for the new Ministerial arrangements which must take place ". It is not easy to describe the effect which this declaration produced in a popular assembly, scarcely an individual of which did not hear it with lively sentiments of exultation, or of concern, both of which were heightened by surprise. No painter could have done justice to the expression depictured in many countenances.'

The adjournment having been agreed on, the House broke up at such an early hour that ' the housekeeper's room became crowded to the greatest degree, few persons having directed their carriages to be ready before midnight. In the midst of this confusion, Lord North's coach drove up to the door: and as he prepared to get into it, he said, turning to those persons near him, with that unalterable equanimity and good temper which never forsook him, " Good night, Gentlemen, you see what it is to be in the secret! " '

Lord North's resignation ' was a great relief to his mind ', wrote his daughter in her reminiscences, ' for although I do not believe that my father ever entertained any doubt as to the justice of the American war, yet I am sure that he wished to have made peace three years before its termination. I perfectly recollect the satisfaction expressed by my mother and my two elder sisters upon this occasion, and my own astonishment at it; being at that time a girl of eleven years old, and hearing in the nursery the lamentations of the women about " My Lord's going out of power! " . . . I thought going out of power must be a sad thing, and that all the family were crazy to rejoice at it! '

If North was so ' relieved ' at leaving office, why was he so anxious to return to it ? He had a pension of £4,000 a year granted him by his grateful sovereign, he was still Warden of the Cinque Ports, he had a comfortable mansion in Bushey Park. Yet in less than a year we find him entering into negotiations with his old rival Charles James Fox, the Whig leader who was especially odious to the king, with a view to forming a coalition government under the Duke of Portland, another Whig!

For several days in the middle of February 1783 there was much coming and going at North's house in Grosvenor Square, and at length on 16 February it was agreed that the Duke of Portland should be First Lord of the Treasury in the contemplated administration, and that Fox and North should serve under him as joint Secretaries of State.

Just a week later the government of Lord Shelburne resigned, and King George was at his wits' end. He hated the Whigs, Fox in particular, while as for Lord North he thought him a traitor, and spoke of him as one who had repaid his trust and affection with the most shocking ingratitude. For six weeks the king twisted and turned, but at last he submitted to the inevitable. The Duke of Portland formed his administration, with Fox and North as his principal assistants. It is not surprising that George treated North with the barest civility.

Why did North do it ? The matter has never been properly resolved. Wraxall was always most favourably disposed towards him, but now he was at a loss. 'Lord North, it must be reluctantly confessed, however circumstances may justify his union with Fox, on principles of policy, of personal safety, or of necessity, did not perform in this great Drama the most dignified part. After having occupied the post of First Minister, at the head of both the Treasury and the Exchequer, for twelve sessions, it seemed to ordinary observers no little degradation, at more than fifty years of age, to accept the Secretaryship of State for the Home Department, and to take his seat as such, on the Treasury Bench where he had so long presided, now squeezed between Fox and Burke. I own, that I never contemplated him in that situation, without reflections allied to pity . . . Even the compliments and the caresses of his late bitter opponents, now become his coadjutors, always appeared to me, only to sink him in the estimation of the House.'

But North himself, ' with the insignia of the Garter across his breast', gave no signs of ' any painful emotions at the political change that he had undergone. The same cheerful complacency, ready wit, and unaffected good humour, always characterized him under every circumstance.' To a man of his portly build it was inconvenient that his offices at the Treasury were now on the second floor, and once Wraxall caught him complaining, ' when out of breath, of the length of the staircase'. Frequently, too, from the effect of long habit, or from absence of mind, he went straight to his old apartments on the first floor. Nevertheless, ' such was the oblivious felicity and equality of his temper, that these accidents, which would have distressed more irritable men, never externally discomposed him '.

For eight or nine months this unhappy state of affairs continued, during which time King George strove with desperate determination to escape from what he called his ' captivity '. With long-practised skill he undermined his ministers, and bided his time until an alternative Prime Minister was found in the person of young William Pitt.

On 18 December 1783 the principal members of the Government were dining together at Lord North's town house. They were sitting over their port when Mr. Nepean, North's under-secretary at the Home Office, arrived bearing an urgent message from the king. ' Lord North,' this read, ' is by this required to send me the seal of his Department, and to acquaint Mr. Fox to send those of the Foreign Department. Mr. Frazer [the other under-secretary] or Mr. Nepean will be the proper channel of delivering them to me this night; I choose this method as audiences on such occasions must be unpleasant.'

Another version of the incident runs that North had already retired to rest when Nepean made his call. Nepean insisted that even so he must see his Lordship at once. ' Then,' so North is supposed to have said, ' he must see Lady North too.' Whereupon Nepean was shown into the bedroom. North told him where the seals were to be found and then went tranquilly off to sleep. Lovers of a good story will be sorry to learn that this one is now generally discredited.

After this second fall from power, North never held office again, although he remained in the Commons until the death of his father in 1790 removed him to the upper house as Earl of Guilford.

Unfortunate in his political career, North was exceptionally happy in his home life, and we may well conclude this chapter with some more quotations from his daughter's account. First, something about her mother.

Soon after his return to England from his travels on the Continent, Lord North at the age of twenty-three ' was married to Miss (Anne) Speek, of Whitelackington Park, Somersetshire, a girl of sixteen; she was plain in her person, but had excellent good sense; and was blessed with singular mildness and placidity of temper. She was also not deficient in humour, and her conversational powers were by no means contemptible; but she was contented to be a happy listener during [her husband's] life, and after his death her spirits were too much broken down for her to care what she was.

' Whether they had been in love with each other before they married I don't know, but I am sure there never was a more happy union than theirs during the thirty-six years that it lasted. *I never saw an unkind look, or heard an unkind word passed between them; his affectionate attachment to her was unabated, as her love and admiration for him.*'

Coming now to her father, Lady Charlotte sets down her recollections of his ' style of conversation and character in private life '.

' His wit was of the most genuine and playful kind; he related remarkably well, and liked conversing upon literary subjects; yet so completely were all these ingredients mixed and amalgamated by good taste, that you would never have described him as a sayer of *bon mots*, or a teller of good stories, or as a man of literature, but as a most agreeable member of society and truly delightful companion.

' His manners were those of a high-bred gentleman, particularly easy and natural . . . He used frequently to have large parties of foreigners and distinguished persons to dine with him at Bushey Park. He was himself the life and soul of these parties. To have seen him then, you would have said that he was there in his true element. Yet I think that he had really more enjoyment when he went into the country on a Saturday and Sunday, with only his own family, or one or two intimate friends: he then entered into all the jokes and fun of his children, was the companion and intimate friend of his elder sons and daughters, and the merry, entertaining playfellow of his little girl, who was five years younger than any of the others. To his servants he was a most kind and indulgent master; if provoked by stupidity or impertinence, a few hasty, impatient words might escape him, but I never saw him really out of humour . . .

' In the evenings, in Grosvenor Square, our house was the resort of the best company that London afforded at that time . . . Mr. Fox, Mr. Burke, Mr. Sheridan . . . habitually frequented our drawing-room: these, with various young men and women, his children's friends, and whist-playing ladies for my mother completed the society. My father always liked the company of young people, especially of young women who were sensible and lively; and we used to accuse him of often rejoicing when his political friends left his side, and were succeeded by some lively young female.

' In the year 1787 Lord North's sight began rapidly to fail him, and in the course of a few months he became totally blind, in consequence of a palsy on the optic nerve. His nerves had always been very excitable, and it is probable that the anxiety of mind which he suffered during the unsuccessful contest with America, still more than his necessary application to working, brought on this calamity, which he bore with the most admirable patience and resignation, nor did it affect his general cheerfulness in society. But the privation of all power of dissipating his mind by outward objects or of solitary occupation could not fail to produce at times extreme depression of spirits, especially as the malady proceeded from the disordered state of his nerves. These fits of depression seldom occurred, except during sleepless nights, when my mother used to read to him, until he was amused out of them, or put to sleep.

' Lord North, when he was out of office, had no private secretary even after he became blind, his daughters, particularly the two elder, read to him by turns, wrote his letters, led him in his walks, and were his constant companions. In 1792 his health began to decline; he lost his sleep and his appetite; his legs swelled, and symptoms of dropsy were apparent. He expired on the 5th of August, 1792 . . .'

12

EARL OF SHELBURNE

WHEN LORD NORTH's twelve years' administration was brought to an end in March 1782, it was followed by the all too short one of the Marquess of Rockingham. On 1 July 1782, the day that Rockingham died, King George wrote to the young Whig nobleman Lord Shelburne, inviting him to become First Lord of the Treasury and form a government.

Although he is almost always referred to as such, Lord Shelburne was born William Fitzmaurice, his family name was changed to Petty when he was a boy, and he ended up as the Marquess of Lansdowne.

By descent he was much more of an Irishman than an Englishman. For hundreds of years his ancestors had been prominent among the Anglo-Irish nobility in Ireland. He tells us about them in one of the autobiographical pieces that he left behind him. After stating that he himself was born in 1737 in Dublin, he goes on to say that he spent the first four years of his life ' in the remotest parts of the south of Ireland, under the government of an old grandfather who reigned, or rather tyrannized, equally over his own family and the neighbouring country, as if it was his family, in the same manner as I suppose his ancestors, Lords of Kerry, had done for generations since the time of Henry II, who granted to our family 100,000 acres in those remote parts in consideration of their services against the Irish, with the titles of Barons of Kerry . . . Both title and estates descending through so many generations from father to son in a country quite uncivilized, peopled by Catholics, reduced by frequent rebellions, and laws passed in consequence, my ancestors necessarily exercised an absolute power over a great tract of country, and the more so as they had in general preserved their loyalty and their attachment to the English Government.'

This grandfather of his was Thomas Earl of Kerry and twenty-first in the succession of feudal lords. He married Anne Petty, ' a very ugly woman ', only daughter of Sir William Petty, the celebrated economist and inventor whom Charles II made surveyor-general of Ireland, in which capacity he amassed a great fortune.

Petty's widow was created Baroness Shelburne, and in due time this title and the Petty fortune devolved on her son John Fitzmaurice, who was Lord Shelburne's father. He took the name of Petty in consequence of his inheritance, and in 1753 was created Earl of Shelburne in the peerage of Ireland and some years later Baron Wycombe in that of Great Britain.

Shelburne was four when his old bully of a grandfather died, and he reverted to the care of his parents. His father had lived so long in a ' state of slavery and feudal habits ' that he never got over it. He had ' an uncommon plain understanding ', but he had no notion of governing his children ' except by fear '. His mother, on the other hand, was ' active to excess, and enterprising as far as her talents would carry her : one of the most passionate characters I ever met with, but good-natured and forgiving when it was over—with a boundless love of power, economical to excess in the most minute particulars, and persevering, by which means she was always sure to gain her ends of my father, who, upon the whole, loved a quiet life '. All the same, ' If it had not been for her continual energy my father would have passed the remainder of his life in Ireland, and I might at this time be the chief of some little provincial faction.'

It is easy to believe him when he says that in these circumstances: ' I had no great chance of a very liberal education; no great example before me; no information in my way, except what I might be able to acquire by my own observation or by chance; good-breeding within my own family, which made part of the feudal system, but out of it nothing but those uncultivated, undisciplined manners and that vulgarity which make all Irish society so justly odious all over Europe.'

But now in the course of his depressing relation, Shelburne introduces ' one illustrious exception ' in the person of his aunt, Lady Arabella Denny. ' If it was not for her, I should have scarce known how to read, write, or articulate, to being able to do which I am indebted, perhaps for the greatest part of the little reputation I have lived to gain in the House of Lords. It was to her alone I owed any alleviation of the domestic brutality and ill-usage I daily experienced at home. She was the only example I had before me of the two qualities of mind which most adorn and dignify life— amiability and independence.' To Lady Arabella's ' virtues, talents, temper, taste, true religion, and goodness of every kind ' he found it impossible ' to do sufficient justice, any more than to the unspeakable gratitude I owe her '.

Down to the end of his life Shelburne was wont to complain of the ' miserable education ' he had been given. He was sent to an ' ordinary publick school ', had a spell under a narrow-minded tutor, and then at fifteen was allowed to proceed on his own to London, where he picked up ' what acquaintance offered '. Often he was in such straits that he would have starved but for being helped out by kindly aunts and cousins.

When his father was made a peer, his fortunes improved; and bearing now the courtesy title of Lord Fitzmaurice, he proceeded to Christ Church, Oxford. At twenty a commission was obtained for him in the Foot Guards, and he saw active service in the Seven Years War. He fought bravely at Minden in 1759, and on his return to England was promoted to colonel and appointed aide-de-camp to the young George III. This brought him into close contact with Lord Bute, who was not long in discovering that he had in him the makings of a successful intermediary. He employed him in some of his negotiations with Henry Fox (Lord Holland), one of the leaders of the Whig party, and unfortunately Shelburne conducted himself in such a way as to lead Fox to complain to Lord Bute. Bute is said to have excused Shelburne with the remark that his conduct had been nothing more than a ' pious fraud '. Whereupon Fox rejoined, ' I can see the fraud plainly enough, but where is the piety ? '

In this way originated that reputation for double dealing that dogged Shelburne throughout his life.

When he was still overseas with his regiment, Shelburne was elected M.P. for Chipping Wycombe, a family borough which his father had represented before he became a peer. He was re-elected at the general election in 1761, but his father died a few weeks later and he succeeded to his seat in the House of Lords as Lord Wycombe.

At the early age of twenty-six, through Bute's influence, Shelburne was appointed in 1763 President of the Board of Trade in Grenville's administration, but he resigned after a few months. By this time he had fallen out with Bute and had also lost the favour of the king, so that he was deprived of his appointment at court. For the time being he retired from politics, and busied himself in the congenial pursuits of an immensely wealthy and highly cultured country gentleman. At Bowood Park, his magnificent seat in Wiltshire, he employed ' Capability ' Brown, the most esteemed landscape architect of the day, in laying out the extensive grounds, and he set about enriching his library with a splendid collection of historical and literary MSS. which on his death were purchased for the British Museum.

At Bowood and his mansion in London he shone as a most genial and generous host. Most of the distinguished men of the time felt honoured to receive his invitations. Among them was Benjamin Franklin, and years afterwards Shelburne wrote to the great American to remind him of the time when they ' talked upon the means of promoting the happiness of mankind, a subject far more agreeable to their natures than the best concerted plans for spreading misery and ruin '.

In 1765 Shelburne married Lady Sophia Carteret, the only child of that Carteret who had been for so many years Sir Robert Walpole's colleague and eventual rival.

Perhaps it would have been better for Shelburne's reputation if he had continued to occupy himself with his books and gardens but his friends would not let him be. On his breakfast-table he found such letters as this from Lord Weymouth: ' I am glad you still like retirement ... though I am sure that your mind is too active to let the great events of the world pass without taking some part in them ', and this from Lord Sandwich: ' Have you done with those silly manuscripts ? ' He refused an invitation from Lord Rockingham, but when in 1766 Chatham offered him the post of Secretary of State in the administration that he was forming—one of the most important posts in the Cabinet, offered to a man who was still on the right side of thirty—Shelburne felt he could not but accept. Very shortly he was recognized as Chatham's chief lieutenant and personal representative in the Government.

But then Chatham disappeared from view, and Shelburne found Grafton, only a couple of years his senior, a much more difficult superior. Furthermore, he was strongly opposed to the policy of using force to bring the American colonists to heel. Grafton at length resolved to get rid of him, but he met an unexpected obstacle. ' Lord Shelburne's removal ', wrote Chatham, ' would never have his consent or concurrence ... He had a great regard and friendship for him and considered that his abilities made him necessary to the office he was in, for the carrying out of the King's business.' For the present he was allowed to remain where he was, but Chatham was on the point of resigning himself, whereupon Shelburne became deprived of his powerful protection.

Shelburne's meteoric rise, when he was still so young and inexperienced, had raised up against him a host of jealous rivals; added to which, he was now exposed to the most vicious attacks in the newspapers. In the *Public Advertiser* for 18 October 1768 there appeared a squib, popularly ascribed to John Wilkes, purporting to describe a masquerade given at the Opera House a week earlier. In this, Grafton, Chatham, and several other ministers had their parts, but the most prominent character was one whose features were described as being ' too happily marked to be mistaken. A single line of his face will be sufficient to give us the heir apparent of Loyola and all the College. *A little more of the devil my lord if you please about the eyebrows; that's enough, a perfect Malagrida, I protest.*'

Malagrida was an Italian Jesuit who had been burnt alive at the stake on a charge of having, while confessor to the Marchioness of Tavora, encouraged her to make an attempt on the life of the king of Portugal. The nickname of Malagrida became indissolubly attached to Shelburne, and in many a caricature he was represented in the guise of a Jesuit.

The day after this malicious piece had appeared, the same newspaper published another of the ' Letters of Junius ', above the signature of ' Atticus '. Readers were reminded that ' the Earl of Shelburne had initiated himself in business by carrying messages between the Earl of Bute '—who though he had fallen from office some years before was still the object of the most malevolent gossip —' and Mr. Fox, and was for some time the favourite of both '. He was a young man who ' before he was an ensign thought himself fit to be a general, and to be a leading minister before he ever saw a public office '; as for his life ' it was a satire on mankind '. Even Chatham's patronage was called in question. Chatham had introduced him ' into the most difficult Department of State, and left him there to shift for himself'—something which, in Atticus's view, ' was a masterpiece of revenge '. And yet the young man, ' unconnected, unsupported, remains in office without interest or dignity, as if the income were an equivalent for all loss of reputation. Without spirit or judgment to take an advantageous moment for retiring, he submits to be insulted as long as he is paid for it . . .'

But in point of fact Shelburne had decided to resign. Without according Grafton the satisfaction of dismissing him, Shelburne on that same day requested an audience of the king and returned to his Majesty the seals of his office.

For many years after this, Shelburne was out of office, although he continued to be actively interested in politics. His wife, a young and attractive woman, died in 1771, and he was deeply affected by her loss. For some months he travelled on the Continent, in France and Italy for the most part. At Paris he mixed freely in the society of the *Philosophes*, and made friends with the brilliant mistresses of the literary *salons* and such eminent economic and political thinkers as the Baron d'Holbach, Morellet, and Turgot. These contacts helped to clarify his ideas about such things as free trade and the necessity for religious toleration. He was a considerable thinker himself, often of a daring originality. The ' Old Whigs ' had always looked upon France as Britain's natural enemy, and had made Anglo-French rivalry the basis of their foreign policy. But Shelburne took pains to understand the French, and he carried back home a sincere appreciation of their efforts to substitute for the *ancien régime* a society inspired by the most liberal principles. Thus it happened that when the French Revolution broke out, Shelburne regarded it with a sympathetic understanding that was rare in the British governing class.

When Chatham died in 1778, Shelburne became the acknowledged leader of those Whigs who had constituted his small following. A year later he married again; his second wife was Lady Louisa Fitzpatrick, daughter of the Earl of Upper Ossory, and like him descended from the old Irish nobility.

All through Lord North's long premiership, Shelburne was one of the leaders of the Opposition. He made a formidable showing, as will be gathered from Wraxall's portrait of him. ' No individual in the Upper House,' he writes, ' attracted so much attention from his accomplishments, talents, and extensive information on all subjects of foreign or domestic policy, as the Earl of Shelburne. In the prime of life, and in the full vigour of his faculties, he displayed, whenever he rose to speak, an intimate knowledge of Europe, together with such a variety of matter, as proved him eminently qualified to fill the highest official situation . . . His acquaintance with the Continent was minute and accurate, the result of ocular inspection on many points, corrected by reflexion; and improved by correspondence or communications with foreigners of eminence, whom he assiduously cultivated and protected.' Nor was he ' less versed in all the principles of Finance and of Revenue, than in the other subjects of political study that form a statesman '.

Shelburne's house, ' or more properly to speak, his palace in Berkeley-square, which had formerly constituted the residence of the Earl of Bute, formed at once the centre of a considerable party, as well as the Asylum of taste and science. It is a fact that, during the latter years of Lord North's administration, he retained three or four clerks in constant pay and employment, under his own roof, who were solely occupied in copying statements of accounts. Every measure of Finance adopted by the First Minister, passed, if I may so express myself, though the Alembic of Shelburne House, where it was examined and severely discussed.' There, opposition M.P.s met to settle their plan of action, Dr. Price and Mr. Baring ' produced financial plans or made arithmetical calculations, meant to controvert and overturn or to expose those of the first Lord of the Treasury ', and Dr. Priestley, eminent as a Unitarian divine and scientific discoverer, lived under Shelburne's personal protection and ' prosecuted in the midst of London his philosophical and chemical researches '.

Wraxall goes on, ' in his person, manners, and address, the Earl of Shelburne wanted no external quality requisite to captivate or conciliate mankind. Affable, polite, communicative, and courting popularity, he drew round him a number of followers or adherents. His personal courage was indisputable. Splendid and hospitable at his table, he delighted his guests by the charms of his conversation and society. In his magnificent library, one of the finest of its kind in England, he could appear as a Philosopher, and a man of letters. With such various endowments of mind, sustained by rank and fortune, he necessarily excited universal consideration, and seemed to be pointed out by Nature for the first employments.'

A fine portrait so far of a most attractive man, but there is a darker side to it. ' The confidence which his moral character inspired did not equal the reputation of his abilities. His adversaries accused him of systematic duplicity and insincerity. They even asserted that unless all the rules of Physiognomy were set at defiance, his very countenance and features eloquently indicated falsehood . . .'

Gainsborough, it is said, once tried to draw Shelburne's portrait, but after the second attempt flung away his pencil. ' Damn it! ' he said, ' I never could see through varnish, and there's an end! '

This was Shelburne's reputation, and he was never able to disprove it or live it down. And yet it was to Shelburne that King George turned when at last he had permitted Lord North to resign. Shelburne on this occasion declined the premiership, but agreed to serve under Rockingham as a Secretary of State with responsibility for American affairs. When a few months later Rockingham died, King George again asked Shelburne to be Prime Minister, and Shelburne felt he could hardly refuse a second time. Immediately on receipt of the king's letter, he acquainted his Cabinet colleagues with its contents, and asked whether they would continue to serve under him ? Most of them said yes, but Fox and his friends contemptuously refused. They maintained that in the existing political situation, the invitation should have come from the Cabinet and not the king, and that in any case they preferred the Duke of Port-land. Furthermore, while acknowledging Shelburne's great gifts and experience, they distrusted him profoundly as a man, and did not hesitate to say so. Shelburne was not greatly concerned: he had managed to secure the young William Pitt as his Chancellor of the Exchequer, and he was delighted with his acquisition.

Early in July 1782 the new administration made its bow, headed by Shelburne in the Upper House and Pitt in the Lower. Shelburne was his customary magnificent self, but even among the peers his Anglo-Irish origins and connections made him appear foreign, while in the House of Commons his personal following can have numbered hardly a dozen. Although he was nominally a Whig and was heading a Whig government, the Whig leaders rallied round Fox and from the outset showed him no mercy. Leading the pack was Edmund Burke, who assailed Shelburne in a speech of the utmost virulence. Shelburne, he declared, was ' a man that he could by no means confide in, and he called heaven and earth to witness, so help him God, that he verily believed that the present ministry would be fifty times worse than that of the noble lord [North]. who had lately been reprobated and removed . . . He meant no offence, but he would speak an honest mind. If Lord Shelburne was not a Catiline or a Borgia in morals, it must not be ascribed to anything but his understanding.'

Shelburne announced his programme, and it was an excellent one. Peace on honourable terms with the Americans, retrenchment in the public expenditure, a reduction in the number of political places and pensions, the rebuilding of Britain's commerce after the shattering blows of the American war . . . Shelburne had feared in his most desponding moments that the grant of American independence would mean the sunset of the British Empire, but now he indulged the hope that her sun would rise again in a brighter morning.

If only Shelburne had not been so widely mistrusted. Very largely the fault lay in his own nature. He seems to have been constitutionally incapable of explaining himself fully and fairly, of saying what he meant in a way that ordinary people could under-stand. The famous lines in *The Rolliad* (a collection of Whig political satires directed in 1784 against William Pitt and his fol-lowers) are said to be merely a versification of one of the speeches that Shelburne actually delivered:

A noble Duke affirms I like his plan:
I never did, my lords!—I never can.
Shame on the slanderous breath which dares instil

That I, who now condemn, advis'd the ill.
Plain words, thank Heaven, are always understood;
I could approve, I said—but not I would.
Anxious to make the noble Duke content,
My view was just to seem to give consent,
While all the world might see that nothing less was meant.

Some progress was made in the negotiations with the Americans, and quite a lot of dust was raised by the new brooms in Whitehall and Westminster. But early in 1783 Shelburne seems to have been confirmed in his suspicions that the king was playing a double game. ' George III ', he was heard to say in after years, ' had one art beyond any man he had ever known, for that by the familiarity of his intercourse he obtained your confidence, procured from you your opinion of different public characters, and then availed himself of this knowledge to sow dissension.' He felt that the king had tricked him, and after several defeats in quick succession he suddenly handed the king his resignation, on 24 February 1783.

The coalition ministry of North and Fox followed, under the nominal premiership of the Duke of Portland, but within a year this had disappeared and young William Pitt strode triumphantly into office. Shelburne, we may be sure, had confidently expected that he would be given a high appointment in the new administration, both on account of his proved abilities and experience and the fact that he had been the favourite disciple of Chatham, the new Prime Minister's father. But Pitt had resolved otherwise. He had the deepest respect and regard for Shelburne, but he simply dared not run the risk of including a man of such dubious personal character in his Cabinet. Shelburne was most sorely offended, but Pitt did his best to soften the blow. Through his good offices Shelburne was created in 1784 Marquess of Lansdowne (after Lansdowne Hill, near Bath, where he had an estate), and he was also promised a dukedom if ever again that dignity should be conferred outside the Royal Family.

Shelburne was still under fifty, in the prime of his faculties and the maturity of his experience, but he never held office again, although more than once it was offered to him. ' The fact is ', he told the House of Lords some years after his retirement from the premiership, ' that throughout my life I have stood aloof from parties. It constitutes my pride and my principle to belong to no faction, but to approve every measure on its own ground free from all connection. Such is my political creed . . .' It was a creed, it may be remarked, that made a strong appeal to the young Disraeli:

in his novel *Sybil* he describes Shelburne as ' the ablest and most accomplished statesman of the eighteenth century . . . the first great minister who comprehended the rising importance of the middle class '.

In 1789 Shelburne lost his second wife. The latter part of his life he spent mostly at Bowood, and when we have been obliged to note so much to his disadvantage it is a pleasure to read the quaint tribute that the old philosopher Jeremy Bentham said about him. ' The master of Bowood . . . is one of the pleasantest men to live with that ever God put breath into. His whole study seems to be to make everybody about him happy—servants not excepted; and in their countenances one may read the effects of his endeavours. In his presence they are as cheerful as they are respectful and attentive; and when they are alone, you may see them, merry, but at all times as quiet as so many mice. To such a poor devil as I, they are as respectful and attentive as if I were a lord.'

Looking back on Shelburne in his long golden evening we see him as the enlightened statesman, the ardent lover of political liberty, the disciple of Adam Smith, the friend of Bentham and Benjamin Franklin, the splendid patron of letters and the arts and the practical sciences, the benevolent landlord, the benefactor of the poor, the staunch friend. He died at Lansdowne House in Berkeley Square on 7 May 1805, at the age of sixty-eight, and was buried in the family vault in the church at High Wycombe.

13

DUKE OF PORTLAND

When in 1783 Lord North and Fox were looking around for a 'great name' to head their coalition ministry they settled on the Duke of Portland. At that time the Duke was considered to be 'the leader of the narrowest section of the Whig party', as Lord Edmund Fitzmaurice put it. Nearly a quarter of a century afterwards he was Prime Minister a second time, but on this occasion he was 'chief of the most Tory of Tory administrations'. This struck Lord Edmund as being a 'singular distinction', and we may well agree.

William Henry Cavendish-Bentinck was the great-grandson of the Dutch statesman Hans William Bentinck, who was the most trusted friend and companion of William of Orange, accompanied him to England in 1688, and after the Glorious Revolution was rewarded with the English earldom of Portland. The second earl was created a duke in 1716 by George I for his staunch support of the Hanoverian dynasty. The second duke was the future Prime Minister's father; the latter's mother was Lady Margaret Cavendish Harley, daughter and heiress of the second Earl of Oxford.

William Henry was born in 1738, and as the eldest son he was styled the Marquess of Titchfield. He went to Eton and Christ Church, Oxford, and in 1761 he entered the House of Commons as member for the Herefordshire borough of Weobley. But his father died in the same year and his heir was translated to the House of Lords as the third Duke of Portland. Four years later he married Lady Dorothy Cavendish, the only daughter of the Duke of Devonshire who had been Prime Minister for a short time ten years previously. It was at this point that the family assumed the additional surname of Cavendish.

In Lord Rockingham's first ministry of 1765 he held the appointment of Lord Chamberlain, but after a year he was out of office. For the next sixteen years he was in opposition, and he spared no effort or expense in combating the Tories and the 'King's friends'. When Rockingham returned to power in 1782 he made Portland Lord Lieutenant of Ireland, and in the following year, in the North-Fox coalition, Portland became Prime Minister.

Horace Walpole was very surprised. ' Nobody recollected that he had been Lord Chamberlain in Lord Rockingham's first administration,' he wrote. ' From that time he had lived in the most stately, but most domestic privacy, often in the country, latterly in Burlington House. His character was unimpeached, but he had never attempted to show any parliamentary abilities, nor had he the credit of possessing any . . . His brief Lord Lieutenancy in Ireland had not raised his reputation, and men profanely sneered at him as " a fit block to hang Whigs on ", as the centre of a gang of " toad-eaters " [sycophants], and as a " heavy-breeched Christian " who wanted " a shove ".'

These uncomplimentary remarks probably do Portland something less than justice. But if he was more than a ' convenient cipher ', he had no opportunity of demonstrating it, since the Government was ignominiously kicked out in December of the same year, 1783, when the young William Pitt took over the administration.

For the next few years, Portland sat among the Whig peers on the Opposition side, but when the great war with the French Republic began he formed the opinion that it was his patriotic duty—and many of his Whig friends thought likewise—to give his support to Pitt. In 1794, just after his wife's death, he accepted the post of Home Secretary and proved to be a capable administrator. He remained at the Home Office until 1801, and then until 1805 he was Lord President of the Council. By this time he had learned how to work with the Tories and no one was really surprised when in March 1807, after Lord Grenville's short Whig administration had come and gone, Portland was appointed First Lord of the Treasury and Prime Minister for the second time.

All the same, he might not have been chosen if he had not taken the unusual step of suggesting it to his Majesty himself, and this when Grenville was still in office. King George was deeply concerned over Grenville's proposals for Catholic Emancipation and Portland was well aware of this; in a letter to the king he said that he felt sure that persons might be found who would be able to carry on his Majesty's business '. . . with talents and abilities equal to those of your present ministers. If your Majesty should suppose ', he went on, ' that in the forming of such an administration, I can offer your Majesty any services, I am devoted to your Majesty's commands; but while I say this I feel conscious that my time of life, my infirmities, and my want of abilities, are not calculated for so high a trust.'

Mock modesty, or simple good sense ? On balance, it was

probably the latter, since we hear of the duke expressing the fear 'not that the attempt to perform this duty will shorten my life, but that I shall neither bodily nor mentally perform it as I ought'. So, at the end of March 1807 'old Dame Portland', as Byron put it, 'fills the place of Pitt'.

As Prime Minister he did not do any better the second time than he had done during his first premiership, but he managed to struggle along for two years and a half without any serious mishaps. The worst that could be said of him was that he was unable to exercise proper control over his Ministers, most of whom did pretty well as they pleased. But the responsibilities of office proved too much for the old duke. In August 1809 he had a paralytic stroke, and he resigned shortly after. He retired to Welbeck, and died there on 30 October, after weeks of pain borne with a stolid fortitude.

14

WILLIAM PITT

IF EVER THERE WAS A MAN destined for a great career in Parliament it was William Pitt—called William Pitt the Younger to distinguish him from his father, the great statesman who eventually took the title of Earl of Chatham.

William Pitt, wrote Lord Rosebery in his short but luminous biography 'went into the House of Commons as an heir enters his home; he breathed in it his native atmosphere—he had, indeed, breathed no other; in the nursery, in the schoolroom, at the university, he lived in its temperature; it had been, so to speak, made over to him as a bequest by its unquestioned master. Throughout his life, from the cradle to the grave, he may be said to have known no wider existence. The objects and amusements, that other men seek in a thousand ways, were for him all concentrated there. It was his mistress, his stud, his dice-box, his game-preserve; it was his ambition, his library, his creed. For it, and it alone, had the consummate Chatham trained him from his birth'.

Born at Hayes in Kent on 28 May 1759 he was the son of William Pitt the Elder and his wife Hester Grenville. He was the second son —fortunately for him, since if he had been the eldest he would have succeeded in due course to his father's earldom and the doors of the House of Commons would have been shut in his face. Even as it was, there was a time when his elder brother's life hung on a thread, and William's political rivals and enemies gloated over the prospect of his imminent removal from the scene of his triumphant exercise of power.

One of his first recorded sayings dates from 1766, when his father made the astonishing decision to become Earl of Chatham. 'I am glad I am not the eldest son,' the seven-year-old boy remarked; 'I want to speak in the House of Commons like Papa.'

The year in which he was born was that year of victories when Britain, under the direction of his mighty sire, strode steadfastly along the road to Empire. But when he was old enough to take note of what was going on around him his father was, for most of the time, a splendid ruin. When the boy first knew him he was a remote figure mysteriously hidden away behind doors which opened only to his mother, as at all hours of the day and night she carried basins of chicken broth to the invalid within. When he was permitted to enter the room, he saw an apparently old man, huddled in his chair, groaning with the pains of gout and muttering imbecilities. Occasionally, however, the clouds lifted, and little William was taken on his father's knee, and they read books together, and the old man made much of the boy who, he was firmly persuaded, would add fresh lustre to the name he bore.

In his boyhood Pitt seemed to be always sickening for something, and his father decided that he had not the stamina to submit to the rough and tumble of education at Eton. Instead he was taught at home by a tutor, and soon gave astonishing signs of precocity. 'Eager Mr. William', 'the Counsellor', and 'the Philosopher', are among the nicknames he was given by his doting parents and friends. Dr. Addington, his father's favourite physician, prescribed a tonic of port wine, and it certainly seems to have done him good. At any rate, he acquired a taste for it that never left him.

Encouraged and aided by his father he read the classics and was specially fond of Thucydides, the English philosopher John Locke and the Scottish David Hume, Shakespeare and Milton, and Adam Smith. When *The Wealth of Nations* came out in 1776 he read it through from cover to cover, and was converted to the Free Trade doctrine.

Not many years later when he became Prime Minister he met Adam Smith who was greatly impressed by his young disciple. 'What an extraordinary man Pitt is,' he remarked once; 'he understands my ideas better than I do myself!' One day when Smith was invited to dine at the house of Henry Dundas, one of Pitt's ministers, he was the last to arrive. When he entered the room all the other guests stood up to greet him. 'Be seated, gentlemen,' he urged in apologetic tones. 'No,' rejoined Pitt, 'we will stand till you are first seated, for we are all your scholars.'

In 1773, when he was fourteen, Pitt was entered at Pembroke Hall, Cambridge. In a letter to the senior tutor Chatham wrote that 'he is of tender age, and of a health not yet firm enough to be indulged to the full in the strong desire he has to acquire useful knowledge . . . Too young for the irregularities of a man, I trust he will not, on the other hand, prove troublesome by the puerile sallies of a boy. Such as he is, I am happy to place him at Pembroke; and I need not say how much of his parents' hearts goes along with him.'

At the university Pitt led the austere life of a student. He never missed chapel or lectures unless he were ill. He played no games, and had no interest in sport. His tutor was a Mr. Pretyman—years later he changed his name to Tomline—who became his friend for life; before he was thirty Pitt had the satisfaction of getting his former preceptor made bishop of Lincoln and dean of St. Paul's. 'The preceptor showed his gratitude,' comments Macaulay, 'by writing a life of his disciple which enjoyes the distinction of being the worst biographical work of its size in the world.' At seventeen Pitt, as a nobleman's son, was admitted M.A. without having to submit to the indignity of passing an examination.

Pitt had few friends at Cambridge, and not many acquaintances. He kept himself very much to himself, and he was never seen at evening parties. When his father was about to make an important speech, Pitt went to London and watched the performance from a seat in the gallery. With strained attention he made a careful note of every gesture, every trick of oratory; he admired, and resolved to copy. On that tragic occasion when Chatham made his last appearance in the House of Lords, Pitt and his brother-in-law Lord Mahon were his supporters, and a few weeks later Pitt was the chief mourner when his father's body was interred with imposing cere-monial in Westminster Abbey. Only twenty-eight years later the same grave opened to receive his own mortal remains.

Chatham had been too proud to become rich, and when he died the family inheritance was hardly sufficient to maintain the dignity of the new earl, William's elder brother. William had little more than three hundred a year of his own, and had, therefore, to think about a career. He took chambers in Lincoln's Inn and was called to the bar in 1780, the year he came of age. He joined the Western circuit, but in the autumn of that year there was a general election and Pitt offered himself as candidate for the university of Cambridge. He was at the bottom of the poll, but immediately afterwards the Duke of Rutland, who had been one of his school-friends at Eton, solicited a seat for him from Sir James Lowther, a great northern magnate who was the happy possessor of no fewer than nine bor-oughs. Lowther was quite agreeable to launching so promising a young man on a parliamentary career, and Pitt was brought into the House of Commons as M.P. for Appleby.

On taking his seat early in 1781 Pitt attached himself to that small section of the Whigs headed by Lord Shelburne, his father's friend and supporter. A month later, on 26 February 1781 he made his maiden speech in the House. It was in support of Burke's plan of economical reform in the public administration. Wraxall was there, and heard him.

Great expectations had been formed of Pitt, he tells us, and 'a sort of anxious impatience for his coming forward pervaded the assembly; which was strongly impressed from common report, with a belief of his hereditary talents and eloquence'. He more than fulfilled expectations. Although ' he then wanted three months to have completed his twenty-second year', he exhibited 'the same composure, self-possession, the imposing dignity of manner, which afterwards so eminently characterized him when seated on the Treasury Bench ... the same nervous, correct, and polished diction, free from any inaccuracy of language, or embarrassment of deportment, which, as First Minister, he subsequently displayed.'

Burke was moved to tears at his performance. ' He isn't a chip of the old block,' he declared, ' but the old block itself.'

That the success which so astonished and pleased his hearers was no flash in the pan was soon made plain. Pitt spoke again and again that session, and it is significant that his speeches were nearly all devoted to the subjects of *peace*—with America and her allies; *retrenchment*—in the public expenditure; and *reform*—in the system of parliamentary representation.

When Lord North made way for Rockingham in February 1782, the new Prime Minister offered Pitt a post in his government. It was only a small one—the vice-treasurership of Ireland—but it was the one his father had held at the outset of his career, and moreover it was very well paid. Without a moment's hesitation the slender stripling turned it down. He let it be known that he would accept no office which did not carry with it a seat in the Cabinet, and shortly afterwards he told the House of Commons so.

Some who heard him were offended at what they deemed his presumption, but outside the House there were very many more who saw in his words and action a reminiscence of the independent spirit of his father. Here was a young fellow with his own way to make, living hand to mouth in scruffy chambers in the Temple, a barrister looking for briefs—and he had turned down a position with next to no work attached to it and with a salary of £5000 a year!

Within three months, Rockingham was dead, and it was Shelburne's turn to form an administration. Fox and his friends refused to serve under him, and he was on the look out for fresh talent. He was determined to have Pitt and offered him the Chancellorship of the Exchequer, with the lead of the House of Commons. This time Pitt accepted, to Shelburne's delight. The new cabinet minister was just twenty-three years old.

Shelburne's ministry had too little support in the House of Commons to last, but a good beginning was made with peace negotiations with America, in which Pitt played a useful part. It is on record that while King George was willing to restore Gibraltar to Spain in return for substantial concessions, Pitt was resolute in refusing to consent to the cession of the great fortress. The months passed, and then early in 1783 those long-standing enemies Fox and North came to terms. A few days later they joined in a censure motion on the Government, objecting to the peace terms, and this was carried by a majority of sixteen. Pitt did poorly on this occasion. He even had the bad taste to taunt Sheridan—the distinguished dramatist who was one of Fox's principal followers—with his connection with the stage.

For some unexplained reason, Shelburne did not at once resign, and on 21 February the battle was renewed. Again a motion of censure was before the House, and Fox led the attack. While Fox was speaking Pitt, who was feeling unwell, stood in the doorway just behind the Speaker's chair, holding open the door with one hand while he was being sick into the basin he held in the other. When Fox sat down, Pitt put down the basin and entered the chamber to make one of the great speeches of his life. He spoke for nearly three hours. He defended the peace with America as a work of necessity, and then, towards his conclusion, he rounded on the coalition which was contemplated. ' If this ill-omened and unnatural marriage be not yet consummated,' he declaimed, as the cheers of his supporters rolled up round him in a tumultuous roar, ' I know of a just and lawful impediment; and, in the name of the public weal, *I forbid the banns!* '

But once again the ministers were left in a minority, and Shelburne handed in his resignation. He may have recommended Pitt as his successor, but in any case King George sent for the young man and made him the offer of the first seat at the Treasury Board. How astounded his Majesty must have been when the splendid offer was respectfully declined! It was repeated, and again declined. Pitt was persuaded that the time was not quite ripe. For five weeks the king shopped around for a chief minister who might save him from Fox and his allies, but at length he had to bow to the inevitable. The Duke of Portland became Prime Minister, while Fox held the reins of power. Pitt returned to his practice at the bar.

During the parliamentary recess that summer, Pitt went abroad.

for the only time in his life. He was accompanied by his future brother-in-law Edward Eliot and his dearest friend William Wilberforce. For six weeks they stayed at the archbishop's palace at Rheims, where Pitt took lessons in French, and was brought into close acquaintance with a young French cleric, the Abbé de Perigord. Ten years later, when they met again, Pitt was Prime Minister and the abbé had been transformed into Talleyrand, the accredited envoy of the French Republic.

Moving on to Paris, the young Englishman was received with marked respect and attention, as the son of the great Chatham. In accordance with court etiquette, King Louis XVI was prevented from entering into conversation with a foreigner, but Queen Marie Antoinette did her best to penetrate the barriers of Pitt's cold manner and still imperfect knowledge of her language. The courtiers made much of him, and it is said that he narrowly escaped marriage with fascinating young Mlle. Necker, only child of the great Finance Minister, who was to become the celebrated authoress Madame de Stael.

In the autumn of 1783 Pitt returned to England, and when Parliament met in November he took his place in the forefront of the battle with the coalition. Fox and his colleagues maintained a jaunty confidence in their massive majority, but King George had been tapping the political barometer and had read the signs aright. He again approached Pitt, and now he was given definite assurances that the young man was ready.

On the evening of 18 December North and Fox received the king's peremptory demand that they should deliver up the seals of their offices, and within twelve hours of having obtained them the king sent for Pitt. The next afternoon Pitt strode into the House of Commons and took his seat on the front bench as First Lord of the Treasury and Chancellor of the Exchequer. He was twenty-four, the youngest man ever to become Prime Minister.

Somehow or other he succeeded in forming a government, of which all the senior members except himself were in the House of Lords. The men who had been supplanted looked on his efforts with amusement, even derision: after all, they still had their majority in the House. In sixteen divisions the Government were defeated, but Pitt was undismayed. He knew that public opinion was declaring itself with irresistible force in his favour. The people were sick of the old gang, who had lost the war with America and had so recently made it perfectly plain that the only thing they really cared about was office and its plums. Furthermore, he had the happy consciousness that the king was with him. Time after time King George was urged to dismiss his ministers, but he indignantly refused. Rather than admit Fox and his friends into office again he would quit England for his principality of Hanover.

All the same, Pitt's position was decidedly precarious. He was young, inexperienced, his friends were few and his opponents many and well established. But in the House he showed no sign of nervousness. His manner was imperturbable, even haughty. His confidence mounted as time passed. Addresses of support poured in from all parts of the country. London offered him the freedom of the city in a golden casket, and when he went to Guildhall to receive it his progress through the streets was a triumphal procession. In the ranks of the opposition there were the first signs of wavering, as the time-servers and place-hunters strove to secure their retreat.

Then it became known that the Clerkship of the Pells had fallen vacant. It was a sinecure, and it was worth £3,000 a year for life. Everyone expected Pitt to take it for himself as a matter of course, and there would have been few to blame him if he had. But Pitt appointed to the post Colonel Barré, an old friend and supporter of his father who had fallen on evil days and was stricken with blindness.

Macaulay hails this as a most happy stroke of policy. 'About treaties, wars, expeditions, tariffs, budgets, there will always be room for dispute,' he writes. 'The policy which is applauded by half the nation may be condemned by the other half. But pecuniary disinterestedness everybody comprehends. It is a great thing for a man who has only three hundred a year to be able to show that he considers three thousand a year as mere dirt beneath his feet, when compared with the public interest and the public esteem. Pitt had his reward. No minister was ever more rancorously libelled; but, even when he was known to be overwhelmed with debt, when millions were passing through his hands, when the wealthiest magnates of the realm were soliciting him for marquisates and garters, his bitterest enemies did not dare to accuse him of touching unlawful gain.'

After three months Pitt advised the king to dissolve parliament. He had judged the matter to a nicety. In the general election that followed Pitt's supporters, Tories and 'King's friends', were returned in overwhelming numbers. A hundred and sixty of the Coalition M.P.s—'Fox's martyrs' they were styled—lost their seats, and Fox himself was hard put to it to secure election for Westminster.

Pitt himself had been feeling increasingly uncomfortable as member for a pocket borough and he allowed his name to go forward again for the university of Cambridge. This time he was returned at the head of the poll. But he was not ungrateful to his former patron: within a very short while, Sir James Lowther was made Earl of Lonsdale.

The question of parliamentary representation had in fact been a matter of concern to Pitt from the beginning of his career. He saw the need for reform, and this—an issue regarded without sympathy by most of his contemporaries—was to prove a stumbling block on more than once occasion.

As Wraxall says; ' It forms an object of the most natural curiosity minutely to survey him at this most critical period of his life ', and there is no better man to answer that curiosity than Wraxall himself, since this former follower of Lord North went over to Pitt and observed his career at close quarters for a number of years.

Pitt, he writes, at this time ' was tall and slender, but without elegance or grace. His countenance, taken as a whole, did not display either the fine expression of character, or the intellect of Fox's face, on every feature of which his mind was more or less forcibly depictured. It was not till Pitt's eyes lent animation to his other features, which were in themselves tame, that they lighted up and became strongly intelligent . . . In his manners, Pitt, if not repulsive, was cold, stiff, and without suavity or amenity. He seemed never to invite approach, or to encourage acquaintance; though, when addressed, he could be polite, communicative, and occasionally gracious. Smiles were not natural to him, even when seated on the Treasury Bench; where, placed at the summit of power, young, surrounded by followers, admirers and flatterers, he maintained a more sullen gravity than his Antagonist [Fox] exhibited, who beheld around him only the companions of his political exile, poverty, and privations.

' From the instant that Pitt entered the doorway of the House of Commons, he advanced up the floor with a quick and firm step, his head erect and thrown back, looking neither to the right nor to the left; nor favouring with a nod or a glance, any of the individuals seated on either side, among whom many who possessed five thousand a year, would have been gratified even by so slight a mark of attention. It was not thus that Lord North or Fox treated Parliament; nor from them would Parliament have so patiently endured it; but Pitt seemed made to command, even more than to persuade or to convince, the Assembly that he addressed.'

In the field of parliamentary eloquence; ' Fox's oratory was more impassioned, Pitt's could boast greater correctness of diction.' From Fox's finest specimens of oratory, much might have been taken away without injuring the effect, but ' to Pitt's speeches nothing seemed wanting, yet was there no redundancy. He seemed, as by intuition, to hit the precise point, where, having attained his object, as far as Eloquence could effect it, he sat down.' Fox's method was different. He calculated that one-third of his audience was always either absent or at dinner or asleep, so that ' after speaking at great length, and sometimes apparently summing up, as if to conclude ', he began again when he saw ' a considerable influx of attendance . . . regardless of the impatience of those whose attention was already exhausted '. Pitt, for his part, never condescended to avail himself of such a practice. He neither lengthened his speeches nor cut them short, from any other consideration than the proper development of his ideas. Old members calculated that whenever Fox was on his feet for three hours, Pitt would require no more than two in which to answer him. ' In all the corporeal part of oratory, he observed likewise more moderation and measure than Fox, who on great occasions, seemed . . . to dissolve in floods of perspiration. The Minister [Pitt], it is true sometimes warmed with his subject, and had occasionally recourse to his handkerchief: but, rather in order to take breath, or to recall his thoughts, by a momentary pause, than from physical agitation.'

When Pitt took office the most experienced parliamentarians had given his ministry a life of only a few weeks, or months at most. As things turned out he was continuously in office for seventeen years—the longest innings of any Prime Minister with the single exception of Sir Robert Walpole.

From now on, Pitt's story is the history of England. His administration may be divided into two almost equal parts. The first part covers the period from the close of 1783 to the autumn of 1792, and the second from that time to early in 1801. These seventeen years constituted his first administration; as we shall learn, he formed a second administration in 1804, which was ended by his death in 1806.

Pitt's admirers will take the greatest pleasure in viewing the first part of his first administration. Those were the years when Britain was at peace, and he displayed a masterly ability in repairing the damage inflicted on the economy by the American War of Independence. They were years of exceptional tranquillity and prosperity. At the head of a nominally Tory government, Pitt showed a liberal spirit. Shortly before taking office he made the striking declaration, ' Necessity is the plea of every infringement of human freedom. It is the argument of tyrants; it is the creed of slaves.' His domestic policies were enlightened, and he kept well within the bounds of constitutional practice. He encouraged trade and commerce, especially with France, the country which, according to the accepted Whig notion, was our traditional enemy. He repaired the national finances after the losses of the American war. He had tried under Rockingham and again under the coalition to introduce some re- forms into parliamentary representation, and he brought forward another measure when he was Prime Minister in 1785. He would doubtless have tried again but for the French Revolution, which made even the most moderate-minded men look askance at consti- tutional changes. He was deeply concerned with the good govern- ment of Ireland, if it were not for the royal obstinacy he would have relieved the Roman Catholics of the worst of their statutory disabilities. One thing more must be mentioned in this connection, his unfailing support of his friend Wilberforce's noble efforts to end the infamous traffic in Negro slaves.

' I well remember,' wrote Wilberforce in one of his letters, ' after a conversation with Mr. Pitt in the open air at the root of an old tree at Holwood '—Pitt's country home on the edge of Keston common, in Kent—' just above the steep descent into the vale of Keston, I resolved to give notice, on a fit occasion, in the House of Commons, my intention to bring forward the abolition of the slave- trade.' It was Pitt's government which in 1788 passed an Act aiming at the regulation of the ' middle passage ' across the Atlantic from Africa, and four years later he assailed the slave trade in a speech which has been ranked as the finest instance of his oratory. Just as the first rays of the morning sun came through the windows of the House of Commons he burst into a prophetic vision of the civilization that should dawn upon Africa, and drew on Virgil for a magnificent peroration.

This may be regarded as the swan song of Pitt the liberal states- man. The French Revolution had been in progress for three years already and Pitt had ignored it as long as he could. As late as the spring of 1792 he was repealing taxes and reducing the strength of the armed forces, and he told the House of Commons that further reductions might be confidently anticipated. He hated war with all his soul, and he deluded himself into believing that the fires of revolution would shortly burn themselves out. ' Unquestionably there never was a time in the history of this country,' he said, ' when from the situation of Europe we might reasonably expect fifteen years of peace than at the present moment.'

Right up to the last, Pitt strove desperately for peace, and he risked his personal popularity in the process. Maret, the French secret agent in London, wrote afterwards that even after the news of the execution of the French king had reached England, and the people were in a torment of rage and horror, Pitt was still striving anxiously against the tide of war. 'There is something pathetic,' writes Lord Rosebery, 'in this flash of light thrown on the lonely figure, clinging to hope with the tenacity of despair. As it fades, the darkness closes, and the Pitt of peace, prosperity, and reform disappears for ever.'

That is finely put, and we should bear it in mind when we read Macaulay's bitter denunciation of the man who, 'if he had been so fortunate as to die in 1792, would now have been associated with peace, with freedom, with philanthropy, with temperate reform, with mild and constitutional administration', yet 'lived to associate his name with arbitrary government, with harsh laws harshly executed, with alien bills, with gagging bills, with suspensions of the Habeas Corpus Act, with cruel punishments inflicted on some political agitators, with unjustifiable prosecutions instituted against others, and with the most costly and sanguinary wars of modern times. He lived to be held up to obloquy as the stern oppressor of England, and the indefatigable disturber of Europe.'

As a wartime Prime Minister, Pitt was as big a failure as he had been a success in the years of peace. Chatham would have gloried to stand in his son's shoes, but Pitt's face was one of lengthening misery. Under him the British army became a laughing-stock on the Continent as it was chased ignominiously from pillar to post, and the navy was driven into revolt. He picked the wrong men, and as often as not gave them the wrong jobs to do. He was grossly extravagant, and to raise the funds that he squandered in subsidies to foreign allies the people at home were taxed and taxed. Who can put a proper valuation in terms of public health and social happiness, on the Window Tax which he imposed and increased time after time ?

So many were the disappointments, the reverses, the disasters of this second phase of his administration, that it is a wonder how he managed to keep going. Any other minister would have been hurled from office, drowned in a sea of disgrace and popular detestation. But in spite of everything, the people still continued to believe in him; the king still trusted him, although he was never at ease with him as he had been with Lord North; and he kept his majority together with the most lavish distribution of titles, appointments, decorations, and other ' honours '.

In the end it was not mismanagement that brought his first ministry to a close, but his proposals to deal with disaffection in Ireland. He wished to grant the Roman Catholics some relief, and King George took fright. He had examined his Coronation Oath, and been reminded that he had sworn most solemnly to maintain the Protestant religion as he had received it. Pitt's urgings proved too much for the old gentleman's mental stability. Whereupon Pitt very rashly promised his royal master that the matter should never be raised again in his Majesty's lifetime. If in so doing he had counted on the king's early demise he had grossly miscalculated, since the king outlived him by fourteen years. In the spring of 1801 Pitt resigned after agreeing upon Addington as his successor.

For three years he was out of office. Most of his time he spent at Walmer Castle, the official residence of the Lord Warden of the Cinque Ports, to which post he had been appointed in 1792. This carried with it a salary of £3000 a year, and he badly needed the money. For this man, who had been in charge for years of the national finances as Chancellor of the Exchequer, was never able to balance his own budget or keep his expenditure in bounds. He was heavily in debt—indeed was never out of it. When it was learnt that writs were out against him and that he was in danger of arrest, the merchants of the City offered him a free gift of £100,000. He declined it, just as he declined a gift of £30,000 from the king's Privy Purse. But he did condescend to accept a loan of some £12,000 from a few personal friends, and this kept the duns off his doorstep. His debts continued to accumulate, however, and there is surely something shameful in the allegation that the collectors of taxes found more difficulty in collecting them from the Prime Minister than from any other inhabitant of the city of Westminster. Even his household bills were in arrears for months or years, and Wraxall says that frequently the tradesmen were kept quiet only with fresh orders. Thus when Pitt was unable to pay the amount owing for repairs to his coach, he ordered a new coach.

Truly an extraordinary state of affairs, and all the more extraordinary when it is remembered that Pitt was in receipt of more than £10,000 a year—£5000 as First Lord of the Treasury, nearly £2500 as Chancellor of the Exchequer and £3000 as Warden of the Cinque Ports. In present-day figures this would be equivalent to at least £30,000 a year. What on earth did he do with the money?

From what we are told, he had no expensive vices. He liked a game of cards occasionally, but he was careful to avoid those gambling-tables which reduced his great rival Fox to beggary. He did not attend race meetings, and had no interest in field sports. He was very fond of reading, but was no collector of fine books and manuscripts as, for instance, Lord Shelburne, or his cousin Thomas Grenville, to whom the British Museum library became so indebted. He was not a patron of the arts, nor for that matter very much interested in them. Like his father, he took a pride in his gardens, and spent large sums in planting trees and otherwise embellishing them. The amount spent in this was, however, chicken-feed compared with the costs of his domestic establishment, and this is one cause of his perpetual financial embarrassment on which we can put a finger with absolute certainty.

When he first went to live at 10 Downing Street his sister, Lady Harriet Pitt, kept house for him, and it is said that she was successful in keeping the household expenses within reasonable bounds. But in 1785 she got married, and after that her brother's affairs fell into the utmost disorder. Not until 1803 was Pitt's table again presided over by a woman—and Lady Hester Stanhope was certainly not one to make a virtue of economy.

This would seem to be a favourable opportunity for turning from an examination of Pitt's finances to the more interesting question of his relationship with women. He seems to have been quite exceptional in that age of sexual licence. Not only was he a bachelor, but he maintained a high standard of moral behaviour, which if not a matter of reproach at least gave rise to much surprised comment. A curious indication of the way in which it was regarded is afforded by Wraxall.

Although he was in the flower of his youth when he was placed at the head of the administration, he writes, Pitt exhibited a coldness, indifference, or apathy towards woman, on which 'his enemies dwelt with malignant, though impotent, satisfaction, while his friends laboured with equal pertinacity to repel the imputation':

'In order to justify him from such a supposed blank in his formation,' Wraxall continues, 'his adherents whispered, that he was no more chaste than other men, though more decorous in his pleasures; and they asserted that he made frequent visits to a female of distinguished charms who resided on the other side of Westminster Bridge; but I never could learn from any of them her name or abode.'

As mentioned earlier, when as a young man he paid his first and only visit to the Continent, he was supposed to have paid his addresses to Mlle. Necker, afterwards Mme. de Stael. According to one version of the story he proposed, and was rejected; according to another it was the young lady's father, M. Necker, who proposed the match, and that Pitt replied that ' he was already married—to his country '. Lord Brougham, in his essay on Pitt in his *Statesmen of the Time of George III*, rejects the answer, ' unless it was a jest ', but grants that there was some foundation of the story.

Years later he did form an attachment which has been called the only love story in his life. This was in 1796 when he was in his thirty-eighth year, and the young lady he had set his heart on was Eleanor Eden, one of the six daughters of his friend and colleague Lord Auckland. He had known the girl from her childhood, since Lord Auckland had a country estate, Eden Farm, not far from Pitt's Holwood. She is described as a handsome and winning girl, full of life and sympathy, intelligent too, and she was just twenty.

Writing to a friend in December 1796 Burke reported that, ' The talk of the town is of a marriage between the daughter of Lord Auckland, and Mr. Pitt, and that our statesman, our *premier des hommes*, will take his Eve from the Garden of Eden.' A few weeks later, Pitt wrote to the girl's father, that ' whoever may have the good fortune to be united to her is destined to more than his share of human happiness ', but ' whether I could have any ground to hope that such might have been my lot . . . I am compelled to say that I find the obstacles to it decisive and insurmountable '. Lord Auckland in reply urged him to think the matter over before arriving at a final decision, but Pitt wrote by return of post to say that he had ' not lightly nor easily sacrificed my best hopes and earnest wishes to my conviction and judgment ', and begged Auckland ' to spare me and yourself the pain of urging it further '.

Why Pitt refused to put himself forward as a suitor for Lady Eleanor's hand has been frequently discussed. The reason usually given is that he did not think it fair to ask her to marry a man who was so pecuniarly embarrassed. This does not ring altogether true, and other excuses that have been offered, that he was so very shy and also so busy, are no better perhaps; plenty of shy men have made a success of marriage, and plenty of busy men have been able to spare at least some time for their wives. It may seem more likely that there was some constitutional deficiency in Pitt's makeup, and that he could not bear the thought of bringing pain and disillusion on a girl for whom he had the deepest respect and perhaps love.

Two years afterwards, Lady Eleanor became engaged to be married to Lord Hobart, and when her father informed Pitt of the fact, in a letter in which he described her as ' a beautiful and good creature, with every advantage of a strong mind and right principles', Pitt sent his ' most cordial good wishes '. But it is said that years later he showed a reluctance to admit Lady Eleanor's husband, who had become Earl of Buckinghamshire, into his Cabinet.

If there was a woman with whom Pitt was really at his ease it must have been his niece, Lady Hester Stanhope, daughter of the Earl of Stanhope and his wife Hester, Pitt's sister. When she received the invitation to preside over Pitt's household, she was a young woman of twenty-six; and her niece, the Duchess of Cleveland, describes her as possessing a very fine figure and the air and gait of a queen, a skin of dazzling fairness, bright blue eyes, and a countenance brilliant with animation and intelligence. This description may be supplemented with what Earl Stanhope, Lady Hester's nephew, says about her in his life of Pitt.

' With considerable personal attractions, the Lady Hester of 1803 combined a lively flow of conversation, and an inborn quickness of discernment. Her wit was certainly even then far too satirical, and too little under control. She made even then many enemies, but she also made many friends. Mr. Pitt was on some occasions much discomposed by her sprightly sallies, which did not always spare his own Cabinet colleagues. But on the whole her young presence proved to be, as it were, a light in his dwelling. It gave it that charm which only a female presence can give. It tended, I believe, far more than his return to power, to cheer and brighten his few—too few—remaining years.'

With her and her young brothers Pitt sometimes unbent to an almost unbelievable extent. Thus in the ' life ' of General Sir William Napier we read how in 1804 when as a youth of eighteen he was staying in Pitt's home at Putney, where Lady Hester's young brothers were also staying, ' Mr. Pitt liked practical fun, and used to riot in it with Lady Hester, Charles and James Stanhope, and myself.' On one occasion the young people were determined to blacken his face with burnt cork, and the fray was just beginning when a servant announced that Lord Castlereagh and Lord Liverpool had arrived to see him on urgent business. ' Let them wait in the other room,' said Pitt, and then, catching up a cushion he belaboured his assailants in glorious fun. ' We were, however, too many and too strong for him, and after at least ten minutes' fight, got him down and were actually daubing his face, when, with a look of pretended confidence in his prowess, he said, " Stop, this will do; I could easily beat you all, but we must not keep those grandees waiting any longer ". His defeat was, however, palpable, and we were obliged to get a towel and basin of water to wash him clean before he could receive his grandees. Being thus put in order, the basin was hid behind the sofa, and the two lords were ushered in.'

Pitt had to put up with a great deal from Lady Hester's ' dazzling indiscretions ', as Lord Stanhope called them. When sometimes his friends expressed their surprise, Pitt would answer, ' I let her do as she pleases; for if she were resolved to cheat the Devil, she would do it.' There can be no doubt that she meant a great deal to him, and almost his last thought on his death-bed was for her. ' Where is Hester ? ' he inquired; ' Is Hester gone ? Dear soul, I know she loves me.'

Lord Stanhope tells us that Lady Hester, for her part, was intensely proud of being called ' Pitt's niece ', and she ' treasured up every word and look that recalled those golden days, to warm her heart in her loveless, solitary, forsaken old age '.

Pitt was out of office for three years, from the spring of 1801 to that of 1804. As mentioned earlier, they were spent principally at Walmer, but he made occasional excursions to Bath for his health's sake, and to London. For many months at a time he was not seen at Westminster. He was not forgotten, however, and in May 1802 he received what Lord Rosebery describes as the greatest compliment ever paid to an English statesman. A motion of censure on his administration was not only defeated by an overwhelming majority, but the House of Commons proceeded forthwith to put on record ' that the Right Hon. William Pitt has rendered great and important services to his country, and especially deserves the gratitude of this House '.

Almost immediately afterwards it was his birthday, and his friends and admirers resolved to celebrate it in some outstanding fashion. A dinner was held—the first of a series which continued for a genera-tion—and for this first banquet the young Canning composed a set of verses in which appeared the title under which Pitt became so generally celebrated:

And oh if again the next tempest should rise,
The dawnings of peace should fresh darkness deform,
When we turn to thy hopeless retirement our eyes,
We shall long for *the Pilot that weathered the Storm.*

The 'next tempest' was not long in coming. In May 1803 the war with France was renewed, and a few days later Pitt returned to the House of Commons. His reappearance created a sensation. There were two hundred new members who had never heard him, many had never even seen him; and as he walked up to take his seat there was a great outburst of emotion. 'Pitt! Pitt!' was the almost universal cry, and the demonstration was repeated at the conclusion of the speech that he proceeded to deliver. But for a year yet Addington's ministry stumbled along, and Pitt spent most of the time at Walmer, raising and drilling a corps of 3,000 volunteers against the threat of a French invasion. He took his responsibilities as Lord Warden most seriously, and unless the wind was in a quarter unfavourable to an invasion attempt he never left his post.

More than once during his retirement he had been approached by Addington with a view to his joining the government. The last occasion was shortly before the renewal of the war. Pitt, although he was getting increasingly bored with his comparative inaction, refused even to discuss the proposed appointment. 'And which of the secretaryships was offered to you?' inquired Wilberforce. 'Really,' replied Pitt with a harsh laugh, 'I had not the curiosity to inquire.'

But at length the Addington administration died an unlamented death, and the king called on Pitt to form a government for the second time. He did so on 12 May 1804, but from the beginning he was hampered by 'the dull, obstinate, unforgiving, and, at that time, half-mad' old king, as Macaulay describes him. Pitt had wanted to form a government of all parties, and all parties were willing to join in. But the king positively refused to accept Fox as one of the Secretaries of State and Pitt, fearing that the king might become completely insane, concurred in his senseless objection.

For Pitt's sake one might almost wish that he had not answered the call. His health was failing, his nerves were constantly on edge, and it would not be surprising that he should have increasing resort to the bottle. Hoppner painted his portrait at this time; and Wilberforce, when he saw it, remarked on 'His face anxious, diseased, reddened with wine, and soured and irritated by disappointments. Poor fellow, how unlike my youthful Pitt!'

All through that spring and early summer Napoleon was with his *Grande Armée* at Boulogne, waiting for the arrival of Villeneuve's fleet that might give him command of the Channel for those twelve hours that were all he needed. But Nelson's ships kept watch and ward, and when August had come and still no Villeneuve, the

Emperor suddenly struck camp and marched his legions hot-foot across the Continent to face the Austrians whom Pitt's subsidies had put into the field. The news of Napoleon's crushing victory at Ulm was a dreadful blow for Pitt, but he did not flinch. Then came the tidings of Trafalgar, and of Nelson's death in the moment of victory.

The day after the news, so glorious and so sad, reached London Pitt rode to the Guildhall to attend the Lord Mayor's banquet. Once more, and for the last time, he was given a hero's triumph. There were many in Fleet Street and the Strand and up Ludgate Hill who recalled his father's progress through those same streets in the year of victories, and now they dragged the son's chariot and roared their acclamations.

At the banquet in Guildhall, the Lord Mayor proposed a toast to Pitt as the ' saviour of Europe '. There must have been a sour taste in Pitt's mouth as he rose to speak in reply, but in what was to prove his last speech he expressed himself with a noble simplicity. It was probably the shortest speech he ever delivered, and certainly the best remembered and treasured in men's minds. ' I return you many thanks for the honour you have done me,' he said. ' But Europe is not to be saved by any single man. England has saved herself by her exertions, and will, as I trust, save Europe by her example.'

A month later he set out for Bath, seeking health in the same place and the same way as his father had done forty years before; and while there he received the news of Napoleon's victory of victories at Austerlitz. The shock of the tidings shattered his already failing constitution. He struggled back to London, and took up residence in Bowling Green House, on the edge of Putney common, which he had rented; and there, having grown steadily weaker and more emaciated, he died on 23 January 1806.

Several reports of his ' last words ' found currency, and all have been questioned, with the exception of his affectionate message to Lady Hester. The one most generally accepted is James Stanhope's, given in Lord Stanhope's more or less official life. In this we are told that he sometimes cried out ' Hear, hear! ' as if in the House of Commons. Then, ' At about half-past two he ceased moaning, and did not speak or make the slightest sound for some time. I feared he was dying; but shortly afterwards in a much clearer voice than he spoke in before, and in a tone I shall never forget, he exclaimed, " Oh, my country! How I leave my country! " From that time he never spoke or moved, and at half-past four expired without a groan or struggle. His strength being quite exhausted, his life departed like a candle burning out.'

Decidedly different is the version for which Benjamin Disraeli was responsible. When he was a young M.P. he used to dine often at the House of Commons, where he was generally served by a grim old waiter who was believed to be the repository of much political lore. One day this venerable domestic happened to be in an unusually communicative mood.

'You hear many lies told as history, sir,' he said; 'do you know what Mr. Pitt's last words were?' 'Of course,' said Mr. Disraeli, 'they are well known ... "O my country ..."' 'Nonsense,' said the old man. 'I'll tell you how it was. Late one night I was called out of bed by a messenger in a postchaise, shouting to me outside the window. "What is it?" I said. "You're to get up and dress and bring some of your meat pies down to Mr. Pitt at Putney." So I went; and as we drove along he told me that Mr. Pitt had not been able to take any food, but had suddenly said, 'I think I could eat one of Bellamy's meat pies". And so I was sent for post-haste. When we arrived Mr. Pitt was dead. Them was his last words ...'

When Pitt died he was heavily in debt, and the House of Commons voted £40,000 to meet the demands of his creditors. Pensions were also awarded of £1,200 a year to Lady Hester Stanhope and £600 a year to each of her two sisters.

A month after his demise, Pitt was buried with stately ceremonial in Westminster Abbey. The grave was dug adjoining Chatham's and, said Wilberforce with fine feeling, as the coffin was lowered into the ground, 'The statue of the father seemed to look with consternation at the vault that was opening to receive his favourite son.'

15

HENRY ADDINGTON

WHEN THE NINETEENTH CENTURY DAWNED, William Pitt was still Prime Minister, but it had run only a few weeks when he was supplanted by an old friend of his who had found more favour with the king. This was Henry Addington, a commoner and the first of our Prime Ministers who came direct from the middle class.

For many generations the Addingtons had been settled in Oxford-shire, where they had a small estate at Fringford. Very little is known about them; they had no aristocratic connections, and in their ancestry they could boast of not a single knight or even a M.P. The first of the family to make a name for himself was Anthony Addington, the future Prime Minister's father. He was a physician in Reading, and married the daughter of the headmaster of the local grammar school; but after a time he decided that he could do better for himself in a wider sphere. He moved to London, where his professional skill and reputation soon secured him some influential patients. Among them was Lord Chatham, and for twenty years he was Chatham's personal physician, his confidential adviser and friend. In 1767 when Chatham showed signs of going out of his mind, King George urged him to call in some other medical adviser, but Chatham peremptorily refused to put his trust in anyone but Dr. Addington.

The Opposition took this as a sure sign that Chatham was indeed mad. Yet the trust was not misplaced, for Chatham got better and in a grateful letter attributed his recovery to Addington's 'judicious sagacity and kind care'. It was also Dr. Addington who prescribed port wine in quantity for the young William Pitt, who was always ailing as a child and youth; and here again the good doctor's prescription worked. Years later Addington was called in to attend King George when he became temporarily insane, and he succeeded not only in assisting his recovery but won his complete confidence.

Dr. Addington's son Henry, the future Prime Minister, was born in 1757 and was therefore William Pitt's senior by a couple of years. He was sent first to a school at Cheam and then transferred to Winchester, after which he proceeded to Brasenose College, Oxford.

He looked forward to a career in the law and was duly entered at Lincoln's Inn. At the age of twenty-four he married Ursula Hammond, daughter of a gentleman of Cheam, and started his legal practice from a house in Southampton Street.

But he was not destined to be a lawyer. From his boyhood days he had been very friendly with young William Pitt, who was grateful to Dr. Addington for having recommended those frequent doses of port wine and who was now just beginning to make his mark in politics. Pitt was on the look out for some personal supporters in the House of Commons; he suggested to Henry Addington that he should think seriously of making politics his career, and offered to help him find a seat. Addington fell in with this suggestion, and through Pitt's aid was returned as M.P. for Devizes in 1784.

For the next five years Addington was an industrious if not specially distinguished member, and he did all that Pitt required of him. He also made a close study of parliamentary procedure, with the result that when in 1789 a new Speaker had to be chosen in succession to Pitt's cousin William Grenville, who had been taken into the Government after only five months in the chair, Pitt thought that Addington was just the right man for the job. Addington had no ambitions in that direction, but when the king expressed his approval he agreed to stand and was duly elected. He performed the duties so well that he retained the chair for twelve years, in three Parliaments.

Up to this time Speakers had had to rely upon certain fees and perquisites, but soon after Addington's election the salary of the Speaker was fixed at £6000 a year.

Addington was thus very well off, and his circumstances were further improved when in 1790 his father died and he came into the family property. He was able to buy a small estate at Woodley, near Reading, where at the time of the invasion scare he raised a troop of yeomanry. King George visited him at Woodley to inspect it.

A few years later he was offered a post in the Government, but he preferred to remain where he was for the present. He kept on very good terms, however, with Pitt, and they spent a good deal of time in one another's company. But although he liked his glass he was no hard drinker, as Pitt was, and it is recorded that he sometimes felt it necessary to tell the Prime Minister, ' Now, Pitt, you shall not have another drop,' although Pitt's eloquence would usually induce him to allow just one more bottle.

When in the spring of 1801 Pitt proposed to grant some relief to the Roman Catholics, who then laboured under numerous political disabilities, King George refused his consent, pleading that it would be contrary to the oath he had taken at his coronation to preserve the Protestant religion. When Pitt persisted, the king begged Addington to do his best ' to open Pitt's eyes to the danger of agitating the question '. Pitt refused to budge, whereupon the king invited Addington to take over the premiership in his place. ' Where am I to turn for support if you do not stand by me ? ' he asked plaintively.

Addington at once consulted Pitt, who advised him to accept. On 14 March 1801 Addington received the seals as First Lord of the Treasury and Prime Minister, and also as Chancellor of the Exchequer. So pleased was the king with the way things had worked out that he appointed his new Prime Minister deputy ranger of Richmond Park, with the occupation of the mansion of Royal Lodge. Addington held this very enjoyable position for forty years.

As Speaker, Addington had earned everybody's good opinions, but as Prime Minister he soon showed his incapacity. As Lord Rosebery explains it, this ' son of the respected family physician, who had prescribed colchicum to the elder and port to the younger Pitt, carried into politics the indefinable air of a village apothecary inspecting the tongue of the State '. For a time Pitt helped him along; but then Pitt's attitude changed and his supporters made things difficult. In the newspapers Addington was referred to scornfully as ' the Doctor ', and Canning, one of Pitt's bright young men, wrote spiteful little verses about him,

> Pitt is to Addington
> As London is to Paddington.

Addington began to see the red light. War with France was expected early in 1803, and he felt quite incompetent to conduct it without Pitt's assistance. He invited Pitt to join his administration, but when this was scornfully declined, he offered to serve under him. Pitt hardly bothered to reply. He was now quite willing to stage a come-back, but it would be on his own terms. Addington hung on for a time after war with France was declared, but when his majority dropped to below forty he decided to resign. On 10 May 1804 he returned his seals of office to the king, and was promptly succeeded by Pitt.

The king offered him an earldom for himself and a pension for his wife, but he begged to be excused. But he did accept for his son of sixteen the very lucrative sinecure of the Clerkship of the

Pells, and obtained very comfortable little places for several of his relations. Only a year later, however, he was back in the Cabinet at Pitt's invitation, and early in 1805 he was created Viscount Sidmouth. Six months later Pitt died, but Addington accepted office in the Whig administration of Lord Grenville. After this collapsed, he remained out of office until 1812 when he became Home Secretary in Lord Liverpool's government, which post he continued to hold for nearly ten years. As such he displayed a most reactionary temper, and in consequence became one of the best-hated men in the country. He suppressed the Luddites and other working-class movements with cruel vigour, he applauded the Peterloo massacre and passed the Six Acts, he suspended Habeas Corpus, he prosecuted harmless Socialist theorists and trade unionists and sought to secure their conviction by the employment of spies and provocators. Lord John Russell described Lord Sidmouth as 'the incarnation of prejudice and intolerance'.

He held office in six administrations and over a period of nearly thirty years; Canning once said that he was like the smallpox that everyone was obliged to have at least once in their lives. He was replaced at the Home Office by Peel in 1822 but he was a member of Liverpool's cabinet for two years more. Then he retired, on the very comfortable pension of £3000 a year.

The first Lady Sidmouth died in 1811, and in 1823 he married the Hon. Marian Scott, only daughter of Lord Stowell. On the latter's death twelve years later Sidmouth inherited his very large fortune, whereupon he had the grace to relinquish his pension. In his later years he took little part in politics—although he attended the House of Lords to cast his vote against the Reform Bill in 1832— and enjoyed a reputation for piety and good works. The younger generation of politicians looked with feelings approaching awe on this survivor from the great age of Fox and Burke and the young Pitt. He lived well into Victoria's reign, not dying until 1844 when he had reached the age of eighty-five. He was buried in the churchyard at Mortlake.

16

LORD GRENVILLE

A FEW WEEKS after Pitt's death, a new administration was formed under Lord Grenville, who was Pitt's first cousin and for many years had attached himself to his coat tails to good purpose. According to its friends the new ministry contained ' all the talents, wisdom, and ability of the country ', whence its opponents in derision dubbed it the ' Ministry of All the Talents '. It did not last long, a little over a year, and it foundered on the same rock which had sunk Pitt's first government. When King George demanded from Grenville an assurance that he would initiate no measures for the relief of the Roman Catholics, Grenville handed in his resignation. His colleagues were not at all pleased at having to resign with him, when their party had been so many years in the political wilderness. Sheridan, better remembered as a playwright than as a politician, expressed their opinion very well when he remarked, ' I have known many men knock their heads against a wall, but I never heard before of a man collecting bricks and building a wall for the express purpose of knocking out his own brains against it.'

William Wyndham Grenville was a member of the greatest and most successful of the Whig clans. His father was the George Grenville who was Prime Minister in the early years of George III; his mother was the daughter of Sir William Wyndham, and the Wyndhams were also of political usefulness. He was born on 25 October 1759, five months after his cousin William Pitt, and after Eton and Oxford followed Pitt into Lincoln's Inn in 1780. But when Pitt started out on his political career Grenville thought he might well do likewise. In 1782 he had no difficulty in getting returned M.P. for Buckinghamshire, a seat within the family's patronage, and before he had been in the House of Commons for a year, Lord Shelburne appointed him Chief Secretary for Ireland. Under the Fox-North Coalition he, like Pitt, was out of office for a few months, but when Pitt became Prime Minister in 1783 he was quick to get his cousin appointed a Privy Councillor and made him Paymaster-General, one of the best paid appointments under Government. Two years later he was transferred to the Board of

Trade as Vice-President, and here his capacity for solid business found full scope.

This was only the beginning, however. For a few months in 1789 he served as Speaker of the House of Commons—this when he was only twenty-nine, making him the youngest man to hold the great office since the reign of Edward III—and then in 1790 he was appointed Secretary of State for the Home Department, i.e. Home Secretary, and he was raised to the peerage as Lord Grenville. In the next year he became Foreign Secretary, which post he held until 1801, when he resigned along with Pitt. For some years he was out of office, until January 1806 when, as we have seen, he was made Prime Minister. And if it is complained that he was not a very successful one, we should remind ourselves that it was his government which passed the Act abolishing the trade in Negro slaves.

To look at, he was a good old English bulldog of a man—broad faced, square jowled, strongly built, suggesting brute courage and tenacity. There was never any question of his abilities. In a character-sketch Lord Brougham pays tribute to his sound sense, steady memory, and vast industry, his thorough acquaintance with business, complete mastery of the art of politics, and perfect familiarity with political economy. He had also an extensive knowledge of classical literature, and wrote Greek and Latin verses which bore testimony to his taste, formed on ' those chaste models '. As a speaker his ' eloquence was of a plain, masculine, authoritative cast, which neglected if it did not despise ornament, and partook in the least possible degree of fancy, while its declamation was often equally powerful with its reasoning and its statement '.

Of course, he had *some* faults of character. ' His firmness was apt to degenerate into obstinacy; his confidence in the principles he held was not unmixed with contempt for those who differed from him. His unbending honesty and straightforward course of dealing with all men and all subjects not infrequently led him to neglect those courtesies which facilitate political and personal intercourse.'

With Whigs and Tories he was almost equally popular. While he pleased the former with his sturdy independence of the Court, the latter were gratified by his ' studiously regular life ' and ' the well-known and steady attachment of himself and his family to the principles and the establishment of the Church of England '.

When in March 1807 he resigned the premiership, he had no regrets. As he wrote to his brother Lord Buckingham; ' The deed is done and I am again a free man, and to you I may express what it would seem like affectation to say to others, the infinite pleasure I derive from my emancipation.' He never again held office, although several invitations were made to him. He was still under fifty; and looking back over his career, in the course of which he had filled four of the highest offices in the State, he must have felt that political life had nothing more to offer. Occasionally he spoke in the House of Lords and more often than not expressed a moderately liberal attitude. Thus in 1813 he strongly supported Sir Samuel Romilly in his proposal to abolish the capital penalty for shop-lifting. 'For strength of reasoning, for the enlarged views of a great statesman,' said Romilly of that occasion, 'for dignity of manner and force of eloquence, Lord Grenville's was one of the best speeches that I have ever heard delivered in Parliament.'

Nearly thirty years of life were left to him, and most of them he spent on his small estate at Dropmore, in Buckinghamshire, which he had purchased soon after Pitt had appointed him to the office of Auditor of the Exchequer, one of the richest at his disposal. The salary was £4000 a year, the duties were by no means onerous, and there was the distinct advantage that the appointment was one of those unaffected by a change of ministry. Grenville enjoyed it for forty years, until his death.

On the solid foundation of this pleasant sinecure, Grenville married in 1792 Anne Pitt, daughter of Lord Camelford, Chatham's nephew, and the union proved to be not only a very happy but a profitable one, since his wife was a substantial heiress. At Dropmore he built a fine house and surrounded it with beautiful gardens, where he planted avenues of trees and filled the beds with rare plants and shrubs. He was also an enthusiastic and knowledgeable collector of books, prints, and old masters, classical marbles and fine china, as well as being a scholarly man of letters. He died on 12 January 1834, at the age of seventy-four.

17

SPENCER PERCEVAL

IN ONE RESPECT, Spencer Perceval was unique. He is the only one of Britain's Prime Ministers who met a violent death. This was on a May evening in 1812 when a man with a grievance, though not specially against him, shot him through the heart in the lobby of the House of Commons.

Spencer Perceval was born in London on 1 November 1762, the second son of the second Earl of Egmont by his second wife. The Percevals were an old Somersetshire family who had long been settled in Ireland, but the first and second earls being Irish peers were enabled to sit in the House of Commons, and each in turn played a small part in English politics at Westminster.

Perceval's father died when he was a boy of ten, and his eldest half-brother succeeded to the peerage. He was sent to Harrow and then to Trinity College, Cambridge, where he graduated M.A. in 1781. His mother, who had been created Baroness Arden, died two years later, and his elder brother succeeded to the barony and the considerable fortune that went with it. He, as a younger son, had only a private allowance of £200 a year, and had to make his own way in life. He chose the Law, studied at Lincoln's Inn, and was called to the bar in 1786, going on the Midland circuit.

One of those who knew him well at this time was Samuel Romilly, years afterwards so justly celebrated as a lawyer and a law reformer but then, like Perceval, a brief-hungry young barrister. Perceval, so Romilly recollected, was a welcome addition to the barristers' table. As he put it, ' With very little reading, of a conversation barren of instruction and with strong invincible prejudices on many subjects, yet by his excellent temper, his engaging manners and his sprightly conversation, Perceval was the delight of all who knew him.'

In 1790 Perceval married Jane, daughter of Sir James Spencer Wilson of Charlton, near Woolwich, a very pretty and charming girl. Her elder sister had become the wife of Perceval's brother Lord Arden some years before, but Perceval was nothing like so good a match and there was a good deal of family opposition to be overcome. It was a love-match, and for the first few years the young couple found it difficult to make ends meet. They had five children in the first six years of their marriage, and Perceval was glad indeed when an influential relation got him the appointment of Surveyor of the Maltings and Clerks of the Irons—a strange-sounding post under Government and a complete sinecure; but attached to it there was salary of £120 a year.

After a time the briefs began to come in, through family influence to begin with, and in 1792 he was one of the counsel employed by the Crown in the prosecution of Thomas Paine, who was charged with being ' a wicked, malicious, seditious, and ill-disposed person, greatly disaffected to our Sovereign Lord the King ', and two years later he was engaged in the ' treason ' trials involving Thomas Hardy and his associates in the London Corresponding Society. Pitt took notice of him, and offered him a post in his Government on terms that would have ensured his financial independence, but Perceval declined on the ground that the terms offered ' would be much too great for any service I could render to the Public, and that you could not grant them with any degree of credit to yourself, or indeed without the inexcusable profusion of the public money '. Such a display of personal dignity and concern for the public interest was rare; Pitt was much impressed and resolved to keep him in mind.

Under Addington, Perceval was Attorney-General; and when Pitt formed his second administration in 1804 he was retained. Grenville would have liked him in his Cabinet, but Perceval was too much of the unbending Tory to serve under a Whig. But when the Tories returned to office in 1807 under the Duke of Portland he was made Chancellor of the Exchequer, with the leadership of the House of Commons. As such, he was the effective head of the Government, and in 1809 he succeeded Portland as Prime Minister, while still retaining his post at the Treasury.

As Prime Minister he continued for some two years and a half, and there is nothing in the record of those years which reflects much credit on him. He had cold feet over Wellington's expedition in the Peninsula, and failed to keep him supplied with the men and equipment that he needed. At home he was faced with an explosive situation; the attempt to blockade the Napoleon-dominated Continent did as much harm—probably more—to British commerce as it did to the enemy's, besides provoking the United States into war in 1812. Manufacturers in England were severely hit, and great unemployment and social unrest ensued. In 1811 there occurred the first of the Luddite riots, in which bands of half-starved mechanics and factory hands set out to smash the new machines which they believed were destroying their livelihood. Perceval and the governing class could think of nothing better than stern repression, while the landed proprietors grew richer and richer and the farming class waxed fat on the profits of their cornfields.

From all that we may learn of Perceval's character, he was plainly unfitted to lead a great nation in these explosive conditions. Lord Brougham, who as a young Whig M.P. sat opposite Perceval in the House of Commons and observed him narrowly, describes him as ' a man of very quick parts, much energy of character, dauntless courage joined to patient industry, practised fluency as a speaker, great skill and readiness as a debater; but of no information beyond what a classical education gives the common run of English youths. Of views upon all things the most narrow, upon religious and even political questions the most bigoted and intolerant, his range of mental vision was confined in proportion to his ignorance on all general subjects.' Within that sphere, however, ' he saw with extreme acuteness—as the mole is supposed to be more sharp-sighted than the eagle for half a quarter of an inch before it; but . . . beyond what he could descry nothing whatever existed; and he mistrusted, dreaded, and even hated all who had ampler visual range than himself'.

Nevertheless, ' he possessed many qualities, both of the head and the heart, which strongly recommended him to the confidence of the English people. He never scared them by refinements . . . and he shared largely in all their favourite national prejudices. A devoted adherent of the Crown, and a pious son of the Church, he was dear to all who celebrate their revels by libations to Church and King. . . . Add to this . . . a temper which, though quick and even irritable, was generally good, a disposition charitable and kind where the rancour of party or sect left his nature free scope. From all sordid feelings he was entirely exempt . . . and only suffering his ambition to be restrained by its intermixture with his fiery zeal for the success of his cherished principles, religious and civil.'

This, then, was the man who met his fate at 5.15 on the afternoon of 11 May 1812 in the lobby of the old Houses of Parliament at Westminster.

Brougham was not a witness of the assassination, although he was close by. The House of Commons had been considering, at his instigation, those ' unjust and preposterous ' Orders in Council which in four years ' instead of collecting all the trade of the world into England, had effectually ruined whatever Napoleon's measures had left of our own'. A motion had been carried some weeks before for examining the question in a committee of the whole House; and on the afternoon in question Brougham was examining his first witness of the sitting.

Perceval should have been present, and a messenger sent to find him met the Prime Minister as he was walking towards the House, arm in arm with his colleague Mr. Stephen. On receiving the message, Perceval quickened his pace, and he had reached the lobby and was about to enter the chamber when a man named John Bellingham suddenly stepped out from behind a pillar and discharged a pistol into his breast. He staggered on for a few paces, and then fell forward on his face, murmuring as he did so the one word, ' Murder!'

Some of those standing by hurried to his assistance, among them a M.P. named Smith who exclaimed ' It is the Prime Minister!' They carried him into the Speaker's apartments. Very shortly a surgeon—Mr. Lynn, of Great Smith Street, who had been urgently summoned—arrived, and after a brief examination pronounced him dead. A pistol-ball fired at close range had gone through his heart. During the night the body was conveyed to No. 10 Downing Street, where Mrs. Perceval and their eleven children were overwhelmed with grief.

Meanwhile the assassin had been arrested. He had made no attempt to escape, and when seized and placed on a bench by the fireplace said, ' My name is Bellingham. It is a private injury—I know what I have done—it was a denial of justice on the part of the Government.' After a preliminary examination by magistrates in a room upstairs, he was taken away to Newgate. The trial opened *four days* later, on 15 May at the Old Bailey. Brougham was one of the counsel for the defence.

When the case for the prosecution had been completed, Bellingham gave evidence. The reports are far from clear, but there is no doubt that he was a man with a grievance, and hardly less doubt that he was out of his mind. It emerged that he was a bankrupt Liverpool merchant who had been in prison. Eight years before he had been engaged in business in St. Petersburg and had suffered some injustice at the hands of the Russian authorities. The British ambassador, Lord Leveson-Gower, had failed to secure him redress. He had come back to England and petitioned various Government departments, and even the Prince Regent, to no avail. He had been pushed about from office to office in Whitehall, until one exasperated official had told him to ' resort to whatever measures he thought fit '.

He had considered that as an invitation to take justice into his own hands, and that is what he had done. He wished to make it quite plain, however, that he had nothing against Mr. Perceval personally: ' If he had been so fortunate as to meet Lord Leveson-Gower, instead of that truly amiable and highly lamented individual Mr. Perceval, he is the man who would have received the ball ! '

Bellingham must have appeared to many in court as a man driven mad by his grievances, and his counsel brought witnesses to prove insanity; but the accused absolutely refused to countenance this line of defence. The Lord Chief Justice summed up, and the jury took only a quarter of an hour to reach a verdict of Guilty. The Recorder thereupon passed sentence of death on Bellingham, and orders were given that his body should be anatomized.

The sentence was carried out on the morning of 18 May in front of Newgate prison. Bellingham died bravely, in a mood of religious resignation. When the body was taken down, it was placed in a cart and taken to St. Bartholomew's hospital, where it was privately dissected.

Lord Brougham summed up the matter in a paragraph that was bitter in its scorn. ' The wretched man . . . never attempted to escape; but was taken, committed, tried, condemned, executed, dissected, all within one week from the time that he fired the shot. So great an outrage upon justice never was witnessed in modern times; for the application to delay the trial, until evidence of his insanity could be brought from Liverpool, was refused; and the trial proceeded, while both the court, the witnesses, the jury, and the people, were under the influence of the feelings naturally excited by the deplorable slaughter of one of the most eminent and virtuous men in any rank of the community.'

18

EARL OF LIVERPOOL

THE MOST INTERESTING THING about Lord Liverpool is that he was Prime Minister for just on fifteen years without a break. In 1812, when he succeeded Spencer Perceval, Napoleon was well on his road to Moscow and Wellington was bloodily occupied in the Peninsula. He was Prime Minister when Waterloo was fought and won, and he was still Prime Minister when Napoleon died in St. Helena. Only Walpole and the Younger Pitt had a longer spell of uninterrupted power.

Born in 1770, the year in which Lord North started his administration, his name was Robert Bankes Jenkinson. He was the son of Charles Jenkinson, a prominent Tory politician in George III's reign who was created Lord Hawkesbury in 1786 and ten years later Earl of Liverpool.

Robert Jenkinson's mother, daughter of a captain in the Royal Navy, died at his birth, and he was brought up by his father at Addiscombe Park, near Croydon. At fourteen he went to Charterhouse as his father had done before him, and thence he proceeded to Christ Church, Oxford, where if he did not shine as a scholar he made some very useful friendships, among them George Canning, who was destined to follow him in the premiership. Jenkinson and Canning founded a college debating society, and every Tuesday evening, sporting a uniform of brown coat with velvet cuffs and collar and buttons bearing the initials of the most celebrated orators of Greece and Rome, they met in one of the members' rooms and spouted to their hearts' content.

On leaving Oxford Jenkinson went on a Grand Tour of the Continent, and he was present at the storming of the Bastille in 1789. He was still abroad when he was elected M.P. for Appleby, the same borough which some years earlier had provided Pitt with his first seat in Parliament, and under the same Lowther family auspices. But he very shortly exchanged Appleby for Rye, and it was as member for this little Sussex town that he eventually took his seat in the House of Commons in 1790. As a Tory he gave his un-

Son of a highly successful mill owner, Sir Robert Peel was the first representative of the manufacturing interest to become Prime Minister. Under him the old Tory party became transformed into Conservatives.

Lord John Russell (above), was immensely proud of his Whig ancestry and might himself be called the last of the long line of Whig Prime Ministers. For more than fifty years he was in Parliament, and never wavered in his support of political and religious liberty.

Lord Palmerston (left). In 1809 he was appointed Secretary at War by Spencer Perceval, and thenceforward for more than fifty years he had a seat in almost every Cabinet. He was Prime Minister for the first time at the age of seventy, and Prime Minister when he died just before his eighty-first birthday.

Above: The House of Commons as it appeared on 5 February 1833, on the occasion of moving the address to King William IV in answer to the speech to the throne on the opening of the first reformed Parliament. Sir George Hayter was ten years in painting this picture, and the great majority of the 373 figures may be identified. In the chair is the Speaker, Charles Manners-Sutton. Lord John Russell, on the front Government bench, is reaching out to the dispatch-box. Among the Peers grouped on the left are Lord Grey (Prime Minister), Lord Melbourne, and the Earl of Ripon (Lord Goderich). Below: Lord Palmerston, when Prime Minister, addressing the House of Commons on the Commercial Treaty with France in 1860.

hesitating support to William Pitt, then in the bright dawn of his premiership.

His maiden speech was on foreign affairs and Pitt was delighted with it. ' Not only was it a more able first speech than had ever been heard from a young member,' he declared, but it ' was so full of philosophy and science, strong and perspicuous language, and sound and convincing arguments, that it would have done credit to the most practised debater and experienced statesman that ever existed.' When every allowance has been made for Pitt's desire to say something really nice about the maiden effort of an old colleague's son, we are left with the impression that it was something quite out of the ordinary.

In 1792 Jenkinson was again on the Continent, first at Brussels, and then at Coblenz, where he had a close view of the French emigrés and their Austrian and Prussian allies. The young man was clearheaded enough to see that they were a poor lot, and he was not in the least surprised when the army of invasion that moved into France with the intention of overthrowing the revolutionary regime soon staggered to a halt and was then driven back in disorder across the Rhine.

Towards the end of the year he was back at Westminster, where he wholeheartedly approved of Pitt's repressive measures. But war with France had now begun and Jenkinson, as an officer in the yeomanry, had to accompany his regiment, the Cinque Ports Fencible Cavalry, as it moved from place to place about the country. In 1796 he was at Dumfries, and his letters home gave a rather mixed picture of Scottish customs. ' The style of living here is rather gross ', he wrote in one of them, ' though very hospitable. The servants are few and very dirty; but there is a great quantity of meat put upon the table, and after dinner the bottle passes rather quicker than I like.'

Then in 1795 he married Lady Louisa Harvey, daughter of the Earl of Bristol who was also Bishop of Derry. In the following year his father was advanced to the earldom of Liverpool, whereupon Jenkinson assumed the courtesy title of Lord Hawkesbury. Furthermore, he was appointed to the very lucrative office of Master of the Mint—the salary was £3000 a year—which his father had held under Lord North.

When Pitt resigned office in 1801 he advised his friends and supporters to give their support to his successor, Henry Addington, and in Addington's administration Lord Hawkesbury featured as Secretary of State for Foreign Affairs. He was very young for the post, not much over thirty, and it is hardly surprising that he was no match for Napoleon and Talleyrand when they sat down to discuss the terms of the proposed peace treaty. Hawkesbury was severely blamed for agreeing to the restoration of practically all the conquests that Britain had made in the course of eight years of war. In answer to his critics he argued that ' It was wise to spare the resources and spirit of Britain as much as possible; they had been in some degrees strained by the long duration of the war, and required to be cherished by peace'; and when the matter was put to the vote, the Government received a massive vote of confidence. All the same, it was not a very auspicious opening to his career as a Cabinet minister, and when Pitt returned to power in 1804 he transferred Hawkesbury to the Home Office. His courtesy title had now been converted into one of Baron in his own right, and he was given the leadership of the Government peers in the House of Lords.

When Pitt died in 1806 George III offered the premiership to Lord Hawkesbury, but he preferred to continue as Home Secretary. The offer was repeated in 1807 and again in 1809, but still Lord Hawkesbury—or Lord Liverpool as he now was, his father having died in 1808—declined the promotion. Under Spencer Perceval he was Secretary of State for War and the Colonies. Then Perceval was struck down, and at length Lord Liverpool emerged from the negotiations as First Lord of the Treasury. He formed his first Cabinet in June 1812. Addington, now Lord Sidmouth, the former Premier, was Home Secretary, and among the other members of Lord Liverpool's governments were an extraordinary number of future Prime Ministers—Peel, Palmerston, Canning, Goderich, and the Duke of Wellington.

For nearly fifteen years Lord Liverpool remained Prime Minister. He had been offered the post when he was thirty-six, and he accepted it when he was forty-two. He led the Tories in four general elections, and won every one.

He was unremarkable in appearance. As a young man he was considered handsome, possessed as he was of a tall and slender figure and with a rather engaging air about him. But his neck was reputed to be the longest in Europe—something which is well brought out in Lawrence's painting of him; and he had a flickering eyelid which proved a godsend to the scribbler who made ' blinking sun ' rhyme with Jenkinson. Nor had he any pretensions to being an orator. As a member of Canning's circle expressed it, in debate he looked ' as if he had been on the rack three times, and saw the wheel preparing for the fourth '.

One is tempted to say that he was without much personality—and here it may be recalled that Disraeli, in his political novel *Coningsby* (1844), refers to him as ' the Arch-Mediocrity, who presided, rather than ruled, over a Cabinet of Mediocrities ', and declares that ' in the conduct of public affairs his disposition was exactly the reverse of that which is characteristic of great men. He was peremptory in little questions, and great ones he left open.' And yet, he did manage to remain Prime Minister for fourteen momentous years. How did he manage it ?

Undoubtedly he was possessed of some excellent qualities. As enumerated by his Victorian biographer Professor Yonge these were: a calm and sound judgment, shrewd insight into the characters of the men with whom he had to deal, extensive information (he had filled every secretaryship of state—something never done before by any Minister—and so was well acquainted with the details of every department of the administration), unsullied integrity, undeviating freedom from jobbery, and a rare scrupulousness in the distribution of patronage, lay and ecclesiastical. Add to these unfailing tact, unvarying courtesy and affability, and a temper that remained un-ruffled by even the wildest storms of political passion, and we have gone some way towards understanding Lord Liverpool's tenacious grip on the premiership.

In himself Liverpool was not a bad fellow, but as Prime Minister he must have come pretty near deserving the detestation in which he was held by most men who stood for liberty and progress. Long after Waterloo had been fought and won, he maintained at full blast all the machinery of repression that Pitt had devised, and without Pitt's excuse. He was Prime Minister at the time of the Peterloo massacre, when on a day in August 1819 a crowd of Lancashire operatives and their wives and children were charged by the yeomanry, eleven persons being killed and many hundreds wounded. It has been said that he disapproved of the magistrates' calling in the military, but as they had done so he felt obliged to cover them with his authority. It was his Government which passed the ' Six Acts ', suspended Habeas Corpus in time of peace, prosecuted Trade Union-ists, clapped Radical journalists into gaol, put rioters on trial for high treason, employèd spies and *provocateurs* in industrial disputes, and made the advocacy of even the mildest and most necessary reforms a criminal offence. For these things that he did, or permitted others to do, he was execrated in his lifetime and has been remem-bered with contumely.

The best that a defending counsel can do is to remind us that as a boy Lord Liverpool had seen London terrorized by the Gordon rioters, and as a young man had watched the storming of the Bastille by the Paris mob. These recollections left their mark, and must have led him to the conclusion that a weak government deserves all that it gets. And there is another thing that is all too often forgotten: he had no police forces to maintain the King's Peace. When there was rioting the soldiers had to be called in: there was no one else to do the job.

Now to take a further glance at the sparse records of Liverpool as a human being. His wife died in 1821, and a year later he married Mary Chester, niece of Lord Bagot, the ceremony being performed in the chapel at Hampton Court Palace. We learn that in 1825 Lady Liverpool succeeded in inducing her husband to take her on a holiday trip to the Netherlands, which she had not seen since she was a girl, before the revolutionary deluge. But this was quite exceptional. As the Duke of Buckingham wrote, ' Lord Liverpool had no habits of any but official employment ', and ' duty ' came first with him wherever they might be living; at Fife House, Combe Wood, or Walmer Castle, which was Liverpool's official residence as Lord Warden of the Cinque Ports.

On the morning of 17 February 1827 his servants found Lord Liverpool lying paralysed and unconscious beside his breakfast-table, clutching in one hand a letter from Mr. Canning that had arrived by the morning's post but which contained nothing that could have caused him any distress. The simple truth was that he had driven himself too hard. Now a stroke left him a physical and mental wreck.

' The moment it was known every sort of speculation was afloat as to the probable changes this event would make in the Ministry. It was remarked how little anybody appeared to care about the *man*; whether this indifference reflects most upon the world or upon him, I do not pretend to say.'

This humane comment comes from the pages of *Greville's Diary*, a book which will be extensively drawn upon in the next few chapters. Charles Cavendish Fulke Greville was the best informed and perceptive reporter of the contemporary scene. A grandson on his mother's side of the Duke of Portland who was twice Prime Minister, he was clerk to the Privy Council from 1821 to 1859 and was intimate with statesmen of both political parties. He began writing his journal in 1818, and the last entry in the last of the scores of red-covered copy books is dated 13 November 1860.

' I close this record,' he wrote with characteristic modesty, ' with great regret that I did not make better use of the opportunities I have had of recording something worth reading.' In point of fact, his memoirs have long been recognized as among the best things of their kind. The first part, containing the Journals of the reigns of George IV and William IV, was published in 1874, and Queen Victoria wrote to her Prime Minister to say how *horrified* and *indignant* she was at this dreadful and scandalous book of Mr. C. Greville's, and Disraeli hastened to reply that it was ' a social outrage '. The final volumes came out in 1887, and Mr. Gladstone took a juster view of their contents. ' There can be no doubt,' he said, ' as to Greville's most conspicuous gift. It is a power of drawing characters with ease, with life, with a fullness never diffuse, and a fairness hardly ever at fault and sometimes conspicuous.' Greville, who had had the acumen to spot the young Gladstone as ' the ace card of the pack ', would have been pleased at that.

After a few weeks it was realized that Lord Liverpool would never get better, and in April 1827 Canning succeeded him in the premiership. Liverpool lingered on for many months. ' Pressure on the brain ' was the doctors' diagnosis, and a pathetic account was rendered by Lady Liverpool to Stephen Lushington, an official of the Treasury. Occasionally the pressure would subside, she told him, and reason would then resume a limited power. But after a short respite the stricken man would feel the pressure coming back again. He ' puts his hand to his forehead, and in a state of pain and forgetfulness says, " I am but a child ", and in sorrow sheds most plenteous tears '.

The end of this death in life came on 4 December 1828. Lady Liverpool survived her husband until 1846. There were no children of either of Lord Liverpool's marriages.

19

GEORGE CANNING

WHEN LORD LIVERPOOL was so peremptorily withdrawn from public view, he was succeeded in the premiership by a man who was in almost every respect of character in pronounced contrast. Liverpool was dull, plodding, unadventurous, but decidedly long-lasting. George Canning, on the other hand, was brilliant, erratic, dashingly self-confident, and, as it turned out, desperately short of time. If we take the count from when he completed his Cabinet, he was Prime Minister for only a hundred days, the shortest term of all.

George Canning was born in London on 11 April 1770 of Irish, or Anglo-Irish parents. There were Cannings who were prosperous merchants in Bristol in the middle ages, but the founder of his branch of the family was one of the English emigrants who were settled in Ulster in Queen Elizabeth's reign. In 1618 James I granted them the manor of Garvagh in the county of Londonderry, where they resided for generations as small country squires, or squireens, to use the Anglo-Irish term. In the middle of the eighteenth century the head of the family was one Stratford Canning, a man of coarse, overbearing disposition, who had three sons. The eldest was George, the future statesman's father, who, having fallen in love with a beautiful but penniless girl of whom his father disapproved, was turned out into the world to make his own way. He went to London, where he was called to the bar at Lincoln's Inn in 1764; but the violence of his political opinions—he was a strong supporter of John Wilkes and a loud-tongued critic of the Government's American policy—did him no good at his profession. Before long he was head over heels in debt, and had to write home for assistance to meet his liabilities. Then in 1768 he committed the further imprudence of marrying an eighteen-year-old girl from Connaught, Mary Anne Costello by name, who like his earlier love was beautiful but without a penny to her name. Soon his debts accumulated afresh, and as a last resource he set up as a wine-merchant. This too proved an utter failure, and in 1771 he died, worn out with worries and disappointments. This was just a year after the birth of his son George.

The young widow was left practically destitute, but she was a woman of fine character and resource, and she formed the notion of going on the stage to keep herself and her boy. She appeared in productions at Drury Lane and Covent Garden, where at first her beauty and sad story aroused the interest of playgoers. But she was nothing much of an actress, and before long she could get engagements only in the provincial theatres. Then she took up with an actor-manager named Reddish, by whom she had several children. His forte was stage-villain parts, and it is said that he was as bad in real life as he was on the boards. He drank heavily; and years after Mary Canning had left him, died in a lunatic asylum at York.

Poverty and sometimes actual want, harsh treatment, disreputable companions—these must have been George's lot, and an actor friend of Mrs. Canning's named Moody, when he first met the boy, concluded that he was ' on the way to the gallows '. He might indeed have ended up there but for this kind-hearted fellow. Moody learnt from Mrs. Canning that George had an uncle, Stratford Canning, who was a successful merchant in the City. He presented the boy's case to such good effect that the old grandfather in Ireland agreed to make the boy an allowance of £200 a year, while Stratford Canning took him into his own home at Putney and practically adopted him.

George was now properly provided for, but we may well ask what happened to his mother. That admirable woman, it would seem, was left to carry on as best she could, with an ever-growing number of children to look after. In 1783 she married an Exeter linen-draper named Hunn, who before long went bankrupt. Whereupon she arranged for him to go on the stage with her, although he must have known even less about acting than shopkeeping. Before long he died, leaving her with another five children to support. She continued as an actress, until in 1801 her son, George Canning, arranged to have transferred to her a pension of £500 a year to which he had become entitled in consequence of his official employment. The gallant lady was thus enabled to retire at last from the theatre, and she spent the remainder of her life in the neighbourhood of Bath. Canning visited her whenever he could, and he wrote to her regularly every week. His affection for his mother is, in fact, one of the most engaging traits in Canning's character. She lived to see him acclaimed the most distinguished statesman of his time, and died only a short time before him.

★   ★   ★

Canning was about eight years old when he was transferred to his uncle's care. Until that time his schooling had been neglected to say the least, but now he was sent to Hyde Abbey, a private school at Winchester kept by Dr. Richards, a pedagogue who wielded the rod with gusto. Canning bore him no malice, or it may be that he was the Doctor's favourite, for when he had come to place and power he appointed Richards to a prebendary's stall in the cathedral.

During the holidays the boy stayed with his uncle and aunt in their house at Putney. Stratford Canning was a staunch Whig, and under his roof George made the acquaintance of other important figures in Whig society. Fox himself is supposed to have urged that the boy should be sent to Eton, where Canning stayed for six years from 1782, and did well there, winning a number of prizes and becoming top of the school. He also helped to launch and was the chief contributor to a school magazine called *The Microcosm*, and shone in the debating society. But while so active in these directions, he showed no inclination for the usual boyish amusements and pursuits. Years afterwards, Wilberforce was told by a former schoolfellow of Canning's at Eton that he 'never played at games with the other boys', but he was 'quite the man, fond of acting, decent and moral'.

Leaving Eton in 1788 when he was eighteen Canning went on to Christ Church, Oxford, where again he showed his superiority in Greek and Latin. More to the point, he made quite a name for himself as a debator, and he was a founder member of that society of which, as we have noted earlier, the future Lord Liverpool was also a member. In 1791 he got his degree and took the coach for London.

On arrival there he started reading for the bar at Lincoln's Inn, but he was very soon deserting his law studies for the drawing-rooms queened over by the great ladies of Whig society, to which he was admitted on the strength of his Oxford reputation as a smart-tongued young man of promise and his uncle's connections in political circles.

At Oxford he had been a 'horrible Whig', and had inveighed against the policies of William Pitt. When the French Revolution broke out, he hailed it as the dawn of an infinitely brighter and happier age, and at the Radical clubs that met in such popular hostelries as *The Hardwicke* and the *Crown and Anchor* his spirited denunciations of tyranny were received with rapturous shouts. But before long he began to have doubts. As he explained in a letter to his friend Lord Boringdon, while the French 'were struggling for their own liberty . . . my opinion, my hopes, and my prayers went with them, and I exulted in the defeat of their enemies; but now I find them a very different people, victorious everywhere . . . not oppressed, attacked, and insulted, but insolent beyond all bounds, professing universal oppression, and proving to demonstration that the best blessing of Heaven, when put into bad hands, as liberty into theirs . . . may be converted into a plague for the disquiet and destruction of all mankind '. For them, in this character, he had now ' contempt, dread, and execration '.

This was written in 1792, when he had already broken with his Whig friends and patrons. He had written to Pitt, offering his services, and in August the Prime Minister had received him at Downing Street in the most friendly fashion. From that moment Canning was Pitt's most devoted supporter. A seat in Parliament was the next step. The Duke of Portland offered to bring him in for one of his boroughs, but Canning said he did not wish to be under an obligation to any other man than Pitt. The Prime Minister told his managers at the Treasury to see what they could do, and in July 1793 Canning was returned unopposed as M.P. for the borough of Newtown in the Isle of Wight.

Of course he was bitterly assailed for this ' desertion'. The disgust of his former friends and associates was given expression in an epigram by Fox's friend, Colonel Fitzpatrick:

> The turning of coats so common is grown
> That no one would wish to attack it,
> But no case until now was so flagrantly known
> Of a schoolboy turning his jacket.

But, it may be asked, if in those days a turncoat was so commonly met with, why should such a novice as Canning be singled out for special opprobrium ? There were plenty of other Whigs doing the same. With much more reason might Canning be blamed for the indecent acrimony with which he proceeded to attack in the columns of a satirical weekly called The Anti-Jacobin those Whigs who still adhered to Fox instead of hurrying to jump on to Pitt's bandwagon.

Early in the next year he made his maiden speech, and although it was not quite so good as his reputation had led people to expect it made a favourable impression. Later on he developed into one of the greatest of Parliamentary orators; Lord Aberdeen, who had an extensive knowledge of the subject, declared that he preferred Canning's oratory to that of such splendid performers as Fox and Pitt. His appearance, too, was prepossessing, for he was a handsome young fellow, with an ample forehead, oval face, penetrating eyes and rather scornful lip, and hair that was raven black until it was powdered into a dusty grey. But what most was to his advantage was the Prime Minister's obvious partiality, and the relationship between them developed into one of sincere affection. Pitt, it was remarked, seemed to look upon Canning almost as a son.

Canning's first experience of office was in 1796, when Pitt appointed him Under Secretary at the Foreign Office, then presided over by Lord Grenville. Since the Minister was in the House of Lords it fell to Canning to represent the department in the House of Commons, but he found the office work boring after a time and thought the job was hardly worthy of his talents. After three years of what he described as ' such slavery as never was slaved ' he was given the much better paid post of joint Paymaster-General and sworn of the Privy Council.

Shortly afterwards, he made a highly advantageous marriage. His bride was Miss Joan Scott, a daughter of Major-General John Scott of Balcomie in Fifeshire; and not only was she politically very well connected—her sister was Lady Titchfield, wife of the Duke of Portland's heir—but she was exceedingly well off. It is said that she brought Canning a fortune of a hundred thousand pounds. She was a few years younger than he and it was, it would seem, a case of love at first sight. He met her for the first time at Walmer Castle, when he was staying there as Pitt's guest—the Prime Minister was then Lord Warden of the Cinque Ports—and whether or not Pitt actually arranged the meeting, he certainly encouraged Canning's suit. As Hookham Frere, Canning's most intimate friend, wrote, ' Pitt regarded the marriage as the one thing needed to give Canning the position necessary to lead a party . . . Had Canning been Pitt's own son, I do not think he could have been more interested in all that related to this marriage.' The wedding took place on 8 July 1800 and Pitt was there with Frere, who was best man. ' After the ceremony,' says Frere, Pitt ' was so nervous that he could not sign as a witness, and Canning whispered to me to sign without waiting for him.'

Mrs. Canning was of a very retiring disposition and never attempted to shine as a Society hostess. But she was devoted to her husband, and he paid innumerable tributes to her good sense and other excellent qualities. She acted as his secretary, writing his letters for him and making copies, and he used to try out his speeches on her before going down to the House. Always in his letters the references to her are deeply affectionate: ' Joan—my chief means of happiness' is typical. By her he had three sons and a daughter. The eldest boy was crippled in body and mind, and died when he was nineteen; the second became a lieutenant in the Royal Navy; and the third was the Lord Canning who was Governor-General of India at the time of the Mutiny in 1857 and earned the noble nickname of 'Clemency Canning'. The daughter, Harriet, was a splendid creature, beautiful and impulsive, ever eager to defend her father against calumny and abuse; she married the Marquess of Clanricarde, and became the ancestress of the earls of Harewood.

When Canning was appointed to the Pay Office he seemed well on the way to a successful political career, but within a few months Pitt took it into his head to retire and Canning felt obliged to follow his patron's lead. He opposed the Addington government, sneering at its leader as 'The Doctor', and did his best to further Pitt's return to office. In May 1802 he induced Pitt to preside at the inaugural dinner of the Pitt Club, and for the occasion he composed the set of verses about 'the Pilot who weathered the storm' which have been mentioned in an earlier chapter.

On Pitt's return to the premiership in 1804 Canning was appointed Treasurer of the Navy—a post which was nothing like so important as he felt he deserved. But his intimate relationship with Pitt survived, though it had been affected to some degree by Pitt's sudden withdrawal from office in 1801. Canning was with Pitt the night before he died, and he was deeply grieved. Immediately after the funeral he wrote to his wife, 'It is all over, dearest Love. I have seen poor Pitt laid in his grave, and I feel somehow a feeling of loneliness and dismay which I have never felt so strongly before. I wish I had been able to get into my chaise and go down and shelter myself with my own dear Love at South Hill'—the house near Bracknell, in Windsor park, where he loved to play the farmer. And six years later, in a speech at Liverpool to those who had recently become his constituents, he declared that 'To one man, while he lived, I was devoted with all my heart and all my soul. Since the death of Mr. Pitt I acknowledge no leader.'

This statement provides the key to an understanding of his political career, so chequered in its various stages. He was not cut out to be a sound party man. He proved an uneasy and unreliable colleague. He was too clever for the ordinary run of politicians, whichever side of the party fence they were on. The Whigs were prepared to forgive his juvenile desertion and Lord Grenville in 1806 went so far as to offer him a post in his administration, which was declined. As for the Tories, to whom he was nominally attached, there is truth in what Byron wrote in *The Age of Bronze* (1823) about Canning,

> Who, bred a statesman, still wast born a wit,
> And never, even in that dull House, couldst tame
> To unleaven'd prose thine own poetic flame;
> Our last, our best, our only orator,
> Even I can praise thee—Tories do no more:
> Nay, not so much—they hate thee, man, because
> Thy spirit less upholds them that it awes . . .

When Lord Portland became Prime Minister in 1807 he made Canning his Foreign Secretary, in which capacity he showed plenty of energy and enterprise. It was he who decided on Spain as the battlefield on which Napoleon's power might be undermined, and he gave his full support to the selection of Wellesley as the commander of the British armies in the Peninsula. His most remarkable stroke was the dispatch of an expeditionary force to Denmark—a country with which Britain was not then at war—which bombarded Copenhagen and seized the Danish fleet, thereby preventing its falling into Napoleon's hands. But his relations with Lord Castlereagh, the War Minister, were always strained, and in 1809 the two men fought a duel on Putney Heath. Canning was wounded in the thigh, but shot a button off Castlereagh's coat. Honour was thus satisfied, but Canning in particular was much criticized for his part in the disgraceful affair.

Before that year was out Portland resigned, and Canning was in great hopes of succeeding him as Prime Minister. It was a deep disappointment when Spencer Perceval was chosen instead. For a number of years he was out of high office, and he was as much to blame as anyone for his long exclusion. His greatest blunder was in 1812 when Lord Liverpool, who had become Prime Minister on Spencer Perceval's assassination, offered him the Foreign Office, on the understanding that Castlereagh should lead the House of Commons. In these circumstances Canning refused the offer—and it was not long before he realized what a fool he had been. He was quite glad to receive in 1816 the comparatively minor appointment of president of the Board of Control (the predecessor of the India Office), and as a member of Liverpool's government he supported to the full all the repressive measures that characterized it. For although inclined to a liberal policy in foreign affairs, he was a hardened reactionary on most domestic issues. Thus he was strongly opposed to any measure of parliamentary reform. The exception to this attitude was his advocacy of Roman Catholic emancipation—and this did him no good with the Tories.

When George IV became king in 1820 Canning left the Government because he disagreed with the proposal to proceed against Queen Caroline on charges of adultery; but in 1822 his old rival Castlereagh cut his throat in a fit of insanity and Canning was offered the vacant post of Foreign Secretary.

Such a wonderful second chance comes to few men, and Canning made the most of it. He ticked off His Majesty's Minister at Lisbon for his slovenly penmanship, and also for including packets of tea with his official correspondence. He brought a breath of fresh air blowing down the dusty corridors, and occasionally his old gay humour asserted itself. The most celebrated instance of this is the dispatch which he sent to the British Minister at The Hague to advise him that because the Dutch had been difficult in some commercial matters a levy of twenty per cent was about to be imposed on Dutch shipping. When deciphered, the message read:

> Sir,—In matters of commerce the fault of the Dutch
> Is giving too little and asking too much.
> With equal protection the French are content,
> So we'll clap on Dutch bottoms just twenty per cent.
> *Chorus.* Twenty per cent, twenty per cent.
> *Chorus of English Customs House Officers.* We'll lay
> on Dutch bottoms just twenty per cent.

As Foreign Secretary, Canning was brilliantly successful. He asserted Britain's independent attitude towards the Holy Alliance of the despotic emperors of the Continent. He supported the Greeks in their struggle to throw off the Turkish yoke. When Spain seemed likely to fall under French control, he furthered the efforts of the Spanish colonies in South America to achieve their independence as democratic republics; as he expressed it in the most memorable of his phrases, 'I called the New World into existence to redress the balance of the Old.'

When Lord Liverpool had a stroke early in 1827, Canning was laid up with a severe chill that he had caught at the Duke of York's funeral, when he had been obliged to stand for hours in the middle of the night on the cold flagstones of St. George's chapel at Windsor. But he recovered himself sufficiently to make a determined bid for the succession.

No one had a better claim to the premiership, and yet strong influences were brought to bear against his appointment. The king did not like him, and Wellington and the ultra-tories distrusted him. For weeks there was much wrangling behind the scenes, and it was only on 10 April that Canning at last kissed the king's hand as Prime Minister, First Lord of the Treasury, and Chancellor of the Exchequer. But he had yet to form a government; most of Liverpool's Cabinet agreed to serve under him, but Wellington and Peel were among those who declined. To a considerable extent he was obliged to rely on Whig support, and Lord Melbourne, one of the more prominent members of that party, was given the post of Chief Secretary for Ireland. It was a month before his ministry was complete.

Canning's administration was given a rough passage in both Houses. As the official opposition, the Whigs under Lord Grey were very naturally opposed to everything he did, but far worse were the Tories who sided with Wellington. Canning, wrote Greville, ' was the only statesman who had sagacity to enter into and comprehend the spirit of the times, and to put himself at the head of that movement which was no longer to be arrested. The march of Liberalism (as it is called) would not be stopped, and this he knew, and he resolved to govern and lead, instead of opposing it ' but ' the Tories—idiots that they were, and never discovering that he was their best friend—hunted him to death with their besotted and ignorant hostility '.

Whether Canning would indeed have answered expectations in this respect is, perhaps, an open question. When he declared his policy, he offended far more than he pleased. He was known to favour Catholic emancipation, but he came out strongly against Parliamentary reform.

On 1 June, as Chancellor of the Exchequer, he introduced his Budget. Three weeks later, on the Corn Amendment Bill, he made what proved to be his last speech in the House of Commons. The young Benjamin Disraeli heard it from a seat in the gallery, and many years afterwards he said that he could recall ' the lightning flash of that eye and the tumult of that ethereal brow. Still lingers in my ear the melody of that voice.'

Parliament rose at the beginning of July, but Canning had to continue at high pressure. Among his last actions were the signing of the treaty which gave freedom to Greece, and the opening of negotiations with Brazil for the abolition of the slave trade. Mentally he was as alert as ever, but he had never properly recovered from the chill he caught some months earlier. The Duke of Devonshire invited him to make himself at home at his comfortable villa at

Chiswick, and he gratefully accepted the kind offer. He went to see the king at Windsor on 30 July, and George remarked how ill he looked. Canning replied that ' he did not know what was the matter with him, but that he was ill all over '. As he drove through the castle gates on his way back to London there was, so it was reported, death in his looks.

When he got back to Chiswick he took to his bed and for a week lingered in the most dreadful agony. The king sent his own doctor to see him, and his diagnosis was inflammation of the liver. Towards the end he lost consciousness, but the watchers at his bedside thought they caught the names Greece, Spain, Portugal, and England from his lips. Then he murmured his wife's name. She had been tending him with the utmost devotion, but now, realizing that the end was near, she collapsed in a faint and was carried from the room. Early on the morning of 8 August 1827 Canning died.

Grief and consternation were the mingled emotions when the news became known. A grave in Westminster Abbey was made ready; and though the funeral was private in accordance with Canning's own expressed wish, and the rain descended in torrents, immense crowds assembled to watch the simple procession go past. The coffin was placed in a vault opposite that containing the remains of William Pitt, the man whose friend and disciple Canning had been most proud to be. Years later, Canning's son, the great Viceroy of India, was laid in a grave beside his.

20

VISCOUNT GODERICH

SANDWICHED between the two famous figures of Canning and the Duke of Wellington comes Lord Goderich, who is perhaps the nearest approach to a nonenity in the list of Prime Ministers.

Disraeli called him ' a transient and embarrassed phantom ', and this is an apt enough description of a man who was Prime Minister for not much more than four months, during which time he never met Parliament, and who used to say of himself that he was not really Prime Minister, ' on the contrary: quite the reverse '.

Robinson his family name was. When he was Premier he was Viscount Goderich, and later on he was made Earl of Ripon. He was born in 1782 and christened Frederick John Robinson. He was the second son of the second Lord Grantham, who had been Secretary of State in Lord Shelburne's administration and who died in 1786. The first Lord Grantham, Goderich's grandfather, had also been an active politician; he was Secretary of State under the Duke of Newcastle and as leader of the House of Commons had aroused Chatham's contemptuous hostility—although his royal master had thought fit to reward his services with a peerage.

Frederick Robinson was at Harrow with Aberdeen and Palmerston, two future Prime Ministers, and from there went on to St. John's, Cambridge. His family connections smoothed the path for him. After serving as private secretary to his cousin, Lord Hardwicke, then Lord Lieutenant of Ireland, he was found a seat in Parliament and as a good Tory given several small appointments in successive ministries. In 1814 he married Lady Sarah Hobart, daughter of the Earl of Buckinghamshire. Lord Liverpool in 1818 made him President of the Board of Trade with a seat in the Cabinet, and in 1823 he was made Chancellor of the Exchequer. In this position he did better than was generally expected of him, and his budget forecasts were usually couched in such optimistic terms that he got the nickname of ' Prosperity Robinson '. He attached himself to Canning, and when Canning became Prime Minister in 1827 he appointed Robinson Secretary for War and the Colonies and at the same time procured him a peerage. Robinson's choice of title—

Goderich—is somewhat intriguing: it has been suggested that it reflects his subconscious regard for piety and wealth.

Four months later, Canning died. The Duke of Wellington was his obvious successor in the premiership, but George IV wanted someone likely to prove more amenable and Goderich was the man he chose. He took office in the first week of September 1827 and succeeded in persuading most members of Canning's Cabinet to continue serving under him. But very shortly his incapacity was made manifest.

Greville had suspected it all along. When Goderich had been Chancellor of the Exchequer, the diarist had noted that he was ' a fair and candid man, and an excellent Minister in days of calm and sunshine, but not endowed with either capacity or experience for these stormy times, besides being disqualified for vigorous measures by the remissness and timidity of his character '. A week later he had come to the conclusion that he was ' obviously unequal to the present crisis ' since his mind was ' not sufficiently enlarged, nor does he seem to have any distinct ideas upon the subject; he is fighting in the dark '. Then on 15 December we read: ' The Ministry is at an end. Goderich resigned either by letter to the king yesterday or at the Council on Thursday. They have been going on ill together for some time. Goderich has no energy, and his colleagues are disgusted at his inefficiency, and at the assumption by the king of all power in disposing of patronage.'

This was not the end of his parliamentary career, however. In 1830 Lord Grey invited him to join his Whig government as Secretary of War, and two years later Goderich was made Lord Privy Seal, created Earl of Ripon, and given the Garter. According to what he told Greville, he had agreed to remain in the Cabinet without taking any office. But Lord Grey had insisted on his taking the Privy Seal, and threatened to resign if he did not. ' He was at last *bullied* into acquiescence, and when he had his audience of the King, his Majesty offered him anything he had to give. He [Goderich] said he had made the sacrifice to please and serve him, and would take nothing. An earldom—he refused; the Bath— ditto; the Garter—that he said he *would* take. It was then discovered that he was not of rank sufficient, when he said he would take the earldom in order to qualify himself for the Garter, and so it stands.'

In 1834 Lord Ripon, as he now was, left the Grey government out of disagreement with some of their proposals for Ireland, but from 1841 to 1846 he had a place in Sir Robert Peel's Conservative administration. This was his last period of office, but he had spent thirty years in successive administrations—Tory, Canningite, Whig, Conservative—and for twenty of those years had had a seat in the Cabinet. He died in 1859, at the age of seventy-six.

21

DUKE OF WELLINGTON

SUCH IS WELLINGTON'S FAME as a soldier that it may come as a surprise to find his name in the list of Prime Ministers. In point of fact, however, he spent more years in the Cabinet than commanding armies in the field, and for most of his life he was closely concerned with political affairs.

On that June evening in 1815, when, galloping along the ridge at Waterloo he waved his cocked hat and launched his sorely tried squares and cavalry brigades on the staggering columns of Napoleon's last throw, he was only forty-six. There remained to him thirty-seven years more—years which in retrospect may have the appearance of an anti-climax. And yet, it may be that posterity has done him something of an injustice. On at least one occasion he saved England from a bloody revolution; and in the latter part of his long life, as indeed throughout it, whether as a soldier or as a statesman, he gave the most splendid demonstration of what seems to have been his supreme quality, his devotion to what he considered to be his duty.

The future Duke of Wellington was Arthur Wellesley, fourth son of Garrett Wellesley, first Earl of Mornington, and his wife Anne Hill, who was a daughter of Lord Dungannon. He was born on 1 May 1769; at least that is the date given by his mother, who might be expected to know, and he always kept 1 May as his birthday. But it may be that the correct date is 29 April, since the entry of his christening in the register of St. Peter's church, Dublin, is dated 30 April. The place of his birth is also uncertain. Generally it is stated to have been in Upper Merrion Square, Dublin. But some authorities prefer Dangan Castle, the family's country seat in the county of Meath, and one writer has maintained that his birth took place on board ship between Holyhead and Kingstown.

The Duke was a member of the Anglo-Irish aristocracy, but his ancestors, Protestants in religion and staunch upholders of English rule, were not in any way remarkable. The family's original name had been Colley, but the Duke's grandfather assumed the name of Wesley in 1728 when he succeeded to the estates of one Garrett

Wesley, who was a kinsman of the famous Methodists John and Charles Wesley. In the Duke's early letters he signs himself Wesley, but in 1798 or thereabouts the family decided to adopt the spelling of Wellesley, which seems to have been the ancient form of the name.

When the Pelhams were governing the country, Richard Colley, the Duke's grandfather who had changed his name to Wesley, was made an Irish peer and in 1760 his son, the Duke's father, was made Earl of Mornington. He seems to have been an amiable sort of fellow, more interested in music than in politics. Trinity College, Dublin, awarded him a doctorate and he was professor of music there for a number of years. Improbable as it may sound, it is interesting to note that Wellington himself played the violin in his young days.

Lord Mornington was celebrated not only for his music but for 'kindness and hospitality', and he also went in for expensive improvements. As a result he got so heavily in debt that he found it advisable to quit Ireland for London, where he died in 1781 at the age of forty-five, leaving his widow to cope with a family of eight children in what her class considered to be straitened circumstances. Her favourite was Richard Wellesley, the eldest son, and she pushed his career with all the influence she could collect. He sat in the Irish House of Peers as Lord Mornington and in 1784 acquired a seat in the House of Commons as M.P. for a pocket borough. He supported Pitt, who made him a Lord of the Treasury, and in 1797 he was appointed Governor-General of the British possessions in India and given an English peerage as Lord Wellesley.

Arthur Wellesley was nine years his junior. He was sent to Eton, as his eldest brother had been, but unlike him did not shine as a scholar. He was inclined to be reserved, and a feeling of inferiority made him aggressive. His mother had no great opinion of him; she spoke of him as that 'ugly boy Arthur', and when it came to choosing his career decided on the army, since he was 'fit only for powder'. He did not want to be a soldier; he would have preferred being a banker, as his mother's father had been. But with an allowance of only £125 a year he could not pick and choose and he was sent off to a French military school at Angers, where he learnt the rudiments of his profession, made a number of friends—some of whom were destined to die on the guillotine, got on well with the mademoiselles, learnt French, and—it is pleasing to be told—earned the devotion of a small terrier named Vic.

On his return to England, his brother's influence got him a commission as an ensign (junior officer or subaltern) in the army, and by the same means he was speedily promoted lieutenant, captain, and major. Then in the spring of 1793 enough money was scraped together to buy him the lieutenant-colonelcy of the 33rd Foot, later the Duke of Wellington's Regiment. In the summer of 1794 he led his battalion very capably in the far from glorious campaign in Flanders, and then in 1796 he went to India with his regiment as full colonel. There he found the fullest scope for his military talents in the succession of wars in which the British were engaged. His brother was now Governor-General, and they worked together to their mutual advantage.

Returning to England in 1805 Arthur, now Major-General Sir Arthur Wellesley, found himself something of a hero, at a time when heroes were pretty thin on the ground. Since no further military employment was available he accepted in 1807 the appointment of Irish Secretary in the Duke of Portland's administration and went off to Dublin.

By this time he was a married man. His bride was the Hon. Catherine Pakenham, sister of the Earl of Longford. He had first met her when he was twenty-four and she a girl of twenty. They had fallen in love, he had proposed and was accepted, but then Lord Longford had refused his consent to their marriage, pointing out that Wellesley had little more than his army pay and this would not be enough to keep a wife on. So Wellesley had sailed away to India, leaving his Kitty to her dreams. Very likely he hardly gave her a thought while he was in the east, but on his return he learned, quite by chance and to his great surprise, that she was still single, and all because of him. Perhaps he felt flattered; in any case, he sought her out, proposed afresh—since that is what his code of honour as a gentleman prompted him to do—and they were married in 1806. No doubt he congratulated himself on having done the 'right thing', but his experience of women was now far more extensive and varied than when he had first proposed to her. She was so very much the lady, and her dewy-eyed innocence must have grated on his susceptibilities. But although they were separated for years at a time they remained on good terms.

Very soon after his marriage, Wellesley was on active service once more, first in Denmark and then in Portugal. He returned to the Peninsula in 1809, and for the next five years was in command of the British troops and their allies in the series of campaigns which goes under the name of the Peninsular War. Sometimes he had to retreat, but only to fight on another and a better day; in fact, he never in all those years lost a pitched battle.

Wellesley's rewards kept in step with his growing fame. Following upon his victory at Talavera in 1809 he was created Baron Douro (after the river which had to be crossed before the main action) of Wellesley and Viscount Wellington of Talavera. Wellesley, it may be noted, is a small place in Somersetshire from which the family took their name in the first place, and Wellington is the nearby market town, some seven miles from Taunton. In 1812 he was created Earl of Wellington, and later in the same year a marquis. When the war had been brought to its triumphant conclusion, he was made Duke of Wellington; and there was nothing higher to give him after his crowning victory at Waterloo.

A vast number of other honours were heaped upon him by his grateful country and her allies; and in accordance with the somewhat disreputable custom which has survived to our own days, he was also well rewarded financially. In 1812 Parliament voted him a grant of £100,000, and in 1814 a further grant of £400,000. Then in 1817 the estate of Stratfieldsaye, in north Hampshire, was bought from Lord Rivers for £263,000 and presented to him by the nation. Years later the trustees of his parliamentary grant purchased for him the freehold of Apsley House in Piccadilly—often referred to, incorrectly, as ' No. 1, London '—which the Duke bought from his brother Lord Wellesley on his return from India. The Duke extended the house and gave it a facing of Portland stone, and grumbled at having to meet the expense.

From 1815 to 1818 Wellington was commander-in-chief of the Allied army of occupation in France, in which position he exerted himself on the side of moderation. He then returned home, and sank into the comparative obscurity of Master-General of the Ordnance in Lord Liverpool's administration, although in his case the post carried with it a seat in the Cabinet.

From time to time he was employed on some government mission, and in 1827 he was appointed Commander-in-Chief. But he had become something of a back number by August 1827 when Canning died. Upon the fall of Goderich's administration in the following January he was called upon by George IV to form an administration. He was not at all keen on doing so and he was not the king's first choice; but it was an order and like a good soldier he obeyed. This was towards the end of January in 1828.

Wellington was Prime Minister for the better part of three years. He gravely disappointed the high Tories by agreeing to the repeal of the Test and Corporation Acts, which for generations had restricted the employment of Nonconformists in the public service; and he was bitterly criticized when, at the instance of Sir Robert Peel, his principal lieutenant, he put the Roman Catholic Emancipation bill on the statute book. The Duke admitted he had changed his mind, but the alternative as he saw it was civil war, and as he told the House of Lords, ' if I could avoid, by any sacrifice whatever, even one month of civil war I would sacrifice my life to do it '.

What did upset him, however, was the charge made by Lord Winchilsea, that ' under the cloak of some outward zeal for the Protestant religion ' he was carrying on ' insidious designs for the infringement of our liberties, and the introduction of Popery into every department of state '. Wellington demanded an apology and when this was not forthcoming, challenged Winchilsea to give him ' that satisfaction which a gentleman has a right to require, and which a gentleman never refuses to give '. So it was that at eight o'clock on the morning of 21 March 1829 in Battersea Fields (now Battersea Park) the Duke fought his first and only duel. He fired, and missed, presumably with intention, and the earl fired into the air. After which Lord Falmouth, the earl's second, declared that his lordship was now ready to make a proper apology. The matter was soon arranged; and with a curt ' Good morning, my lords ', the Duke mounted his horse, and rode briskly away.

In June of the following year the king died, and the ensuing general election returned a number of supporters of the Parliamentary Reform proposals put forward by Lord Grey and his Whigs. Wellington completely misjudged the situation. He thought the cry a purely fictitious one, worked up by Radicals, agitators, and suchlike riff-raff. When he was challenged on the matter by Lord Grey, he told the House of Lords that he was ' fully agreed that the country possesses at the present moment a Legislature which answers all the good purposes of legislation, and this to a greater degree than any Legislature has ever answered in any country whatever '. In conclusion he stated that not only was he not prepared to bring forward himself any measure of Parliamentary reform but ' as long as I hold any station in the government of the country, I shall always feel it my duty to resist such measures when proposed by others '.

From being a national hero the Duke became overnight the most unpopular man in the country. A few days later his Government was defeated in the House of Commons and he handed in his resignation. He was succeeded in the premiership by Lord Grey, who very shortly introduced his Reform Bill.

Wellington resisted it as long as he thought that there was anything to be gained by further resistance, but when the creation of new peers in sufficient number to carry the Bill was agreed to by King William, he advised his followers in the Upper House to let the bill go through. There is no doubt that his action was a timely and a statesmanlike one, since revolution was only just round the corner. But his reputation had taken a severe mauling. Twice his windows at Apsley House had been smashed by the mob, and he had to protect them with steel shutters which he kept in place for the rest of his life. Even when the bill had become law, and on the anniversary of the battle of Waterloo, he was hooted as he rode through the London streets. 'A rum day to choose,' he commented to a friend as he entered the forecourt; then, touching his hat to his pursuers, 'Good morning . . .'

Now in his early sixties, Wellington had still twelve years of active political life ahead. In 1834 when William IV took it into his head to dismiss Lord Melbourne he invited the Duke to form an administration in his place. The Duke declined in favour of Sir Robert Peel, but while Peel was making his way home from Italy Wellington was gazetted First Lord of the Treasury and sworn in as a Secretary of State. For three weeks he was virtually dictator and did very well. On Peel's arrival, he became Foreign Secretary in his Cabinet; and when Peel became Prime Minister again in 1841 the Duke acted as Tory leader in the House of Lords and gave the administration his most loyal support, although the abolition of the Corn Laws went very much against the grain with him. But chief among his political principles was what he often expressed in the words, 'The Queen's government must be carried on.'

After Peel left office in 1846, Wellington retired from active politics. In his latter years he became a sort of father-figure, occupying a position which Greville describes as 'eminently singular and exceptional', a position which raised him far above any other subjects of the crown and was only a little below that of royalty.

'The whole royal family', Greville goes on, 'admitted him to a peculiar and exclusive familiarity and intimacy in their intercourse with him, which, while he took it in the easiest manner, and as if naturally due to him, he never abused or presumed upon. No man was more respectful or deferential . . . but at the same time he always gave them his opinions and counsels with perfect frankness and sincerity, and never condescended to modify them to suit their prejudices or wishes. Upon every occasion of difficulty, public or private, he was always appealed to, and he was always ready to come forward and give his assistance in his characteristic, plain, and straightforward manner.'

One of the Duke's last public appearances was at the opening of the Great Exhibition in 1851, when he walked in the procession led by the Queen and Prince Albert. He went back to Walmer Castle, his official residence as Lord Warden of the Cinque Ports, where he died peacefully in his armchair on 14 September 1852.

Greville was at Doncaster for the races when he heard of the old Duke's passing. Doncaster was probably the only place in the kingdom, he wrote a few hours later in his journal, where the sensation caused by the news was not absorbing and profound since it came through on the morning of the St. Leger, but everywhere else the excitement and regret were unexampled, and the way the newspapers handled the news was admirable. So full and well-informed were the obituaries that they left little or nothing to be said, except for those ' minute traits of character and peculiarities about the Duke which it was impossible for mere public writers and men personally unacquainted with him to seize '. Greville, who had known the Duke well for many years, proceeded to fill the gaps.

' In spite of some foibles and faults, he was, beyond all doubt, a very great man—the only great man of the present time—and comparable in point of greatness to the most eminent of those who have lived before him. His greatness was the result of a few striking qualities—a perfect simplicity of character without a particle of vanity or conceit, but with a thorough and strenuous self-reliance, a severe truthfulness, never misled by fancy or exaggeration, and an ever-abiding sense of duty and obligation which made him the humblest of citizens and the most obedient of subjects.

' The Crown never possessed a more faithful, devoted, and disinterested subject . . . [He] would at any time have sacrificed his ease, his fortune, or his life, to serve the Sovereign and the State.

' Passing almost his whole life in command and authority, and regarded with universal deference and submission, his head was never turned by the exalted position he occupied, and there was no duty, however humble, he would not have been ready to undertake at the bidding of his lawful superiors . . . He was utterly devoid of personal and selfish ambition, and there never was a man whose greatness was so *thrust* upon him . . .'

Having delineated the Duke as a public figure, Greville added some personal details to his sketch. ' The Duke was a good-natured, but not an amiable man; he had no tenderness in his disposition, and never evinced much affection for any of his relations. His nature was hard, and he does not appear to have had any real affection for anybody, man or woman, during the latter years of his life, since

the death of Mrs. Arbuthnot, to whom he probably was attached.'
Elsewhere Greville states that this lady, the wife of the Duke's
private secretary, had ' lived in the most intimate relations for many
years' with the Duke ' and in whom he certainly confided. Domestic
enjoyment he never possessed, and, as his wife was intolerable to
him, though he always kept on decent terms with her, at least,
ostensibly, he sought the pleasure of women's society in a variety
of capricious *liaisons*, from which his age took off all scandal: these
he took up or laid aside and changed as fancy and inclination
prompted him. His intimate friends and adherents used to smile at
these senile *engouements*, but sometimes had to regret the ridicule to
which they would have exposed him if a general reverence and
regard had not made him a privileged person, and permitted him
to do what no other man could have done with impunity.

' In his younger days he was extremely addicted to gallantry, and
had great success with women, of whom one in Spain gained great
influence over him, and his passion for whom nearly involved him
in serious difficulties. His other ladies did little more than amuse
his idle hours, and subserve his social habits, and with most of them
his *liaisons* were certainly very innocent. He had been very fond of
Grassini, and the successful lover of some women of fashion, whose
weaknesses have never been known, though perhaps suspected.
These habits of female intimacy and gossip led him to take a great
interest in a thousand petty affairs, in which he delighted to be mixed
up and consulted. He was always ready to enter into any personal
matters, intrigues, or quarrels, political or social difficulties, and to
give his advice, which generally (though not invariably) was very
sound and good; but latterly he became morose and inaccessible,
and cursed and swore at the people who sought to approach him,
even on the most serious and necessary occasions . . .

' Partly from a lofty feeling of independence and disinterestedness,
and partly from indifference, he was a very bad patron of his
relations and adherents, and never would make any application for
their benefit. The consequence was that he was not an object of
affection, even to those who looked up to him with profound
veneration and respect.

' He held popularity in great contempt, and never seemed touched
or pleased at the manifestations of popular admiration and attachment
of which he was the object. Whenever he appeared in public he
was always surrounded by crowds of people, and when he walked
abroad everybody who met him saluted him; but he never seemed
to notice the curiosity or the civilities which his presence elicited.'

Never had there been such a demonstration of national grief as that displayed at Wellington's funeral on 18 November 1852. His body was conveyed on a specially constructed triumphal car, still to be seen in the crypt of St. Paul's cathedral, from Chelsea Hospital where it had been lying in state, to St. Paul's where it was interred beside Nelson's beneath the dome. The sculptor Alfred Stevens was commissioned in 1856 to design a monument to stand in the cathedral, but this was not completed until 1894.

22

EARL GREY

FOR NEARLY HALF A CENTURY after Pitt formed his administration at the close of 1783 the Whigs were out of office. They formed the opposition to a succession of Tory governments, and a pretty feeble opposition it was for much of the time. Many of them joined Pitt, and only a small band of faithfuls clung together until the long night of exile came to an end. When they did at last emerge from their bleak obscurity the Whigs in a few years of tremendous effort laid the foundations of our present parliamentary democracy.

The credit for this achievement should largely go to the Northumbrian squire who is usually styled Lord Grey, although he did not come into the title until middle life. For forty years he kept his vision undimmed. Although his footsteps sometimes faltered his was the eventual triumph.

Charles Grey was the eldest surviving son of General Charles Grey, one of the Greys of Howick who took their appellation from the old peel-tower or fortified manor house of Howick on the North Sea coast not far from Alnwick in Northumberland. He was born on 13 March 1764 at his father's house at Falloden, rather nearer to Alnwick than Howick, the latter being then in the occupation of Sir Henry Grey, the head of the family who was the General's elder brother.

The Greys have been established in Northumberland for hundreds of years. General Grey, his father, had distinguished himself in the Seven Years' War before his son was born; later on he was one of the most successful of the British commanders in the war with the colonists in America, and later still helped to demolish the French empire in the West Indies. When Napoleon threatened invasion, the veteran soldier took command of the southern district of England, and at the peace of Amiens in 1802 was rewarded with a peerage.

At the age of six Charles Grey was sent to a boarding-school at Marylebone and spent three miserable years there. In after life he always spoke of it ' with the utmost horror '. The sort of place it was may be gauged from the fact that a few days after his arrival in London he was taken to see a batch of Jews hung for forgery at

Tyburn. So that he should not miss anything of the spectacle he was hoisted on the shoulders of a tall grenadier, and even as an old man he would wake in a cold sweat from a nightmare of recollection.

From nine to seventeen, when his father was on active service in America, he was at Eton, and proceeded thence to King's College, Cambridge, where he won prizes for English composition and public speaking. Leaving Cambridge in 1784 he went abroad on the Grand Tour, and was still travelling on the Continent when in July 1786 he was returned as one of the two M.P.s for the county of Northumberland. On entering the House of Commons he joined that section of the Whigs that was headed by Charles James Fox, partly because of his naturally liberal sympathies but also because he belonged to the territorial interest which was being threatened by the young William Pitt's government.

Grey's first speech in the Commons was in 1787, and it is nothing to his credit that it was an attack on the commercial treaty that Pitt was negotiating with France. The speech seems to have been a good one; Henry Addington, the future Prime Minister, wrote to his father that, ' A new speaker presented himself to the House, and went through his first performance with an *éclat* which has not been equalled to my recollection. His name is Grey. He is not more than twenty-two years of age; and he took his seat only in the present session. I do not go too far in declaring that in the advantage of figure, voice, elocution, and manner, he is not surpassed by any member of the House; and I grieve to say that he was last night in the ranks of the Opposition, from whence there is no hope of his being detached.'

From all accounts, Grey was a strikingly handsome man, in youth, in middle age, and when grown old. Addington, as we have just seen, was impressed. Lord Byron, years later, spoke of Grey's ' patrician thoroughbred look ', and in 1831 the diarist Thomas Creevey described him as ' the best dressed, the handsomest, and apparently the happiest man in all his royal master's dominions '.

Like many young and eager spirits of his generation Grey hailed the French Revolution with enthusiasm, but his transports were soon modified. He was no Radical, either then or later. He had read Thomas Paine's *The Rights of Man*, and told the House of Commons that he considered ' the rights of man as the foundation of every government, and those who stand against those rights as conspirators against the people ', but he was ' not a friend of Paine's doctrines ' for all that. He was a reformer, not a revolutionary, and it was because of this that he was not at all attracted by the

London Corresponding Society being formed by the London shoe-maker Thomas Hardy, which had for its principal objectives universal suffrage and annual parliaments. Grey thought that the times were not propitious for such sweeping changes, and in the spring of 1792 he was prominent in the formation of the Society of Friends of the People, which was a much more moderate and respectable body. In their manifesto the ' Friends of the People ' advocated nothing more explicit than ' a more equal representation of the people in Parliament, and a more frequent exercise of their right of electing their representatives '. Later they issued a Report on the State of Parliamentary Representation which disclosed that more than 300 of the 513 M.P.s returned by constituencies in England and Wales owed their seats to ' proprietors ', who numbered 71 Lords and 91 Commoners; that a little over 11,000 voters returned a clear majority of M.P.s in England and Wales; that 51 constituencies had fewer than 50 voters each; that Scotland (with a total of 2,643 voters) returned 45 members, while a single English county (Cornwall) returned 44; and that Cornwall had more M.P.s than the two most populous counties—Yorkshire and Middlesex—put together. Fur-thermore, that seats in Parliament were bought and sold quite openly, and that the price of one ' was better known than the price of a horse '.

Grey, charged with bringing these facts to the notice of the House of Commons with a view to their being investigated by a committee to be appointed for the purpose, might as well have saved his breath. All the old arguments for maintaining the ramshackle fabric of ' rotten boroughs ' were trotted out by defenders of the old order; and by 282 votes to 41 the Commons decided that they had not the least wish to have any inquiry made into the way in which they had obtained their seats.

By this time, Pitt had taken fright at the excesses across the Channel. Repression was made Government policy, and with a view to striking terror into the hearts of the reformers Thomas Hardy and eleven other prominent members of the Corresponding Society were arrested in 1794 and put on trial for high treason.

Grey had never been a member of that society and thought many of its activities misjudged but he took the Hardy prosecution as a danger-signal, in spite of having excellent reason for keeping out of trouble just then since he had become engaged to Miss Elizabeth Ponsonby, the charming, eighteen-year-old daughter of William (later Lord) Ponsonby. ' The first trial, which will be Hardy's, comes on Tuesday,' he wrote to his betrothed. ' I believe I shall

attend it in order to learn how to conduct myself when it comes to
my turn. You see by these new constructions of treason, they have
found a much better way of disposing of obnoxious persons than by
sending them to Botany Bay and one which will save both you and
me a great deal of trouble.'

Grey did attend the trial when it opened at the Old Bailey on
28 October 1794 and his next letter to Miss Ponsonby was written
from his seat in court. ' I am writing from the Bench, with a Judge
at my elbow, who I am not quite sure does not think I ought to be
in Mr. Hardy's place at the Bar . . . They are now examining one
of the Government spies who has been employed to frequent a
meeting at Sheffield, and who is exhibiting a shocking sense of
infamy.' Then in a third note he tells the girl, ' I have no power,
nor do I believe the English language affords words sufficiently
strong, to express my abhorrence of the whole proceeding. If this
man is hanged there is no safety for any one. Innocence no longer
affords protection to a person obnoxious to those in power, and I
do not know how soon it may come to my turn.'

For eight days, Hardy's trial went on. Scott, Lord Chancellor in
the Tory governments almost continuously from 1801 to 1827, did
his damnedest to prove the charge, and Erskine surpassed himself
in the defence. Chief Justice Eyre summed up, and the jury—Tories
to a man—retired to consider their verdict. They were out for
three hours, and filed slowly back into their box amid an ' awful
silence and suspense '. Their foreman delivered their verdict—but
in so weak a voice that he could not be heard, and he fell down in
a faint. But stronger voices repeated his words: ' Not guilty! '

In London that night there were wild rejoicings in the streets,
and the demonstrations were repeated when in due course several
others of the accused men were put on trial and similarly acquitted.
Whereupon the prosecutions of the remainder were dropped.

Pitt had been checked—but he had not been stopped, and in the
next year or so practically all the vaunted freedoms of the Englishman were put in abeyance. Only in the House of Commons might
a man still speak his mind, because of parliamentary privilege, and
even there the atmosphere soon became too stifling and oppressive
for Fox and Grey and their little band of democrats. In the winter
of 1797 the Foxites constituting the official Opposition became so
disheartened that they decided to withdraw from the House
altogether.

Grey joined in this pusillanimous decision, but not before he had
made one more attempt to obtain some measure of parliamentary

reform. In May 1797 he introduced a bill which proposed the abolition of a number of rotten boroughs and the enfranchisement of a number of 'new towns', and that the vote should be extended to all householders, a term which was left undefined. Grey must have thought he had done very well when 91 M.P.s followed him into the lobby as against 256 for the Government.

The Whig Seccession, as it was called, lasted until 1800, when Grey and his friends resumed their attendance at Westminster. His heart was not there, however, but in his home. Immediately after the Hardy trial he had married Miss Ponsonby, on 18 November 1794. A few years later his uncle, who was a confirmed bachelor, decided to live in London, and made over to him the old house at Howick.

It was a delightful place, and the Greys were very happy there. Between 1797 and 1819 Elizabeth bore her husband ten sons and five daughters and they were all educated at home by a succession of tutors and governesses. And what a cheerful crowd they were! No stiff and starched formality, but they called one another by pet variations of their Christian names. Grey himself was always 'Car' in the family circle.

From such pleasant surroundings, Grey found it more and more difficult to tear himself away. Howick was several days distant from London by post-chaise, and even when he was prepared to make the journey the state of the roads, not to mention the weather, was such as to deter his wife—and he never travelled without her if he could help it.

Among Fox's letters to him at Howick is one dated January 1805, in which Mrs. Grey is begged 'not to think of letting you come alone, or that at least she will follow very soon after. God knows when you are in town without her you are unfit for anything, with all your thoughts at Howick . . . in a constant fidget and misery.'

During those years he often felt desperately discouraged. 'I feel more and more convinced of my unfitness for a pursuit which I detest,' he wrote to his wife from London in 1804, 'which interferes with all my private comfort, and which I only sigh for an opportunity of abandoning decidedly and for ever. Do not think this is the language of momentary low spirits; it really is the settled conviction of my mind.' Elizabeth encouraged him to persevere, and blamed him for harping on a subject which, as she wrote to her 'Dearest Charles' at a much later date, 'is a very sore one with me, and adds very much to the depression for which you scold me so unmercifully'. So he had to resign himself to the political treadmill

Benjamin Disraeli had just astonished the town with his satirical novel *Vivian Grey* when Maclise made this drawing of him (left). The young dandy with his rings and flowered waistcoat and behind him his hookah, suggestive of his Turkish travels, contrasts strongly with the mature statesman painted by Millais (below). Mrs. Disraeli, who as an old lady was created Viscountess Beaconsfield, was something of a beauty in her young days (below left). On the fly-leaf of his novel *Sybil* Disraeli paid tribute to her as 'a perfect wife'.

Millais painted this fine portrait of W. E. Gladstone in 1879, when the 'G.O.M.' was on the eve of his second premiership. The photograph of Mrs. Gladstone was taken at about the same period. Below: Hawarden Castle, in Flintshire, which was Gladstone's much-loved home and where he died in 1898.

in London, the long hours listening to interminable debates, the thick air, the smell of guttering candles and of lamps burning the midnight oil.

In 1806 there came a change for the better. After twenty years in the House of Commons he had his first experience of office. In Lord Grenville's 'All the Talents' ministry he was First Lord of the Admiralty from February to September 1806, and on Fox's death became Foreign Secretary and Leader of the House. As such he had the satisfaction of piloting through Parliament the bill for the abolition of the slave trade that William Wilberforce had sponsored. But in the spring of the next year, Grenville made way for the ex-Whig, now Tory, Duke of Portland, and Grey returned to the Opposition benches.

This year of office was all Grey had until he became Prime Minister, and that lay more than twenty years in the future. To make matters worse his father, who had been given a peerage in 1801 in recognition of his military services and in 1806 granted an earldom (whereupon Grey assumed the courtesy title of Lord Howick) died in 1807 and Grey forthwith became a peer himself. He found the House of Lords an even less congenial place than the House of Commons. 'What a place to speak in!' he complained to his wife. 'With just enough light to make darkness visible, it was like speaking in a vault by the glimmering of a sepulchral lamp to the dead. It is impossible I should ever do anything there worth thinking of.'

When Perceval was forming his Ministry in 1809 he approached Grey and Grenville to join, but the overtures came to nothing. Further approaches were made to Grey under the Regency, but he had formed a strong dislike and distrust of the Prince Regent since his repudiation of his marriage with Mrs. Fitzherbert and had no wish to serve in a Cabinet under his rule.

After Waterloo Grey became more and more detached. He condemned the repressive measures of the Liverpool government, but only a few weeks after Peterloo we find him warning a friend against associating too closely with the Radicals. 'Is there one among them with whom you would trust yourself in the dark ?' he inquired; and he gloomily prophesied that 'if you place yourself in their trammels, depend upon it, if a convulsion follows, I shall not precede you many months on the scaffold, which you will have assisted in preparing for us both'.

Inertia seemed to have become second nature with him. He was isolated. The young men in both parties who were beginning to call themselves Liberals looked upon him as a lost leader. He suffered the loss of friends, the defection of supporters. He infuriated such eager spirits as his son-in-law Lambton with his attitude of resigned pessimism. ' Oh, yes,' he would say, ' Reform is bound to come—but not in my time—or even in yours! '

Liverpool, Canning, Goderich, Wellington . . . George IV gave place to William IV. Toryism was in decline, beginning to stink in the nostrils of decent men. There were mutterings of an approaching storm. Reformers began to take heart. Great new influences were at work on public opinion. On 16 November 1830 the Duke of Wellington resigned the premiership, and the new king's advisers were at his elbow and all saying the same thing ' Send for Lord Grey! '

On the next afternoon King William did send for him, and invited him to form an administration. And he accepted—this man of sixty-six, who had been in office for only a twelvemonth and that twenty-four years before; this left-over from the great age of Fox and Burke and Pitt, this political Rip van Winkle, this ease-loving and easy-going aristocrat.

He took his elevation as though he had expected it all along. He was still handsome, as well-dressed and well-groomed as ever, dapper, cultured in speech, suave in manner, serenely confident. His mind, too, was settled. As a young man he had championed Reform when to do so was to run the risk of the gallows. Through all the years since he had kept the faith, however doubtful he may have been at times. Now his hour had struck, and he was ready. The people wanted Reform, did they? Well, they should have it.

Within four days he had formed his Ministry, and its quality may be gauged from the fact that it contained four future Prime Ministers—Melbourne, Russell, Palmerston, and Stanley (Derby)—and one former one, Goderich, while Lord Brougham was Lord Chancellor. Hardly had it been completed when plans were set afoot for the introduction of a measure of parliamentary reform. On 1 March 1831 the Reform Bill was introduced into the House of Commons by Lord John Russell.

' Nothing talked of, thought of, dreamt of, but Reform,' wrote Greville in his *Journal* a week later. ' Every creature one meets asks, What is said now ? How will it go ? What is the last news ? What do *you* think ? and so it is from morning till night, in the streets, in the clubs, and in private houses.'

In the early hours of 23 March the Bill was given its second reading by a majority of *one*—'in the fullest House that ever was known—

303 to 302 ', noted Greville. When Lord Grey was told the news he remarked calmly, ' I have kept my word with the nation '.

This was only the beginning of what proved to be a long drawn-out battle, however. A month later General Gascoyne's motion, ' that the number of representatives for England and Wales ought not to be diminished ', was carried against the Government, and Grey at once resolved to appeal to the country.

A general election was the last thing the Tories wanted since they knew they would fare badly, and in the House of Lords they put down a notice of an address to the Crown against dissolving Parliament. The Ministers were resolved to prevent this, and Grey got the king to go down to the House and prorogue Parliament in person the same day.

' This *coup d'état*,' wrote Greville, ' was so sudden that nobody was aware of it till within two or three hours of the time, and many not at all. They told him [the king] that the cream-coloured horses could not be got ready, when he said, " Then I will go with anybody else's horses." Somebody went off in a carriage to the Tower, to fetch the crown, and they collected such attendants as they could to go with his Majesty.' In both Houses there were extraordinary scenes. In the Commons Peel was speaking ' in the midst of every sort of noise and tumult ' when the guns announced the arrival of the king and Black Rod knocked at the door to summon members to the Upper House, where the proceedings were ' if possible still more violent and outrageous . . . as much like the preparatory days of a revolution as can well be imagined '.

Greville goes on: ' The King ought not properly to have worn the crown, never having been crowned; but when he was in the robing-room he said to Lord Hastings, " Lord Hastings, I wear the crown; where is it ? " It was brought to him, and when Lord Hastings was going to put it on his head he said, " Nobody shall put the crown on my head but myself." He put it on, and then turned to Lord Grey and said, " Now, my Lord, the coronation is over." George Villiers said that in his life he never saw such a scene, and as he looked at the King upon the throne with the crown loose upon his head, and the tall, grim figure of Lord Grey close beside him, with the sword of state in his hand, it was as if the King had got his executioner by his side . . .'

The general election resulted in an increased majority for the Government, and the Reform Bill was reintroduced, passed through all its stages in the House of Commons without any difficulty, and sent up to the Lords. At about five o'clock in the morning of 8

October Lord Grey rose to wind up the debate on the second reading.

'I had no desire for place,' he told his fellow peers, ' and it was not sought after by me; it was offered to me under such circumstances that nothing but a sense of duty could have induced me to accept it. I have lived a life of exclusion from office—I had no official habits—I possessed not the advantages which those official habits confer—I am fond of retirement and domestic life, and I lived happy and content in the bosom of my family. I was surrounded by those to whom I am attached by the warmest ties of affection. What, then, but a sense of duty could have induced me to plunge into all the difficulties, not unforeseen, of my present situation ? What else, in my declining age,

> " What else could tempt me on these stormy seas,
> Bankrupt of life, yet prodigal of ease ? " '

The Lords were unmoved, however, and a delaying motion was carried by forty-one votes. ' I stood in a group with Grey and Holland,' wrote John Campbell, later to become Lord Chancellor; ' the latter was a little excited, but Grey was tranquil and smiling, as if they had been dividing on a Road Bill. There was no cheering, as with us in the Commons upon a great division, and no stranger would have imagined that a measure was decided that might occasion the land to be deluged in blood.'

During that winter blood was shed in many English cities, as great crowds rioted on behalf of ' the Bill '. It would have flowed in torrents but for the statesmanship of the Prime Minister. Grey kept his head when men all around were losing theirs, and managed to keep a potentially revolutionary situation under control.

Shortly before Christmas in 1831 a fresh Bill was introduced into the Commons and passed its third reading on 25 March 1832 with a majority of 116. It went to the Lords, and Lord Grey moved its adoption. The second reading was carried on 14 April by a majority of nine, but in May the Ministers were defeated on a delaying motion of Lord Lyndhurst's by a majority of thirty-five.

Two days later, on 9 May Lord Grey resigned. Amid tremendous public excitement, Wellington and Lyndhurst tried to form a ministry but were unsuccessful. Whereupon Grey was reinstated, and on 17 May got the king's signature to the following: ' The King grants permission to Lord Grey and to his Chancellor, Lord Brougham, to create such a number of peers as will be sufficient to insure the passing of the Reform Bill, first calling up peers' eldest sons.'

This small sheet of paper has been called the Magna Carta of responsible government. A great revolution had been carried out. Henceforth the House of Commons, acting through the Prime Minister and his Cabinet, was the principal political force in the Constitution. It is Lord Grey's testament.

In the event, Grey did not have to exercise the power given to him: the threat was sufficient. When the document was shown round, a number of peers, acting under the leadership of the Duke of Wellington, abstained from voting on the third reading and the Bill was passed on 4 June 1832 by 106 votes to 22, giving the Ministers a majority of 84. It received the royal assent three days later.

With the Reform Bill safely on the Statute Book, Grey's government proceeded to tackle a number of other great reforms, including the abolition of slavery in the British dominions, the reform of the Poor Law, and the Factory Act of 1833. Then things began to get difficult in the Cabinet, and Grey concluded that it was now right for him to retire. On 9 July 1834 he resigned the premiership, and for the eleven years that were left to him he lived quietly and happily with his family at Howick. There he died on 17 July 1845.

23

VISCOUNT MELBOURNE

WHEN LORD MELBOURNE was invited by William IV to form a Government, he told his private secretary, Thomas Young—described by Greville as ' a vulgar, familiar, impudent fellow, but a man of indefatigable industry, and a man who suits Melbourne '—that ' he thought it a damned bore; and that he was in many minds what he should do—be Minister or no '.

Young rejoined, ' Why, damn it, such a position never was occupied by any Greek or Roman, and, if it only lasts two months, it is well worth while to have been Prime Minister of England.'

' By God, that's true,' said Melbourne, ' I'll go.'

This was in July 1834, when Melbourne was in his middle fifties. He was born William Lamb, at Brocket Hall, in Hertfordshire (or at Melbourne Hall, in Derbyshire—the accounts differ) on 15 March 1779. He was the son of Peniston Lamb, the first Viscount Melbourne, and his wife Elizabeth Milbanke, daughter of a Yorkshire baronet; but there was a persistent rumour that his real father was George Wyndham, third Earl of Egremont, who at the relevant time was Lady Melbourne's regular lover. Greville states quite definitely that this was so, and adds that Melbourne resembled Lord Egremont ' in character and manner, as he did remarkably in feature '. Melbourne himself, however, always denied the rumour.

The Lambs were newcomers to the peerage. The founder of the family fortunes was one Matthew Lamb, an attorney at Southwell, in Nottinghamshire, who in the first half of the eighteenth century built up a large and lucrative practice among the landed gentry. His son, also Matthew, was a highly successful lawyer in London, who bought himself a seat in Parliament, acquired a baronetcy, purchased Brocket Hall in Herts, and when he died left a fortune of nearly a million pounds. With such substantial backing his son Sir Peniston Lamb can have experienced little difficulty in obtaining first an Irish barony, and then in 1781 a viscounty. In 1815 he was created Viscount Melbourne in the English peerage. He was the future Prime Minister's father—unless we believe the story about Lord Egremont.

Much more is told us about his mother, and a good deal of it is scandalous. Married at seventeen, and coming from a family considerably higher in the social scale than her husband's, the first Lady Melbourne was a woman of decided character, hard and domineering, ambitious for social advancement, and sexually promiscuous. She was a fine figure of a woman, voluptuously formed, handsome rather than beautiful, and attractive to men. But she was intelligent enough to be reasonably discreet, and her parties at the Melbourne family mansion in Piccadilly attracted the cream of political and literary society, and she played the hostess to perfection. The Lambs were Whigs, and Melbourne House was a centre of the Whig party. Among the most welcome guests was the young Prince of Wales, later George IV, who from an admirer of her ladyship was before long promoted to lover.

William Lamb was sent to Eton and then to Trinity College, Cambridge, achieving no great distinction. Since he was the second son he was expected to follow a profession, and naturally enough he chose the law. He was called at Lincoln's Inn and went on the Northern Circuit. He had one brief, and only one. It was at the Lancashire sessions and was marked a guinea. In after years he used to say that the appearance of his name on that bit of official paper gave him the highest feeling of triumphant satisfaction that he ever experienced.

But he was not cut out to be a lawyer, and he made no serious efforts in that direction. Very good looking, wealthy, remarkably intelligent, and naturally lazy—it was hardly to be expected that he should spend his time in dingy chambers in the Temple or being bored by the interminable wrangles in the courts at Westminster. Infinitely more pleasant and rewarding were the great houses where he was always a welcome guest—the splendid palace at Petworth, where old Lord Egremont always made much of him, Holland House where the Whig *élite* were so agreeably at home, Carlton House where the Prince Regent held his vulgar court, and Lord Bessborough's villa at Roehampton, where he fell increasingly under the spell of an elf-like little creature who occasionally flashed him a glance that made his heart go pitapat.

Her name was Lady Caroline Ponsonby, and she was Lord Bessborough's youngest daughter. Lamb would have liked to propose to her, but as a younger son he had not much to offer, compared with other possible suitors for her hand. She was so pretty, so lively, so clever—not for nothing was she nicknamed ' Sprite ', ' Ariel ', and the ' Fairy Queen '. But in 1805 Lamb's elder brother died and he became the heir. He was now an eligible suitor and when he proposed marriage he was accepted. They were married on 3 June 1805, when he was twenty-six and she nineteen.

To begin with their union was almost romantically happy. The young couple had no home of their own but Lady Melbourne placed a suite in Melbourne House at their disposal. In 1807 a child was born to them. 'Caroline was brought to bed about an hour ago', wrote the proud father to Lady Holland, 'of a very large boy for so small a woman.' He was their only child. The boy was mentally and physically deficient; although he lived to be thirty-one and outlived his mother, he never grew up. This was the tragedy of their married life. If Lady Caroline had a family to look after, she might never have developed her own form of mental instability— what Mr. Torrens, one of the earliest of Melbourne's biographers, styled her unceasing activity. 'Painting, music, reading, writing verses, patronizing plays, taking part in private theatricals, dreaming romantically, and talking in a way to make people stare; riding on horseback, often coquetting, sometimes quarrelling (she hardly knew what it was about) with her husband, trying to please her father-in-law, who thought her a fidget, and trying to please the child, whose wistful gaze of incurious wonder made her for the moment staid and sad. These, and a world of intermingling trifles, filled up her time.'

As the years passed, she became even more wilful, more demanding, more passionately self-seeking and self-regarding, while her husband developed an armour of indolent acquiescence with all her whims. All the same her flightiness, her deficiencies in decorum, her shocking flings at the by no means strict conventional behaviour of their circle must often have been a sore trial to him. The most deplorable and notorious of her escapades was her infatuation with Lord Byron.

In 1811 the poet returned from Greece, bringing with him the opening cantos of *Childe Harold*. Lady Caroline managed to get hold of a proof copy. She shivered in ecstasy as she read them, and felt sure that she recognized in him a soul to match her own. She obtained an introduction to him, and wrote in her diary that he was 'mad, bad, and dangerous to know', which was as good as saying that she was determined to get to know him really well. For more than nine months, so she said, 'he almost lived at Melbourne House'.

Lady Caroline had as little concern for her husband's reputation as for her own. She besieged Byron in his rooms, attached herself to him at balls and parties, waited for him afterwards in the street and invited him to see her home in her carriage. She wrote him the most imprudent letters. She offered him her jewels if he were short of cash. She almost begged him to elope with her.

At first Byron was flattered and intrigued. He found her immensely attractive—even though she was inclined to be skinny and he liked his women plump. He described her as ' the cleverest, most agreeable, absurd, amiable, perplexing, dangerous, fascinating little being that now lives, or ought to have lived two thousand years ago '. But before long he got tired of her; and when she was slow to accept her dismissal treated her with that ostentatious cruelty which he reserved for women who made a nuisance of themselves.

Meanwhile Lady Melbourne had been doing her best to protect her son's reputation. She made up to Byron herself to distract his attention and it was she who suggested that a niece of hers, Lady Isabella Milbanke, who was a considerable heiress, would make an admirable match for him. Byron came to think so, too, and married her in January 1815—to the astonishment of his friends and the furious disgust of Lady Caroline.

A year of marriage was as much as Byron could stand, and in 1816 he quitted England, never to return. Lady Caroline was still infatuated with his memory, however, and she now took a strange, disastrous revenge. She wrote a novel, *Glenarvon*, in a month of hot scribbling, and got it published. The book was a best-seller for several weeks, and everybody who was anybody in society amused themselves in detecting the originals of the chief characters. The heroine was Lady Caroline, without a doubt; Lord Avondale, the heroine's husband, was William Lamb; and Glenarvon—why, of course, he was Byron.

Already a separation between Lamb and his wife had been under discussion, and now the legal machinery was set in motion. The agreement was ready for signature. All the parties were assembled at Brocket, and at the last moment Lamb was not to be found. His brother went upstairs in search of him, and found him and Lady Caroline seated side by side in the most loving fashion, and she was feeding him with thin slices of bread and butter.

Greville says that he got acquainted with Melbourne about this time, when ' the irregularities of his wife had partly estranged him from her, though they were not yet separated, and he was occasionally amused by her into condonation of her amours, and into a sort of half-laughing, half-resentful reconciliation. They lived in this queer way. He, good-natured, eccentric, and not nice; she, profligate, romantic, and comical. Both were kept together, as they had been brought together, by the influence and management of their common relations and connexions.'

In one respect, at least, Melbourne was better situated than his wife, since he had found an infallible resource. Greville continues: 'It was during this period that he devoted himself with ardour to study, and that he acquired the vast amount of miscellaneous knowledge with which his conversation was always replete, and which, mixed up with his characteristic peculiarities, gave an extraordinary zest and pungency to his society.' This taste for reading and information, which the circumstances of these years confirmed into a habit, continued unbroken to the end of his life. ' He lived surrounded by books, and nothing prevented him, even when Prime Minister . . . from reading every new publication of interest or merit . . .'

So the strange pair resumed their life together. It is only fair to say that there is a letter of Lady Caroline's to her friend Lady Morgan which puts a rather different complexion on the matter. ' He cared nothing for my morals,' she wrote of her husband; ' I might flirt and go about with what men I pleased. He was privy to my affair with Lord Byron, and laughed at it. His indolence rendered him insensible to everything. When I ride, play, and amuse him, he loves me. In sickness and suffering he deserts me. His violence is as bad as my own.' And yet in other letters she referred to her husband as the best and kindest of men.

The years passed, until one morning in 1824 she happened to see Lord Byron's funeral going past the park gates. This was the first she had heard of Byron's death, and it gave her a fearful shock. For a time she was very ill, and when she had recovered somewhat her conduct was more outrageous than ever. A separation had now become inevitable, and Lamb insisted that everything possible should be done to make his wife's life as happy and easy as might be. She was to spend most of her time at Brocket, keeping old Lord Melbourne company, while Lamb lived in London. She wrote to him from time to time, and not long after their separation she sent him some verses she had composed, of which one stanza runs:

> Passion and pride and flatt'ry strove,
> They made a wreck of me,
> But oh! I never ceased to love,
> I never loved but thee . . .

A year or so later she became dangerously ill with dropsy, and in 1828 she died at the age of forty-three. ' Send for William ' were almost her last words; ' he is the only person that never failed me.' Nor did he fail her then.

* * *

All this time Lamb, in the lazy, lounging fashion in which he usually did things, had been following a political career. In 1806, the year following his marriage, he was elected M.P. for Leominster and took his seat in the House of Commons as one of the supporters of Lord Grenville, the Whig Prime Minister, since most of his family were Whigs and his wife was connected with the great Whig houses of Spencer and Cavendish. The recent marriage of his sister Emily with Lord Cowper had also enlarged his Whig relationships. But he was always inclined to take an independent line, as when his support of Roman Catholic emancipation incensed the Tories, and his support of the Liverpool government disgusted the Whigs.

Not until 1827 was he given any post in the Government. Canning was forming his administration, and he suggested to King George that Lamb should be found a place. ' William Lamb,' rejoined the king, who had known Lamb from old Melbourne House days, ' William Lamb: put *him* where you please.' So Lamb became Chief Secretary for Ireland, which post he held for a year until he resigned with the other Canningites from Wellington's too-Tory government.

In Dublin Castle, the seat of government in Ireland, he was not able to do very much, but did that little with great good humour which ingratiated him with the Irish of all classes. He was an excellent talker, a quality much appreciated in Ireland; and he also got on very well with the ladies—too well, indeed, with a certain Lady Brandon. Shortly after his return to London he was sued by Lord Brandon for damages on the ground of improper intimacy with his wife. Melbourne (as he now was, since his father had died) employed a good lawyer, and the Lord Chief Justice who tried the case told the jury that ' nobody could give one word of proof against Lord Melbourne ', and directed that the case should be non-suited.

Melbourne was now fifty, and after a quarter of a century in politics had precious little to show for it. But in 1830 Lord Grey took office, and he at once made overtures to the Canningites, of whom Melbourne was one of the most important. Melbourne was offered the Home Office, and accepted it without demur, although he was not particularly keen on parliamentary reform.

As it happened, he was not called upon to play any large part in the struggle, being fully occupied with the affairs of his own department.

The country was in a very disturbed state. In the manufacturing districts of the north and midlands there was much unemployment, and the workpeople were banding together to destroy the machines which they blamed for their distress. In the agricultural areas, especially in the southern counties, things were just as bad, if not worse. The farm labourers had been goaded beyond endurance by their scandalously low wages and shocking housing conditions, and gangs were moving about the country at night, burning hayricks, breaking threshing-machines, and pillaging farmhouses. Melbourne gave his full support to the local magistrates and landlords, and generally displayed a most insensitive attitude towards the genuine grievances of the labourers. Following the disturbances, in which not a single person had been killed or seriously injured by the rioters, special commissions were set up under Melbourne's authority to try the many hundreds who had been arrested. Nine men and boys were hanged, 457 were transported, and another 400 were imprisoned.

Melbourne was Home Secretary when six farm labourers living in the Dorsetshire hamlet of Tolpuddle were arrested on a charge of having administered illegal oaths in connection with the formation of a local branch of the Friendly Society of Agricultural Labourers. At Dorchester assizes in March 1834 the men were put on trial, found guilty, and sentenced to seven years' transportation. Within a month they were at sea on their way to Botany Bay. Melbourne was showered with protests at this perversion of justice, but he uttered not a word of criticism or reproof; on the contrary, he stated that ' the law had been most properly applied ', and congratulated the authorities on the way in which they had handled the matter. Only after four years of agitation were the ' Tolpuddle Martyrs ' reprieved and allowed back to England.

This unsympathetic reaction to labour problems is the harder to understand when it is known that Melbourne maintained close relations with Francis Place, ' the Radical tailor of Charing Cross '. Melbourne had known Place since 1819, when he had helped his brother George Lamb to obtain election for Westminster. He got his coats and breeches from Place's establishment, and on one occasion Melbourne was so slow in settling his account that Place told his solicitor to take out a summons, ' to see what that will do, but, damn it, nothing further '.

In the summer of 1834 Lord Grey resigned the premiership.

Acting on his advice King William sent for Lord Melbourne, who became Prime Minister on 16 July. His colleagues in the Cabinet accepted his elevation as a matter of course. As Lord Durham, Grey's son-in-law, put it, ' Melbourne is the only man to be Prime Minister, because he is the only one of whom none of us would be jealous.'

Melbourne's premiership on this occasion lasted for only five months. In November he went down to see the king at Brighton, where he was in residence at the Royal Pavilion, to consult him about a Cabinet appointment. To his surprise the king informed him that while he had nothing against Melbourne personally, he had decided that a change of ministers was desirable. Melbourne took his dismissal in quite good part, however. When he got back to town he went off to the theatre, roaring with laughter—which his colleagues, who had lost their jobs, thought very unfeeling of him.

Peel was sent for, and succeeded in forming a ministry which stayed in office until April of the following year although he had no majority in the House of Commons. Then a series of defeats enforced his resignation, and the king had to swallow his pride and send for Melbourne again. In April 1835 Melbourne formed his second administration, with Lord John Russell as Home Secretary and Lord Palmerston at the Foreign Office. As a Prime Minister Melbourne did not cut much of a figure, and in the following year his personal reputation took a further battering when he was involved in another unsavoury divorce case.

In his entry for 11 May 1836 we find Greville writing: ' Great talk about Melbourne's affair with Mrs. Norton, which, if it is not quashed, will be inconvenient. John Bull fancies himself vastly moral, and the Court is mighty prudish, and between them our off-hand Premier will find himself in a ticklish position.'

Mrs. Norton, born Caroline Sheridan, was the playwright's granddaughter. She was a tall brunette, with fine dark eyes and a voluptuous figure—the acid-tongued parson Sydney Smith called her a ' superb lump of flesh '. In 1827, when she was nineteen, she married George Norton, nine years her senior. Norton was a Tory M.P. before the Reform Bill deprived him of his seat, and he was chronically hard up. The Sheridans were Whigs and well known to Melbourne, and Caroline sought to improve their situation. She wrote to Melbourne when he was Home Secretary, and begged him to do something for her husband. As a result, Melbourne gave Norton an appointment as a metropolitan police magistrate with a salary of £1,000 a year.

It was in answer to her letter that Melbourne first stepped across the threshold of Mrs. Norton's little house in Storey's Gate. He found it, and its mistress, very much to his taste. For six years the friendship pursued its dangerous course, between the middle-aged statesman and the brilliant young married woman who continued living under her husband's roof as wife and mother. But in 1835 there was a terrible scene between husband and wife, and Norton decided to seek a divorce.

In those days, before the passing of the Divorce Act of 1857, a marriage might be dissolved only by a long and expensive process involving a special Act of Parliament. A husband (not a wife) petitioning for such an Act was required to sue for a separation and bring an action for damages against the alleged seducer of his wife. This is what Norton now decided to do, and out of his wife's numerous admirers he settled upon Lord Melbourne as the most suitable person to proceed against.

That the intended victim was Prime Minister in a Whig government struck some of Norton's Tory associates as being extraordinarily fortunate.

On 22 June 1836 the case of the Hon. George Norton v. the Lord Viscount Melbourne for criminal conversation was heard at the law courts before Lord Chief Justice Tindal, and on the next morning *The Times* devoted more than four of its eight pages to a full report of the proceedings—over twenty columns of closely printed text.

Counsel for Norton opened with a long story based in the main on the evidence of Mrs. Norton's servants. Lord Melbourne had visited the house in Storey's Gate on a number of occasions, almost always when Norton was absent on his court duties. When he arrived he was shown into Mrs. Norton's room, the blinds were lowered and the door locked. Mrs. Norton had been seen to go upstairs to her bedroom with her dress and hair disordered; and having put herself to rights, come downstairs again to him in the drawing-room. Servants told how they had seen them holding hands, and one of the maids testified that his Lordship kissed Mrs. Norton on the cheek. A former footman, who had been given the sack for drunkenness, said that on one occasion he had been sent out to buy some theatre tickets for his mistress. He returned to find Lord Melbourne sitting in a chair in front of the fire, elbows on knees and his head in his hands, regarding Mrs. Norton who was lying on the floor before him, with her head on the hearth-rug. He had thought her dress was somewhat disarranged.

The things that servants see! And how little they did see, protested the Attorney-General, Sir John Campbell, who was leading for the defence. He tore the servants' evidence to shreds: one of the maids had been dismissed for immoral conduct; other witnesses had been paid handsomely for saying what they had been told to say. Was a woman to be supposed guilty of adultery because she had gone upstairs to wash her hands? Then the story of that drunken old reprobate the footman—could it be believed that if the act of adultery had taken place the lady would have continued in that unbecoming posture on the hearth-rug? Surely the most profligate woman in the world would not have behaved in so unconcerned a manner. And Lord Melbourne had been visiting at Storey's Gate for six years; if Mr. Norton had been angry when he came home and found him there, why did he say in effect, 'Stay and eat our mutton at my table; stop and take pot-luck, and in the evening we will go to Covent Garden and see the play'?

In his summing-up the Lord Chief Justice said that in his opinion there had been 'great familiarity and the closest intimacy'. But the jury disregarded that and lost no time in reaching a verdict for the defendant. Whereupon there were cheers in court, and his Lordship protested angrily about such disgraceful behaviour . . .

'The town has been full of Melbourne's trial,' wrote Greville, 'great exultation at the result on the part of his political adherents, great disappointment on that of the mob of low Tories, and a creditable satisfaction among the better sort; it was, in point of fact, a triumphant acquittal.' The king, too, expressed his satisfaction; but some of Melbourne's friends were heard to say that he had been d——d lucky to get away with it, and he really should be more careful in future.

If the case had gone the other way Melbourne would of course have had to resign. He had indeed offered to do so before the case opened—but the Duke of Wellington had pooh-poohed any such idea. All the same, it did him no good, and it was generally recognized that his Government was in low water and before long must surely sink. But King William was taken ill, and died soon after two o'clock on the morning of 20 June 1837.

For Melbourne this was the best thing that could have happened. It worked a complete change in his fortunes, both personal and political. Almost exactly a year after the scandalous allegations of the Norton case he received the charge of the highly impressionable and by no means unattractive young girl of eighteen who had so suddenly attained the throne.

Upon the accession of Queen Victoria, writes Greville, Melbourne 'found himself placed in the most curious and delicate position which any statesman ever occupied. Victoria was transferred at once from the nursery to the throne—ignorant, inexperienced, and without one human being about her on whom she could rely for counsel and aid. She found in her Prime Minister and constitutional adviser a man of mature age, who instantly captivated her feelings and her fancy by his deferential solicitude, and by a shrewd, sagacious, and entertaining conversation, which were equally new and delightful to her. She at once cast herself with implicit confidence upon Melbourne, and, from the first day of her reign, their relations were marked by an intimacy which he never abused; on the contrary, he only availed himself of his great influence to impress upon her mind sound principles of constitutional government, and truths of every description that it behoved her to learn.

' It is impossible to imagine anything more interesting than the situation which had thus devolved upon him, or one more calculated to excite all the latent sensibility of his nature. His loyal devotion soon warmed into a parental affection, which she repaid by unbounded manifestations of confidence and regard. He set himself wisely, and with perfect disinterestedness, to form her mind and character, and to cure the defects and eradicate the prejudices from which the mistakes and faults of her education had not left her entirely free . . . He never scrupled to tell her what none other would have dared to say; and in the midst of that atmosphere of flattery and deceit which kings and queens are almost always destined to breathe, and by which their minds are so often perverted, he never scrupled to declare boldly and frankly his real opinions . . . and to wage war with her prejudices and false impressions with regard to people or things whenever he saw she was led astray by them. He acted in all things an affectionate, conscientious, and patriotic part, endeavouring to make her happy as a woman, and popular as a queen.'

The queen's own *Journal* bears out all that Greville said. In the entry for 20 June, the day she became Queen, we read, ' At 9 came Lord Melbourne, whom I saw in my room, and of *course quite alone*, as I shall *always* do all my Ministers. He kissed my hand, and I then acquainted him that it had long been my intention to retain him and the rest of the present Ministry at the head of affairs, and that it could not be in better hands than his. He again then kissed my hand. . . . He was in full dress. I like him very much, and feel confidence in him. He is a very straightforward, honest, clever and

good man . . .' That evening Melbourne came again and she had
' a very important and very *comfortable* conversation with him ', and
noted that ' Each time I see him I feel more confidence in him; I find
him very kind in his manner too . . .' Throughout the Coronation
ceremony, ' My excellent Lord Melbourne stood very close to me
. . . he gave me *such* a kind, and I may say fatherly look '; and when
it was all over, and she was sitting down after dinner, feeling ' a little
tired on my feet ', he ' turned round to me with the tears in his eyes,
and said *so* kindly: " And you did it beautifully—every part of
it . . ." To hear this, from this kind impartial friend, gave me great
and real pleasure '.

The very next morning she sent him a note: ' The Queen is very
anxious to hear if Lord Melbourne got home safe, and if he is not
tired, and quite well this morning. Lord Melbourne will be glad
to hear that the Queen had an excellent night, is not the least tired,
and is perfectly well . . .'

In letter after letter, she expresses her concern for his health. She
worried about him if he caught a cold; she charged him with attending too many dinners and eating things that did not agree with him,
and staying out too late. ' The Queen anxiously hopes Lord Melbourne has slept well, and has not suffered from last night ', runs
one of her letters to him in 1839; ' It was very wrong of him not
to wish the Queen good-night, as she expected he would in so small
a party, for she *saw* that he did *not* go away immediately after supper.
When did he get home ? It was a great pleasure to the Queen that
he came last night. We kept up the dancing till three, and the
Queen was much amused, and slept soundly from four till half-past
ten, which she is ashamed of. She is quite well, but has got a good
deal of cold in the head; she hopes to see Lord Melbourne at two.'

For four years Melbourne continued to hold this ' most curious
and delicate position '. He lived at Windsor Castle, submitting to
a daily routine which he must have often found irksome. He of
all men appeared to be the last to be broken in to the trammels of
a Court, wrote Greville, but ' never was such a revolution seen in
any one's occupations and habits. Instead of indolently sprawling
in all the attitudes of luxurious ease, he is always sitting bolt upright;
his free and easy language interlarded with " damns " is carefully
guarded and regulated with the strictest propriety, and he has exchanged the good talk of Holland House for the trivial, laboured,
and wearisome inanities of the Royal circle.'

After the queen's marriage to Prince Albert—which Melbourne
entirely approved of—his position can hardly have been the same

as when he was the only man in the queen's life; but all the same, it was a very intimate relationship which lasted until August 1841, when a succession of defeats in Parliament brought about Melbourne's resignation.

On the evening of his resignation he went down to Windsor to see her at her special request. He tried to put a bright face on their parting, but admitted that it would be very painful to leave her. She, too, was upset, but not so badly as two years before, when Melbourne had been only temporarily displaced. Then she had protested against ' this dreadful change ', and had ' begged him still ever to be a father ' to her. Now she had a husband to support her. ' For four years,' said Melbourne, ' I have seen you every day; but it is different now from what it would have been in 1839. The Prince understands everything so well, and has a clever, able head.' The queen saw him again the next morning before he left the castle, and again he spoke in warm terms of her husband. ' You said when you were going to be married,' he reminded her, ' that he was perfection, which I thought a little exaggerated then. But really now I think that it is in some degree realized.'

Very naturally, the queen wished to do honour to her departing Prime Minister, and he was offered the Garter. But Melbourne did not wish it. As he explained to Mr. Anson, Prince Albert's private secretary, ' The Prince has been urging me to accept the Blue Riband before I quit office, and I wished to tell you that I am very anxious that this should not be pressed upon me by the Queen; it may be a foolish weakness on my part, but I wish to quit office without having any honour conferred upon me; the Queen's confidence towards me is sufficiently known without any public mark of this nature. I have always disregarded these honours, and there would be an inconsistency in my accepting this. I feel it to be much better for my reputation that I should not have it forced upon me. Mr. Pitt never accepted an order . . .'

' What does he want now,' Melbourne is reported to have asked about a peer who was pestering him for some honour; ' is it a Garter for the other leg ? '

When Peel took over as Prime Minister, the queen told him that she felt she could not break off all correspondence with Lord Melbourne, as strict constitutional etiquette might have enjoined, and Peel very heartily acquiesced. So she continued to correspond with the old man, and had him to stay at Windsor from time to time, when she made a point of sitting next him at dinner and keeping him amused with her talk. Greville has preserved a dinner-table incident soon after Peel's conversion to Free Trade. 'It was at dinner, when Melbourne was sitting next to the Queen. Some allusion was made to passing events and to the expected measure, when Melbourne suddenly broke out, " Ma'am, it is a damned dishonest act ". The Queen laughed, and tried to quiet him, but he repeated, " I say again it is a very dishonest act ", and then he continued a tirade against abolition of Corn Laws, the people not knowing how to look, and the Queen only laughing.'

Lord Melbourne spent most of his time after his retirement at Brocket. Sometimes when he looked through his accounts he concluded that he was very hard up—quite mistakenly, it appears—and then the queen lent him money to tide him over. Occasionally there was a sprightly letter from Mrs. Norton in his morning's post, for this was a friendship that endured.

But after so many years at the head of affairs he was sorely put out when in 1846 Lord John Russell told him, in the nicest possible fashion, that he could not offer him a post in the Government he was forming. Occasionally he went up to London, and Greville draws a pleasant picture of him at Holland House or at Lady Palmerston's, where 'he loved to lounge and sprawl at his ease, pouring out a rough but original stream of talk, shrewd, playful, and instructive'. But then he would return to Brocket, with its gloomy memories, and sometimes he would quote lines from Milton's *Samson Agonistes*:

> My race of glory run, and race of shame,
> And I shall shortly be with them that rest,

and applied them to his own situation.

Lord Melbourne died at Brocket on 24 November 1848, ' without suffering pain ', wrote Greville, ' but having had a succession of epileptic fits the whole day, most painful and distressing to his family collected about him '. He was buried at Hatfield.

24

SIR ROBERT PEEL

SIR ROBERT PEEL belonged to the new aristocracy of wealth which was created by the Industrial Revolution. The founder of the family fortunes was his grandfather, Robert Peel, who started life as a yeoman farmer in the neighbourhood of Blackburn, as his ancestors had been for generations, but was quick to see and take advantage of the opportunities that lay in the development of machine industry in cotton spinning and calico printing.

His son, another Robert, was born in 1750 and lived until 1830. He was a man of great energy, enterprise, and inventiveness. He worked hard, lived frugally, and ploughed his profits back into the business. He did not marry until he was thirty-three, when his bride was Ellen Yates, the eighteen-year-old daughter of his partner in a cotton-printing business at Bury. By the time of his marriage he had prospered greatly, and over the years he built up a colossal fortune which he left to his children in due course. But he also possessed something of a social conscience, which led him to take a practical interest in the humanizing of the industrial system. He was largely responsible for the first Factory Act in 1802, which was intended to improve the lot of the apprentice children employed in the mills of Lancashire and Yorkshire; and when this proved a dead letter he sponsored, with Robert Owen, the Factory Act of 1819, which was concerned with child labour in general.

His fortune made, Robert Peel entered politics as a Tory. He bought Drayton Manor in the neighbourhood of Tamworth, in Staffordshire, and became one of the M.P.s for that borough. As a staunch supporter of William Pitt, and a generous contributor to the Tory party funds, he was rewarded with a baronetcy in 1800.

This great captain of industry was the statesman's father. When his eldest son—named Robert after him—was born at Chamber Hall, Bury, on 5 February 1788, he is said to have gone down on his knees and vowed ' to give his child to the country '. In the *Peel Memoirs* this is expressed rather differently. Soon after Robert was born, his father ' finding himself rising daily in wealth and consequence, and believing that money in those peculiar days could always command a seat in Parliament, determined to bring his son up expressly for the House of Commons. When that son was quite a child, Sir Robert would frequently set him on the table and say, " Now, Robin, make a speech, and I will give you a cherry." What few words the little fellow produced were applauded; and applause, stimulating exertion, produced such effects that, before Robin was ten years old, he could really address the company with some degree of eloquence. As he grew up, his father constantly took him every Sunday into his private room, and made him repeat, as well as he could, the sermon which had been preached . . . When at a very distant day the senator, remembering accurately the speech of an opponent, answered his argument in correct succession, it was little known that the power of so doing was originally acquired in Drayton church.'

From a school at Bury the boy proceeded to Harrow, where Byron and Lord Palmerston were among his schoolfellows. Thence at eighteen he went to Christ Church, Oxford. Even at Harrow, so Byron stated, ' there were always great hopes of Peel amongst us all, masters and scholars ', and at Oxford he took a double first in classics and mathematics, being the first Oxford man ever to achieve that honour. But he was no solitary student. He dressed in the fashion of the day; he boated, played cricket, and rode to hounds, and generally conducted himself as a young man of wealth and station. The sport he cared for most was shooting, and he became an excellent shot. He was never much of a horseman, however.

As soon as he came of age, his father's money obtained for him a seat in the House of Commons as member for the Irish pocket borough of Cashel. His father was in the House at the time as Tory M.P. for Tamworth, and Peel took his place beside him. Only a year later Spencer Perceval gave him the post of Under-secretary for the Colonies and War. Here his official chief was Lord Liverpool, whom he had already served as his private secretary. Liverpool formed a very high opinion of his abilities, and when he became Prime Minister in 1812 he promoted Peel to be Chief Secretary for Ireland.

As Chief Secretary, Peel did all that his masters expected of him. Ireland was a country seething with discontent, teeming with conspiracy, and always on the brink of armed rebellion. The Anglo-Irish governing class had no answer for such a situation other than the severest repression, and at Dublin Castle Peel became so closely

identified with the Orangemen—the association of extreme Protestants that was named after William of Orange—that he was given
the nickname of ' Orange peel '. He was responsible for several
coercive Acts, and in 1814 extended to the whole of Ireland the
police force, later known as the Royal Irish Constabulary, that the
Duke of Wellington had founded when he was Irish Secretary years
before.

In those days there was no stronger opponent of any measure of
Roman Catholic emancipation than Peel, and it was on the strength
of this reputation that in 1817 he was chosen without a contest to
represent the university of Oxford in the House of Commons. His
rival for the nomination was George Canning, but Canning had
shown signs of weakening on the Catholic emancipation issue and
this killed his chances with the Tory dons.

The following year Peel resigned the Irish secretaryship, the work
of which had grown wearisome, and for the next five years he was
out of office although he continued to give general support to the
Liverpool administration. In 1819 he was chairman of a House of
Commons committee appointed to consider the resumption of cash
payments in place of the paper money which had been legal tender
since 1797. This had been proposed in 1811 by Francis Horner, a
Whig member, and on that occasion Peel, prompted by his father,
had voted against it. Now the matter was to be considered afresh.
With characteristic zeal, Peel applied himself to the study of one of
the most difficult subjects in the whole field of economics, and before
long came to the conclusion that cash payments ought to be resumed.
His arguments convinced the committee, and the House agreed. In
1821 golden sovereigns reappeared in people's purses—not to dis-
appear again (and this time for good) until 1914.

This was Peel's first great financial achievement. It was also his
first ' conversion '. There were more conversions to come.

While he was free from official responsibilities, Peel got married.
His wife was Julia Floyd, the twenty-five-year-old daughter of
General Sir John Floyd, a distinguished member of a family of
soldiers. They first met at Lady Shelley's place at Maresfield, in
Sussex, in January 1819 and at first sight she was not favourably
impressed. As she wrote at the time, Peel ' spoke of shooting and
other country pursuits in a condescending manner '. But it was not
long before she detected that his superior airs were a mask for shyness
and deep-seated reserve. Then it was *his* turn to have qualms. Julia
was young and attractive, and he murmured something about her
being perhaps too fond of ' the world '. Whereupon she rejoined

without hesitation, but surely not without a maidenly blush, ' *You* are my world.'

The marriage took place in June 1820, and from first to last it was a completely happy and successful union. She insisted that ' I am *no politician* ', but Peel did not mind that. He had quite enough of politicians outside his home. But she was a sympathetic listener and a good counsellor, and she became his intimate confidante. Reserved though he was with others, he was never so with her, and he found in domestic happiness consolation for all the trials and tribulations of his public life. A number of his letters to her have been preserved, and they tell their own tale. Within a month or two of their wedding he is addressing her as ' My dearest Life ', ' My own dearest tenderest Love ', and ' My own dearest Julia '. She bore him five sons and two daughters, and Peel proved himself a devoted father, with nothing of the heavy Victorian paterfamilias about him. When after thirty years of most happy married life her husband died, Lady Peel wrote, ' He was the light of my life, my brightest joy and pride. I am desolate and most unhappy. Still I am his; our union is but suspended, not dissolved.'

After declining several offers of a place in the Cabinet, Peel at length consented in 1822 to join Lord Liverpool's administration as Home Secretary. Here for the first time he revealed a liberal streak in his composition. The penal law was in an abominable state, savage and merciless in its application, and not all the devoted efforts of Sir Samuel Romilly and Sir James Mackintosh had been able to effect much amelioration. Peel was no creative genius but he had the wit to see what was good in other people's ideas and then carry them into practice. He sponsored five Acts of Parliament which together exempted about a hundred felonies from the death penalty, and before he quitted office in 1827 nearly a hundred Acts relating to the criminal law had been repealed or modified, while those remaining had been consolidated into eight.

Mackintosh was unstinting in his tribute, staunch Whig though he was. Referring in after years to the vast and beneficial changes that Peel had brought about, he said ' that he could almost think that he had lived in two different countries, and conversed with people who spoke two different languages '. After Peel's reforms, there were no more little boys hanged for stealing goods worth no more than a shilling.

On Lord Liverpool's death, Peel retired from the Cabinet rather than serve under Canning. This has been put down to personal rivalry, and there is no denying that Peel and Canning were rivals for the leadership of the Tory party. Relations between them were often strained, and on occasion they went for one another hammer and tongs; years afterwards, at the height of the Corn Laws controversy, Lord George Bentinck accused Peel of having been one of those who 'hunted Mr. Canning to death', although it is said that Canning himself once declared that Peel was the only man who had behaved decently towards him. However this may have been, the two were separated by their opposite opinions on some of the great questions of the day, of which the most important was Roman Catholic emancipation. Canning was in favour of it—and had lost the nomination of the Oxford seat in consequence; Peel was against it, and the university had rewarded him with their confidence. Peel was still maintaining this attitude when Canning died.

The way was now clear for his political advancement, and early in 1828 he became Home Secretary and leader of the House of Commons in the Duke of Wellington's Cabinet—which made him the second man in the Government.

The new administration was Tory, and its policy was to resist reform as long as possible. But the winds of change were now beginning to blow, and very soon they would reach gale force. The most important measure of the session of 1828 was the repeal of the Test and Corporation Acts, proposed by Lord John Russell. Peel voted against the measure, but when the House of Commons passed it he worked for a compromise which the House of Lords agreed to. Encouraged by this success, the reformers then proposed that the laws relative to Roman Catholics should be reviewed. Peel and his friends resisted as before and were again defeated, but this time the Lords sustained them in their attitude.

Then a very strange thing happened: Peel changed his mind. In the speech from the throne at the opening of Parliament in February 1829 the suppression of O'Connell's Catholic Association was the first measure proposed, after which 'His Majesty recommends . . . that you should take into your deliberate consideration the whole condition of Ireland, and that you should review the laws which impose civil disabilities on his Majesty's Roman Catholic subjects.'

Members could hardly believe their ears; they were filled with astonishment, intense indignation or exultation, according to which side of the House they were on. The words were put into the mouth of the king, but everyone knew that it was Peel who was their author—Peel, the man who for years had withstood the grant of the Roman Catholic claims, who had 'hounded Canning into his grave' when he had proposed much the same thing, and who sat for the university of Oxford, the principal stronghold of the Protestant Establishment!

The strangeness was mostly on the surface. Peel was a realist, and long and close study of the problem had almost convinced him that the Catholics' claims must be allowed. O'Connell's dramatic victory in a by-election in county Clare clinched the matter. As a Catholic O'Connell would not, as the law stood, be allowed to take his seat, but it was reported that he would make the attempt. And if he were excluded, then this would be taken as the signal for an insurrection. Peel shuddered at the prospect, and Wellington shared his concern when he was told that the loyalty of the Irish soldiers of the Crown might well be affected.

The two worked in close conjunction, and on 5 March 1829 a bill to grant emancipation to Roman Catholics was introduced into the House of Commons. Peel spoke for more than four hours in its support. 'I have for years attempted to maintain the exclusion of Roman Catholics from Parliament and the high offices of State,' he said; 'I do not think it was an unnatural or an unreasonable struggle. I resign it in consequence of the conviction that it can no longer be advantageously maintained . . . I yield, therefore, to a moral necessity which I cannot control, unwilling to push the resistance to a point which might endanger the establishments which I wish to defend.'

Backed by Wellington's immense prestige, the Bill was carried without too much difficulty. O'Connell took his seat at Westminster. Civil war was prevented. Looking back on Peel's conduct in the affair, he may be seen as a wise, practical-minded statesman. But this is not the view that was taken by many of his Tory associates. For them he was an apostate, he was a man who had betrayed the constitution, and he was made to pay a price.

Just before Parliament assembled, he informed the Vice-Chancellor of Oxford University that he was resigning his seat since he could no longer support the policy on which he had been elected. His friends at once re-nominated him, but after a sharp contest with a Tory of extreme Protestant views he was defeated. A vacancy was thereupon created for him at Westbury, which seat he exchanged in 1830 for his father's old seat at Tamworth.

Roman Catholic emancipation was the second of Peel's notable 'conversions'. With it out of the way he was able to concentrate on his duties at the Home Office, and in 1829 he created the Metropolitan Police Force. To begin with, the men in blue were far from popular, and the nicknames of ' Peelers ' and ' Bobbies ' were not intended as compliments. But before long the Metropolitan Police had become a model for police forces throughout the country, and it remains as a monument to Peel's administrative genius.

In 1830 the long reign of Toryism came to an end, and Lord Grey formed his Whig administration. In the same month Peel's father died, and he succeeded to the baronetcy and an income of over £20,000 a year. He was now in opposition, and it fell to him to lead the fight against the new Reform Bill. But his attitude towards the proposals, although generally critical, was not outrageously so. He resisted the measure as long as he thought it politic to do so, and he was able to win back the support of those Tories who had been alienated by his change of front on the matter of Roman Catholic emancipation. But once again he was converted. Was it worth while running the risk of armed strife to save the ' rotten boroughs ' ? He thought not, and the Duke of Wellington agreed with him. Between them, they managed to put the brake on the extremists, and the bill went through.

When at the ensuing general election the Tories suffered very heavy losses, there were many to blame Peel. But he stood his ground, and consolidated his position as leader of a party which was now shedding the old, obnoxious name of Tory in favour of ' Conservative '. He applied himself to reorganizing it after its defeat, and succeeded in giving it a new and much more attractive image, while growing in stature and authority himself.

As early as 1834 we find Greville writing that ' Peel's is an enviable position; in the prime of life, with an immense fortune, *facile princeps* in the House of Commons, unshackled by party connexions and prejudices, universally regarded as the ablest man, and with (on the whole) a very high character, free from the cares of office, able to devote himself to literature, to politics, or idleness, as the fancy takes him. No matter how unruly the House, how impatient or fatigued, the moment he rises all is silence, and he is sure of being heard with profound attention and respect.'

Much sooner than might have been expected, he had his reward. When Lord Grey resigned in the summer of 1834, King William invited Peel to form a coalition government with Lord Melbourne. He refused, but a few months later the king took it into his head to dismiss Melbourne and summon Peel to take his place, and this though the Whigs still had a majority in the House of Commons.

Peel was travelling on the Continent at the time, and his exact whereabouts were unknown in England. A young gentleman-usher to the queen named James Hudson was entrusted with letters from the king and the Duke of Wellington, and told to find Peel and deliver them with all speed. Hudson pushed his horses as fast as they would go, and in nine days arrived at Rome where he had learnt Peel was staying. Peel received him with cold formality, and having read the letters and ascertained the nature of Hudson's mission, coolly informed him that if he had taken another route he might have made the journey in a day less. This was on 25 November. Peel left Rome the next day, and reached London early on 9 December. He waited on the king at once, and promptly accepted the office of First Lord of the Treasury, to which he added that of Chancellor of the Exchequer.

The new Prime Minister determined to dissolve Parliament at once, in the hope of securing a majority in the House of Commons, and he issued to his constituents at Tamworth a statement of what he stood for and what he hoped all the Conservative candidates would likewise support. This Tamworth Manifesto, as it came to be called, made it clear that the new Conservatism was very different from the old Toryism. The Reform Bill was accepted as ' a final and irrevocable settlement of a great constitutional question, which no friend to the peace and welfare of this country would attempt to disturb '. Then, as to ' the spirit of the Reform Bill ... if it be meant that by adopting it we are to live in a perpetual vortex of agitation . . . promise the instant redress of anything which anybody may name an abuse . . . abandon altogether that great aid of Government, more powerful than either law or reason, the respect for ancient rights . . . if this be the spirit of the Reform Bill I will not undertake to adopt it. But if it implies merely a careful review of institutions, civil and ecclesiastical, undertaken in a friendly temper, combining, with the firm maintenance of established rights, the correction of proved abuses and the redress of real grievances—in that case, I can for myself and colleagues undertake to act in such a spirit and with such intentions . . .'

At the general election, the Conservatives won a number of seats in the counties, but not sufficient to give them a majority in the House. Peel was defeated six times in succession, and then resigned on 8 April 1835. Melbourne resumed his premiership, and Peel returned to the leadership of the Conservative opposition, striving— on the whole, very successfully—to heal the party's divisions and build up its strength until the time came for it to return to government. So completely did he assert his personal ascendancy in the House that in the course of a debate in 1839 one of the Radical members said, amid applause, that 'the right hon. member for Tamworth governs England'.

But for the accession of the young queen in 1837 his turn might have come earlier than it did, and two years later he was indeed asked to form an administration but failed because the queen refused to accede to his not unreasonable request that some of the ladies of her bedchamber (most of whom belonged to great Whig families) should be changed. But in 1841 the Conservatives had a majority of ninety at the general election; Lord Melbourne resigned the premiership; and in August Peel became Prime Minister for the second time, now with full power.

The Cabinet he proceeded to form was one of the most able and distinguished of the century, what with the Duke of Wellington leading the House of Lords; Lord Aberdeen, a future Prime Minister, at the Foreign Office; Stanley, another future Prime Minister as the Earl of Derby, at the Colonial Office, and Sir James Graham as Home Secretary; while among the holders of minor posts was W. E. Gladstone. Years afterwards Gladstone described it as 'a perfectly organized government, because its legislative acts tended greatly, and almost uniformly, to increase the well-being of the country, and to strengthen the attachment of the people to the Throne and the laws'.

In making up his list, however, Peel left out Benjamin Disraeli. The omission was deliberate, and it turned out to be about the biggest mistake that Peel ever made.

The new Prime Minister was faced with no easy task. Foreign affairs were in a mess, since relations with France and the United States were strained, and England was becoming engaged in two of those disgraceful little wars—in the present instance, with China and Afghanistan—with which the annals of Queen Victoria's reign are cluttered. In the domestic sphere things were no better. The country was in a very depressed state. Trade was at a low ebb, with consequent widespread unemployment. Wages were low and getting lower, profits were stagnant, and taxation while sufficiently high to cause grumbling at all levels bore most heavily on the poorer classes. Not only were imported luxury goods taxed, but severe imposts were levied on the necessaries of life. In particular the duties on imported corn, which had been imposed in 1815 at the conclusion of the great and terribly expensive wars with France, were still maintained, with the result that the working man's loaf cost much more than it would otherwise have done. But there were few among even the Whigs to argue that the Corn Laws ought to be abolished, while the Conservatives were united in supporting them as absolutely essential to Britain's economic health and social stability.

Peel was an exception, however. He was no doctrinaire economist any more than he was a hidebound party politician. He was a consummate opportunist, who preferred to keep an open mind and was quite prepared to change it if he decided that circumstance demanded it. In other words, he was open to conversion, and this is what happened now, although the process was not the result of a sudden, blinding light from heaven but one of slow but steady feeling of the safe way through the rocks and quicksands of destiny.

The Budget of 1842 was an epoch-making one. Although Peel was not Chancellor of the Exchequer it bore all the marks of his genius for financial arrangement. First, an income tax of 7d. in the pound was imposed, in order that the possessors of property should contribute their fair and full share towards balancing the national accounts, which were in a deplorable state of almost constant deficit. Then a start was made with reforming the tariff, in course of which the duties were removed or substantially lowered on a great number of articles imported from abroad. In the five years he continued in office, Peel continued this policy of liberalization, reducing the duties on over a thousand articles of common consumption and totally abolishing them on six hundred more.

This commercial and fiscal policy was strikingly successful. The deficit was cured, trade statistics surged upwards and the income tax brought in much more than had been estimated, and the rapidly growing middle classes were given a fillip. Nor were the working classes left out. Since Peel's accession to power he had come to cast his gaze beyond the moneyed and propertied classes from which most of his support came, and to include in his purview those vastly larger working classes on which in the final resort the health and strength of the nation depended.

Even in 1842 he was a free trader, without perhaps fully realizing it. As his early strokes of liberating policy bore fruit, he became one more and more. As his mind moved slowly along new channels, the country as a whole was increasingly aroused by the propagandist activities of the Anti-Corn Law League that had been founded in 1839, and which under the inspired direction of Richard Cobden and John Bright demanded the complete abolition of the Corn Laws. Peel reduced the import duties on corn, and was prepared to reduce them further when his hand was forced by the failure of the potato crop in Ireland in 1845, owing to the attacks of a terrible blight. Half the population of Ireland was entirely dependent on the potato for their staple food, and before long millions were facing famine and starvation. To avert unprecedented disaster, a large importation of wheat was necessary, and Peel decided that the ports must be thrown open to receive corn from whatever quarter it might be obtained although (so Wellington testified) it cost him agony to arrive at the decision. At first he hoped that a gradual modification of the Corn Laws would be sufficient, but on 15 October we find him writing; 'The remedy is the removal of all impediments to the import of all kinds of human food—that is, the total and absolute repeal for ever of all duties on all articles of subsistence.'

Slow as was his custom to make up his mind, he was resolute enough when once he had done it. He submitted his proposals to the Cabinet, and only two of its members—Gladstone and Aberdeen —were prepared to support him, all the others being hostile to a lesser or greater extent. When he was quite sure that he could not carry them with him he handed his resignation to the queen. This was on 6 December 1845.

Lord John Russell, the Whig leader, was sent for. He had recently emerged as a complete free trader, but he proved unable to form a Government. Lord Stanley, who was recognized as the leader of the Protectionists among the Conservative party, was then ap-proached, and he too failed. Whereupon Queen Victoria sent for Peel and begged him to resume his premiership, reconstruct his ministry, and secure the abolition of the Corn Laws. Peel was quite agreeable. 'I am ready to kiss hands as your Minister tonight,' he told the queen. 'I believe I can collect a ministry which will last long enough to carry free trade, and I am ready to make the attempt.' When he said this (Lord Aberdeen reported long afterwards) he had only two men on whom he could rely, but one of the first to join him was the old Duke of Wellington. 'The Queen's government must be carried on,' said the Duke; 'we have done all that we could for the landed interest. Now we must do all we can for the Queen.' In the event, all the Ministers except Stanley agreed to serve again under Peel.

The session of 1846 was one of the most memorable in Parliamentary history. Not until the Home Rule debates of a generation and two generations later was there such an outburst of fury. Writing in February, the Prince Consort observed; 'Here we are in the middle of the Corn debate. Peel is abused like the most disgraceful criminal. He shows boundless courage and is in the best of spirits; his whole faculties are roused by the consciousness that he is at this moment playing one of the most important parts in the history of his country.' It is not pleasant, however, to be denounced as ' turn-coat ', ' traitor ' and the rest by one's own former supporters, and the majority of the Conservative members roared their approval and appreciation of the venomous onslaughts of Disraeli, who now avenged his exclusion from Peel's government. Prince Albert must have seen the Prime Minister in one of his most confident moods; there were other times when, his biographer Thursfield reports, Peel sat on the Treasury bench ' in visible agony, while his alienated followers watched the spectacle in vindictive silence, unmoved at the tragedy, not displeased with the retribution, nor ashamed of the instrument which inflicted it '.

Peel stuck it out, and the bill passed all its stages in the House of Commons and was sent up to the Lords. There it was passed on 25 June. The many months of struggle were at an end, and Peel had triumphed. But on that very night, an Irish measure was being discussed and men of all parties united against the Ministry. Peel was defeated, and forthwith resigned.

He had no regrets for the part he had played. He knew full well that whatever Disraeli and his men might say in the House, in the country at large his name was being spoken with gratitude and respect and reverence. In his speech announcing the resignation of his Government he said; ' I shall leave a name censured, I fear, by many who, on public grounds, deeply regret the severance of party ties—deeply regret that severance, not from interested or personal motives, but from the firm conviction that fidelity to party engage-ments, the existence and maintenance of a great party, constitutes a powerful instrument of government. I shall surrender power severely censured by others who, from no interested motive, adhere to the principle of Protection, considering the maintenance of it to be essential to the welfare and interests of the country. I shall leave a name execrated by every monopolist who, from less honourable motives, clamours for Protection because it conduces to his own individual benefit. But it may be that I shall leave a name sometimes remembered with expressions of goodwill in the abodes of those whose lot it is to labour and to earn their daily bread with the sweat of their brow, when they shall recruit their exhausted strength with abundant and untaxed food, the sweeter because it is no longer leavened with a sense of injustice.'

As he left the House on the day of his fall, crowds of people stood on the pavements to see him go by. The queen offered him the Garter, and any other honour he might care to name. He respectfully refused, and he begged her most strongly never to invite him to take office again. To him his resignation was ' the greatest relief from an intolerable burden ', and he retired to Drayton where he passed his days with his wife and children so happily that, as he expressed it, ' I have every reason to forgive my enemies for having conferred upon me the blessing of the loss of power '.

Peel lived for nearly four years after his retirement. His last appearance in the House of Commons was on 28 June 1850, when he spoke against Lord Palmerston's bellicose foreign policy. As he walked home in the early morning of the next day, he remarked to the friend who accompanied him that he felt at peace with all the world. Lady Peel had stayed up as usual to greet him on his return.

After a few hours' rest he attended a meeting of the Commissioners of the proposed Great Exhibition, and then in the afternoon he went for his customary ride. After leaving his name at Buckingham Palace, he proceeded along Constitution Hill, where his horse suddenly became restive and Peel was thrown violently to the ground. He was picked up, placed in a passing carriage and driven to his house in Whitehall Gardens. He was laid on a sofa in the sitting-room, too ill to be taken upstairs to bed. He stayed there in great agony for three days. His clavicle was fractured, and there were other injuries which the physicians were unable to treat because of the terrible pain. He recovered sufficiently to receive the sacrament from the hands of Bishop Tomlinson, and a few minutes after eleven on the night of Tuesday, 2 July 1850, he ceased to breathe. He was in his sixty-third year, and had spent more than forty years in Parliament. He was buried in the church at Drayton Bassett. Lady Peel died in 1859.

The grief at his death was profound among all classes both at home and abroad, where he had long been considered to be the greatest Liberal statesman of the age. When the House of Commons met the next day the adjournment was moved at once, and Gladstone seconded the motion in a most moving tribute. A year or two later Disraeli, who had been so largely responsible for his fall from power, wrote *his* tribute. ' Not the greatest Minister that this country has ever produced . . . we cannot recognize him as our greatest orator . . . But what he really was . . . is the greatest Member of Parliament that ever lived.'

25

LORD JOHN RUSSELL

'LITTLE JOHNNY' was what they called him—and he was indeed small in stature, so small that when he rose to speak in the House of Commons little could be seen of him above the brassbound boxes on the table. But he knew how to make up for his lack of inches. Standing as far back from the table as he could, with his arms folded across his chest and speaking in tones that were slow and confident and slightly nasal, he displayed a manly resolution, a dauntless front. ' He is a marvellous little man,' wrote Charles Greville, ' always equal to the occasion, afraid of nobody, fixed in his principles, clear in his ideas, collected in his manner, and bold and straightforward in his disposition.' For more than fifty years he was in Parliament, and ever in the forefront of the battle for civil and religious liberty.

For the greater part of his life he was Lord John Russell, although when he formed his second administration he had been created an earl. He came of one of the oldest and most aristocratic of English families, but from his ancestors he inherited a tradition of ardent liberalism. He was the third child of a Lord John Russell who succeeded his brother in 1808 as sixth duke of Bedford. He was born in his father's London house in Hertford Street, Mayfair, on 18 August 1792. His father, like all the Russells for generations, was a Whig; he had joined the Friends of the People with Lord Grey, and during Lord Grenville's short ministry had served as Lord Lieutenant of Ireland. Lord John's mother—she was Georgiana Byng, daughter of Viscount Torrington—died in 1801, but two years later his father married Lady Georgina Gordon, daughter of the Duke of Gordon, who proved a most kindly stepmother.

Lord John's education was, as he put it, ' broken and disturbed '. To begin with, he was sent, ' in the usual English way, to a very bad private school at Sunbury ', and then between ten and eleven he was transferred to the great public school of Westminster. But he did not stay there long enough to reach the upper school. ' The hard life of a fag—for in those days it *was* a hard life—and the unwholesome food disagreed with me so much that my stepmother insisted that I should be taken away and sent to a private tutor.'

Brought up in a political atmosphere, he soon showed signs of an interest in public affairs. At Woburn, the stately home that was his father's principal seat, he met the great men of the Whig party, including Fox, whose more splendid qualities made a deep impression on the boy. He started keeping a journal, and from its pages we may learn that as a thirteen-year-old schoolboy he had begun to think for himself. In 1805 Lord Melville, Pitt's chief lieutenant, was impeached for gross breach of duty as Treasurer of the Navy but was acquitted by his peers. 'What a pity,' wrote the boy, ' that he who steals a penny loaf should be hung, whilst he who steals thousands of the public money should be acquitted!'

When the time came for him to go to a university his father ruled out Cambridge, where John's elder brother had gone, since in the Duke's opinion the chief studies of the youths there seemed to be ' the sciences of horse-racing, fox-hunting, and giving extravagant entertainments '. Instead, Lord John was sent to study at Edinburgh, where he lived in the house of Professor Playfair, who held the chair of mathematics in the university. In after years, he referred to the professor as ' one of the most delightful of men and a very zealous lover of liberty '.

In 1808, when he was sixteen, Lord John was taken by Lord and Lady Holland on a trip through the Spanish peninsula, even though that part of the world was being overrun by Napoleon's troops. The following year he went there again, on his own, to visit his brother William who had been wounded at the battle of Talavera and was in hospital in Cadiz. With two other youths he paid another visit in 1812, and while at Minorca he received a letter from his father informing him that the member of Parliament for the family's pocket borough of Tavistock had recently died, and that he meant to use his influence to obtain the seat for his son. Lord John hurried home, and as soon as he set foot in England he learnt that he had been already elected M.P. for Tavistock. This was early in 1813, when he was not yet of age.

On entering the House of Commons, he joined the small band of Whigs who constituted the opposition, but his health was poor and prevented him from attending regularly. That autumn he made another continental excursion, in course of which he had the unforgettable experience of being received by the temporarily banished Napoleon in the island of Elba.

For some little time after his return to England, Lord John absented himself from Westminster, partly because of his ill-health but also because of the apparent hopelessness of being able to make any headway against the overwhelming majority of Lord Liverpool's Tory administration. So dispirited did he become, that he had thoughts of abandoning his parliamentary career altogether and devoting himself to literature, in which field he had had some success. But his friends urged him never to think of such a thing, and Thomas Moore, the poet, addressed to him a *Remonstrance*:

> What! *thou*, with thy genius, thy youth, and thy name—
> Thou, born of a Russell—whose instinct to run
> The accustomed career of thy sires, is the same
> As the eaglet's to soar with his eyes on the sun! . . .
>
> Oh no, never dream it—while good men despair
> Between tyrants and traitors, and timid men bow,
> Never think for an instant thy country can spare
> Such a light from her darkening horizon as thou!

Perhaps Moore's verses had their effect, or Lord John may never have had any real intention of abandoning the fight. In any case, he soldiered on. He made his first important speech in favour of parliamentary reform in 1819, and two years later had his first small success when Parliament accepted his motion that the decrepit little Cornish borough of Grampound should be disfranchised and its two members transferred to the great and populous county of Yorkshire. Then in 1828 he was able to secure the repeal of the Test and Corporation Acts which since the reign of Charles II had discriminated against the Nonconformists.

In 1830 he introduced a bill which would have conferred the right of returning members to Parliament on Manchester, Birmingham, and Leeds, the three largest unrepresented towns in the country. This very reasonable proposal was rejected by Wellington's government, but a few months later the Whigs took office, and Lord John was given a post as Paymaster-General. He was also called on to assist in drawing up the Reform Bill, and when it was ready he was chosen to introduce it into the House of Commons. So on 1 March 1831, Lord John advanced to the table and began to explain the Government's intentions.

Supposing, he said, a foreigner, who had heard of Britain's wealth, civilization, and renown, should come to England to make a study of her institutions, would he not be astonished if he were taken to a green mound, and informed that it returned two members to the British Parliament; if he were shown a stone wall, and told that it also sent two members, or if he walked into a park, without the vestige of a dwelling, and was told that it, too, sent two members? But how much more would he be astonished if he were carried into the north of England, where he would find large, flourishing towns, full of trade, activity and intelligence, magazines of wealth and manufactures, and were told that these places sent *no* representatives to Parliament!

Having thus prepared the ground, he proceeded to list the boroughs which it was proposed should be disfranchised, in order that a corresponding number of seats should be given to the new centres of population which were without any representation in the House.

'Never shall I forget the astonishment of my neighbours,' wrote J. C. Hobhouse, later Lord Broughton, in his *Recollections*, 'as Lord John Russell developed his plan. Indeed, all the House seemed perfectly astounded; and when he read the long list of boroughs to be either wholly or partially disfranchised, there was a sort of wild ironical laughter. Lord John seemed rather to play with the fears of his audience; and, after detailing some clauses that seemed to complete the scheme, smiled and paused, and said, " More yet ".'

In the face of mounting disorder, Lord John carried on manfully to his conclusion. The Government, he made it clear, had reached the decision that ' no half-measures would be sufficient; no trifling, no paltry reform, could give stability to the Crown, strength to the Parliament, or satisfaction to the country '. Even though he had not used the term, he had announced a revolution, and sat down to excited roars of cheering from his supporters on the benches behind him and the jeers and taunts of those opposite who were enraged at the prospect of losing their political privileges and possessions.

For a year and more the struggle went on, as we have seen in the chapter on Lord Grey, and throughout Lord John Russell was the doughty leader of those who would be content with nothing less than ' the Bill, the whole Bill, and nothing but the Bill! ' He introduced three Reform Bills in quick succession, and finally the last of the series received the royal assent in June 1832.

This was his finest hour, even though years afterwards he became Prime Minister on two occasions. For a time he was about the most popular man in England, and the dominant figure in the Cabinet. 'Lord John,' remarked the Duke of Wellington once, ' is a host in himself.' But before long his colleagues were complaining that he was too opinionated, too self-assertive, too intent on getting his own way; he was altogether too exuberant for their taste, and besides, he could not always be relied upon to follow the line that had been agreed. Thus in 1834 he spoke against the Government on a question of reforming the Protestant Church in Ireland, and Grey was so disgusted that he resigned the premiership. This was the occasion described by Lord Stanley in the words, ' Johnny has upset the coach '.

On Melbourne succeeding Grey, he asked Lord John to take on the leadership of the House of Commons. He was quite willing: as he said, more in joke than in earnest perhaps, ' If I were offered the command of the Channel Fleet, and thought it my duty to accept, I should not refuse it '. The remark got out, and brought a good deal of ridicule on Lord John's head. It was by no means the only *faux pas* he was guilty of. Another was some years later, when he declared that he regarded the great Reform Bill as a final settlement and would take no further steps in that direction—after which he was given the nickname of ' Finality Jack '.

Lord John did not get the leadership of the House when first offered it, because King William thought him too inexperienced, but a year later Melbourne had his way and Lord John was appointed not only leader of the House but Home Secretary.

Here we may break in on Lord John's political progress to say something of his private life. In 1835, the year in which he became Home Secretary, he got married when he was forty-three. His bride was Adelaide, daughter of Thomas Lister and widow of the second Lord Ribblesdale; she brought with her four young children by her first husband, and in 1836 she bore Lord John a daughter. In October 1838 she bore a second daughter, but died on 1 November. ' We have all been much distressed by the melancholy and untimely death of poor Lady John Russell,' wrote Queen Victoria to her uncle King Leopold of the Belgians on 6 November; ' she was safely confined on the 20th of October with a little girl, who bears my name, and seemed to be going on very well, but on Wednesday she began to sink from weakness, not disease, and died at 3 o'clock on Thursday. It is a dreadful blow to *him*, for he was *so* attached to her, and I don't believe two people ever were happier together . . . he is *dreadfully* beat down by it, but struggles manfully against his grief, which makes one pity him more.'

With six children to look after—the eldest twelve and the youngest, as Queen Victoria noted, a fortnight, it is hardly surprising that Lord John should before long be on the look-out for a second wife. His choice fell on Lady Fanny Elliot, second daughter of the Earl of Minto who was First Lord of the Admiralty. Lord John had been a frequent visitor at her father's house at Putney and at the Admiralty, and she had come to admire him as a political hero. But she was twenty-five and he was nearly twice her age, with a houseful of young children. She was rather dismayed when in the summer of 1840 he began to show signs of a personal interest in her. In September of that year he visited them at Minto, and on his last evening, she noted in her diary, ' in wishing me good-bye he said quite enough to make me tell Mama all I thought . . . I could see that she was very glad I did not like him in that way. I am sure I do in every other.' Lord John left behind him a letter containing a proposal of marriage, and she replied at once with a firm but very appreciative ' no '.

Whereupon Lord John wrote to her: ' Dear Lady Fanny,—You are quite right. I deceived myself, not from any fault of yours, but from a deep sense of unhappiness, and a foolish notion that you might throw yourself away on a person of broken spirits, and worn out by time and trouble. There is nothing left to me but constant and laborious attention to public business, and a wretched sense of misery, which even the children can never long drive away . . .'

' A very, very sad note from Lord John in answer to mine,' wrote Lady Fanny in her diary, ' so kind, but oh! so sad.' For a day or two she tried to put the matter out of her mind as something that had been settled once and for all, but then she was writing, ' Though I do not think, I dream . . .' Miss Lister, Lord John's sister-in-law, wrote to her praising him to the skies. Her parents' objections on account of Lord John's age seemed to be weakening. The newspapers got hold of the story, and spoke of the marriage as being practically agreed upon. The young woman was in a torment of indecision.

Meanwhile Lord John had let it be known, in the kindest possible manner, that he had not given up hope, although he took care not to see her too often. At length, after much family consultation and seeking of Divine guidance (for Lady Fanny was sincerely religious) she resolved that if he asked her again her answer would be different. He did ask her again, and she accepted him. They were married in the drawing-room of Minto House on 20 July 1841.

The union was an exceptionally successful one. The new Lady John Russell—well-educated, deeply cultured, most seriously minded—had no ambition to shine in society but devoted herself to the care of her husband, their children—she added three sons and a daughter to the collection—and their home. In 1847 Queen Victoria, knowing that Lord John was not too well off, offered him as a ' grace and favour ' residence Pembroke Lodge in Richmond

Park, and this was their home for the rest of their life together. It was a delightful place, large and rambling and comfortable, surrounded with lovely grounds on the wooded slopes above the little village of Petersham. We may well believe Lady John when she tells us that those were ' happy days . . . the hours of work so cheerfully got through, the hours of leisure so delightful '.

In the same summer as his marriage, Lord John Russell went out of office with Melbourne, and throughout Peel's administration was leader of the Whig opposition. The agitation for the abolition of the Corn Laws was soon in full swing, and Lord John precipitated events by a bold declaration to his constituents in the City of London —where he had come to rest after a number of electoral vicissitudes, and which returned him to Parliament at every election until he became a peer—in favour of abolition at the earliest possible date.

A ministerial crisis followed, Peel took his decision, and was immediately abandoned by a large part of his following. Whereupon Lord John, very much to his own surprise, received a summons to Windsor and was invited by the queen to form a government. On this occasion he was unable to do so and Peel had to return to office, but six months later Peel was defeated and Lord John was sent for again. This time he was successful and on 6 July 1846 he kissed hands as Prime Minister. After thirty-three years in the House of Commons, he had reached the top.

He was Prime Minister for nearly six years, and a pretty gruelling experience it must have been. Very soon the queen was complaining to him of the way in which the Foreign Secretary, Lord Palmerston, had become a law unto himself; she urged that he should be kept in better order—which was easier suggested than done. Lord John had more than enough to keep him fully occupied in domestic matters, what with a terrible famine raging in Ireland, a grave trade depression, and in all the manufacturing districts large numbers of people unemployed, living in abominable housing conditions, and suffering from poverty, malnutrition, and cholera epidemics. Of the measures passed by his Government the most worthy of remembrance is the great Factory Act of 1847, which provided among other things that the normal working day in factories of women and young persons should not exceed ten hours.

Meanwhile Palmerston was showing himself more and more obstreperous, and in December 1851 he went too far even for the too indulgent Russell. When he expressed approval of Louis Napoleon's *coup d'état* in Paris, the Prime Minister was constrained to ask for his resignation. A few weeks later Palmerston had the immense satisfaction of giving what he called his ' tit for tat for Johnny Russell ', when he carried an amendment against the Government on the Militia Bill. Russell thereupon resigned.

For the next ten months Lord Derby was Prime Minister, until in December 1852 Lord Aberdeen formed his Coalition government. The queen urged Lord John Russell to join it, relying upon what she termed his ' patriotic sacrifice of personal interests and feelings '; while Prince Albert noted that Lord John, despite ' a temporary and undeserved unpopularity, remained the first man in the country, and might be Prime Minister again '. Russell became leader of the House of Commons and Foreign Secretary, but he did not shine in either capacity. Then came the Crimean War, of which he strongly disapproved. He was blamed for much of the bungling that proved so costly in human life and suffering, and in January 1855 he resigned when a motion of censure was threatened. His resignation precipitated the fall of the Aberdeen government.

For the first time in his life Lord John was really unpopular, and he remained out of office for four years. However, he was happy enough in his home and his literary activities, for by now he had become well established as an author of books on political history and social subjects. He returned to the Government in June 1859, when he became Foreign Secretary in the administration formed by his old rival Lord Palmerston, and in 1861 was raised to the peerage as Earl Russell, since his age and indifferent state of health made it necessary for him to seek relief from the heavy work in the House of Commons. The year following he was given the Garter.

Russell's management of foreign affairs was not particularly successful. Indeed, his old antagonist Lord Derby declared his opinion that ' the foreign policy of the noble earl . . . may be summed up in two truly expressive words—meddle and muddle. During the whole course of his diplomatic correspondence, wherever he has interfered—and he has interfered everywhere—he has been lecturing, scolding, blustering, and—retreating.'

Earl Russell was still at the Foreign Office when Palmerston died on 18 October 1865. The next day the queen wrote to him. ' The melancholy news of Lord Palmerston's death reached the Queen last night,' she said. ' This is another link with the past that is broken, and the Queen feels deeply in her desolated and isolated condition how, one by one, tried servants and advisers are taken from her.' She went on, ' The Queen can turn to no other than Lord Russell, an old and tried friend of hers, to undertake the arduous duties of Prime Minister, and to carry on the Government.'

When thus appealed to, Russell could not refuse, although he was now seventy-three and feeling his years. He proceeded to form an administration, in which Gladstone was Chancellor of the Exchequer and the most active figure. At once they decided to bring in a new Reform Bill—Russell's last attempt in this direction had been in 1860—and Gladstone introduced a measure in the spring of 1866. The scheme fell flat, however, and Derby and Disraeli nipped in with their own more sweeping and popular proposals. In June the Government was defeated on the committee stage of their Bill, and Russell promptly resigned, although the queen insisted that she could see no necessity for it.

Earl Russell was glad to go. 'John so well and happy that my joy in his release becomes greater every hour', wrote Lady Russell a few days later, and she told her sister Lady Dunfermline that he was in excellent spirits and that they both felt as if fetters had been struck from their minds and bodies. Russell never held office again, although it was offered to him. In the first years of his retirement they were able to revisit Switzerland and Italy, but then the old man returned to Pembroke Lodge and never left it. He died there on 28 May 1878, when he was not far off eighty-six, and was buried among his ancestors in the little village church at Chenies, in Buckinghamshire. Among his last words recorded by his wife were, 'I have made mistakes, but in all I did my object was the public good.' Lady Russell died on 17 January 1898, soon after her eighty-second birthday, and was buried beside him.

26

EARL OF DERBY

THE FOURTEENTH Earl of Derby, who flourished in the middle years of Queen Victoria's reign, enjoyed the distinction of three terms as Prime Minister. But the three premierships did not amount to four years in all.

The earldom dates from 1485, when it was conferred on the Lord Stanley who by changing sides at the critical moment of the battle of Bosworth enabled Henry Tudor to win the crown. But the Stanleys were very important people long before that. In course of time they accumulated vast estates in Lancashire, and at Knowsley, just outside Liverpool, they had a magnificent country seat. There Edward Stanley, the future Prime Minister, was born on 29 March 1799, the eldest son of the Lord Stanley, who in 1834 became the thirteenth earl.

Stanley was educated at Eton and Christ Church, Oxford, where he distinguished himself as a classical scholar and gave promise of his future eminence as an orator. It is said that as a youth he was given lessons in elocution by his grandfather's second wife, who as Miss Elizabeth Farren had been celebrated as an actress.

The Stanleys were by tradition Whigs, and in 1820 Edward Stanley was returned as M.P. for the borough of Stockbridge. Years later he told the House of Lords how his election had been managed. ' It so happened,' he said, ' that a West Indian proprietor of high Tory principles found himself, as West Indian proprietors sometimes did —even before the passing of Negro emancipation—in pecuniary difficulties. He was the possessor of property, however, which included a borough, over which he had absolute and entire control. It happened, also, that a wealthy Whig peer was desirous of increasing his political influence, and he requested me, then a young man, and without the slightest connection with the borough in question, or with the neighbourhood—to accept the seat which was to be placed at my disposal. And so far, my Lords, was the complaisance of the Tory proprietor of the borough carried, that he not only vacated his seat in the middle of the session but also went down in person and introduced to the constituency, whom he had sold, the nominee of the Whig peer to whom he had sold them.' He concluded this account with the confession that a few years afterwards, when he had become a strong supporter of Lord Grey's Reform Bill, he had been 'guilty of such ingratitude' as to vote that the borough in question should be among those to be extinguished altogether.

For four years he was a silent member. His maiden speech was delivered early in the session of 1824 in the debate on the bill for lighting Manchester with gas. This would hardly seem to offer much opportunity for flights of oratory, but Hansard reported that the speech was characterized by 'much clearness and ability', and one of the most experienced members in the House, Sir James Mackintosh, declared that it 'afforded the strongest promise that the talents which the hon. member had displayed in supporting the local interests of his constituents would be exerted with equal ardour and effect in maintaining the rights and interests of the country'. Thus encouraged, Stanley exerted himself to excel, and before long he was acknowledged to be one of the finest speakers in the House.

In 1824 Stanley visited Canada and the United States—an unusual itinerary for aristocratic travellers of those days—and on his return he married Miss Emma Caroline Wilbraham, whose father a few years later was created Lord Skelmersdale.

Parliamentary reform was now becoming the great question of the day and Stanley, as a Whig, naturally was in favour of it. To improve his situation he exchanged his 'rotten' borough for the comparatively sound one of Preston. Soon afterwards he accepted office as Under-secretary for the Colonies in Canning's administration, and he kept it under Goderich but refused to serve under the Duke of Wellington. Then in 1830 the Whigs came in under Lord Grey and Stanley was given the important post of Chief Secretary for Ireland. He showed a firm hand at Dublin, but it was at Westminster that he really made his mark. In the great debates on the successive Reform Bills he developed a slashing style of oratory which aroused intense enthusiasm among his supporters.

It was some time later that Disraeli compared him with the dashing leader of the Royalist cavalry in the Civil War. 'The noble lord is the Prince Rupert of Parliamentary discussion; his charge is resistless, but when he returns from the pursuit he always finds his camp in the possession of the enemy.'

It may be doubted, however, whether Stanley was ever particularly interested in reform itself. What really interested him was the battle, not the rights and wrongs of a speculative question. He fought to win, just as when he betted on a horse-race—which he very often did, since like his grandfather, the founder of the Derby, he was an ardent patron of the Turf—he did so not to make money but to enjoy the satisfaction of having picked a winner. When it became clear to him that the Reform Act was being taken as the prelude to other reforms he started to jib; nor did his promotion to the Colonial Secretaryship make him any more comfortable. In May 1834 he resigned his office, and in the following year joined the Tories under Peel. At the time his secession was regarded as a serious blow to the Government, but on balance they probably gained as much as they lost. Stanley had made himself obnoxious to many, with his heedless rhetoric and the (possibly quite unconscious) air of superiority that he so often displayed. With his slight and graceful figure, his handsome, high-bred features, and the cutting brilliance of his oratorical style, he was very much the aristocrat—and there was now an increasing number of members of the House of Commons who deeply resented aristocratic exhibitions and pretensions.

As is so often the way with turncoats, Stanley proceeded to attack his late colleagues with special animosity. The language he employed in one speech at this time has been often quoted as an excellent specimen of his powers of vigorous but coarse expression.

If the House did not think he was descending too low, he said, he would say that he had never witnessed anything like the principle on which the Government was acting, except among a class of persons not generally received into society but who were commonly to be met with at country fairs, the instruments of whose calling were a small deal table and four or five thimbles. Their skill was shown in dexterously shifting a pea, placing it first under one thimble and then under another, and calling upon the bystanders to bet which of the thimbles it was under—the deluded individuals who speculated on the manoeuvres of the juggler being sure in the end to lose their money.

The illustration was a low one, he admitted, but he thought the House would agree with him that the self-same principle adopted by the thimble-rigger was to be traced in the plan then being put forward by his Majesty's government.

Towards the close of 1834 Stanley—now known by the courtesy title of Lord Stanley, since his grandfather had died and his father had succeeded to the earldom—was invited by Sir Robert Peel to join his Conservative ministry. He declined on that occasion but in Peel's second administration in 1841 he appeared as Colonial Secretary, the same position he had held under Lord Grey as a Whig. But long and late hours in the House of Commons proved too irksome to him, and in 1844 he was moved up to the House of Lords as Baron Stanley of Bickerstaffe.

When Peel declared in favour of Free Trade, however, Stanley resigned, since 'Protection, in his opinion, was necessary for the maintenance of the landed interest and the colonial system, the two pillars on which he conceived the British Empire to rest'. From 1846 he was generally considered to be the leader in the House of Lords of those Conservatives who adhered to Protection, while Lord George Bentinck and Disraeli led them in the Commons. Early in 1851 he was invited to form a Government, but was unable to do so. The next year the queen sent for him again, and this time he was successful in forming a Conservative administration. He was now Earl of Derby, following his father's death in 1851.

This first Government of Lord Derby's, formed in February 1852, was facetiously termed the 'Who ? Who ? administration', because the Duke of Wellington, who was now very deaf, kept on asking 'Who ? Who ?' when the names of the new Ministers were read out in the House of Lords.

Benjamin Disraeli was his Chancellor of the Exchequer, but for the rest Derby was well justified in speaking of them as his 'team of young horses' and 'raw troops'. But he would allow no one to make fun of them but himself. 'Come, now, Lord Derby,' said a marchioness who had the reputation of being clever, sharp-tongued and well-versed in politics, ' who are all these people you have got around you ? Who are so-and-so and so-and-so ? What is so-and-so ? Is he a real man, or only a puppet ? '

'As to whether he is a real man or not,' Lord Derby replied, ' I can only assure your ladyship that he has had three wives. . . .' Her ladyship did not stay to hear the rest.

The first Derby ministry lasted only from February to December in 1852, when Disraeli's budget brought about its defeat. Lord Derby formed a second administration in February 1858 which managed to keep in office until June of the following year, although as before there was no Conservative majority in the House of Commons. During the session of 1858 it contrived to pass two measures of worthwhile reform; a bill to remove Jewish disabilities, and a bill transferring the government of India, following the suppression of the Mutiny of 1857, from the old East India Company to the Crown. The general election of 1858 again denied Derby a majority and he resigned immediately after a vote of no confidence. He was in opposition again for the next seven years.

With more leisure, Derby was now able to devote himself to those classical studies which had always been so congenial to him. In 1852 he had been elected Chancellor of the university of Oxford in succession to the Duke of Wellington and perhaps it was with some idea of proving himself worthy of his new distinction that he now put forth his best efforts as a scholar and an author. His first venture was a poetical rendering of some of the Odes of Horace, and this was followed by a volume of translations of poems in several languages, ancient and modern. These were well received and, so encouraged, he published in 1864 his translation of Homer's *Iliad* in blank verse, which proved so successful that six editions were called for in four years.

Until 1865, when he sold his racing stud, Lord Derby was the most prominent patron of the Turf. He was the life and soul of the great race meetings, and he was probably never happier than when he was presiding over the dinners in the Jockey Club rooms at Newmarket. Greville, who fully shared Lord Derby's enthusiasm for racing and sometimes profited by his tips, furnishes us with a fascinating picture of the Earl at a race-meeting at Newmarket in April 1851, a few days after he had been invited to form a Government.

'If any of his vociferous disciples and admirers, if some grave members of either House of Parliament, or any distinguished foreigner who knew nothing of Lord Stanley but what he saw, heard, or read of him, could have suddenly found themselves in the betting-room at Newmarket on Tuesday evening and seen Stanley there, I think they would have been in a pretty state of astonishment. There he was in the midst of a crowd of blacklegs, betting men, and loose characters of every description, in uproarious spirits, chaffing, rowing, and shouting with laughter and joking. His amusement was to lay Lord Glasgow a wager that he did not sneeze in a given time, for which purpose he took pinch after pinch of snuff, while Stanley jeered him and quizzed him with such noise that he drew the whole mob around him to partake of the coarse merriment he excited. It really was a sight and a wonder to see any man playing such different parts; and I don't suppose there is any other man who would act so naturally, and obey all his impulses in such a way, utterly regardless of appearances, and not caring what anybody might think of the minister and the statesman so long as he could have his fun.'

It was a common thing for Lord Derby after a long debate in

the House of Lords to take the night mail train to the north, arriving in time to see his horses gallop over the downs at break of day. He was a very successful breeder and in twenty-two years won nearly a hundred thousand pounds. He never succeeded in his great ambition to win the Derby, but in 1858, when he was Prime Minister, his horse *Toxophilite* was first favourite and was just beaten at the post.

In the interval between his second and third premierships occurred the great cotton famine in Lancashire, when owing to the civil war then raging in America the supplies of cotton were interrupted and many thousands of operatives were soon on the verge of destitution. There was absolutely no public provision in those days for the unemployed, and resort had to be made to charity. From the beginning Lord Derby, as the outstanding landowner in the county, took the lead in raising the necessary funds, and made a handsome donation himself. He acted as chairman of the Relief Committee, and unstinted tributes were paid to his energy, generosity, and business management.

He became Prime Minister for the third time in July 1866, in succession to Lord Russell who had resigned after the defeat of Gladstone's Reform Bill. Disraeli as Chancellor of the Exchequer was the dominating figure in Derby's Cabinet, and in this matter of parliamentary reform he pushed his leader much farther along the road than he had ever dreamed of going. He introduced a new Reform Bill, which in its final form conferred the franchise on all householders in borough constituencies, and in the counties to occupiers of premises of the rateable value of £12 per annum and over. The bill passed through the House of Commons with ease, since most of the Whigs or Liberals joined the Conservatives in supporting it, and the House of Lords, too, passed it on Lord Derby's recommendation.

In his speech on the third reading he said that he hoped the measure would put an end to the agitation for parliamentary reform that had been going on for so long, and then described it in a phrase which became famous. ' No doubt we are making a great experiment,' he said, ' and *taking a leap in the dark*, but I have the greatest confidence in the sound sense of my fellow-countrymen, and I entertain a strong hope that the extended franchise which we are now conferring upon them will be the means of placing the institutions of this country on a firmer basis, and that the passing of the measure will tend to increase the loyalty and contentment of a great portion of her Majesty's subjects.'

In conversation with his colleagues he used another phrase, much more colloquial and idiomatic, which is also remembered: 'We have dished the Whigs!'

The Bill received the royal assent in August 1867, and thereby the electorate was increased from 1,136,000 to 2,448,000. (The great Reform Bill of 1832 had added fewer than 500,000, although this represented a virtual doubling of the electorate as it was.)

In January 1868 Lord Derby became seriously ill, and it became clear to his colleagues—sooner than it did to him—that he ought to resign. The queen thought so too, and she advised it the more readily since his successor was bound to be her favourite Disraeli. Derby resigned on 25 February, and was followed immediately by Disraeli as Prime Minister. He retired to Knowsley, and there died on 23 October 1869 at the age of seventy, and his body was interred in the little village church there as he had desired.

27

EARL OF ABERDEEN

LORD ABERDEEN, who formed the Coalition Government in 1852, was the first Scotsman to become Prime Minister since Lord Bute, ninety years before. He had all of what are considered the typically Scottish qualities. He was cautious, level-headed, shrewd —canny, to use the Scottish term—and very serious minded. But he had his critics, who maintained that he sometimes carried them to the point where virtue becomes defect.

Born at Edinburgh on 28 January 1784, he was George Hamilton Gordon, the eldest of the six sons of Lord Haddo, the eldest son and heir of the third Earl of Aberdeen. Lord Haddo never succeeded to the earldom since he died in 1791, ten years before his father—whereupon George Gordon became Lord Haddo in his turn.

On her husband's death Lady Haddo moved to England, taking her young family with her. George received his earliest education at private schools near London, until he was sent to Harrow at his grandfather's expense. In 1795 his mother, too, died, and young George Gordon made a respectful application to his grandfather for assistance. He was rebuffed, whereupon he had the good sense to make a personal appeal to Henry Dundas, later Lord Melville, who was an old friend of the family and was at that time all-powerful in Scotland as Pitt's chief representative there. Melville at once responded to the boy's appeal, and took the whole family of seven children—of whom the eldest, George, was eleven and the youngest only four—under his guardianship. Furthermore, he introduced them to Pitt, and for years the six boys and their sister lived at either Melville's house or Pitt's. On leaving Harrow, George Gordon expressed a wish to go on to Cambridge, but his grandfather refused to finance what he regarded as a useless extravagance. Again the youth had recourse to his powerful friends, and when Pitt had told Lord Aberdeen that he ' did not concur with his Lordship in considering that rank superseded the necessity for education ', the old earl was shamed into advancing the requisite funds. George Gordon thereupon proceeded to St. John's College, Cambridge, in 1800, and he had been there only a year when his grandfather died and he succeeded to the earldom.

At Cambridge Lord Aberdeen, as we should now call him, studied hard, read a great deal, and became something of a classical scholar. He was still at the university when the Peace of Amiens in 1802 made the Continent available to English travellers, after it had been closed to them by ten years of war. Lord Aberdeen seized the opportunity, and in the autumn of that year visited Paris where he had the honour of dining more than once with Napoleon, then First Consul; he subsequently extended his travels not only to Italy but to Greece and Constantinople. Everywhere he went he made a close study of the antiquities, and while in Athens he did a little archaeological digging, in course of which he discovered, or rediscovered, the amphitheatre on the hill known as the Pnyx. This explains Lord Byron's reference in one of his poems to ' The travell'd thane, Athenian Aberdeen '.

On returning to England, Aberdeen lived as before with his patrons. He came of age in 1805, when he travelled north to Aberdeenshire to take possession of his inheritance. He had not been there since he left it as a boy of eight and was not prepared for what he found. The ' appalling badness ' of Haddo House, he wrote to a friend in England, was ' only equalled by the desolation of the exterior, while the backward condition of agriculture, the miserable dwellings and half-savage habits of the peasantry, the ignorance and coarseness of the gentry, the inclement climate, and the ugliness and monotony of the country—bare and treeless— were very unlike his dreams and filled him with dismay. So depressing was the prospect that the young earl played with the idea of giving the property away, and when that proved impractic- able, of becoming an absentee landlord. But after days of mental conflict and indecision he arrived at the conclusion that it was his duty not to abandon the territorial possessions to which he owed his place in the world, not to desert the people living on his estates but to help them toward a more comfortable and civilized existence. Having so decided, he devoted himself for years to schemes of improvement. As his son, Sir Arthur Gordon, tells us in his short biography of his father, ' he drained, he planted, he built. Tracts of moorland became fields of corn, new schools rose in every parish, new buildings on every farm.'

In 1805 Lord Aberdeen married. His bride was Lady Catherine Hamilton, eldest daughter of the Marquess of Abercorn. He idolized her; in his eyes she was ' the most perfect creature ever formed by the power and wisdom of God '. She bore him three daughters; then she fell into a decline and after a long and painful illness died early in 1812. From the day of her funeral to the day of his death Lord Aberdeen, his son informs us, constantly wore mourning for her.

Until the time of his wife's death he had been too happy in his domestic life to accept any kind of official employment, although his friends in high places often offered it. But in the spring of 1813 he agreed to go to Austria as a kind of Government emissary, with a view to persuading the Emperor Francis I to desert his son-in-law Napoleon and throw in his lot with the Allies. Taking a very roundabout route, since most of the Continent was then under occupation by French troops, he arrived at length at Prague, where he met the Emperor and found him in a very accommodating mood. Then he accompanied the Austrian army in its march towards France, and what he saw on this occasion filled him with an absolute abhorrence of war that never left him.

In letters home to his sister-in-law Lady Maria Hamilton he described his experiences. Thus on the day following the battle of Leipzig, in which Napoleon had been defeated, he entered the city in the wake of the departing French troops. ' How shall I describe the entrance to this town ? For three or four miles the ground is covered with bodies of men and horses—many not dead, wretches wounded, unable to crawl, crying for water, amidst heaps of putrefying bodies. Their screams are heard at an immense distance, and still ring in my ears. The living, as well as the dead, are stript by the barbarous peasantry, who have not sufficient charity even to put the miserable wretches out of their pain. It must be owned that a victory is a fine thing, but one should be at a distance to appreciate it.'

And again, ' the most affecting sight I think that I ever beheld I have seen today. Houses were burning; the owners of these cottages in the deepest misery, and their children playing around, quite delighted with the fire which consumed the whole property of their parents, and condemned them to cold and hunger. Here is a mixture of innocence and wretchedness which goes to the heart. I do not know when I have felt more severely the wretchedness of mankind.'

When the campaign was over, Aberdeen represented Britain at the peace congress and signed on her behalf the Treaty of Paris. For his services he was created a British peer with the title of Viscount Gordon, and admitted a member of the Privy Council.

For some years he was able to devote himself to his family and estates and in 1815 he married again. His second wife was the widow of Lord Hamilton, his first wife's brother. She had young sons, and the two families were brought up together at Bentley Priory near Stanmore, north of London, which was the Abercorn country house.

When the Duke of Wellington formed his Tory government in 1828 Lord Aberdeen received the appointment of Chancellor of the Duchy of Lancaster and then was given the much more important post of Foreign Secretary. He was Colonial Secretary in Peel's Tory government of 1834–5, and was again Foreign Secretary in Peel's administration of 1841–6. Although he was ranked among the Tories, he displayed a liberal attitude towards Catholic Emancipation and Parliamentary reform and fully supported Peel in his abolition of the Corn Laws. At the Foreign Office he steadfastly adhered to the policy of non-intervention in continental disputes, but supported the cause of Greek independence and established excellent relations with Louis Philippe's government in France.

For the next six years Aberdeen was out of office, and although after Peel's death in 1850 he was recognized as the leader of the Peelites—as those Conservatives who had followed Peel's lead in the abolition of the Corn Laws were now styled—he played no great part in politics. The whole period between the end of one parliamentary session and the commencement of the next he spent in Scotland, where Haddo was now a splendid advertisement of his foresight and business management; he was never so happy as when he was there. In the biographical sketch mentioned earlier, his son gives a delightful picture of the round of days in those pleasant times.

Rising early, ' his Lordship ', as he was called even in the family circle, invariably took a short walk, accompanied by one of his sons, before meeting his family and guests over the breakfast-table. After breakfast he wrote in his own room till the departure of the post. He then saw his bailiff, who presented him with a ' daily state ' of the servants employed in the house, on the home farm, in the gardens and grounds—often exceeding a hundred—and issued his orders for the day. As twelve o'clock struck, he descended the broad flight of steps which led from the drawing-room to the terrace, to meet the head gardener who stood in readiness at the foot. Together they made a tour of the terrace and garden. Arrived at the end of the lime avenue, he was joined by the head forester, who accompanied him on a tour of the plantations.

On Saturdays this routine was varied. On that morning, at noon, Lord Aberdeen made his appearance not on the drawing-room steps but on the corresponding flight on the other side of the house, and there he received all who wished to speak to him on any matter of business, complain of some grievance, ask advice on some personal or domestic matter, or to give information. He spoke to each man or woman in turn, and took notes of what was said. This ' sitting in the gate ', to employ the old term, was a survival of the days when the laird administered justice to his followers, and Lord Aberdeen was among the very last of the Scottish nobility to practise it.

These Saturday morning levees were never without attendants, but there was always a specially large assembly on the first Saturday after Lord Aberdeen's return from England, since it was not unusual for a man to say that he had no particular matter to bring to his lordship's attention but just wished to see his face again.

In the afternoon, Lord Aberdeen's favourite amusement was to be driven in a light pony carriage at a smart pace to outlying parts of his huge estates, and he was thus enabled to keep in close touch with the improvements that were always in hand.

On Sundays of course he and his family and most of the staff went to church. There was but one service, at midday, and a procession of vehicles was formed to convey the household to the church in the village. The minister and the congregation assembled outside the church to await his lordship's party, and as soon as the lumbering old coach, holding six inside, drew up at the door the villagers hurried to take their seats and the minister made his way through the crowd to the pulpit, mounted the stairs, hung up his hat on the peg provided, and proceeded to read the metrical psalm with which the service was always begun. At the close of the service, the minister, after pronouncing the blessing, turned to Lord Aberdeen's pew and ' made a low bow, which was returned with equal gravity and depth of obeisance by his lordship standing '. On Sunday afternoon the whole family and any guests took a ' solemn walk ' to the top of a hill in the deer park, round the lake in the grounds, and into the kitchen garden. After dinner, the day was concluded by the assembly of the whole household in the library for prayers read by his lordship, many of them of his own composition.

This placid existence was interrupted in 1852 when the queen called on Lord Aberdeen to form a government. The old party system was being transformed: the Whigs were becoming Liberals, and the Tory party was split between the Conservative Protectionists under Lord Derby and Disraeli, and the Peelites who acknowledged the leadership of Lord Aberdeen. The latter was so very much a middle-of-the-road man that he seemed the obvious choice to head a coalition. He accepted the royal commission, and formed an apparently strong government, which included Lord John Russell and Lord Palmerston from the Whigs, and Gladstone and himself from the former Tories who had become Peelites.

On every hand he was congratulated on having got together so promising a team, and no one was more gratified than the queen. ' Our Government is very satisfactorily settled,' she wrote to her uncle, King Leopold of the Belgians. ' To have my faithful friend Aberdeen as Prime Minister is a great happiness and comfort to me personally.'

On the other hand, Sir James Graham, who was the leader of the Peelites in the House of Commons and took office himself in the ministry as First Lord of the Admiralty, described the Government as a powerful team that would require good driving. ' There are some odd tempers and queer ways among them; but on the whole they are gentlemen, and they have a perfect gentleman at their head, who is honest and direct and will not brook insincerity in others.'

If England had remained at peace the ' perfect gentleman ' would no doubt have succeeded to everyone's satisfaction; but unfortunately the country became involved in the Crimean War. He did his best to avoid it, and when it had become inevitable thought he should resign. As he wrote to a friend some years later, ' You are quite right in supposing that I look back with satisfaction to the efforts made by me to preserve peace. My only cause of regret is that when I found this to be impossible I did not at once retire, instead of allowing myself to be dragged into a war which, although strictly justifiable in itself, was most unwise and unnecessary.'

Aberdeen *might* have made a first-rate Prime Minister if the country had remained at peace, but beyond any doubt he was quite unfitted to lead the country in war.

The state of military unpreparedness that was disclosed—the incompetence of generals whose only recommendation had been their aristocratic connections—the mismanagement of the commissariat— the shocking sufferings of the wounded in the make-shift hospitals, which Florence Nightingale's noble efforts could go only a small way to alleviate—all these together provided ample material for a massive indictment.

It was urged then, as it has been urged since, that the conditions in the Crimea were no worse than those which, for example, Wellington's soldiers had to endure in the Peninsula. But for the first time in our history a British army was accompanied to the front by newspaper correspondents—and that made a tremendous difference. In his dispatches to *The Times*, Howard Russell proved himself the soldiers' best friend. While he paid full tribute to their courage, he exposed the horrible conditions prevailing in the base camps and in the hospitals. The revelations made tens of thousands of British breakfast tables shake with honest wrath and indignation, and the Aberdeen government was soon floundering in a storm of opprobrium. Lord John Russell, the Foreign Secretary, resigned rather than stay to face a vote of censure which he knew he and his colleagues were unable to meet, and just a week later, on 30 January 1855, Lord Aberdeen presented himself at Windsor Castle and tendered the resignation of himself and the whole Government.

The queen was very upset; and regardless of the obloquy with which Aberdeen was being covered, she insisted in bestowing on him the Garter as a most signal indication of royal favour. She also wrote him a personal letter, concluding ' with the expression of her warmest thanks for all his kindness and devotion, as well as of her unalterable friendship and esteem . . .'

Lord Aberdeen refused all offers of continued employment in politics and retired to Haddo, which he quitted only for an occasional visit to London to attend the House of Lords. He died in London, at Argyll House, St. James's, on 14 December 1860, aged seventy-six, and was buried in the family grave in the ruins of the old church at Stanmore.

28

VISCOUNT PALMERSTON

HENRY JOHN TEMPLE, Viscount Palmerston, became Prime Minister for the first time when he was seventy, and for the second time when he was seventy-five. He was called ' The Evergreen Premier ' among other things, complimentary and otherwise, in the course of his almost unequalled career of long public service. Perhaps the most popular name given him was ' Old Pam '—a term of affection, for the people loved him with all his faults, and perhaps the more because of them.

Born in 1784 ,when the young William Pitt had hardly commenced his premiership, he remained very much alive until the October day in 1865 when, as Prime Minister himself, he died at Broadlands, with an opened dispatch-box on his table and a half-finished letter lying on his desk.

He sprang from an old family which had been originally English but had been established for some generations in Ireland. His great-grandfather was a brother of the famous Sir William Temple, diplomatist, man of letters, friend of William III and patron of Dean Swift. His grandfather was made an Irish viscount (Palmerston is the name of a village near Dublin) by Walpole in 1722, and his father, the second viscount, made his home at Broadlands, near Romsey in Hampshire. The second viscount sat for forty years in the English House of Commons as member for a pocket borough, travelled on the Continent a good deal, spent his money freely and entertained hospitably, cultivated letters and the arts, and with his wife—born Mary Mee, daughter of a wealthy citizen of Bath and both good-looking and well-dowered—cut a fine figure in Society.

Generally it has been stated that the future Prime Minister was born at Broadlands, but it now seems to be established that it was at his father's London house in Park Street, Queen Anne's Gate, Westminster, that he first saw the light on 20 October 1784.

As a child he accompanied his parents on their trips abroad, and in 1795 was sent to Harrow where he was not very good at his books but showed himself a jolly little fellow with lots of pluck. At sixteen he went to Edinburgh to attend the classes of the celebrated Scottish philosopher Dugald Stewart, and in the three years he spent there, he wrote later, 'laid the foundation of whatever useful knowledge and habits of mind I possess'. In 1802 his father died, and at the age of seventeen he became Viscount Palmerston.

It should be made clear that this was a title in the peerage of Ireland. If it had been an English title he would have been precluded from sitting in the House of Commons, but as it was there was no such bar.

The following year Palmerston proceeded to St. John's College, Cambridge, and he was a student there when his mother died, to his bitter grief.

At the university he paid much more attention to politics than to classical studies, and in January 1806, when he had only recently come of age and had not yet taken his degree, he decided to stand for Parliament as Tory candidate for the University. He canvassed energetically—and came last in the poll. He stood again for the same seat in 1807 and was again beaten, but this time by only four votes. 'I did not expect so many voters,' he said, 'and at some future time I may meet with greater success.'

The time was not long in coming. At the age of twenty-two he was appointed a junior lord of the Admiralty through the influence of Lord Malmesbury, who had been one of his guardians during his minority, and shortly afterwards he was found a seat in the House of Commons as member for Newtown, in the Isle of Wight—the same seat that had been occupied by Canning at the outset of his career. It was in the gift of Sir Leonard Holmes, and in his journal Palmerston noted that 'One condition was, that I would never, even for an election, set foot in the place—so jealous was the patron lest any attempt should be made to get an interest in the borough.'

Early in 1808 he delivered his maiden speech. Canning was now Foreign Secretary, and he was being called over the coals for his action in ordering the seizure of the Danish fleet to prevent its falling into the hands of Napoleon. This was just the sort of spirited action that was to appeal to Palmerston in later years when he stood in Canning's place, and he spoke strongly in his defence. 'You will see by this day's paper,' he wrote to his sister from the Admiralty on 4 February 1808, 'that I was tempted by some evil spirit to make a fool of myself for the entertainment of the House last night; however, I thought it was a good opportunity of breaking the ice, although one should flounder a little in doing so, as it was impossible to talk any very egregious nonsense upon so good a cause.'

Having broken the ice, he spoke occasionally, when he had something useful to say, but he was never a fine speaker. Even when he had been years in the House, his style was slipshod and untidy, with innumerable hums and haws, noisy throat-clearings and much flourishing of his pocket-handkerchief, and he might be guilty of sucking an orange. But his dogged, determined manner, his bulldog tenacity and obvious love of a scrap—what Greville was to call his ' bow-wows '—made men sit up and listen. Furthermore, he always managed to convey the impression that here was a man who was able to do things, and see that others did them.

This was the case even when he was a very young man, quite new to the game, as is evidenced by the letter that he received at Broadlands one morning from Spencer Perceval, the Prime Minister. Would he come up to town immediately, as he had a proposal to make which Lord Palmerston might find agreeable ?

' I went up to him, and he offered me the Chancellorship of the Exchequer.' Palmerston says he was a good deal surprised at so unexpected an offer, as well he might be. Most young men in politics would have jumped at it, but not Palmerston. He asked Perceval if he might have a little time to think it over and consult his friends; whereupon the Prime Minister told him that if he did not fancy the Treasury he might be able to offer him the War Office instead.

This is what he chose. ' Of course, one's vanity and ambition would lead one to accept the brilliant offer first proposed,' he wrote to Lord Malmesbury, ' but it is throwing a *great stake*, and where much is to be gained, *very much* may also be lost. I have always thought it unfortunate for anyone, and particularly a young man, to be put above his proper level, as he only rises to fall lower.'

So in 1809, at the age of twenty-five, Palmerston became Secretary at War. *At* War, be it noted, not *for* War. The latter was a quite separate post, the holder of which was responsible for policy and field operations; the Secretary *at* War was in charge of the office, the business side of the department. ' I think I shall like it very much,' Palmerston wrote soon after his appointment. ' There is a good deal to be done, but it is some satisfaction to have some real business to do.'

Palmerston dealt with the business so successfully that he was at the War Office for not far short of nineteen years without a break. Prime Ministers came and went—Spencer Perceval, Liverpool, Canning, Goderich, Wellington. While every other post in the Government changed hands time after time, Palmerston stayed put.

He was clearly the right man in the right job, and it should not be forgotten that in the earlier years of his tenure it was his responsibility to keep Wellington in the Peninsula supplied with everything— guns and ammunition, food and uniforms, stores, equipment of all kinds—necessary to maintain his army as a fighting force in the field of war.

When he had been appointed, Palmerston had understood that holidays would be hard to arrange, and for most of the time he kept rigidly to his desk. Occasionally, however, he was able to get away for a few weeks to Broadlands and even to Ireland, where he had estates near Sligo. His first visit was in 1808, and he found his property consisted of a largely uncultivated tract of country, about two miles by six. He laid plans for making roads and reclaiming the bog-lands, for building houses, a little manufacturing village, a pier and a small port, and proposed to introduce a Scottish farmer to teach his tenants how to make a living. All these things took years to carry out, but he kept at it. Nearly twenty years later he was recording that he had started two schools (but was at war with the priest, who forbade his flock to send their children), that his harbour was nearly completed and his linen factory doing well. All the same, the prospect was generally depressing, since there was some-thing very like civil war going on between the English government and the Roman Catholic population. He came to the conclusion that some measure of Roman Catholic emancipation was absolutely essential, and this at a time when Wellington and Peel, his party leaders, were rigidly insisting on no concessions.

For the present, however, he was content to continue with his duties at the War Office, making an occasional speech in the Commons, and enjoying his position in society. He was never without plenty of invitations to dinner and parties, for he had the knack of making himself agreeable, and he was quite a favourite with the ladies, who playfully dubbed him ' Cupid '. He also had his estate at Broadlands to look after, his racing stables, and his country pursuits.

During Lord Liverpool's long administration he was offered in turn the posts of Chief Secretary for Ireland, an Indian governorship, and the Postmaster-Generalship accompanied by an English peerage. He declined them all: he was quite content with the War Office.

So far as party ties went he was still a Tory, but in 1826 he was opposed at Oxford by a Government-supported candidate, and kept his seat mainly through Whig support. ' I told Lord Liverpool,' he said afterwards, ' that if I was beat I should quit the Government.

This was the first decided step towards a breach between me and the Tories, and they were the aggressors.'

When Canning became Prime Minister in 1827 he sent forPalmerston and offered him the post of Chancellor of the Exchequer, with a seat in the Cabinet. This time Palmerston was willing, but the offer was withdrawn. Would he care to go to India as Governor-General ? No, he would prefer to stay where he was. Goderich, when he succeeded to the premiership, made the same offer of the Treasury, and again it fell through. So Palmerston was still at the War Office when the Duke of Wellington became Prime Minister in 1828. But after a few months the Canningites in the Government decided to break loose because of the Duke's ultra-Toryism, and Palmerston, who was one of the principal members of the group, decided to quit with them.

The truth of the matter was that he was no longer a Tory. He had supported Roman Catholic emancipation when Wellington and Peel held out against it, and now he was feeling his way towards the necessity for some measure of parliamentary reform. He was not quite ready to join the Whigs, but, he told his brother, ' I like the Whigs much better than the Tories, and agree with them much more '.

After twenty-one years as a Minister, Palmerston was now out of office. But not for long. When in November 1830 Lord Grey set about forming his Whig government, he at once made an approach to Palmerston. Was he right in thinking that Lord Palmerston was prepared to support a Reform Bill ? Yes, he was. Was he prepared to serve in a Whig Cabinet ? What as—shall we say as Foreign Secretary ? Why, yes, he would, with pleasure . . .

In fact, it was just the job for him. He had always taken a very keen interest in foreign affairs; he could express himself perfectly in French, had a working knowledge of Italian, and could read German; he had travelled a good deal on the Continent, and had made innumerable friends there; his experience at the War Office had made him a master of international business. For most of the eleven years from 1830 to 1841 he remained at the Foreign Office, and he was immensely successful. He took a leading part in securing the independence of Belgium, supported constitutional government in Spain and in Portugal, worked harmoniously with Louis Philippe's France, and strove to protect Turkey from being absorbed by Russia. With truth it has been said of him, that in those eleven years he ' raised the prestige of England to a height which she had not occupied since Waterloo '.

A few days before Christmas in 1839 Palmerston took the plunge into matrimony. He had left it rather late: he was fifty-five, an age when he had reached the status of a gay old bachelor. The woman he chose was the dowager Lady Cowper, only three years younger than he was, and we have met her before, since she was the Emily Lamb who was Lord Melbourne's sister. From the time of her debut she was one of the Queens of Society—beautiful, accomplished, decidedly clever and immensely attractive. ' What a fool she would have made of me if she had been a few years younger, had she thought it worth her while!' mused Lord Byron once.

When she was eighteen she was married to Earl Cowper, and at once took her place as a great hostess, attracting to her soirées and dinner-parties and dances all who were fair and famous. Palmerston as a young and rising politician was a welcome guest both at the Cowpers' London house and their country seat of Panshanger in Hertfordshire. They became great friends; perhaps they were more than friends, and some of the gossip that linked their names may have been near the truth. She bore her husband three children, and their daughter Emily married in 1830 Lord Ashley, who lives so very deservedly in history as the most eminent and devoted of Victorian philanthropists, the seventh Earl of Shaftesbury.

Earl Cowper died in 1837, and eighteen months later Palmerston married his widow. The wedding was at St. George's, Hanover Square, on 16 December 1839; Lord Melbourne, the Prime Minister, and the bride's son and daughter and Palmerston's brother and brother-in-law signed the register.

It proved a wonderfully happy and successful match. The new Lady Palmerston blossomed into a fresh flowering of grace and beauty and she was devoted to her husband. To the end of their life together her letters began, ' My dearest love '. She employed her wit and charm in encouraging his friends and in conciliating those who had taken umbrage at his words or deeds. She was always ready to defend him against his detractors. She acted as his private secretary, making copies with her own hand of the letters he had written. She backed him up in everything, and he, for his part, trusted her implicitly. When he became Prime Minister she was heard to complain that ' I would rather my husband was only Foreign Minister or Home Secretary, for since he became Prime Minister I see nothing of him. He never comes to bed till 4 or 5 o'clock.' But she took the greatest pride in his achievements.

Throughout Peel's administration, Palmerston remained in opposition, but he supported wholeheartedly Peel's free trade measures and the abolition of the Corn Laws. When the dreadful famine struck Ireland he went to see how his tenants were faring, and he exerted himself in enabling as many of them as he could to emigrate to the United States and Canada. He studied the arrangements for their passage, and stipulated that ' Every man and woman shall have a hot tumbler of the best Jamaica rum-punch after dinner on Sundays or oftener.' But alas, the temperance enthusiasts got wind of the proposal and made a fuss, and Palmerston had to amend his instructions. The rum that had been taken on board for the punch was to be sold at Quebec; and instead, ' every man, woman, and child is to have a cup of hot coffee with a biscuit every day after dinner '. We are not told what the emigrants thought of the changed arrangements.

When Lord Russell was forming his ministry in 1846 he invited Palmerston to return to the Foreign Office, although he was rather nervous of what he might do there. Palmerston gladly accepted, and proceeded to carry out his duties with his customary energy and aplomb. Very early he made it perfectly clear where he stood, and where he thought Britain ought to take her stand. When in 1849 Richard Cobden expressed himself in favour of submitting international disputes to arbitration, Palmerston disagreed. He agreed with Mr. Cobden, he told the House of Commons, in feeling the utmost dislike, ' and I may say horror ' of war in any shape, and this was the opinion of the vast mass of Englishmen. But, he went on, ' that which I wish to guard against—the impression that I wish should not be entertained anywhere, either in this country or out of it—is that, while there is in England a fervent love of peace, an anxious and steady desire to maintain it, there should not exist the impression that the manly spirit of Englishmen is dead; that England is not ready, as she is ever, to repel aggression and resent injury . . .'

Palmerston was never the man to turn the other cheek, and his sometimes high-handed policies met with frequent opposition in the House of Commons.

In 1848, the year of revolutions on the Continent, Palmerston did not disguise his sympathies with the peoples, in Italy and elsewhere, who were struggling to be free.

There was a famous incident in 1850 when the Austrian general Haynau visited England. Haynau was reported to have suppressed nationalist risings in Hungary with savage cruelty, including the flogging of women. In the course of his stay in London he visited

Barclay Perkins' brewery, and the draymen gave him such a rough reception he had to be rescued by the police. The Austrian minister demanded satisfaction for this insult but Palmerston coolly refused any such thing. 'The people of this country are remarkable for hospitable reception of strangers,' he said, 'but General Haynau was looked upon as a great moral criminal; and the feeling in regard to him was of the same nature as that which was manifested towards the Mannings '—a man and his wife who had been recently executed for an atrocious murder—' with this only difference, that General Haynau's bad deeds were committed upon a far larger number of victims.'

Whatever his Cabinet colleagues may have thought, the people roared their approval of ' Old Pam's ' spirit.

A few months later, in the summer of 1850, occurred what became known throughout the world as ' the Don Pacifico case '.

Don Pacifico was a Jew, a native of Gibraltar, whose house in Athens had been sacked in broad daylight by a mob headed by the sons of the Greek Minister of War. Don Pacifico was a dubious character, but he *was* a British subject, and that in Palmerston's eyes was enough. Palmerston demanded redress of the wrong that had been done him, and to others in similar cases; when the representations had been treated with contempt he ordered the British fleet into the Piraeus where certain vessels were seized and held.

There was a great outcry in Parliament. In the House of Lords, where there was a permanent Conservative majority, a motion of censure was proposed by Lord Stanley and passed. But in the House of Commons a Radical M.P., J. A. Roebuck, moved that ' the principles on which the foreign policy of Her Majesty's government has been regulated have been such as were calculated to maintain the honour and dignity of this country, and in times of unexampled difficulty to preserve peace between England and the various nations of the world '. A four nights' debate ensued, and on the second night Palmerston rose to make his defence. He spoke for four hours and thirty-five minutes. His ' Em ' was in the gallery, and her eyes never left his face for a moment.

Standing at the table, sturdily erect, his chest well out, and with not a tremor in his voice, he presented his case. He reviewed the course of events. He paid a splendid tribute to the British people and to the Constitution under which they were enabled to live in happiness and freedom. He acknowledged that it was ' a noble thing to be allowed to guide the policy and to influence the destiny of such a people'. He uttered not a word of apology or regret.

After four hours he was drawing to his conclusion. ' I therefore fearlessly challenge the verdict which this House, as representing a political, a commercial, a constitutional country, is to give on the question now brought before it—whether the principles on which the foreign policy of her Majesty's government has been conducted, and the sense of duty which has led us to think ourselves bound to offer protection to our fellow-subjects abroad, are proper and fitting guides for those who are charged with the government of England ' —the packed House was still, every eye was turned on the doughty, frock-coated figure—' or whether, as the Roman in days of old held himself free from indignity when he could say *Civis Romanus sum*, so also a British subject, in whatever land he may be, shall feel confident that the watchful eye and strong arm of England will protect him against injustice and wrong.'

Later in the debate Peel spoke—for the last time in the House as it proved—and although his speech was critical he confessed that Palmerston's had been ' a most able and temperate speech ', one that ' made us proud of the man who delivered it '. Then Disraeli joined in the attack, and Gladstone excelled himself in lofty indignation. But there was no getting away from that tremendous *Civis Romanus sum*, and when the vote was taken the Government were home and dry by forty-six votes.

Greville, no great admirer of Palmerston as a rule, could not forbear from joining in the chorus of praise, even though he held that ' an attentive and calm perusal ' of Palmerston's speech must reveal its insufficiency as an answer and a defence. But ' it was a wonderful effort to speak for nearly five hours without ever flagging, and his voice nearly as strong at last as at first ', and the speech was ' admirably arranged and got up, entirely free from the flippancy and impertinence in which he usually indulges, full of moderation and good taste, and adorned with a profusion of magnificent and successful clap-traps '.

But there was no doubt about it, ' the success of the speech has been complete, and his position is now unassailable '. The newspapers had carried Palmerston's brave words into every home and he became a popular idol. Probably it was now that, for the first time, Palmerston must have realized that the premiership was not beyond his reach.

But in the Cabinet he was distrusted, and at Windsor the queen and Prince Albert were often shocked and indignant. The queen

'The People's William', as Gladstone was called at the height of his popularity, walking through London on the arm of Lord Hartington, later Duke of Devonshire. This sketch is by the cartoonist Harry Furniss. Below left: Lord Salisbury, who was thrice Prime Minister at the head of Conservative and Unionist administrations. Below right: A. J. Balfour, Lord Salisbury's nephew, and his successor in the premiership on his retirement in 1902. Years later Balfour won fresh laurels as an 'elder statesman'.

The cartoon by Bernard Partridge (right) shows Mr. Asquith and his chief lieutenant D. Lloyd George engaged in a game of parliamentary football with the House of Lords. Lloyd George reached the heights of his tempestuous career when he led the British delegation to the Peace Conference in 1919, at the conclusion of the Great War that he had done so much to win. The photograph above shows him in Paris with Premier Orlando of Italy, Premier Clemenceau of France, and President Woodrow Wilson of the U.S.A.

A HANDY CUSTODIAN.

Asquith "YES, WE OUGHT TO GET PAST THE OTHERS PRETTY EASILY, BUT THAT'S THE FELLOW I'M AFRAID OF."

disagreed strongly with his liberal policies, his encouragement of a new order in foreign arrangements. *She* was interested in dynasties, in royal and princely houses, nearly all of which were intimately connected with her by ties of blood or marriage; *he* was concerned with peoples and nations striving to liberate themselves from age-old thraldoms. The queen remonstrated again and again with Lord John Russell, and implored him to keep his subordinate in order. She claimed as her right that she should at least be shown the foreign dispatches before they were sent off, and Palmerston was induced to agree. But before long he was reasserting his personality and policy, and while he always treated her Majesty with proper respect he had no compunction about telling her when he thought her views ran counter to what he considered to be the country's best interests. Inevitably he went too far.

When Prince Louis Napoleon, whom he had known well for many years, executed his *coup d'état* in Paris in December 1851 Palmerston expressed something like approbation to the French ambassador, without thinking it necessary to consult the queen or the Prime Minister beforehand. Whereupon Lord John, as kindly as he could, told Palmerston that he must relieve him of his office.

' *Palmerston is out !*—actually, really, and irretrievably out,' wrote Greville in his journal on 23 December, and added that he nearly dropped off his chair when he heard the news.

Out he was, but he didn't seem to mind very much. He had a very pleasant chat with his successor, Lord Granville. ' Ah, how are you, Granville ? Well, you have got a very interesting office, but you will find it very laborious; seven or eight hours' work every day will be necessary for the current business, besides the extraordinary and the parliamentary, and with less than that you will fall into arrears! '

Palmerston went down to Broadlands and enjoyed himself in the hunting field; in visiting his trainer, playing billiards and making himself agreeable to his wife's unending stream of guests. But he was only biding his time, and he did not have to wait long for his revenge. In February 1852 he moved an amendment to the Militia Bill which was carried, and Lord John Russell forthwith resigned. ' I have had my tit-for-tat with Johnny Russell! ' remarked Palmerston in high good humour.

Lord Stanley—or Lord Derby as he was now—was called upon to form an administration, and he made one last effort to persuade Palmerston to return to the Tory fold. He offered him the Chancellorship of the Exchequer, although the queen was strongly against it. Palmerston, thinking, no doubt, of the number of times he had been offered that same post before, declined. In less than a year, Derby had to make way for Lord Aberdeen, and of course Palmerston received an invitation to join the coalition. Not as Foreign Secretary, however: that went to Lord John Russell. It was the Home Office for Palmerston, and he accepted it with pleasure.

As was his way, he flung himself into his new responsibilities with enthusiasm. Before long he was writing to his brother; 'I shall be able to do some good at the Home Office. I am shutting up all the graveyards in London, a measure authorized by an Act of last session and absolutely required for the preservation of the health of the town. There is a company who are going to make two great tunnels under London, fifty feet below the surface . . . These tunnels are to be the receptacles into which all the sewers and the drains are to be discharged, so that nothing is to go into the Thames; and the contents of those tunnels are at the point of termination to be dried and converted into manure, to be sold to agriculturists as home-made guano. I shall try to compel at least the tall chimneys to burn their own smoke, and I should like to put down beer-shops, and to let shopkeepers sell beer like oil, or vinegar, or treacle, to be carried home and drunk with wives and children.'

In 1853 there was another cholera outbreak, and the Scottish clergy wrote to the Home Secretary urging that the Government should proclaim a national day of fasting and humiliation. Lord Palmerston didn't think much of the proposal. 'The best course which the people of this country can pursue to deserve that the further progress of the cholera should be stayed', he advised the petitioners, 'will be to employ the interval between the present time and the beginning of the next spring in planning and executing measures by which those portions of their towns and cities which are inhabited by the poorest classes . . . may be freed from those causes and sources of contagion which, if allowed to remain, will infallibly breed pestilence and be fruitful of death, in spite of all the prayers and fastings of a united, but inactive people.'

When the Crimean War was being fought Palmerston was at the Home Office, and so his public image remained untarnished, his popularity unaffected. Early in 1855 Lord Aberdeen's well-meaning but bungling ministry petered out, and the queen had to look for a new premier. She applied to Lord Derby, nothing doing; to Lord John Russell—no better. Greville watched the game being played. Very soon, he noted in his journal, ' the Queen will play her last card, and have recourse to *the man of the people*!—to Palmerston, whom they are crying out for, and who, they fondly imagine, is to get us out of all difficulties '. At length, very much against her will—and Prince Albert's—she sent for Palmerston. He came, bursting with vitality and good humour, and on 4 February he was writing to inform her Majesty that he thought ' he could undertake with a fair prospect of success to form an Administration which will command the confidence of Parliament and effectually conduct public affairs in the present momentous crisis '. On 10 February the Ministry was complete.

' Palmerston Prime Minister!' confided John Bright to his journal four days later. ' What a hoax! The aged charlatan has at length obtained the great object of his long and unscrupulous ambition.' Disraeli, who saw his hopes dashed once again, was even more embittered. ' An impostor,' he described the new Prime Minister to a sympathetic lady correspondent, ' utterly exhausted, and at the best only ginger-beer, and not champagne, and now an old painted pantaloon, very deaf, very blind, and with false teeth, which would fall out of his mouth while speaking, if he did not hesitate and halt so in his talk . . .'

Meanwhile Palmerston was proceeding with confidence, although even he felt a bit surprised. He wrote to his brother; ' A month ago, if any man had asked me to say what was one of the most improbable events I should have said my being Prime Minister. Aberdeen was there, Derby was head of one great party, John Russell of the other, and yet, in about ten days' time they all gave way like straws before the wind, and so here am I writing to you from Downing Street as First Lord of the Treasury.'

When Palmerston's ministry was formed, wrote Lord Morley in his life of Gladstone, ' everybody took it for granted that [it] would be temporary. Mr. Gladstone gave it a twelvemonth at most. As it happened, Lord Palmerston was in fact, with one brief interruption, installed for a decade. He was seventy-one; he had been nearly forty years in office . . . he had served under ten Prime Ministers . . . He was not more than loosely attached to the Whigs, and he had none of the strength of that aristocratic tradition and its organ, the Bedford sect. The landed interest was not with him. The Manchester men detested him. The church in all its denominations was on terms of cool and reciprocated indifference with one who was above all else the man of this world.' On the face of it, these were grave disadvantages. But there was another side to the picture. Morley went on; 'The press he knew how to manage. In every art of parliamentary sleight of hand he was an expert, and he suited the temper of the times, while the old maxims of government were tardily expiring, and the forces of a new era were in their season gathering to a head.'

There was something else he knew—knew better, perhaps, than any other of the generations of statesmen who were his contemporaries. He knew his Englishman—the fellow whom he described as ' a fat man with a white hat in the twopenny omnibus '.

And so the rather battered old chap who had been something of a Regency buck came to preside over the England of railways and Free Trade and bouncy crinolines.

Palmerston's first ministry lasted for just over three years, during which time he brought the Crimean War to a successful conclusion and weathered the storm of the Indian Mutiny. He did so well that the general election of 1857 gave the Liberals, as his following was now generally styled, a great majority. (Palmerston himself, however, had been a Tory and had become a Whig, and was hardly to be called anything else.) Things seemed to be going so well with him that he remarked once that, like the Roman Consuls in a Triumph, he ought to have somebody to remind him that as a minister he was not immortal. In fact the reminder soon came, for on 19 February 1858 a combination of parties procured his defeat on a matter of no great importance and he resigned.

For a year Lord Derby was Prime Minister, but early in 1859 he suffered a defeat on a franchise bill and appealed to the country.

Since 1835 Palmerston had been sitting for Tiverton, and he always went down there to meet his constituents, even when he was unopposed, as he was on this occasion. There was a Radical butcher, Rowcliffe by name, who always turned up at the hustings to give his lordship a ' bit of his mind '. Palmerston always enjoyed these occasions, and gave as good as he got.

The Liberals won the election, and on 18 June 1859 Palmerston was installed as Prime Minister for the second time. His Government contained representatives, for the first time, of all the Liberal elements in Parliament—Whigs, Radicals, Liberals, Peelites, and plain Palmerstonians. Gladstone was Chancellor of the Exchequer, and thus definitely joined the Liberal party. Palmerston remained Prime Minister for the rest of his life.

' The constancy with which he attended the sittings of the House of Commons ', wrote the Duke of Argyll (Queen Victoria's son-in-law) in his small book on Palmerston, ' was the wonder of more youthful and more restless members. Hour after hour he sat on the Treasury bench, the day-light from the high-placed windows or the gas-light from the ceiling of the chamber falling on his grey locks, which were always carefully brushed forward in the old fashion . . . During a " great night " it was curious to see how apparently unmoved and passive he remained during all the phases of the debate, his face in repose, his eyes looking steadily in front of him, often half-closed, his frock-coat buttoned neatly across him, his gloves always on his hands, his neat trousers of a light-toned cloth strapped down to his neat boots. Not a turn of the arguments used escaped him, and yet, when at the end he rose to conclude the debate, it did not follow that he would reply point by point. On the contrary, important points were sometimes avoided, or he would play round them, and, with the jaunty fun and half mocking raillery he knew so well how to use, he would " pitch into " an opponent . . . and then he would call upon his friends to vote in some effective passage which combined English common sense with the concise phraseology born of long knowledge and the ring of an undoubted patriotism and honesty of conviction, which told on his party and ensured him the majority he expected.'

Until he was nearing eighty, Palmerston showed few of the usual signs of old age and none of decrepitude. He rose and shot when he was at Broadlands, went out to dinner and delighted in playing the host. A pretty face never lost its attraction with him, and he mixed easily with men and women of all classes and ages. Every day when he was in town he might be seen coming down the steps of Cambridge House in Piccadilly, mount his old grey and set off on his ride. He was a familiar figure to thousands of Londoners; they waved to him as he ambled past, and he courteously acknowledged their greeting with a finger to his hat.

In the spring of 1865 he had a specially nasty attack of the gout, but he was well enough to go down to Tiverton for his last election. The country people welcomed him with their usual warmth and again he was returned unopposed. And the country, invited again to vote ' Pam for Premier ', did just that.

After leaving Tiverton he went to Brocket Hall, his wife's country house which had belonged to her brother, Lord Melbourne. The gout was still troubling him but he enjoyed the young company assembled there and was able to get out for a ride or a drive. He still worked at his red dispatch-boxes, brought down to him from Downing Street, and still wrote letters in that flowing penmanship that Gladstone said was one of the most perfect things he had known.

The last of the many stories told about him comes from these closing weeks. There were some high railings opposite the front door, and one morning he was seen to go straight up to them and, after casting a glance round to see that no one was looking, climb deliberately over the top railing down to the ground; after which he turned round, climbed back again, and went back indoors. He had just wanted to prove to himself that he was not done for yet.

But on Thursday, 12 October, he woke feeling poorly, although he and ' Em ' went out for a drive in the carriage later. He came home with a cold, was put to bed, dawdled over his undressing and insisted on taking his bath as usual. On the Monday he was well enough to breakfast off two mutton-chops and a half-glass of old port, and expressed surprise that he ' should have lived so long without discovering what a good breakfast it is '. The next day he was not so well, but he lingered on until he was within a couple of days of his eighty-first birthday. The last words attributed to him are so much in keeping that we may well believe he actually said them. ' Die, my dear doctor ? That's the *last* thing I shall do ! '

He died on the morning of 18 October 1865. In his will he had stated that he wished to be buried at Romsey Abbey, beside his ancestors, and arrangements had been made to that effect when Gladstone insisted on a public funeral and a grave in Westminster Abbey. Lady Palmerston's consent was obtained on the understanding that a place should be preserved for her by his side.

So on 29 October Lord Palmerston's body was buried in Westminster Abbey. ' The crowds were immense,' wrote Lord Shaftesbury afterwards, ' but in wonderful order; silent, deeply reverential . . . Such a scene has seldom been seen . . . The people loved the man, his open simplicity, his imperturbable good humour, his incapability of resentment, his readiness to stand up, at all times, for what he thought to be right . . . Every man regarded him as a personal friend . . .'

29

BENJAMIN DISRAELI
(EARL OF BEACONSFIELD)

BENJAMIN DISRAELI was the most *improbable* of Prime Ministers. No one could have invented such a character, and in his novels he never created one so full of strangenesses and contradictions as he was himself.

No distinguished lineage lay behind him, and he had no powerful friends to give him a start. You will look in vain for his name on the panels at Eton or Harrow, and he never dawdled as a youth along the banks of Isis or of Cam. Until he was not far off middle age his reputation was shady and raffish. Before he was a politician he was an author, and when he came to present his Budgets people complained that they were fiction, too. When at length he had made a beginning in politics men found it hard to decide which party he really belonged to, and he seems never to have been quite sure himself.

But this is only part of the story. The literary lounger wrote novels that have become part of our intellectual heritage. The impecunious speculator lived to become the leader of the men of wealth and landed property. The political adventurer succeeded in climbing, not once only but twice, what he called the ' greasy pole '. The outrageous Radical became the Conservative statesman. The skilled practitioner in liaisons became the devoted husband of an adoring woman, and—more extraordinary—the intimate counsellor of the queen who was regarded as the embodiment of Victorian respectability.

This man, whose obviously Hebrew countenance stares out from painting and photograph, with its sallow skin creased into a sardonic smile, the heavy-lidded eyes, the prominent nose, the thick lips, the greasy locks of dyed hair—he was a legend in his lifetime; and on his birthday his admirers still pay tribute to his memory with posies of primroses which may, or may not, have been his favourite flower.

Benjamin Disraeli was born on 21 December 1804, at his father's house in King's Road, Bedford Row (since renamed 22 Theobald's Road), in the Gray's Inn district of London. He was the second child and eldest son of Isaac D'Israeli (as he originally spelled it: he dropped the apostrophe when Benjamin was a child), a Jewish man of letters in comfortable circumstances. Isaac's father was an Italian Jew who was engaged in the straw-bonnet trade, and who migrated to London in 1748, where he did well as a stockbroker. The story that his ancestors on his father's side had been Jews expelled from Spain in 1492 at the instigation of the Inquisition, and had thereupon removed to Venice where they flourished for generations as merchants, seems to have been one of Benjamin's inventive flights. Isaac was not in the least interested in business, and as soon as he came into his father's money he devoted himself to his books. He left all the cares of everyday life to his wife, born Maria (or Miriam) Basevi, who like him came from a respectable family of Italian Jews.

Although Isaac Disraeli was a Voltairean freethinker, he retained some slight connection with his ancestral faith, and Benjamin was duly circumcised at the synagogue of Spanish and Portuguese Jews in Bevis Marks. As a small boy he was sent to a dame's school at Islington, and then to a boarding-school at Blackheath kept by a Nonconformist minister. In 1816 Isaac Disraeli's father died and he succeeded to his father. He moved to a large house in Bloomsbury Square, and made a final break with Judaism, in which step he was encouraged by his wife, who regarded it with detestation. In consequence, all the children were baptized into the Church of England, in Benjamin's case the date and place being 31 July 1817, at St. Andrew's, Holborn.

Although the boy may not have realized it at the time, this was one of the most important events in his life. If he had remained a professing Jew he could not have become a member of Parliament when he did, since it was not until 1858, when he had been a M.P. for more than twenty years, that Jews were permitted to take a suitably modified oath of allegiance.

At the age of thirteen the newly-baptized Benjamin was sent to a fresh school, one at Walthamstow kept by a Unitarian minister. In 1821, when just seventeen, he was articled to a firm of solicitors in Frederick's Place, Old Jewry, but after four years there he was entered at Lincoln's Inn to study for the other branch of the law. But he liked neither the one branch or the other.

What, then, did he want to be? There is a passage in his first novel *Vivian Grey* which must be an autobiographical reflection. ' The Bar!—pooh! Law and bad jokes till we are forty, and then with the most brilliant success the prospect of gout and a coronet. Besides, to succeed as an advocate I must be a great lawyer, and to be a great lawyer I must give up my chances of being a great man. The "services" in war time are fit only for desperadoes (and that truly am I), and in peace time fit only for fools. The Church is more rational. I should certainly like to act Wolsey, but the thousand and one chances are against me, and my destiny should not be a chance.'

When he tackled his father on the subject he was told to ' beware of trying to be a great man in a hurry '. But he *was* in a hurry. He felt that youth was the golden age, and that it was slipping from him. Why, he was twenty already—and Byron was only twenty-five when he blazed like a new star in the literary firmament, and Pitt—he was Prime Minister at twenty-four!

While he was in this undecided state he attempted to make a fortune on the Stock Exchange. With some young friends, as inexperienced as himself, he played the ' bull ' in South American mining shares, committing himself to dangerously large financial obligations. For a time all went well. John Murray, the eminent publisher who was one of his father's friends, employed him at this time as a go-between in the negotiations concerning the establishment of a new daily newspaper that would rival *The Times*. *The Representative*, as the new paper was called, at Disraeli's suggestion, was launched early in 1826. Then disaster struck. *The Representative* proved a failure and after six months publication ceased; and the bottom dropped out of the mining-shares market. Disraeli did not sell out in time, and was left with the most crippling liabilities. This was the beginning of that chronic financial embarrassment from which he was never able to extricate himself completely.

Without a job and head over heels in debt, Disraeli now burst on the world as an author. *Vivian Grey* appeared in the shops in April 1826; and although it was slammed by the more sober reviews it had a startling success. It was the novel of the season; everybody talked about it and quite a number of people read it; ' keys ' were published to the real-life characters who were satirized in its lively, witty, and deliciously naughty pages.

All the same, the book did him little good. Some in his father's circle of friends were gravely offended, and Disraeli acquired a reputation for loose-living cynicism which took him years to live down, if indeed he ever did. A succession of worries and perpetual strain brought about a nervous breakdown. The next two or three years were spent at Bradenham, the fine old house not far from High Wycombe amid the Buckinghamshire beechwoods that his father had taken, and there he wrote a sequel to his first novel, several short stories, and another novel, *The Young Duke*, for which Colburn, who had published *Vivian Grey*, paid him £500.

On the strength of this Disraeli set out on a grand tour of the Mediterranean countries, in the course of which he and his travelling companion William Meredith, the fiancé of his sister Sarah, visited not only the usual tourist haunts but penetrated into the Balkans, Constantinople, Jerusalem, and Egypt. In Cairo, Meredith died with tragic suddenness of smallpox, and the shock almost prostrated Disraeli. As for Sarah, she lived henceforth to promote her brother's happiness and success in his career.

Returning to England late in 1831, Disraeli established himself in rooms in St. James's and embarked on the life of a man about town. He was twenty-seven now, and no nearer achieving whatever it was he intended to be. But he stood out from the crowd on account of his good appearance, exotic dress, affected conversation, and his reputation as a successful novelist and adventurous traveller in out of the way places. The best people were inclined to give him the cold shoulder, but the 'Blessington set' welcomed him with open arms. At the mansion in Kensington Gore, Disraeli met the still beautiful Lady Blessington and her lover Count d'Orsay, and a host of literary celebrities, including the Mrs. Norton whose name was before long to be so closely connected with Lord Melbourne's.

Women, of course, found him fascinating. His sister was always on the look out for the right sort of girl for him to marry, but he was not yet thinking of marriage. He was quite sure he would not marry for love, in any case, since he had observed that the men of his acquaintance who had done so either beat their wives or abandoned them . . .

For the present he preferred mistresses, and in particular Lady Henrietta Sykes, the wife of a complaisant Berkshire baronet with one house in Gloucester Place and another in the country at Basildon. Disraeli's affair with her blazed up in the summer of 1833 and did not fizzle out until 1836. She is described as a 'fine woman, very pleasant and good natured', strong-willed and passionately possessive. But mistresses are apt to be expensive, and Disraeli was chronically hard up. Beyond what his father allowed him he had to rely on the fruits of his pen, and although he wrote novel after novel the fruits were disappointing. He had resort to money-lenders and bill-brokers and in consequence the burden of his debts weighed him down more and more.

Politics seemed to offer him a way of escape from his embarrassments, besides providing glorious opportunities to shine. Members of Parliament were not paid in those days but they were often put in the way of nice little jobs which yielded a steady income and demanded little effort in return. Furthermore, for the successful—and of course he would be *that*—there was always the chance of a seat in the Cabinet, with a substantial salary and a whole heap of what we might style fringe benefits.

One day in the summer of 1834 he called on Mrs. Norton at her house in Storey's Gate. Lord Melbourne was there, as he so often was, and she introduced him. Melbourne was quite taken with Disraeli, and in particular liked his free and easy way of talking. 'Well, now, Disraeli,' he inquired, 'what do you want to be?' Disraeli had his answer ready: 'I want to be Prime Minister.'

Melbourne shrugged his shoulders. 'No, no,' he said, 'there's no chance of that in our time. It is all arranged and settled. The next Prime Minister will be Stanley.' (The future Lord Derby, three times Prime Minister.) 'If you *are* going into politics, and mean to stick to it, you will do very well. You have ability and enterprise . . . but you must put all these foolish notions out of your head; they won't do at all. Stanley will be the next Prime Minister, you'll see.'

By this time Disraeli was fully resolved on a political career. The only question was which party should he join? To begin with, he called himself a Radical, and as such he stood above the portico of the 'Red Lion' in High Wycombe in June 1842 and, as he put it, 'gave it them for an hour and a quarter . . . I made them all mad. A great many absolutely cried. I never made so many friends in my life, and converted so many enemies. All the women are on my side, and wear my colours—pink and white.' This was a by-election, the last fought on the old unreformed register, and there were only forty or fifty entitled to vote. Disraeli's opponent was Colonel Grey, the Whig Prime Minister's son, and when the result was declared it showed, Grey—20; Disraeli—12.

Disraeli was not disheartened; at least he had made a beginning. He stood again for Wycombe a few months later, and was again at the bottom of the poll, although this time he collected 119 votes. In 1834 he stood yet again at Wycombe, and was again defeated. But he had had some Tory support, and when he made his fourth attempt he stood as a Tory for Taunton in 1835, where he obtained 282 votes to 452 cast for the Whig candidate.

This Taunton contest got him talked about, which was what he wanted. The newspapers reported him as having referred in one of his speeches to Daniel O'Connell, the Irish leader who was then an ally of the Whigs, as an 'incendiary and a traitor'. O'Connell retaliated by calling Disraeli a 'miscreant', one whose 'life is a living lie', a Jew who 'possesses just the qualities of the impenitent thief that died upon the cross, whose name I verily believe must have been Disraeli'.

Resolved to show that 'he could not be insulted even by a yahoo without chastising it', Disraeli jibed at O'Connell as an 'hereditary bondsman who had forgotten already the clank of his fetters', and challenged him to a duel. Whereupon the police seized Disraeli one morning when he was still in bed and carried him off to Bow Street, where he was bound over in £500 to keep the peace. If his part in the affair was nothing to boast about, he had, he declared to his sister, 'shown pluck'.

After Taunton another year or two ensued of apparently aimless drifting around the clubs and drawing-rooms, often accompanied by Henrietta Sykes. She devoted herself to pushing his interests, and it was at her dinner-table that he met Lord Lyndhurst, who had been Lord Chancellor in several Tory governments and was to be again under Peel. Lyndhurst was the first big figure in the political world whom Disraeli encountered on easy terms, and he became his personal secretary.

About this time another lady began to take a hand in determining his future. In April 1832 at a dinner-party given by his fellow novelist and great friend Bulwer Lytton, Disraeli had been introduced to a Mrs. Wyndham Lewis, wife of the Tory M.P. for Maidstone, who had expressed a particular desire to meet one about whom she had heard so much. In a letter to his sister, Disraeli described her as 'a pretty little woman, a flirt and a rattle, indeed gifted with a volubility I should think unequalled'. She had told him, 'she liked melancholy men', and he had answered that he had no doubt about it.

This does not sound very promising, and Disraeli may well have found her a bit of a bore at first. But during the next few years they met on a number of social occasions, and he also met her husband. Apparently Disraeli got on well with him, for in 1837, when a second Conservative candidate was being looked for to run in harness with Wyndham Lewis—Maidstone was a two-member constituency—Disraeli was chosen. The election proved a horribly expensive one and added greatly to Disraeli's load of debt, but this time he was successful. He ran second to Wyndham Lewis, but he was a couple of hundred votes ahead of their Whig opponent.

Disraeli had fought five elections in five years and he was in at last. 'What fun,' he wrote to his sister, 'and how lucky after all I should esteem myself.'

That autumn the Wyndham Lewises visited them at Bradenham, and in November Disraeli took his seat in the chamber he had so often looked down upon from the gallery. On 7 December 1837 he delivered his maiden speech—surely the most celebrated in parliamentary history.

'Mr. Disraeli made his first exhibition the other night,' wrote Greville in his journal, 'beginning with florid assurance, speedily degenerating into ludicrous absurdity, and being at last put down with inextinguishable shouts of laughter.'

'I made my maiden speech last night,' is Disraeli's own account, in a letter to his sister, 'rising very late after O'Connell, but at the request of my party and with the full sanction of Sir Robert Peel. I state at once that my *début* was a failure—not by my breaking down or incompetency on my part, but from the physical power of my adversaries . . . I fought through all with undaunted pluck and un-ruffled temper, made occasionally good isolated hits when there was silence, and finished with spirit . . . My party backed me well, and no one with more zeal and kindness than Peel, cheering me re-peatedly, which is not his custom.'

Just before his voice was drowned by the organized clamour, Disraeli uttered these words, or something like them. 'I have begun several things many times, and I have often succeeded at the last, though many have predicted that I must fail as they have done before me. I sit down now, but the time will come when you *will* hear me.'

A week after he had been howled down he was on his feet again, talking about the Copyright Bill, and this time he was loudly applauded. Copyright was something he was well qualified to speak on. In the remainder of the session he spoke frequently, and often to good purpose. Then in the spring of 1838 his friend and colleague Wyndham Lewis died, and his personal life was invaded by a strange new complication.

Disraeli and Mrs. Wyndham Lewis had become very good friends. She was considerably older than he and treated him with a motherly concern; 'my political protégé', she called him. But there had developed between them something more than a common interest in politics. Disraeli had broken with Henrietta Sykes some years before, and he was not looking for a fresh mistress—and Mrs. Wyndham Lewis would have been most unlikely to oblige even if he had. But they were obviously on such excellent terms that soon people were talking, and Disraeli cannot have been much surprised when (so the story runs) his friend Count D'Orsay suggested, half in jest and half in earnest, that he might do worse than marry the lady . . .

Well, why not ? Mary Anne was forty-six to his thirty-four, but she was vivacious and attractive, retaining the good looks which had been hers when as a girl she had won the affections of the wealthy South Wales industrialist Wyndham Lewis. She was also very well off, since her husband had left her their house in Grosvenor Gate and property bringing in between £4,000 and £5,000 a year. This income was only a life interest, but Disraeli did not know that.

Very soon he found out, but by this time it made no difference; he forgot all his cynical reservations about marrying for love. She put him off, pleading that it was not a year since the funeral. He pressed his suit, and she got very angry. She called him a selfish bully, and reminded him of the money she had lent him to fight the election at Maidstone. He flung out of the house, and wrote her an enormously long letter of reproach and resignation.

But it all turned out happily. Mary Anne called him back, tearfully insisted that she had only been concerned for their good name, begged him to forgive and forget. Like the hero and heroine in one of his romantic novels they fell into one another's arms. They were married at St. George's, Hanover Square, on 28 August 1839.

When they had been married for so many years that she must have found it hard to believe that she had been for twenty-three years the wife of another, she used to remark with a touch of half-mischievous complacency, 'Dizzy married me for my money—but if he had the chance again he would marry me for love!'

The first part of her boast can hardly have been true, but the second most certainly was.

Mary Anne was one of the nicest of the Prime Ministers' wives. Certainly it is difficult to write about her without admiration and affection. She was not high born or well educated. She called herself a dunce, and Disraeli gleefully recalled her remark that she never could remember which came first, the Greeks or the Romans. In her dress she often chose the wrong colours, and she was always dropping clangers in conversation.

Once when they were staying at some country house, and the next bedroom was occupied by Lord Hardinge and his wife, she remarked casually at breakfast next morning; 'Oh, Lord Hardinge, I consider myself the most fortunate of women. I said to myself when I awoke this morning, " What a lucky woman I am! Here I have been sleeping between the greatest orator and the greatest warrior of the day!" ' Lady Hardinge did not look at all pleased.

And one evening when the ladies in the drawing-room began discussing certain men possessed of fine figures, she made the startling remark, ' Oh, you should see my Dizzy in his bath! '

When he first obtained high office she sent him a note. ' Bless you, my darling! Your own happy, devoted wife wishes you joy. I hope you will make as good a Chancellor of the Exchequer as you have been a husband to your affectionate Mary Anne.' And when he carried through his Reform Bill in 1867 he hurried home from the party at the Carlton Club to Mary Anne who was waiting up for him with the lights full on as she always insisted, at 3 o'clock in the morning. A pie from Fortnum & Mason's was on the table, a bottle of champagne lying ready in the bucket.

' My dear,' said Dizzy, as he plunged his fork into the pie and raised his glass to his seventy-five-year-old spouse, ' you are more like a mistress than a wife! '

One evening they had driven to the House of Commons together. It was to be a big occasion, he had an important speech to make, and he was worried. As he shut the carriage door her hand was caught. Knowing how upset he would be if he were aware of the mishap, she bore the pain until he was out of earshot before calling the footman to release her.

On the fly-leaf of *Sybil*, his best novel, he wrote the dedication: ' To one whose noble spirit and gentle nature ever prompt her to sympathise with the suffering; to one whose sweet voice has often encouraged, and whose taste and judgment have ever guided, its pages; the most severe of critics, but—a perfect wife! '

At the general election of 1841 the Conservatives under Peel gained a big majority, and Disraeli, who had been returned for Shrewsbury, confidently expected that he would be offered some appointment in the Government. When days passed and no letter came, he so far humbled himself as to write to Peel, pointing out that from the moment he enrolled himself under his banner he had been obliged ' to struggle against a storm of political hate and malice few men have experienced ', and that he had been sustained ' under these trials only by the conviction that the day would come when the foremost man in the country would publicly testify that he had some respect for my ability and character. I confess to be unrecognized at this moment by you appears to me to be overwhelming, and I appeal to your own heart—to that justice and magnanimity which I feel are your characteristics—to save me from an intolerable humiliation.'

Mrs. Disraeli also wrote to Peel, of course without her husband's knowledge. 'I beg you not to be angry with me for my intrusion, but I am overwhelmed with anxiety. My husband's political career is for ever crushed, if you do not appreciate him . . . Do not destroy all his hopes, and make him feel his life has been a mistake . . .'

But no offer came. Peel could find no place in his administration for one whom he still regarded as a political adventurer. And bitterly he must have regretted it when, not long after, Disraeli turned upon him with a tongue envenomed not only with political disagreement but personal resentment.

For the present Disraeli kept his thoughts to himself, and proceeded to develop a line of his own as the spokesman of a small group of Conservative M.P.s who were known as 'Young England'. What may be called the text-book of the group is Disraeli's novel *Coningsby; or, The New Generation*, which was published in 1844. The book is perhaps the best political novel in the English language. Its background is the England of Grey's and Melbourne's administrations, and many of the characters are drawn from life. The original of the great nobleman Lord Monmouth was Lord Hertford who also appears in Thackeray's *Vanity Fair* as Lord Steyne; and Rigby, the professional M.P. who sat for one of his lordship's boroughs and managed his parliamentary interest, was John Wilson Croker, who for a generation had been one of the chief wirepullers in the Conservative party machine. Then there is that precious pair Tadpole and Taper, whose names have passed into everyday speech as standard specimens of the party hack.

'A sound Conservative government,' said Taper, musingly. 'I understand: Tory men and Whig measures.'

Coningsby was a great success, three editions being called for in as many months, and 50,000 copies being sent to America. Disraeli followed it up with *Sybil; or, The Two Nations* in 1845. The two nations are the rich and the poor, and not even Mrs. Gaskell did anything better in the descriptions of life in the new towns and industries. The story is as rubbishy as most of Disraeli's fire, but the background is beyond challenge. He took immense trouble to get his facts right. He went up to Manchester and toured the factories, and made a most careful study of the great Government reports that were appearing in the eighteen-forties. In *Sybil* there are scenes and episodes which might have been taken word for word from the report of the Midland Mining Commission of 1843. All in all the book is a compelling indictment of the social and political systems of the day, but it ends on a note of hope. ' We must prepare for the coming hour. The claims of the Future are represented by suffering millions; and the Youth of a Nation are the trustees of Posterity.'

These books greatly increased Disraeli's literary reputation, and they contributed not a little to getting him known as a parliamentary figure. But although he now had a full house when he rose to speak he was still nothing more than a back-bencher, and he realized that he would be nothing more as long as Peel held the reins of power.

When the session of 1845 opened Disraeli was forty—and in *Coningsby* he had written of ' that fatal thirty-seven '! But his hour was about to strike. Before the year was out he had fought his way to the front, and his tongue had done it—that biting, malicious tongue with which he assailed night after night the greatest figure in Parliament, and made him wince and squirm.

So, the Prime Minister had decided on the abolition of the Corn Laws, had he ? It was not the first time he had adopted the principles and policies of his opponents. ' The right hon. gentleman has caught the Whigs bathing,' Disraeli jeered, ' and has run away with their clothes.' Even those seated behind Peel could not refrain from laughing, and some joined in the cheers.

In an unguarded moment, Peel ventured to quote Canning's famous line, ' Save, O save me from the candid friend! ', neglectful of the charge that had been brought against him that he, as a young Tory member, had been one of those who hunted Canning into his grave.

' The theme—the poet—the speaker—what a felicitous combination!' said Disraeli when he rose to reply. ' Its effect in debate must be overwhelming; and I am sure, if it were addressed to me, all that would remain would be for me thus publicly to congratulate the right hon. gentleman, not only on his memory, but on his courageous conscience.'

A few days later Disraeli was after Peel again. With insolent solicitude he begged the House not to be impatient with the Prime Minister. ' There is no doubt a difference in the right hon. gentleman's demeanour as Leader of the Opposition and as Minister of the Crown. But that is the old story. You must not contrast too strongly the hours of courtship with the years of possession. I remember the right hon. gentleman's Protection speeches. They were the best speeches I ever heard. But we know in all these cases when the beloved object has ceased to charm, it is useless to appeal to the feelings.' In 1828 it had been Protestantism that had ceased to charm, and Peel had urged the repeal of the laws against the Roman Catholics. Now it was Protection that was to be abandoned, and by the same Minister. But Disraeli would have none of it. Turning on Peel he flung out the challenge, ' Dissolve, if you please, the Parliament whom you have betrayed, and appeal to the people, whom I believe mistrust you. For me there remains this at least, the opportunity of expressing my belief, that *a Conservative government is an organized hypocrisy*!'

On speeches such as this Disraeli rode to triumph, and in 1846 he tasted the sweet revenge of bringing about Peel's fall. The Conservative party was shattered, and only a rump formed themselves into an opposition, Disraeli amongst them. But of them was shortly to become the recognized leader in the House of Commons.

Lord Melbourne was still alive, and when he received the news of Disraeli's election to the Conservative leadership his mind harked back to that conversation in Mrs. Norton's drawing-room. ' By God! ' he exclaimed, ' the fellow will do it yet! '

Of course Disraeli was lucky in that most of the leaders of the party followed Peel in his conversion and were before long working in partnership with the Liberals. But he was chief of those who had refused to abandon the faithful, landed gentry for the most part. Disraeli himself didn't possess an acre, but steps were taken now to repair that unfortunate deficiency. The estate of Hughenden Manor, near High Wycombe, was on the market. The price asked was £35,000 which was quite beyond Disraeli's means, burdened as he was with debts which are said to have amounted to £20,000. But his friends Lord George Bentinck and his brothers offered him a loan of £25,000, which with £3,000 he got from his father's estate and what Mary Anne was able to provide enabled him to complete the purchase. In 1848 the Disraelis took possession and henceforth this was his home. He was a country gentleman at last, and to complete his satisfaction he was elected M.P. for the county of Buckinghamshire.

Four years later he had his first experience of office, when Lord Derby formed his first administration. He offered Disraeli the posts of Leader of the House of Commons and Chancellor of the Exchequer. Disraeli had to confess that ' this was a branch of which I had no knowledge ', but Lord Derby brushed aside his objections. ' You know as much as Mr. Canning did,' he said; ' they give you the figures.' It was a minority government, and was in office for only a few months. But Disraeli did well at the Treasury and led the House of Commons with an affable efficiency. And there was one *very* important person on whom he made an excellent impression. It was one of his duties as Chancellor to compose the nightly letter to the queen reporting on the day's doings in Parliament, and she commented on his interesting style.

Out of office again at the end of 1852, Disraeli had no responsibility for the Crimean War, but did his duty as a keen and conscientious critic. In 1858 Derby became Prime Minister for the second time, and he appointed Disraeli to the same positions as before. He had no chance of doing anything spectacular, since there was a permanent majority in the House of Commons against him. But he did his best to ' educate ' his party, as he put it, and to bring them into line with modern thinking. The chief barrier to their success had been their holding on to the policy of Protection, but Disraeli told them plainly ' Protection is dead and buried '. Reform was again beginning to be talked about, and he proceeded to introduce a Bill which would have conferred the vote on doctors, university graduates, ministers of religion, schoolmasters, and persons with £60 in a savings-bank account. These proposals were denounced by John Bright as ' fancy franchises ' and the Bill was rejected, as were the Conservatives at the next general election.

More years followed on the Opposition front bench, and then in 1866 he was for the third time Chancellor of the Exchequer and Leader of the House in Lord Derby's last government. The Liberals under Russell and Gladstone had recently introduced a Reform Bill which Disraeli had been largely responsible for getting rejected. With a masterly sense of timing, he now proceeded to introduce a Reform Bill of his own, of a much more sweeping and democratic character than the one just thrown out. This was carried, and the Conservatives might claim the credit of having enfranchised the working men of the towns.

Disraeli enjoyed a great personal triumph when the Bill was passed. He was over sixty now but as resourceful as ever—' diabolically clever ' Gladstone said—and with his party united behind him. He was a great national figure and his queen, the ' widow of Windsor ', was always so glad to see him.

With her, indeed, his success was complete. Not since Lord Melbourne had Victoria had a chief minister so much to her taste. Melbourne's task was perhaps the easier: it was a virginal young mind he was charged to guide and instruct in the principles of statecraft and royal behaviour. But the queen whom Disraeli served was a matronly widow, stubborn in her convictions, demanding in her ways.

Disraeli was always fond of elderly ladies, and he approached Victoria like a lover his mistress. He slobbered over the hand she held out to him, he was almost touched to the point of tears when she offered him a chair ' because of his gout ', he oozed compliments.

' You have heard me called a flatterer, and it is true,' he once confessed to Matthew Arnold. ' Everyone likes flattery; and when you come to Royalty you must lay it on with a trowel.' How different from Mr. Gladstone! He, the queen complained, addressed her as though she were a public meeting. ' Mr. Gladstone harangues her about the policy of the Hittites or the harmony between the Athanasian creed and Homer,' reported Lord Russell; but Disraeli ' used to engage her Majesty in conversation about water-colour drawing and third cousinships of German princes.' Once Disraeli admitted to Lord Esher, ' I never deny; I never contradict; I sometimes forget '.

Early in 1868 Lord Derby told the queen that his health was now so poor that he ought to think about retiring. She had already come to the same conclusion, it seemed, and she pushed him into carrying it out. She sent for Disraeli, as Derby had recommended, on 26 February. The news was announced in the House of Commons, and on the 27th Disraeli went down to Osborne House in the Isle of Wight where the queen was staying, and kissed her pudgy little hand as her Prime Minister. The queen wrote to her daughter, the Crown Princess of Prussia, a few days later that he had bent himself almost double over her hand and murmured, ' In loving loyalty and faith '.

When he got back to town Disraeli was surrounded by jubilant friends who thumped his back and shook his hand again and again. ' Yes,' he said complacently, ' I have climbed to the top of the greasy pole.'

' If only your sister had been alive to witness your triumph, what happiness it would have given her! ' remarked his intimate friend Sir Philip Rose, who was also his solicitor. (Sarah Disraeli had died in 1859.) ' Poor Sa,' rejoined Disraeli; ' poor Sa! Yes, we have lost our audience.'

But Mary Anne was still with him, an old lady now, bent and shrivelled and suffering from cancer of the stomach, although she had not told him that yet. Never in her life had she been so happy and proud as when at the great reception at the Foreign Office, surrounded by everybody who was anybody in the London of the day, she watched her Dizzy walking about the room with the Princess of Wales on his arm, while she herself was escorted by the Prince, the future Edward VII.

This was but a brief period of glory, however, for Disraeli's government soon encountered heavy weather and he found it necessary to go to the country, whereupon the Liberals under Gladstone were returned with a big majority. Disraeli resigned on 1 December 1868. The queen offered him an earldom, and he declined with expressions of gratitude. But there *was* something he would like: would her Majesty confer a peerage on his wife? And so Mary Anne became Countess of Beaconsfield in her own right, and within a few days was using letter-paper marked with a large B surmounted by a coronet. And how proud she was when she signed her letters to him, ' Your own devoted Beaconsfield '!

Disraeli returned again to the Opposition front bench, where he was confronted night after night by the triumphant Gladstone. As a relief from parliamentary boredom he put the finishing touches to *Lothair*, his last novel but one, which like most of its predecessors is about immensely rich young noblemen and fascinating ladies, and their comings and goings in the high society of Church and State. The book appeared in 1870 and was an immense success— ex-Prime Ministers don't write novels every day—not only in Britain but in the United States where, an admirer wrote to inform him, it was not at all unlikely that a notice of the book had appeared in each of the country's five thousand newspapers.

Much of his time was spent down at Hughenden, where his wife was slowly dying. She was eighty-one and he sixty-eight, but theirs was a relationship that mocked the passing of time. She died on 15 September 1872, and Disraeli was desolate. When he could bring himself to look through the papers in her desk he found a letter she had addressed to him in 1856.

' My own dear Husband,' it began, and after asking that they should be buried in the same grave, went on, ' And now God bless you, my dearest, kindest! You have been a perfect husband to me . . . Farewell, my dear Dizzy. Do not live alone, dearest. Some one I earnestly hope you may find as attached to you as your own devoted Mary Anne.'

For many months Disraeli was deeply depressed. Many women had a part in his life, for women were necessary to his existence. But there was only one Mary Anne.

Two years later, the ' exhausted volcanoes ' as he called the Liberal ministers sitting on the Treasury bench, gave a final rumble and went out. At the general election that followed the Conservatives had a large majority, and on 18 February 1874 Disraeli became Prime Minister for the second time; he remained in office for a full six years. But he was seventy, feeling his age and frequently laid up with attacks of gout, so he was obliged to leave most of the work to his subordinate ministers, Lord Salisbury in particular. Then in 1876, at the queen's suggestion, he was translated to the House of Lords as Earl of Beaconsfield. This, surely, was as high as he could climb ? 'I am dead,' he is reported to have said when leaving the House after his first sitting; 'dead, but in the Elysian Fields.'

If we consult the records of his second administration, we shall read about his purchase of a controlling interest in the Suez Canal in 1875, his proclamation of the queen as Empress of India in the following year, and then his extraordinary success at the Berlin Congress of 1878, when—war with Russia averted, Cyprus gained for the British Empire, and Turkey given a last chance of survival— he came back to England, bringing with him 'Peace with Honour'. Glittering strokes of policy these may have been, but in the balances of human welfare they are as nothing compared with the great measures of social progress which his government got placed in the Statute Book. Indeed, in the long list of Victorian administrations there is none to better Disraeli's second in this respect. And no one who has read *Sybil* will be at all surprised.

He was the first of our statesmen to recognize the existence of that political animal who seems so inexplicable to the Marxist theoretician—the Conservative working-man; in fact, he may claim a large part in having brought him into being, since it was his first government that gave him the parliamentary vote, and his second strengthened the position of trade unions in the national life. The Public Health Act of 1875 was a landmark in sanitary legislation, and other salutary measures passed by his Government included Acts for furthering the building of working-class houses, the regulation of the sale of food and drugs, and the enforcement of the Plimsoll line on merchant vessels.

At the general election in 1880 the political pendulum swung the other way, and in April a Liberal government took office under Gladstone. Lord Beaconsfield went into retirement, and at his age he knew that this time it was for good. In a letter to 'Madam and most beloved Sovereign' he wrote; 'Your Majesty is graciously pleased to ask whether I am alone. I have not seen, I may say, a human being since I returned from Westminster, a month ago; but

I have never had a dull moment. Solitude suits me, and so long as I can look at trees and books, I have always agreeable companions.' But inactivity bored him, and a month or so later he was writing to tell her that he had 'found it necessary to seek some relief in literary composition . . . a weakness, but one which organically, it seems, I cannot resist'. He felt sure that she would be interested—had he not in conversation sometimes spoken of 'We authors, Ma'am' ?—and he concluded with saying that the book would not be published for about a month but he hoped to be able to send a copy somewhat sooner, to her 'Who is the Sovereign not only of my person, but of my heart'.

The book in question was *Endymion*, the last of his novels, and in its pictures of political life of the times of Melbourne and Peel it is as clever and entertaining as any of its predecessors. Longmans paid him £10,000 for it, a sum such as had never been paid for a work of the kind.

That winter was a bitterly cold one, and for days Beaconsfield would lie on his sofa at Hughenden, trying to keep warm. In early spring he managed to get up to London, where he spoke occasionally in the House of Lords and dined with the Prince of Wales and other old friends. Towards the end of March he caught a chill, and took to his bed in his house in Curzon Street. His last letters to the queen were scrawled in pencil. She sent him primroses from Osborne by special messenger, wired every day from Windsor for the latest news, and would have visited him but for fear of exciting him overmuch.

On 31 March, as he lay in bed, he corrected the proofs for Hansard of his last speech in the Lords: 'I will not go down to posterity talking bad grammar,' he muttered. His last words are said to have been, 'I had rather live, but I am not afraid to die'.

Just before the end he rose from his pillows and assumed the posture so characteristic of him when about to make a speech in the House. He murmured something which the waiting friends could not catch, slipped back, and fell into the sleep from which there was no waking on 19 April 1881.

Gladstone, as Prime Minister, offered a public funeral and a grave in Westminster Abbey, but Beaconsfield's executors insisted on carrying out the terms of his will. He was buried in a grave just outside the little church in Hughenden park, between his wife and Mrs. Bridges Williams, an eccentric lady, his friend and Mary Anne's, who had insisted on leaving him a fortune. It was a simple funeral, but the Prince of Wales was there among the mourners, and

on the coffin was a wreath of fresh primroses from the queen,
bearing the words, 'His favourite flower,' and there was another,
also from her with the inscription, 'A token of true affection,
friendship, and respect'.

30

WILLIAM EWART GLADSTONE

THE GRAND OLD MAN, or G.O.M. for short: this was how they referred to Gladstone in the seventies and eighties and early nineties of the last century, and surely no popular appellation was better deserved.

For more than sixty years he was a member of the House of Commons. Between 1843 and 1892 he sat in ten Cabinets, and over four of them he presided as Prime Minister. When he first caught the ear of the House he was a beardless youth, with an earnest, intelligent countenance, dark and rather prominent eyebrows, and a fine head of jet-black hair; and still, in his eighties, when reduced to a bag of bones, his eyebrows beetling and his eyes glaring and bloodshot, his hair sparse and straggling, his thin neck emerging from an enormous winged collar, he rode the parliamentary storms in triumph. And his voice, a wonderful instrument, never lost its power of producing the noblest and most compelling music, fit accompaniment to the grandeur of his themes.

At length he died, an old, old man of nearly ninety, and tributes were paid to his memory such as few men have been given and fewer still have come anywhere near to deserving. At Westminster it fell to two of his stoutest opponents to declare the final verdict. Mr. Balfour, the leader in the House of Commons, spoke of him as ' the greatest member of the greatest deliberative assembly that the world has seen '. In the House of Lords, the Prime Minister, Lord Salisbury, came nearer to the heart of the matter. Mr. Gladstone, he said, would leave behind him ' the memory of a great Christian statesman ', he had provided an example, ' to which history hardly furnishes a parallel, of a great Christian man '.

William Ewart Gladstone was born on 29 December 1809, at No. 62, Rodney Street, Liverpool, the fourth son of John (afterwards Sir John) Gladstone by his second wife, Anne Robertson. He was named after William Ewart, a great friend of his father and like him an immigrant Scot and a prominent merchant of the city.

The family name was originally Gledstanes or Gladstones, and geneaologists have traced it back to a very early period in Scottish records. Gladstone himself described his forefathers as borderers, and said that whatever their status may have been in earlier times he had been unable to find any traces of their gentility later than the latter part of the seventeenth century. His grandfather, Thomas Gladstones, originally of Biggar in Lanarkshire, made his way to Leith, where he set himself up in a modest way as a corn-dealer. He had sixteen children and the eldest was John Gladstones, who was Gladstone's father. He was a man of stirling character, forceful and enterprising. At the age of nineteen he joined his father's business at Leith, and four years later, having saved £500, he moved to Liverpool where he was admitted into partnership by two corn-merchants. Soon after that he dropped the final ' s ' from his name, because it sounded awkward in the name of the firm. The business was mainly with the East Indies but in time John Gladstone became the owner of extensive sugar and coffee plantations in Jamaica and British Guiana (or Demerara, as it was called in those days). These were worked by negro slaves, a fact which was to cause a lot of bother to Gladstone at the outset of his parliamentary career.

John Gladstone was not only a highly successful merchant but an active citizen who became, as his son proudly recalled, a foremost member of the community. He took a great interest in politics. As a young man he was a Whig, but when he got on in the world he became a Canningite Tory, and took the lead in inviting Canning to stand for Liverpool in 1812. He himself sat in Parliament as a Tory from 1818 to 1827, and as an old man his services to the party were rewarded with a baronetcy on the recommendation of Sir Robert Peel. At about the same time as he changed his political allegiance he quietly abandoned the Presbyterianism in which he had been brought up and joined the Church of England.

Anne Robertson, Gladstone's mother, came from Dingwall, and was of Highland stock. Gladstone was, therefore, of unmixed Scotch origins, half Lowland borderer, half Highland clansman. ' I am not slow to claim the name of Scotsman,' he declared, when he had risen to become a great man in politics; ' not a drop of blood runs in my veins except what is derived from a Scottish ancestry.'

Among the earliest of Gladstone's recollections was Canning's staying at his father's house in Liverpool in 1812. ' Much enter-taining went on,' he related in an autobiographical fragment, ' and on the day of a great dinner I was taken down to the dining-room . . . set upon one of the chairs, standing, and directed to say to the company, "Ladies and gentlemen".'

In September 1821, when just on twelve, he was sent to Eton where he spent the next six years. The headmaster was Dr. Keate, a sadistic little bully who was known to have flogged over eighty boys on a single summer's day and in his old age expressed regret that he had not flogged a great many more. Gladstone was lucky: he got only one flogging, and was so happy at Eton that to him it was always 'the queen of all schools', even though he did not learn very much there.

From Eton he proceeded in the autumn of 1828 to Christ Church, Oxford. Here he studied hard and became an excellent classical scholar. At his finals in 1831 he came out a double first in classics and mathematics, twenty-three years after Peel had done the same thing.

Even as a schoolboy he had distinguished himself in the debating society at Eton, but it was at the Oxford Union, of which he became President, that he first displayed those powers of speech which were to win him his commanding position in the State. Very possibly he would never have become a politician but for a speech that he delivered at the Oxford Union in May 1831. In the light of his subsequent development it is interesting to learn that it was in support of a motion condemning the great Reform Bill as constituting a threat 'to change the form of the British Government, and ultimately to break up the whole fabric of society'. To the young men who heard it his speech seemed incomparably splendid, and when he had finished, one of them reported, 'we all of us felt that an epoch in our lives had occurred'.

On the strength of this dazzling performance the Duke of Newcastle, father of Gladstone's Eton friend Lord Lincoln, offered to use his influence to bring him in as Tory member for the borough of Newark. Gladstone found the proposal 'stunning and overpowering', but his conscience—that inconvenient conscience that was never to leave him alone—made him hesitate. Had not the Duke of Newcastle once declared Canning to have been 'the most profligate minister the country had ever had', and did he realize with what feelings of reverence Gladstone regarded him? He consulted his father, and the shrewd old Liverpool merchant made short work of his objections. Canning was dead, so what on earth did it matter *what* the duke had said about him? As for Gladstone's further fear that there were strings attached to the offer, his Grace had laid down no conditions and, furthermore, had most generously offered to go halves in the election expenses.

Gladstone's conscience being thus put at rest, he accepted the duke's offer, and at the general election—the first to be held after the passing of the Reform Bill—of December 1832, he was returned as one of the two members for Newark, virtually as the nominee of one of the biggest borough-mongers in the country. But the expense! During the contest the pubs had been kept open day and night, beer had flowed like water, and as early as the second day Gladstone's agent had told him that practically every man in the place was drunk. In the event the bill came to twice the £1,000 that had been first estimated. Gladstone was appalled, not only at the expense in which he had involved his father but at a system of representation which could result in a state of general intoxication.

At the opening of the 1833 session he took his seat in the House of Commons—the old house, that was burnt down in the following year—as a member of the Tory opposition under Peel. His first speech of any note was in defence of his father against allegations that his agent in Demerara had worked some of the slaves to death, but it is only fair to note that he did not defend slavery as an institution. It was something which had begun in crime, an atrocious crime (he admitted) but emancipation of the slaves before they had been prepared for it by proper instruction would be bound to have the most ruinous effects on the colonies, the country, and the slaves themselves. When he sat down he was warmly congratulated, not least by Lord Stanley, the Colonial Secretary, who said that he had never listened to any speech with greater pleasure.

When the emancipation bill became law in 1834, Gladstone's father received £75,000 in compensation for his 1609 Negro slaves who were liberated.

While steadily gaining in acceptance as a speaker, Gladstone also gave his full support to his party in the divisions. Some of the votes he cast point the difference between what he was then and what he later became. He supported the most repressive measures in Ireland. He voted against the admission of Jews to Parliament and of Dissenters to Oxford and Cambridge. He supported the Corn Law. He opposed the property tax and agreed to the window tax. He resisted a move for the abolition of flogging in the army save for mutiny and drunkenness. He voted against the ballot in parliamentary elections—a reform which his own Government carried forty years later. On the other hand, he voted with Lord Ashley, later Lord Shaftesbury, against postponing the beneficent policy of factory legislation.

So useful a party member had he proved himself that in 1834, when Sir Robert Peel was forming his first administration, he was appointed a junior lord of the Treasury, and after a few months

Peel transferred him to the Colonial Office as under-secretary. Here his official chief was Lord Aberdeen, so that it fell to Gladstone to represent the department in the House of Commons. Within a few months, however, Peel was compelled to resign, and for the next six years Gladstone was one of the Opposition.

Those years were taken up with his parliamentary duties, with several love affairs which came to nothing, and in writing and getting published a book on the relations of Church and State, in which he argued that since the Church of England possessed the monopoly of religious truth only its members were entitled to enjoy and exercise the full powers of citizenship. Such high-falutin notions found few sympathisers, and Gladstone had sense enough to realize, soon enough, that he had made a blunder. And yet the book may not have done him much real harm. Macaulay thought it of sufficient importance to make it the subject of an enormously long notice in the *Edinburgh Review*, in which, while dismissing Gladstone's argument as specious nonsense, he was unusually polite to Gladstone himself. He described him as ' a young man of unblemished character and of distinguished parliamentary talents, the rising hope of those stern and unbending Tories, who follow, reluctantly and mutinously, a leader [Sir Robert Peel], whose experience and eloquence are indispensable to them, but whose cautious temper and moderate opinions they abhor '.

When the book appeared Gladstone was in Italy, and at Rome he happened to come across an English family—the widowed Lady Glynne, with her sons Sir Stephen (Whig M.P. for Flint Burghs) and Henry, and her daughters Catherine and Mary—with whom he had become increasingly friendly in England. He and Sir Stephen had been friends at Eton and Oxford, and Gladstone had stayed at Hawarden Castle, the family seat in Flintshire. Already he had been attracted to Catherine Glynne, a charming young girl, about two years younger than he was, tall and slender, with brown hair, sapphire-blue eyes, and warm-tinted complexion, and now the attraction turned into something much deeper. The party went on to Naples, and Gladstone made the ascent of Vesuvius with the two girls, after which they all returned to Rome. There on a January evening in 1839, when they were viewing the Colosseum by moonlight, Gladstone was able to catch Catherine on her own for a few moments, and he seized the opportunity to speak of his love.

Perhaps the girl had expected a somewhat warmer approach, but she asked for time to consider the matter. The next day he sent her a long and terribly involved letter—one sentence runs to 141

words and takes up a whole paragraph—containing a formal proposal of marriage. She replied most kindly and appreciatively, but
said that if he insisted on an immediate answer it would be in the
negative. Weeks and months passed, and she kept on putting him
off, until he was almost off his head with worry. June came, they
were in London, and he felt that he could not bear the suspense much
longer. Then one evening he met her at a garden party given by
Lady Shelley at Parson's Green. They strolled by the river, and he
told her that he had wanted to be a clergyman but was now resolved
on showing that a politician's life could be a truly Christian one,
and she delighted him with the information that she had read his
book and had copied out several passages in order to learn them by
heart. Almost overwhelmed by such a demonstration of trustful-
ness, he proposed again, and this time the answer was yes.

A few days later the twenty-one-year-old Lord Lyttelton became
engaged to Catherine's sister Mary, and it was decided that there
should be a double wedding. This took place at Hawarden parish
church on 25 July 1839, and was the occasion for much local
rejoicing. Sir Francis Doyle, who was Gladstone's best man, wrote
a poem for the double event, and among the stanzas referring to
Catherine are these:

> High hopes are thine, oh! eldest flower;
> Great duties to be greatly done;
> To soothe, in many a toil-worn hour,
> The noble heart which thou hast won.
>
> Covet not then the rest of those
> Who sleep through life unknown to fame;
> Fate grants not passionless repose
> To her who weds a glorious name.
>
> He presses on through calm and storm
> Unshaken, let what will betide;
> Thou hast an office to perform,
> To be his answering spirit bride . . .

Most girls might have been put off by such a prospect, but not
Catherine. For all the nearly sixty years of their life together she
was as perfect a wife as even Gladstone might hope for.

She belonged to what may be described as the Whig aristocracy.
She was a granddaughter of George Grenville, the Prime Minister
who passed the Stamp Act, and niece of Lord Grenville, Prime

Minister in 1806; her great-aunt was wife to Chatham, and William Pitt was a cousin. Thus she was related by birth to four Prime Ministers and was destined to become the wife of a fifth.

Born into the landed gentry, Catherine Glynne was not an intellectual but a bright and cheerful lover of country-house life, an excellent horsewoman and expert in the then very popular ladies' sport of archery. Every morning throughout her long life she took a cold bath. She had the great gift of making friends easily, and keeping them. In the years 1840 to 1854 she bore her husband eight children, seven of whom survived. She was not particularly interested in politics; but when, soon after their marriage, her husband asked her which she would prefer—to know nothing of the great matters of State in which he might become involved and so be entirely free from all responsibility, or to know everything and be bound to secrecy—she unhesitatingly chose the latter.

Whereas Gladstone was the soul of method, neat in his habits, as thrifty of his time as of his money, the woman he married was just the reverse, and she used to tease him with the remark that it was good for him that he should have such an untidy, unmethodical wife. And yet she was very much the mistress in her own house. She managed their domestic life with an easy efficiency, and tended him with a motherly devotion. Laughingly, she used to tell him that while no doubt he knew how to govern the country, he had much better leave the times of the trains to her. She encouraged him to take his daily exercise, such as chopping down trees in Hawarden park, and in bad weather she made sure that he was always well wrapped up. There was always something hot for his supper when he came home late from the House. She accompanied him whenever he had an important speech to make, and observed him from the Speaker's gallery. With her own hands she prepared the egg-flip which he sipped in the pauses of his long-sustained oratory. She protected him from bores, and firmly shut the door on intruders.

As sincerely religious as he was, she was much more cheerful about it. Together they strove to make their union a truly Christian marriage. He was absolutely devoted to her, as she was to him, but she had none of his inhibitions about showing it. In her letters she addressed him as ' My own darling ', ' dear old thing ', ' my precious thing ', and ' my dear old oak ', and she might conclude with some such assertion as ' I would go the world's end for you . . .'

*   *   *

Two years after they were married, Gladstone received an appointment in Peel's second administration. It was nothing much, only Vice-President of the Board of Trade, and he was bitterly disappointed. He had expected a post with a seat in the Cabinet, and he was given a very minor post connected with trade, a subject of which he knew next to nothing. Peel urged him to accept, however, and pointed out that the head of the department would be a peer, Lord Ripon (the man who as Lord Goderich had been Prime Minister in 1827), and so all the business of representing the department in the House of Commons would fall upon his shoulders.

Years afterwards Gladstone described to John Morley how he felt about the proposal. ' I was totally ignorant both of political economy and of the commerce of the country. I might have said that my mind was in regard to all those matters a " sheet of white paper ", except that it was doubtless coloured by a traditional prejudice of Protection, which had then quite recently become a distinctive mark of Conservatism. In a spirit of ignorant mortification I said to myself at the moment: the science of politics deals with the government of men, but I am set to govern packages.'

Peel knew him better, perhaps, than he knew himself, and Gladstone had not been long at the Board of Trade when he discovered that ' packages ' were nothing like so uninteresting as he had supposed. In fact, we find his wife confiding in her diary that ' He works hard all the time at home, and it is a little dreary sometimes.'

Within a few months, Ripon had been transferred to another position in the Government, and Gladstone succeeded him as President of the Board of Trade and entered the Cabinet, this when he was only thirty-three. As such he proved himself Peel's ablest (and most sincerely admiring) lieutenant, and his mind followed his leader's in the slow transition from Protection to Free Trade.

In the great struggle over the Corn Laws, Gladstone played only a minor part, but in his own department there were reforms for which he was very largely responsible. In 1843 he secured the removal of restrictions on the export of machinery, and in the following year the first Telegraph Act was passed. Even more important was his work in connection with the railways, of which an immense extension was about to take place. He was responsible for two Acts of Parliament which stand out in the history of railways. The first, in 1843, laid down that there must be some form of State supervision of railway development and working; the second, in the next year, required that every railway company should

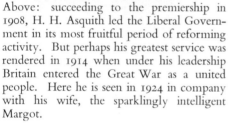

Above: succeeding to the premiership in 1908, H. H. Asquith led the Liberal Government in its most fruitful period of reforming activity. But perhaps his greatest service was rendered in 1914 when under his leadership Britain entered the Great War as a united people. Here he is seen in 1924 in company with his wife, the sparklingly intelligent Margot.

Britain's first Labour Prime Minister was J. Ramsay MacDonald, (above right), the story of whose rise from the humblest origins to the highest position in the state is full-charged with the elements of romance, splendid achievement, and final pathos. Twice he headed Labour governments, and then in 1931 became Prime Minister in an all-party administration.

Right: Stanley Baldwin was never so happy (at least he so declared) as when he was able to exchange the clamours of Westminster for the peace and quiet of his native Worcestershire. Three times Prime Minister, he reached a vast new public in his broadcast talks, charged as they were with homely wisdom and expressions of pride in the English heritage.

Never, surely, has a Prime Minister had such a welcome as Neville Chamberlain's on his return from the Munich conference in 1938. War had seemed inevitable and imminent—but now it was 'Peace with honour!'

Surrounded by a wildly enthusiastic crowd, he flourishes the scrap of paper, bearing his signature and Hitler's, on which is expressed 'the desire of our two peoples never to go to war with one another again'.

run at least one train each day, stopping at every station if required, on which there should be good covered seating accommodation for third-class passengers at a fare not in excess of one penny per mile. These 'Parliamentary trains', as they came to be called, proved of immense advantage to the travelling public.

Early in 1845 Gladstone resigned from the Government because of his objection to the proposal to increase the annual grant made to the college at Maynooth outside Dublin where men were trained for the Roman Catholic priesthood. To resign over so small a matter was regarded as an act of political prudery. Disraeli expressed the opinion that Gladstone's political career was over, and Peel complained to a friend that 'really I have great difficulty sometimes in comprehending what Gladstone means'. Gladstone regretted his step almost as soon as he had made it, and he voted for the bill's second reading. He remained on good terms with his former colleagues, and when Peel reconstituted his ministry for the specific purpose of carrying Free Trade he offered Gladstone the post of Colonial Secretary, which he was quite glad to accept. But as a new Cabinet minister he was obliged to seek re-election, and the Duke of Newcastle made it quite plain that he would no longer get his support at Newark. As a Conservative Free Trader, Gladstone found great difficulty in finding a seat, and it was not until the general election of 1847 that he was returned as the junior of the two members for Oxford University. Thus it happened that he was out of the House of Commons, though still a minister, when the abolition of the Corn Laws was being achieved.

When Peel's government came to an end, Gladstone followed his leader into political eclipse. He was ranked among the Peelites, who at first under Peel and then, after Peel's death, under Lord Aberdeen, supported a policy of liberal conservatism of which Free Trade was a principal feature. But, as he stated years later, 'the whole lifetime of the Parliament of 1847–52 was one during which my political life was in abeyance'. This was because he was pre-occupied with trying to preserve the Glynnes from having to go bankrupt as a consequence of heavy losses incurred in a small mining venture in Staffordshire. Towards the close of 1847 there was a great crisis, when it seemed as though Hawarden Castle would have to be sold, but now Gladstone stepped into the breach. For those five years 'the whole conduct of the seemingly all but hopeless struggle to maintain the estate, and repair the disaster fell on me'. But he did not complain, since the time was in no wise wasted: the business 'supplied, in fact, my education as Finance Minister'. In the end he succeeded, but only after a quarter of a million of his own money had been employed in the work of rescue. Many years later Gladstone paid off the balance of the debts, and the property became his.

For fifty years Hawarden Castle was his home, the place where he enjoyed unbroken domestic happiness. As year followed year, he loved the place more and more, and until he was an old man his favourite—indeed, his only—exercise was a spell of tree-felling and wood-chopping in the thousand acres of surrounding parklands.

In part it was a very natural desire to escape for a while from the Hawarden entanglement that led Gladstone to take his family on holiday to Naples in the autumn of 1850. The trip was to have the most momentous consequences. At that period Naples was ruled over by Ferdinand II, King of the Two Sicilies, who two years earlier had earned the nickname of 'Bomba' because of his inhuman bombardment of his kingdom's principal towns when they revolted against his tyranny. Gladstone must have known of this, but he was not particularly concerned until one day his friend James Lacaita, the legal adviser to the British Embassy, took him to the courtroom where Poerio, one of the leaders of the abortive rising, was on trial.

Gladstone was horrified at the way the trial was conducted, and even more so at the sentence that was passed—twenty-four years' imprisonment *in irons*. He proceeded to make his own investigations, and discovered that there were thousands of men and women imprisoned in the Neapolitan gaols in conditions of cruelty and degradation whose only crime was having dared to resist an abominable tyranny. As a result of what he saw and heard his whole life was changed.

He returned to England in a state of Vesuvian eruption. At the station in London he was met by Sir James Phillimore, an old friend, who was the bearer of a letter from Lord Stanley asking him to call on him at once in connection with the Conservative ministry he was attempting to form. Gladstone could hardly be bothered to listen; he stuffed the letter into his pocket and drive off to his home in Carlton House Terrace. There another messenger arrived, begging him to call on Stanley without delay. 'I did not like to stickle, and went,' Gladstone wrote in his diary. 'He told me his object was that I should take office with him—*any* office.' But when he learnt that Stanley was contemplating a small duty on imported corn he turned the invitation down.

Then he went to Lord Aberdeen, the leader of the Peelites, and urged him to take up the question of the prisoners at Naples. Aberdeen was ' as always, kind, just, moderate, humane ', and agreed to see what could be done by way of private remonstrances—although, to tell the truth, he was not at all anxious to get involved in the matter. How often had he criticized Lord Palmerston for interfering in the affairs of other countries, and now he was being urged to do just that very thing!

Gladstone waited anxiously and with growing impatience for any outcome to Lord Aberdeen's intervention; he could not bear the thought of those poor people rotting their lives away in Bomba's dungeons. After four months had gone by he sent to the printers a pamphlet he had written with the title, *A Letter to Lord Aberdeen*.

The pamphlet appeared at the beginning of July 1851, and it was followed before the month was out by a second *Letter*. Not since the days of the French Revolution had there been so dramatic an appeal to public opinion. What is this Government of the King of the Two Sicilies ? Gladstone demanded, and he gave the answer: ' *It is the negation of God erected into a system of government !* '

The sensation was profound. At one stroke Gladstone had become not only a national but a world figure. Everywhere, the lovers of freedom hailed his name and begged him to become the champion of peoples rightly struggling to be liberated from their oppressors. No one was more pleased than the Home Secretary, Lord Palmerston. He gave orders that copies of the *Letters* should be sent to the British representatives at every court in Europe, and when the Neapolitan envoy in London protested he refused to accept delivery of what he described as a ' flimsy tissue of bare assertions and reckless denials, mixed up with coarse ribaldry and commonplace abuse ', and warned the Neapolitan government that unless they set to work to correct the manifold and grave abuses to which Mr. Gladstone had drawn their attention their ' long-continued and widespread injustice would assuredly bring upon them a violent revolution '. And when Gladstone was criticized in the House of Commons, Palmerston gave him solid support. The right honourable gentleman was to be commended, he maintained; for instead of seeking amusements, diving into volcanoes and exploring excavated cities, he had visited prisons, descended into dungeons, examined cases of illegality and injustice, and had then sought to arouse the public opinion of Europe against them.

Gladstone cannot have been altogether pleased with Palmerston's jaunty congratulations, and he noted that the applause was coming in the main from the Liberal benches. Surely the Conservatives ought to have been equally concerned? He pondered these things in his heart . . .

* * *

Early in 1852 a weak Conservative administration was formed under Stanley, now Lord Derby, with Disraeli as Chancellor of the Exchequer. Disraeli's first budget was eagerly awaited; he knew that the Government were doomed, but he resolved to go down fighting. His speech on 16 December 1852 was a *tour de force*, and when he resumed his seat he was given an ovation.

Gladstone rose at once to answer him. Most men there thought that he could not possibly outshine Disraeli's brilliant performance. A great thunderstorm was raging without, but no one noticed the flashes of lightning or heard the tremendous rolls of thunder. Disraeli's speech, ran *The Times* report, had been in every respect worthy of his oratorical reputation, full of telling hits, pointed and bitter retorts, invective pushed to the limit of virulence, but Gladstone's was pitched throughout in a high tone of moral feeling. ' When he concluded the House might well feel proud of him, and of themselves.'

From that hour Gladstone was recognized as being in the direct line of succession with the greatest masters of parliamentary eloquence, with Chatham and Burke, Fox and Pitt. His speech also marked the beginning of the duel between him and Disraeli that went on for a quarter of a century.

They were not friends to begin with, and over the years their relationship descended into jealous rivalry and intense distrust and hostility. Looking back at the close of his career, Gladstone assured John Morley that ' for all the deterioration in our public life, one man, and one man alone, is responsible—Disraeli. He is the grand corrupter . . .' This was mild, however, with what Disraeli said of him. In a letter to Lord Derby written in 1876 Disraeli wrote: ' Posterity will do justice to that unprincipled maniac Gladstone— extraordinary mixture of envy, vindictiveness, hypocrisy, and superstition; and with one commanding characteristic—whether preaching, praying, speechifying or scribbling—never a gentleman!' A year or two later he described him as ' a sophistical rhetorician, inebriated with the exuberance of his own verbosity'.

When the division was taken on that December morning the Conservative government were defeated, as Disraeli had expected them to be. Lord Derby thereupon resigned, and Lord Aberdeen formed his coalition ministry. In this Gladstone was Chancellor of the Exchequer, and soon it was his turn to produce a Budget.

For weeks beforehand he toiled at his desk, thirteen, fourteen, fifteen hours a day. When his proposals were laid before the Cabinet some of the members jibbed, but he carried the doubters with him. On the Sunday beforehand he went to church as usual, and read Dante, but then ' I was obliged to give several hours to my figures '. The next day he walked and went for a drive with Mrs. Gladstone, and then at half-past four went to the House. ' Spoke four and three-quarter hours in detailing the financial measures,' his diary records, ' and my strength stood out well, thank God.' This simple entry relates to one of the great parliamentary performances of the century.

What men said about the Budget is not so important as what it proposed. The great work that Peel had begun eleven years before was carried forward almost to completion. Nearly a hundred and forty customs duties were extinguished, and a hundred and fifty lowered. The tea duty was to be reduced in stages over three years from 2s. to 1s. a lb. The duty on soap, which had contributed so largely in keeping the people dirty, was swept away, although it had been bringing in over a million a year. A uniform receipt-stamp was introduced. The duty on insurance policies was reduced from half a crown to sixpence on the hundred pounds. Advertisements in the newspapers were relieved of duty. Gladstone also declared his intention of reducing the income-tax, then standing at sevenpence in the pound, by gradual stages until at the end of seven years he hoped to be able to abolish it altogether.

Gladstone's budget, wrote Greville in his Journal, ' has raised him to a great political elevation, and, what is of far greater consequence than the measure itself, it has given the country the assurance of a *man* equal to great political necessities, and fit to lead parties and direct Governments '.

But for the outbreak of the Crimean War Gladstone might well have succeeded in getting rid of the obnoxious income-tax. But as it was, he had to find the money to pay for a war with which he was in little sympathy. In 1854 he doubled the income-tax and raised the duties on spirits, sugar, and malt. To his wife he wrote, ' War! War! War! I fear it will swallow up everything good and useful.'

In the coalition government, Gladstone was sitting with Liberals, but he still maintained some sort of connection with the Conservatives. And yet, when Lord Derby offered him office in 1855 and again in 1858 he declined. He remained out of office until 1859, when Lord Palmerston invited him to join the administration he was in process of forming, in any capacity he liked to name.

Only a few days before Gladstone had voted with Disraeli and the Conservatives in support of the Derby government, and he had never disguised his opinion of Palmerston as a wily old opportunist. On one occasion, indeed, he had described him as the worst Minister that ever was. But now, as he wrote later, ' Never had I an easier question to determine than when I was asked to join the [Palmerston] government. I can hardly now think how I could have looked any one in the face, had I refused my aid (such as it is) at such a time and under such circumstances.'

Of course he was bitterly assailed by those he was leaving. It was supposed that he had made a careful calculation, that since Palmerston and Lord John Russell, the Liberal leaders, were both years older than he was the time would soon come when he might become not only leader of the party but Prime Minister. Such suspicions do Gladstone a grave injustice. What really decided him might be contained in one word—Italy.

Just at that time the war of Italian liberation had begun, and all Gladstone's hopes were concentrated on victory for Garibaldi. Now at length those poor fellows in the Neapolitan prisons might be avenged! Throughout his long career Palmerston had been the professed champion of European liberalism—the principle of Nationality—while Derby and the Conservatives had been lukewarm at best. In joining Palmerston, Gladstone was convinced that he would be doing God's will. On 18 June 1859, then, he kissed hands as Chancellor of the Exchequer in the Palmerston administration.

It was the parting of the ways for Gladstone, although there was little or nothing in the nature of a conversion. On domestic issues there was little difference between Palmerston and himself, while on the paramount issue of foreign policy they were completely at one. But no doubt about it, henceforth the man who had been in his youth the ' rising hope of the stern and unbending Tories ' was the acknowledged leader of the forces of Liberalism.

For the next six years he managed the country's finances with a masterful efficiency and vigour. His Budget statements became red-letter days in the parliamentary calendar. ' Just as Macaulay made thousands read history who before had turned from it as dry and repulsive,' wrote John Morley in his classic ' life ', ' so Mr. Gladstone made thousands eager to follow the national balance-sheet, and the whole nation became his audience, interested in him and his themes and in the House where his dazzling wonders were performed.'

The Budget of 1860 that opened the new series was described as 'epoch-making' and 'the great Budget'. Gladstone nearly worked himself to death in preparing it, so that his emaciated condition alarmed his friends. But the speech with which he introduced it on 10 February 1860 was acknowledged as one of the most extraordinary triumphs ever witnessed in the House of Commons. 'Spoke 5–9 without great exhaustion,' he noted in his diary afterwards; 'aided by a great stock of egg and wine '—the concoction in a bottle that Mrs. Gladstone had prepared with her own hands. 'Thank God!' the entry concludes; 'Home at 11. This was the most arduous operation I have ever had in Parliament.'

While the income-tax was raised to 10d., in order to pay for equipping the navy with ironclads and for a military expedition to Peking, Gladstone was able to eject 'our old friend Protection' from 'those holes and corners in which he had found pretty comfortable shelter and good living ', so that duties on only 48 articles were left on the tariff, and those were for revenue purposes. Free Trade was victorious all along the line.

As Chancellor of the Exchequer, Gladstone looked upon himself as 'the trusted and confidential steward of the public ', as one who 'is under a sacred obligation with regard to all that he consents to spend '. What he called the spirit of expenditure was anathema to him. 'Economy is the first and great article of my financial creed ', he declared. And again; 'It is the mark of a chicken-hearted Chancellor when he shrinks from upholding economy in detail, when because it is a matter of only two or three thousand pounds, he says that it is no matter. He is ridiculed, no doubt, for what is called candle-ends and cheeseparings, but he is not worth his salt if he is not ready to save what are called candle-ends and cheeseparings in the cause of the country.'

This was ' Gladstonian finance' in action, and a fine thing it was in some respects. Year after year the burden of taxation was steadily reduced, and the cost of living went down. Gladstone was delighted when he was able to introduce the halfpenny postcard, and one of the proudest of his achievements was the establishment in 1861 of the Post Office Savings Bank. This excursion into State enterprise was very much the exception, however. Gladstone had no conception of the State as being the instrument of social progress, and he had some excuse when we remember the inadequacy of the governmental machinery. There was no Civil Service such as we understand the term until he introduced it in 1870. Nevertheless, there is a good deal of truth in Lloyd George's assertion that Gladstone, although much the biggest figure in our political history, had no social consciousness.

All the same, as the years passed he grew much broader-minded and more generous in his democratic expression. At a time when it was considered undignified for a statesman to appear on a public platform he developed a remarkable gift for popular oratory. Starting in Lancashire, he addressed large audiences of working men and encouraged them to take a practical interest in the way they were governed. The stricter sort of church people also noted with alarm that he was getting on quite good terms with Nonconformists, and they were horrified when he made his proposal for the disestablishment of the Anglican church in Ireland. These tendencies did him no good with his constituents at Oxford, and it was hardly surprising that at the general election in 1865 he lost his seat.

Fortunately, he had taken the precaution of getting himself nominated also for a division of Lancashire, and on the very day the university threw him out he addressed an audience of six thousand in the Free Trade Hall in Manchester. ' At last, my friends,' he declaimed, ' I am come among you, and I am come among you *unmuzzled*.' The enthusiasm was terrific, and he was elected as the third of the constituency's three members, the others being Tories.

A few weeks later Lord Palmerston died, Earl Russell succeeded him as Prime Minister, and Gladstone took over the leadership of the House of Commons while remaining as Chancellor. A further measure of parliamentary reform had been decided upon, and Gladstone introduced a bill, the terms of which pleased nobody and frightened a great many, so that it had to be withdrawn. It was in the course of the debate on the second reading that Gladstone made the striking declaration, ' You cannot fight against the future! Time is on our side. . . .'

Russell's government resigned on 28 June 1866, and he was followed in the premiership by Lord Derby at the head of a Conservative ministry. Then Disraeli, as leader of the House of Commons, proceeded with what Gladstone denounced as ' diabolical cunning ', to introduce and carry a Reform Bill which was far more sweeping and generally popular than the Gladstonian measure. Gladstone's bill would have added about 400,000 men to the electoral register; Disraeli's added over twice that number, so that the total electorate came to not far short of two and a half millions.

But if Disraeli had hopes that the new electors would cast their votes for the Conservatives who had enfranchised them he was disappointed. At the general election that was held in November 1868 the Liberals won a great victory, although Gladstone himself was beaten in Lancashire. As on the earlier occasion, however, he had been nominated for a second seat, this time at Greenwich, and here he was successful.

As soon as the result of the election was known Disraeli, who had succeeded Lord Derby as Prime Minister nine months earlier, tendered his resignation. The queen sent forthwith for Gladstone, who since Earl Russell's retirement had been the Liberal party leader.

The summons from Windsor reached him on the afternoon of 1 December 1868, when he was cutting down a tree in Hawarden park. 'I was standing by him,' wrote Mr. Evelyn Ashley afterwards, ' holding his coat on my arm while he in his shirtsleeves was wielding an axe to cut down a tree. Up came a telegraph messenger. He took the telegram, opened it and read it, then handed it to me, speaking only two words, " Very significant," and at once resumed his work. . . . After a few minutes, the blows ceased, and Mr. Gladstone, resting on the handle of his axe, looked up and with deep earnestness in his voice and with great intensity in his face, exclaimed, " My mission is to pacify Ireland." He then resumed his task, and never said another word until the tree was down.'

Gladstone had no difficulty in forming his Government, with himself as First Lord of the Treasury, Robert Lowe as Chancellor of the Exchequer, and John Bright (Cobden's associate in the Anti-Corn Law League of a generation before), as President of the Board of Trade. Gladstone always spoke of this Cabinet as one of the best instruments for government that was ever constructed. Certainly it was responsible for some reforms of the greatest importance. As he had resolved, Gladstone's first efforts were concentrated on ' pacifying Ireland ', and he carried through a bill for the disestablishment of the Irish Church and several measures for the reform of land tenure.

More productive of permanent good was the bill introduced by W. E. Forster providing for the establishment throughout the country of a national system of elementary education. This bill did *not* make education either free or compulsory, but it provided for the setting up of school boards to fill the gaps that existed in the voluntary system of mainly parochial schools. It became law in 1870, and it would have been a much better measure than it was but for the sectarian squabblings of the supporters of Church and Chapel.

Other measures of outstanding importance were the Ballot Act of 1872 and the abolition by royal warrant of the purchase of commissions in the Army and Navy. But before long there were signs of popular reaction against the spate of legislation. In October 1873 Disraeli was writing that the Gladstone administration had ' harassed every trade, worried every profession, and assailed or menaced every class, institution, and species of property in the country ', and that the country was making up its mind to bring ' this career of plundering and blundering ' to a close. After some discomforting divisions, Gladstone decided on dissolving Parliament. At the general election the Liberals suffered a severe reverse, and on 17 February 1874 Gladstone resigned.

*   *   *

This first premiership of Gladstone's might have been far more pleasant and profitable if he had succeeded in retaining the queen's friendship and trust. Until some years after the Prince Consort's death she liked him well enough, because the Prince had done the same. But even while he was Chancellor of the Exchequer there were occasions of disharmony, and as early as 1862 we find Mrs. Gladstone urging her husband to ' *pet* the Queen, and for once believe you can, you dear old thing '. Gladstone was not much of a courtier, however, and he began to find the queen more and more difficult to handle.

A profound believer in monarchy as a Divinely ordained institution, he also held the view that the queen owed a duty to her subjects. He could not but be aware of the growing republican agitation, in which Joseph Chamberlain was then prominent, and he urged upon the queen that instead of burying herself away in widow's weeds at Windsor or Balmoral she should show herself and take an active interest in the welfare of her people.

Then there was the question of the Prince of Wales—that ' unemployed youth ', as he was sometimes unsympathetically described. Gladstone suggested that he should be given something to do, and the job he favoured was Lord Lieutenant of Ireland. He also proposed that the Prince and his charming consort, Princess Alexandra, might deputize for the queen sometimes, at courts and other social and official functions. The queen took all these suggestions in very bad part. She resented them as intrusions, and when Gladstone still insisted on putting them forward she started complaining of his manner of approach. The Prime Minister, she grumbled, spoke to her as though he was addressing a public meeting.

As time passed, relations between the queen and the Prime Minister deteriorated further. Gladstone suspected that some of his political rivals, Disraeli in particular, were not above trying to prejudice her against him; and there was one very special activity of Gladstone that might well lead to suspicious gossip.

It would seem that soon after his marriage Gladstone embarked on a personal crusade, a mission of rescue among the women of the London streets. For forty years he made it his practice, at least one evening in each week whenever possible, to patrol that part of the West End that lies between Piccadilly, Soho, and the Thames Embankment. To begin with, he waited to be accosted, but as he grew accustomed to the habits of his quarry it was he who very often did the accosting. He would speak to the girl with kindness and courtesy, inquire into her circumstances, and then, without a word of unctuous moralizing or reproof, invite her to accompany him home, where his wife would be waiting to offer her supper and a bed. Then in the morning they would be in a position to discuss ways and means whereby she might be restored to a useful and respectable life.

Very often, as may well be supposed, his advances were rebuffed and the woman turned from him in distrust or indignation. But in innumerable others he was successful. Over the years he spent a very large sum of money on this work of human salvage.

Of course, there were occasional incidents of acute embarrassment and even attempted blackmail. Time after time Gladstone's friends remonstrated with him about his nocturnal excursions, pointing out the extreme danger there was to a man in his position of having his actions misconstrued and misrepresented. Gladstone listened, and sometimes promised to be more circumspect in future. But in fact it was not until 1886 that, following upon further representations from Lord Rosebery, he agreed to cease his rescue work altogether.

If the queen *did* hear some whisper of these extraordinary goings on, it would not be surprising if it contributed to her feelings of unease and lack of confidence.

* * *

Gladstone took his political reverse much to heart. He was now in his middle sixties, and he decided that the time had come for him to retire from active politics. He refused the peerage that the queen offered him, and resigned the leadership of the Liberal party though he still remained a M.P. He—and everybody else—would have been amazed if they had been told that more than twenty years of the most sustained political effort lay ahead.

Gladstone might have remained in retirement if in the spring of 1876 the Bulgarians had not risen against their Turkish oppressors, and almost at once been suppressed with what was described as atrocious cruelty. The news of what was happening in the Balkan villages and valleys penetrated to Gladstone's library at Hawarden, and the man who had been outraged by the cruelties of King Bomba was again stirred to tremendous wrath and indignation. In August he started work on a pamphlet, and finished it in a week. It was rushed through the press and came out in early September.

The Bulgarian Horrors and the Question of the East, as it was called, took the public by storm. It was the *Letters to Lord Aberdeen* over again, only more so. Forty thousand copies were sold in the first three or four days, two hundred thousand by the end of the month. Not until the exposures of German atrocities in Belgium in 1914 was there anything like it. ' Basest and blackest outrages upon record within the present century, if not within the memory of man . . . foul Satanic orgies . . . abominable and bestial lusts . . . scenes at which Hell itself might almost blush . . .' From the record of torture and violation and massacre Gladstone moved on to a tremendous exhortation. ' Let the Turks now carry away their abuses in the only possible manner, namely by carrying off themselves . . . from the province they have desolated and profaned.'

Just as he had a quarter of a century earlier, Gladstone succeeded in arousing public interest and even the public conscience; there was no question of his returning to the peace and quiet of Hawarden. Disraeli, who had endeavoured to pour cold water on the agitation, was compelled to act, and at Berlin he achieved what he called ' peace with honour'. Gladstone scoffed at the pretension, and resolved to challenge the Government on their record of foreign intervention, in support of the Turks in Europe, in Afghanistan, and against the Zulus in South Africa.

After the general election of 1874 Gladstone had resolved not to stand again for Greenwich, and he now sought a new political base. A safe seat was offered him in Edinburgh, but he was in fighting mood and he declined it. Instead he accepted an invitation to become Liberal candidate for the county of Midlothian, then held by a Conservative. The Midlothian Conservative was described to Gladstone as a Tory of the hardest and narrowest type, so that the fight was likely to be fierce.

The campaign that followed was perhaps the most dramatic in our political history. Leaving Liverpool with his wife and daughter on 24 November 1879, Gladstone proceeded to Edinburgh. ' The journey,' he entered in his diary, ' was really more like a triumphal procession.' Nothing like it had been seen before in Britain. It was a bleak winter day, but the stations where the train stopped were crowded, hundreds gathered at bridges and crossings just to see the express roar through. At Carlisle there was a public reception, and at Hawick and Galashiels great multitudes were gathered to hear him on this first of ' whistle-stops '. When he reached Edinburgh, after nine hours of it (to quote Morley's account), ' the night had fallen upon the most picturesque street in all our island, but its whole length was crowded as it has never been crowded before or since by a dense multitude, transported with delight that their hero was at last among them '. Gladstone entered in his diary that night, ' I have never gone through a more extraordinary day '.

With Lord Rosebery as his host, Gladstone spent the next weeks in an almost unbroken succession of public engagements. People came from as far away as the Hebrides to hear him speak. Where there were six thousand seats in a hall there were applications for forty or fifty thousand. In speech after speech, Gladstone addressed farmers, peasants, weavers, villagers, artisans—and he never talked down to any of them. His language was the same as in the House of Commons, and much of what he told them must have been beyond their comprehension. But one thing they understood: his appeal to their moral judgment. After he had urged that they should seek to preserve the world's peace, foster the strength of the empire by wise laws, and avoid needless and entangling engagements, he went on to demand that our foreign policy should be inspired by such love of freedom as had marked Canning, and Palmerston, and Russell, to acknowledge the equal rights of all nations. ' Remember,' he thundered, ' that the sanctity of life in the hill villages of Afghanistan, among the winter snows, is as inviolable in the eye of Almighty God as can be your own. Remember that He who has united you as human beings in the same flesh and blood, has bound you by the law of mutual love; that mutual love is not limited by the shores of this island, is not limited by the boundaries of Christian civilization . . .'

On the return journey the scenes of unparalleled enthusiasm were repeated. They got back to Hawarden on 3 December, and Gladstone's niece wrote that Mrs. Gladstone had at once taken to her bed but that Uncle William was ' as fresh as paint '.

The general election did not come until March 1880. From first to last Gladstone was captain-general of the Liberal hosts. In a series of discourses spread over a fortnight ' I have hammered with all my poor might at the fabric of the present Tory power'. The campaign was remarkable in that now the two great parties were ranged against each other as nationally organized and directed bodies—on the one hand the National Union of Conservative Associations, founded in 1872, and on the other the National Liberal Federation, founded in 1877. Gladstone also detected a clear-cut division of the electorate such as had never been seen before.

' The great trial proceeds, gentlemen,' he said in one of his campaign speeches. ' We have great forces arrayed against us. Apparently we cannot make our appeal to the aristocracy, excepting the distinguished and enlightened minority . . . whose feelings are with those of the people . . . I am sorry to say we cannot reckon upon what is called the landed interest, we cannot reckon upon the clergy of the established church either in England or in Scotland, subject again and always to the most noble exceptions . . . We cannot reckon upon the wealth of the country, nor upon the rank of the country, nor upon the influence which wealth and rank usually bring . . .' But, he went on, ' above all these, and behind all these, there is something greater than these—there is the nation itself! '

From the classes, then, Gladstone turned to the masses, and he had his reward. He himself was returned at Midlothain by 1579 votes to 1368 for his Conservative opponent, Lord Dalkeith. For a fortnight the results were coming in, and soon Gladstone was entering in his diary, ' The triumph grows and grows; to God be the praise! ' The final results gave the Conservatives under Lord Beaconsfield about 240 seats against the Liberals with 347 and 65 Irish Nationalists. Beaconsfield resigned before the meeting of the new Parliament, and the question was, who should be Prime Minister ?

On the face of it, Gladstone was only a private member, but Lord Granville, the Liberal leader in the House of Lords, and Lord Hartington, his opposite number in the Commons, were in no doubt that Gladstone must resume the Liberal party leadership and become Prime Minister.

The queen was horrified at the idea. As she expressed herself in a letter to Sir Henry Ponsonby, her private secretary, ' She will sooner *abdicate* than send for or have anything to do with that *half-mad fire-brand* who would ruin everything, and be a Dictator.' But she had no choice. The general election had been a duel between the two greatest political personalities of the day; the People had been asked to choose between them, and they had made their choice. So Gladstone was summoned to Windsor, and on 23 April 1880, we find the entry in his diary, 'At 6.50 I went to see the Queen, who received me with perfect courtesy, from which she never deviates . . . All things considered, I was much pleased. I ended by kissing her Majesty's hand.'

Gladstone's second administration makes nothing like so fine an impression on the pages of history as his first. He was over seventy, and although full of vigour found himself at sea when he had to face a multitude of great and pressing issues, at home and abroad. A third Reform Bill was put on the Statute Book, which added two millions to the electoral rolls and established something like universal adult male suffrage. But there were troubles in Egypt and the Sudan, and Gladstone was blamed (not least by the queen) for the death of General Gordon at Khartoum; there was war with the Boers in South Africa, and Ireland was once again on the brink of insurrection as Parnell mustered the forces of Nationalism. In the end it was Ireland that brought about Gladstone's fall. In June 1885 a temporary combination of Conservatives and Parnellites defeated the Government on an amendment to the Budget, and on 9 June 1885, Gladstone resigned.

Lord Salisbury was called to the premiership, although there was still a Liberal majority in the House of Commons. The queen urged Gladstone to accept an earldom, but he declined. That winter Salisbury dissolved Parliament, and at the general election—the first fought on the expanded register—the Liberals were returned with 333 members, while the Conservatives had 251 and the Irish Nationalists led by Parnell had 86. Towards the end of January 1886 Lord Salisbury resigned, and on the 30th Gladstone was called upon to form his third administration. Already he had come to the conclusion that since the voice of the Irish people had declared in favour of Home Rule, this must be given to them. To begin with, he sought a solution on non-party lines, but when agreement with the Conservatives proved impossible he decided to go it alone.

Gladstone's conversion to Home Rule created a great political storm. He was assailed with the utmost bitterness, hooted in the streets, hissed and jeered at in Parliament, given the cold shoulder in society. The Liberal party was split down the middle. A large section, including Lord Hartington, Joseph Chamberlain, and John Bright broke away, and eventually were allied with the Conservatives as Liberal Unionists. From this disastrous schism the Liberals did not recover for nearly twenty years. Absolutely convinced as he was of the rightness of his policy Gladstone pushed on, and early in April 1886 he introduced the first of the series of Home Rule for Ireland bills.

In the course of the ensuing debates, Gladstone spoke five times, the last being on 8 June 1886 when he wound up for the Government on the second reading. 'The unflagging veteran,' runs John Morley's account, 'was almost as white as the flower in his coat, but the splendid compass, the flexibility, the moving charm and power of his voice, were never more wonderful. The construction of the speech was a masterpiece, the temper of it unbroken, its freedom from taunt and bitterness and small personality incomparable.' Towards the close he rose to heights of oratory that even he never surpassed. 'Ireland stands at your bar expectant, hopeful, almost suppliant . . . Think, I beseech you; think well, think wisely, think, not for the moment, but for the years that are to come, before you reject this bill.'

The question was put, the sand-glass was turned on the table, and the ministerial whips had still not given up hope. When the votes were cast, however, there were 313 for the Bill and 343 against. Ninety-three Liberals had gone into the lobby against the Bill.

'As I passed into his room at the House with Mr. Gladstone that night,' wrote Morley, ' he seemed for the first time to bend under the crushing weight of the burden that he had taken up.'

Parliament was dissolved two days later, and there ensued a most bitterly contested general election, from which there emerged only 191 Gladstonian Liberals, with 85 Irish supporters, whereas the Conservatives had 316 together with 78 Liberal Unionists. On 20 July 1886 Gladstone resigned, and Lord Salisbury became Prime Minister again.

Now in his seventy-seventh year, Gladstone might have been expected to retire, but instead he took his place as leader of the Opposition in the House of Commons. Six years passed, and the time for a general election came round again. Gladstone girded himself for battle, to the queen's amazement and disgust. As she wrote to her private secretary in June 1892, ' the idea of a deluded excited man of 82 trying to govern England and her vast Empire with the miserable democrats under him is quite ludicrous. It is like a bad joke!' The election was fought, and although Gladstone was denied the massive majority that he had confidently expected he *had* a majority, for the final results gave 270 Liberals, 81 Irish

Nationalists, and 4 Labour members, as opposed to 269 Conservatives and 46 Liberal Unionists. A motion of no-confidence in the Salisbury government was moved by Asquith in the House of Commons on 11 August 1892; it was carried, and Salisbury resigned at once. Four days later Gladstone was kissing the queen's hand at Osborne House in the Isle of Wight—Prime Minister for the fourth time.

The queen noticed that he was 'greatly altered and changed, not only much aged, walking rather bent, with a stick, but altogether; his face shrunk, deadly pale, with a weird look in his eyes, a feeble expression about the mouth, and the voice altered!' And throughout the interview Victoria did not utter one sympathetic word.

Although he knew well enough that with such a slender majority behind him he had not the smallest chance of overcoming the opposition of the House of Lords, he introduced a new Home Rule for Ireland bill. This passed through all its stages in the House of Commons—albeit with depressingly small majorities—but was rejected by the House of Lords on 9 September 1893 by the crushing majority of 419 votes to 41.

Gladstone realized then that his attempt to pacify Ireland had ended in complete failure, but he urged his Cabinet to dissolve and go to the country with the battle-cry of the People versus the House of Lords. But they knew full well that the country was sick of the whole business. Then there was trouble within the Cabinet, with Gladstone fiercely opposing the new Naval estimates. In January 1894 he left England for a holiday in Biarritz with his wife and daughter Mary Drew. Everyone expected the news of his retirement, but the old man kept them all on tenterhooks. On returning to London he had an audience with the queen at Buckingham Palace on 28 February and gave her an intimation of his approaching resignation. 'She was at the highest point of her cheerfulness,' he noted sadly.

On 1 March 1894 he presided over his last Cabinet, and told them of his intention. There was an emotional scene, through which (reports Morley, who was there) 'Mr. Gladstone sat composed and still as marble.' He spoke some 'words of acknowledgment and farewell', and 'then, hardly above a breath, but every accent heard, he said, " God bless you all " ... rose slowly and went out of one door while his colleagues filed out of the other '. In his diary Gladstone noted, ' a really moving scene ', but he afterwards was heard to refer to ' that blubbering Cabinet '.

A little later that same afternoon he delivered what was to prove his last speech in the House of Commons. It was a fighting speech, an exhortation to battle with the House of Lords, and it went down well. Then at the close of business he got up and slowly walked away from the assembly he had first addressed sixty-one years before.

Three days later at Windsor, on 3 March he had his last audience with the queen. He carried her a letter in which he had stated that at eighty-four he was sensible of a diminished capacity for prolonged labour, although this in itself would not have justified his praying to be relieved from the restraints and exigencies of official life. But his deafness had become a serious inconvenience and, graver still, there was an obstruction of vision arising from cataract in both eyes. The queen offered him a seat when he entered the room, and they had a conversation which was ' neither here nor there '. She seems to have offered him not a single word of thanks for the years of honourable and devoted service.

Four years were left to him after his retirement, and he spent them mostly at Hawarden, although he was able to attend the opening of the Kiel Canal in 1895 and spent holidays at Cannes and Biarritz. He did not stand for re-election to the House of Commons at the general election held in 1895. The Armenian massacres brought him out of his retirement briefly, and at Liverpool, in September 1896 he spoke for an hour and twenty minutes in denunciation of Abdul Hamid, the Sultan of Turkey—' the great assassin ', he called him. His last speech of all was in August 1897, to the members of the Hawarden Horticultural Society. Shortly afterwards there were signs of a cancerous growth behind the cheek-bone, which spread to the palate, and until the end he suffered dreadful pain. He died on the early morning of 19 May 1898, with his family kneeling round his bed and his son Stephen reading the prayers for the dying.

The news was telegraphed to Westminster, and both Houses of Parliament adjourned immediately. On the next day noble tributes to his memory were paid by Lord Salisbury and Lord Rosebery in the Lords and Balfour and Harcourt in the Commons. A State funeral was ordered; and on 28 May, after his body had lain in state in Westminster Hall for three days, during which enormous multi-tudes filed past in simple reverence, it was buried in a grave in the north transept close beside the statues of Peel and Disraeli. The pall-bearers included the Prime Minister, Lord Salisbury; Lord Rosebery; the Prince of Wales and the Duke of York. On Mrs. Gladstone's death two years later, she was laid beside him.

' Never has so wide and honourable a pomp all over the globe,' wrote John Morley, ' followed an English statesman to the grave.'

*   *   *

On a day in September 1877, Gladstone addressed the boys of Hawarden grammar school. ' Be inspired with the belief,' he told them, ' that life is a great and noble calling; not a mean and grovelling thing that we are to shuffle through as we can, but an elevated and lofty destiny.'

That is what he thought a man's life ought to be—and that was how he lived it.

31

MARQUESS OF SALISBURY

LORD SALISBURY was the last of Queen Victoria's Prime Ministers, and by no means the least distinguished. He held the premiership three times, for nearly fourteen years in all. He was also the last of Britain's Prime Ministers to hold the office while a member of the House of Lords.

Three hundred years before, his ancestor, William Cecil, the great Lord Burghley, was Queen Elizabeth's First Minister; and Burghley's son, Sir Robert Cecil, held the same position under the queen and her successor James I. He was created Earl of Salisbury in 1605. The seventh earl received the marquessate in 1789. His son, the second marquess, was the future Prime Minister's father. He married a Miss Gascoyne, daughter of a wealthy City merchant, and her marriage settlement brought large estates in Lancashire and Essex to be added to the Salisburys' extensive patrimony.

Lord Robert Arthur Talbot Gascoyne-Cecil was born at Hatfield House, the Jacobean mansion in Hertfordshire which was built by Sir Robert Cecil in 1611, on 3 February 1830. He was the third son of the marriage, but the second son died in infancy, and the eldest, who bore the courtesy title of Lord Cranborne, suffered from a nervous debility which caused his death, prematurely senile, before he was fifty.

Lord Robert Cecil, as he was known until his brother's death, started school when he was six. It was a private establishment and a dreadful place: once he referred to his life there as ' an existence among devils '. In 1839, when his parents were abroad during what proved to be his mother's last illness, he passed some months at Brixham in charge of the Rev. Henry Lyte, the author of ' Abide with me ' and other well-known hymns, and it was Mr. Lyte who encouraged him to take an interest in geology and botany—subjects which remained among his favourite studies even up to old age.

The next year he went to Eton, where he was always lonely and frequently miserable. He got on well enough with the masters, whose only complaint was that he showed a ' mischievous spirit of negligence ' about his clothes and books, but the boys bullied him incessantly. 'You see,' he wrote home once, 'my age is so much against me, for the boys in my part of the school are three years, if not more, older than myself. Then besides, I am not strong nor healthy . . .'

At first his father was inclined to think that the boy was making mountains out of molehills, but when Robert had just turned fifteen Lord Salisbury withdrew him from Eton, and he spent the next two years at Hatfield, happy in the great library or wandering about the countryside with a packet of sandwiches in his pocket, looking for specimens to add to his botanical collections. Early in 1848 he went into residence at Christ Church, Oxford, but after two years there his health broke down.

For eighteen months he lived mostly at Hatfield, until the family doctor diagnosed a 'complete breakdown of the nervous system' and prescribed a long sea voyage. In the summer of 1851 he left England in a sailing-ship bound for the Cape. He passed three months there, and then went on to Australia, where he visited the goldfields near Adelaide. After this he was for six months in New Zealand. Everywhere he went he made a careful note of the people; he mixed with all sorts and conditions of men, and women, and the information he got at first-hand was of inestimable value to him in after years when he became responsible for the direction of Britain's colonial and imperial policy.

When about to start back for England he sent his father a letter that must have made the old gentleman very cross. 'I am afraid I shall arrive in England just in time for the London season—to be stewed and bored at dinners and parties, after the usual destiny of us unfortunate white slaves—I look forward to returning to London after staying in these unconventional places with great horror . . . I can't at all reconcile myself to the idea of shaving again.' But the trip had done him good. 'The voyage has quite answered its end in giving me health. I am scarcely ever unwell, unless I sit up late . . .'

What worried him most when he got back to England was not his health but what he was to do with his life. The first thing he thought of was the House of Commons: '. . . undoubtedly it is the sphere in which a man can be most useful, but my chances of getting into it are practically none'. The Bar, then, as his father had suggested ? It did not appeal to him in the slightest, 'writing for the newspapers would be preferable to the Bar . . .'

As things turned out, he was worrying himself unnecessarily, for in the summer of 1853, only a few months after he returned to

England, a parliamentary vacancy occurred at Stamford, a small borough that was practically in the pocket of Lord Exeter, the head of the elder branch of the Cecil family. His lordship offered to use his influence on behalf of his young cousin, and in August Lord Robert was elected M.P. without opposition. He remained M.P. for Stamford until his father's death in 1868 removed him to the House of Lords, and in those fourteen years he never had to fight an election.

When he entered the House of Commons, Lord Aberdeen was Prime Minister, and party politics were at their dullest. Lord Robert sat as a Conservative, and the Conservatives were in opposition where they were to remain for most of the next twenty years. Late nights and bad air brought about a return of his poor health and he was not interested in much of what was going on. He spoke seldom; and although Disraeli, leader of the Conservatives in the Commons, spoke in complimentary terms of his performances he remained in very low spirits. They sank still lower when his father, who was an enthusiastic amateur soldier, offered him the colonelcy of the Middlesex Militia. 'I detest all soldiering beyond measure,' he told his father. 'As fas as taste goes, I would sooner be at the tread-mill.'

The marquess took his refusal in very bad part, and called in the doctor again to see if he could discover what was really wrong with the young man. Dr. Ackland's report was disconcerting. 'Very great care would have to be taken of Lord Robert if he were not to develop into a hypochondriac . . .' This might very well have been his fate if he had not met Miss Georgina Alderson, and had the good sense and strength of character to insist on marrying her, very much against his father's wishes.

At this period of his life Lord Robert was inclined to be scared of women, especially of such young ladies as might aspire to become marchionesses. His appearance, his thin and lanky figure—so different from what it became in later years, his constant stoop, his shortsightedness, awkward movements, and atrocious carelessness in dress, may well have rendered him unattractive with the other sex, and he was clever enough to realize it. But Georgina Alderson seemed to be different. She was the daughter of a Baron of the Exchequer, what today would be a High Court judge, and several years older than he. She is described as being not particularly pretty, but she was a vivid, vital person, very energetic, intensely interested in people rather than in causes, a brilliant conversationalist, and as deeply religious as he was, High Church but not bigoted. It was their common interest in church history that led to their forming an intellectual friendship; they corresponded about books and discussed questions of history, theology, and politics. Before long friendship blossomed into love.

As already indicated, Lord Salisbury was not at all pleased when he heard of his son's attachment. Lord Robert had no means other than the allowance his father made him, and with numerous other children on his hands his father had strained his resources in putting him into Parliament. He had expected that Lord Robert would remain single until he was in a position to keep a wife, but here he was proposing at twenty-six to make a love-match with a young lady with only £100 a year of her own. Lord Robert had quite made up his mind, however. All he would agree to was a probationary period of six months, and as soon as that was passed they were married, on 11 July 1857.

By the standards of his class the young couple were not very well off, but they were certainly not poverty-stricken. He had £300 a year from his mother's fortune and £100 a year his father continued to allow him, and she had her own hundred. He was very soon able to make their income up to £700 a year by contributing to the magazines and journals. Between 1860 and 1873 he wrote more than thirty articles for the *Quarterly Review*, and obtained not only cash but widespread recognition as a writer. He applied for several official appointments, including the clerkship of the Privy Council that the diarist Charles Greville had held for so long, but in 1865 his elder brother died and he assumed the title of Lord Cranborne as the immediate heir. This great improvement in his personal fortunes was reflected in his political situation, for in the following year Lord Derby gave him his first Cabinet appointment, as Secretary of State for India.

After nine months he was so disgusted with what he regarded as Disraeli's opportunist Reform Bill—he denounced it as ' an outrage on political morality '—that he resigned his post, but in the spring of 1868 his father died and he succeeded as Marquess of Salisbury, with all the prestige and possessions that went with the historic title. He now moved into the House of Lords, where he enhanced his reputation as a capable if not inspiring speaker and as a good manager of parliamentary business. He was no die-hard; nor did he fancy himself as a great aristocrat. Thus he supported a bill which would have enabled the queen to confer a number of life-peerages on persons of distinction—a reform which had to wait until our own time.

When Disraeli became Prime Minister again, in 1874, he at once invited Salisbury to join his government. Salisbury spent three days thinking it over. He distrusted Disraeli as a politician and disliked him intensely as a man. But in the end he agreed to serve as Secretary for India as before. It proved a momentous decision. At first relations between the two men were not good and Salisbury's tongue sometimes ran away with him. In one of his speeches he referred to 'the bluster of the House of Commons', and Disraeli was so nettled that he called him 'a master of gibes and flouts and sneers'. But Disraeli was remarkably conciliatory, and there developed between them a sincere respect and regard.

On Lord Derby's resignation of the Foreign Office in 1878 Lord Salisbury was appointed to his place, and so it happened that he accompanied his chief to Berlin to play his part in the famous Congress. Disraeli was delighted with his junior's 'consummate mastery of detail', and indeed the greater part of the spadework of the conference was done by Salisbury. After his return in triumph, Disraeli was offered the Garter by his grateful queen, but he declined to accept it unless Salisbury got one too.

Lord Salisbury made a highly successful Foreign Secretary, firm but temperate, not countenancing any dangerous adventures but intent upon maintaining Britain's power and prestige abroad and not letting slip any opportunity of adding to the rapidly expanding British Empire. In 1880 the Liberals returned to power and Salisbury lost his office, but in the next year on Lord Beaconsfield's death he was chosen to lead the Conservative opposition in the House of Lords. He did so well, and in particular made so favourable an impression upon the queen, that when in June 1885 Gladstone resigned, the queen summoned Salisbury to Balmoral and invited him to form a ministry.

Salisbury demurred at first, since he felt that Sir Stafford Northcote, the leader of the Conservative party in the House of Commons, had a prior claim. Besides, he would have much preferred returning to the Foreign Office. At last however he agreed, provided he might combine the Foreign Secretaryship with the post of Prime Minister. By a most unusual arrangement, Northcote was appointed First Lord of the Treasury and was elevated to the House of Lords as Earl of Iddesleigh.

This first ministry of Lord Salisbury's did not last long, only a matter of some six months, but he was Prime Minister again from July 1886 to August 1892, in succession to Gladstone once more, and for the third time from June 1895 to August 1902, when he finally retired.

The eighteen-eighties were dominated by the Home Rule controversy, in which Salisbury and Gladstone were the perpetual protagonists. Salisbury strongly opposed Gladstone's proposals for a separate Irish parliament, and in this he was supported by a strong body of Liberals who became known as Liberal Unionists and were so generally satisfied with his leadership that they entered into an electoral alliance with the Conservatives. In his third Cabinet some of their leaders were given places, notably Joseph Chamberlain who became Colonial Secretary. Salisbury again took the Foreign Office in addition the premiership, and Arthur Balfour was First Lord of the Treasury.

Lord Salisbury was the first of Queen Victoria's Prime Ministers who was younger than she was, and it is said that she considered him about the best. Certainly they got on very well; he never toadied to her but spoke to her as man to man, if the phrase may be allowed. She was of great help to him in his duties as Foreign Secretary, since there were some aspects of continental life with which she was far better acquainted than he was. Foreign royalties, for instance: most of them were related to her, and she knew, none better, all the ramifications of their family trees and their tangled relationships. He deeply respected—revered would probably be a better word—her as a woman. He found her opinionated and occasionally obstinate, but absolutely to be relied on in all circumstances. Whenever he was asked by a newcomer to the Court how she should be approached, his only advice was, ' Always speak the truth to the Queen '.

On the occasion of both of the queen's jubilees, the Golden Jubilee in 1887 and the Diamond Jubilee ten years later, Lord Salisbury was Prime Minister. The first was marked by an innovation which must have owed something to that interest in imperial affairs which had been aroused by his trip to the Cape and Australia and New Zealand as a young man. He invited representatives of the queen's overseas dominions to meet in London, and the conference held in the spring of 1887 was the first of the kind. There was a second conference in 1897, and at a banquet in the Imperial Institute at South Kensington Salisbury spoke with pride of ' the triumph of a moral idea in the construction of a great political organization ', an empire sustained entirely upon ' the basis of mutual goodwill, sympathy, and affection '.

On the home front Lord Salisbury's administrations were responsible for a good deal of useful if not spectacular social legislation. Two measures may be singled out for mention. In 1891 fees in elementary schools were abolished, so that elementary education, which had been compulsory since 1870, was now free. The second reform was in the field of local government. In 1888, it has been estimated, there were more than 27,000 independent local authorities of one kind or another which had the right of levying a rate on the English rate-payer. There was no system about it; it was a chaos, a jungle; something which had grown up and multiplied over the centuries. A tidying up operation was urgently required, and in 1888 a Local Government Act covered England and Wales with a network of sixty-two administrative counties, while sixty and more of the largest towns were constituted county boroughs, each enjoying almost complete independence in local affairs. The good work was extended by the Rosebery government in 1894, when an Act was passed which established in every county a comprehensive system of urban, rural, and parish councils.

In the closing years of the nineteenth century Lord Salisbury was supreme in the political scene. Gladstone had finally retired, and the Liberals were at sixes and sevens. At the elections in 1895 and 1900 the Conservatives had majorities such as had not been seen since 1832. In the favour of the sovereign and of the great majority of her subjects, Lord Salisbury had no rival.

From whatever way we look at him, he was a big man. Big in frame—six feet and four inches tall and massively built, big in intelligence, big in capacity and performance, big in moral stature.

Born an aristocrat, he disliked his title but never dreamed of a world in which titles would not count. He was no democrat. He laughed at political equality: 'it is not merely a folly', he wrote, 'it is a chimaera'. In every country, he maintained, there are some men destined to rule, whether by right of birth, or intellectual power and culture, or even wealth. Yet he was no reactionary Tory; he was a true Conservative, believing that changes must come, but they must be slow and gradual and a natural development of what has gone before. If he believed in a ruling class he also believed that rank and great possessions brought with them great responsibilities and should be paid for, as it were, in public service. He certainly lived up to this belief in his own career.

Religion was the foundation of his life and work. He was a lifelong member of the Church of England, and was as regular in attendance at public worship as his circumstances allowed. And his daughter Lady Gwendolen Cecil tells us, in her life of her father, that unless prevented by some actual physical necessity his weekly Communion was never foregone. Books of theology were among his favourite reading, but he also read Darwin and Professor Huxley and works of Biblical criticism—without their having the least effect on his complete trust in the fundamental doctrines of Christianity.

Hatfield House is one of the most famous of Britain's stately homes, and he enjoyed living there although he left the domestic arrangements entirely to his wife. It was she who supervised the succession of hospitalities, while he withdrew whenever he could to his great library with its double doors and the laboratory and workshop where he messed about with chemicals and scientific experiments, sometimes with results that startled his family out of their wits. He installed an electric-lighting system, the power coming from a sawmill on the little River Lea a mile and a half distant, and for a time dinner was an exciting and tantalizing experience as the lights flickered and sank and occasionally went out altogether, because, he explained, the wind was blowing tree branches against the overhead wires. Long before the telephone was a commonplace he had one installed, and his guests had to learn to avoid tripping over the wires that trailed across the floor. He detested huntin' and shootin' and fishin', but played tennis and billiards and loved a country walk, always keeping his eyes open for something of botanical interest. He strongly disliked official receptions, but was an excellent host at home. His shortsightedness led him into ludicrous situations; and as for his dress, his daughter remarks diplomatically that ' dress never was his strong point '.

Lord Salisbury's last premiership carried him well into the new century and a new reign, but for some years before his resignation he was obviously breaking up. The death of his wife from a stroke in 1899 was a grievous blow, and it came at a time when he was sorely perturbed by the outbreak of war in South Africa. He stayed on as Prime Minister until the war was over, and talked of seeing the new king crowned.

But his relations with Edward VII had never been cordial, and he could never hope to be on such excellent terms with him as he had been with his mother. In the end he went to Buckingham Palace on 11 July 1902 and tendered his resignation. Then, on doctor's orders, he went for a holiday on the Continent and so missed the Coronation which took place during the next month. On his return he retired to Hatfield, and there, at sunset on 22 August 1903, he died at the age of seventy-two. A grave in Westminster Abbey was offered, but his family knew and respected his wishes, and he was buried in Hatfield churchyard beside his wife.

32

EARL OF ROSEBERY

LORD ROSEBERY is perhaps the greatest of the ' might have beens ' in the list of Prime Ministers. Gladstone once called him ' the man of the future ', and to one of his biographers he was ' the man of Promise '. But the future disappointed and the promise faded, and it was left to Winston Churchill to contain his career in a trio of sentences. ' At first they said " He will come." Then for years " If only he could come." And finally, long after he had renounced politics for ever, " If only he would come back." ' But he never did.

Archibald Philip Primrose, who became the fifth Earl of Rosebery and was Prime Minister for fifteen months in 1894–95, was born on 7 May 1847 at No. 20 Charles Street, Berkeley Square, which was the family's London home. He was the elder son of Lord Dalmeny —the courtesy title held by the eldest son of the Earls of Rosebery— and grandson of the fourth Earl. His mother was Lady Catherine Stanhope, celebrated as one of the most beautiful women in society.

The Primroses had owned estates in Perthshire and Midlothian for centuries. In the civil wars of the seventeenth century they were Royalists, and suffered for it; but after the Restoration they found fresh openings for profit and advancement. A Scottish peerage came their way in 1700, and three years later the head of the house was made an earl. When Archibald was four his father died and he succeeded to the title of Lord Dalmeny. Two years later his mother married again, her husband being Lord Harry Vane who became Duke of Cleveland. He was enormously rich, and he used to rent great country houses, including Brocket, the old home of Lord Melbourne, where the Primrose children lived with their mother and stepfather in conditions of expensive grandeur.

At the age of thirteen he proceeded to Eton, where he was given a remarkably high place for a new boy, this being largely attributable to his love of reading. His tutor at Eton was William Johnson, who called himself William Johnson Cory after inheriting a small estate. He was a distinguished classical scholar and perhaps the best of Eton masters. Johnson worked hard to make a scholar out of young Primrose, and he succeeded. But in his half-term letters to Lady Harry he commented on her son's reluctance to work, and to a colleague he described the youth as ' one of those who like the palm without the dust '.

The phrase got around and was widely quoted, but Winston Churchill thought it was unfair. Rosebery, he asserted, was capable of very hard work and long hours of concentration both on politics and literature, but ' the dust had never come his way '.

When he was nineteen, young Dalmeny was entered at Christ Church, Oxford, where his money and his sporting tastes made him a very popular figure. He did little work there, however. He bought a racehorse, with which he hoped to win the Derby; but the college authorities informed him that an undergraduate was not allowed to keep a racehorse and he must dispose of it forthwith. Rather than do so, Dalmeny left Oxford in the spring of 1869, before he had taken his finals. His mother and family were strongly disapproving, and it was not long before he himself recognized what a silly young fellow he had been.

For the next few years racing seems to have been his chief interest. He registered his racing colours (primrose and rose hoops, rose cap) at the Jockey Club, and became a well-known figure on all the racecourses up and down the country. He gambled quite heavily, sometimes winning large sums and as often losing. He bought a house at Epsom—' The Durdans '—so as to be within easy reach of the downs. But he mixed with the best society and was a prominent member of the Marlborough House set which revolved round the Prince of Wales and Princess Alexandra. He also showed considerable interest in politics and thought of trying for a seat in the House of Commons, but in 1868 his grandfather died and he became Earl of Rosebery. He took his seat in the House of Lords, and spoke occasionally. His speeches were unusually literate and he had a graceful manner and appearance. While not a dogmatist, in politics or anything else, he showed a partiality for the Gladstonian Liberals.

One of the sayings most often attributed to Lord Rosebery is that he had three ambitions in life: to marry an heiress, to become Prime Minister, and to win the Derby. He always denied having said any such thing, but in fact he did all three, and in that order.

The first must surely have been the easiest, although it is hard to understand why a young man with an income of £40,000 a year should wish to marry an heiress. Until well on in the eighteen-seventies Rosebery was a Prince Charming. He was a welcome guest at the great country houses, and occasionally he was summoned to Balmoral by the queen. As it happened, he remained a bachelor until he was thirty, and then his choice fell on a Jewess, Hannah Rothschild, the only child of Baron Meyer de Rothschild, one of the wealthiest and most distinguished members of the English branch of the Rothschild family. Baron Meyer had a splendid mansion, Mentmore, near Leighton Buzzard, where he indulged his tastes for collecting works of art and items of historic interest. He was also a breeder of racehorses on the grand scale, and he won most of the big races.

Rosebery was introduced to Miss Hannah at Newmarket in 1868, and the introduction was effected by Mrs. Disraeli. She was then seventeen—a lonely, shy, introspective girl, who found it difficult to get on well with young men, probably because she suspected that they were chiefly interested in her money. Almost from the first she found Rosebery immensely attractive. For years they met at Mentmore and on social occasions, and it is surprising that the affair took such a long time to develop. A principal reason may have been the opposition that might be expected from the Jewish community, if it were proposed that their richest heiress should marry a Gentile. Indeed, when the engagement was announced the comments in the Jewish press were decidedly critical.

Until the death of Baron Meyer in 1874 the relationship was friendship only, but about that time Rosebery seems to have begun to contemplate making a proposal of marriage. The Baroness favoured his suit, but she died, too, three years later, and Hannah was left an orphan. Rosebery then decided to employ a go-between, as is the custom in Jewish families, and early in 1878 Rosebery made a formal proposal and was immediately accepted. One of the first to be informed of his choice was Gladstone, who replied by return of post offering his warmest congratulations.

Rosebery's sister, Lady Leconfield, was equally delighted with the news, but their mother was absolutely aghast. Rosebery's relations with her had never been easy, and now she wrote to say how unhappy she was to learn that he proposed to marry one ' who has not the faith and hope of Christ '. She went on to say that while she was prepared to ' receive the future Lady Rosebery with all the kindness and consideration that are her due ', she and her husband the Duke would not be able to attend the wedding unless it were in church, and that she assumed that it would be a very quiet one.

The wedding took place on 10 March 1878, and so far from being quiet it was one of the great events of the London season. There were two ceremonies. The first was in the Board-room of the Jewish Guardians in Mount Street, and was attended only by a few close friends and representative tenants of the two families. The second, in Christ Church, Doen Street, Piccadilly, was very different. Neither his mother nor his stepfather were present, but his sister Lady Leconfield was. The bride was given away by Lord Beaconsfield, the Prime Minister, and the Prince of Wales was among those who signed the register and he also proposed the bridal toast at the wedding-breakfast.

The marriage turned out to be a very happy and successful one, although Rosebery sometimes found his wife excessively fond. Sir Edward Hamilton, who as Gladstone's private secretary was likely to know such things, described Hannah Rosebery as ' one of those born to direct; and with this birthright she had in a notable degree the faculty of getting other people to work and of quickening their energies '. This was just what Rosebery needed. In the same year as his marriage he agreed to stand as the Liberal candidate for the rectorship of Aberdeen University, and he defeated his Conservative opponent by the small but sufficient majority of three votes. His victory marked him out as a leader of Liberalism in Scotland, and his status was immensely enhanced when in 1879, largely because of his backing, Gladstone was chosen as Liberal candidate for Midlothian. J. M. Barrie, who was a student at Edinburgh at the time, reported that ' Gladstone and Rosebery were the father and son of the Scottish people '.

When Gladstone formed his second administration in 1880 he invited Rosebery to join it, but it was only after much persuasion that Rosebery agreed in 1881 to serve as under-secretary at the Home Office. He held the post for only two years, and then resigned apparently because Gladstone had not created a Secretary for Scotland, a post which Rosebery might have thought he was specially qualified to fill.

While out of office he and his wife went on a tour of Australia, in course of which he became deeply impressed by the immense potentialities for good in the developing British Empire. In a speech at Adelaide in 1884 he employed a phrase which years afterwards was given official recognition. ' These are no longer colonies in the ordinary sense of the term,' he said. ' This is a nation . . . but does this imply separation from the Empire ? God forbid! There is no need for any nation, however great, leaving the Empire, because the Empire is *a Commonwealth of Nations.*'

Soon after his return to England, Rosebery was made First Commissioner of Works and Lord Privy Seal, and then in 1886 Gladstone promoted him to the much more important position of Foreign Secretary. Six months was insufficient to enable him to do very much in this capacity, but he left office with a greatly increased reputation. Then in 1888 the London County Council came into being, and Rosebery was induced to stand as Independent candidate for one of the City division seats. He was elected, and at once was chosen to be chairman of the Council. He proved an excellent choice. John Benn, leader of the Progressives (the majority party) pronounced him to be ' the best possible first chairman of the greatest municipal body in the world ', and he was elected again in 1892. A practical expression of his great interest in the welfare of Londoners was his gift of a fine swimming-pool to the People's Palace at Mile End.

But in 1890 he suffered a shattering blow. His wife died of a sudden attack of typhoid fever when not yet forty and after only eleven years of marriage, and he was left with four young children— two sons, two daughters—to bring up. For ever afterwards he used notepaper with a heavy black border, and he kept 18 November, his wife's death-day, as a day of solitary fasting and solemn remembrance.

Deprived of his wife's constant help and encouragement, Rosebery seemed to have lost all interest in politics. When Gladstone in 1892 offered him the post of Foreign Secretary again, Rosebery went off in his yacht so as to make himself inaccessible, and when he was contacted he drove Gladstone nearly frantic with his objections. Rosebery asserted that he was suffering from insomnia, and now that his wife was dead he wanted nothing other than solitude, since all his ambition was buried in her grave. But the queen wished to see him at the Foreign Office, and at length the Prince of Wales managed to persuade him to accept.

As on the previous occasion, he displayed tact and firmness, and won good opinions at home and abroad. But the Cabinet was at sixes and sevens, Gladstone was almost in his dotage, and in March 1894 he resigned the premiership.

The question was who should succeed him ? The most obvious claimant was Sir William Harcourt, who had been a Liberal M.P. since 1868, had held high office in previous governments, and was now Chancellor of the Exchequer and leader of the House of Commons. But he was a man of difficult temper, and his colleagues in the Cabinet vowed that they would not have him for Prime Minister at any price. The queen decided the matter, and with an exceptional use of her prerogative summoned Lord Rosebery to

Windsor and invited him to become Prime Minister and form an administration.

Rosebery was constrained to accept, and on 3 March he informed the Cabinet that ' under great pressure and under a strong sense of various disabilities' he had done so, and he trusted that in these circumstances his colleagues would afford him their ' cordial co-operation '.

If he really expected this, he certainly did not get it. Many Liberals objected to him as a peer. Harcourt was disgruntled, although he continued to serve as Chancellor. Campbell-Bannerman at the War Office, John Morley as Irish Secretary, Asquith as Home Secretary, and Lord Kimberley as Foreign Secretary were often at loggerheads, and between them they made the Prime Minister's life a misery. Gladstonian Liberalism was just about burnt out, but it gave a few expiring flickers. An impossibly ambitious programme was put out, including Home Rule for Ireland, ' mending or ending' the House of Lords, the disestablishment of the Church in Wales, payment of M.P.s, and a local veto on liquor sales.

The Government were entirely dependent on the Irish members for their majority, and quite early on Rosebery blundered when in a platform speech he gave an assurance that there would be no Home Rule for Ireland unless and until the majority of members for English constituencies were in favour of it—which was as good as saying that it was to be postponed indefinitely.

Rosebery became increasingly uncomfortable. A fixture in the Lords, he could not keep control of what was going on in the lower house. The queen bossed him unmercifully, and was quite clearly looking forward to the time when he would have to make room for Lord Salisbury. He suffered horribly from his insomnia, and he had a particularly nasty bout of influenza. By-elections went against the Government, and in the Commons a motion of censure was carried on Campbell-Bannerman's administration at the War Office. This provided Rosebery with the excuse he was looking for, and on 23 June 1895 he went down to Windsor and tendered his resignation. In their final interview the queen bestowed on him the Thistle, the distinctively Scottish order of chivalry. That night he wrote in his diary, ' To London—free '.

By this time he had achieved the third of the ambitions attributed to him. On 6 June 1894 his horse *Ladas* stormed ahead to win the Derby, and the vast crowd at Epsom roared their delight—at least he had done something no Prime Minister had done before! The next year he again had the proud experience of leading in the Derby winner—this time *Sir Visto*; and in 1905, with *Cicero*, he won the great race for the third time.

Rosebery retained the leadership of the Liberal party until 1896, when he formally resigned, having had more than enough of disunion and dissension. During the Boer War he headed a body of Liberals who supported the Salisbury Government in the prosecution of the war, in contrast with those under Campbell-Bannerman who were hailed as pro-Boers. For years afterwards there was talk of his becoming leader of a reunited Liberal party, but he was done with politics, although he liked to be consulted as an elder statesman.

As a man of letters Rosebery enjoyed a deservedly high distinction, chiefly as the author of biographical studies of the young Chatham, William Pitt, Peel, Lord Randolph Churchill (Winston's father), and of the last phase of Napoleon.

More and more, as he grew old, he lived in his children, and it was a bitter blow when his younger son, the brilliantly gifted Neil Primrose, died of wounds in Palestine during the First World War. A month before the Armistice in 1918 Rosebery had a stroke, but he recovered and lived on until he was over eighty.

When he felt that his end could not be far off he sent his servant out to buy a gramophone, and gave him instructions that when death was obviously near he should put on the record of the Eton Boating Song. This was done, and perhaps the haunting strains that he had loved as a boy were the last sounds to fall upon his ear. He died at The Durdans, Epsom, on 21 May 1929; and to most of those who read the lengthy obituary notices in the newspapers his was not even the echo of a once great and famous name.

33

ARTHUR JAMES BALFOUR

WHEN LORD SALISBURY RETIRED from the Premiership in the summer of 1895 his nephew slipped into the vacant seat with the greatest of ease. Since the time when as a young man he had accompanied Lord Beaconsfield and his uncle to Berlin in 1878 he had been carefully groomed for the position; when the opportunity came he had established himself as the heir apparent with not a rival in sight.

Arthur James Balfour was born on 25 July 1848 at Whittingehame, his father's fine house in East Lothian, in the lowlands of Scotland. He was a Scot, but not a Celt, for the Balfours traced their descent from a thane or chieftain of Saxon or Danish blood who had emigrated from Northumbria into the lowlands in the eleventh century. The Whittinghame branch of the family was founded by Arthur's grandfather, James Balfour, who made a fortune in India, at first in the service of the East India Company and then as a contractor of Naval stores. Soon after returning to Scotland in 1812 he married a daughter of the Earl of Lauderdale, bought the estate of Whittingehame and built a mansion. His son, James Maitland Balfour, became a railway director and was a Conservative M.P. for some years in Peel's time; he married Lady Blanche Cecil, the eighteen-year-old daughter of the second Marquess of Salisbury and sister of the third who became Prime Minister on three occasions.

Arthur was their first son; there were four more sons later and three girls. He was named James after his father and Arthur after the Duke of Wellington, who was a great friend of Lady Blanche's mother.

When Arthur was eight his father died, and he was brought up by his mother. She was a woman of fine character, an excellent manager of people and possessions, reasonably well educated, a lover of reading, deeply religious, and at the same time brightly amusing. It was she who introduced him to Milton and Lord Macaulay and Jane Austen and many another of the classical authors.

When he was ten, Arthur was sent to a preparatory school at Hoddesdon, not far from the Cecils' home at Hatfield, where he

323

usually spent his holidays with his Cecil cousins. Then at thirteen he proceeded to Eton, where the future Lord Rosebery, his senior by a year, had gone a year earlier. Leaving Eton at eighteen, he was entered at Trinity College, Cambridge, as a fellow commoner, a term applied in those days to a class of undergraduates who because of their birth and wealth enjoyed among other privileges the right of dining at high table with the fellows.

At Trinity his friends were drawn chiefly from the younger dons, and among those who attracted him most were John Strutt, later Lord Rayleigh, the eminent physicist, and Henry Sidgwick, who won distinction as a philosopher. Both these became his brothers-in-law, Strutt marrying his sister Evelyn and Sidgwick his sister Eleanor (Nora) who, it may be noted, was principal of Newnham College for women at Cambridge from 1892 to 1910. Through Strutt, Arthur obtained admittance to scientific circles, and Sidgwick guided his studies in the moral sciences.

It was at Cambridge, too, that Balfour was able to indulge his taste for music, Handel's oratorios in particular. He did not go in much for the usual sporting activities but he played tennis to keep himself fit—' real' tennis, although he took up lawn tennis in the 1880s when it was just coming into vogue, and continued to play until he was an old man. Altogether, he recalled in later life, his time at Cambridge was ' a period of almost unmixed satisfaction '.

In his last year there he came of age and entered into possession of the fortune which his grandfather had founded, his father had increased, and his mother had carefully husbanded. He was a very rich man, even by mid-Victorian standards, and could indulge his tastes to the full. They were not those of the normal Scotch laird; he was not interested in salmon-fishing or grouse-shooting or even deer-stalking, although he did this occasionally. He loved good company, good talk, and playing the host at Whittingehame and at No. 4 Carlton Gardens in the most aristocratic quarter of the West End, which became his London home. He was a very welcome guest at the country houses which then lay so generously scattered over the social landscape. His personal attractions were more than considerable. He was tall and handsome, and dressed with a careless but obviously expensive good taste. He talked and wrote brilliantly, and he had a dry sense of humour.

Women were drawn to him, and to the end of his days he delighted in feminine company. Mary Gladstone, the statesman's second daughter, was so obviously attracted that there was talk of marriage between them. Balfour did not return her affection, however, for he had fallen in love with her cousin Mary, or May, Lyttelton, one of the daughters of Lord Lyttelton and his wife who was a sister of Mrs. Gladstone. In 1874 there may have been a formal engagement, but in the beginning of 1875 May Lyttelton was taken seriously ill with typhoid fever, and in March she died. Although no announcement of any engagement had been made, Balfour sent a ring to one of May's brothers, with the request that it should be placed in the girl's coffin. At the funeral Balfour broke down, and for weeks afterwards he seems to have lived in a mood of dumb despair.

There were to be other women in Balfour's life. One lady in particular was associated with him in popular gossip—Mary Wyndham, the third Mary in his life, whom he had known shortly before her marriage in 1883 at the age of eighteen to Lord Elcho, the Earl of Wemyss's heir. For a number of years this affair ran its sometimes dangerous course, until at length it subsided into a friendship which endured through Balfour's life. But there was never another May Lyttelton. For whatever reason, Balfour remained a bachelor to the end.

At the beginning of 1874 Balfour was returned unopposed as Conservative M.P. for Hertford, the constituency in which Hatfield was situated and which was, of course, largely under the influence of the Cecil family. His uncle, Lord Salisbury, on becoming Foreign Secretary in 1878 made Balfour his parliamentary private secretary, and in this capacity he accompanied Beaconsfield and Salisbury to the Congress of Berlin. Two years later the Conservatives were defeated, and Balfour had to fight really hard to retain his seat at Hertford. In the new House of Commons, Balfour sat below the gangway, as though to emphasize his independence, and for the next few years he was closely associated with what was facetiously called the Fourth Party (the others being Conservatives, Liberals, and Irish Nationalists), which consisted of Lord Randolph Churchill, Sir Henry Drummond Wolff, and Sir John Gorst. It was not really a party, as he explained to his uncle; today it would be called a ginger-group. Its members were gadflies, and Balfour was the gad-fly in chief. Reading the nasty and often insulting things he said about Gladstone it is hard to believe that only a short time before he had basked in the old Prime Minister's friendship.

The motion that brought about the fall of the Gladstone ministry was drawn up in Balfour's London home. In the Salisbury administration that followed, Balfour was Secretary for Scotland, with eventually a seat in the Cabinet. Then in March 1887 he was offered and accepted the Irish Chief Secretaryship, which at that juncture, when the Home Rule question was assuming a paramount importance and urgency, was one of the most prominent, and certainly the most dangerous post in the Cabinet.

The appointment of ' Pretty Fanny ', as Balfour was superciliously styled, to govern Ireland was received with something like stupefaction in political circles. Some said that the Prime Minister must have gone mad, others that he had been carried away by family partiality. But Salisbury knew what he was doing. He had himself declared that what Ireland was most in need of was ' government ', and he was quite convinced that Balfour was the man to give it. Balfour hurried off to Dublin, weighed up the situation, and then sped back to Westminster with a policy of stern repression which he got Parliament to approve. Then he returned to Ireland to carry it out.

Hardly a day went by without his being threatened with shooting, or a knife in his back, or some horrible mutilation. His desk was piled with anonymous screeds couched in the most blood-curdling terms. One of these he kept as a souvenir. ' Bloody Balfour,' it began, and went on: ' I write to inform you that your days are numbered. You bloody ruffian . . . If no one will shoot you I will. I will send you down to hell. Remember you bloody curr, your long legs will be shot off. Blood for blood . . .'

At Westminster, the Liberals under Gladstone and their Home Rule allies raged against the Irish Secretary, but even his opponents could not but admire the fine courage, the imperturbable temper, and the exquisite irony with which Balfour met the abuse, the threats, the howlings-down. ' Personal abuse has made my political fortune,' he wrote to his young friend Margot Tennant, who became Mrs. Asquith.

When W. H. Smith—founder of the famous bookstall firm—died in 1891, Balfour was chosen to succeed him as First Lord of the Treasury and Leader of the House of Commons. Political commentators were quick to remark on the situation in which the Conservative forces in the House of Lords and the House of Commons were led by uncle and nephew; nothing like it had been seen, they pointed out, since those founders of Cecil greatness, Lord Burghley and his son Sir William Cecil, ruled England together under another queen, three hundred years before.

The next year Gladstone returned to office, and he was followed as Liberal Prime Minister by Lord Rosebery. Then in 1895 the Conservatives triumphed at the general election, and in the third

Salisbury administration Balfour was appointed First Lord of the Treasury and Leader of the Commons as before. These positions he continued to hold until Lord Salisbury retired from the premiership in July 1902, whereupon Balfour stepped into his uncle's shoes as a matter of course.

For three years and a half he was Prime Minister, and it can hardly be said that the experience was a happy or successful one. He did not get on very well with King Edward: his Majesty once complained that his manner was too *condescending*. He had an unruly lot of ministers, and very soon Joseph Chamberlain, who was Colonial Secretary, launched out on a raging, tearing campaign in support of what he called Tariff Reform, which turned out to be suspiciously like Protection under a new name. Ritchie, the Chancellor of the Exchequer, was a convinced Free Trader, and the Cabinet meetings in which he and Chamberlain clashed must have been a sore trial to Balfour, who found it next to impossible to make up his mind between the sets of confusing arguments.

Then there was education. Balfour had an entirely genuine belief in the virtues of national education, and in 1902 he had introduced a Bill which proposed the abolition of the School Board system that had been set up under the Act of 1870 in favour of one in which the county councils became the local education authorities, responsible for providing and maintaining a comprehensive network of primary and secondary schools. The Bill was most strenuously resisted by the Nonconformists on the ground that they as ratepayers might be called upon to contribute towards the support of schools that had been established by the Church of England. In the end the Bill became law, but only in face of an agitation which was continued for years and contributed very largely to the Conservative defeat at the polls in 1906. It was the Education Act of Balfour's government, however, which laid the foundations of the educational system which has endured to our own time.

Much less controversial was the conclusion of the *Entente cordiale* with France in 1903. This ought indeed to have been considered much more critically than it was, since it represented the abandonment of Britain's time-honoured and well-tried policy of ' splendid isolation ' from continental quarrels that Lord Salisbury had insisted upon. Balfour, it seems, looked upon the *Entente* as a means of settling old disputes rather than a new alliance, but he lived to see it denounced as a contributory factor to the First World War.

With his party and his government bitterly divided, confronted by problems clamouring for solution and without the foggiest notion of how they might be resolved, suffering reverses in the lobbies and by-election defeats, Balfour at length determined to resign, which in December 1905 he did. Campbell-Bannerman thereupon formed his administration and went to the country.

The general election resulted in the most crushing Conservative defeat. Almost twenty years of Conservative domination were ended at a stroke. Balfour had inherited a majority of well over a hundred, but in the new House he was left with a dispirited remnant —a total of 157 in a House of 670 members—many of whom disputed his leadership and more still blamed him for the electoral disaster.

Balfour himself was among the defeated, being rejected at Manchester by a majority of two thousand votes. He was shortly after returned for the City of London at a conveniently arranged by-election, and he was confirmed in the leadership of the party. But his position became increasingly difficult and tiresome, and in November 1911 he resigned the leadership.

This was by no means the end of his political career, however; indeed, it may be said that it was in his later years that he attained to his full stature. From 1915, when he joined Asquith's coalition government as First Lord of the Admiralty, until 1929 when he retired after five years as Lord President of the Council under Baldwin, Balfour had a seat in almost every Cabinet.

Not much that he did was specially noteworthy in these years, but an exception must be made in respect of his successful advocacy of the establishment in Palestine of a ' national home for the Jewish people '. Although it was issued with the full authority of the Cabinet, the so-called Balfour Declaration was made in a letter Balfour wrote to Lord Rothschild and signed as Foreign Secretary on 2 November 1917. The Declaration, it should be noted, was a calculated political move to enlist world Jewry on the side of the Allies against the Central Powers, but it is true to say that Balfour had an intense sympathy with the Jewish people in their age-old struggles against persecution and suppression. At the same time, he was not anti-Arab; in many speeches he urged that Jews and Arabs should work together to construct a society in which both races and religions should have free and equal participation.

Balfour was called ' a politician among philosophers, and a philosopher among politicians '. No statesman was more convinced of the vast importance of theoretical and practical science, and particularly in his latter years as Lord President of the Council he strove to promote the application of science to industry. His was a penetrating, probing, intensely inquisitive intelligence, and it is worth mentioning that he took an almost lifelong interest in Spiritualism, without ever becoming a believer. He was a founder member of the Society for Psychical Research in 1882, and its President ten years later. As regards his religion, his writings, e.g. *A Defence of Philosophic Doubt* (1879), *The Foundations of Belief* (1895), and *Theism and Humanism* (1915), reveal him as a philosophic Theist, and he was a regular churchgoer.

For a man who professed indifference to honorary distinctions he did pretty well. He was elected Chancellor of Cambridge University and President of the British Association. In 1916 he was awarded the Order of Merit, and in 1922 that of the Garter, with the intimation that an earldom would be his if he cared to accept it. He did care and after a few months as Sir Arthur Balfour he became Earl of Balfour.

When the Baldwin government came to an end in 1929, Balfour's official career ended with it. He retired to Fisher's Hill, his brother Gerald's house at Woking, where he passed the remaining months of his life—listening to gramophone music, greeting old friends, engaging in sprightly talk, receiving bits of political gossip, and taking an occasional look at his investments, which he had never had time to watch over properly.

As an old man not far short of eighty-two, grown feeble in body but with a mind still capable of flashing gleams of intelligence, he died on 19 March 1930. An Abbey funeral was offered as a matter of right, but he was buried, as he had wished, in the family ground beside the church at Whittingehame.

34

SIR HENRY CAMPBELL-BANNERMAN

AT THE TURN OF THE CENTURY, the premiership was almost a Scots monopoly. Gladstone, Rosebery, Balfour, Campbell-Bannerman—the odd man out was Salisbury. Campbell-Bannerman was the third Scotsman in succession to become Prime Minister in a Liberal Government. This was in 1905, when the Liberals under his leadership won the greatest electoral triumph in their history.

' C.B.'—the initials are a convenient shorthand and were very generally employed—was the descendant of Scottish peasants who for generations had been settled in Menteith, in south-east Perthshire, until in 1803 James Campbell (as we shall see, the Bannerman was added later), was obliged to sell his farm because a neighbouring landowner wished to add it to his park. He moved with his wife and nine children to Glasgow, where he opened a grocer's shop in Gallowgate and then a year later moved to the Saltmarket, where he dealt in general provisions. Times were hard, however, the shop had to be given up, and the sons had to push out on their own. The eldest went to America and stayed there, but James, William, and Alexander found various employments in Glasgow.

The brother we are principally concerned with is James, since he was the future Prime Minister's father. At the age of twenty he became a partner in a tailoring business, but this failed and for the next four years he was a clothier on his own, during which time he was able to put by enough to pay off all the debts incurred in his earlier venture. Then in 1816 he joined his brother William in opening a warehouse supplying goods to hawkers and other small traders. In the next year this became the firm of J. and W. Campbell, and it was soon doing well. James Campbell was the senior partner, and in 1822 he was sufficiently well off to marry Miss Janet Bannerman, daughter of a prosperous Manchester manufacturer. About 1830 he acquired Kelvinside House—a large, pleasant eighteenth-century dwelling situated on the banks of the little river Kelvin in what was then a rural neighbourhood; and here, on 7 September 1836, was born the Campbell's second son and youngest child, who was named Henry.

James Campbell did not die until 1876, when he was eighty-six. He is described as a man of immense industry and a strong will. In addition to running a large and constantly expanding business he was prominent in local affairs. For many years he led the Conservatives in the town council, and in 1840 he was elected Lord Provost. As such he was one of the Scottish municipal dignitaries who were honoured with knighthoods on the occasion of the birth of the Prince of Wales. In 1837 and 1841 he stood for Parliament but was unsuccessful. He remained prominent in the local party, however, and lived long enough to see Henry become a Liberal M.P.—something which gave him a feeling of fatherly pride, however much he may have deplored his son's choice of party.

At the age of eleven, Henry Campbell was sent to Glasgow High School, where he remained until he was just on fourteen. Then he accompanied his brother James, who was ten years his senior, on a business trip to the Continent. The idea was that he should improve his knowledge of French, which would be very useful when the time came for him to join the family firm. This was in 1851, so on the way home the brothers put in a day at the Great Exhibition in Hyde Park.

In that same year Henry was entered at Glasgow University, where at seventeen he won the Cowan gold medal for Greek. Then from 1854 to 1858 he was at Trinity College, Cambridge, living quietly and not achieving any academic or sporting distinction. In one of his early speeches in the House of Commons he remarked that Oxford and Cambridge were places where a few young men were given a minimum of education at a maximum of expense.

Returning to Glasgow, he was given a desk in the business, and after two years he was made a partner, even though he disliked the work and dodged it whenever he could. In 1860, when he was twenty-four, he married Miss Charlotte Bruce, daughter of Major-General Sir Charles Bruce, officer commanding the troops at Edinburgh. He had first met her at his brother James's wedding, and it was a case of love at first sight.

So many Prime Ministers have been lucky in love that it seems hardly necessary to say that this union was no exception. The new Mrs. Campbell was not very interested in politics, but she was a soldier's daughter, and C.B. had no more resolute and courageous supporter than his Charlotte. When she spoke of her husband, Lady Campbell-Bannerman used to say, ' Henry is a good man, how good no one knows but myself '.

By this time Henry Campbell had become a Liberal in politics and his thoughts turned more and more towards the possibility of a parliamentary career. In 1868 he took the plunge and stood as an independent Liberal at a by-election at Stirling Burghs. He was defeated, but at the general election later in the year he stood again and this time was successful. He remained M.P. for Stirling Burghs for the rest of his life.

Before the election he had given an undertaking that if he were successful he would devote the whole of his time to his parliamentary duties. His father and brothers put no obstacles in his way, and he retired from active participation in the business although he retained a substantial financial interest.

When he entered the House of Commons, Gladstone was Prime Minister, and Campbell gave him his enthusiastic support. His speeches were not very frequent to begin with, and they remained rather pedestrian performances throughout his career. Gladstone had his eye on him as a fellow Scot but more because of his business experience, and in 1871 C.B. was appointed Financial Secretary at the War Office.

In that same year his uncle Henry Bannerman, who had succeeded to the Manchester business, died and left him a property in Kent on the condition that he assumed the name of Bannerman.

Out of office between 1874 and 1880 when the Conservatives were in power, he returned to his former place at the War Office when Gladstone formed his second administration. In 1882 he was transferred to a similar post at the Admiralty, and then two years later was made Chief Secretary for Ireland. This was a notoriously exacting post, but C.B. managed pretty well. Parnell, the leader of the Irish Home Rulers, commended him for ' letting things alone— a sensible thing for an Irish Secretary ', and Healy, another of the Irish M.P.s, said that he governed Ireland with Scotch jokes.

When the Liberal party split over Gladstone's Home Rule policy, C.B. threw in his lot with Gladstone, and in 1886 was appointed (apparently on the suggestion of Queen Victoria, who had come to think rather highly of him) Secretary of State for War with a seat in the Cabinet.

Very soon he was out of office again, but he returned to the War Office in 1892 under Gladstone and continued under Rosebery until 1895, when a motion was carried alleging that C.B. had failed to ensure that the Army had a sufficient supply of cordite. The adverse vote brought about his resignation, which was immediately followed by that of the Rosebery government.

There was widespread regret at his departure from the War Office. Soldiers and civil servants were agreed that he had done a good job, and they particularly appreciated his sense of humour. The workers in the Ordnance factories remembered that it was he who had obtained for them a forty-eight-hour week. The queen was so pleased with him that she made him G.C.B.

At this time Sir Henry thought of letting his name go forward in the election of Speaker of the House of Commons; but his Liberal colleagues urged him to continue in active politics, and in 1899 they showed their regard by electing him to the party leadership.

This soon proved to be a decidedly hot seat. When war broke out in South Africa the Liberal party were bitterly divided. One section, who became known as Liberal Imperialists and included Asquith, Haldane, and Edward Grey, were inclined to support the Salisbury government; but the more radical element rallied round Campbell-Bannerman and his young lieutenant, David Lloyd George, in denouncing the policies that had led up to the war and urging that peace should be made as soon as possible. As might be expected, C.B. and his following were dubbed pro-Boers, and the Conservative government forthwith plunged the country into a general election—the so-called khaki election—in hopes of cashing in on patriotic sentiment. When the electors were warned that 'a vote for the Liberals is a vote for the Boers' it is remarkable that the Liberals lost no more than a handful of seats, although C.B. was among those who had their majorities severely reduced.

By that time, the close of 1900, it was thought that the war was as good as won, but in fact it dragged on for two more years, as the Boer commandos were always 'on the run' but never seemed to get caught. To contain their activities Kitchener, the commander of the British forces, embarked on a scorched-earth policy, burning the crops and homesteads of the Boer farmers and rounding up their women and children into concentration camps, where numbers of them died of disease and hardship.

C.B. denounced this policy in the strongest terms, in Parliament and on public platforms throughout the country, and in one of his speeches he used the phrase, 'methods of barbarism', which aroused intense opprobrium. He was urged to soften the remark or explain it away, but with typical stubbornness he refused to budge and even went out of his way to repeat it. With the result that in a crucial division in June 1901, fifty Liberals ostentatiously refrained from supporting him in the lobby, and there was talk of getting him removed from the party leadership.

But when the war was over he soon succeeded in re-establishing his position, and in the years of the Balfour administration he was able to rally the Liberals and form them into a united party, full of fight and vigour. He was confirmed in the party leadership, and on 5 December 1905, the day after Balfour had offered his Government's resignation, Sir Henry Campbell-Bannerman was received by King Edward at Buckingham Palace and invited to form an administration. He accepted forthwith, and went off to draw up his list of ministers.

This did not prove so straightforward a matter as he may have hoped. It was soon made clear to him that he was not everybody's choice: some of the Liberal Leaguers would have preferred Rosebery, and although they were quite prepared to serve under C.B. they were strongly of the opinion that, considering his age and his indifferent health, he would be well advised to accept a peerage and go to the House of Lords, leaving the leadership of the House of Commons to Asquith.

Campbell-Bannerman was taken aback, and very much hurt. He recalled that at their recent interview King Edward had made much the same suggestion, and he wondered if his Majesty had been influenced against him. He promised to think the matter over, which everybody understood to mean that he would consult ' the Authority ', as he whimsically styled his wife. Lady Campbell-Bannerman arrived in London from Scotland the day following his appointment, and when she heard what was going on she put her foot down.

Through all the lean and hungry years of opposition her Henry had kept the Liberal flag flying, and now, in the hour of victory, his colleagues wanted to put him on the shelf! He was too modest, she told him, too self-effacing; he must stand up, and fight!

In fact that is what he had already resolved to do, and when it came to the crunch he experienced no difficulty. Asquith offered his assistance, and Grey and Haldane thereupon hastened to come to terms. The Prime Minister presented his list to King Edward on Sunday, 10 December 1905, and the next morning the new Ministers went to the Palace to kiss hands.

Campbell-Bannerman was Prime Minister and First Lord of the Treasury; and it should be noted that now, for the first time, the Prime Minister received official recognition—after the office had been in existence since Walpole's time—and given a place in the Order of Precedence (in England, following Royalty, the two Archbishops, and the Lord Chancellor). Asquith was Chancellor of the Exchequer, Sir Edward Grey Foreign Secretary, Herbert Gladstone Home Secretary, John Morley Secretary of State for India, Haldane Secretary of State for War, Lloyd George President of the Board of Trade, and the veteran Labour leader John Burns President of the Local Government Board. Way down among the under-secretaries appeared the name of Winston Churchill. In the light of history, the administration appears as the most distinguished of modern times.

Now the election campaign opened, and Campbell-Bannerman led the Liberals into battle. He was not far off seventy, and his health was giving cause for anxiety, but he displayed a power of leadership, which even his best friends had hardly suspected. He was never much of a speaker, but wherever he went he had huge audiences, and, except for a few Suffragettes, who now for the first time made themselves seen and heard, he was received with tremendous enthusiasm.

Polling began in the middle of January and went on for a fort-night, as was the rule in those days. The very first results showed which way the tide was moving, and in the end the Liberals were returned 377 strong; in addition there were 53 Labour members and 83 Irish Nationalists who were generally their allies. The Conservatives totalled 157 only, so that the Government majority was 356. It was indeed a landslide.

For two years Campbell-Bannerman was Prime Minister, and from the outset he must have realized that his age and increasing infirmity of body were against him. But there was no lack of spirit in the way in which he faced the House and laid down his pro-gramme. King Edward had come to have a sincere regard for C.B. and was resolved to give him his support.

Before long, however, the Prime Minister's health was giving rise to increased anxiety; then in the summer of 1906 Lady Camp-bell-Bannerman, who some years before had suffered a paralytic stroke, was taken seriously ill when they were staying at Marienbad, where they had been going for years. She died on 30 August, and the old man was heartbroken. ' Now I am alone in the world,' he wrote to one of his closest friends. ' But with God's help, I will go on, as she would have had me go on, until such forces as I possess without her I can muster, fail altogether . . .'

For another year or so he carried on, presenting a brave face to the world. He took his seat on the front bench in the House of Commons whenever he was able, but he was obliged to leave most of the fighting to his lieutenants, Asquith in particular. An Education Bill was introduced, but was killed by the House of Lords. The Trade Disputes Act of 1906 strengthened the position of trade unions in the eyes of the law. Responsible government was restored to the Boer republics. These and all the other measures of his government the Prime Minister supported with an ability and energy that surprised his opponents and shamed those of his supporters who had doubted his staying power. And there was no doubt that the public at large had a most genuine affection for him. But early in 1908 he was clearly breaking up. The doctors diagnosed heart trouble, and occasional fainting-fits caused consternation among his staff. On 12 February he spoke in the House of Commons for the last time, and that evening he took to his room at No. 10 never to leave it again.

For two months he lay there ill, getting steadily worse, and for six weeks the Government was virtually without a Prime Minister. King Edward and the Cabinet were most anxious not to do anything that would cause him any distress, but on 3 April Sir Henry wrote a formal letter of resignation.

'That's the last kick,' he told his secretary as he laid down his pen; and then, noting his distress he added, 'My dear fellow, I don't mind. I've been Prime Minister for longer than I deserve.' He was too ill to be moved from No. 10, and it was there that he died, on 22 April 1908.

There was a grand memorial service in Westminster Abbey, and in the House of Commons Asquith paid a most powerful tribute to one who 'was stricken down in the midst of his work, a martyr, if ever there was one, to conscience and duty . . .' On 26 April C.B. was buried beside his wife in the churchyard at Meigle, the little village in the vale of Strathmore close to Belmont Castle, which for over twenty years had been his much loved home.

Above the grave was placed a stone tablet for which he had chosen the inscription; it is in Italian, from Tasso's *Jerusalem*, and has been rendered; 'And he led her to where was his aged wife, who with heart at one with his had made Heaven for him.'

C.B. was much more of a cosmopolitan than most British politicians. He spoke perfect French and was fluent in Italian. From 1872 he and his wife used to spend six weeks during the summer recess on the Continent, always including a stay at Marienbad, where Dr. Ott, the celebrated spa doctor, was a personal friend.

Belmont Castle, his home in Scotland, was nothing like so stately a home as the name suggests. He bought it in 1887 and largely rebuilt it, making it a most comfortable place to live in. He delighted in visiting the stables—he kept carriages but never a motor—and the extensive gardens. Almost always he had a dog or dogs at his heels. His special pleasure was in his trees. No tree might be touched without his permission. When he got back to Belmont after a stay in London he would walk round the grounds and bow to his special favourites, and wish them good morning.

He had other quaint habits. He had a collection of walking-sticks, and on choosing one for his morning stroll he would apologize under his breath to the others for having to be left behind. In his bureau was a drawer into which he slipped the stubs of pencils, since, he said, they were old friends who ought to be properly cared for when their day was done.

In the early days at Belmont he used to do a little shooting, but in later years he left that to his guests; he liked living things too much to be happy in killing them. He loved to see the rabbits gambolling on the lawn in front of his window, and absolutely forbade that they should be trapped, or even wired off.

In his dress he was always very neat, a bit of a dandy in fact. A wealthy man, and a most generous one, he also practised the Scottish virtue of thrift, and kept strict accounts of his expenditure. He got on very well with Edward VII after he became Prime Minister. On one occasion a picture was published in the illustrated papers of King and Prime Minister in earnest conversation at Marienbad; his Majesty was striking his hand in his palm and C.B. was listening gravely. It was widely supposed that they were discussing possible developments in the Balkans, but when C.B. was shown the picture he remarked; ' Would you like to know what the King was saying to me ? He wanted to have my opinion whether halibut is better baked or boiled ! '

35

HERBERT HENRY ASQUITH

MR. ASQUITH, as he was known for nearly the whole of the forty years that he spent in Parliament, was a Yorkshireman, born at Morley in the West Riding on 12 September 1852. His father, Joseph Dixon Asquith, was engaged in the woollen industry as a weaver or wool-spinner, and is described as a cultivated man, pious and agreeable, but somewhat lacking in business initiative. His mother, Emily Willans, was more forceful, and like her husband came of Puritan Nonconformist stock. The local Congregational chapel was the centre of their life.

Asquith himself recalled that his early years were passed in simple comfort and semi-rural surroundings, first at Morley and then at Mirfield, and that he spent a great deal of time in going to chapel and Sunday school and reading sermons. It was the ordinary existence of the lower middle-class Nonconformist, and in after life he looked back upon it with little interest and no regrets.

Joseph Asquith died in 1861, leaving his wife in very poor circumstances with four young children to care for. Her father, William Willans, a man of some business standing in Huddersfield as a woolstapler, came to the rescue, and the whole family were transferred to Huddersfield. The two boys, Henry and his elder brother Willans, then aged respectively eight and nine, were sent for a short time to a local day school and then in the autumn of that same year to a boarding-school at Fulneck, near Leeds, that was run by the Nonconformist denomination known as the Moravians.

But in 1863 the grandfather died and there was another family upheaval. Mrs. Asquith moved south, to St. Leonards, and her brothers assumed responsibility for her boys' education. They were entered as day boys at the City of London school, then established in Milk Street, Cheapside. Lodgings were found for them at Pimlico and later in Islington.

Soon after their arrival at the school, Dr. Edwin Abbott was appointed headmaster, and this distinguished scholar and fine teacher was quick to appreciate Henry's extraordinary capabilities. He encouraged him in every way, and in 1869, at the age of seventeen, the youth won a classical scholarship to Balliol College, Oxford, of which the great Benjamin Jowett had just become master. Asquith's career at Balliol was one continued triumph, and after winning a number of prizes and scholarships he was elected a fellow of the college in 1874. This furnished him with a small but regular income over the next seven years, when he was greatly in need of it.

'Asquith will get on,' pronounced Jowett, 'he is so direct.' Oxford was indeed the making of him, and he bore away with him not only a fund of sound scholarship but a great reputation as a speaker. He distinguished himself at the debates of the Oxford Union, and became its President. An academic career lay open but his heart was already in politics and he decided to read for the Bar. He was called at Lincoln's Inn in 1876, and then for the next six or seven years toiled desperately hard as a brief-hungry young barrister in Fig Tree Court in the Temple. To help make ends meet he became a contributor to the *Spectator*, *The Economist*, and other journals, and he also did a good deal of lecturing for the Law Society.

While he was still struggling to build up a practice, he took the highly venturesome step of getting married. His bride was Helen Melland, daughter of a prosperous Manchester physician, whom he had met while staying with his mother at St. Leonards. He was eighteen when he fell in love with her and she was fifteen, and they had to wait for five or six years before even getting engaged. But at length, in August 1877, they were married and set up house in John Street, now Keats Grove, in Hampstead. In the next dozen years five children were born to them, and they were chronically hard up. But Mrs. Asquith's private income of a few hundreds a year and what he could make at the Bar and with his writing enabled them to maintain a reasonably high standard of comfort and culture.

That Asquith felt pretty confident of the future is shown by the fact that in 1886, when he received an invitation to stand as Liberal candidate for East Fife at the forthcoming general election, he posted his acceptance the same day. A few days later he issued an election address, in which he made it clear that he was a Liberal of the advanced Gladstonian persuasion, and in due course he was returned at the head of the poll. He continued to represent East Fife without a break until 1918.

When he entered the House of Commons, Lord Salisbury was Prime Minister at the head of his Conservative administration. From the first Asquith displayed what was called a front-bench style. The old Gladstone's eagle eye fastened upon him, and in

1892 Asquith was appointed Home Secretary in Gladstone's fourth and last Government—an extraordinarily rapid promotion for a man of forty who had had absolutely no previous experience of office.

But while Asquith seemed to be striding ahead to a great future his domestic happiness was suddenly laid in ruins. In August 1891 he took his wife and children on holiday to Lamlash in the Isle of Arran, and while there Mrs. Asquith was taken ill with typhoid. After lying dangerously ill for three weeks she died, when she was only thirty-five. In mid-September Asquith took his children back to a home made desolate.

' I was only eighteen when I fell in love with her,' he wrote to a friend in a letter that is printed in the official life of him by J. A. Spender and his son Cyril Asquith, ' and we married when we were little more than boy and girl. In the cant phrase, our marriage was " a great success "; from first to last it was never troubled by any kind of sorrow or dissension; and when the sun went down it was in an unclouded sky.'

Asquith buried himself in his work. He was Home Secretary for three years, and he earned the reputation of being the best one of modern times. He was responsible for appointing the first women factory inspectors and for an excellent Factory Act (1895); he showed a firm hand in industrial disputes. But at the general election in 1895 the Liberals were defeated, and after three years as a Cabinet minister Asquith returned to his practice at the Bar—the first ex-Cabinet minister to do such a thing.

In the meantime he had married again. His second wife was Miss Margot (Margaret) Tennant, a daughter of Sir Charles Tennant, Bart., who had made a great fortune as a company promoter and financier. They first met in 1891 at a dinner at the House of Commons. Until then she had not even heard his name, but she was drawn to him because in dress and appearance, reserved demeanour and intelligent interests, he seemed so very different from the men of her own gay and pleasure-loving set. After dinner they walked on the terrace, leant on the parapet and looked at the river, and talked and talked far into the night, until a policeman came to tell them that the House had been up for some time.

When she found out that he was married, she asked the Asquiths to dinner, and she visited them at Hampstead on a number of occasions. Of Helen Asquith she wrote years afterwards in her *Autobiography* that ' she was so different from me that I had a longing for her approval '. She was gentle, pretty, and unambitious, and spoke of her home and children in a way that seemed to exclude her from ' a life of political aggrandizement, which was from early days the life that captivated my imagination '. When Margot congratulated her on having married a man who was bound to achieve the highest political distinction, Mrs. Asquith calmly rejoined that *that* was not what she coveted for him. As Margot drove home to Grosvenor Square she felt so shaken that she wondered if her ambition for Asquith's success was wrong.

' Different ' she was from both husband and wife. She belonged to ' society '—not the aristocratic *élite*, it is true, but the ostentatiously wealthy, the new rich. She was outrageously frank, never minding what she said or to whom she said it. She was a fine and daring rider to hounds, she danced very well, she could draw and play the piano ' with a touch of the real thing ', she could hold her own with ease among the politico-literary coterie of ' the Souls ', and could appreciate the finer points of her friend Arthur Balfour's literary style. After riding, the thing she cared for most was writing, and it is in her volumes of autobiography that she revealed herself, so brilliant and wayward, so spiteful and charitable, so irritating, and above all, so courageous.

Courage she certainly needed, when at length she agreed to marry the middle-aged widower with his houseful of young children. ' It is not possible to be a leader of fashion and to do your duty to the five children,' warned her old friend Dr. Jowett. Some of her circle thought she was far too frivolous a person to marry such a famous man as Mr. Asquith, but others, including Mr. Gladstone and Arthur Balfour, were content to let her make her own decision. On 10 May 1894, at St. George's, Hanover Square, the twenty-six-year-old Miss Margot Tennant married the forty-one-year-old Mr. Asquith. A grand affair it was, too, with four Prime Ministers— past, present and future—Gladstone and Rosebery, Balfour and Asquith himself—putting their names to the marriage-register. And, to quote Margot's own summary, ' We kept together in an inseparable clasp of confidence and love.'

As for the five children, she took them in her stride. As Lady Violet Bonham Carter (Baroness Asquith) revealed in a broadcast, she filled them ' with admiration, amazement, amusement, affection, sometimes (even as children) with a vague sense of uneasiness as to what she might, or might not do, next '. Before long she had added to the family two children of her own, Anthony and Elizabeth (Princess Bibesco).

*   *   *

For ten years after the collapse of the Rosebery administration in 1895 the Liberals were in opposition. Asquith had his place on the Opposition front bench, but with a large and growing family to support he had to cultivate his practice at the Bar—which he did to such good effect that before long he was making between five and ten thousand a year. Until the Boer War he gave his support to Campbell-Bannerman as the Liberal party leader, but then he joined the Liberal League and on one famous occasion refused to follow C.B. into the lobby. But when Joseph Chamberlain launched out on his raging, tearing campaign in support of Tariff Reform there was no more doughty propounder of the case for Free Trade than Asquith, whether in Parliament or on platforms up and down the country.

Then came the general election of 1905, in which the Liberals won so massive a victory. Asquith was among those who urged that the new Prime Minister, Campbell-Bannerman, should retire upstairs to the House of Lords, when the leadership of the House of Commons would have fallen on Asquith's shoulders; but when C.B. proved obstinate he refused to press him, and he had no qualms about accepting the post of Chancellor of the Exchequer in the government that was formed.

As such, he introduced three Budgets. The first, in 1906, was necessarily a humdrum affair; the second was notable for the innovation of a different rate of tax on earned and unearned income; and the third provided for the payment of Old Age Pensions. Judged by modern standards these were niggardly: 5s. a week to persons over the age of seventy with no more than 8s. a week of their own. But for great numbers of old folk that 5s. made all the difference, and Asquith's measure may be seen as the first step towards the establishment of the Welfare State.

But by the time Asquith introduced his third Budget he was no longer Chancellor of the Exchequer but Prime Minister.

For months past Campbell-Bannerman had been a very sick man, and most of the work had fallen to Asquith as his second-in-command. On 27 March 1908, C.B. called Asquith to No. 10 Downing Street and told him that he knew he was dying. They talked together for over an hour, and as they parted C.B. shook him warmly by the hand and thanked him for having been ' so wonderful a colleague, so loyal, so disinterested, so able '. His final words were: ' You are the greatest gentleman I have ever met. This is not the last of me. We will meet again, Asquith.'

A few days later King Edward, who was holidaying at Biarritz, received his Prime Minister's resignation, and he at once summoned Asquith to come and see him with a view to his forming a government.

The news that Asquith had been sent for leaked out and there was some unfavourable comment. The king was generally blamed for not having cut short his holiday and proceeding to London, and *The Times* characterized the appointing of a Prime Minister on foreign soil as ' an inconvenient and dangerous departure from precedent '. But Asquith did not seem to mind. Dodging the reporters hovering round his dootrstep in Cavendish Square, he gave a wave to his wife and drove to Charing Cross. Arrived at Biarritz, he presented himself to his Majesty at his hotel on 6 April. He had put on a frock coat, he wrote to tell his wife, and the king was similarly attired. ' I presented him with a written resignation of the office of Chr. of the Exr., and he then said, " I appoint you P.M. and 1st Lord of the Treasury," whereupon I knelt down and kissed his hand. *Voilà tout!* He then asked me to come into the next room and breakfast with him . . .'

On his return to London, Asquith formed his government. With only slight reshuffling it was the same brilliant team that Campbell-Bannerman had put together, but Lloyd George took Asquith's former place at the Exchequer, and Winston Churchill was promoted from an under-secretaryship to the presidency of the Board of Trade.

For the next three years Asquith was preoccupied with the struggle to overcome the Lords' veto. Since Gladstone's first ministry the Upper House, with its permanent Conservative majority, had been a thorn in the flesh of Liberal governments; but in 1909 they went too far when they rejected Lloyd George's budget. Not since 1688 had the House of Lords refused to pass into law the financial provisions made by the House of Commons, and Asquith promptly denounced their action as ' a breach of the constitution and a usurpation of the rights of the House of Commons '. Parliament was promptly dissolved, and in January 1910 a general election was fought mainly on the issue of ' Peers v. the People '. The Liberals were returned to power but with a much-reduced majority—in fact, henceforth Asquith was dependent on the Irish members to keep him in office.

Undeterred, however, he proceeded to introduce the Parliament Bill, which provided that the House of Lords should be deprived of their power to reject ' money bills ', and that other Bills, if passed by the House of Commons in three sessions spread over three years, would receive the royal assent even without the approval of the Lords. On this being rejected, as was to be expected, by the upper house, Asquith appealed to the country again in December 1910, and the general election resulted in a net gain to the Government of one seat. The Parliament Bill was again introduced, and Asquith then revealed that he had obtained the consent of the new king, George V, to the creation if necessary of a sufficient number of new peers to get the Bill through the House of Lords. The fury of the Conservatives was unbounded. Asquith was accused of having acted the bully in the royal closet; and when on 24 July 1911 he rose in the House of Commons to move that the Lords' amendments be rejected, he was howled down.

The next morning the speech he had been prevented from delivering was printed in all the newspapers. The Parliament Bill was submitted again to the House of Lords and this time wiser counsels prevailed. Although a number of ' die-hards ' under Lord Halsbury persisted in their opposition, a number of Conservative peers abstained and a number more voted with the Government, so that the Bill was passed on 10 August by 131 votes to 114.

With the passing of the Parliament Act the House of Commons obtained at last that predominance over the House of Lords for which it had been struggling for centuries. The Lords still possessed their veto, but it was a much limited one, and since then it has been even further restricted. Asquith in fact had achieved a great constitutional revolution, and he promptly took advantage of it to introduce a bill providing for the grant of Home Rule to Ireland.

By the spring of 1914 the bill had passed the House of Commons twice and had been twice rejected by the House of Lords; now the time had come for its third, and final, submission. The Ulstermen, fully backed by the Conservatives at Westminster under Bonar Law and Sir Edward Carson, prepared for armed resistance. In March 1914 there was the Curragh incident, when a number of British Army officers in the great camp outside Dublin gave notice that they would resign their commissions rather than be employed against Ulster. The War Secretary, General Seely, blundered badly, and Asquith had to take over his post while still continuing as Prime Minister. This had a steadying influence, but civil war was still an imminent possibility when the assassination of the Austrian archduke at Serajevo set in motion the chain of events that led to the outbreak of the First World War.

Britain declared war on Germany on 4 August 1914, and it was largely due to Asquith's leadership that she did so as a united people, feeling convinced that her cause was wholly just. In the light of history this may be seen as Asquith's greatest achievement.

Until May 1915 the Liberal government remained in office, but then Asquith thought it desirable to bring the Conservatives into active participation. He thereupon proceeded to form a Coalition, of which he was Prime Minister but in which places were found for the Conservative leaders—Balfour, Bonar Law, Austen Chamberlain, Lord Curzon, and Carson—and also for Arthur Henderson as the representative of Labour.

The Coalition was not a success. The Liberal and Conservative sections failed to pull together, and the Government as a whole became increasingly unpopular with the general public. As the war dragged on and there seemed to be little to show for the heavy casualties on the various fronts and the inconveniences and deprivations at home, the newspapers became more and more loud voiced in their criticisms, and Lord Northcliffe's journals in particular, *The Times* and the *Daily Mail*, made a dead set at Asquith, charging him with ignorance, indifference, dilly-dallying, and downright incompetence. A remark of his, ' Wait and see ', that he had made years before in connection with the Parliament Bill, was now resurrected and given the widest circulation. Thus George Robey, then at the height of his fame as a music-hall performer, introduced a verse into one of his most popular songs in which the Prime Minister was supposed to have answered his critics with advice which ended:

> Just stem this tide of ignorant conjecture,
> Remain inert and dormant just like me,
> And cultivate spontaneous acquiescence,
> In other words, Wait and See !!!

Cruel caricatures of the Prime Minister appeared in the papers, and there was a loud outcry aginst the ' old gang '. In her autobiography Mrs. Asquith tells how her husband was alleged to have had shares in Krupps, the great German armaments firm; that her daughter was engaged to a German general—or it may have been an admiral; and that she herself was wont to ' feed Prussian prisoners with every dainty and comestible, and play lawn tennis with them at Donnington Hall—a place whose very whereabouts is unknown to me '. For one specially virulent libel she sued a London newspaper and was awarded £1000 in damages.

As 1916 wore on the outlook got steadily worse. The battle of Jutland gave a nasty shock to public opinion when it was revealed as something less than a victory. There was the Easter Rising of Sinn Feiners in Dublin, which was suppressed only after savage street fighting. Then in June, Lord Kitchener, who had been elevated into a kind of national father figure, was drowned in H.M.S. *Hampshire* when on the way to Russia. Asquith appointed Lloyd George to fill his place at the War Office—much to Mrs. Asquith's dismay. 'We are out,' she wrote in her diary; 'it can only be a question of time now when we shall have to leave Downing Street.'

But the climax of horror in that year of massive disappointment and disaster was the battle of the Somme, in which the flower of Britain's manhood were driven to the slaughter under generals who excelled in bloody-mindedness if in nothing else. It was a terrible blow to Asquith when his eldest son, Raymond—he had four other sons in the Army—was killed in September when he was leading his men over the top. This son, whose academic record outshone even his father's, was the apple of his eye. 'Whatever pride I had in the past,' Asquith wrote at the time, 'and whatever hope I had for the far future—by much the largest part of both was invested in him. Now all that is gone . . .' He was so crushed by the news that it was weeks before he was able to get back his bearings, and in fact after Raymond's death he was never the same man again.

As the year drew to its close, there were indications of a definite move against the Prime Minister. The newspapers stepped up their campaign against him, and on every hand it was coming to be recognized that there must be a radical change in the direction of the war. It says much for Asquith's hold on his colleagues that at first there was no idea of his being displaced. The opposition centred round Lloyd George, who had been achieving some loudly publicized successes at the Ministry of Munitions and now at the War Office. A prime mover behind the scenes was Sir Max Aitken (soon to be made Lord Beaverbrook), who was in the intimate counsels of Bonar Law. Lloyd George now came out with the proposal that there should be set up a War Committee of three or four members which would be charged with the active direction of the war. The Prime Minister would not be a member of this executive council, but he would still retain 'supreme and effective control of War policy'. Asquith seemed at first to fall in with this suggestion, but on Monday, 4 December, *The Times* came out with a leading article attacking Asquith in most insulting fashion, giving the impression that he was being relegated to a subordinate position in his own

Government. Asquith then backed out from his understanding with Lloyd George, whereupon the latter, with many expressions of personal attachment and esteem, tendered his resignation.

Asquith's Liberal colleagues hastened to assure him of their unflinching support; but to his surprise, dismay even, the Conservative leaders showed an inclination to take a different line; in fact they gave it as their opinion that he ought to resign—or accept their resignations. At seven o'clock on the evening of Tuesday, 5 December 1916, Asquith went to Buckingham Palace and placed his resignation in the king's hands.

Why he chose this course is still a matter of dispute, but one of the explanations is that he thought that the king would send for Bonar Law and Lloyd George in turn, and when both had proved unable to form a ministry, he would be recalled to office with greatly increased power and prestige. If this is what he thought, he miscalculated badly. Bonar Law and the other Conservative chiefs fell over themselves to serve in a Lloyd George administration, and on 7 December Lloyd George kissed hands as Prime Minister.

Asquith was offered a post in the new ministry but he refused to serve under Lloyd George, or, indeed, under Bonar Law or Balfour. King George offered him the Garter, but he respectfully declined. After having been Prime Minister for eight years and 241 days— the longest premiership since Lord Liverpool's—he took his seat on the Opposition front bench. He played no important part in the House until May 1918, when he committed a strange blunder. Without taking the elementary precaution of checking his facts, he moved that a Select Committee should be appointed to inquire into allegations made by Sir Frederick Maurice, Director of Military Operations at the War Office, that the Western Front had been starved of troops. Lloyd George strongly repudiated the charge, and insisted on treating Asquith's motion as one of ' no confidence '. In the ensuing division only 106 Liberals voted with Asquith. The incident was a most damaging blow to his reputation, and had the direst effects on his own political fortunes and those of the Liberal party of which he remained the leader.

Following the Armistice, there came a rather half-hearted suggestion from Lloyd George that Asquith should join the Government in some capacity, but this came to nothing, as likewise Asquith's hint that he might perhaps be included as one of the British representatives at the Peace Conference. Then came the general election, in which those who had supported Asquith in the Maurice debate were denied the ' coupon ' that was dished out by Lloyd George and

Bonar Law to their supporters. The result was a foregone conclusion. Only twenty-six members of the new House of Commons were Asquithian Liberals, and Asquith himself was defeated at East Fife after thirty-two years of unbroken service.

He took it badly. He was now sixty-six, and it might have been supposed that after such a deep personal humiliation he would think it time to retire from active politics. But Parliament was his life; and after many months when he was in almost complete eclipse, cold-shouldered by his former supporters, denied a public platform, and generally regarded as a has-been, he made a triumphant return to the House of Commons at a by-election in 1920 as Independent Liberal M.P. for Paisley.

When Asquith re-entered the House of Commons he soon concluded that it was the very worst he had known, full of hard-faced businessmen who seemed to have done very well for themselves out of the war. Things were not much better after the fall of the Coalition in 1922. Following upon a good deal of unseemly manoeuvring, the two wings of the Liberal party—Asquith's and Lloyd George's—were combined under Asquith's nominal leadership, but it was an uneasy conjunction and the rift between the two men was never properly closed. In 1924 the Liberals held the balance between the Conservatives and Labour, and Asquith took the responsibility of putting Labour in. He defended his action on the ground that Labour must govern some time, and under what better conditions could the experiment be made than the present, when MacDonald and his men would hold office only on condition of their good behaviour ?

But before the year was out MacDonald had come to grief, and at the general election the Liberals were almost wiped out. Asquith was again among the defeated, losing his seat at Paisley in a straight fight with a Labour opponent by over two thousand.

This was the end of the road for him, politically speaking. He was seventy-two, and there was little likelihood of his ever being able to return to the House of Commons. King George came to his assistance. In a most generously phrased letter he wrote that he thought Mr. Asquith's absence from Westminster was ' a national loss ', but that he felt strongly that after so long and eminent a career it was not fitting that he should be subjected to the strain and uncertainty of further electoral contests. In these circumstances, ' *it would give me great pleasure* ', he said, to confer on him a peerage. After some deliberation and consultation, Asquith was created Earl of Oxford and Asquith.

The new peer took his seat in the House of Lords, but he was no more comfortable there than he had been in the latter-day House of Commons. This is understandable, for in him the great line of politicians who were also fine classical scholars came to an end. Sometimes he was styled the ' last of the Romans ', and indeed he would have looked well in a toga—better, perhaps, than in the conventional black coat and waistcoat and striped trousers, generally baggy at the knees, that was his customary garb.

There was certainly a good deal of the patrician about him, notwithstanding the modest circumstances from which he sprang. He loved the pleasures of good society, and the kind of establishment that his wife preferred—with plenty of servants, including a butler, a big motor-car, and the constant flow of hospitality. He smoked a pipe, and he also liked his glass—a fact that was sometimes too obvious when he returned to his seat in the House after dinner. He was a great reader, from solid treatises on history and philosophy to Dickens and Scott and P. G. Wodehouse. He was also an untiring letter-writer, especially when, as Winston Churchill phrased it, ' his letters were addressed to brighter eyes than peer through politicians' spectacles '.

Sport did not appeal to him. He played golf, billiards, and chess, but what he liked best was a quiet evening at the bridge-table. He enjoyed country-house life, and in the most stormy period of his career sometimes laid himself open to criticism by going away for a long weekend.

In his personal character, he displayed some of the most distinctively Roman virtues—piety, which may be rendered as equivalent to patriotism, gravity and equanimity, resolution and absolute devotion to his duty as he saw it. At his best, his oratory ranked him among the great masters of parliamentary eloquence.

The short remainder of Asquith's life was spent mostly at his country house, The Wharf, on the banks of the Thames at Sutton Courtenay, in Berkshire. Early in 1927 he had a stroke which deprived him of the use of one leg, and he had to be pushed around in a wheel-chair. Occasionally he was well enough to be taken for a ride in a motor-car, which had always been one of his most appreciated pleasures. Towards the end his mind began to fail. He died on the evening of 15 February 1928, and was buried in the churchyard at Sutton Courtenay. His wife survived him until 1945.

In due course a memorial tablet was erected to Asquith in Westminster Abbey, on a pillar facing the statues of Gladstone and

Beaconsfield, Peel and Canning. On it are inscribed lines from
Milton's *Paradise Lost*, chosen by his family:

> Unmoved
> Unshaken, unseduced, unterrified,
> His loyalty he kept, his love, his zeal;
> Nor number, nor example, with him wrought
> To swerve from truth, or change his constant mind.

36

DAVID LLOYD GEORGE

LLOYD GEORGE was a Welshman of Welshmen, the first of his race to become Prime Minister. And yet it was not the fresh air from the Welsh hills that first filled his lungs but the muggy atmosphere of Manchester.

His birthplace was No. 5 New York Place, a little brick house in an alley off a back street, and the date of his birth was 17 January 1863. His father, William George, was the son of a Pembrokeshire hill farmer, but being clever and of a roving disposition he had gone out into the wider world as a school teacher. He held posts at private schools in London, Liverpool, and at several places in Wales; and he was teaching at Pwllheli, in Caernarvonshire, when he met and married Elizabeth Lloyd, daughter of the village shoemaker at Llanystumdwy, near Criccieth. But at the time of David's birth— he was the second child of the marriage, the first being a girl, Mary —William George was headmaster of a National school in a Manchester district. After only three months, however, his health broke down and he took his wife and their two children back to Pembrokeshire, where he rented a small farm near Haverfordwest. There he caught a chill one day while working in his garden, and after a week's illness, died of pneumonia in 1864, when he was only in his middle forties.

Left a widow at thirty-six, and with two little ones to provide for—and another on the way—Mrs. George was almost penniless. Fortunately she had a brother to whom she could turn—Richard Lloyd, who was carrying on the shoemaking business at Llanystumdwy that their father had established years before. 'Come, Richard,' was her simply-worded appeal, and he came at once. He settled their small affairs, and then took his sister and her two children back with her to his village. There shortly afterwards Mrs. George bore a third child, who was named William after his father.

Llanystumdwy was the first place that Lloyd George remembered, and throughout his long life it was never far from his thoughts. It was, and it is still, a grouping of small stone cottages, set astride the road to Criccieth, with the little river Dwyfor, here crossed by a triple-arched bridge, running through it on its way to the sea. And not far away to the north are the heights of Snowdonia, now blue-black in the sunshine and now wrapped in cloud, that played so large a part in Lloyd George's glowing oratory.

The Lloyds' dwelling was a typically Welsh cottage, with kitchen, tiny parlour and scullery on the ground floor and three bedrooms above. Next door was the workshop where Richard Lloyd and one or two assistants did the shoemaking and cobbling. He was a bachelor, and the home was managed by his mother who had been a widow for a quarter of a century. This Rebecca Lloyd, who was Lloyd George's grandmother, was also a good business woman, but she died when he was a child and he was brought up by his mother and uncle.

Very early David Lloyd George became aware of the existence of two Waleses. One was Wales of the landowners and landlords, the clergyman and his curate, the schoolmaster and the doctor and the better-off shopkeepers. They spoke English as a rule, prided themselves on their English ways and connections, and were regular attendants at the parish church of the Anglican establishment. When election time came round they voted solidly for the Conservative candidate.

The other Wales was peopled by the peasantry, the small traders and shopkeepers, the shepherds and cowhands and farm labourers, the blacksmith and baker and shoemaker, who spoke Welsh as a matter of course, went to chapel, and usually voted Liberal. When they dared, that is: Richard Lloyd was about the only Liberal in the village who was bold enough to admit the fact, for the landlords had a nasty habit of turning a tenant into the street if he had ventured to cast his vote in a way they didn't approve.

David Lloyd George was never in any doubt which was *his* Wales. Welsh was the first language he heard spoken at the fireside and the shoemaker's bench, and three times every Sunday, and on Wednesday evenings as well, he was taken to the little chapel of the Disciples of Christ (a stricter version of the Baptists) on the hill behind Criccieth. It was through listening to the Welsh preachers that he came to understand what power and majesty might be expressed in words.

When he was between three and four he was sent to the village school; it was attached to the church, but there was none other. The headmaster was an excellent teacher, and encouraged David in his simple studies. He taught him the Church Catechism and the three R's; and he had a wonderful way of telling the Bible stories so that they seemed to come alive. David showed such promise that he was allowed to stay on at school for a year or two beyond twelve, the usual school-leaving age.

But the best part of his education was what he was able to gather from the slender collection of books that he found on his uncle's shelves. Very early he fell under the spell of Macaulay and Thomas Carlyle and John Ruskin, and of the novelists Victor Hugo was perhaps his favourite. Hardly less important were the conversations that he heard in his uncle's workshop. Richard Lloyd was a deeply, if not widely, read man, and he took an intelligent interest in politics. It was in those lamp-lit surroundings that David Lloyd George first heard of Gladstone, and what the Liberalism was that Gladstone stood for.

When he left school—it was when he was just on fourteen—the question of his future came up. The boy was clever, beyond a doubt: he was a good talker, full of life and spirit. He might be a teacher, perhaps? They would have preferred the pulpit—but the Disciples had no paid ministry, and the boy had to earn his living . . . Then his mother recalled a lawyer in Liverpool who had been a very good friend to her at the time of her husband's death. He had been a good man: why should not her David become like him? So the Law it was.

Money was the first obstacle, but they decided to spend their slender savings on the boy's fees and apprenticeship. Then there was the preliminary examination. French was required—and they knew no one who had a word of it. Uncle Lloyd was undaunted. He took in the weekly parts of *Cassell's Popular Educator*, bought a second-hand French grammar and dictionary, and studied them at odd moments during the day. Then in the evenings by candlelight he imparted to his nephew what he had learnt. Towards the end of 1877 Lloyd George passed the preliminary examination of the Law Society at Liverpool, when he was not yet fifteen, and in January 1879 he was articled to Mr. Casson, of Messrs. Breese, Jones & Casson, Solicitors, of Portmadoc, in whose offices he had already spent some months as a junior clerk. No better place could have been found for the acquiring of an intimate knowledge of the life of the ordinary people, and Lloyd George let no opportunity slip. Mr. Breese was a prominent local Liberal, and encouraged his pupil in political activities. Lloyd George became quite celebrated for his powers of speech, in court and the Portmadoc debating society and in the various chapel occasions, and he also began contributing to the local newspapers.

Going to London in November 1881—his first visit there—to take an examination, he made his way to the Houses of Parliament. It was a Saturday and the House was not in session; but he recorded his impressions, ' I will not say but that I eyed the Assembly in a spirit similar to that in which William the Conqueror eyed England on his visit to Edward the Confessor, as the region of his future domain. O Vanity!'

Two years later he was in London again, this time to take his final examinations. Again he visited the House of Commons, but on this occasion a debate was in progress; he heard Gladstone speak and then Randolph Churchill reply. ' I hated him for assailing the Old Man, but I thoroughly enjoyed his speech; it was *splendid*.'

Lloyd George passed the examination with honours, and as a fully fledged solicitor returned to Criccieth, where his family were now living; the shoemaking business had been given up owing to his uncle's ill health and his mother was making ends meet by letting lodgings to visitors in the summer. Now it was Lloyd George's turn to shoulder the responsibility, and having refused an offer of a managing clerkship in his old firm he put up his brass plate on the front door of their home: *D. Lloyd George, Solicitor*. His office was in the back parlour.

Almost at once he began to make his mark in the courts and in private practice. While he refused to take cases unless he were pretty sure of winning them, he made it clear that he was afraid of no man—landlord or parson or influential politician. He was often intentionally rude, and his audacity knew no bounds. His engagement book was crammed with invitations to address meetings of every kind; Liberal associations, chapel congregations—he sometimes preached, temperance organizations, anti-tithe agitations, meetings of the farmers' union which he started.

With plenty of work coming in he felt himself in a position to take a wife, and on 24 January 1888 he married Margaret Owen, daughter of a prosperous farmer on the outskirts of Criccieth. Her parents were doubtful of her choice but she had made up her mind. She proved just the sort of wife that he needed at that time—serene and steadfast, level-headed and a good manager, large-hearted and devoted. Their first son was born in 1889, and another son and three daughters were to follow.

Now the rising young lawyer made his first bid for public office. The Local Government Act of 1888 established a system of county councils in place of the local squirearchy. The first elections for the new bodies took place early in the following year, and Lloyd

George stood as a Liberal for a seat on the Caernarvon County Council. He was elected, and immediately on taking his seat was chosen as one of the first aldermen. He remained an alderman for the rest of his life.

At about the same time he was nominated as prospective Liberal candidate for the parliamentary constituency of Caernarvon Burghs, and almost at once he had to go into battle. The Conservative M.P. for the Burghs died suddenly, there was a by-election, and Lloyd George appealed to the electorate on an advanced Liberal programme—Home Rule for Ireland, but justice for Wales too; disestablishment and disendowment of the Anglican Church in Wales; taxation of land values; enfranchisement of leaseholders; graduated taxation, and a ' free breakfast table '—i.e. no taxes on imported food. On 11 April 1890, he was elected M.P. by the narrow majority of eighteen votes—and he was returned at every election for Caernarvon Burghs for fifty-five years without a break.

Six days later he took his seat in the House of Commons, a young man of twenty-seven, black-haired and blue-eyed, slightly built but graceful in his movements, and gifted with a Celtic eloquence. He spoke for the first time on 13 June and his maiden speech evoked glowing tributes. After that he spoke often, and almost as often he took a line of radical independence. He was a Liberal—but he never forgot, or let others forget, that he was a Welshman. For the first fifteen years of his parliamentary career his chief concern was to promote the welfare of the principality.

On his arrival in London, Lloyd George rented rooms in the Temple and later in Gray's Inn, but after a while he took a house on Wandsworth Common, where his wife and children joined him. M.Ps. received no salaries or expense allowance in those days, and he was generally hard up. Eventually he established a branch of his practice in London, while his brother William and his uncle Richard carried on the office at Criccieth. More than once he was offered a company directorship, but although two or three hundred guineas a year for doing very little would have been exceedingly useful he always refused.

Fortunately his constituents thought so highly of him that in 1895, when he was faced with his third election in five years, they agreed to his request that in future they should shoulder his election expenses.

On the outbreak of the Boer War in 1899, Lloyd George ranged himself unhesitatingly with Campbell-Bannerman. He opposed the war tooth and nail, and incurred immense unpopularity as a result. Whenever he appeared on a public platform there was likely to be a rough house. There was one famous occasion, on 18 December 1901, when at Birmingham Town Hall the mob got out of hand and he had to be smuggled out of the hall by a back entrance disguised in a policeman's cape and helmet. Even in his own constituency at Bangor he was burnt in effigy, although at the khaki election of 1900 he not only held his seat but added a hundred to his majority.

During the Balfour administration Lloyd George was prominent in the fight against the Education Bill, which he opposed because of what he considered its unfairness to Nonconformists, and against Chamberlain's Tariff Reform proposals, which would involve increases in the cost of living. Then Balfour resigned and Campbell-Bannerman succeeded to the premiership and formed his administration, in which Lloyd George had his place as President of the Board of Trade. He was just on forty-three, and had been in the House of Commons for fifteen years. A few weeks later he was fighting at Caernarvon for the fifth time, and this time he was more than twelve hundred votes ahead of the Conservative.

At the Board of Trade Lloyd George did excellently. Among the measures he managed to get passed were an Act for controlling the registration of foreign patents, a Companies Act enforcing a measure of publicity for accounts, a strengthened Employers' Liability Insurance Act, and the Merchant Shipping Act of 1906 which constituted something in the nature of a Seamen's Charter. With these substantial achievements to his credit, it was not unexpected that when Asquith succeeded Campbell-Bannerman as Prime Minister in the spring of 1908 he appointed Lloyd George to be Chancellor of the Exchequer.

This was the key position in a government which had embarked on what came to be styled the Liberal Experiment. From now on Lloyd George stood out as a Social Reformer, the principal mover in the efforts to use the powers of the State to improve the condition of the people.

In the summer of 1909 Lloyd George went to Germany, Austria, and Belgium to make a first-hand study of the social legislation which had been introduced in those countries. The German achievement impressed him most, and in particular the system of national insurance inaugurated by Bismarck a quarter of a century earlier. On his return to England he set about preparing a Budget in which provision should be made for the establishment of something similar in Britain.

The People's Budget, as it came to be called, was introduced by Lloyd George in the House of Commons on 29 April 1909—a date which could be marked as the birthday of the Welfare State. The Chancellor spoke for four hours, and his performance was no more than passable; indeed, as a parliamentary occasion it was a failure. He was nervous, his speech was long-winded, and he made the mistake of reading it. But what he said was much more important than the way in which he said it.

At the outset he explained that he had to find the money for two main objects: first, naval estimates sufficient to keep the Royal Navy in a reasonable state of superiority over our rivals, and, secondly, a great programme of social reforms. He then proceeded to explain the principles of his insurance scheme, one which should be compulsory, contributory, largely comprehensive, and practically universal.

How were these things to be paid for? By a modest increase in income tax—it was raised from 1s. to 1s. 2d. in the £, and a heavy increase in death duties on estates of over £5000 in value. A super-tax of 6d. in the pound on incomes above £5000 per annum. Additional taxes on spirits and tobacco. Small taxes on motor-cars and petrol (the Motor Age had now dawned). But what upset the Opposition more than anything else was the comprehensive array of taxes on land—on the unearned increment of land values, un-developed land, and the enhanced value arising at the end of a lease; and on mineral rights, coal in particular.

Just before he sat down Lloyd George declared: ' This is a War Budget. It is for raising money to wage implacable war against poverty and squalidness. I cannot help believing that before this generation has passed away, we shall have advanced a great step towards that good time when poverty, and the wretchedness and degradation which always follows in its camp, will be as remote to the people of this country as the wolves which once infested its forests.'

For seventy-two days the Finance Bill was under discussion in the House of Commons. There were several all-night sessions. It passed its third reading on 4 November 1909 by 379 votes to 149, and was sent upstairs to the House of Lords. On 30 November the Lords took the unprecedented step of rejecting it—by 350 votes to 75.

Throughout the summer and autumn Lloyd George had been conducting a spirited campaign in support of his proposals. His speeches were masterpieces of vituperation, the most notorious being one he delivered at Limehouse on 30 July to an audience of 4000 poor East Enders assembled at the ' Edinburgh Castle ' public house, in which he declaimed against the landlords as rapacious parasites. After the landlords, it was the turn of the dukes, who had waxed so grossly fat on the unearned increment of their properties in the West End. And in a final burst of rhetorical exuberance he demanded, ' Who is going to rule the country ? The King and the Peers ? or, the King and the People ? '

This proved rather too much for Edward VII and he sent a letter to Mr. Asquith, the Prime Minister, complaining of the introduction of the king's name into political controversy. Lloyd George sent his Majesty a letter in which he offered to explain his financial proposals (which in fact he had already done at earlier interviews), and King Edward wrote in reply that while he gave ' the Chancellor of the Exchequer every credit for the patience and perfect temper he had shown, under considerable provocation, during the debates on the Budget ', he felt it his duty to ' express to him his fear that Mr. Lloyd George was departing from the best traditions of his high office, traditions that had always been invariably observed by his distinguished predecessors '.

In consequence of the Lords' action Asquith dissolved Parliament and there was a general election in January 1910, in which the Liberals were again returned to power but with a much reduced majority. The Budget of the previous April was then reintroduced, passed rapidly through the House of Commons, and was passed by the House of Lords on 28 April 1910 without a division.

A year later Lloyd George introduced his National Insurance Bill. It was in two parts. The first part provided that the great majority of manual workers between the ages of sixteen and seventy who were earning less than £160 a year should be compulsorily insured against sickness by the joint contribution of themselves, their employers, and the State. The contributions, paid weekly and recorded by stamps on insurance-cards, were 4d., 3d. and 2d. respectively, and thus (the Chancellor explained, without convincing everybody) the worker would be receiving ' ninepence for fourpence '. Part 2 provided for workers engaged in certain trades in which the incidence of unemployment was especially heavy (building, shipbuilding, mechanical engineering, construction works, vehicle building, etc.) to be further compulsorily insured against unemployment.

An immense agitation was worked up by the Northcliffe and other Conservative newspapers against the scheme. Stamped insurance cards (a complete novelty in those days in this country) were denounced as a German invention, and readers were asked to sympathize with the duchesses who protested that never, no never, could they be compelled to lick stamps. But Lloyd George rode the storm and this first instalment of State measures against poverty and its accompanying ills was passed into law.

Among the propertied classes Lloyd George was as unpopular as he had been in Boer War days, but the great mass of the lower-middle and working classes gave him their enthusiastic support. He was not a Socialist, and he hoped and intended that his progressive measures would spike the guns of the rising Labour party. He was ranked among the Liberals; but in his hands the old and rather dry Liberalism of *laissez-faire* days was transformed into something warm and enterprising and full of promise. ' Radical ' would be perhaps a more appropriate word for him.

When the Finance Bill of 1909 had been passed Asquith proceeded to introduce the Parliament Bill with a view to putting a curb on the House of Lords' veto. The fight that ensued was long and bitter, and Lloyd George flung himself into it with gusto. None of Asquith's Ministers worked harder than he, none put the Government's case more persuasively—or more provocatively, none could equal his skill to sway the masses. Especially strong was his hold on the Nonconformist vote. The ' Nonconformist conscience '— then something which had to be taken into account—seemed to be in his pocket. Was he not a Nonconformist himself? How powerfully he campaigned against Demon Drink and the brewers! It was reported that he had conscientious scruples against playing golf on Sundays with his friends at Walton Heath. When in London he and his family attended the Welsh Baptist church in Castle Street, near Oxford Circus, and it had been noticed how intently he listened to the sermon and how vigorously he joined in the hymns. They were not to know—or if they did they pretended not to—that the tongues of scandal had been clacking about him since his youth.

When he was fighting his first election, his chances were put in jeopardy by the report that he had recently fathered a child on a sprightly widow at Caernarvon. The matter was hushed up, but the smallness of his majority may be taken as a reflection of what was said. Thenceforth the rumours were persistent. No doubt about it, he had a way with women. He found them irresistible, just as they very often found *him* irresistible. More than once his name came up in the reports of divorce proceedings and this could not be kept from his wife; his home was distracted by divided loyalties. Fortunately Mrs. Lloyd George stuck by him: if she hadn't he would have been ruined.

And yet, when he did arrive at the brink of disaster, it was not the result of an amorous escapade but of a financial scandal.

Early in 1912 there were unpleasant rumours. Lloyd George and several other Liberal ministers, it was said, had taken advantage of their knowledge that the Postmaster General (Herbert Samuel) was negotiating with the Marconi Company for the establishment of a chain of wireless stations to speculate in the Company's shares. The rumours were untrue, but it must be admitted that there were good grounds for suspicion. It has to be understood that there were *two* Marconi companies, an English and an American; it was the former which had put in the successful tender, and Lloyd George and his friends were stating only the truth when they asserted that they had never owned a share in it. What they might have said and *should* have said was that they had bought a number of shares in the American company, which though operating quite independently was more than half-owned by the English company.

The rumours continued to grow, there were frequent references to the 'Marconi scandal' in the press, in this country and on the Continent, and at length it was raised in the House of Commons. Lloyd George offered his resignation to the Prime Minister, but Mr. Asquith stood by his subordinates most loyally. A Select Committee was appointed, on strict party lines, and its sittings continued until well on into 1913. When it reported, it was to exonerate the accused ministers from all charges of corruption or unfaithfulness to public duty. In the course of the debate that followed the presentation of the report Lloyd George declared, with hand on heart: 'I am conscious of having done nothing wrong which brings a stain upon the honour of a Minister of the Crown. If you will, I acted thoughtlessly, I acted carelessly, I acted mistakenly, but I acted innocently, I acted openly and I acted honestly.' The report was adopted, after a motion of censure had been rejected in a division almost entirely on party lines.

All the same, Lloyd George was extremely lucky to get away with it, even taking into consideration the fact that his flutter in Marconis had left him with a loss of £500. If the verdict had gone the other way his career would have ended in dust and ashes. As it was, some of the mud that had been flung at him stuck, and could never be rubbed off completely.

*　　　　*　　　　*

When 1914 dawned, Lloyd George was still at the Treasury, engaged in a long wrangle with Winston Churchill over the Naval estimates.

The First Lord of the Admiralty wanted a stronger Navy, but Lloyd George persisted in an inability to see why. In an interview reported in the *Daily Chronicle* on New Year's Day he protested against what he described as the ' overwhelming extravagance of our expenditure on armaments '. There was really no necessity for it. ' The Navy is now, according to all impartial testimony, at the height of its efficiency. If we maintain that standard no one can complain, but if we go on spending and swelling its strength, we shall wantonly provoke other nations.'

As the fateful year drew on he maintained this attitude. On the afternoon of Sunday, 29 June, he had been working on a speech he was to deliver to a meeting of City bankers when he drew out of the red despatch-box that had been just brought in the telegram announcing the assassination of the Austrian archduke at Serajevo. ' This means war,' he said, as he handed it to his personal secretary Miss Stevenson to read; but she was sure that what he meant was another war in the Balkans, not a world-wide conflagration. He was not a Pacifist, but he hated war with all his heart and mind and soul and did everything in his power to avert it. Up to the last his attitude in the Cabinet was undecided, and it remained undecided until the brutal invasion of Belgium made up his mind for him. After *that* there was no further hesitation. For Britain there was only one course open: fight—and keep on fighting until German militarism was utterly defeated.

Lloyd George's handling of the financial arrangements was masterly. On his orders the Bank Holiday which fell on Monday, 3 August, was extended to three days, and when the banks reopened on the 6th there were no more golden sovereigns and half-sovereigns. In their place were strange-looking pieces of printed paper called Treasury notes. The whole financial resources of the country and Empire were mobilized for the war effort.

At first there was much talk of ' Business as usual ' and the war being over by Christmas; but if Lloyd George ever indulged in such comfortable imaginings he soon awoke from them. On the last day of 1914 he was writing to the Prime Minister protesting against the prevailing policy, or rather complaining that there didn't seem to be one. On 1 January 1915 he circulated a memorandum in which he argued for some fresh measures to break the developing stalemate of trench warfare on the Western Front. When conflict arose between the Westerners, who would put all the available resources into the struggle in France and Flanders, and the Easterners, who urged that the enemy flank might be turned by an attack through Turkey and the Balkans, Lloyd George expressed himself in favour of the latter. In this he was overruled, then and later.

But very shortly it was not strategy but supply that aroused his most earnest and constant concern. The war, he concluded, was being fought by Boer War generals on Boer War lines. There was a shortage of everything, but most especially of shells. On 15 April Asquith agreed to the appointment of a Munitions of War Committee with Lloyd George as chairman, but a few days later there was a political crisis out of which emerged the first Coalition government. In this Lloyd George was head of the new Ministry of Munitions. He did not want to leave the Treasury and hoped to return to it before long, but (he told Sir George Riddell, the proprietor of the News of the World, who was one of his closest friends and advisers), 'I had to do it. They all wanted me to, and the King was anxious that I should.'

For thirteen months he was Minister of Munitions. He had to start from scratch, with an office in Whitehall Gardens furnished with a couple of chairs and a table. 'We were an orphan department,' writes Miss Stevenson, 'no one wanted us—everyone resented us.' Under his dynamic direction the ministry expanded into the largest industrial establishment the world had seen, a mighty network employing over 25,000 persons spread over a vast array of hotels, clubs, houses, bungalows, and anything else with a roof over it that could be acquired. Whereas the Government contracts had been going to a small number of selected firms, Lloyd George threw them open to all who could show that they knew how to deliver the goods. He brought the whole industrial system under State control. He enlisted the support of hosts of industrialists, the great majority of whom gave their services free. He aroused the patriotism of the workers in factories and mines and workshops, and induced them to put their cherished trade practices into cold storage for the duration of the war. He devoted much attention to the welfare of the labour force and insisted upon improvements that generations of trade-union activity had failed to win. Perhaps his most outstanding achievement was the enlistment of the woman-power of the nation to an altogether unprecedented degree. None of the other nations engaged in the war, on the one side or the other, came near to equalling Britain in this respect.

At 5 o'clock in the afternoon of 5 June 1916 H.M.S. Hampshire, in which Lord Kitchener, who since August 1914 had been Secretary of State for War, struck a mine off the Orkneys and sank within a few minutes, carrying with her nearly everyone on board. Lloyd

George heard the news the next day when he entered the Cabinet Room at No. 10. The Prime Minister, Sir Edward Grey, Mr. Balfour and Sir Maurice Hankey were sitting at the table, 'all looking stunned by the tragedy'. A month later, on 6 July, he agreed to fill the vacant place at the War Office. He was not anxious to move from the Ministry of Munitions, but he had to acknowledge that his work there was practically done: the machine had been created and was functioning satisfactorily, so that there would be no more shell scandals. But at the War Office he would be concerned not with supplying the forces in the field but in their direction, and for some time past he had been far from satisfied with the way in which the war was being run. However, he took the job, and for five months fought military stubbornness, political wirepullers and incompetent generals. His best achievement was the appointment of Sir Eric Geddes to take charge of the transport arrangements behind the Western Front, which had fallen into such a mess that the munitions the factories at home were now pouring out were unable to reach the men in the line.

The Battle of the Somme had begun on 1 July, and at the end of the first day of fighting the British killed and wounded reached the unparallelled figure of 57,000 men. As the weeks and months went by and the awful battle continued the Somme became, as Churchill described it, 'the graveyard of Kitchener's army'. Lloyd George was appalled at the slaughter: it was not only horrible but senseless. The more he thought about it the more he became convinced that the supreme direction of the war was at fault. He came to the conclusion, as he writes in his *War Memoirs*, that 'Mr. Asquith did not possess the qualities that make a great War Minister'.

Courage, composure, judgment—Asquith possessed all these to a superlative degree. He gave leadership to the nation which if not rousing and vigorous was dignified. 'But a War Minister must also have vision, imagination and initiative—he must show untiring assiduity, must exercise constant oversight and supervision of every sphere of war activity, must be in continuous consultation with experts, official and unofficial, as to the best means of utilizing the resources of the country in conjunction with Allies for the achievement of victory. If to this can be added a flair for conducting a great fight, then you have an ideal War Minister.'

As early as the spring of 1916 Lloyd George was having conversations with persons who shared his critical opinion of the Prime Minister. Prominent among these were some of his Conservative colleagues in the administration—Balfour, Bonar Law, Carson,

Curzon; but the newspaper magnates—Northcliffe, Aitken (Lord Beaverbrook), and Riddell—were also brought in to the discussions, and played a most powerful part in the ensuing events. On 1 December Lloyd George saw Asquith and put to him the proposal that there should be set up a small executive committee to run the war.

At this stage Lloyd George had no wish to supplant Asquith in the premiership, but he can have left the Prime Minister in no doubt that he intended to secure the chairmanship of the proposed War Council for himself. Even so, Asquith appeared ready to fall in with the proposal, until on 4 December *The Times* published an article eulogizing Lloyd George and referring to Asquith in contemptuous terms. Not surprisingly, the Prime Minister was greatly upset. He concluded—wrongly, as it turned out: the article had been written by the editor, Geoffrey Dawson—that it had been inspired by Lloyd George, who strongly denied having had any responsibility for the article. But the damage was done: Asquith stiffened his attitude, and refused to fall in with the proposition that had been put to him.

The next day Lloyd George took up the challenge. In a letter to the Prime Minister he reminded him that more than once he had asked to be released from his responsibility for a policy with which he was in thorough disagreement, but at the Prime Minister's urgent personal request he had remained in the Government. But he had always felt, and felt deeply, that he was in a false position inasmuch as he could not defend in a wholehearted manner the action of a Government of which he was a member. But, he went on, ' We have thrown away opportunity after opportunity, and I am convinced, after deep and anxious reflection that it is my duty to leave the Government in order to inform the people of the real condition of affairs, and to give them an opportunity, before it is too late, to save their native land from a disaster which is inevitable if the present methods are longer persisted in. As all delay is fatal in war, I place my office without further parley at your disposal . . .'

The crisis thus precipitated moved swiftly to its conclusion. On the evening of that same day Asquith went to Buckingham Palace and tendered his resignation, probably expecting that he would shortly be invited to form a fresh administration—without Lloyd George. But Lloyd George had now reached a definite understanding with Bonar Law and his Conservative colleagues. When invited by his Majesty to undertake the formation of a Government Bonar Law declined and recommended instead that Lloyd George should be sent for. On Thursday, 7 December 1916 Lloyd George kissed hands as Prime Minister.

On leaving the Palace he went back to the War Office, where Miss Stevenson was waiting for him in his room. He told her what had taken place, and then she heard him mutter, half to himself, ' I wonder if I can do it? '

Forming an administration was not so difficult. Most of the Liberal ministers declined to serve under him, but the Conservatives switched from Asquith to Lloyd George with the greatest of ease. A War Cabinet was speedily formed, consisting to begin with of Lloyd George, Lord Curzon, Bonar Law, Lord Milner, and Arthur Henderson; General Smuts was included a few weeks later. On 19 December he made his first speech in the House of Commons as Prime Minister, and opened with the solemn admission, ' I appear before the House of Commons today with the most terrible responsibility that can fall on the shoulders of any living man.'

Lloyd George was not exaggerating. On every hand there were appalling difficulties to face. The War was going badly, and for many months there seemed to be small sign that Lloyd George was going to prove a better War Minister than Asquith had been. Nineteen-sixteen had been a terrible year, but nineteen-seventeen was as bad, if not worse. On the Continent the Kaiser's armies seemed everywhere triumphant. Scores of German U-boats almost succeeded in cutting Britain's life-lines. The food situation at home became increasingly critical. Russia collapsed, and hundreds of thousands of German troops were released to bring a mighty reinforcement to the Western Front. In March 1918 Hindenburg and Ludendorff launched a terrific offensive against Haig's lines; for the British armies it was indeed a matter of ' backs to the wall '.

It was then that Lloyd George really proved himself. For a long time past he had wanted to replace Haig by a commander with a fresher mind, but the generals had been too firmly entrenched to let him have his way. But in the hour of disaster he was able to secure at long last unity of command, and Foch became general-issimo of the Allied armies in France. Then Lloyd George made the strongest personal appeals to President Wilson to speed the despatch of American troops to the battlefield. By early August the German High Command knew that the war was lost, and in November they were suing for an armistice.

On the afternoon of 11 November 1918 Lloyd George rose from his seat in the House of Commons and gave the news that the whole world had been waiting for. ' At eleven o'clock this morning came to an end the cruellest and most terrible war that has ever scourged mankind. I hope we may say that thus, this fateful morning, came to an end all wars. This is no time for words. Our hearts are too full of gratitude to which no tongue can give adequate expression. I will, therefore, move: " That this House do immediately adjourn until this time tomorrow, and that we proceed, as a House of Commons, to St. Margaret's, to give humble and reverent thanks for the deliverance of the world from its great peril ".' Then, with Asquith on one side of him and Bonar Law on the other, the Prime Minister led the way, through delirious crowds, to the church across the way.

* * *

In that hour Lloyd George touched the topmost peaks of fame and power. What came after must, inevitably, have the appearance of a decline, as the years descended through disillusion and disappointment into a wearied old age.

The general election at the end of 1918 was a pretty squalid affair, when the platforms resounded with cries of 'Hang the Kaiser!' and 'Make Germany pay!' The Lloyd George-Bonar Law coalition won a tremendous victory at the polls; practically every candidate who had been given the ' coupon ' by the two leaders was returned, so the Government had a majority of about 263. But the Coalition Liberals numbered only 133 as against about 330 Coalition Unionists (Conservatives) and 48 Unionists who stood as supporters of the Coalition but without the label, so that from the outset, Lloyd George was the prisoner of the Conservative-Unionist party, and he had to do a lot of things that were against his Liberal leanings.

The most memorable feature about this election was that women —some women: those over thirty, who were householders or the wives of householders—had the right to vote, this having been accorded by the Representation of the People Act passed some months earlier.

During the first half of 1919 Lloyd George was mainly occupied with the Paris Peace Conference. With President Woodrow Wilson of the U.S.A., Clemenceau, the French Premier, and Orlando, the Italian Premier, he constituted the Big Four, which remade the map of Europe and a good bit of the world outside. The Treaty of Versailles was signed on 28 June 1919, and once again Lloyd George was the centre of almost universal acclamation. ' Versailles ' was not so bad as it has often been made out to be, but in its clauses there was precious little assurance of ' no more war '.

On his return from Paris, Lloyd George was met by King George V at Victoria station, and drove with him to Buckingham Palace through wildly enthusiastic crowds. On 5 August the king conferred on him the Order of Merit.

The glory soon faded, however, for at home there were problems sufficient to daunt even the ' Welsh wizard '. Lloyd George had the satisfaction of obtaining the disestablishment of the church in Wales, which had been among the very first items in his political programme, but Ireland was a very different matter. At the general election in 1918 the old Irish Nationalist party had been almost wiped out, and their place taken by the Sinn Feiners who proceeded to proclaim an Irish republic. Lloyd George tried force to begin with, and for years a terrible civil war raged in the distracted country, composing a tale of ambush, murder, and ferocious outrage that shamed both sides. Lloyd George publicly declared that he would ' never negotiate with assassins ', but in the end circumstances were too strong for him. In the autumn of 1921 it became clear that he was ready to ' shake hands with murder '. A conference was held in London, and when it was on the verge of breakdown Lloyd George surpassed himself as a negotiator. At midnight on 6 December 1921, an agreement was signed between the British and the Irish delegates which gave southern Ireland a measure of independence that would have astounded Gladstone. It was not Lloyd George's fault that the Sinn Fein extremists under De Valera repudiated the treaty, and there followed months of war between the Irish factions before the Free State was firmly established.

In Britain there was widespread depression after the hectic expansion of the war period. Great numbers of workers were unemployed, and there were prolonged strikes in the basic industries. The class war became a very real thing. The fine promises Lloyd George had made about making the land one fit for heroes to live in were found impossible to carry out, and the Prime Minister's popularity sagged with every month that passed.

Then in the summer of 1922 there was a tremendous outcry about the sale of honours, something that had been going on for a long time but was brought to a head by the publication of the list of Birthday Honours. It was alleged that titles and awards were being distributed on an unprecedentedly lavish scale, and it is on record that during the Lloyd George administration 26 peerages, 130 baronetcies, and 481 knighthoods appeared under the heading of ' Business ', while the Press received 5 peerages, 5 baronetcies, and 37 knighthoods. The general opinion was that many of the honours had been distributed in return for hard cash, which had gone into a special fund under the personal control of the Prime Minister.

In the end, however, it was an issue of foreign policy that brought the Coalition down, and Lloyd George with it. In October the war-weary British public suddenly awoke to the fact that there was a distinct possibility of a renewal of the war against the Turks, now under the dynamic leadership of Kemal Ataturk. There was an immense feeling of revulsion, and Lloyd George was denounced as a war-monger. In fact there was no war, and Lloyd George played a statesmanlike part in preventing it, but his public image had taken such a battering that the Conservative party managers in the country came to the conclusion that he had outlived his usefulness as a vote-catcher. The Conservative M.Ps. were summoned to a meeting at the Carlton Club in London on 19 October, and by a vote of 186 to 87 it was resolved that the Conservative party should fight the next election on its own.

This was the end of the great wartime Coalition. At 5 o'clock on the afternoon of the Carlton Club meeting Lloyd George drove to Buckingham Palace and tendered his resignation. 'I am sorry he is going,' wrote George V in his diary, 'but some day he will be Prime Minister again.'

Lloyd George, we may be pretty sure, thought so too. After all, he was not yet sixty, and seventeen years of office without a break had raised him to a position of commanding eminence among contemporary politicians. Not long before he had been ranked with Chatham and Pitt, and a turn of Fortune's wheel might provide a 'come-back'. His health was good, his vigour unimpaired, his courage undaunted, his spirit unbroken. Never again, however, was he to hold office.

If we look for reasons, we may start with Lloyd George's own personality. Power tends to corrupt, as Lord Acton said; and in Lloyd George's case if it did not actually corrupt it certainly went to his head. As the Coalition Government went stumbling down the slope the Prime Minister became more autocratic, more arrogant, more caustic in his criticisms of the men who were his subordinates and who had to make his policies work.

But a more important reason was the fact that he had no great party behind him. The Liberals never forgave the slaughter of the 1918 election, and although in the next few years some sort of reconciliation was patched up between him and Asquith and the Liberal party machine, there could be no putting back the clock.

In particular, the existence of the Lloyd George Fund soured the relationship and militated against successful co-operation. Lloyd George kept the Fund entirely under his own control. He maintained that it was made up of contributions that had been made to him personally, for the advancement of policies which he stood for and the donors approved of, and furthermore, that a large part of it was derived from the profits he had made in some highly successful newspaper deals. The Liberal candidatures in the elections of the nineteen-twenties were financed largely out of his fund, and since he paid the piper he thought it only right that he should call the tune.

As for the Conservatives, they deeply resented the 'betrayal' of the Irish loyalists when Lloyd George agreed to the establishment of the Free State, and they had had more than enough of his nimble mind and his opportunist way of doing things. With relief they turned to the austere Bonar Law and then to the companionable Baldwin. A working alliance with Labour might have seemed a possibility, and indeed there were moves in that direction. But Lloyd George and Ramsay MacDonald would have proved uneasy partners; besides, Lloyd George was no Socialist but a Radical who jibbed at doctrinaire solutions of practical problems.

All the same, there was at least a possibility of Lloyd George's return to power up to the 1929 general election, and perhaps that of two years later. Alone among the statesmen of his day and generation he had a vision of a revivified Britain. He summoned to his aid experts in every field, and under his auspices and financed by his Fund there appeared a series of blue-prints outlining reforms which if they could have been implemented would have prevented untold economic loss and social distress: *Land and the Nation* (1925), *Coal and Power*, *Towns and the Land*, and, most valuable of all, *Britain's Industrial Future* (the 'yellow book', from the colour of its cover) in 1928, which was condensed into a best-selling pamphlet, *We Can Conquer Unemployment*.

In 1931 he might have been included in the National Government, but as bad luck would have it he had only recently undergone a serious operation for a prostate condition and was incapacitated. At the general election the Liberals made a most disappointing showing, and Lloyd George's own following in the House of Commons was reduced to a family party of three—his son Gwilym, his daughter Megan, and his son's brother-in-law Goronwy Owen. In 1935, on his seventy-second birthday, he launched a programme for a new deal on the Roosevelt model, and later in the year formed a Council of Action in which Liberals and some Labour men joined and also a sprinkling of forward-looking young Conservatives. Baldwin was sufficiently impressed to suggest to his colleagues that it might be as well to find a place for the fiery demogogue, but Ramsay MacDonald demurred, and Neville Chamberlain, who had most painful recollections of the months he had spent in Lloyd George's administration during the war, made it quite clear that he would never agree to sit in the Cabinet with him.

A year later, on 18 June 1936, when the National Government announced its abandonment of sanctions against Mussolini, Lloyd George electrified the House of Commons by a terrific onslaught on what he considered to be a collection of fainthearts. ' I have been in this House nearly half a century,' he declaimed; ' I have never heard a British Minister, speaking on behalf of the Government, say that Britain is beaten—Britain and her Empire beaten—and that we must abandon the enterprise we have in hand.' Then turning on the apprehensive front bench he said, ' Tonight we have had the cowardly surrender, and *there* are the cowards! '

A few months later Lloyd George accepted Hitler's invitation to visit Germany, and he was greatly impressed by what he was shown of the constructive achievements of the Nazi regime. Hitler appealed to him as a man of action, and for a time he seems to have fallen under the Fuehrer's spell.

Then came the Second World War, and in the House of Commons on 8 May 1940, when the expedition to Norway had ended in fiasco, the old man raised his voice for the last time against inefficiency and worse in high places. When the Prime Minister referred to his ' friends ', Lloyd George delivered a speech that sealed Chamberlain's fate. ' It is not a question of who are the Prime Minister's friends. It is a far bigger issue. He has appealed for sacrifices. The nation is prepared for every sacrifice so long as it has leadership. I say solemnly that the Prime Minister should give an example of sacrifice, because there is nothing which can contribute more to victory than that he should sacrifice the seals of office.'

Within a few hours Chamberlain had resigned, and Churchill was forming his administration. He immediately invited Lloyd George to accept a place in his Cabinet, but Lloyd George was too old, or too weary, or he had concluded that the new Government was going to prove too much of a one-man show. Lloyd George's last speech in the House of Commons was on 11 June 1942, when he congratulated the Government on having effected a treaty with

Soviet Russia; if it had been effected earlier, he commented grimly, the war might not have happened.

*　　*　　*

Not long before he quitted office on the fall of the Coalition Lloyd George bought sixty acres of heath and scrub at Churt, near Farnham in Surrey, and here he built a house and established a farm on which he raised stock and poultry but went in particularly for fruit. Here he lived for most of the succeeding years, although Dame Margaret Lloyd George—she had been created a Dame Grand Cross of the Order of the British Empire in 1920—kept the family home going at Criccieth. As a practical farmer, Lloyd George was remarkably successful, and he took the greatest pride in his results.

At Bron-y-de ('slope of the south'), as the house at Churt was named, Lloyd George wrote his *War Memoirs* between 1931 and 1934; they were published in six volumes, and he received £50,000 for the British rights—and another £9,000 for *The Truth about the Peace Treaties* which appeared later in two volumes. For more than twenty years, until after the beginning of the Second World War, he was a regular and highly paid contributor to American newspapers. During those years he was able to indulge in a good deal of foreign travel, including several trips to the United States.

Early in 1941 Dame Margaret had a fall and broke her hip. Lloyd George set off from Churt for Criccieth as soon as he heard the news, but his car got stuck in snowdrifts in the Welsh mountains; and although half the countryside turned out to give a hand in digging him out he arrived too late to see her. She died on 20 January, and he stayed on at Criccieth until after the funeral. Among the large number of messages of sympathy he received was one from Mr. and Mrs. Churchill, paying tribute to 'that great woman who embodied all that was most strong and true in the British race'.

Lloyd George returned to Churt, and resumed his farming activities. Then on 25 October 1943 he married Miss Frances Stevenson at a register-office near Guildford.

More than thirty years had passed since her life had been joined with his. It was in 1911, when she was teaching at a girls' school in Wimbledon, that she was recommended to Lloyd George, then Chancellor of the Exchequer, as a suitable person to give his daughter Megan some private coaching in her studies. In her autobiography, *The Years that Are Past* (1967), she tells how, 'nervous and pale, and looking, I think, much younger than I was'—she was twenty-three—she knocked at the door of No. 11 Downing Street, and was shown up to the drawing-room where she met Lloyd George for the first time, and at once experienced 'a magnetism which made my heart leap'. That summer she spent some very happy months with the Lloyd George family at Criccieth, and on their return to London Megan became a pupil at the school where she taught. Lloyd George got into the habit of calling there to see his daughter, letters were exchanged, and a deep and sincere friendship developed. She told him that she wanted to give up teaching for an office job, and he offered her a post on his staff at the Treasury. Although, as she explains, she was very innocent and inexperienced for her age, she had become much too fond of him not to understand what he had in mind. Before the matter was settled she went on holiday to Scotland, and there she received an urgent letter from him, saying that something terrible had happened, and that he *needed* her. The 'something' terrible was the Marconi scandal.

On returning to London, she reached her decision, and 'a heart-shocking one' it was for her, 'due to my upbringing and the opinions I held regarding any woman who *lived* with a man to whom she was not married . . .'

When at length they were married, 'a deep contentment possessed me; contentment, but not the thrills of the usual bride. Our real marriage had taken place thirty years before.'

At the end of 1944 Mr. and Mrs. Lloyd George left Churt for Llanystumdwy, where years before Lloyd George had bought a farmhouse called Ty Newydd. There he delighted in showing his wife the scenes of his boyhood and in meeting the few surviving friends of those long distant days. He was still M.P. for Caernarvon, but a general election could not be long postponed and this time there was no doubt that he would meet stern opposition from Labour. A defeat after so many years would have broken the old man's heart; and when Mr. Churchill begged to be allowed to submit the name of his almost lifelong friend for a peerage, Lloyd George wired back, 'gratefully accept'. So his name appeared in the New Year's honours list as Earl Lloyd-George (with a hyphen) of Dwyfor.

Only a few more months were left to him. He grew steadily weaker, more frail and weary. Once again he turned to the old favourites among his books, Macaulay and Dickens' novels. On 26 March 1945 he died, when his wife was holding one of his hands and his daughter Megan the other.

Four days later his body was placed on a waggon and drawn by friends to where his grave had been made ready, in a place he himself had chosen—high on the bank of the little river Dwyfor and looking towards Snowdon. People came in their thousands from all parts of Wales to see Wales's most famous son make his last journey. And so they buried him there; and on his grave they placed a huge stone, one taken from the river bed and on which he had often sat as a small boy.

37

ANDREW BONAR LAW

AFTER HE HAD ATTENDED Bonar Law's funeral in Westminster
Abbey as one of the pall-bearers Asquith is reported to have remarked, contemplatively, ' It is fitting that we should have buried
the unknown Prime Minister by the side of the Unknown Soldier.'

In truth Bonar Law was never such a great popular figure as, for
instance, his colleague Lloyd George. But he was by no means the
insignificant sort of fellow that Asquith's remark might seem to
imply; and in his life, parliamentary and private, there were
moments of drama and periods of sustained excitement, times when
passion or pathos broke through the mask of melancholy resignation.

Bonar Law was the first ' colonial' to become Prime Minister. He
was born in New Brunswick, which was then one of the British
colonies in North America. This was on 16 September 1858, and
the place was the small township of Kingston on the Richibucto
river, where his father, Rev. James Law, was minister of the local
congregation of the Free Church of Scotland. Many of the New
Brunswickers were Scotch immigrants, but James Law was an
Ulsterman, born at Coleraine in the county of Londonderry, the
son of a prosperous farmer whose ancestors had crossed the sea from
Scotland in the seventeenth century. He went out to New Brunswick in 1845, and was minister at Kingston for thirty-two years.
He returned to Coleraine because of ill health and died there in 1882.
This family connection with Ulster goes some way towards explain-
ing Bonar Law's championship of those counties in the great Home
Rule controversy.

Bonar Law's mother was Annie Kidston, born in Halifax, Nova
Scotia, although her father was an iron-merchant in Glasgow. She
died when Bonar was two, and her sister Janet then came out from
Scotland to look after her brother-in-law and his children.

Of the two names given him at his christening, Bonar Law hardly
ever used the first. As regards the Bonar, it might be supposed that
this was given him in honour of the Scottish preachers of that name,
who were distinguished figures in the Free Church of Scotland in
the first half of the last century; but it would seem that this was not

so. Mrs. Law wanted to name the boy Robert after Rev. Robert McCheyne, another eminent Scottish divine, but she already had one son named Robert. McCheyne's life, however, had been written by Andrew Bonar, and so she chose *his* name as the next best thing. ' This is a curious way of getting a name,' Bonar Law is said to have told an inquirer, ' but my father gave me that account of it.'

Life in the little lonely wooden homestead was frugal. The minister's stipend being insufficient to keep a family, Mr. Law had a small farm in the surrounding fields. Little Bonar had to rough it, but he never went without. He was sent to the village school, and gave a hand in the home and on the farm, and might have grown up to be a farmer if his father had not married again. This was in 1870, when Bonar was twelve, and his stepmother was a New Brunswick schoolmistress. Miss Janet now came to feel that she was no longer wanted; she told her brother-in-law that she would like to go back to Scotland, and she offered to take Bonar with her on the understanding that he should be brought up by her Glasgow relatives and given a good start in life. James Law was not one to stand in the boy's way, so Bonar accompanied his aunt back to Scotland and never saw New Brunswick again.

Arrived in Glasgow, he went to live with his aunt in her house at Helensburgh, overlooking the Firth of Clyde. Here life was comfortable, in the solid Scottish fashion, for the Kidstons were very well off. After some terms at a small boarding-school at Hamilton, he proceeded at the age of fifteen to Glasgow High School. After only a year, however, he left school for a desk in the Glasgow office of the merchant bankers, Messrs. William Kidston & Co., which was run by his aunt's cousins. The hours were long and the work monotonous, but he was treated as one of the family rather than as an ordinary clerk. Every morning he caught the 7.10 train from Helensburgh that arrived at Glasgow's Queen Street station at around eight. A short walk took him to his office, where he took off his coat, rubber-banded his sleeves, and got down to his figures. He used to lunch at a coffee-house near by, and as often as he could got in a game of chess afterwards. Then back to the office and work again until it was time to catch the train for home.

In his spare time he went to evening classes at the university, and filled in the gaps in his education with omnivorous reading. Carlyle was his favourite author, but Gibbon ran him close. When Austen Chamberlain once confessed that he had never been able to get through the *Decline and Fall*, Bonar Law protested that *he* had read it three times from beginning to end. Already he had begun to take an interest in politics. He joined the Glasgow Parliamentary Debating Society, and often took part in the debates as one of the Conservative spokesmen. He was not then, or later, a brilliant speaker, but he had a hard slogging style, and he always knew his facts and figures.

To keep himself fit, he did a lot of walking in the hills around Helensburgh, and he also played an excellent game at lawn tennis. Later he became a reasonably good golfer. Chess was his favourite indoor relaxation but he also enjoyed whist, and then bridge when it became popular. He never went to a concert if he could help it, and the theatre bored him to distraction. He was never in the least what is called a convivial man. Although he always had drinks available for his guests, he was himself a complete teetotaller. To the end of his life he would go to bed on a glass of milk and a piece of gingerbread. But he was a confirmed smoker, and Lloyd George tells us that Bonar Law hated a long lunch or dinner, not only because he was an unappreciative eater but because it delayed the moment when he could light his pipe.

Although it belongs to a much later period, there is a story told of Bonar Law by Lloyd George that seems to fall into place here. It was during the First World War, and they were driving together along the coast road near Cannes. The sky was cloudless, and the Mediterranean a lovely blue. L.G. turned to his companion and inquired if he didn't think it beautiful? ' I don't care much for scenery,' rejoined Bonar Law, in his rather toneless voice. L.G. tried again. He had been to the opera the night before, and he mentioned how beautiful Mozart had sounded. ' I don't care much for music,' was Bonar Law's comment. Still not quite flattened, L.G. then called attention to some very pretty ladies who were on their way to play golf. ' Women don't attract me,' was the laconic comment. Thoroughly exasperated at all this disdain for the attractions of life L.G. then said; ' Will you tell me what it is that you *do* care for? Scenery—music—women—none of them has any meaning for you. What is it that you *do* like? ' 'I like bridge,' was the reply.

When Bonar Law had been with the Kidstons for about a dozen years the partners, who were now getting old, sold their business to the Clydesdale Bank. But Bonar Law was well provided for. At the age of twenty-seven he was given a partnership in William Jacks & Co., an important firm in the iron trade. For the next fifteen years he was a prominent figure in Glasgow's Royal Exchange, buying and selling as a middleman the raw material of Scotland's heavy industries. His life was very much as it had been when he was a junior, but he now caught the 4.10 back to Helensburgh, which gave him time for a round of golf or a game of tennis, before his evening meal followed by a few hands at bridge.

In 1891 when he was thirty-two he married Annie Pitcairn Robley, the twenty-four-year-old daughter of a Glasgow shipbroker who was a neighbour at Helensburgh. They spent their honeymoon in Paris, and on their return settled down to a very happy domestic life in a large house in Helensburgh. Six children were born to them in the next few years, four sons and two daughters.

By this time he was well established in business, and besides had been made financially independent by two legacies of £30,000 each left him by two of the Kidston old ladies. Now he was in a position to set about a career in politics, and in 1900 he was chosen as Unionist or Conservative candidate for the Blackfriars division of Glasgow, a seat then held by a Liberal. At the general election Bonar Law won the seat, converting a Liberal majority of about five hundred into a Unionist one of exactly a thousand. He was now forty-two.

At Westminster he found the aristocratic element in the Unionist leadership decidedly alien, but he was very strongly drawn to Joseph Chamberlain, a business man like himself and engaged in the same business. The veteran statesman went out of his way to make himself agreeable, and before long Bonar Law was being taken as Chamberlain's most devoted and capable disciple. At the launching of the Tariff Reform campaign he ranged himself behind Chamberlain and spoke often in support of his proposals, always with a formidable array of statistics that stood up to challenge. Although no orator he was forceful, pugnacious, resolute, not afraid of a scrap, and also, for a politician, remarkably honest. In the circumstances it is not surprising that when he had been in the House only eighteen months he was appointed Parliamentary Secretary to the Board of Trade.

In the Conservative débacle of 1906 Bonar Law lost his seat at Glasgow, being defeated by George Barnes, a leading figure in the up-and-coming Labour party. But he was much too useful a man to be left out in the cold; within a few months the Conservative party managers had engineered a vacancy at Dulwich, and for this safe seat he was duly returned. For the next three years he steadily improved in performance and reputation, and in the bitter turmoil of the 1909 session he played a conspicuous part. Then he was overwhelmed by a domestic tragedy: his wife died suddenly, and he was so stricken with grief that he seriously contemplated giving up politics altogether. But his many friends in the House of Commons joined in persuading him to carry on, and his sister, Miss Mary Law, agreed to come down to London to keep house for him and his children. About this time, too, he made a firm and enduring friendship with Max Aitken, later Lord Beaverbrook, who was a native of New Brunswick like himself. Aitken had made his pile in Canada and was now bent on a political career in England. In 1910 he had been elected Unionist M.P. for Ashton-under-Lyne, and very early in their acquaintanceship he accepted it as his mission to ' give Bonar a shove '.

Bonar Law, then, continued in Parliament, and as year followed year his standing in the party, in the House and in the country steadily improved. So much so that when in 1911 Balfour resigned the Conservative party leadership Bonar Law allowed Aitken and his friends to put his name forward. There were two other nominations, Walter Long and Austen Chamberlain, both men of high reputation and experience, but a deadlock ensued between them and Bonar Law slipped in as the third man who was acceptable to all. ' The fools have stumbled on their best man by accident,' was Lloyd George's comment.

' You are a great man now,' Max Aitken told Bonar Law as they left the Carlton Club together after the election; ' you must talk like a great man, behave like a great man.' Bonar Law pursed his lips. ' If I am a great man,' he said, ' then a good many great men must have been frauds.'

As leader of the Conservatives in the Commons he was now leader of the Opposition to Asquith's Liberal government. Very soon he showed his mettle. He was a hard-hitter, one who let his comments rip regardless of fine feelings and susceptibilities. His speeches aroused fierce passions. He assailed Lloyd George's budget as ' pure and unadulterated Socialism ' and hit out at its author as a tricky Welsh jobber; he sneered at Asquith, and charged Winston Churchill with changing his coat too often. He was the principal figure in innumerable parliamentary storms. He attacked the Insurance Bill, championed the Lords in their long struggle with the Commons, resisted the disestablishment of the Welsh Church, and stood shoulder to shoulder with Carson and the Ulstermen in their determination to resist Home Rule, by force of arms if need be.

Then came the war, and he at once approached Asquith and offered him his party's full support in its prosecution. When the first Coalition was formed in 1915 Bonar Law was given the not very important post of Colonial Secretary, but as the leader of the Unionist wing in the Coalition he held a key post, and his position was fortified by his increasing admiration for Lloyd George's abilities and drive. When it became clear to almost everybody that Asquith must be replaced, Bonar Law played a decisive role in the manoeuvres that brought about a change of government. When Asquith resigned on 5 December 1916, Bonar Law could have had the premiership if he had wanted it, but in the prevailing circumstances he had decided that Lloyd George was the man for the job and offered to serve under him. So it was arranged. Lloyd George became Prime Minister, and Bonar Law received the appointments of Chancellor of the Exchequer and Leader of the House of Commons, with a seat in the War Cabinet.

Stanley Baldwin once declared that Bonar Law's co-operation with Lloyd George during the war years was 'the most perfect partnership in political history'. It sounds extravagant, but Lloyd George's account in his *War Memoirs* is most generously appreciative. 'For nearly five years,' he wrote, 'Mr. Bonar Law's friendship for me and mine not only survived but grew from year to year. When ill-health drove him from collaboration and companionship, I felt the separation more deeply than any I have endured during my political life.'

And yet, 'there never were two men who constituted such a complete contrast in temperamental and mental equipment'. They had nothing in common except a lowly origin and a stern puritan upbringing, but these early influences differentiated them completely from the other leading figures with whom they had to work— Balfour, Curzon, Churchill, Grey, Milner, who might have been 'reared in another planet'. Bonar Law was by temperament, Lloyd George explains, a pessimist, who generally took a gloomy view of the world and its ways. That is one of the reasons why Asquith, a temperamental optimist, disliked him so. At the beginning and often at the end of an interview he would murmur, 'There is lots of trouble ahead!' When any project was placed before him, his first impulse was to dwell on its difficulties and dangers. Because of this, Lloyd George used to make it his practice to try out his schemes on Bonar Law first.

Immediately after breakfast Lloyd George would walk along the corridor that connected No. 10 with No. 11 Downing Street, where Bonar Law had his official quarters, 'for a smoke and a talk with Bonar'. After a preliminary survey of the morning's news and the day's business Lloyd George would unfold the plans he had been turning over in his mind. Bonar Law would listen, puffing away at his pipe, and then come out with all the objections imaginable, for ' he had an incomparable gift of practical criticism '. Sometimes the force of his arguments induced the Prime Minister to change his plans or drop them altogether, but if they stood up to Bonar Law's objections he felt he could go ahead in complete confidence. And ' once I had secured his consent, I had no more loyal supporter '.

Two of Bonar Law's sons were killed in the war. Charles, his second son, fell at the battle of Gaza in April 1917, and then a few months later James, his eldest son, who was a fighter pilot in the R.F.C., was shot down in France. Bonar Law was so crushed by this double blow that Beaverbrook thought it might give him some relief if he were to go to France and meet his son's comrades in the squadron and hear how proud they were of him. This Bonar Law did, and for two hours he sat alone, sunk in a sombre reverie, in the cockpit of a plane such as his son had flown.

When the war came to an end, Bonar Law and Lloyd George concerted their plans for a joint appeal to the country. The Coalition was returned to power with a great majority, and in the new administration that Lloyd George proceeded to form Bonar Law—who now represented Central Glasgow—was Lord Privy Seal and Leader of the House of Commons. In effect he was deputy Prime Minister. Throughout 1919 he worked at very high pressure, and with Lloyd George absent for so much of the time at the peace conference in Paris, practically the whole burden of domestic affairs fell on his shoulders. The year following gave him little relief; and in March 1921 he was so overstrained and in such poor health that he felt obliged to announce his withdrawal from public life.

For eighteen months he was in retirement, except for occasional attendances at Westminster. He thoroughly enjoyed his rest and freedom from worry, as he put it, and was soon able to report that he felt better than he had done for four years past. As 1922 wore on he became increasingly disturbed by the way things were going. When Britain seemed on the verge of war with Turkey, Bonar Law wrote a strong letter of protest that was published in Northcliffe's *The Times* and Beaverbrook's *Daily Express*, in which he made the point that, the country's financial and social condition being what it was, ' we cannot alone act as the policeman of the world '. His attitude made a strong appeal to the rank-and-file Conservatives who wanted to break loose from the Coalition, and he was given a tremendous reception when he put in an appearance at the famous meeting held at the Carlton Club on 19 October 1922. He spoke in favour of the Conservatives fighting the next general election as an independent party, and his speech was most enthusiastically received. The resulting vote sounded the death-knell of the Coalition, and that same afternoon Lloyd George drove to Buckingham Palace and tendered his resignation and his government's. Within a matter of minutes, Lord Stamfordham, King George's secretary, was on the phone to Bonar Law asking him to come to the Palace forthwith.

To Lord Stamfordham's great surprise, Bonar Law demurred, on the ground that he was not yet elected leader of the Conservative party, and the most he would agree to do was to pay his Majesty a courtesy visit. But on 23 October, at a specially called meeting of Conservative M.Ps., candidates, and peers, Lord Curzon nominated, and Stanley Baldwin seconded, Bonar Law's election to the party leadership. This was carried with acclamation. Bonar Law then drove at once to the Palace, where he formally kissed hands as Prime Minister and First Lord of the Treasury.

The next day he announced the members of his Cabinet. It was not a very inspiring list, since most of the Conservative leaders who had held office in the Coalition refused to abandon Lloyd George at that juncture. Winston Churchill, who was one of these, referred disparagingly to the new administration as a ' second eleven '.

A week later Bonar Law published his election manifesto. Its keynote was ' Tranquillity ', and it concluded with the remark that ' the nation's first need, in every walk of life, is to get on with its own work, with the minimum of interference abroad and of disturbance at home '. This seems to have been what the electors wanted, for the Conservatives won the general election with an overall majority of 77.

Some little time afterwards Stanley Baldwin declared that it was really Lloyd George who had won the election for the Conservatives, and he had done it with just six words. ' There is a vast new electorate in the country,' said Baldwin. ' There are millions of voters unattached to any party, and up and down the country they were wondering what they wanted and for whom they were to vote. One morning they opened their papers and read that Lloyd George had said of Bonar Law that he was " honest to the verge of simplicity ". And they said, " By God, that is what we have been looking for ".'

For the first few weeks things ran smoothly, but in the spring of 1923 Bonar Law ran into trouble over Curzon's foreign policy and

Baldwin's negotiations for the settlement of Britain's war debt to America. Then in April the Prime Minister's health again gave rise to great anxiety. He was suffering from an affection of the throat, which was eventually diagnosed as cancer of an inoperable type.

The seriousness of his condition was carefully kept from him, but there is reason to suppose that he knew it, although he maintained an attitude of stoical calm. He offered to resign, and was dissuaded only with difficulty. On the advice of Lord Horder, his physician, he agreed to see what a sea voyage might do, and in early May he set out on a trip to the Mediterranean. But after a week or two he was in such pain that he decided to return home overland. He arrived back in London on 19 May, and at Victoria station the crowd stood silent in sympathy as the obviously stricken man walked slowly to his car. He was driven back to his home at No. 24 Onslow Gardens, and within a few hours his resignation was announced. This was on 20 May, when he had been Prime Minister for only 209 days—one of the shortest premierships on record.

After a stay at Brighton, Bonar Law was brought back to London, and he died on 30 October 1923. In his will he had expressed the desire that he should be buried beside his wife in the cemetery at Helensburgh, but the family bowed to the universal wish that he should be laid to rest in Westminster Abbey. After cremation at Golder's Green and a service at St. Columba's, Pont Street, the Scottish Presbyterian church where his family were wont to worship, the ashes were interred in the Abbey on 5 November. The Prince of Wales was one of the pall-bearers, and the others were the Speaker of the House of Commons, Mr. Baldwin, the Prime Minister, Balfour, Asquith, Carson, Austen Chamberlain, Ramsay MacDonald, Beaverbrook, and Lord Edmund Talbot, one of Bonar Law's oldest friends and political associates.

In the course of an eloquent tribute in the House of Commons a week later, Mr. Baldwin said that there was no doubt that Bonar Law gave his life for his country, just as much as if he had fallen in the Great War.

38

STANLEY BALDWIN

ONLY A WEEK before he succeeded Bonar Law as Prime Minister, Stanley Baldwin had jocularly expressed the hope of being able to return to his home in Worcestershire ' to read the books I want to read, to live a decent life, and to keep pigs '.

Did he mean it ? Certainly he looked a sturdy countryman, and that he loved the country is clear from everything that he wrote, and almost everything that he said.

Born at Bewdley, Worcestershire, on 3 August 1867, he was the only child of Alfred and Louisa Baldwin. His father was one of a family whose members, originally Shropshire yeomen, had turned to the iron industry in the early days of the Industrial Revolution and done quite well at it. Their chief works were a foundry at Stourport where they made cast-iron, and a forge at Wilden where they made wrought-iron. As a young man Alfred Baldwin became proprietor of the latter. He lived close to the works, ' among his own people ' as they used to boast. He was a fine specimen of the Victorian employer. He knew all his workpeople by their Christian names, and entered into all their family joys and sorrows. He prospered, as he deserved to prosper, so that at the time of his death he was not only chairman of Baldwins Ltd., a combination of the family firms that he had brought about in 1902, but of the Great Western Railway, a provincial bank, and a colliery company. In 1892 he was elected Conservative M.P. for a Worcestershire division, and he was returned at every election up to his death in 1908. One thing more should be said about him—he was a sincerely religious man, a Wesleyan Methodist who had become a Churchman, one who all through his life looked upon his business not just as a means of making money but as a sacred trust.

Mrs. Baldwin was also a remarkable character in her own individual way. As her maiden name of Macdonald indicates, she came of Scottish Highland stock, although there were also Welsh and Irish ingredients in her make up. Youngest but one of the seven children of a Wesleyan minister, she was brought up in a home where there was often not enough money to go round but which was bright with intelligence and artistic expression. One of her sisters married the famous Victorian painter Burne Jones, and another the equally celebrated Edward Poynter. Yet a third sister married J. L. Kipling, so that Rudyard Kipling was Stanley Baldwin's first cousin. It was on a visit to some friends of her parents who lived at Stourport that Louisa Macdonald met the young ironmaster Alfred Baldwin, who was four years her senior. They fell in love, married, and for nearly forty-two years lived in what their grandson, Mr. A. W. Baldwin, in his book on his father, describes as a ' perfect union of man and wife '.

Stanley was named after his mother's grandfather, Rev. Jacob Stanley, another Wesleyan minister. His childhood was a very happy one, for though he had no brothers and sisters to play with there were heaps of cousins on both sides of the family.

At some date, too early to be remembered, he started taking an interest in books, an interest which never left him. In his speech to the English Association in 1927 he recalled himself as a small boy, ' reading all day in that most comfortable attitude, lying on his stomach on the hearthrug in front of the fire '. By the time he was nine he had read aloud to his aunt Edith, who came to keep house for the Baldwins when Mrs. Baldwin was for long an invalid, a number of Scott's novels; he knew the *Pilgrim's Progress* by heart, had browsed a good deal in Malory's *Morte d'Arthur*, fallen under the spell of Grimm's Fairy Tales (' which I still think the finest collection ever made '), made a beginning with Shakespeare through Lamb's *Tales*, and been thrilled to the marrow by Dickens's *A Tale of Two Cities*.

Shortly before his eleventh birthday he was sent to Hawtrey's preparatory school at Slough, and by the end of three years there was top boy. Then in the autumn of 1881, when he was fourteen, he proceeded to Harrow, instead of to Eton as most of Hawtrey's boys did, and as he would have much preferred. This turned out to be a rather unfortunate choice. Stanley was accused of some boyish prank, for which he was flogged severely by the headmaster, Dr. Butler, before he had been given an opportunity to explain. The insensitive way in which he was treated left an indelible mark on his character, and he did not do anything like so well at his lessons as had been expected. Nor were things much better when from Harrow he proceeded to Trinity College, Cambridge, for to his dismay he encountered Dr. Butler there as the newly appointed master. After three years he left with a not very good degree in history.

After many years of the most contrasting political fortunes, Winston Churchill was called to the premiership in 1940, when Britain was threatened with the most terrible and crushing disasters. Then it was demonstrated once again that Britain in her hour of direst extremity can bring forth a leader. For five years Churchill was the indomitable captain, the personification of the people's spirit to endure, to ' hang on ' till victory be won. Above: as a principal founder of the Grand Alliance he sits next to Stalin and President Roosevelt at the Yalta conference in 1945. Right: photographed by Karsh of Ottawa in a characteristic mood of stern resolution.

As an old soldier himself—did he not charge with the Lancers at Omdurman and make a dramatic escape from the Boers in South Africa?—Churchill loved to mix with the fighting men whenever the occasion offered. But for King George's direct orders to the contrary, he would have joined the invading armada on D-Day. Above: he is shown (inevitable cigar in mouth) thoroughly enjoying the opportunity of sitting in Hitler's chair, discovered in the ruins of the Fuehrer's bunker after the capture of Berlin.

Churchill's second premiership came to its honourable conclusion in April 1955, and here we see him, his fingers giving the V for Victory sign, bidding farewell to the crowd from the steps of No. 10 Downing Street.

In after life he had not much good to say of the academic education he had received. The education that did him most good, he asserted, was what he had obtained after he had gone into business, on railway journeys and at odd moments during the day, and through his reading when he got home at night.

On coming down from Cambridge, he played with the idea of becoming a parson, but at length decided to join his father in the family firm. Here he was fortunate. 'It was a place where I knew, and had known from childhood, every man on the ground,' he told the House of Commons in 1925; 'a place where I was able to talk with the men not only about the troubles in the works, but troubles at home, and their wives. It was a place where strikes and lock-outs were unknown. It was a place where the fathers and grandfathers of the the men then working there had worked, and where their sons went automatically into the business. It was also a place where nobody ever " got the sack ", and where we had a natural sympathy for those who were less concerned in efficiency than is this genera-tion, and where a large number of old gentlemen used to spend their days sitting on the handles of wheelbarrows, smoking their pipes.' And yet, he claimed, it was not an inefficient community, although it was the last survival of a type of works which ultimately became swallowed up in some great combination.

When he was twenty-five Baldwin married Miss Lucy Ridsdale, whom he had met while staying with his Burne-Jones uncle and aunt at their home in Rottingdean. The wedding took place in Rottingdean church on 12 September 1892, and in the next dozen years there were six children born to them—four daughters and two sons. For ten years they lived at Dudley Hall, near Stourport, but in 1902 they moved, because of their growing family, to Astley Hall, which Baldwin first rented and eventually bought. The house had a small park and about a hundred acres of farmland which were let to a tenant farmer. But Baldwin was able to keep a few cows and pigs and poultry, and liked to think of himself as a practical farmer, although he seldom ' put his hand to the plough ' himself.

Baldwin's first attempt to enter Parliament was in 1906, when he stood as Conservative or Unionist for Kidderminster. He was un-successful; but two years later, when his father died, he was chosen to take his place as member for the Western, later known as the Bewdley, division of Worcestershire. He continued to represent it until he was made a peer.

For a number of years he was an undistinguished back-bencher, regular in his attendance, speaking seldom but sensibly, on subjects he understood as a practical man of business. In 1916 Bonar Law, who had known his father, appointed him his Parliamentary Private Secretary, and the following year he received his first government post, as Financial Secretary to the Treasury.

As a young man he had held a commission in the Volunteers, but he was too old to serve in the army during the war. All the same, it left its mark on him. He was overwhelmed by the thought of the lost generation, and this may help to understand his reluctance to contemplate the possibility of another war, even more deadly than the last. Staying at home and making money out of war contracts pricked his conscience; he thought that these profits were tainted, they were blood-money, and he decided on a step that would go some way towards relieving his conscience and at the same time contribute something to the country's financial solvency.

In *The Times* of 24 June 1919, there appeared a letter above the initials F.S.T. It opened with a reference to the way in which the people rallied to save the nation in 1914, and went on to describe the crisis of another kind that faced them now, on the eve of the conclusion of peace. 'How can the nation be made to understand the gravity of the financial situation; that love of country is better than love of money? This can be done only by example, and the wealthy classes have today an opportunity of service which can never recur. They know the danger of the present debt; they know the weight of it in the years to come. They know the practical difficulties of a universal statutory capital levy. Let them impose upon themselves, each as he is able, a voluntary levy. It should be possible to pay to the Exchequer within 12 months such a sum as would save the taxpayer 50 millions a year. I have been considering this matter for nearly two years, but my mind moves slowly; I dislike publicity, and I hoped that someone else might lead the way. I have made as accurate an estimate as I am able of the value of my own estate and have arrived at a total of about £580,000. I have decided to realize 20 per cent of that amount or, say, £120,000, which will purchase £150,000 of the new War Loan, and present it to the Government for cancellation . . .'

The letter aroused small interest at the time, and very few people followed the example that had been put before them. Not until some years later did it come out that F.S.T. stood for Financial Secretary to the Treasury and that Stanley Baldwin was the writer of the letter.

In the spring of 1921 Baldwin was promoted to President of the

Board of Trade in Lloyd George's administration. He performed his duties admirably, but confessed to feeling uncomfortable when surrounded by so many allegedly first-class brains. As the months passed he became increasingly distrustful of Lloyd George, feeling that he was corrupting the public tone and that his foreign policy might well lead to a revival of the war. Then came the meeting of Conservative M.P.s at the Carlton Club on 19 October 1922, and Baldwin put up an astonishing performance. In a most vigorous speech he denounced Lloyd George, championed Bonar Law, and urged that the party should fight the coming general election as an independent force. His eloquence carried the day, and he emerged as the man who had smashed the Coalition. He had his reward. In Bonar Law's Cabinet he was given the post of Chancellor of the Exchequer.

As such, it fell to him to negotiate a settlement of the war debt with America, and when he came back from Washington he was severely criticized, not least by Bonar Law, the Prime Minister, for agreeing to terms which were regarded as much too onerous. Baldwin put up a good businessman's defence. When he went to Washington, he told the House of Commons on 16 February 1923, he was resolved to show the world that one country at least stood by the sanctity of contracts and by its bond.

There was something else in this speech that made his hearers sit up and had an impressive impact on the world outside. The night before a Communist member had spoken of the time when his party would take over the government of the country. Baldwin scoffed at the notion. ' No gospel founded on hate,' he declared, ' will ever seize the hearts of our people—the people of Great Britain. It is no good trying to cure the world by spreading out oceans of bloodshed. It is no good trying to cure the world by repeating that pentasyllabic French derivative, " Proletariat ". The English language is the richest in the world in thought. The English language is the richest in the world in monosyllables. Four words, of one syllable each, are words which contain salvation for this country and for the whole world, and they are " Faith ", " Hope ", " Love ", and " Work ".'

Not since Gladstone, perhaps, had words of such solemn exhortation been heard in the House of Commons, and they awoke a sympathetic response. It was realized that Baldwin was outlining a policy, the kind he would pursue if he were ever in a position to do so. His opportunity was not slow in coming. On 20 May Bonar Law was compelled to resign through ill-health, and it was not the high and mighty Lord Curzon who succeeded to the premiership but the comparatively insignificant Stanley Baldwin.

'It is a strange experience,' remarked the old ex-premier Lord Rosebery when he was informed of it, 'to realize that the Prime Minister of Great Britain is a man of whom one has never heard.'

This was the first of Baldwin's three premierships, and it lasted for less than a year. Bonar Law, when Prime Minister, had given a pledge that there would be no protection of British industries, and Baldwin, having become convinced that some measure of protection was necessary if the unemployment problem were to be solved, decided that he was in honour bound to consult the country first. He therefore went to the country in December 1923, in order to be relieved from the promise Bonar Law had given. 'I think Baldwin has gone mad,' wrote Lord Birkenhead to Austen Chamberlain; 'he simply takes one leap in the dark, looks round, and then takes another.'

At the general election the Conservatives suffered a reverse, and in January 1924 Baldwin resigned and became leader of the Opposition to the first Labour government. But in the following October Labour lost the election, and Baldwin became Prime Minister for the second time, but backed now by a large Conservative majority in the House of Commons.

This second administration lasted from November 1924 to May 1929. Baldwin's hold on his party was now so undoubted that those Conservative leaders who had remained with Lloyd George after the fall of the Coalition now returned to the fold. Baldwin managed to fit most of them in Cabinet posts, and his most surprising appointment was Winston Churchill as Chancellor of the Exchequer. But the chief laurels were won by Austen Chamberlain, the Foreign Secretary, at Locarno.

Baldwin was not particularly interested in foreign affairs, and his knowledge of the Continent hardly extended beyond Aix-les-Bains, the French spa to which he and his wife were in the habit of resorting each year to take the waters. What concerned him most deeply was the relationship of Capital and Labour, Employers and Employed, and in speech after speech he pleaded for a new spirit of co-operation in industry. Altogether typical was his successful appeal to the House to reject a bill introduced by one of his own supporters which aimed at limiting the financial support given by trade unions to the Labour party. 'There are many in all ranks and parties,' he concluded, 'who will echo my prayer: "Give peace in our time, O Lord".'

The General Strike occurred a year later, and the steady, almost imperturbable way in which Baldwin handled a possibly revolutionary situation, and even more, perhaps, his refusal in the hour of triumph to take a conqueror's advantage, immensely enhanced his standing with the nation as a whole. As one of the weekly reviews put it; 'Without any calculation, without any ambitious intent, without any effort of self-centred will, he has leapt into a position such as no Prime Minister had occupied since the days of William Pitt.'

In no small measure, Baldwin's popularity with the common folk was owing to his mastery of the then novel technique of the radio broadcast. Not particularly effective as a speaker on public platforms or in the House of Commons—unless he was really roused—he was right in his element when addressing little groups of two or three gathered round the fire in their own homes. No Prime Minister has ever surpassed him in this simple, almost fatherly and certainly good-neighbourly approach.

This was the high watermark of Baldwin's political career. As a statesman he could draw on a great fund of goodwill, the contributions of men and women of all parties—and of none. Party strife was at a low ebb, and in industry there was a real possibility of masters and men pulling together for the good of all. Unfortunately it was a false dawn, and the blame for it must be laid very largely at Baldwin's door. His Government did some good things, such as the Widows, Orphans, and the Old Age Pensions Act of 1925, and the grant (in 1928) of the parliamentary franchise to women on the same terms as men, but Baldwin's personal share in these things was small. Having appointed his Ministers, he was well content to leave them alone to carry on their jobs. ' Why come to me?' he would say; 'I have perfect confidence in you.' No Prime Minister has had a better record of attendances in the House of Commons; for hours on end he would sit on the Treasury Bench, taking his ease, saying little and apparently finding the pages of *Dod's Parliamentary Companion* most interesting reading.

By constitution he was easy-going—some would say indolent—and his energies seem to have been drained by the effort of countering the General Strike. While it is going too far to assert, as was asserted, that ' Baldwin might have done anything—and did nothing', there is substance in Lloyd George's charge that his Government degenerated into one that was ' torpid, sleepy, and barren'. In these circumstances, it was not surprising that the Conservatives lost the general election of May 1929. Baldwin at once resigned, and Ramsay MacDonald took his place as Prime Minister.

As leader of the Opposition, Baldwin was ineffectual, and before long there was a move to replace him in the Conservative party leadership, a move that was strongly supported by the press lords, Beaverbrook and Rothermere. But when Baldwin had his back to the wall he could fight. At the Conservative party assembly in 1930 he produced a letter from Lord Rothermere (which he had been given permission to quote) in which that nobleman stated that unless he were made acquainted with the names of at least eight, or ten, of his most prominent colleagues in his next Ministry, he would withdraw the support of his newspapers. 'A more preposterous and insolent demand was never made on the leader of any political party,' declared Baldwin; 'I repudiate it with contempt, and I will fight the attempt at domination to the end.' For the time being Baldwin rode the storm, but then lethargy supervened, and in the spring of 1931 there was open mutiny in the Conservative ranks. He talked to Mrs. Baldwin of retiring from public life to the peaceful pleasures of Astley Hall, but this defeatist mood soon passed. A critical by-election was in progress at St. George's, Westminster; the Conservative candidate had withdrawn on the ground that he could not support his leader, and the press peers were giving full backing to an independent. Baldwin offered to resign his own seat and stand at St. George's, but Duff Cooper was then chosen. Breaking an old convention that party leaders do not speak at by-elections, Baldwin addressed a great meeting at the Queen's Hall, and made victory sure with a speech in which he castigated the press lords in unforgettable terms. 'What the proprietorship of these papers is aiming at is power, and power without responsibility, the prerogative of the harlot throughout the ages.'

A few months later, Britain was swept by the economic blizzard. MacDonald resigned and was promptly reinstated as Prime Minister, but now as the head of a National Government. Baldwin might have had the premiership for himself, but he adopted what was generally regarded as a truly patriotic course and agreed to serve under MacDonald as deputy leader while holding the position of Lord President of the Council. As such he continued for four years until in June 1935 he changed places with the rapidly deteriorating MacDonald and became Prime Minister for the third time.

Baldwin was now nearly sixty-eight, and the years were beginning to tell. Much better had it been for his personal happiness and his place in history if he had refused the king's invitation and gone into retirement then, and not a couple of years later. But his name was still a superlative vote-catcher, as was demonstrated afresh in

November 1935, when at the general election the National Government was given a resounding vote of confidence.

Early in 1936 George V died, and Baldwin was deprived of his powerful support and steady friendship. The new sovereign was young enough to be his son, and the gap between their ages soon made itself apparent. But Baldwin's prepossessing concern was with Britain's position in competition with Hitler's Germany. Baldwin was so much a man of peace that he found it impossible to appreciate anything like the full gravity of the situation. When Hitler was steadily re-arming Germany in complete defiance of the limitations imposed by the Treaty of Versailles, Baldwin dragged his feet in Britain's rearmament, although he was under constant pressure from Churchill and his friends to create and maintain an Air Force at least as strong as Hitler's.

In Winston Churchill's *The Gathering Storm* the story of these disastrous years is told as only he could tell it, but of course from his standpoint. The most damning item in the indictment is a speech of Baldwin's delivered in the House of Commons on 12 November 1936. In this Baldwin spoke with what he himself called ' an appalling frankness '. He recalled that the difference of opinion between Mr. Churchill and himself was ' in the years from 1933 onwards ', and he continued to remind the House how often he had ' stated that a democracy is always two years behind the dictator. I believe that to be true. It has been true in this case.' He went on, ' You will remember at that time the Disarmament Conference was sitting in Geneva. You will remember at that time there was probably a stronger pacifist feeling running through this country than at any time since the war. You will remember the election at Fulham in the autumn of 1933, when a seat which the National Government held was lost by over 7,000 votes on no issue but the pacifist . . . My position as the leader of a great party was not altogether a comfortable one. I asked myself what chance was there—when that feeling that was given expression to in Fulham was common throughout the country—what chance was there within the next year or two of that feeling being so changed that the country would give a mandate for rearmament? Supposing I had gone to the country and said that Germany was rearming, and that we must rearm, does anybody think that this pacific democracy would have rallied to that cry at that moment? I cannot think of anything that would have made the loss of the election from my point of view more certain . . . '

As Churchill commented when reprinting this passage, ' This

was indeed appalling frankness. It carried naked truth about his motives into indecency. That a Prime Minister should avow he had not done his duty in regard to national safety because he was afraid of losing the election was an incident without parallel in our Parliamentary history.' Churchill unhesitatingly allows that Baldwin was not moved by any ignoble wish to remain in office; on the contrary, he was at the time most desirous of retiring. What dictated his policy was the fear—well-grounded—that if the Socialists came into power they would do even less than the National Government had done. But, Churchill argues, this was no defence and did less than justice to the spirit of the British people.

Maybe Churchill overstated his case, maybe Baldwin expressed himself badly: the matter may be argued indefinitely. But no doubt about it, 1936 was a most difficult year for Baldwin, since there was not only this question of Rearmament but before the end of the year there was the Abdication crisis. Baldwin handled this with gentlemanly consideration and effectiveness, and it is good to learn that he and the ex-king parted on good terms. He remained in office until the Coronation of George VI, and then, on 28 May 1937, tendered his resignation. He was given the Garter, and a few days later created Earl Baldwin of Bewdley. Then he withdrew to his home of Astley Hall, with everybody's good wishes for a long and happy retirement.

That was not to be, however, not after the first year or two. When the war he had so long anticipated with mounting dread came at last, and Britain's nakedness before her foes became plain for all to see, men wanted a scapegoat and they turned on the old statesman with a fury as insensate as it was cruel. He had been slothful, deliberately misleading, stubborn in his ignorance, he had betrayed the country in the interests of his party . . . After Dunkirk the abusive letters poured through his letter-box, and the poor old man, as he opened them with fumbling fingers—he had no secretary —was desperately wounded. He looked at the newspapers, listened to the news on the wireless, and read Jane Austen and all the other old favourites. He smoked almost as much as before, and went for an occasional stroll through the country lanes. His wife died in 1945, and his widowed eldest daughter came to keep house for him. Some time in the night of 13 December 1947 he died. A grave in Westminster Abbey was offered, but it was decided that his ashes should be laid beside those of his wife beneath the nave of Worcester cathedral.

39

JAMES RAMSAY MacDONALD

LOOK DOWN THE LIST of Britain's Prime Ministers, and the one who comes nearest to the American traditional term of ' log cabin to White House ' was James Ramsay MacDonald.

As his name cannot fail to have told us, he was a Scotsman. He was born on 12 October 1866, at Lossiemouth, a quiet little place inhabited by fisherfolk and farm-hands near the Moray Firth on the north-eastern cost of Scotland. His birthplace was a typical ' but and ben ' cottage of the Scottish peasantry, two roomed (one up and one down), with a thatched roof, floor of stone flags, and tiny windows filled with bottle-glass.

This was the home of his grandmother, Mrs. Isabella Ramsay, a crofter's daughter who had married the village baker, but had been deserted and left to bring up their four children on her own. Somehow she managed it, by working in the fields and at herring-gutting and making clothes for the local women and children. The youngest of the family was Anne, a girl who was said to have been the most attractive and intelligent of the lot. Early in 1866 she was working as housekeeper at a farm in the parish of Alves, not far from Elgin, where she was courted by the head ploughman, John MacDonald, a handsome and sturdy young Highlander from the Black Isle of Ross. For some reason they never married, and when the girl found herself pregnant she went home to her mother to bear her child. Nothing more is told us of John MacDonald, but the future Prime Minister always bore his surname.

Notwithstanding its geographical situation, Lossiemouth is considered to be a Lowland town, and Ramsay's mother was probably of Saxon stock. More certainly, his father was a Celt. He was, then, a blend of the two Scottish breeds and cultures, and this was often clear enough in his character and conduct, when the mystic seemed to be contesting for supremacy with the matter-of-fact rationalist. Very likely the accident of his birth contributed to the sensitivity which was one of his most marked characteristics; he must also have owed much to the example of his stout-hearted and high-principled grandmother.

As a little lad of five or thereabouts he was sent to the local school attached to the Free Kirk which his grandmother attended. Then after a year or so he was transferred to the Board School at Drainie, where in return for fees of 8d. a month he was taught the three R's, Euclid's propositions and the elements of Latin. Already he had devoured the small collection of books on his grandmother's shelf, including *Pilgrim's Progress*, Burns's poems, and of course the Bible. A consumptive watchmaker in the town introduced him to *Pickwick Papers* and Shakespeare, and the dominie at Drainie gave him the run of his bookshelves where MacDonald made the acquaintance of Carlyle and John Ruskin, and a book which had a tremendous vogue at that time, Henry George's *Progress and Poverty*, in which most of the ills of society are traced to the private ownership of land.

Once, years afterwards, MacDonald was asked at a dinner-party of distinguished people, what had been his university. ' *Cassell's Popular Educator*,' he replied.

The dominie at Drainie thought so well of him that he persuaded his mother and grandmother to let him stay on as pupil teacher, at a salary of £7 10s. a year. The two devoted women were delighted, and although the money would hardly keep him in clothes and books they insisted in fitting him out with a new suit to wear on his first day at his new post.

But their ambitions for him extended far beyond Lossiemouth, and they encouraged him to look for a job in the south. He studied the advertisements in the *Scotsman*, and after drawing many a blank was offered in 1885 a post as assistant to a clergyman in Bristol who wanted a bright lad to help in the running of a boys' club. It lasted only a few months, but Bristol happened to be one of the very few places in Britain at that time where there was some sort of Socialist organization. MacDonald joined the local branch of Hyndman's Social Democratic Federation, and served his apprenticeship as a Socialist ' agitator ', speaking at street corners and in back-street halls, although the Marxist Socialism that he was required to preach was never really to his taste.

After a few months back in Lossiemouth, he set off again, this time for London. For weeks he tramped the city streets, looking for a job, any sort of job. He nearly starved, and was down to his last shilling when he was taken on by the newly formed Cyclists' Touring Club to address envelopes at 10s. a week. A little later he obtained a post as clerk in a warehouse at 15s. a week, and now, he claimed in after years, he ' lived like a fighting cock '. His staple food was oatmeal, which he had sent him from home; he couldn't afford tea, but discovered that hot water was just as good once you had got used to it; and his midday dinner was a twopenny beefsteak pudding at Peace & Plenty's establishment in Aldersgate Street. Somehow or other he managed to keep himself alive, send money home to his mother, pay his fees for evening classes at the Birkbeck Institute, and save a little into the bargain.

Before long his wages at the warehouse were raised to £1 a week, with a stool in the counting-house, but he had now set his heart on winning a scholarship at South Kensington to qualify as a teacher, and for many weeks he stayed in his lodgings, working at his books for twenty hours a day, morning, afternoon, and night. For days he never went out. The result was that even his peasant's constitution was undermined, and he had to go back to Lossiemouth to be nursed back to health.

By 1888, when he was twenty-two, he was back in London, and now had a stroke of good fortune. Somehow he made the acquaintance of Thomas Lough, the wealthy and popular Liberal candidate for Islington who made him his private secretary at £75 a year. He held this post until 1891, and it was a most useful introduction not only to the mechanics of politics but to the life of the cultured and leisured classes.

MacDonald did not follow the Liberal road, however, but joined all the Socialist organizations he came across, including the Fabian Society and the Independent Labour Party, both of them in their hot and eager youth. In Scotland he had contributed to the local newspapers, and now in London he wrote for the *Echo*, an evening newspaper, and other journals. Such was the knowledge he had contrived to pick up, he was commissioned to write a number of articles for the *Dictionary of National Biography*.

All his spare time was devoted to Socialist propaganda, and at the general election of 1895 MacDonald made his first appearance as a parliamentary candidate, standing on behalf of the Independent Labour Party at Southampton. He polled only 886 votes: all the same the election was to prove of marked consequence in his life.

Shortly before the election in May 1895, MacDonald had been lying ill in St. Thomas's hospital in London, and while there he received one day a letter, signed M. E. Gladstone, enclosing a small contribution towards his election fund. He wrote in acknowledgment, and discovered that the sender was a woman, one Miss Margaret Ethel Gladstone, the daughter of a distinguished scientist (no relation of *the* Mr. Gladstone) who was also well known for his social and religious activities.

Brought up in an atmosphere of middle-class piety and comfort, well-educated and cultured and most serious-minded, Miss Gladstone had become dissatisfied with the life she was required to lead and had taken up social work in Hoxton, one of the poorest of the London districts. Then she had drifted into politics, and almost unconsciously had become a Socialist of sorts. One Sunday evening she had heard MacDonald speak at a small Labour club, and had been instantly impressed. Hence the small donation.

The acquaintance thus begun soon ripened into friendship. She went to his meetings, and accompanied him to the British Museum where they spent hours together in the reading-room. On the steps of the Museum he proposed to her, and was at once accepted. She had some money of her own, her origins and upbringing had been very different from his, and he was still nothing more than a struggling journalist and a mostly unpaid political propagandist. But they were in love, and in November 1896 they were married, and made their home in a flat at No. 3 Lincoln's Inn Fields, in the heart of London.

Mrs. MacDonald's first anxiety, her husband tells in the short memoir he wrote of her, was that their home should be open, and ' once every three weeks or so our rooms were crowded with men and women busy in the service of Labour and Socialism '. She served on innumerable committees, but always put the emphasis on the personal relationship. She had a genius for making people feel at home. Sometimes a friend might suggest that she did not pay sufficient attention to her appearance, and indeed she was indifferent to dress. Her domestic arrangements were inclined to be slapdash, and it was sometimes suspected that bananas were the MacDonalds' staple food. Within a few years she bore six children, and they played around her or sat on her knee as she worked at her desk or banged away at her typewriter.

The companionship of this remarkable woman meant everything to MacDonald. It is not too much to say that his marriage was the making of him. Through her he was admitted to the middle class, and her small private income gave him a comfortable feeling of independence. It was on her money that they were enabled to take those holidays abroad which meant so much to both of them.

With her encouragement and support he now forged ahead in the Labour movement. For three years (1901–1904) he was a member of the London County Council. In 1900 he became secretary of the Labour Representation Committee out of which emerged the Labour Party in 1906; he held the post until 1912, after which he was the party treasurer until 1924. At first the secretaryship was unpaid and the only office was a room in his flat, but in 1904 he was given a salary of £250 a year, out of which he was expected to pay £100 a year to an assistant.

In 1900 he stood at the general election as Labour candidate for Leicester. But he had made himself notorious as an opponent of the Boer War, and he was unsuccessful. But in the great landslide of 1906 he was returned as the junior of the town's two M.P.s. The other was a Liberal, and MacDonald owed his election to Liberal support.

Old Mrs. Ramsay had died some years before, but his mother was still alive, hale and hearty. The news of her Jamie's triumph reached Lossiemouth late at night, and she had gone to bed; but jubilant townsfolk rattled at her window to give her the news.

From the first MacDonald made his mark in the House of Commons: ' a born Parliamentarian ', was Balfour's description of him. He made frequent speeches, and developed a gift for oratory. His good looks and gentlemanly bearing added to his attractiveness. With his wife he travelled widely—to South Africa, India, the United States, and the Continent many times. He held his seat at Leicester at the two elections of 1910, and in 1911 was elected chairman of the Labour parliamentary group. Already it was whispered that he might be found a place in the Liberal government.

But about this time he suffered a succession of personal bereavements. Early in 1910 the MacDonalds' son David sickened and died, and a few days later MacDonald's mother died at Lossiemouth: her son had built her a new house and she overtaxed her strength in getting it to rights. The MacDonalds' youngest child was born in December 1910, and before she was properly recovered Mrs. MacDonald exhausted herself in visiting a sick friend. On 20 July 1911, her forty-first birthday, she went to Leicester to investigate the running of some industrial schools, and next morning lunched with her husband at the House of Commons to meet a Negro professor. That afternoon they went to their country cottage at Chesham Bois, in Buckinghamshire, for the weekend, but she complained of pains and tiredness and MacDonald took her home to their flat. For weeks she lay in bed, and then on 8 September 1911 she died. ' She was called to sleep whilst it was still day,' wrote her husband in his most moving record, ' and before the chilly shadows of night came up with dew-wet arms to enfold her.'

Three years later, in December 1914, a memorial to Mrs. MacDonald was unveiled in Lincoln's Inn Fields. It consists of a granite seat surmounted by a bronze group of Mrs. MacDonald with her arms stretched out over the heads of a merry band of little children; the inscription reads that the seat was placed there in memory of one who ' spent her life in helping others '.

By this time Britain was at war with Germany. On 5 August 1914 MacDonald resigned from the chairmanship of the Parliamentary Labour party when its members refused to follow him in opposing the grant of credits for carrying on the war. Whereas most of the Labour leaders joined with Arthur Henderson and George Barnes in supporting the national war effort, MacDonald was a most persistent critic, with the result that he became about the most unpopular man in the country. Throughout the war years his position was a most distressful one. Friendships of a lifetime were disrupted. In London and many other places the platforms were closed to him, or if he attempted to make a speech he was howled down by the angry crowd. His expulsion from the Lossiemouth golf club was a small matter, but it rankled all the same. He was viciously attacked in the popular newspapers, and the cruellest blow of all was when Horatio Bottomley published in his weekly *John Bull* a copy of MacDonald's birth certificate. ' Thank God my mother is dead,' MacDonald told J. H. Thomas, the railwaymen's leader, ' for this would have killed her.'

In the prevailing climate of opinion it is not surprising that at the general election of 1918, MacDonald—charged with being a pro-German, a Bolshevik, a traitor, a loose-liver and an atheist—and furthermore being deprived of Liberal support—was rejected at Leicester by over 14,000 votes.

This is not surprising, but what is surprising is that in spite of everything MacDonald was able to retain the respect and perhaps the affection of great numbers of Labour supporters, including many who did not approve in the least of his attitude towards the war. In the spring of 1921 he stood as Labour candidate in a by-election at East Woolwich and was narrowly defeated, but at the general election of 1922 he won easily the miners' stronghold of Aberavon, in South Wales. Immediately on his return to the House of Commons he was elected chairman and leader of the Parliamentary Labour Party—very largely because of the enthusiastic support of the Clydesiders—and since the Labour M.P.s now outnumbered the Liberals he became automatically leader of the Opposition. Then at the general election of 1923, while the Conservatives under Baldwin remained the largest party with 258 seats, Labour had 191 as against the Liberals with 158.

When Baldwin faced the new House of Commons, a vote of no confidence was carried against him on 21 January by a combination of Labour and Liberals, and he resigned the next day. 'At 12.15,' wrote King George in his diary for 22 January 1924, 'I held a council, at which Mr. Ramsay MacDonald was sworn in as a member. I then asked him to form a Government, which he accepted to do. I had an hour's talk with him, he impressed me very much; he wishes to do the right thing.' The entry concludes: 'Today 23 years ago dear Grandmama [Queen Victoria] died. I wonder what she would have thought of a Labour Government!'

Later in the afternoon, after the House of Commons had adjourned, MacDonald went to the Palace again, kissed hands on his appointment as Prime Minister, and handed the king a list of his proposed ministers. In addition to the premiership he assumed the responsibilities of Foreign Secretary; J. R. Clynes was deputy leader, and Philip Snowden Chancellor of the Exchequer; and near the bottom of the list was the name of Mr. Attlee, who was under-secretary at the War Office.

Some unfavourable comments were voiced by sterner Socialists concerning the haste with which the new Prime Minister got himself rigged out in Court dress, complete with sword. Some ladies, too, were worried about Miss MacDonald: would she know how to behave at court? Would she know the right sort of dresses to wear? Miss Ishbel soon put them in their place. 'I have already chosen my frocks,' she said 'and I think I know how to behave at court . . .'

This first administration of Ramsay MacDonald's was short and not very noteworthy. The Prime Minister's handling of foreign affairs was on the whole surer than his touch with domestic issues. But the Government was in office only on sufferance of the other parties, and by the autumn it was in trouble. MacDonald decided on an appeal to the country. The general election was fought in October, and Labour's chances, never very bright, were practically destroyed by the publication, shortly before polling-day, of the so-called Zinoviev letter, or 'the Red letter', from which it appeared that the prominent Soviet leader had been endeavouring to interfere in Britain's internal affairs. MacDonald—than whom it would have been difficult to find a more pronounced opponent of the Soviet system—had already ordered a note of protest to be handed to the Russian Chargé d'Affaires in London, but the matter was handled badly and the public came to the conclusion that the Government were being too soft with the Russians. On polling-day they registered their disapproval, and the first Labour Government was swept out of office. Labour lost 49 seats, and Baldwin had a majority of 225.

Five years of Conservative rule followed, until in the spring of 1929 Baldwin sought a renewal of his mandate. But the electorate were not impressed by his slogan of 'Safety first'; they were in the mood for a change, and at the general election Labour won 287 seats—thus becoming for the first time the largest party in the House of Commons. MacDonald had stood for Seaham, a Durham mining constituency, and he achieved a great personal triumph, being returned with the record majority of 28,794 over his Conservative opponent.

On 5 June MacDonald motored down to Windsor, where King George, who was recovering from an illness, received him in his bedroom. They discussed the various appointments, and the king raised an interesting point; how far MacDonald was satisfied in his own conscience that his party were justified in calling themselves a Labour party ? How many of them had ever done a day's manual work in their lives ? MacDonald replied that at least *he* had. He then kissed hands as Prime Minister for the second time.

At first he had thoughts of taking the Foreign Office in addition to the premiership, as he had done on the previous occasion, but eventually Henderson was appointed to this key post. Snowden became Chancellor of the Exchequer as before, and history was made with the appointment of Miss Margaret Bondfield as Minister of Labour—the first woman to become a Cabinet minister. She was also the first woman Privy Councillor.

As in 1924, MacDonald was heading a minority government, and at any moment he might be dislodged by a combination of Conservatives and Liberals. Henderson had some successes at the Foreign Office, but the domestic record was pretty barren. Then the economic blizzard began to blow. The number of unemployed, which stood at round about a million when MacDonald took office in 1929, had risen to more than two and a half millions by the beginning of 1931, and the cost of paying unemployment benefit put the nation's finances in the red. An economy committee under the chairmanship of Sir George (later Lord) May reported in July that there would be a deficit of £120 millions within a year, and proposed substantial cuts in Government expenditure and a large increase in taxation. MacDonald pressed on his colleagues a number of economies, most of which were very reluctantly agreed to. But there was a majority in the Cabinet against a proposed reduction of

10 per cent in the unemployment benefit; and to add to the Prime Minister's difficulties the Trades Union Congress showed themselves most unco-operative.

Meanwhile Britain's economic plight had been advertised to the world, and there was a flight from the pound as foreign investors withdrew their gold balances from London. An application for a large loan from America met the response that the Budget must be balanced before the money would be forthcoming.

The attitude of the New York bankers stiffened the opposition in the Cabinet, and on Sunday, 23 August, after a meeting of the Cabinet, MacDonald, looking ' scared and unbalanced ' as the report put it, hurried to Buckingham Palace and informed the king that his colleagues could not agree on the policy to be adopted, and that in these circumstances he had no alternative than to tender his resignation.

But King George did not see it in that way. He told MacDonald that in his opinion he was the only man able to lead the country through the crisis, and urged him to reconsider the matter. This MacDonald agreed to do, but only on the understanding that his Majesty should take Mr. Baldwin and Sir Herbert Samuel, the leaders of the Conservative and Liberal parties respectively, into consultation. So at 10 o'clock the next morning the king held a conference at Buckingham Palace with the Prime Minister, Baldwin, and Samuel, out of which emerged the plan that a National Government should be formed, with MacDonald remaining as Prime Minister.

At midday MacDonald met his colleagues in the Cabinet Room at No. 10, and put the proposal to them. It was not to be a coalition in the generally accepted sense, he explained, but a ' Cabinet of individuals ' formed to see the crisis through. He invited those who felt so inclined to join him, but he suggested that the junior ministers at least might do better to follow the party line. The announcement caused consternation, and MacDonald was almost deserted. Only Snowden, Thomas and Sankey (Lord Chancellor) were prepared to follow him into the new administration.

MacDonald thereupon set about the formation of a National Government—according to Snowden ' with an enthusiasm which showed that the adventure was highly agreeable to him ', but according to his own version, feeling quite sure that he was committing political suicide.

By the evening of the next day MacDonald was able to submit to the king a list of names to constitute a Cabinet of ten members—

four Conservatives, two Liberals, and four Labour. These were sworn in on 26 August. The great majority of MacDonald's former colleagues went into opposition under Henderson but Malcolm MacDonald, the Prime Minister's son, insisted on throwing in his lot with his father.

Immediate steps were taken to balance the Budget, and millions of dollars were borrowed from New York. But when these credits were used up the crisis was renewed, and on 21 September the Government which had been formed to save the pound was compelled to admit defeat, when Britain went off the gold standard.

MacDonald's original idea seems to have been that the National Government should be a purely temporary administration, and that when the crisis had been surmounted the party system should operate as before. But Baldwin was quite happy with the way things were going, and he was able to induce MacDonald to agree to the National Government going to the country to seek a ' doctor's mandate '.

The ensuing general election campaign was unequalled for bitterness. From one end of the country to the other MacDonald was denounced by his old-time friends and associates as a Judas, one who had betrayed for his own unworthy ends all that he and they had stood for over the years. But the result was a foregone conclusion. The National Government won an overwhelming victory at the polls, for of the 615 members of the new House of Commons no fewer than 544 were its supporters. MacDonald had tempted fortune by standing again for Seaham, which had long been regarded as a Labour stronghold, but he triumphed with a majority of nearly 6,000 over his Labour opponent.

Following the election MacDonald reconstituted his government, forming his fourth administration. His own National Labour group numbered only a dozen, including his son Malcolm, who was given a Cabinet post; and he might well be described as the prisoner of his allies. He pressed on with a programme of retrenchment and reform, however, and until Hitler came upon the scene supported the cause of international disarmament.

But his own position was far from being an enviable one. To the Labour party he was very much the ' lost leader ' of Browning's poem. For so many years they had ' loved him so, followed him, honoured him ', and then he had left them—not, it is true, for ' a handful of silver ' or ' a riband to stick in his coat ', but for the companionship of courtiers and men of place and wealth and power, the patronage of his former enemies, the blandishments of his

Sovereign. They remembered (or so they said) that even as a young man he had been intensely ambitious, seeking his own advancement, jealous of rivals and suspicious of friends. When he had become Prime Minister, it had gone to his head. If only his wife had lived, she would have kept him on the right track! Instead of spending his days on the Front Bench he had held court in his room behind the Speaker's chair; and when he should have been in the House answering questions he was off to Lossiemouth to play golf or hob-nob with the admiring locals, or he was spending long weekends in the delightful surroundings of Chequers.

Before long MacDonald began to show signs of the most serious overstrain, both physical and mental. The long hours he spent at his desk—for whatever they said to the contrary, he was a tremendous worker; the incessant worries of his situation; the separation from old friends, and the difficulty he experienced in making new ones; the often foul-mouthed abuse with which he was showered; increasing dissensions in his Cabinet—all these things took their toll. Once his oratory had held great audiences spellbound, but now he wandered off into unintelligible maunderings. Once he had commanded attention, and even those who hated his opinions could not refrain from admiring his guts. But now he was declining into a drivelling relic.

At length things came to such a pass that his colleagues in the Government took alarm, and induced him to retire. On 7 June 1935 he resigned the premiership and took the sinecure office of Lord President of the Council. But not all the fight had gone out of him, and at the general election in the following November he had the temerity to stand again for Seaham. This time he went down in defeat: the figures being Emanuel Shinwell (Labour), 38,380; Ramsay MacDonald (National Labour), 17,882; Labour majority, 20,498.

At a by-election in January 1936, he was elected M.P. for the Scottish Universities, but he was a ghost of his former self. In the autumn of 1937 he went on a voyage to South America, and he died suddenly at sea on 9 November. His body was brought home; and after a funeral service in Westminster Abbey his ashes were buried beside those of his wife in the churchyard of Spynie, near his home on the edge of the moor at Lossiemouth.

40

NEVILLE CHAMBERLAIN

FOR MORE THAN SIXTY YEARS the Chamberlains were one of the most important political families in England. First there was Joseph Chamberlain (1836–1914), a Londoner who made a fortune manu facturing screws in Birmingham, entered Parliament in 1876 as Radical M.P. for Birmingham, and might well have become Prime Minister if he had not broken with Gladstone over Home Rule. As it was, he held office as a Liberal Unionist in the governments of Lord Salisbury and A. J. Balfour. Then there was his son Austen Chamberlain (1863–1937), who was Chancellor of the Exchequer under Balfour and again under Lloyd George; a member of Lloyd George's War Cabinet, and as Foreign Secretary under Baldwin negotiated the Locarno Pact of 1925, and thereupon became Sir Austen. Like his father he was well in the running for the premier-ship, but just failed to make it. Finally, there was Joseph's younger son Neville Chamberlain.

Arthur Neville Chamberlain was born at his father's house in Edgbaston, Birmingham, on 18 March 1869. His mother was Florence Kenrick, Joseph Chamberlain's second wife and his first wife's cousin; she died when Neville was six, so that he had only hazy recollections of her. At the age of eight he was sent to a pre-paratory school at Southport, where he was reasonably happy, and then to another at Rugby, where he was miserable. He entered Rugby School in 1882, which was even worse; in after years he used to say that he hated the place. Leaving Rugby in 1886, when he was seventeen, he did not go to Cambridge as his brother Austen had done but studied metallurgy and engineering design at Mason College in Birmingham. On leaving there he was ap-prenticed to a firm of accountants in Birmingham but in 1890, now twenty-one, his father sent him out to the West Indies to manage an estate of 20,000 acres he had bought on the island of Andros, in the Bahamas, with the intention of growing sisal on a large scale. For six years Neville wrestled with the problems of an unsuitable soil, unskilled and unsuitable labour, transport difficulties, and marketing the crop. In the end the venture proved a complete flop, and

Joseph Chamberlain decided to wind it up when he was £50,000 out of pocket.

Neville returned home to Birmingham in 1897, when he was not far off thirty, and went into business on his own account, buying a small engineering firm which specialized in making berths for emigrant ships. But like his father he began to take a keen interest in local affairs. He became chairman of the General Hospital, and in 1911 was elected to the City Council as a Liberal Unionist. Because of his business experience he was at once appointed chairman of the Town Planning committee. In 1914 he was made an alderman, and the following year was elected Lord Mayor. Now he flung himself into war work, but in 1916 he had the satisfaction of opening the Birmingham Municipal Savings Bank, the first of its kind. He served a second term as Lord Mayor in 1916.

In all these activities Chamberlain was most warmly supported by his wife. She was Miss Anne (Annie) Vere Cole, and when they were married—at St. Paul's, Knightsbridge in January 1911—she was twenty-eight and he was within a few weeks of forty-two. Daughter of an army officer who had died in India when she was a little girl, she was brought up by her grandparents in very comfortable circumstances at West Woodhay, and this difference in social background made her friends fear that a middle-aged Birmingham business man was hardly the most suitable match for her. But they had many tastes in common; a love of music and art, of books and flowers. As much as Chamberlain she loved the country-side and life in the country. She would accompany him on his walks—at least for part of the way: Chamberlain was a prodigious walker; she understood his enthusiasm for shooting and, later, fishing; she could take an intelligent interest in his botanizing and bird-watching and collecting butterflies and moths.

Before the year of their marriage was out a daughter was born to them, and a son followed in 1914. In the surroundings of a happy home Chamberlain unbent to a degree that would have surprised those who knew him only as the reserved and rather solemn public figure. From the outset of their marriage Mrs. Chamberlain was her husband's constant companion, helper, and encourager. Every success he was able to achieve he put down to her. 'I'd never have done it without Annie,' was his frequent tribute.

Chamberlain's renown as first citizen of Birmingham was responsible for his appointment, at the close of 1916, as head of the department of National Service that Lloyd George had just set up. This proved a most unpleasant experience. Chamberlain had a headquarters given him, in St. Ermin's hotel, Westminster, but he had no staff to speak of and no clear instructions. Lloyd George seems to have taken an almost instant dislike to him, and all his references to Chamberlain in his *War Memoirs* are disparaging. 'A vein of self-sufficient obstinacy in the new Minister contributed to the difficulties that baffled all our endeavours,' he writes, and there was a general feeling that the department 'was being run in a narrow spirit of unimaginative officialism and that its limbs were bound in a tangle of red tape'. After seven months Chamberlain had had enough, and Lloyd George accepted his resignation with the chilliest of acknowledgments.

Chamberlain went back to Birmingham feeling pretty sore and fully determined never to have any further dealings with Lloyd George. All the same there was something about the life at Westminster that appealed to him, and he began to give serious thought to the possibility of a career in politics. At the general election of 1918 he stood as Unionist, or Conservative, candidate in the Lady-wood division of Birmingham, and on the strength of his family name and personal reputation had an easy victory over his Labour opponent.

Early in 1919 he took his seat in the House of Commons, when he was within a few weeks of his fiftieth birthday. But although he was such a late starter he made exceptionally rapid progress. When the Coalition government fell in 1922 and Bonar Law succeeded Lloyd George as Prime Minister, he appointed Chamberlain Postmaster-General. A few months later he was transferred to the Ministry of Health, where he produced a workmanlike Housing Act. Baldwin confirmed him in his appointment, and after three months promoted him to Chancellor of the Exchequer. Chamberlain was surprised, as he might well be, but immensely gratified. In little over a year he had graduated from back-bencher to the second post in the Government.

As things turned out, he was at the Treasury for only four months. The Chamberlains moved into No. 11 Downing Street at the beginning of October and spent the next weekend at Chequers, but then Baldwin decided on a general election in which the Conservatives suffered a severe reverse. The Chamberlains moved out of No. 11 and the Snowdens moved in. But in October 1924 there was another general election, and this time Baldwin's Conservatives won a great victory.

At this election, however, Chamberlain had a very narrow victory. As before, he stood for Ladywood, but over the years this had become a distinctly marginal seat and now the Labour candidate was Sir Oswald Mosley, then the darling of the left. When the votes were counted, the result was such a near thing that four recounts were required. To begin with, Chamberlain was in by 30 votes; then by 15, then by 7. The third recount showed him out by 2. A fourth was demanded, and at 4.30 a.m. this gave him a majority of 77.

Baldwin set about forming his administration, and Chamberlain was one of the first to be summoned for consultation. ' Needless to say I want you to go back to the Treasury,' Baldwin began. Chamberlain said nothing, whereupon (Chamberlain noted in his diary) ' he asked me what I should like and I said I had given the matter full consideration and would like to go back to Health '. And so it was arranged.

Chamberlain had chosen wisely. The five years (1924–1929) he spent as Minister of Health under Baldwin were by far the most satisfactory of all those he spent in Parliament. Indeed, good judges have pronounced him to have been the best Minister of Health the country has ever had. This may be attributed in large measure to his experience in local government. No other Conservative Prime Minister has approached him in this respect.

Within a few weeks of taking office he had drawn up a programme of work, comprising twenty-five measures of greater or lesser importance, and he never had fewer than six and sometimes had ten or more in the pipeline. By the end of his term, twenty-one of these had reached the Statute Book. Special mention should be made of the Rating & Valuation Act of 1925, which reduced the number of rating authorities from 15,546 to 1,767 and achieved something like a uniform rating system throughout the country; and the Local Government Act of 1929, which abolished the Boards of Guardians, made extensive alterations in local government areas and functions, and effected a revolution in local government finance. This Act consists of 138 sections with 12 schedules, and *The Times* described it as ' one of the outstanding legislative achievements of the twentieth century '.

At the same time, it must be said that Chamberlain's zeal for administrative efficiency sometimes led him to adopt an overbearing attitude that his opponents found offensive. Once Baldwin had to tell him that when he spoke in the House of Commons he gave the impression of ' looking upon the Labour Party as dirt '. Of course Chamberlain did not think so, but as with other deeply sensitive men opposition aroused a combative streak in his nature, and he expressed himself badly and too provocatively. Labour hostility was something he always had to reckon with, and in the end it was a factor in his downfall.

From 1929 to 1931 Chamberlain—sitting now for Edgbaston: he had seen the red light at Ladywood—was out of office, but then he was given a place in the National Government as Chancellor of the Exchequer. As such it fell to him to introduce on 4 February 1932 the Import Duties Bill. It was the 'great day in my life', he told his sister, for it marked the victory of the Tariff proposals that his father had introduced a generation before. The Bill was passed, and the Protectionist revolution was crowned at the Ottawa Conference later in the year.

Chamberlain continued at the Treasury after Baldwin changed places with Ramsay MacDonald. By now he was generally regarded as the natural heir to the premiership, and but for the Abdication crisis he would probably have become Prime Minister a year or so earlier. But on 28 May 1937, immediately after Baldwin's resignation, Neville Chamberlain kissed hands as First Lord of the Treasury and Prime Minister. Two days later we find him writing to one of his sisters; ' It has come to me without my raising a finger to obtain it. But I should never have been P.M. if I hadn't had Annie to help me . . .'

As a matter of course he was promptly elected leader of the Conservative party, and in his speech of acceptance he mentioned that he had ' reached an age when most people are thinking of retiring from active work' (he was sixty-eight). But, he went on, he had led ' a sober and temperate life' and as a result was ' sound in wind and limb'. They laughed and cheered, and his premiership seemed to have made a propitious beginning. Very shortly, however, he was caught up in a great crisis. For him there were to be no more opportunities for economic advance and social improvement. Instead there opened before him the road to Munich.

Chamberlain's name has become so indissolubly connected with the policy of Appeasement that it tends to be forgotten that in his successive budgets as Chancellor he made provision for increased armaments on such a scale as to arouse the intense hostility of the Labour and Liberal oppositions, who denounced him as a warmonger, while the support he received from his own side was often lukewarm. But while resolved upon repairing the gaps in the nation's defences he was also determined to do everything in his power to avert a war which must cause the death of millions and perhaps the destruction of Western civilization.

How to prevent it? Most people muttered something about Collective Security, but Chamberlain was convinced that the Dictators were not to be stopped by passing pious resolutions in the League of Nations Assembly at Geneva. He thought that Hitler had something of a case, as long as he confined himself to demanding the return to the Reich of former German territories and even the incorporation of adjoining areas where there was a large German population. As for Italy, he refused to condemn Mussolini out of hand for endeavouring to obtain colonies into which the surplus Italian population might be decanted. He strongly opposed the Italian invasion of Abyssinia, but when the conquest had been practically accomplished he was the first Cabinet minister to condemn the continuation of sanctions against Italy as ' midsummer madness', and it was largely because of his insistence they were abandoned. In taking up these attitudes he considered that he was acting the part of a reasonable man, and perhaps his greatest mistake lay in thinking that he had reasonable men to deal with.

However that may be, at some stage or other he took the decision to see what his personal diplomacy might do. His first approaches were to Mussolini.

Through his sister-in-law Lady Chamberlain, Sir Austen's widow, who spent much of her time in Rome, he had maintained some form of unofficial contact with Count Ciano, the Italian Foreign Minister: and now, in the early part of 1938, he urged upon Anthony Eden, his Foreign Secretary, that official talks should be opened with Mussolini in the hope of detaching him from his association with Hitler. Eden thought the proposal inopportune, to say the least, and when the Prime Minister persisted, Eden resigned. In his place Chamberlain proceeded to appoint the more amenable Lord Halifax, and in April 1938 an Anglo-Italian agreement was concluded at Rome.

So far, so good, Chamberlain may have thought; but now he was forced into a confrontation with Hitler. As the summer of 1938 drew on into autumn the Czechoslovak crisis worsened, and war seemed inevitable. Then at the eleventh hour the world was startled by the spectacle of an elderly gentleman setting out in an aeroplane to beard Hitler in his fastness at Berchtesgaden. The Fuehrer was so taken aback that he received him with reasonable courtesy; but when a week later Chamberlain put in a second appearance, this time at Godesberg, he was obliged to submit to the grossest insolence and humiliation. Chamberlain was disgusted and disheartened, and his mood found expression in his broadcast to the people after his return to London.

' How horrible, fantastic, incredible, it is,' he said, ' that we should be digging trenches and trying on gas-masks here because of a quarrel in a far-away country between people of whom we know nothing!' After this shockingly insensitive reference to Czecho-slovakia, he went on; ' I am myself a man of peace in the depths of my soul . . . but if I were convinced that any nation had made up its mind to dominate the world by fear of its force, I should feel that it must be resisted. Under such a domination, life for people who believe in liberty would not be worth living; but war is a fearful thing, and we must be very clear before we embark upon it that it is really the great issues that are at stake.'

When he rose to address the House of Commons on 28 September it was to report the failure of his mission. While he was speaking Lord Halifax passed to him a note just received to the effect that Hitler had invited the Prime Minister, together with Mussolini and M. Flandin, the French Premier, to meet him at Munich. When Chamberlain announced this to the House it was received with unrestrained relief.

Early the next morning Chamberlain set out on his third flight, ' to see what I can make of this last effort '. To the enthusiastic crowd that saw him off at Heston he quoted the old childhood rhyme, ' If at first you don't succeed, try, try, try, again ', and expressed the hope that when he returned he would be able to say with Hotspur in Shakespeare's play, ' Out of this nettle, danger, we pluck this flower, safety.'

So he went to Munich, and Czechoslovakia was thrown to the Nazi wolves. And when on 6 October the Prime Minister came back—when he flourished before the reporters at the airport the scrap of paper bearing his signature and Hitler's, on which it was written that ' we regard the agreement signed last night . . . as symbolic of the desire of our two peoples never to go to war with one another again ' he was given the reception of a conquering hero. A message from the king was handed to him: ' Come straight to Buckingham Palace, so that I can express to you personally my most heartfelt congratulations on the success of your visit to Munich.' All the way from Heston to the Palace the roads were lined by cheering crowds, and when he and Mrs. Chamberlain appeared on the balcony between the king and queen he was given a tremendous ovation. Later that night he spoke to a delirious crowd from a window in Downing Street, and he was so carried away by the occasion that he ventured to make a comparison between his home-coming and Lord Beaconsfield's return from the Berlin Congress in 1878. ' This is the second time in our history,' he said, ' that there has come back from Germany to Downing Street peace with honour. I believe it is peace for our time.'

So he believed, and nearly everybody else believed it at the time. All the Dominion premiers hastened to send their congratulations. In the next three weeks Chamberlain received 40,000 letters from well-wishers, and his wife a further 12,000. Gifts poured in, including tulips from Holland, cases of wine from France, fishing-rods and salmon-flies. In the eyes of millions all the world over, and not least in Germany, he was the man who had saved the world from war.

But it was a false hope. Less than a year later, at 11.15 a.m. on 3 September 1939, the man who had brought back peace with honour was broadcasting from the Cabinet Room at No. 10 to announce that the British ultimatum to Germany had expired and that Britain was therefore at war. At noon he was reporting to the House of Commons the failure of all his hopes. ' It is a sad day for all of us,' he said ' For none is it sadder than for me. Everything that I worked for, everything that I had hoped for, everything that I believed in during my public life has crashed into ruins this morning. There is only one thing left for me, and that is to devote what strength and powers I have to forwarding the victory of the cause for which we have to sacrifice so much. I cannot tell what part I may be allowed to play myself, but I trust I may live to see the day when Hitlerism has been destroyed and a restored and liberated Europe has been re-established.' But in this, too, he was destined to be disappointed.

When the war began, Chamberlain was already a sick man, although he did not realize it. He clung to office, and was not deterred when the Labour and Liberal leaders refused to serve under him in a Coalition government. He did, however, secure the return of Winston Churchill to the Admiralty; and Churchill served him most loyally, although often with misgiving. Chamberlain's popularity had started to dwindle, and to be called ' the man of Munich ' was a masterpiece of obloquy.

For seven months the ' phoney war ' dragged out its wearisome course, and Chamberlain's image was further affected by fatuous remarks about Hitler having ' missed the bus '. Then came the Norway fiasco, and the tide of criticism became a flood. In the House of Commons on 7 May he was exposed to a motion of censure, not for the mismanagement of the Norway expedition so much as for the unpreparedness of the nation's defences, the woeful deficiencies that had been disclosed in planes and equipment, the general lack of drive, for most of which, however unfairly, he was held personally responsible. Lloyd George lashed him unmercifully; Sir Roger Keyes (in the full dress of an Admiral of the Fleet) voiced the deep concern of the men in the fighting services; Attlee denounced him on behalf of the Labour opposition and Sir Archibald Sinclair did the same for the Liberals, and finally Leopold Amery, a Conservative ex-minister, rounded on him with Cromwell's tremendous words when dismissing the Rump Parliament in 1653: 'You have sat here too long . . . Depart, I say, and let us have done with you. In the name of God, go!'

On the second day of the debate Herbert Morrison announced that the Opposition would divide the House against the Government. Chamberlain rose and angrily called upon 'my friends in the House—and I have friends in the House . . . to support us in the lobby tonight'. This appeal to party loyalty only made matters worse, although Churchill defended the Prime Minister in a speech in which he commented grimly, 'I hope he has some friends. He certainly had a good many when things were going well!' The vote was taken, and it was found that the Government majority, normally in the region of 200, had fallen to 81.

This convinced Chamberlain that the time had come for the formation of a National Government, and on the afternoon of 9 May he invited Mr. Attlee and Arthur Greenwood to No. 10, and put to them the question whether the Labour party would be prepared to join in such a government either under himself or someone else (he had in mind Lord Halifax). The Labour leaders went away to consult their executive, and on 10 May they told him that Labour would serve in a national government—but not under him. Chamberlain at once drove off to Buckingham Palace and handed his resignation to King George.

'The King was as nice as possible,' he wrote to tell his sister, 'and expressed what I know were very genuine regrets as well as his own pleasure at my remaining in the new Government.' Churchill, too, was deeply appreciative. 'My first act in coming back from the Palace,' he wrote, 'is to write and tell you how grateful I am to you for promising to stand by me, and to aid the country at this extremely grievous and formidable moment . . .'

In the Churchill government Chamberlain held the post of Lord President of the Council. But almost immediately after his retirement from the premiership he was experiencing acute abdominal pains, and in July he had an operation for a cancerous growth. This seemed at first to have been successful, but in September he had a relapse and his doctor, Lord Horder, broke the news to him that he had only a few months to live. He resigned his Cabinet post on 30 September, and the king offered him a peerage and the Garter. But Chamberlain respectfully declined the one and the other. He would prefer, he said, 'to die plain "Mr. Chamberlain" like my father before me'.

Chamberlain's last days were spent at Heckfield, near Reading. Sometimes he was able to take a walk in the country lanes, but mostly he stayed indoors in his wife's constant companionship, and finding relief from the depressing war news in reading again and again the old favourites on his bookshelves. The last book on the table beside his bed was George Eliot's *Middlemarch*. He died on 9 November 1940, and a few days later there was a funeral service in Westminster Abbey at which the members of the War Cabinet were the pall-bearers. Then his ashes were deposited in a grave not far from Bonar Law's.

In the House of Commons on 12 November Winston Churchill pronounced a sombrely eloquent valediction.

'Whatever else history may or may not say about these terrible, tremendous years, we can be sure that Neville Chamberlain acted with perfect sincerity according to his lights and strove to the utmost of his capacity and authority . . . to save the world from the awful, devastating struggle in which we are now engaged . . . When contrary to all his hopes, beliefs, and exertions, the war came upon him, . . . there was no man more resolved to pursue the unsought quarrel to the death. The same qualities which made him one of the last to enter the war, made him one of the last who would quit it until the full victory of a righteous cause was won. . .' In conclusion the Prime Minister paid tribute to 'the gracious and charming lady who shared his days of triumph and adversity with a courage and quality the equal of his own'.

Mrs. Neville Chamberlain died in London in 1967, at the age of eighty-four.

41

SIR WINSTON CHURCHILL

'I suppose you don't know why I have sent for you?' said King George VI, as Winston Churchill entered his room at Buckingham Palace. Churchill, 'adopting his mood', replied, 'Sir, I simply couldn't imagine why.' The king laughed and said, 'I want to ask you to form a Government', and Churchill said he would certainly do so. In this brief, matter-of-fact encounter on 10 May 1940 was born one of the greatest ministries in Britain's hundreds of years of parliamentary history.

For days past, crowded days of political crisis—as Churchill wrote in his splendidly distinctive prose in *The Gathering Storm*—his pulse had not quickened at any moment: he took it all as it came. But as he went to bed at 3 a.m. he was conscious of a profound sense of relief. 'I felt as if I were walking with destiny, and that all my past life had been but a preparation for this hour and this trial . . .'

It had all begun nearly sixty-six years before, when in one of the scores of bedrooms at Blenheim Palace the wife of Lord Randolph Churchill gave birth—on St. Andrew's day, 30 November 1874—to a son, who was christened Winston Leonard Spencer-Churchill He was a seven months' child: he was always in a bit of a hurry.

Churchill was born to a great name, if not to great possessions. He was a direct descendant of the John Churchill who became Duke of Marlborough and won undying renown as the greatest captain of his age. His father, Lord Randolph Churchill, was the third son of the seventh Duke of Marlborough, and in the seventies and eighties of the last century was considered to be the most promising and capable of Conservative politicians—until in 1886, when Chancellor of the Exchequer in Lord Salisbury's government, he suddenly took it into his head to resign, and, greatly to his surprise and chagrin, his resignation was accepted. In his own phrase, he 'had forgotten Goschen', who stepped into his place at the Treasury, and he died in 1895 a prematurely old and disappointed man.

Lady Randolph was an American, daughter of Leonard Jerome, a prominent man of business in New York, and for many years she reigned as one of the queens of London society. She lived until 1921, when her son had already made his mark as a politician. Winston was devoted to her. ' My mother always seemed to me a fairy princess,' he wrote in *My Early Life*; ' a radiant being possessed of limitless riches and power.'

Winston's earliest recollections were of Ireland, when Lord Randolph was serving in Dublin as secretary to his father who was the Lord Lieutenant. On a day in 1878 the Duke unveiled a statue to Lord Gough, and the three-year-old boy carried away with him clear and vivid impressions of the occasion—the great black crowd, scarlet soldiers on horseback, and the brown shiny sheet that his formidable grandpapa pulled away.

Churchill was ' first menaced with Education ', as he put it, in the person of ' a sinister figure described as a Governess '. This was when they were still living at the Little Lodge in Dublin. In 1880 the family returned to England, Gladstone having appointed a new Lord Lieutenant, and Churchill was sent in the next year to an expensive boarding-school at Ascot—where the headmaster was a ferocious flogger. Churchill's two years there were miserable, and the only bright spot was when his father gave him a copy of *Treasure Island*, which he devoured with delight. There followed two years at a boarding-school in Brighton kept by two ladies, and then, at the age of twelve, he went to Harrow. There he remained in the fourth form three times as long as anyone else; but this was not perhaps a bad thing, since he learned English so thoroughly as a result of having to spend so much time on it. His father suggested that he should go into the Army, and after twice failing the entrance examination he managed to gain admittance to Sandhurst, thanks largely to an excellent crammer. Here he did excellently, and in 1895, soon after his father's death, he was commissioned in the 4th Hussars at Aldershot.

Almost immediately he took advantage of a few months' leave to go to Cuba as an observer attached to the Spanish army then engaged in fighting an insurrection, and he paid for his expenses by acting as special correspondent for the *Daily Graphic*. Not long after returning to England, he embarked in 1896 with his regiment for India, where he was very soon on active service on the North-West Frontier. That winter, when he was almost twenty-two, ' the desire for learning came upon me '. He had plenty of spare time on his hands in Bangalore when the day's parades were over, and he went in for reading on a grand scale. Someone had told him that his father had read Gibbon with delight, and Lieutenant Churchill sent home for a complete set of the *Decline and Fall* and proved for himself how right his father had been. After Gibbon he want on to Macaulay, Plato, Darwin—to Lecky's *Rationalism in Europe* and *European Morals* and Winwood Reade's *Martyrdom of Man*. Another book that was greatly to his taste was Bartlett's *Familiar Quotations.*

At Bangalore he also became an author, writing an account of his experiences on the N.W. Frontier (*The Story of the Malakand Field Force*) and also a novel, *Savrola,* which in later years he advised his friends not to read. Then in 1898 he was able to wangle a transfer to the 21st Lancers in Egypt, and arrived in time to charge with them against the Dervishes in the battle of Omdurman. This campaign he described in *The River War,* which was immediately successful on its publication in 1899. So successful, indeed, was he as a journalist that he was able to resign the queen's commission and turn his attention to politics. In the summer of 1899 he stood as Conservative candidate in a by-election at Oldham, a purely working-class constituency, but this time his luck was out. 'Never mind,' wrote Mr. Balfour, who had been his father's friend, 'it will all come right, and this small reverse will have no permanent ill effect upon your political fortunes.'

Very soon, however, Churchill had other things to think about. By October it seemed likely that war was coming in South Africa, and Churchill was fully resolved to be there. Such was his reputation as a military reporter that the *Morning Post* appointed him their chief war-correspondent (£250 a month, all expenses paid), and on 11 October he sailed from Southampton in the same boat as Sir Redvers Buller, the British commander-in-chief. Churchill was afraid that the war would be over before they got there, but when they landed at the Cape the news was of defeats and disasters and he soon had his fill of adventure. Going up country from Durban he joined an armoured train, which was ambushed and he was taken prisoner, his captor being Louis Botha, then an unknown Boer commando but destined to become before many years had passed the first Premier of South Africa and a firm friend of the British. Churchill was imprisoned in Pretoria, but managed to escape and after an extraordinary journey reached Delagoa Bay in Portuguese territory. When he got back to Durban he found himself a popular hero.

For some months more he remained in South Africa, long enough to be present at the battle of Spion Kop, the relief of Ladysmith and the occupation of Pretoria. When he returned to England his

Clement Attlee (right), the first Prime Minister to head a Labour government possessed of full power, acknowledges the plaudits of supporters on the night of his party's overwhelming victory at the polls. During his six year's premiership he presided over the establishment of the Welfare State and he played a principal part in the grant of Indian independence.

For six years from 1957 the premiership was held by Mr Harold Macmillan, seen below with Mr Selwyn Lloyd (Foreign Secretary and then Chancellor of the Exchequer in his Government) at the funeral of the Labour leader Mr Aneurin Bevan in 1960. On his retirement in 1963 he devoted himself to writing his memoirs and presiding over the publishing house of Macmillan.

Harold Wilson, seen in the upper picture on an election tour with Mrs Wilson (hands folded on lap), was only forty-eight when he became Prime Minister in 1963—the youngest Premier for more than a century. The lower picture is of the historic Cabinet Room in No. 10 Downing Street.

name was on everybody's lips. The Khaki Election was about to begin; Churchill was adopted again at Oldham, and he won the second seat in the two-member constituency by a majority of 230.

Parliament was to meet in early December, but Churchill had been booked for a lecture tour in the United States and had to get this over before he could make his appearance at Westminster. The tour proved so successful that he was able to hand £10,000 to a knowledgeable friend for him to invest to the best advantage. This and his earnings as a writer and war-correspondent made him financially independent for some years to come.

At length he was able to take his seat, and on a night in February 1901 he rose to make his maiden speech. He was dreadfully nervous and not made any the more comfortable on being told that he was to follow ' a rising young Welshman, a pro-Boer, and one of our most important bugbears, named Lloyd George'. But once he was on his feet, courage returned, and he ' got through it all right '. He ventured to make a joke at the Irish members' expense, and being Irish they laughed. But when he went on to say, 'The Boers who are fighting in the field—*and if I were a Boer, I hope I should be fighting in the field*—', he saw a ruffle upon the Treasury Bench below him and Joseph Chamberlain said something to his neighbour. After the debate he was warmly congratulated, and among those who came up to give him a warm handshake was Lloyd George.

Chamberlain kept a suspicious eye on him, and not without reason. Churchill had demonstrated his independence, and before long he was speaking against the Conservative party line and even going into the lobby with the Liberals. Then in the summer of 1903 Chamberlain came out with his Tariff Reform proposals, and Churchill was among those Conservatives who declared their continued support for Free Trade. When it seemed clear that the Protectionists were winning in the Cabinet Churchill decided to throw in his lot with the Liberals, and on 31 May 1904 he crossed the floor of the House and took his seat next to Lloyd George. Bitterly reviled by his old friends and warmly welcomed by his new ones, Churchill played an active part in the closing scenes of the Balfour administration, although he was mainly occupied in putting the finishing touches to his biography of his father, a book which won acclaim as one of the best pieces of political portraiture in the language. Then at the end of 1905 Balfour resigned, Campbell-Bannerman formed his ministry, and in this Churchill appeared as Under-Secretary of State for the Colonies. A month later he stood as Liberal candidate for North-West Manchester and was triumphantly returned. Three years later, in 1908, when Asquith succeeded to the premiership he appointed Churchill President of the Board of Trade, with a seat in the Cabinet. As such he had to submit himself for re-election. He was defeated at N.W. Manchester, but soon found a fresh seat at Dundee.

Also in 1908 Churchill got married, to Miss Clementine Ogilvy Hozier, the twenty-three-year-old daughter of Colonel Sir Henry Montague Hozier, K.C.B., and his wife Lady Henrietta Blanche, daughter of the seventh Earl of Airlie. The wedding took place at St. Margaret's, Westminster, on 12 September and, as he wrote on the last page of his *My Early Life*, they 'lived happily ever afterwards'. They had five children: Diana (1909–63, who married Duncan Sandys, M.P.); Randolph (1911–68, eminent as a journalist and his father's biographer); Sarah (who had a career on the stage); Marigold Frances (who died in childhood); and Mary (who married Christopher Soames).

At the Board of Trade Churchill was responsible for some very useful social legislation, including the establishment of Labour Exchanges, a measure directed at sweated labour, and the creation of the Port of London Authority. After two years he was promoted to the Home Office, where again he proved an enlightened and vigorous administrator. In particular he concerned himself with the welfare of prisoners and ex-prisoners; indeed, he gave a powerful impetus to the penal reform movement as a whole.

Then, in 1911, the Kaiser sent a German gunboat to Agadir in Morocco. Churchill was already deeply concerned over the continued increases in the German navy; and when in October Mr. Asquith, the Prime Minister, asked him whether he would like to go to the Admiralty, he jumped at the chance. For the next three years he worked untiringly on carrying out the mandate he had been given, to get the fleet ready for war with Germany. He created an efficient Naval General Staff. He insisted upon a great extension of the naval building programmes. Lloyd George complained that Churchill was always coming to him with his 'Look here, David,' and then ' declaim for the rest of the afternoon about his blasted ships '. Almost all the new ships—submarines, destroyers, light cruisers, fast battleships—were oil-burning, and arrangements were concluded with the Anglo-Persian Oil Company for the supply of the new fuel. He displayed a remarkable judgment in the choice of commanders. Then on 1 August 1914, as soon as the news came of Germany's declaration of war on Russia, Churchill on his own responsibility sent out orders for the immediate mobilization of the

Fleet, and this while the Cabinet were still trying to make up their minds. At 11 p.m.—12 by German time—on 4 August the British ultimatum to Germany expired, and on his direction the war telegram which meant 'Commence hostilities against Germany' was flashed from the Admiralty to all the ships and establishments under the White Ensign. After which he walked across Horse Guards Parade to the Cabinet Room at No. 10 and reported to the Prime Minister and the assembled Ministers 'that the deed was done'.

Under the protection of the Royal Navy, the British Expeditionary Force was transported to France without the loss of a ship or a man. There followed the great battle of the Marne, and then the Germans raced to obtain possession of the Channel ports. In a desperate bid to forestall them Churchill himself organized and accompanied an expedition to Antwerp, which delayed the fall of the city for five days, sufficient for Calais and Boulogne to be preserved from the invaders.

This dashing adventure was followed early in 1915 by his plan to seize the Dardanelles by a combined military and naval expedition and so knock Turkey out of the war and open up a sea route to Russia, Britain's hard-pressed ally. The plan, never properly thought out and prepared for, was deplorably mismanaged, and Churchill had made so many enemies, political and in the services, that he became the scapegoat. When the Coalition government was formed in May 1915 the Conservatives imposed the condition that Churchill should not be a member, except in the very minor office of Chancellor of the Duchy of Lancaster. Six months of idleness and frustration proved as much as he could stand, and in November he resigned his sinecure and went over to France as an officer attached to the 2nd Grenadiers. A month later he was made colonel of a battalion of the Royal Scots Fusiliers, and took over his command in the trenches at Ploegsteert—or Plug Street, as it was popularly called. He served in the line until the autumn of 1916 when, his battalion having been absorbed in another, he returned to England and engaged once more in politics.

When Lloyd George formed his government in December of that year he would have gladly found a place in it for Churchill but the Conservatives were still obdurate. However, in February 1917, the report of the Dardanelles Commission was published, and Churchill's name was so far cleared that in May Lloyd George was able to appoint him Minister of Munitions. After the general election at the end of 1918 he was transferred to the War Office, and it fell to him to arrange for the orderly demobilization of the army's millions.

Unfortunately for his reputation, and his country's, Churchill had developed what Lloyd George calls a ' morbid detestation of the Russian Revolution ', and he was responsible for an armed intervention in support of the White Russian leaders, Koltchak and Denikin, that was much against Lloyd George's wishes and aroused intense opprobrium. This ill-starred adventure increased the suspicions of those who thought Churchill a fire-eater, and their suspicions seemed to have been confirmed when he came out as a strong supporter of military action against the Turks in 1922. Then came the fall of the Coalition. Churchill sided with those ministers who decided to stick by Lloyd George, but at the crucial moment (he wrote in *The Gathering Storm*) he was prostrated by a severe operation for appendicitis, ' and in the morning when I recovered consciousness I learned that the Lloyd George Government had resigned, and that I had lost not only my appendix but my office as Secretary of State for the Dominions and Colonies ', which he had been holding since the previous year. Very shortly he lost something else, for at the general election he was decisively rejected by the voters at Dundee.

A year later he stood at the general election as Coalition Liberal candidate at West Leicester, and was again defeated. Early in 1924 he tried once more, this time as an Independent anti-Socialist or Constitutionalist in a by-election in the Abbey division of Westminster. For the third time in a row he lost, but now the majority against him was only thirty-four. His political evolution was almost complete, and at the general election in the autumn he stood as Constitutionalist for the Epping division of Essex. Now he triumphed, polling nearly ten thousand more votes than his Liberal opponent, who was the runner-up. Until 1935 Epping returned him by big majorities; and in 1945, after a seat redistribution, he was elected for Woodford.

Following the election, Baldwin proceeded to form his second administration, in which those Conservative leaders who had stayed with Lloyd George returned to the fold and were found posts. Churchill too received a summons to the Prime Minister's room. ' I can offer you the job of Chancellor,' Baldwin opened. ' Of the Duchy ? ' Churchill inquired politely. ' No,' rejoined the Prime Minister, ' of the Exchequer.' Churchill admits that he was surprised, as indeed he might well be, but the Conservative party was dumbfounded.

For the five years of the Baldwin administration he was Chancellor. His first budget contained provisions for pensions for widows and orphans, but its most conspicuous feature was the return to the gold standard—something for which he has been widely criticized. The consequential high prices of British goods in the export market led to great difficulties, and in particular the mining industry was badly hit. The owners reduced wages, the miners struck, and there followed the General Strike in 1926, in which Churchill behaved as a rabid partisan. In particular, his editing of the official news-sheet, the *British Gazette*, came in for some well-deserved condemnation. Then the proposals to grant self-rule to India aroused his hostility—originating, very likely, in his experiences as a young lieutenant in the glorious days of the British Raj. So seriously was he out of step with the Conservative leadership that when the National Government was formed in 1931 he was not offered a place in it.

Through most of the thirties he was politically isolated. He had resigned from the Conservative shadow Cabinet as a protest against the party's support for the Labour government's Indian policy, and he resisted the India Bill through all its stages. During the Abdication crisis he showed a degree of sympathy for King Edward VIII that brought him to the verge of organizing a body of ' King's friends '. Then he was one of the first to realize the full gravity of the Nazi menace. For years his warnings fell on deaf ears, but when the crunch came it was remembered that he had been right. The popular voice demanded his recall to office, and on 3 September, the day war was declared, Chamberlain asked him to become First Lord of the Admiralty once more. He accepted, and forthwith sent word to the Admiralty that he would be arriving at six p.m. As soon as they received it the Board of Admiralty sent out the signal to the fleet, ' Winston is back.'

There ensued the strange, perplexing days of the ' phoney war ', and not the least of his contributions to the war effort were his broadcasts, in which his growling tones brought confidence and courage to millions of homes. And so we come to that 10 May 1940, when he ' walked with Destiny '. Never, surely, in Britain's history had the Hour been so splendidly matched with the Man.

Churchill was sixty-five, and had been in the House of Commons almost continuously for forty years. In the course of his long political experience he had held most of the great offices of State but (he wrote in *Their Finest Hour*, the second volume of his history of the Second World War) the post which had now fallen to him was the one he liked the best. Power for the sake of lording it over fellow-creatures or adding to personal pomp was rightly judged base, ' but power in a national crisis, when a man believes he knows what orders should be given, is a blessing. In any sphere of action there can be no comparison between the positions of number one and numbers two, three, or four.' He was now Number One, and he gloried in it.

The day following his appointment he announced his list of ministers, and profiting from his experience in the First World War, he formed a War Cabinet in which he was not only Prime Minister and First Lord of the Treasury but Minister of Defence and Leader of the House of Commons. Neville Chamberlain was Lord President, Clement Attlee Lord Privy Seal, Lord Halifax Secretary of State for Foreign Affairs, and Arthur Greenwood Minister without portfolio—three Conservatives and two Labour.

The House of Commons was specially summoned for Monday, 13 May, and Churchill presented himself as Prime Minister for the first time and asked for a vote of confidence.

' I would say to the House as I said to those who have joined this Government: " I have nothing to offer but blood, toil, tears, and sweat." We have before us an ordeal of the most grievous kind. We have before us many, many long months of struggle and of suffering.

' You ask what is our policy; I will say: " It is to wage war by sea, land, and air, with all our might and with all the strength that God can give us, and to wage war against a monstrous tyranny, never surpassed in the dark, lamentable catalogue of human crime." That is our policy.

' You ask what is our aim; I can answer in one word: It is victory —victory at all costs—victory in spite of all terrors—victory, however long and hard the road may be; for without victory there is no survival—let that be realized—no survival for all that the British Empire has stood for, no survival for the urge and impulse of the ages, that mankind will move forward towards its goal . . . At this time I feel entitled to claim the aid of all, and I say: " Come, then, let us go forward together with our united strength." '

Faced with these simple issues, expressed in the language of a master of words as well as of action, the House of Commons gave the new Government a unanimous vote of confidence.

In the months that followed, that note of bulldog courage was struck again and again. On the morrow of the miracle of Dunkirk Churchill warned that ' wars are not won by evacuations ' and that

Hitler might very shortly make an attempt to invade England. But what of it ? ' We shall defend our island, whatever the cost may be, we shall fight on the beaches, we shall fight on the landing-grounds, we shall fight in the fields and in the streets, we shall fight in the hills; we shall never surrender . . .' Just as the Battle of Britain was about to begin he brought the House of Commons to their feet with the stirring exhortation, ' Let us, therefore, do our duty and so bear ourselves that if the British Commonwealth and Empire lasts a thousand years men will still say, " *this* was their finest hour ".'

Through all those terrible years and occasions, Churchill ' set the pace ', as his deputy, Mr. Attlee, expressed it. His method of operation was essentially personal, arising out of his quite exceptional knowledge of military matters and equally exceptional experience of government office. The timetable was governed by his personal habits. The mornings he would spend at his desk or in some visit of inspection. After lunch he would sleep soundly for a couple of hours or so. Then, completely refreshed, he would tackle the business of the day. Cabinet meetings were called usually for 11 p.m., and after they were over Churchill would continue until the early hours in consultation with those of his colleagues who had managed to keep up with him.

No Prime Minister can have mixed more freely and easily with the people, or more often. On airfields and military stations, on the invasion beaches and amidst the still burning ruins of the bombed cities, in factories and munition works—here there and everywhere might be seen his cigar and the fingers framed in the V-sign of coming victory. He wanted to see everything that was going on, he wanted to know what everybody was up to. When D-Day dawned it required a direct order from King George to keep him from embarking on one of the bombarding destroyers so that he might see the men fight their way ashore.

No Prime Minister has ever taken the people so much into his confidence as he did. He was no great orator, at least in the Gladstonian sense, but he developed on the wireless a masterly technique of intimate communication. Millions listened to the broadcasts in which he reported on the progress of the war, and his gruff and growling voice had the power of stilling the noisiest bar-parlour. For the most part the language he employed was so simple as to seem ordinary, but he seldom missed including a passage of memory-sticking prose.

Churchill lived on the job. In Horse Guards Parade was built a huge, fortress-like Annexe, which became the nerve-centre of the nation's war organization. Here, above the vast arrangement of underground chambers, he and his wife lived comfortably in a small flat; and to make the place look more homelike Mrs. Churchill hung a few pictures on the walls of the sitting-room. From the roof there was a splendid view of London, and on the nights of the blitz he would go up there and, protected only by a light overhead cover from flying splinters, ' walk in the moonlight and watch the fireworks '.

Very early in the war he received a personal letter from President Roosevelt, inviting him to ' keep me in touch personally with anything you want me to know about '. Churchill responded with alacrity, using the signature of ' Naval Person ', and after he had become Prime Minister, ' Former Naval Person '. The correspondence continued until Roosevelt's sudden death in 1945, and the close personal contact so established was of immense benefit ' to the high causes which we served '. From the first Roosevelt strained neutrality to the limit, and when the news of Pearl Harbour reached London Churchill carried out his promise that in such an event the British declaration of war on Japan would follow ' within the hour '. With Roosevelt he attended the great Allied conferences at Casablanca, Moscow, Teheran, and Yalta, and together they signed the Atlantic Charter in 1941.

Several times during the war years Churchill was stricken with illness and seemed near to death. But his spirit was encased in a body of exceeding toughness, and this, with the devoted attentions of his personal doctor, Lord Moran, pulled him through. Victories —there were not many of them to begin with—did not elate him overmuch; defeats and disasters such as the falls of Tobruk and of Singapore—though they might stagger him for the moment, were quite unable to dim his confidence in final victory. And at length it came, on 7 May 1945, when the Nazi forces surrendered unconditionally.

At 3 o'clock on the afternoon of the next day Churchill announced in an eagerly-awaited broadcast that ' the German war is at an end ', although ' Japan, with all her treachery and greed, remains unsubdued '. They might, however, allow themselves ' a brief period of rejoicing ', and he concluded with the words, ' Advance Britannia! Long live the cause of Freedom! God save the King! '

The broadcast over, the Prime Minister moved through enormous crowds to the House of Commons, where he was given a standing ovation as he entered the chamber. He almost broke down, and there were tears in his eyes as he moved—as his old friend and colleague Lloyd George had moved twenty-seven years before—that the House ' do now attend at the Church of St. Margaret, Westminster, to give humble and reverent thanks to Almighty God for our deliverance from the threat of German domination '.

If Churchill had had his way, the Coalition government would have remained in office until the conclusion of the war with Japan, but his insistence on an early general election led to the withdrawal of the Labour leaders. At noon on 23 May 1945 Churchill tendered his resignation to King George, and four hours later kissed hands as Prime Minister in a caretaker government composed of Conservatives and their Liberal National allies, which it was intended should continue only until the general election had been decided. The date for this was fixed as 5 July, although the votes would not be counted until the 26th, to give time for those of men and women in the services to be included.

The election campaign was very hard fought, and Churchill seemed to emerge in a most disturbing light. Gone was the great national wartime leader, and in his place stood the tub-thumping party politician. In his first broadcast he denounced the Socialism of his opponents as being ' an attack not only upon British enterprise but upon the right of an ordinary man or woman to breathe freely, without having a harsh, clumsy, tyrannical hand clapped across their mouth and nostrils. A free Parliament . . . is odious to the Socialist doctrinaire.' To make matters worse, he descended to personal abuse of the men who had served as his colleagues in the Coalition, and asked his hearers to believe that if the Labour party were returned there would soon be something in the nature of a police state. To which Attlee rejoined that, while he knew that the Prime Minister had ' old-fashioned ideas about what was permissible in elections ', he had never thought that he would have descended to ' such depths of misrepresentation and ingratitude towards men who had shown him such loyalty and consideration '.

In the interval between polling-day and the count Churchill went to Potsdam to consult further war measures with Stalin and President Truman, taking Attlee with him as ' friend and counsellor '. Then he returned to London to await the people's verdict. It was declared on 26 July, and showed a landslide victory for the Labour party. Labour won 393 seats, while the Conservatives and their Liberal National allies were reduced to 213.

Of course, Churchill was deeply wounded, and his feelings found expression in a passage in *The Gathering Storm*. For five years and three months, he wrote, he had wielded in ever-growing measure the chief power in the State, ' at the end of which time, all our enemies having surrendered unconditionally or being about to do so, I was immediately dismissed by the British electorate from all further conduct of their affairs '.

For the next five years Churchill was leader of the Opposition in the House of Commons, a position for which he was not well suited. He was bitterly critical of the proposal to grant independence to India, and he denounced the similar grant to Burma (which had been made part of the British Empire when his father, Lord Randolph Churchill, had been Secretary of State for India) as a 'policy of scuttle'. As a world-statesman, however, he made a much better showing. When on a visit to the United States in March 1946, he delivered a speech at Fulton, in the presence of President Truman, in which, after referring to the ' iron curtain ' which had descended across the continent of Europe, he urged the closest association between Britain and the U.S.A. Then at Zurich a few months later he pleaded for a reconciliation of France and Germany and the creation of a United States of Europe.

After the general election of 1951, which gave the Conservatives a majority of sixteen in the House of Commons, Churchill became Prime Minister for the second time. Within a few months his staunch friend King George VI died suddenly, and it fell to him—an old and sorrowfully bent figure—to receive the young queen at the airport on her return from her trip to East Africa. Shortly after the Coronation he was taken ill and it was widely supposed that he would be shortly retiring. But once again he triumphed over his disabilities and was able to return to the House of Commons. When his eightieth birthday came round he was still in office, and Parliament paid him the signal honour of a reception in Westminster Hall, something unprecedented in its annals.

To Queen Elizabeth he gave the same devoted and loyal service he had rendered to her father and grandfather and great-grandfather. Just before the Coronation in 1953 she bestowed on him the Order of the Garter—an honour which had been offered him by her father in 1945 but which he had then respectfully declined. He accepted it now because its conferment had become the prerogative of the Sovereign. At length, on 5 April 1955, he handed Her Majesty his resignation, the morning after she had dined with him and Lady Churchill at No. 10.

At the general elections of 1955 and 1959 he was returned as the member for Woodford, and he became the ' Father ' of the House of Commons. But in these latter years, though he might still be seen in his seat in the chamber he took small part in the business. In the summer of 1962 he had a fall and broke a thigh bone, and spent some time in Middlesex Hospital. Not long afterwards it was announced that he would not be seeking re-election. Shortly before Parliament was dissolved, the House of Commons, on 28 July 1964, accorded him a supreme tribute, when it passed a motion ' putting on record its unbounded admiration and gratitude for his services to Parliament, to the nation and the world '. He was not in the House that day, but the motion was taken to him at his house in Hyde Park Gate by the party leaders.

Churchill's parliamentary career extended over more than sixty years, longer even than Palmerston's. But he was an author before he had become a politician, and he was still writing in the years that remained to him after his retirement from the parliamentary scene. His first books were vivid pieces of first-hand reporting, covering his experiences on active service in India, Egypt, and South Africa. His biography of his father was published in 1906. After the First World War he wrote *The World Crisis* (4 vols., 1923–29), which was at once recognized as a classic description of the events that led up to the war and marked its course. With the £20,000 that Churchill received for this he purchased the house and estate of Chartwell, near Westerham in Kent, which became his country home for the rest of his life. In the nineteen-thirties, when he was becoming politically isolated, he found solace in writing *Marlborough: His Life and Times* (4 vols., 1933–38) which he embarked upon with the object of clearing the memory of his great ancestor from the aspersions of Lord Macaulay.

When following the defeat of 1945 he was again out of office he devoted himself to the writing of his history of *The Second World War*, of which the first volume was published in 1948 and the sixth and last in 1954. At the beginning of each volume he printed as the ' Moral of the Work ': ' *In War:* Resolution. *In Defeat:* Defiance. *In Victory:* Magnanimity. *In Peace:* Good will.' These were the qualities that he most admired, and in the many hundred pages we may find them exemplified in Churchill's own personality and performance. Not since Julius Caesar wrote his *Commentaries* has there been a comparable instance of a great man of action describing in workmanlike and often splendid prose the momentous events in which he had a commanding part.

Finally, there is his *History of the English Speaking Peoples* (4 vols., 1956–58). He had delivered about half a million words of this to the printers when he was called away to the Admiralty on 3

September 1939, and for the nearly six years of war and for an even longer period when he was occupied with his war memoirs, the book 'slumbered peacefully'. But if there was need for such book before, there was an even greater need for it after the war in which 'for the second time in the present century the British Empire and the United States have stood together facing the perils of war on the biggest scale known among men, and since the cannons ceased to fire and the bombs to burst we have become more conscious of our common duty to the human race'.

Politics, Literature—and still there is Art! It was after his dismissal from the Admiralty in 1915 that Churchill took up painting. Four years later he exhibited a portrait at a London exhibition, but it was landscapes which he came to prefer and in which he excelled. Wherever he went on his wartime journeys he would set up his easel, and some of his happiest efforts were evoked by the burning sun and sands of North Africa. In 1948 the Royal Academy honoured him, and itself, in electing him Hon. Academician Extraordinary, a truly unique distinction that pleased him greatly.

A page or more would be required to list his honours. He became a Privy Councillor in 1907 and a Companion of Honour in 1922. In 1946 he was awarded the Order of Merit. From 1941 he was Lord Warden of the Cinque Ports, and he was an Elder Brother of Trinity House. More than thirty universities conferred on him honorary degrees, and he was made a freeman of more than fifty towns and cities across the globe. The Royal Society elected him a Fellow in 1941, and in 1953 he received the Nobel Prize for Literature. Of the many distinctions granted him by foreign countries the one he esteemed most was the Honorary Citizenship of the U.S.A. which was conferred on him by proclamation at a ceremony in the White House at Washington in 1963—an honour bestowed on no one else in the history of the United States.

Early in January 1965 Sir Winston was taken ill with cerebral thrombosis; and shortly after 8 a.m. on Sunday, 24 January he died 'in peace and without pain' in his London home at Hyde Park Gate. Lady Churchill and his three surviving children were present with him at the end.

At once Britain became a land of mourning. The State Bell at St. Paul's began to toll, flags everywhere were lowered to half-mast, and at night the lights of Piccadilly Circus were extinguished. Messages of condolence and affection poured in from all parts of the world. The queen wrote to Lady Churchill that 'The news of Sir Winston Churchill's death caused inexpressible grief to me and my husband. The whole world is the poorer by the loss of his many-sided genius, while the survival of this country and the sister nations of the Commonwealth in the face of the greatest danger that has ever threatened them will be a perpetual memorial to his leadership, his vision, and his indomitable courage.'

In accordance with the queen's desire, expressed in a message to Parliament, a State Funeral was ordered. The arrangements combined the honours that had been paid to Gladstone and the Duke of Wellington. For three days the body lay in state in Westminster Hall, and a vast crowd moved past it in tribute. Then on Saturday, 30 January, a great funeral procession was marshalled, there was a funeral service in St. Paul's attended by the queen and many other Heads of State, after which the body was conveyed by launch from Tower Pier to Festival Pier, and thence by road to Waterloo station. Here the official ceremony ended, and the coffin, attended by members of the family and personal friends, was conveyed to the little village of Bladon, across the park from Churchill's birthplace at Blenheim. And there, in the churchyard, beside the graves of his father, mother, and brother, they buried ' the greatest Englishman of his time '.

42

CLEMENT ATTLEE

WHEN MR. ATTLEE drove through the gates of Buckingham Palace on the evening of 26 July 1945, the results of the general election were still coming in, but sufficient had been declared to show that Labour had won a sweeping victory. For the first time Labour was *in power*, and not in office on sufferance of the other parties.

Clement Richard Attlee was born on 3 January 1883, the fourth son and seventh child in a family of eight. His father, Henry Attlee, was a partner in a highly regarded firm of solicitors in the City, but the Attlees for some generations previously had been millers and corn-merchants in the neighbourhood of Dorking; two of his uncles were brewers, however, and another was a clergyman. His mother, Ellen Bravery Watson, was the daughter of a gentleman of some private means who was secretary of a company producing reproductions of works of art, and there were also a number of medical men in her family tree.

He was born in Portinscale Road, Putney—in a solid, comfortable, Victorian-style residence in a district which then bordered on the country, with fields and market gardens separating it from Wandsworth and Wimbledon.

The Attlees would not have described themselves as wealthy, but they were very comfortably off. In politics Mr. Attlee was a Gladstonian Liberal, but the rest of the family were inclined to favour the Conservatives. A succession of governesses were responsible for the girls' education, and sometimes Clem was permitted to have a share in their lessons although it was at his mother's knee that he learned to read and write. Every summer they went away for a fortnight at the seaside, until in 1897 Mr. Attlee bought a country house near Thorpe-le-Soken in Essex, where holidays were spent from that time on.

When he was nine Clem was sent to a preparatory school at Northaw Place, near Potter's Bar in Hertfordshire, which was kept by a clergyman-friend of the family. After four years he was removed to Haileybury College, near Hertford, one of the big public schools that catered for the sons of the rising middle class.

He had five years there and on the whole (he recalled years later) they were reasonably happy, although there were periods of black misery. The accommodation was rough, and the lower boys had to ' pig it '. The food was disgustingly served, and the teaching was on the whole pretty bad. He played cricket and rugger, but was not particularly good at either, and he joined the school cadet corps and went into camp at Aldershot. He also joined the school debating society, but was far too shy to speak more than very occasionally and then not at all well.

Leaving Haileybury in 1901, and feeling ' mentally very young ', Attlee went up to Oxford, where he was entered at University College. Here he spent three exceedingly happy years—at least, that is how they looked in an old man's retrospect. He played games with zest, went on the river, walked a good deal, attended debates at the Union but was still far too nervous to speak there, and read studiously for a degree in modern history. He took his examinations in the summer of 1904 and managed to get a good second-class degree.

At this time he would have called himself a Conservative, but in fact he was not specially interested in politics. The Liberals were in the doldrums, and Socialism was hardly heard of.

In 1904 ' this pleasant time ', as Attlee calls his years at Oxford, came to an end and he started work in London reading for the Bar. He spent a year at Lincoln's Inn, passed his examinations without any difficulty, and was called in 1905. But very few briefs came his way, and in any case his interest in the law was tepid to say the least. Then on an evening in October ' there occurred an event which was destined to alter the whole course of my life '. This was a visit to the boys' club in Stepney that was run by old Haileyburians.

From the first he was very interested in the work that was being carried on there, and very shortly he was spending one evening a week at the club, while still living at Putney. The club had a cadet company, and Attlee took a commission in the cadets. Then the club manager resigned, and Attlee was invited to take his place. He consented, and thus began a residence of fourteen years in the East End. Once he had got over his shyness he found the boys excellent company. East London boys are very friendly, he wrote in his autobiographical volume *As It Happened*; ' there is no better way of getting to know what social conditions are like than in a boys' club. One learns much more of how people in poor circumstances live through ordinary conversation with them than from studying volumes of statistics.'

What he saw and heard—the stark poverty, the degradation of unemployment, the general insecurity of life, the stink and squalor, the abominable characters and those who in contrast were flowers in the human dunghill—*shocked* him into Socialism. There was next to nothing of theorizing about it; he may have read Marx, but he was not a Marxist, either then or later. Out of what he actually observed and experienced he became convinced that poverty and malnutrition and unemployment were not inevitable, but things to be fought and overcome.

For a year or so he was secretary of Toynbee Hall, the educational and social settlement in Whitechapel. He joined the Fabian Society and the Independent Labour Party, and became a Socialist propagandist, a ' street-corner agitator '. When Lloyd George's insurance scheme was instituted Attlee was employed as one of the lecturers sent about the country to explain its terms, and for a time he lectured at the London School of Economics which Sidney and Beatrice Webb had founded. This was his apprenticeship in the Labour and Socialist movement, and he confesses that he was a rank-and-file worker with no special ambitions to become anything more, though he did stand, unsuccessfully, for election to Stepney borough council.

Then came the war, and he was convinced not only that Britain was right to fight against German militarism but that it was his duty to enlist and play his part. When he tried to join the army he was told he was too old—he was thirty-one—but he joined the Inns of Court Officers Training Corps and then managed to get a commission in the South Lancashire Regiment. He passed the first winter of the war in camp at Tidworth on Salisbury Plain, and early in 1915 spent some weeks in France helping to train an Indian unit. Then in June his battalion was among those sent to the Dardanelles. He had three or four weeks in the trenches at Helles, but went down with dysentery and was sent to hospital in Malta. Towards the end of the year he rejoined his battalion on the peninsula, and at the Suvla evacuation he was in command of the last party to leave.

After some months in Egypt, he was among those ordered to Mesopotamia. They disembarked at Basra and proceeded in paddle-boats up the Tigris. Early in April 1916 he was wounded in a skirmish at El Hanna, and was sent down river to Basra and thence to hospital at Bombay, and eventually back to England. Now a major, he saw some weeks' service in France in 1918, but fell sick and was evacuated in October to England and was in hospital again.

As soon as he could get his discharge from the army he returned to Stepney and resumed his social and political work. In the autumn of 1919 he had his first experience of public office when he was co-opted to Stepney borough council and appointed mayor. Unemployment was once more devastating the East End, and Attlee led a deputation of Labour mayors to see Lloyd George at Downing Street, but got precious little satisfaction from the Prime Minister. When Attlee's year of office was up, he was elected to the aldermanic bench, and he remained an alderman until 1927.

As mayor, he tells us, he had been somewhat handicapped in his work by being unmarried, although his sister Margaret acted as mayoress on several occasions. This deficiency was now repaired, however. In the summer of 1921 he went on a well-deserved holiday to Italy with a friend, Edric Millar, who had a job in the civil service, and the friend's mother and sister. As the tour proceeded, Attlee formed an attachment for Miss Violet Millar, and a week or two after their return to London he asked her to go to a football match with him. But when the day came the ground was too hard for football, and they went for a walk in Richmond Park instead. During the afternoon Attlee proposed, and was accepted. They were married on 10 January 1922, when Attlee was just thirty-nine, and set up house at Woodford Green in Essex. It proved a very happy and successful union, Mrs. Attlee supporting him in all his activities. In the next eight years they had a son and three daughters.

Attlee's parliamentary career began that same year. At the general election in the autumn that followed upon the collapse of the Lloyd George coalition, Attlee stood as Labour candidate for Limehouse, and succeeded in winning the seat from the Liberal who (with Conservative support) had held it since 1906. The Labour party had 142 M.P.s in the new House, and Attlee was one of those who voted for Ramsay MacDonald as leader of the party in preference to J. R. Clynes, a vote which he afterwards much regretted. MacDonald appointed him one of his parliamentary private secretaries, and it fell to Attlee to support the Labour case in the debate on the King's Speech. He spoke for about twenty minutes, and the argument he advanced in this maiden speech was one that he was hammering away at for many a year to come. In wartime the Government controlled the purchasing power of the nation and decided what things should be produced; why shouldn't they do the same in peace time?

At the general election in the autumn of 1923 Attlee held his seat at Limehouse with an increased majority; and in the government that MacDonald proceeded to form—the first Labour government, although the party was in a minority in the House—Attlee was under-secretary for War. Here his military experience served him well. Before the year was out there was another general election, which proved a severe set-back for Labour, although at Limehouse Attlee's vote was slightly increased. In the new House he developed into one of the Opposition's most capable spokesmen, especially in the debates on Neville Chamberlain's Electricity and Rating & Valuation bills.

Attlee was not included in MacDonald's second administration when it was formed, but in 1930, after Sir Oswald Mosley had resigned his appointment as Chancellor of the Duchy of Lancaster out of disgust with the government's failure to tackle the problem of unemployment, Attlee was appointed instead. Then in 1931 he became Postmaster-General, in which capacity he was able to introduce some useful reforms, particularly in the field of public relations. He found the work at the Post Office fascinating, but he had hardly got into his stride when the economic crisis brought about the fall of MacDonald's government.

Attlee was on holiday with his family at the seaside when the crisis broke, but when matters came to a head he was summoned to Downing Street and heard the Prime Minister declare his intention of forming a National Government to tide over the crisis. As a junior minister, Attlee was one of those whom MacDonald advised against joining him in his new administration, but he was not in the least impressed: he had worked it out that if they *did* join him there would not be anything like enough jobs to go round. In fact, he had become disillusioned with MacDonald. Originally he had thought him a fine fellow, but since he had come to closer quarters with him he had discovered his defects—his ' increasing vanity and snobbery ', and worse still, his habit of telling a junior minister what a poor lot most of the Cabinet were. Attlee's considered verdict was that MacDonald's action constituted ' the greatest betrayal in the political history of this country '.

There ensued the general election of 1931, in which Labour sustained the most crushing defeat in its history. Attlee would not have been surprised if he had been defeated himself, but he was returned at Limehouse with a drop of only a few hundreds in his vote, although his majority was cut from the over 7,000 in 1929 to 551.

Attlee was one of the lucky ones. Only 52 Labour members were returned, and among them George Lansbury was the only one who had held Cabinet rank. Lansbury was elected leader of the parliamentary party, and Attlee his deputy. There followed four years of most arduous effort, in which Attlee, with Lansbury and Sir Stafford Cripps, put up a gallant fight against the National Government with its bloated majority of nearly five hundred. This was the arrangement until October 1935, when Lansbury (a dedicated pacifist) resigned the leadership rather than follow the party line in favour of sanctions against Italy because of her invasion of Abyssinia. Attlee was thereupon elected leader, and as such he led the party through the general election campaign of 1935. Labour won 154 seats, but they still made a poor showing compared with the 387 Conservatives and their 33 Liberal National allies. At Limehouse Attlee won the highest vote he ever had: 14,600 votes, as against 7,355 for his Conservative opponent.

When the new Parliament met, Attlee's succession to the leadership of the Labour parliamentary party was challenged by Arthur Greenwood and Herbert Morrison, and he was elected on the second ballot by 88 votes to Morrison's 44. At all subsequent elections he was elected without a contest.

Compared with Ramsay MacDonald he seemed a rather colourless figure, but throughout his career there was a tendency for people to underestimate him, and especially was this so in the years just before the Second World War. Even after Hitler's ambitions had been proclaimed to the world—even after Mussolini had sent his armies into Abyssinia—he was leading his followers into the lobby against the Service estimates. In his defence it may be urged that the Labour party were committed to collective security under the League of Nations, and they had no confidence in the National Government's foreign policy. Attlee was no pacifist, however: he never was. He had to educate his party, and that they had learnt their lesson was plain enough when war came in 1939, and the Labour Opposition, while refusing to join in a coalition under Chamberlain, offered their full support in the national war effort; and plainer still in May 1940 when, following upon the Nazis' seizure of Norway and Denmark, criticism of the Government became almost general. On 8 May what was equivalent to a motion of censure on the Government was put to the vote, and into the lobby with the Labour members trooped forty Conservatives. The Government majority shrank to eighty-one.

The next day Attlee and Arthur Greenwood were invited by the Prime Minister to call upon him at No. 10. They found him in consultation with Lord Halifax, the Foreign Secretary, and Winston Churchill, the First Lord of the Admiralty. ' It was not a pleasant task to tell a Prime Minister that he ought to go,' wrote Attlee years afterwards, ' but I had no option but to tell him the truth.' Chamberlain then inquired whether the Labour party would be ready to enter a government under some other Prime Minister ? The Labour party was then holding its annual conference at Bournemouth, and the two leaders offered to consult their executive. The next day Attlee was on the 'phone to the Prime Minister, giving the answers to the questions he had put. ' Would they enter a Government under the present Prime Minister ? *No.* Would they come in under someone else ? *Yes.*'

When Attlee got back to London that evening he found that the ' someone else ' was already forming his administration, and wanted to see him forthwith at the Admiralty. He hurried off to meet Mr. Churchill, and in a very short time the great coalition was in being.

With characteristic modesty, Attlee took the post of Lord Privy Seal, but he was generally recognized at Churchill's No. 2, with special responsibility for domestic affairs. Early in 1942 Churchill transferred him to the Dominions Office and at the same time appointed him Deputy Prime Minister—a post hitherto unknown to the Constitution or in parliamentary practice. This was to enable him to act with the Prime Minister's full authority during his frequent absences abroad, but it was also a recognition of Attlee's shrewdly capable management of business in the Cabinet and in the House of Commons.

After victory in Europe had been won, Churchill wished the Labour party to continue in the Coalition until the end of the war with Japan, and Attlee was quite prepared to agree. However, his Labour colleagues decided otherwise, the Coalition was ended on 23 May, and the general election of 5 July 1945 was contested on party lines.

In the interval between the election and counting the votes Attlee accompanied Churchill and Anthony Eden to meet Stalin and President Truman at the Potsdam Conference. He returned to England on 25 July and the next morning went down to Stepney for the count. Of course, he was in, with a majority of 6,789 in a total poll of 10,006, and it was soon apparent that Labour was romping ahead elsewhere. When the last results were to hand it was shown that Labour had 396 seats while Churchill's Conservatives and their allies had 213, the Liberals 12, and ' others ' 19.

On leaving the count at Limehouse, Attlee and his family went to have tea at the station hotel at Paddington. Presently he was told that the Prime Minister was resigning forthwith, and a summons to Buckingham Palace followed. Mrs. Attlee drove him in their small family-car to the Palace, where Attlee was received in audience immediately while Mrs. Attlee waited outside. King George said afterwards that he looked rather surprised when he invited him to form an administration, and Attlee admitted that the extent of the Labour success *had* surprised him. He kissed hands as Prime Minister and First Lord of the Treasury, rejoined his wife and was driven off to a great victory celebration at Westminster Central Hall, where he announced, amid tremendous jubilation, that he had been invited to form a government and had accepted the invitation. After which he looked in at a Fabian Society gathering, and then at length returned home to his house at Stanmore. Not a man given to exaggeration, even he called it ' an exciting day '.

Within the next forty-eight hours he had appointed the men to the key posts in his administration—Ernest Bevin Foreign Secretary, Hugh Dalton Chancellor of the Exchequer, Arthur Greenwood Lord Privy Seal, Herbert Morrison Lord President of the Council, Chuter Ede Home Secretary, Aneurin Bevan Minister of Health, and Sir Stafford Cripps President of the Board of Trade. Attlee himself in addition to being Prime Minister and First Lord of the Treasury was Defence Minister. Then Attlee hurried off again to Potsdam, where the conference of Allied war leaders was still in session, but this time he took with him Ernest Bevin as his chief colleague.

On his return to London he completed his Government, and then took up the most pressing tasks. The war with Japan had to be brought to a successful conclusion, millions of men and women had to be demobilized from the Forces and the munition factories, and an orderly transition from a war economy to one of peace and reconstruction had to be effected. As soon as possible a start was made with the massive programme of social legislation the people had been led to expect.

*   *   *

The years 1945 to 1949 constituted the most important period of social and economic reform since the Liberal experiment of forty years before. They saw among many other things the introduction of the National Health Service, the nationalization and reconstruction of the fuel industries—coal, gas, and electricity, to which was added the new enterprises for the production of atomic energy, nationalization of the railways and a large section of road transport, rebuilding of the bombed cities and towns, vast schemes of slum clearance, the establishment of the first of the New Towns, the creation of National Parks, and the building of hundreds of thousands of new houses.

All in all, what was effected was a social revolution, in which Attlee played a vital part—not so much as an initiator of the various schemes, perhaps, as that of chairman of the nation's board of directors.

For six and a half years Attlee was Prime Minister. The house at Stanmore that had been the Attlees' home since 1931 was sold, and they ' settled into No. 10 Downing Street and found it very comfortable '. This was because, instead of inhabiting the imposing and inconvenient State rooms on the first floor they established themselves in a flat in what had been the servants' quarters in the attics. Mrs. Attlee also saw to the installation of a badly needed modern kitchen.

Actually Attlee saw more of his family during his premiership than ever before, since he was now ' living on the job ', as he put it. He even found enough time to read Gibbon all through. Every morning after breakfast he would walk round the park with his dog at his heels and accompanied by Mrs. Attlee or one of the children, and then be at his desk in the Cabinet Room by 9.30. He then worked right through the day, with intervals for lunch and dinner, and did not get to bed as a rule before twelve. He was a very quick, methodical worker, who made a point of always clearing his desk before the end of the day.

Week-ends were spent mostly at Chequers, which he found ' a most friendly house in which to live '. In the summer the Attlees played tennis and croquet on the lawn, and in the winter took long walks through the beautiful Buckinghamshire countryside. They did a good deal of official entertaining there, and every year on Boxing Day they gave a party at Chequers for the children of his ministerial colleagues and private secretaries. Years afterwards it was recalled how the Prime Minister used to stand on the steps by the open front door and hand to each departing child a bag of sweets.

After five years there was a general election, in February 1950, and although Labour increased its vote by over 1,250,000 its majority in the House of Commons was slashed to ten. Attlee's old constituency at Limehouse had been abolished under the redistribution scheme, but he stood for West Walthamstow, where he scored an easy triumph, having a majority of more than 12,000 over his Conservative opponent.

With such a slender majority in the Commons, Attlee could not expect to do very much, but he struggled on for eighteen months, during which time he suffered the crippling losses of Bevin and Cripps through death. There was also some dissension in the ministry, when Hugh Gaitskell, Cripps's successor at the Treasury, imposed charges to meet part of the cost of supplying false teeth and spectacles under the National Health Service. Aneurin Bevan strongly opposed these in the Cabinet, and the area of dispute was later widened to include the whole question of rearmament. In April 1951 Bevan resigned, and took with him Harold Wilson and John Freeman, two of the ministerial newcomers. In the midst of these disputes Attlee fell ill and had to go into hospital for treatment of duodenal ulcers. When he returned he had to face a harassing situation arising out of the nationalization of the Anglo-Iranian oil-fields in Iran (Persia). King George was due to visit Australia and New Zealand the following year, and Attlee—out of consideration for a monarch with whom he had come to enjoy the most friendly relations—decided that if there were to be a change of government it should take place before the king left the country. In October 1951, then, Parliament was dissolved, and at the ensuing general election—although the Labour vote increased by over 700,000 to nearly fourteen millions, the largest vote given to any political party in our history—the net result was a loss of nineteen seats. Attlee, who had been returned at West Walthamstow with a slightly reduced majority, at once tendered his resignation to the king, and was succeeded as Prime Minister by Winston Churchill. A few days later Attlee was summoned to Buckingham Palace and King George conferred upon him the signal award of the Order of Merit.

Attlee became Leader of the Opposition once again, and for the next four years carried on under conditions of increasing difficulty and strain. It was a still divided Labour party that he led into the general election of May 1955, when Sir A. Eden became Prime Minister, but he made his customary wide-ranging tour of the constituencies, in a car driven by his wife. Notwithstanding his years and poor health he would make up to eight speeches in a single day, and also spoke for his party ' on the air '. But he wore the appearance of a man who was weary of the political strife, no longer looking forward to a morrow of better things. The Conservatives increased their majority to 60.

For some months Attlee continued as Leader of the Opposition, but in August he had a slight stroke, and although he made a complete recovery his retirement was generally expected. It came on 6 December 1955, when he met the members of the Parliamentary

Labour party in Committee Room No. 14 at the House of Commons where he had so often presided, and after a typically brief and modest speech left quietly by a side door. He had been Leader of the party for twenty years.

Next day, Queen Elizabeth offered him an earldom, which, to a good many people's surprise, he accepted; the reason was simple enough—he was still mentally fit, and he saw in the House of Lords an opportunity of rendering further service to his party and the State. In April 1956 the queen conferred upon him the Order of the Garter.

After he left office, Lord Attlee travelled widely, including trips to Russia and China. He made frequent contributions to debate in the House of Lords; and, as had been his way in the Lower House, his speeches were object-lessons in the art of saying a great deal in a few words.

Lady Attlee died in June 1964, at the age of sixty-eight. Lord Attlee then gave up his house in Buckinghamshire and took a flat in King's Bench Walk in the Temple. He could still enjoy his pipe, and he had his books and good friends to visit him. Then there was *The Times* crossword, which it is said he invariably solved. Early in September 1967 he was admitted to Westminster Hospital for what was supposed to be a minor condition, but after a week this developed into pneumonia. In hospital he was frequently visited by his son, Lord Prestwood, and his daughters. He died on 8 October, and on the next day the newspapers carried impressive memorial notices. On 7 November his ashes were interred in Westminster Abbey.

In many of the tributes that were paid to him, in Parliament and the press, the point was made that only later generations will be able to assess Attlee at his full stature. His own summing-up was given in the concluding page of his *As It Happened* (1954): ' Having now exceeded the age of three score years and ten I would say that up to the present I have been a very happy and fortunate man in having lived so long in the greatest country in the world, in having a very happy family life and in having been given the opportunity of serving in a state of life to which I had never expected to be called.'

43

SIR ANTHONY EDEN

IN THE SUMMER OF 1942, when the Second World War was at its height and Mr. Churchill was about to visit Washington, King George asked him whom he would recommend as his successor in the premiership in the untoward event of his death. Mr. Churchill thereupon tendered the advice that in these circumstances His Majesty should entrust the formation of a new government to Mr. Anthony Eden, ' who is in my mind the outstanding minister in the largest political party in the House of Commons and in the National Government over which I have the honour to preside, and who, I am sure, will be found capable of conducting Your Majesty's affairs with the resolution, experience, and capacity which these grievous times require '.

For more than a dozen years after that Anthony Eden—Sir Anthony from 1954—was the great Churchill's heir-apparent. At length in 1955 he succeeded to the position for which he had been so carefully groomed. But the Churchillian mantle proved an uneasy fit, and after a premiership of not much more than a year and a half he slipped away into memoir-writing retirement.

Robert Anthony Eden was born on 12 June 1897 at Windlestone, the family seat of the Edens near Bishop Auckland in Durham. He was the third son, and fourth of the five children, of Sir William Eden, seventh baronet, and his wife Sybil Frances Grey.

The Edens had been prominent in north-country life for many generations, and to the wider world they contributed generals and bishops, ambassadors and administrators, ministers of the Crown and Colonial governors, collecting in the process a couple of baronetcies and three peerages. Somewhere in the family tree appears the Lord Auckland with whose daughter William Pitt the Younger had his one and only love affair. Anthony Eden's father was a wealthy eccentric, a fine rider to hounds who also dabbled in water-colour painting, a man of violent temper and equally violent prejudices, of whom his children stood very much in awe. His mother (who came of the family that produced the Lord Grey of the great Reform Bill of 1832 and Sir Edward Grey who was Asquith's Foreign

Secretary) was a woman of great beauty and charm, and to her Anthony was devoted.

After being taught at home by a German governess, Anthony went to Sandroyd, a preparatory school near Cobham in Surrey. Thence at the age of thirteen he went to Eton, where he stayed for four years and was in no way conspicuous. He was in his final year at school when war broke out, and as soon as possible after his eighteenth birthday he volunteered for the army. In September 1915 he was gazetted a lieutenant in the 21st battalion of the King's Royal Rifle Corps, and went to France with it in May 1916. He served throughout the battle of the Somme and was appointed adjutant of his battalion at the exceptionally early age of nineteen. In the battle of Ypres he was gassed, and in June 1917 he was awarded the Military Cross for gallantry in rescuing his platoon sergeant, who was lying out in no-man's-land desperately wounded. After this Eden was promoted captain and served for some time on the staff of Plumer's Second Army.

On being demobilized in 1919 he decided (not very willingly, but his mother strongly urged it) to go to Oxford, as his ancestors had done for generations. He was entered at Christ Church, and showed originality in choosing Oriental languages for his special study. He took his final examinations in 1922 in Persian and Arabic, and gained a first-class honours degree. At Oxford he led a rather retired existence, and it may be noted that he did not join the Union or any of the political clubs.

Nevertheless, he had already in mind a career in politics, and in November 1922 he stood as Conservative candidate in the strongly Labour constituency of Spennymoor, Durham. He was defeated by over six thousand votes, although he had the satisfaction of pushing the Liberal into third place. At the general election in the following year he was chosen to contest Warwick and Leamington, a traditionally safe Conservative seat, and he was returned with a majority of over fifteen thousand.

Shortly before the election campaign opened Eden had become engaged to Miss Beatrice Beckett, daughter of Sir Gervase Beckett, banker, and a principal proprietor of the *Yorkshire Post*. They were married at St. Margaret's, Westminster, on 5 November 1923 and they had only a couple of days' honeymoon in Sussex before Eden had to return to his electioneering. This romantic circumstance may well have contributed to his popularity, not least with the women voters who had been already most favourably impressed by his handsome bearing and engaging manners.

Only a week after the new House of Commons had assembled, Eden made his maiden speech. It was a plea for a Royal Air Force, large and powerful enough to ' protect this country from the danger of attacks from the air '. A month later he spoke again, and again his subject was in connection with Britain's air forces. A few weeks more, and this time he spoke on foreign affairs, a department with which his name was to become indissolubly associated.

Early in 1925, when Baldwin had become Prime Minister, Eden was appointed a parliamentary private secretary at the Home Office, and that summer through his father-in-law's influence he attended the Imperial Press Conference at Melbourne as the representative of the *Yorkshire Post*, to which newspaper he was already a regular contributor. His experiences in this trip round the world provided him with the material for a book, *Places in the Sun*, which was published after his return, with a commendatory foreword from Mr. Baldwin.

Now recognized as a Baldwin protégé, Eden had another stroke of good fortune in 1926 when he was transferred to the Foreign Office as P.P.S. to Sir Austen Chamberlain, then basking in the success of the Locarno Pact. It was still a modest appointment, the lowest rung in the parliamentary ladder, but it gave him access to the foreign dispatches and he took care to profit from Chamberlain's instruction.

From 1929 to 1931 Eden was out of office, but in August 1931 when the National Government was formed under Ramsay Mac-Donald he became under-secretary at the Foreign Office, at first under Lord Reading (the Sir Rufus Isaacs of Lloyd George days) and then under Sir John Simon. At the general election in October he had a majority at Warwick and Leamington of more than 29,000 over his Labour opponent—one of the largest majorities in the country.

Now began his regular attendance at the League of Nations sessions at Geneva. His good looks, pleasant manner, unfailing affability, his charming smile and his elegant clothes, made him a figure as welcome as he was well known. With Simon he met Hitler in Berlin, and went on his own to talks with Stalin in Moscow, Benes in Prague, Pilsudski in Warsaw, Mussolini at Stresa. In 1934 he was given the post of Lord Privy Seal in MacDonald's administration, and a year later Baldwin had him in mind for Foreign Secretary but appointed him Minister for League of Nations affairs instead. At Geneva he proved an able and zealous advocate of Collective Security under League auspices, and he took a strong line against Mussolini's aggression on Abyssinia. With good reason he was styled the ' Member for the League ', and the ' Sir Galahad of Geneva '.

The general election of November 1935 was fought, and won, on a policy of full support for League principles, but very shortly there occurred the political storm of the Hoare-Laval pact for the recognition of Mussolini's Abyssinian conquest. Sir Samuel Hoare, who had been Foreign Secretary for some months past, was compelled by the force of public opinion to resign; and on 22 December 1935, Anthony Eden—again in accordance with the loudly expressed public demand—was made Foreign Secretary in Hoare's place. He was only thirty-eight: the youngest Foreign Secretary since Lord Grenville in 1791.

For a little more than two years he was Foreign Secretary, years of declining hopes and ever-increasing fears. The Dictators made the running, and the Democracies faltered along behind. Hitler reoccupied the Rhineland, in direct defiance of the Versailles settlement, and got away with it. Mussolini completed his conquest of Abyssinia, and it was a bitter moment for Eden when it fell to him to propose at the League of Nations assembly that sanctions against Italy should be ended, since they had failed completely in the intention. In Spain a most bloody civil war dragged on and on.

When Neville Chamberlain succeeded Baldwin as Prime Minister in May 1937, Eden was confirmed in his post at the Foreign Office. But very soon he discovered that Chamberlain was a very different man to handle than Baldwin had been. He had his own decided views on foreign policy, his own sources of information, his own channels of negotiation. He had come to the conclusion that France was unwilling and Britain unable to fight a European war, and so he embarked on his policy of appeasement.

Eden went along with Chamberlain as long and as far as he could, but Chamberlain's rebuff of President Roosevelt's offer to act as an intermediary, followed by his insistence upon a new and friendly approach to Mussolini, proved too much for him. On 20 February 1938 Eden resigned.

The news reached Winston Churchill late that night over the telephone, and, as he wrote in *The Gathering Storm*, his heart sank, and for once sleep deserted him. There had ' seemed one strong young figure standing up against long, dismal, drawling tides of drift and surrender, of wrong measurements and feeble impulses . . . Now he was gone . . .'

The following day Eden told the House of Commons *why* he had resigned. 'Recent months, recent weeks, recent days,' he said, 'have seen the successive violation of international agreements and attempts to secure political decisions by forcible means. We are in the presence of the progressive deterioration of respect for international obligations.' He went on, 'Of late the conviction has steadily grown upon me that there has been too keen a desire on our part to make terms with others rather than that they should make terms with us. This never was the attitude of this country in the past. It should not, in the interests of peace, be our attitude today . . . I do not believe that we can make progress in European appeasement . . . if we allow the impression to gain currency abroad that we yield to constant pressure.'

When the Munich agreement was debated Eden gave it his modified approval, but he did confess that ' there can be few of us who, whatever our sense of relief, did not feel also a sense of humiliation when we read those proposals . . .' When the division was taken, Eden was one of those Conservative M.P.s who joined Churchill in a demonstrative abstention.

Immediately on the outbreak of war in September 1939 Chamberlain reconstructed his Government. Winston Churchill returned to the Admiralty, and Anthony Eden was appointed Dominions Secretary. When in May 1940 Churchill was called upon to form his government he transferred Eden to the War Office, where he promptly set about the launching of what were named Local Defence Volunteers until Churchill rechristened them the Home Guard. Then in December 1940 he became Foreign Secretary for the second time.

In this capacity he spent the next four and a half years in travel about the continents, attending conferences, smoothing out differences, creating new alliances and cementing old ones. Three times he visited Stalin in Moscow, and he was present at Yalta and Potsdam; he consulted with President Roosevelt in Washington, and was at the birth of the United Nations at San Francisco. One of the most travelled men of his age, he was also beyond a doubt the most widely experienced of Foreign Secretaries. After the National Government was wound up he continued at the Foreign Office in Churchill's caretaker administration until the general election in the summer of 1945 put Labour in power. For the next six years he was in opposition, but when Churchill returned to office in 1951 he immediately reappointed Eden to his old post at the Foreign Office, and also made him Deputy Prime Minister.

As mentioned earlier, Eden was married in 1923. He obtained a divorce in 1950, on the grounds of desertion, and on 14 August 1952 he married a second time. His bride was Miss Clarissa Anne Spencer Churchill, daughter of Major J. S. Churchill (the Prime Minister's younger brother, who had died in 1947) and Lady Gwendeline Bertie, daughter of the seventh Earl of Abingdon. She was thirty-two, had studied at Oxford, and then during the war had worked at the Ministry of Information and in the Foreign Office as a clerk. The marriage took place at Caxton Hall register-office in Westminster. Mr. and Mrs. Churchill were present, and after the ceremony there was a family luncheon party at No. 10.

At the Foreign Office Eden worked tremendously hard, beginning early in the day and finishing late. When the weekend came he was fortunate if he could get away to the cottage at Broadchalke, in the Wiltshire downs, which his wife had bought before their marriage. But wherever he happened to be, the stream of dispatch-boxes was always catching up with him; and now that he was in middle life his health, which had never been robust, gave increasing cause for anxiety. In 1953 he was seriously ill with chronic inflammation of the gall-bladder, and he had three operations, the third in the United States in a hospital in Boston. When he left hospital he spent three months convalescing, accompanied by his wife, at a friend's house in Rhode Island and by the Mediterranean.

After an absence of six months he returned to the Foreign Office, where he found plenty of problems awaiting his attention. First, there was the situation in Egypt, where Colonel Nasser was bent on ending the British occupation of the Suez Canal Zone. In July 1954 Eden concluded the Anglo-Egyptian agreement for the withdrawal of all the British troops—an agreement which was vehemently condemned by the right-wing of the Conservative party as being not so much a sell out as a give away. Next he took the lead in the conference at Geneva which brought the terrible war in Indo-China to an end. After this he went for a short holiday in Austria, but was recalled to deal with the situation arising out of the French opposition to the proposed European Defence Treaty. Eden visited the European capitals, and was able to arrange a nine-power conference in London in September, at which France's objections to German rearmament were overcome and it was agreed that Western Germany should be admitted a member of the North Atlantic Treaty Organization. Eden made success possible by the dramatic announcement of a pledge to keep the British military and air forces on the Continent for the foreseeable future—a pledge that made clear that Britain was now a fully committed member of the concert of Europe.

This action may be said to have crowned Eden's efforts for the establishment of peace in Europe, and his services were recognized by the queen on 20 October 1954 by the award of the Garter.

All this time much of the work of the premiership had fallen to him as a result of Churchill's increasing feebleness. At length Sir Winston handed the queen his resignation, and on the day after, on 6 April 1955, Sir Anthony Eden kissed hands as Prime Minister and First Lord of the Treasury.

High hopes were entertained for his premiership, but before many weeks had passed there were indications of disappointment. Foreign affairs monopolized his attention, and in particular there was the nagging problem of the future of the Suez Canal. On 26 July 1956, Nasser nationalized the Suez Canal Company; and Eden, who had negotiated the Anglo-Egyptian treaty in the belief that Nasser was to be trusted, now felt all the indignation of a man who feels that he has been personally betrayed. The months that followed were filled with proposals that were turned down almost as soon as they were made, and conferences that ended in nothing but talk. Then in the last week of October the hostility of Jew and Arab flamed again into war, and Israeli tanks went racing across the desert towards the Canal.

Four days later, on 31 October, British and French bombers destroyed the Egyptian air forces on the ground; a few days more, on 5 November, British and French airborne troops were dropped on Port Said and until nightfall there was fighting in the streets with the Egyptian garrison. Then an armistice was agreed, and shortly after a United Nations force took over.

The Prime Minister told the House of Commons that these steps had been taken with the object of separating the Israelis and Arabs and preventing the war from spreading. But the result was world-wide consternation and alarm. There were ructions in the Cabinet, and a couple of junior ministers resigned. The House of Commons was in a state of constant uproar. Threats from Moscow—angry protestations from Washington. Palmerston might have got away with it, but this was a hundred years later. On 19 November it was given out that the Prime Minister was suffering from severe strain, and two days later he went to Jamaica to get over it, while Butler and Macmillan strove desperately to clear up the mess. On returning to London in mid-December Eden declared he felt absolutely fit, but here he was being hopelessly optimistic. There came an announcement from his doctors on 9 January 1957, that 'The Prime Minister's health gives cause for anxiety. In spite of the improvement which followed upon his rest before Christmas there has been a recurrence of abdominal symptoms. This gives us much concern because of the serious operations in 1953 and some subsequent attacks of fever. In our opinion his health will no longer enable him to sustain the heavy burdens inseparable from the office of Prime Minister.'

That same evening Sir Anthony had audience with the queen and submitted his resignation from the premiership. Her Majesty offered to create him an earl, as is customary when a Prime Minister retires, but he respectfully declined. Two days later he resigned his seat at Warwick and Leamington and on 18 January left England with Lady Eden for a long holiday in New Zealand.

On their return they made their home at Broadchalke, with occasional trips to their house in St. John, Barbados. Sir Anthony devoted himself to writing his memoirs, of which the first volume, *Full Circle*, was published in 1960; *Facing the Dictators* followed in 1962, and *The Reckoning* in 1965. In 1961 he accepted the renewed offer of a peerage, and took his seat in the House of Lords as Earl of Avon. His son Nicholas—the younger of his two sons by his first wife: the elder, Simon, was killed during the war in 1945, while serving as a pilot officer with the R.A.F. in Burma—adopted the courtesy title of Viscount Eden.

44

HAROLD MacMILLAN

WHEN SIR ANTHONY EDEN resigned from the premiership in January 1957 there were two outstanding ' possibles ' as his successor. One was Mr. R. A. Butler, and he was the man whom most of the newspapers ' tipped '. Since before the war he had held office in successive governments, and in the Eden administration he was Lord Privy Seal and Leader of the House of Commons. The other was Mr. Harold Macmillan, his senior by eight years but of not such wide and extensive ministerial experience, although his present position in the Cabinet was Chancellor of the Exchequer, which has often proved the stepping-stone to the premiership. Right up to the last Butler was pretty generally supposed to be in the lead, but Macmillan had powerful friends working for him in the most influential quarters, with the result that it was he who, on 10 January 1957, received the royal summons to the Palace and was commissioned by her Majesty to form an administration.

Maurice Harold Macmillan—the first Christian name was dropped —was born at 52 Cadogan Place, the London home of his parents, on 10 February 1894. He came of a very well-to-do, upper middle-class family, whose fortunes were built round the great publishing house of Macmillan. The firm had been founded by his grandfather, Daniel Macmillan, who was born in 1813 in the Isle of Arran in such poor circumstances that Harold Macmillan was almost justified in claiming that he was a crofter's grandson. As a boy of eleven Daniel was apprenticed to a bookseller in Irvine, and then at eighteen went to London, where eventually in conjunction with his brother Alexander he opened a bookshop in Aldersgate Street, out of which developed the publishing firm bearing their name. Harold's father, Maurice Macmillan, was Daniel's second son, and he was a director of the firm up to his death in 1936.

Harold Macmillan's mother was Helen Artie Belles, the daughter of a country doctor at Spencer, a small township in Owen County, Indiana. Nellie, as she was always styled, was a remarkable woman, forthright and determined. At nineteen she married a musician but was widowed after six months. She then felt an urge to travel and see something of the world, and in 1876 or thereabouts she went to Paris, where she studied sculpture and exhibited sometimes at the Salon, and also became a concert singer. Very likely it was at Paris that she met Maurice Macmillan, but after their marriage they lived in England, at the town house in Cadogan Place or at Birch Grove House, not far from Horsted Keynes in Sussex. Mrs. Maurice Macmillan survived until 1937. Like Churchill, then, Macmillan was half-American by birth, and proud of the fact.

Macmillan's childhood seems to have been a very happy one. Big houses to live in, both in town and country, with lots of servants and every convenience. Holidays in the summer on the sands at Hunstanton, or at Kingsgate in Kent, and a kindly father who on Sunday evenings would read aloud—from Shakespeare and the poets by preference but also from Scott and Dickens, after which he would read the evening service from the Prayer Book.

At six or seven Harold was sent to a day-school in Sloane Square that was kept by a Mr. Gladstone, and then at nine to Summerfields, a preparatory school at Oxford. In 1906, when he was twelve, he obtained a scholarship to Eton, where he suffered a good deal from various illnesses and nearly died from an attack of pneumonia. For some months he was an invalid, and had to leave the school earlier than usual. But he recovered well enough to proceed in due course on an exhibition to Balliol College, Oxford where (he tells us) ' life was indeed sweet '. In the Easter term of 1914 he took a first-class honours degree, and spent that glorious summer enjoying to the full the ' carefree life of Oxford '. Then, suddenly and un-expectedly, a real bolt from the blue, came the war. Macmillan joined the Artists' Rifles, an officer-training battalion, and was commissioned as 2nd Lieutenant in the King's Royal Rifle Corps. But before long he persuaded his mother to wangle his transfer to the Grenadier Guards, since they seemed likely to be sent to the front quicker.

In August 1915 they went to France, and a month later Macmillan went over the top at the battle of Loos. He was wounded in the head and in the hand, and was sent to hospital in England. Going to France again in April 1916, he spent three months in the Ypres salient, before moving down to the Somme where the tremendous battle was in progress. On the night of 15 September he left his trench with a party of men to try and silence a German machine-gun that was proving nasty. They dealt successfully with the German gunners, but Macmillan was knocked out by a stream of machine-gun bullets in his pelvis. Throughout the day he lay in a shell-hole while the firing continued from both sides. 'Even if I had known of a " better 'ole," ' he wrote in his *Winds of Change*, ' I could not have gone to it.' Fortunately he had in his pocket a copy of Aeschylus's *Prometheus* in Greek, and 'as there seemed nothing better to do, and I could not move in any direction, I read it intermittently'. Two or three times in the day the Germans counter attacked and they looked down on him in his hole, ' but I lay " doggo " and feigned to be dead '. After twelve hours darkness fell and the company sergeant-major, ' a splendid man ', went out with a search party and brought him back. For two years he was in hospital in England, and his wound did not finally heal until 1920.

After the Armistice he stayed on in the Army for a while, since he was in no hurry to enter the family business, and he was so fortunate to receive (through an introduction effected by his mother) an appointment as A.D.C. on the staff of the Duke of Devonshire, who since 1916 had been Governor-General of Canada. Macmillan arrived in Ottawa in March 1919 and stayed there until the following January. These ten months were ' in many ways the happiest in my life ', and it was there that he met and fell in love with the Duke's daughter, Lady Dorothy Cavendish, a warmly attractive and intelligent young woman of nineteen. Early in 1920 they went back to England, and on 21 April were married at St. Margaret's, Westminster. Among those who signed the marriage-register were Queen Alexandra and the Duke of York (later King George VI), who were friends of the Cavendishes, while the Macmillan interest was represented by such famous authors as Lord Morley and Thomas Hardy.

' My wife has sometimes reproached me that she thought she was to marry a publisher,' Macmillan wrote in his autobiography, ' with the prospect of the quiet world of literature and art. Instead, she has been drawn into the hurly-burly of politics . . . However, she accepted with zest what was, after all, on her side, almost a hereditary profession. For my part, I could not have sustained the excitements and frequent disappointments of the early years, or the heavy burdens of the later, without her wise advice and loyal support.'

By hereditary profession is meant, of course, the political life. The Cavendishes were for generations among the most important houses of the Whig aristocracy. Lady Dorothy's grandfather was the Marquess of Hartington of Gladstonian times, and her father (the ninth Duke) became Colonial Secretary in 1922. Through his marriage Macmillan became related to sixteen M.P.s and was introduced not only into the high places of Conservative party politics but the circles of aristocratic wealth and culture.

Soon after his marriage he entered the family firm to learn the trade, and in due course he joined the board of directors. But he was strongly drawn to a career in politics, and in 1923 he went along to the Conservative central office and asked that his name should be put down on their list of candidates. He made it clear that he was not particularly anxious to win—not yet, since he had only just started in business: what he wanted was some useful experience. The party managers soon found him a seat to fight— and a sufficiently hopeless one it seemed—Stockton-on-Tees, a town of heavy industry where unemployment was great and chronic. He had hardly heard of the place and had not the least knowledge of any mechanical or industrial processes other than printing. He went to Stockton in company with his wife, and was both impressed and depressed by what he found. Sooner than he expected he had to face a general election, towards the end of 1923. He put up such a good show—and his wife proved such an effective canvasser—that he came within 73 votes of winning. He returned to London, not disappointed but exhilarated—and carrying with him ' a memory of massive unemployment that began to haunt me then and for many years to come '.

A year later there was another general election after MacDonald's government had come to grief. Macmillan stood again for Stockton, and this time he was successful, with a majority of more than three thousand over his Labour opponent.

Parliament met in December, and Macmillan took his seat among the supporters of Mr. Baldwin, who was now Prime Minister for the second time. Early in the session he attached himself to a group of young members, most of them newcomers like himself, who were known as the Young Conservatives and given the nickname of ' Y.M.C.A.' Notwithstanding his business commitments he was able to attend the House pretty regularly, and he also made a point of going north to visit his constituency two or three times a month. On these trips Lady Dorothy accompanied him as often as not.

Macmillan delivered his maiden speech on 30 April 1925, in support of Neville Chamberlain's budget resolutions. He was generously applauded on that occasion, but he did not make much mark as a speaker—his language was too literary and his manner too donnish. At the time of the General Strike in 1926 he gave a hand at The Times office in doing up bundles of newspapers, but he had a lot of sympathy for the miners and deeply regretted Baldwin's failure to live up to his promises of a new and better order in industry. From now on Macmillan was one of those Conservatives who strove to discover some constructive alternative to *laissez-faire* capitalism.

At the general election of 1929 Macmillan ' became a victim of the general movement against the Government ', and ' the tide swept me away '; in other words, he was defeated at Stockton. For two years he was out of Parliament, but at the general election of 1931 he stood again for Stockton and—with no Liberal in the field, so that he collected most of the Liberal votes—he had a majority of over eleven thousand.

Quite a number of the Young Conservatives were given posts in the National Government, but Macmillan was not one of them. In the new House of Commons he became something of a rebel against Conservative ideology and party discipline. He stood out as an ardent advocate of economic planning, and in *Reconstruction*, published in 1933, he argued strongly that the choice lay between ' orderly capitalism and economic and social disorder '. He developed and expanded this theme in a much larger volume, *The Middle Way*, that appeared in 1938. There was a good deal of resemblance between Macmillan's ideas and Lloyd George's, and Macmillan was prepared to go along with L.G. at least part of the way.

But a greater and more permanent influence was exercised by Winston Churchill, and as the dreary years wore on Macmillan was found more and more often in the Churchillian camp. In the division that followed upon the Munich agreement he abstained, together with the rest of those Conservatives who were included in Eden's and Churchill's groups, and at a by-election at Oxford not long afterwards he supported the independent candidate against the official Conservative.

When war came in September 1939 the Government was partly reconstructed, but there was still no offer to Macmillan. In November he joined a party of volunteers who went to Finland to help the Finns against the Russian invaders, but this war was soon over and he returned to London fuming with indignation at the way in which the Finns had been let down by their allies. Then in May 1940 there was the Norway fiasco, and Macmillan was one of the thirty Conservatives who supported with their votes the censure motion on Chamberlain's administration.

Now Churchill was called to the premiership, and after sixteen years in Parliament Macmillan was given his first post. It was not much—parliamentary secretary to the Minister of Supply—but it was a beginning, and it led to something better. In the summer of 1942 he was made under-secretary at the Colonial Office, and then in the following November Churchill asked him to become Britain's Minister Resident in French North Africa, which the British and Americans had just invaded. Macmillan accepted: at last he was ' in the big stuff ', as he phrased it, and he demonstrated his quality. He got on well with Eisenhower and reasonably so with de Gaulle, and when the Allies invaded Italy Macmillan went with them as Resident Minister at Allied Headquarters. In the last year of the war he was entrusted with many ticklish political assignments in the eastern Mediterranean which he handled with diplomatic skill.

For six weeks in 1945 Macmillan was a Cabinet minister: Secretary of State for Air in Churchill's caretaker administration. At the general election in July he stood for Stockton as before, but he lost the seat to his Labour opponent by more than eight thousand votes. In November a safe seat was found for him at Bromley, in middle-class suburbia on the Kentish fringe of London, and he was sent back to Parliament with a substantial majority.

When he re-entered the House of Commons he found things very much changed. ' I feel like a Rip van Winkle,' he confessed. The new generation of Labour members had little time for his ' planned Capitalism ', and they were inclined to be irritated by his Edwardian elegance and his rather patronizing airs. But he found his feet before long, and he became the Conservative party's chief spokesman on industrial matters. He was a chief architect of the Industrial Charter which they produced, and exerted himself in putting it across.

When Churchill returned to power in 1951 he offered Macmillan the Ministry of Housing. Macmillan had hoped for and expected something better, but when the Prime Minister put the invitation in the form of a challenge—could he build 300,000 houses a year ?— he accepted it, provided he was allowed to run the ministry in his own way. He picked some excellent assistants, brought in some businessmen from outside, and applied business methods to what was after all a business problem. By the end of 1953 the target had been reached, and in 1954 Macmillan was promoted to the Ministry of Defence. But six months later Eden, on becoming Prime Minister, appointed him Foreign Secretary; and at the end of 1955, following the Conservative success at the general election, he became Chancellor of the Exchequer. As such he produced one budget, which was chiefly remarkable for the introduction of the Premium Bonds scheme. Then in the autumn the Suez crisis boiled over.

Macmillan's part in the Suez operation is hard to determine, but it would seem that to begin with Eden had no stronger supporter in the Cabinet than Macmillan, and even when it was all over and Macmillan was engaged in picking up the pieces he resolutely refused to don the white sheet. Why hadn't he tried to stop it ? demanded Harold Wilson; after all, as Chancellor of the Exchequer he was in the best position to know what an intolerable strain it would impose on the country's finances. That is just what he had been greatly tempted to do, Macmillan explained; at his age he might be looking forward to retirement, and all his interests pointed to ' what we used to call appeasement '. Then why hadn't he taken that road ? ' I will tell the House frankly and sincerely, it is because I have seen it all happen before . . .'

Macmillan's attitude towards the Suez operation did him no harm with the Conservative M.P.s and peers. When Sir Anthony Eden resigned, Lord Salisbury and Lord Kilmuir (Lord Chancellor) took soundings, and they soon came to the conclusion that the consensus of opinion was in favour of Macmillan. Lord Salisbury reported accordingly to the queen; and three-quarters of an hour after Salisbury had left the Palace, her Majesty sent for Harold Macmillan and commissioned him to form a government.

This he succeeded in doing. It was supposed by most people that it would be a stop-gap administration. The Conservative party were in disarray, the Cabinet at sixes and sevens, the backbenchers on edge. But in the event Macmillan stayed in office for more than six years—a longer period than any Prime Minister had enjoyed since Asquith forty years before.

Macmillan kept his head and his nerve. He assumed a jaunty manner in the House, and was hail-fellow-well-met in the smoking-room. As chairman in the Cabinet he won golden opinions.

Years passed; two years, three years. The Prime Minister made a lengthy tour of the Commonwealth, visited Khrushchev and Eisenhower and de Gaulle, and through his personal diplomacy brought about something of a thaw in the cold war. He took every opportunity of appearing on T.V., and in this new medium developed a fatherly, fireside-chat technique that recalled Baldwin's performances on the radio a generation earlier.

For the time being he was greatly helped by economic circumstances. The graphs showed an upward swing in industrial production, jobs were so plentiful that employers started complaining about over-employment, wages were good and salaries, too—so that people of all classes went in for buying motor-cars, refrigerators and washing-machines, T.V. sets, and all the other aids to pleasant living in the 'affluent society'. More people than ever before bought their houses through the building societies.

'Let us be frank about it,' Macmillan told an audience at Bedford in July 1957; 'most of our people have never had it so good. Go round the country, go to the industrial towns, go to the farms, and you will see a state of prosperity such as we have never had in my lifetime—nor indeed ever in the history of this country.'

True, the first Macmillan boom, as it was called, was followed by a period of comparative slump, but soon the graphs were on the upturn once more and in October 1959 Macmillan felt that he was justified in appealing to the country for a vote of confidence. And he got it. At the general election the Conservatives and their associates were returned to power with 365 M.P.s as compared with 344 at the previous election, while Labour was reduced from 277 to 258. To win three general elections in succession was something without precedent in our political history, and Macmillan had good cause for satisfaction.

If he had retired then, or not long after, he would have gone down in history as one of the most successful of modern Prime Ministers. But very few Prime Ministers have known the right moment to retire, and Macmillan stayed on.

Soon after the triumph of the general election he went to Africa, where the old-style Commonwealth was under the severest strain in Nigeria and Rhodesia and the Union. At Cape Town he addressed the South African Parliament, and in the course of his speech made use of a phrase that was soon echoing throughout the world. ' *The wind of change* is blowing through the continent . . .' After this he went to America, where he developed a very personal relationship with the new President, J. F. Kennedy—being helped in this by the fact that the President's sister had married Lady Dorothy Macmillan's nephew. Then with a view to ensuring Britain's future as a world industrial power he sent Edward Heath to open negotiations with 'the Six' for Britain's entrance to the Common Market.

Meanwhile at home the situation had greatly changed from the times when people spoke admiringly of ' Supermac ' and ' Mac-Wonder '. The ' never-had-it-so-good ' theme-song began to sound very flat as successive Chancellors of the Exchequer applied the brake to private spending in a series of ' Stop-Go ' budgets, and unemployment mounted to not far short of 900,000. There was another financial crisis. By-elections went against the Government, and Conservative party morale was in a low ebb. With a view to stopping the rot, Macmillan in the summer of 1962 carried out a drastic, even brutal, purge, in which six Cabinet ministers were dismissed.

The next year started badly, when in mid-January President de Gaulle delivered the first of his 'noes' to Britain's application to join the Common Market. There were several spy cases, and the gravest reflections were cast on the state of security in Government departments. Then in June Mr. Profumo, Secretary of State for War, had to resign. In the House of Commons Harold Wilson, who had become Leader of the Opposition in February, delivered a savage attack on the Prime Minister for his alleged insufficient concern for security. In his answering speech Macmillan spoke with disarming candour. He confessed that he had not known sufficient of what was going on: 'I do not live among young people much myself . . . My colleagues have been deceived, and I have been deceived—and the House has been deceived—but we have not been parties to deception.' And he concluded with an appeal to the 'sympathetic understanding and confidence of the House and of the country'.

On this occasion he managed to ride the storm, but very soon the criticisms of his leadership were being voiced loudly and often. He was getting too old for the job, was the cry; he was not far off seventy, and Harold Wilson was forty-seven. Macmillan himself refused to see it, and several times on T.V. he spoke hopefully of leading the Conservatives through one more electoral campaign. But on 8 October on the eve of the Conservative party conference at Blackpool, which he had planned to attend, he had to go into hospital (King Edward VII Hospital for Officers, Marylebone) with prostate trouble. An immediate operation was found necessary, and Macmillan sent a message to the conference at Blackpool through Lord Home that 'it will not be possible for me to carry the physical burden of leading the party at the next general election', and that he hoped it would soon be possible 'for the customary processes of consultation to be carried on within the party about its future leadership'.

A few days later Macmillan had recovered sufficiently from his operation to take a very important part in the 'customary processes'. From where he was in the matron's room at the hospital Macmillan dispatched envoys to take the views of Conservative M.P.s and peers, and he received their reports in due course. Perhaps he was a bit surprised when Lord Home was indicated as the preferred choice, but he acted on it without delay. Just after 9 o'clock on 18 October 1963 he sent his resignation to the queen, and two hours later her Majesty came to visit him in his hospital room. The matter was soon arranged, and soon after the queen's return to the palace it was announced that Lord Home had been invited to form an administration.

Macmillan remained M.P. for Bromley until Parliament was dissolved in the autumn of 1964. On resigning the premiership he returned to his publishing firm, and devoted his leisure to the writing of his memoirs, of which *Winds of Change: 1914–1939* appeared in 1966 and *The Blast of War* in 1968.

Lady Dorothy Macmillan died at Birch Grove in 1966.

45

SIR ALEC DOUGLAS-HOME

WHEN THE EARL OF HOME kissed hands as Prime Minister on 19 October 1963, he was the first peer of the realm to do so since the appointment of Lord Salisbury in 1895. He did not remain a peer very long, however. So strong was the popular feeling against a Prime Minister in the House of Lords that only four days later he took advantage of a very recently passed Act of Parliament and divested himself of his earldom, lordships and baronies, and reverted to the ranks of the commoners.

Alexander Frederick Douglas-Home was born on 2 July 1903 at his family's London house in South Street, Mayfair. He was the eldest of the seven children born to Lord Dunglass, son and heir of the twelfth Earl of Home, and his wife Lillian Lambton, daughter of the fourth Earl of Durham.

The Homes have been part of the chequered history of Scotland since the early Middle Ages, usually as upholders of the royalist cause. In later generations they have been Conservatives, although it is worth mentioning that on both his father's and his mother's side the future Prime Minister was descended from the famous Earl Grey of the Reform Bill. After a period of comparative decline, the fortunes of the family were fully restored in 1832 when the eleventh earl married the heiress of the Douglas estates. The twelfth earl was the owner of more than 100,000 acres, mostly in Lanarkshire and Berwickshire, bringing in a princely income of over £50,000 a year.

The correct pronunciation of the family name has often been in dispute, but it would seem that for generations the Homes themselves have pronounced it as though it were spelled with a 'u' instead of 'o'.

Alec Douglas-Home spent his boyhood chiefly at Springhill, the dower-house of the family, in Berwickshire, on the banks of the Tweed, until on the death of his grandfather the twelfth earl in 1918, when the family removed to their principal seat of The Hirsel, a few miles away near Coldstream, some nine miles from Kelso. On the succession of his father to the earldom Alec Douglas-Home became known by the courtesy title of Lord Dunglass.

An English governess gave him his first education, and then at the age of ten he went to a preparatory boarding-school at New Barnet, on the northern outskirts of London. Thence he proceeded to Eton, where he achieved some distinction as a cricketer, doing particularly well in the Eton v. Harrow match at Lords in 1922.

Eton was followed by three years at Christ Church, Oxford, where he joined the principal university clubs and societies—but not, it may be noted, the Union, the nursery of so many budding politicians—and did not make anything of a show at his examinations. After this he went on a cricketing tour of South America and then returned home to share in the management of the family estates.

Although his father had once stood, unsuccessfully, as a parliamentary candidate, there was not much in the family history to encourage him to take part in politics. But something he had read of Lloyd George's—that the problems of the new age demanded young men with new ideas to tackle them—encouraged him to think of making politics his career. In 1928 he stood as Conservative candidate for Coatbridge, and lost; but in 1931 he stood for the South Lanark division of Lanarkshire and won a great victory, with a majority of nearly nine thousand. He took his seat in the House of Commons among the supporters of MacDonald's National Government, and had the cheerful audacity to announce himself as a ' Clydesider '. At the general election of 1935 he managed to retain his seat, although with a rather smaller majority. Shortly afterwards he was appointed Parliamentary Private Secretary to the Ministry of Labour, and then in 1937 was transferred to serve in the same capacity under Neville Chamberlain, then Chancellor of the Exchequer.

In 1936 he married Miss Elizabeth Hester Alington, second daughter of Dr. A. C. Alington, who had been headmaster at Eton during his time there and was now dean of Durham. The wedding ceremony in Durham cathedral was performed by the Archbishop of York and the bride's father. After a honeymoon trip to the Rhine and Italy Lord and Lady Dunglass made their home at Springhill and in London at a house in Chester Square.

For the next three years Lord Dunglass was in more or less constant attendance upon Neville Chamberlain, who had become Prime Minister in 1937 in succession to Stanley Baldwin. He accompanied him to Munich and back, and Chamberlain took him with him on 10 May 1940, when he went to Buckingham Palace to tender his resignation.

Released from official duties, Lord Dunglass now hoped to join the Lanarkshire Yeomanry on active service, but when he presented himself for medical examination he was turned down. He tried again in the autumn of 1940, but now it was disclosed that he was suffering from a spinal condition with consumptive associations which was traced back to a mishap of some years before, when in trying to uproot a bush on the estate he had fallen against a tree stump and bruised his back. An immediate operation was recommended, and after the operation he was condemned to spend two years on his back, encased in plaster. At length, in the autumn of 1942, he was able to exchange his plaster jacket for a spinal brace, and the next year saw him up and about again. The doctors pronounced him fit, and he congratulated them on having achieved what might have been considered the impossible: ' You have put backbone into a politician! '

In the spring of 1944 he was able to resume attendance at Westminster, and occasionally he took part in the debates in the House of Commons, usually on some matter connected with foreign affairs. At the general election of 1945 he lost his seat at South Lanark, however, and for five years he was out of the House.

At the general election of 1950 he stood as Conservative candidate for Lanark and was successful. But his career in the House of Commons was brought to an end in July 1951, when his father died and he succeeded to his peerages and was automatically removed to the House of Lords. Lord Home, as he now was, thought that this was the end of his political ambitions, but a few months later Churchill appointed him to the new post of Minister of State at the Scottish Office, and he was soon fully occupied with schemes for promoting the welfare of the crofters in the Highlands and Western Isles, hill farming, forestry, and hydro-electric projects.

When Eden became Prime Minister he transferred Lord Home to the Commonwealth Office as Secretary of State. At that time Home had never set foot in any of the territories for which he had become responsible, and he hastened to visit New Zealand, India, Pakistan, and Ceylon. Early in 1957 Harold Macmillan on taking over the premiership made him Lord President of the Council and Leader of the House of Lords, while still retaining his post at the Commonwealth Relations office. Two years later, in July 1960 came his appointment as Foreign Secretary in place of Selwyn Lloyd, who had become Chancellor of the Exchequer.

There had not been a peer as Foreign Secretary since Lord Halifax in 1938, and the appointment was strongly criticized. In the House

of Commons Hugh Gaitskell, the leader of the Opposition, pronounced it as being ' constitutionally objectionable ', and moved a
censure motion. Macmillan did not see why the accident of birth
should deprive him of the services of the ' best man for the job . . .
the man I want at my side '. The censure motion was thereupon
rejected.

Lord Home had been at the Foreign Office for rather more than
three years when in October 1963 the Prime Minister was suddenly
taken ill and had to go into hospital in London for an operation.
The Conservative party conference was in session at Blackpool
when on 10 October Lord Home rose from his seat on the platform
and read out the letter he had just received from Mr. Macmillan
containing the intimation of his forthcoming resignation.

At once began a struggle for the party leadership that was without
precedent. For the second time Mr. Butler seemed to be the most
obvious choice, even more so than in 1957 since he was now First
Secretary of State and Deputy Prime Minister. But in the unseemly
scramble he was pushed aside.

In the earlier stages Lord Home's name was barely mentioned.
But as president of the National Union of Conservative and Unionist
Associations he was inevitably in the limelight, and at the closing
rally at Blackpool on Saturday, 12 October he was given a most
encouraging reception.

The battle now shifted to London. Lord Home was still ' the
reluctant peer ', which is understandable enough. He would have
to relinquish his peerages, and in this matter he must consider his
family as well as himself. He had enjoyed life in the comparatively
calm atmosphere of the House of Lords, and he might well hesitate
before returning to the rough-and-tumble of the House of Commons. The fortunes of the Conservative party were obviously at
a very low ebb, and he would be taking a serious gamble in trying
to restore them. He was sixty, and his health might not be able to
stand the strain. This last matter, however, he was quick to resolve.
On his return to London from Blackpool he submitted himself for
a medical check-up, and also an eyesight test. Both were favourable,
and he thereupon let it be known that he was willing to be drafted,
as the Americans say.

Meanwhile Mr. Macmillan had been directing affairs from his
hospital bed, and from what his informants told him he had come
to the conclusion that Home was the most favoured of the con-
testants. He advised the queen accordingly, and on 18 October it
was announced from Buckingham Palace that Lord Home had been

received in audience and the queen had invited him to form an administration.

Immediately on leaving the Palace, Home embarked on a long series of interviews. Several of his Cabinet colleagues declined to serve under him, but his success was assured when Mr. Butler, in a mood of generous resignation, agreed to take office in his Cabinet as Foreign Secretary. On 19 October, just a week after the Blackpool conference had closed, Lord Home went again to the Palace and kissed hands as Prime Minister.

Only three hours after the announcement had been made, Harold Wilson attacked the new Prime Minister as ' an elegant anachronism '. What (he demanded) could anyone bred and reared in his ' sheltered aristocratic background ' know of the problems of ordinary families—of housing problems, keeping up mortgage payments, the cost of travelling to work, running a home in time of sickness, providing for aged relatives, the problem of simply making ends meet ? Then, on education, what could he know of the agonies of the eleven-plus, or of finding a room in which to do homework ? Above all, how could ' a scion of an effete establishment ' appreciate and understand, and above all, lead the scientific revolution ? ' This is the counter-revolution,' Wilson declaimed in a final thrust. ' After half a century of democratic advance, of social revolution, the whole process has ground to a halt with a fourteenth earl ! '

A few days later the Prime Minister appeared on T.V. and in great good humour brushed aside the objections. When asked by Mr. Robin Day, ' Do you know how the other half lives ? ' he made the reply, ' I think this is inverted snobbery to begin with, and, secondly, I object to the proposition that there are two halves to the nation. When I was in Parliament I represented a constituency where there were miners. I lived among miners for twenty years. I'm a farmer: I know all about the work on the farms. No, it's certainly untrue that I don't know how other people live. Of course I do.' As for his being the fourteenth earl, he supposed the Leader of the Opposition must be the fourteenth Mr. Wilson.

But while his titles were certainly nothing to be ashamed of they constituted a handicap which he took prompt steps to remove. On 23 October he put his signature to a document drawn up in accordance with the Peerage Act 1963, whereby he, ' the Right Honourable Sir Alexander Douglas-Home, Knight of the Most Ancient and Most Noble Order of the Thistle ', disclaimed for his life the earldom of Home, the lordship of Dunglass, the lordship of

Home, and the lordship of Hume of Berwick—all in the peerage of Scotland; the barony of Douglas, of Douglas in the county of Lanark, and the barony of Hume of Berwick, both in the peerage of England. Henceforth he was known as Sir Alec Douglas-Home.

No longer a member of the House of Lords, he was not a member of the House of Commons either. Parliament was due to meet on 24 October, but it was specially prorogued until 12 November, to enable the Prime Minister to secure election. A vacancy was engineered at Kinross and West Perthshire, one of the safest of Conservative seats, and on 6 November Sir Alec was elected with a majority of over nine thousand. On his return to London he was formally elected leader of the Conservative party at a meeting held in Church House, Westminster. Then on 12 November he presented himself at the bar of the House of Commons, which he had quitted twelve years before, and took his seat on the front bench as Prime Minister. Almost immediately afterwards he had to fly to Washington to attend the funeral of the assassinated President Kennedy.

As 1964 opened, Sir Alec made a very favourable impression. So far from being trounced, ' made mincemeat of ', ' torn to shreds ', etc. by the formidable Mr. Wilson, as the latter's followers had confidently anticipated, he at least managed to hold his own. At question-time he showed to special advantage. When the general election was mentioned—and one would have to be held in the autumn at latest—he gave the impression that he was quite looking forward to it and had every confidence in his party's chances.

At length Parliament was dissolved, and the general election was fixed for 15 October. Sir Alec campaigned vigorously—Harold Wilson likewise—so that the contest closely resembled a presidential election in the U.S.A. As the first results came in around midnight it seemed that Labour had won a substantial victory, but the results declared the next morning showed that the Conservatives were holding their own in the counties. The final result was Labour 317, Conservatives and their associates 303, and Liberals 9, showing a Conservative net loss of 56. In the afternoon of 17 October Sir Alec drove to Buckingham Palace and tendered his resignation. He had been Prime Minister for three days short of a year.

At Kinross and West Perthshire he had a majority of nearly twelve thousand. After his resignation he became leader of the Opposition until July 1965, when he was succeeded by Edward Heath. But in the Conservative party and in the country as a whole he continued to play a distinguished part.

46

HAROLD WILSON

HAROLD WILSON, who became Prime Minister in the Labour government that was formed in October 1964, was—at forty-eight —the youngest Prime Minister since Lord Goderich in 1827.

When he was born, on 11 March 1916, his parents were living in Linthwaite, a district on the southern outskirts of Huddersfield in the West Riding of Yorkshire. Not long afterwards they moved to another part of Huddersfield, Cowlersley, near Milnsbridge. He was given the names of James Harold, but the James was soon dispensed with. His father, Herbert Wilson, was an industrial chemist employed in the laboratories of a local factory: his grandfather had kept a draper's shop in Manchester. Harold Wilson's mother, born Ethel Seddon, had been a school-teacher before her marriage, and two of her brothers were also teachers. Harold's sister Marjorie, some years his senior, became a teacher in due course.

The Wilsons were Baptists, and regular in their attendance at the chapel in Milnsbridge. Harold went to Sunday School, and as soon as he was old enough joined the Scout troop. Herbert Wilson took a keen interest in politics, in his young days as a Liberal of a radical type and later as a member of the Labour party. According to his own testimony, Harold became a Socialist at the age of seven. His father was also a loyal supporter of Huddersfield Town football club, and on Saturday afternoons Harold would accompany him to see the matches at their ground in the Leeds Road.

When he was five he started school, at the junior or primary council school in New Street, Milnsbridge. At ten he was taken by his mother on a visit to her brother in Western Australia, which provided him with ample material for a number of school essays. A few months after returning to England he won, at the age of eleven, a scholarship to the Royds Hall secondary school in Huddersfield, where he remained until 1931 when, consequent upon his father having obtained a new job at a chemical works in Bromborough, Cheshire, the family moved there and Harold was entered at Wirral grammar school at Bebington, about two miles away. At

Royds Hall he had done well, but at Wirral he did brilliantly. Mathematics was his best subject, and he could memorize figures and dates with ease. It was reported that he could rattle off the list of Prime Ministers from Walpole to Ramsay MacDonald. As captain of the school in 1933 he moved a vote of thanks at a prize distribution—his first public speech. He played rugger and cricket, but his best sport was long-distance running. On Sundays he attended the Highfield Congregational church at Rock Ferry.

From Wirral, Harold Wilson won an open exhibition in History to Jesus College, Oxford, and went into residence there in the autumn of 1934. At first he studied History, but before long switched to Philosophy, Politics, and Economics. He worked very hard and almost his only relaxation was his cross-country running. He joined the Liberal Club, because the Labour Club was too much under Communist influence, but in 1935 when he was nineteen he was admitted a member of the Labour party. He did not take much part in political or social activities, however, but kept grinding away at his books. He won some prizes for essays, including one on railway history, and then at his final examinations obtained a first-class degree.

He stayed on at Oxford until the war broke out in 1939, first as a lecturer in Economics at New College and then as a fellow at University College. Here the Warden was Sir William Beveridge, who soon appreciated Wilson's qualities and appointed him his research assistant. Beveridge could be a hard taskmaster, and Wilson once said that he had never known what hard work really meant until he had gone to work for him; but he profited immensely from his example, and Beveridge said that Wilson was the most able research assistant he had ever had.

At the beginning of the war, Wilson applied to join the army, but instead he was drafted into the Civil Service as a ' temporary '. He had a clerical appointment at the Ministry of Supply and then in the Economics section of the Cabinet Secretariat. A spell at the Ministry of Labour followed, after which he was transferred to the Ministry of Fuel and Power where he became director of Economics and Statistics. Out of this latter experience he wrote his first book, *New Deal for Coal*, which was published in 1945; this was his first venture into the political field, and it revealed him as a convinced believer in nationalization on both theoretical and practical grounds. By the time the book appeared, Wilson had left the Civil Service and gone back to his lecturing at Oxford. In 1945 he received the O.B.E. in recognition of his war services.

Early in 1940 he had got married. His bride was Miss Gladys Mary Baldwin, who was almost the same age as himself; they had known each other since they were eighteen. She was the daughter of a Congregationalist minister, and as she related years afterwards she had been brought up in ' the pretty strict Puritan tradition, in the rather old-fashioned Nonconformist style ' of ' plain living and high thinking '. She liked poetry—Tennyson was perhaps her favourite—and she occasionally wrote verses herself. In art her taste ran to the Pre-Raphaelites, and in music she took a keen pleasure in choral singing. When she and Harold Wilson first met—it was at the tennis and social club attached to the Highfield church— she was working as a shorthand-typist at Port Sunlight and living in lodgings not far from his home. They became engaged three weeks after their first meeting, but of course marriage was out of the question for a long time, since he was earning nothing at all and was entirely dependent on his scholarship grant.

For six years they saw one another only in the vacations, when Wilson went home to his family at Bromborough. Not until he had obtained a position in the Civil Service, in 1940, were they able to get married. The wedding was in the chapel of the Mansfield theological training-college in Oxford. Their first home was a flat in Oxford but in 1948 Wilson was able to buy a house in Southway, in Hampstead Garden Suburb. Soon after going to live there they joined the local Free Church.

Years later, in 1959, Wilson bought a plot of land on St. Mary's in the Scilly Isles, on which he had a bungalow built. This became their holiday home. Mrs. Wilson in particular loved the place, because, as she has expressed it, ' it is wild and solitary and quiet, and you can walk for miles and just think '.

When he went back to Oxford on being released from the Civil Service, Wilson already had in mind a political career, and he was shortly adopted as prospective Labour candidate for the Ormskirk division of Lancashire. The sitting member was Commander Stephen King-Hall, a popular writer and broadcaster on international affairs, who had been elected unopposed in 1939 on the National Labour ticket but now chose to be an Independent. Since the wartime political truce was now abrogated the Conservatives felt justified in putting up their own candidate, with the result that at the general election in 1945 the anti-Labour vote was split and Wilson won the seat with a majority of more than seven thousand over the Conservative, while the Commander was a bad third.

At twenty-nine Wilson was one of the youngest of the new M.P.s, and he was one of five newcomers to whom Attlee gave posts in his administration, the appointment in his case being Parliamentary Secretary to the Ministry of Works. Thus he was never a back-bencher, but made his appearance on the parliamentary stage as the 'baby' of the ministerial team. Early in August he took his seat in the House of Commons, and on 9 October delivered his maiden speech, when he was called upon to reply to the complaints of a veteran Labour member about the shockingly overcrowded and uncomfortable conditions under which they were required to work.

With characteristic diligence Wilson applied himself to mastering the details of parliamentary procedure, and he proved so effective a spokesman for his department that in March 1947 Attlee promoted him to become Secretary for Overseas Trade. Here his chief concern was to get the flow of exports moving to pay for the imports of food and essential raw materials, and he headed trade delegations to Moscow and Geneva with that end in view. He had been only six months in this position when he was given the much more important appointment of President of the Board of Trade in succession to Sir Stafford Cripps who had become Minister for Economic Affairs. Thus at the extraordinarily early age of thirty-one Wilson became a Cabinet minister—the youngest Cabinet minister for a hundred years at least. At the same time he was admitted a member of the Privy Council.

Wilson took over at the Board of Trade in the dreary and depressing time of post-war rationing, food shortages and indeed the short supply of most things, from steel to women's stockings. It was the golden age of spivs and contact men who flourished in the shady underworld of the black market, while honest traders and manufacturers found it hard to stay in business. At the outset Wilson was regarded as a distinct improvement on his predecessor, the austere and pleasure-denying Stafford Cripps: he was reputed to be agile-minded, forward-looking, and a bit of a hustler. But these favourable impressions soon faded. Wilson was then represented as a doctrinaire Socialist, a don who had not had a day's experience of business or for that matter of politics either; a fanatical nationalizer, a controller who was so much in love with controls that he kept them going long after they were needed.

When challenged in the House of Commons he defended the Government's policy with vigour. Thus in a speech in April 1948 he spoke of ' the decision which we, as a free nation, have taken, that setting aside thoughts of luxury and easy living, we will, as our first task, seek to stand on our own feet, pay our way in the markets of the world, rebuild our war-shattered economy, and lay the foundations of new additions to our production equipment which, in the years to come, will mean a higher standard of living for our people and a new industrial greatness for our nation'. But these promises of a brighter and happier tomorrow as often as not failed in their appeal to those who had to live in a present in which they were short of everything.

A few weeks after making the eloquent exposition just quoted, he addressed an open-air rally at Birmingham, and in the course of his speech tried to explain why he was still not in a position to take children's shoes off the ration. Before he could do that, he said, output must be increased by at least fifty per cent above pre-war production, since at present there were just not sufficient shoes to go round. Then in an unfortunate moment, he went on to remark (so the newspaper report ran) that 'The school I went to in the north was one where more than half the children in my class never had boots and shoes to their feet'.

At once the indignant protests rolled in. Huddersfield was up in arms, and Wilson was accused of talking rubbish. In a letter to the Socialist mayor he then said that he had not been thinking of Huddersfield but of Liverpool, Manchester, and Birmingham. This change of front only made matters worse. Civic heads, teachers, medical officers, social workers rushed into print with hot denials that barefooted school-children had been seen in any of the cities mentioned for at least a generation, and Wilson was kept busy denying a whole lot of things that he had never said. Years afterwards he explained that what he had really said was that a number of boys he had known at school had no shoes but had to wear clogs—and the newspaper reports had omitted the bit about clogs.

As the months passed, charges of mismanagement at the Board of Trade continued to multiply. Thousands of Civil Servants were being employed, it was alleged, not on promoting trade and industry but hampering them by a complicated and extensive system of licences and permits. Wilson protested that these could not be abolished until the economic situation showed a marked improvement, but at length, on the eve of Guy Fawkes Day, he had a bonfire of controls which did away with the need for a vast number of permits and licences a year. On 15 March 1949 he abolished clothes rationing, and fifty million clothing ration-books went into salvage. A few days later there was another bonfire of controls.

At the general election of 1950 Wilson did not stand for Ormskirk —which owing to a boundary distribution had become much more of a middle-class constituency—but for the newly formed Lancashire division of Huyton. This was just as well, since at the election Ormskirk was recaptured by the Conservatives with a big majority. Even at Huyton, Wilson's majority was under a thousand and he owed his success to Liberal intervention.

Returned to office but with a miserably small majority, the Labour government exceeded all expectations in surviving for twenty months. Attlee made some changes in his Cabinet, but Wilson remained at the Board of Trade. The most interesting alteration was the appointment of Hugh Gaitskell as Stafford Cripps's deputy at the Treasury. For some time past Wilson had considered Gaitskell to be his chief rival among the younger men in the Government, and he was intensely annoyed at Gaitskell's advancement. He was more so a few months later, when on Cripps's resignation Gaitskell became Chancellor of the Exchequer, which made him Wilson's superior in the Cabinet. More and more Wilson became drawn to the brilliant but erratic Aneurin Bevan, then Minister of Health, and his feelings were so apparent that he was given the nickname of 'Nye's little dog'. Gaitskell was right wing and Bevan left wing, and Wilson was a left-winger too.

The first real clash between them came in the spring of 1951, when Gaitskell introduced his first, and only, budget. Faced with the necessity of finding the money for massive rearmament, the Korean war, and the mounting cost of the National Health Service, Gaitskell proposed that charges should be made for the supply of dentures and spectacles, and Wilson followed his friend in regarding this as an altogether unwarrantable breach in the National Health Service. Aneurin Bevan resigned from the Government on 21 April and Wilson followed suit two days later. In his speech on 24 April he insisted that he and Bevan had resigned not on a mere matter of teeth and glasses but out of their conviction that the country was being required to embark on a rearmament programme which was quite beyond their material resources.

Wilson had been in the Government for six years when he retired, and for four of those years he had been in the Cabinet. His action was generally considered likely to prove fatal to his prospects, but in fact it did him little harm. The Government was so tottery that it could not possibly last much longer, and his constituency organization accepted his explanations and stood by him. The loss of his salary of £5000 was a serious matter, but he was fortunate in obtaining an appointment as economic adviser to a timber-exporting firm in a large way of business.

The general election came in October 1951; and as had been expected the Labour government suffered a severe reverse. Wilson, however, improved somewhat his showing at Huyton, having a majority—this time in a straight fight with a Conservative—of nearly twelve hundred.

When the new Parliament assembled, Wilson took his seat on the front Opposition bench, and he soon established himself as one of the most vigorous debaters. He spoke often and at great length, filling hundreds of columns of Hansard. His memory for facts and figures was spoken of as phenomenal, and he became recognized as his party's chief spokesman on finance and economic matters. He excelled in putting awkward questions to ministers; his interventions were spiced with wit and barbed with malice, often devastating in their effect.

As in the previous Parliament, Wilson to begin with was numbered among the Bevanites, but as time passed he struck out on a line of his own. He was ambitious, and he neglected no opportunity of getting himself known and talked about. When Bevan in a fit of pique resigned from the shadow cabinet, Wilson stepped into his shoes. He obtained a seat on the national executive of the Labour party. In the House of Commons his knock-about style of oratory won him plenty of cheers—and jeers.

Then came the general election of 1955, which was even more of a setback than the previous one had been. Wilson doubled his majority at Huyton, however, and soon after the new Parliament had met he was appointed chairman of a committee of inquiry into the state of the Labour party's organization. His report was scathing. The party's electoral machine, he wrote, was ' at the penny-farthing stage in a jet-propelled era, and, at that, it is getting rusty and deteriorating with age '. In these circumstances the really surprising thing was ' not that the general election was lost, but that we won as many seats as we did '.

This bit of business expertise enhanced Wilson's reputation, and when Hugh Gaitskell became leader of the Parliamentary Labour Party at the end of 1955 he appointed Wilson as shadow Chancellor. His standing in the House—where he frequently duelled with Macmillan—improved steadily, just as it did in the country at large. In the constituency section election for the National Executive of the Labour Party he topped the poll.

After four years another general election was announced. Wilson was right in the forefront of the battle and he proved an able and attractive exponent of Labour's case on T.V. and on platforms up and down the country. Labour's election campaign seemed to be going quite well, until just after half-way when their spokesmen started making promises that were so extravagant and contradictory and obviously impossible of fulfilment, that even the most dim-witted and gullible of electors could not fail to see through them. Labour if returned to power would carry out a whole series of splendid reforms—and they would do it without any increase in taxation! Wilson's individual contribution to the display was his intimation that the party expected to be able to abolish purchase tax on household essentials, furniture, and clothing, and reduce it on a number of other items. Macmillan seized on this and similar declarations with delight, and accused the Labour leaders, Gaitskell and Wilson in particular, with ' putting forward for electioneering purposes these specious and unworthy plans '.

Labour's hopes were dashed completely, and the Conservatives romped home in their third general election victory in succession. Labour lost nearly twenty seats, and the Conservative majority was increased from about sixty to a hundred. A scapegoat was looked for, and Wilson was specially blamed, although his responsibility was surely not so great as his leader's. But at least he had the satis-faction of holding his seat at Huyton with an increased majority of nearly six thousand.

When the new Parliament met, the Labour Opposition were in a very disappointed and querulous mood. Gaitskell made valiant efforts to give the party a new and more attractive image, but Wilson opposed his suggestion that there should be a new approach to the problems of nationalization, and also took the opposite line in the matter of unilateral disarmament. In the summer of 1960 Aneurin Bevan died, and Wilson stepped into his shoes as the leader of the Left.

In November 1960 Wilson was emboldened to challenge Gaitskell for the leadership of the Parliamentary party; and although he was defeated—the voting was Gaitskell 166, Wilson 81—he was not disgraced. Two years later he stood against George Brown for the deputy leadership, and obtained 103 votes to Brown's 133. In this way he staked out a claim for consideration as the eventual leader of the party. Then on 18 January 1963 Hugh Gaitskell died suddenly.

Wilson was now in a very strong position. With both Aneurin Bevan and Hugh Gaitskell gone, he stood out as the most experi-enced of the Labour leaders in the House of Commons, and he was still on the right side of fifty. In February the Labour M.P.s proceeded to choose their new leader. Three names were on the ballot-papers—Harold Wilson, George Brown, and James Callaghan. Wilson almost won on the first ballot, when the voting was 115, 88, and 41. On the second ballot he had a straight fight with Brown, and he won with 144 votes against 103. He took his success calmly, and at once gave an assurance that he would follow the Gaitskell line down the middle of the road.

Now he was Leader of the Opposition in the House of Commons, and he led his party with skill and tact and vigour. He showed himself most affable to the Gaitskellites; and while still on good terms with his old associates the Bevanites made it clear that he was in nobody's pocket. He soothed George Brown's ruffled feelings, and welcomed him as his deputy. In the summer of 1963 the Conservative government was in a visible state of decomposition, and Wilson exerted himself in advancing the date of the funeral. Macmillan went, and Home took over, with many a gibe from Wilson about 'fourteenth earls' and the like. At last the date of the general election was announced, and on 15 October 1964 Harold Wilson led his party to victory. On the afternoon of the next day he kissed the queen's hand as Prime Minister.

All the same, the result of the general election was about the nearest thing possible, since Labour was left with a majority of four only. But at least the thirteen years of uninterrupted Tory rule had been brought to an end, and Wilson was eager to show that with only a single-figure majority Labour was not only willing but able to rule. For the next eighteen months he walked the political tightrope with extraordinary skill and daring, and especially in the day-to-day management of parliamentary business he displayed consummate mastery. At length the appropriate moment seemed to have arrived for another appeal to the country, and under his leadership Labour entered into the fight with enthusiastic vigour. The general election on 31 March 1966 resulted in the return of 363 Labour M.P.s, while the Tories were reduced to 253 and the Liberals mustered a dozen. In the new House of Commons Labour had a majority of very nearly a hundred.

This was the high noon of Harold Wilson's premiership: what came after is a matter for the history-books, and the time to relate it is not yet. We have reached the end of the long picture-gallery of Britain's Prime Ministers, and we are bound to recognize that No. 46 is only an interim sketch. The full-length study, the finished portrait—that must await the brush marks still to be made by passing time.

CHRONOLOGICAL LIST OF
BRITAIN'S PRIME MINISTERS

REIGN OF GEORGE I (1714–27)

| 1721 | Walpole, Sir Robert | Whig |

GEORGE II (1727–60)

1742	Wilmington, Earl of	Whig
1743	Pelham, Henry	Whig
1754 (1)	Newcastle, Duke of	Whig
1756	Devonshire, Duke of	Whig
1757 (2)	Newcastle, Duke of	Whig

GEORGE III (1760–1820)

1762	Bute, Earl of	Tory
1763	Grenville, George	Whig
1765 (1)	Rockingham, Marquess of	Whig
1766	Chatham, Earl of (William Pitt the Elder)	Whig
1767	Grafton, Duke of	Whig
1770	North, Lord	Tory
1782 (2)	Rockingham, Marquess of	Whig
1782	Shelburne, Earl of	Whig
1783 (1)	Portland, Duke of	Coalition
1783 (1)	Pitt, William (the Younger)	Tory
1801	Addington, Henry	Tory
1804 (2)	Pitt, William	Tory
1806	Grenville, Lord	Whig
1807 (2)	Portland, Duke of	Tory
1809	Perceval, Spencer	Tory
1812	Liverpool, Earl of	Tory

GEORGE IV (1820–30)

1827	Canning, George	Tory
1827	Goderich, Viscount	Tory
1828	Wellington, Duke of	Tory

WILLIAM IV (1830–37)

1830	Grey, Earl	Whig
1834 (1)	Melbourne, Viscount	Whig
1834 (1)	Peel, Sir Robert	Tory
1835 (2)	Melbourne, Viscount	Whig

VICTORIA (1837–1901)

1841 (2)	Peel, Sir Robert	Tory
1846 (1)	Russell, Lord John	Whig
1852 (1)	Derby, Earl of	Conservative
1852	Aberdeen, Earl of	Coalition
1855 (1)	Palmerston, Viscount	Liberal
1858 (2)	Derby, Earl of	Conservative
1859 (2)	Palmerston, Viscount	Liberal
1865 (2)	Russell, Earl	Liberal
1866 (3)	Derby, Earl of	Conservative
1868 (1)	Disraeli, Benjamin	Conservative
1868 (1)	Gladstone, W. E.	Liberal
1874 (2)	Disraeli, Benjamin (Earl of Beaconsfield)	Conservative
1880 (2)	Gladstone, W. E.	Liberal
1885 (1)	Salisbury, Marquess of	Conservative
1886 (3)	Gladstone, W. E.	Liberal
1886 (2)	Salisbury, Marquess of	Conservative
1892 (4)	Gladstone, W. E.	Liberal
1894	Rosebery, Earl of	Liberal
1895 (3)	Salisbury, Marquess of	Conservative

EDWARD VII (1901–10)

1902	Balfour, A. J.	Conservative
1905	Campbell-Bannerman, Sir Henry	Liberal
1908	Asquith, H. H.	Liberal
		(Coalition—1915)

GEORGE V (1910–36)

1916	Lloyd George, D.	Coalition
1922	Bonar Law, A.	Conservative
1923 (1)	Baldwin, Stanley	Conservative
1924 (1)	MacDonald, J. Ramsay	Labour
1924 (2)	Baldwin, Stanley	Conservative
1929 (2)	MacDonald, J. Ramsay	Labour (National—1931)
1935 (3)	Baldwin, Stanley	National

EDWARD VIII (1936)
GEORGE VI (1936–52)

1937	Chamberlain, Neville	National
1940 (1)	Churchill, Winston S.	Conservative (Coalition—1945)
1945	Attlee, Clement	Labour
1951 (2)	Churchill, Sir Winston S.	Conservative

ELIZABETH II (1952)

1955	Eden, Sir Anthony	Conservative
1957	Macmillan, Harold	Conservative
1963	Douglas-Home, Sir A.	Conservative
1964	Wilson, Harold	Labour

BIBLIOGRAPHY

WALPOLE

Memoirs of Sir R. Walpole, Earl of Orford.
Rev. W. Coxe. 3 vols. 1798.
Sir Robert Walpole. A. C. Ewald. 1878.
Walpole. Lord Morley. 1889.
*Sir Robert Walpole: The Making of a
Statesman.* 1956, and *The King's Minister.*
J. H. Plumb. 1960.
   Memoirs of the Reign of George II. By
John, Lord Hervey, Ed. by J. W. Croker.
2 vols. 1848.
Lord Hervey's Memoirs. Ed. by Romney
Sidgwick. 1963.
Memoirs of the Reign of George II.
Horace Walpole, Ed. by Lord Holland.
2 vols. 1822.
Horace Walpole's Memoirs and Portraits.
Ed. by R. Sidgwick. 1963.
The Four Georges. W. M. Thackeray.
1855.
Lord Macaulay's essays on Horace
Walpole, and Chatham
*History of England in the Eighteenth
Century.* W. E. H. Lecky. 8 vols. 1879.

PELHAM

The Pelham Administration. Rev. W. Coxe.
2 vols. 1829.
   Lord Chesterfield's *Characters*, and
Letters to His Son. Ed. by Lord Mahon.
1849–53.
   Memoirs from 1754 to 1758. James, Earl
Waldegrave. 1821.

BUTE

John Stuart, Earl of Bute. J. A. Lovat Fraser.
1912.
A Prime Minister and His Son. Hon. Mrs.
E. Stuart Wortley. 1925.
   Sir N. W. Wraxall's *Historical Memoirs
of my own Time.* Ed. by Richard
Askham. 1904.

GEORGE GRENVILLE

The Grenville Papers. Ed. by W. J. Smith.
4 vols. 1852.

ROCKINGHAM

*Memoirs of the Marquess of Rockingham and
his contemporaries.* Ed. by G. T., Earl of
Albemarle. 2 vols. 1852.

CHATHAM

*History of Rt. Hon. William Pitt, Earl of
Chatham.* Rev. Francis Thackeray. 2 vols.
1827.
Chatham. Frederic Harrison. 1905.
Chatham: His Early Life and Connections.
Lord Rosebery. 1910.
Chatham. J. H. Plumb. 1955.
Chatham and the British Empire. Sir C.
Grant Robertson. 1946.

GRAFTON

*Autobiography of Augustus Henry, 3rd Duke of
Grafton.* Ed. by Sir William Anson. 1898.
   Letters of Junius. Ed. by John Wheble.
1771.
   Political Register. Ed. by John Almon.
1768.

NORTH

Lord North. R. Lucas. 2 vols. 1913.
Lord North. W. Baring Pemberton. 1938.
   Statesmen of the Time of George III. Lord
Brougham. 1839.

SHELBURNE

Life of William, Earl of Shelburne. Lord
Edmund Fitzmaurice. 3 vols. 1875.

PITT THE YOUNGER

Life of William Pitt. Lord Stanhope.
4 vols. 1861.
Pitt. Lord Rosebery. 1891.
*William Pitt: some chapters of his life and
times.* Lord Ashbourne. 1898.
William Pitt. J. Holland Rose. 1911 and
1923.
William Pitt. Sir Charles Petrie. 1935.
Life and Letters of Lady Hester Stanhope.
Ed. by the Duchess of Cleveland. 1897.
Lord Macaulay's essay on William Pitt.

ADDINGTON

Life and Correspondence of Rt. Hon. Henry Addington, First Viscount Sidmouth. Hon. G. Pellew. 3 vols. 1847.

SPENCER PERCEVAL

Life of Rt. Hon. Spencer Perceval, M.P. Sir Spencer Walpole. 2 vols. 1874.

LIVERPOOL

Life of Robert Bankes, 2nd Earl of Liverpool. C. D. Yonge. 3 vols. 1868.
Lord Liverpool and his Times. Sir C. Petrie. 1954.
    The Greville Memoirs. By C. C. F. Greville. Ed. by H. Reeve. 8 vols. 1875–87.
    Leaves from the Greville Diary. Arranged by Philip Morrell. 1929.
    Selections from The Creevy Papers and *Creevy's Life and Times.* Ed. by John Gore. 1948.

CANNING

Life of Rt. Hon. George Canning. R. Bell. 1845.
Political Life of George Canning. A. G. Stapleton. 1831.
George Canning and his Times. A. G. Stapleton. 1859.
Life of Canning. H. W. V. Temperley. 1905.
Canning. Sir Charles Petrie. 1946.
John Hookham Frere and his friends. Gabrielle Festing. 1899.

GODERICH

Life of the First Marquess of Ripon. Lucien Wolf. 2 vols. 1921.
'Prosperity' Robinson: the Life of Visct Goderich, 1782–1859. W. D. Jones. 1967.

WELLINGTON

Life of the Duke of Wellington. W. H. Maxwell. 3 vols. 1862.
Life of Arthur, Duke of Wellington. G. R. Gleig. 1899.
Wellington. Sir J. W. Fortescue. 1925.
The Duke. Philip Guedalla. 1931.
The Duke of Wellington and his friends. Ed. by G. Wellesley. 1965.

GREY

Life and Opinions of Charles, Second Earl Grey. Hon. C. Grey. 1861.
Lord Grey of the Reform Bill. G. M. Trevelyan. 1920.

MELBOURNE

Memoirs of William Lamb, Second Viscount Melbourne. W. M. Torrens. 2 vols. 1878.
Lord Melbourne. Henry Dunckley. 1890.
Lord Melbourne. Lord David Cecil. 1965.

PEEL

Memoirs of Sir Robert Peel. 2 vols. 1856–57.
Sir Robert Peel. J. R. Thursfield. 1904.
Private Letters of Sir Robert Peel. Ed. by George Peel. 1920.

RUSSELL

Lord John Russell. Spencer Walpole. 2 vols. 1885.
Lord J. Russell. Stuart J. Reid. 1895.
Lady John Russell. Desmond McCarthy and Agatha Russell. 1910.

DERBY

Earl of Derby. Stuart J. Reid. 1892.
Lord Derby. T. E. Kebbel. 1893.
Lord Derby. George Saintsbury. 1892.

ABERDEEN

The Earl of Aberdeen. Hon. Sir Arthur Gordon. 1893.

PALMERSTON

Life of H. J. Temple, Viscount Palmerston. Sir H. Bulwer, Lord Dalling. 3 vols. 1871.
Life and Correspondence of Lord Palmerston. E. Ashley. 2 vols. 1879.
Viscount Palmerston, M.P. The Marquess of Lorne. 1892.
Palmerston. Philip Guedalla. 1937.

DISRAELI

Life of Benjamin Disraeli, Earl of Beaconsfield. W. F. Monypenny and G. E. Buckle. 6 vols. 1910–20.
Lord Beaconsfield. J. A. Froude. 1891.
Disraeli. André Maurois. trans. 1928.
Disraeli. Robert Blake. 1966.

GLADSTONE

Gladstone. G. W. E. Russell. 1891.
Gladstone. Herbert Paul. 1901.
Life of W. E. Gladstone. Lord Morley. 3 vols. 1903.
Gladstone. Sir Philip Magnus. 1954.
Catherine Gladstone. Mrs. Drew. 1919.
After Thirty Years. Lord Gladstone. 1946.

SALISBURY

The Marquess of Salisbury. H. D. Traill. 1892.

Life of Robert, Marquess of Salisbury. Lady Gwendolen Cecil. 4 vols. 1921–32.
Salisbury, 1830–1903: Portrait of a Statesman. A. L. Kennedy. 1953

ROSEBERY

Lord Rosebery. The Marquess of Crewe. 1931.
Rosebery. R. R. James. 1963.

BALFOUR

A. J. Balfour: the happy life of the Politician, Prime Minister, Statesman and Philosopher. Kenneth Charles Young. 1963.

CAMPBELL-BANNERMAN

Sir Henry Campbell-Bannerman. J. A. Spender. 2 vols. 1923.

ASQUITH

Asquith. R. B. McCallum. 1936.
H. H. Asquith. J. A. Spender and Cyril Asquith. 1932.
Asquith. Roy Jenkins. 1964.
Fifty Years of Parliament. H. H. Asquith. 2 vols. 1926.
Memories and Reflections: 1852–1927. H. H. Asquith. 2 vols. 1928.
Autobiography of Margot Asquith. Ed. by M. B. Carter. 1962.

LLOYD GEORGE

Life of Lloyd George. Malcolm Thompson and Countess Lloyd George. 1948.
Lloyd George. Thomas Jones. 1951.
Tempestuous Journey: Lloyd George, his life and times. Frank Owen. 1954.
Earl Lloyd George of Dwyfor. Richard Lloyd George. 1960.
Decline and Fall of Lloyd George. Lord Beaverbrook. 1966.
The Years that are Past. Countess Lloyd George. 1967.
Memoirs. David Lloyd George. 6 vols. 1933–36.

BONAR LAW

The Unknown Prime Minister: Life and Times of Andrew Bonar Law. Robert Blake. 1955.

BALDWIN

Stanley Baldwin. G. M. Young. 1952.
My Father: the True Story. A. W. Baldwin 1955.

MACDONALD

Ramsay MacDonald. Vol. 1: 1866–1919. Lord Elton. 1939.
The Tragedy of Ramsay MacDonald. MacNeile Weir, M.P. 1938.
Margaret Ethel MacDonald. J. Ramsay MacDonald. 1912.

CHAMBERLAIN

Neville Chamberlain. Iain MacLeod. 1961.
Life of Neville Chamberlain. Keith Feiling. 1946.

CHURCHILL

Winston Churchill. Lewis Broad. 1946.
Winston S. Churchill. Vol. 1: 1874–1900. Vol. 2: 1901–1914. Randolph S. Churchill.
My Early Life. Winston Churchill. 1930.
The World Crisis. Winston Churchill. 4 vols. 1923–29.
The Second World War. Winston Churchill. 6 vols. 1946–54.
Winston Churchill as I knew him. Lady V. Bonham Carter (Baroness Asquith). 1967.

ATTLEE

Mr. Attlee: an Interim Biography. Roy Jenkins. 1948.
As It Happened. C. Attlee. 1954.
A Prime Minister Remembers. The War and Post-War Memoirs of Earl Attlee. Francis Williams. 1961.

EDEN

Sir Anthony Eden: the Chronicles of a Career. Lewis Broad. 1955.
Memoirs of Sir Anthony Eden. Full Circle, 1960; *Facing the Dictators,* 1962; *The Reckoning,* 1965.
The Rise and Fall of Sir Anthony Eden. Randolph Churchill. 1959.

MACMILLAN

Macmillan: Portrait of a Politician. Emrys Hughes. 1962.
Macmillan: a Study in Ambiguity. Anthony Sampson. 1967.

HOME

The Uncommon Commoner: a study of Sir Alec Douglas-Home. John Dickie. 1964.
Sir Alec Douglas-Home. Emrys Hughes. 1965.

WILSON

Harold Wilson: a Pictorial Biography. Michael Foot. 1964.
Harold Wilson: the authentic portrait. Leslie Smith. 1964.
Harold Wilson: a critical biography. Dudley Smith. 1964.
English Premiers from Sir Robert Walpole to Sir Robert Peel. J. G. Earle. 2 vols. 1871.
The Prime Ministers of Britain, 1721–1921. Hon. Clive Bingham. 1922.
Wives of the Prime Ministers, 1844–1906 Elizabeth Lee. 1918.
The Office of Prime Minister. Byrum E. Carter. 1956.

INDEX

INDEX

484